C000148363

# Street by Street

# BUCKINGHAMSHIRE

## PLUS BERKHAMSTED, HENLEY-ON-THAMES, LEIGHTON BUZZARD, MAIDENHEAD, RICKMANSWORTH, SLOUGH, THAME, TRING, WINDSOR

### Enlarged Areas Aylesbury, High Wycombe, Milton Keynes

Ist edition May 2001



Published by AA Publishing (a trading name of Automobile Association Developments Limited, whose registered office is Norfolk House, Priestley Road, Basingstoke, Hampshire, RG24 9NY. Registered number 1878835).

Mapping produced by the Cartographic Department of The Automobile Association.

A CIP Catalogue record for this book is available from the British Library.

Printed by G. Canale & C. S.P.A., Torino, Italy



Ref: MX091

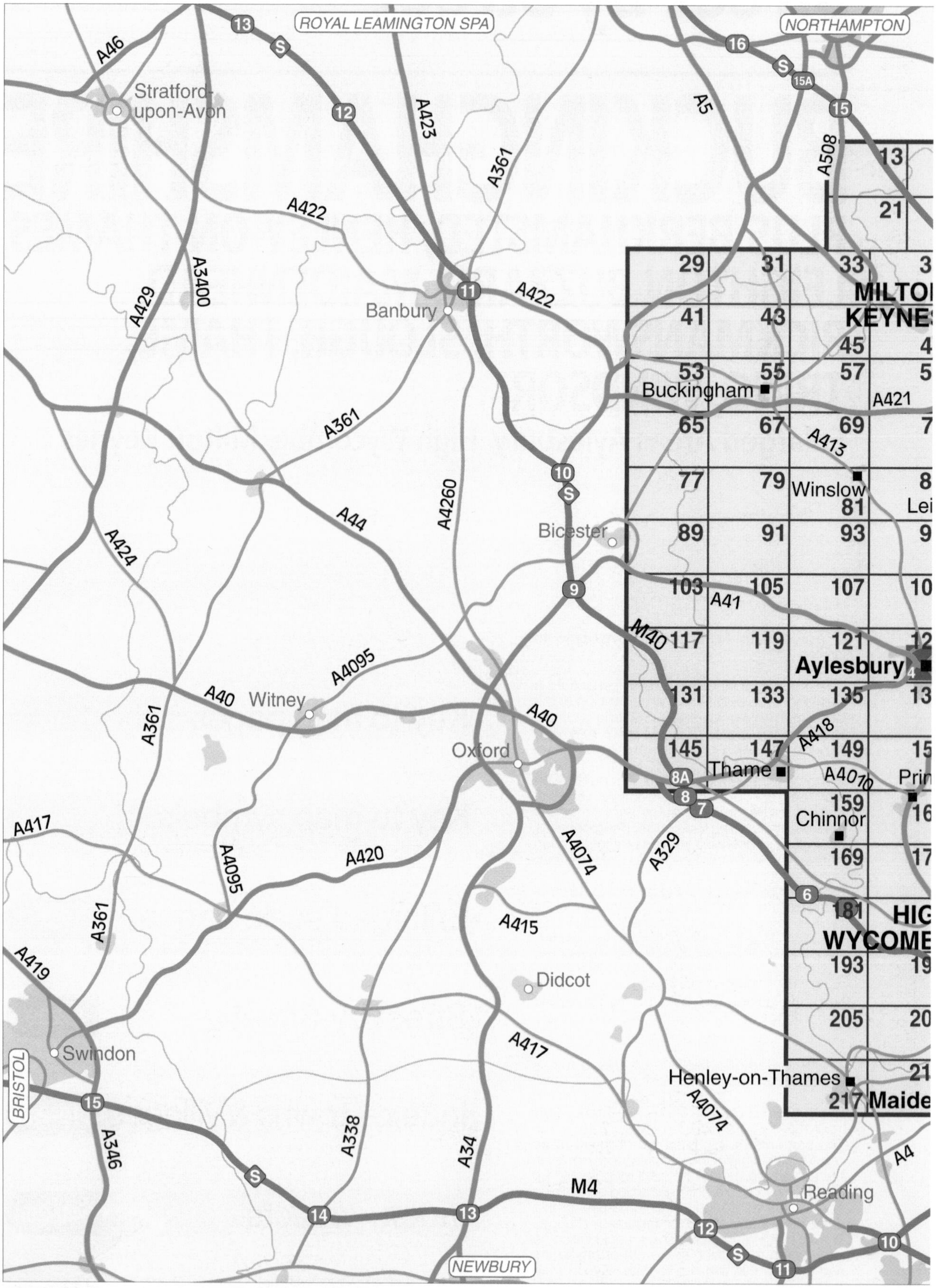

ROYAL LEAMINGTON SPA
NORTHAMPTON
Stratford-upon-Avon
Banbury
Bicester
Witney
Oxford
Didcot
Swindon
Reading
Buckingham
Winslow
Aylesbury
Thame
Chinnor
Henley-on-Thames
MILTON KEYNES
HIGH WYCOMBE
Maide
Prin
Lei
BRISTOL
NEWBURY

A46 A422 A423 A361 A5 A508 A3400 A429 A4260 A44 A424 A4095 A40 A41 M40 A413 A421 A418 A4010 A417 A420 A4074 A329 A415 A419 A346 A338 A34 M4 A4

13 21 29 31 33 41 43 45 53 55 57 65 67 69 77 79 81 89 91 93 103 105 107 117 119 121 131 133 135 145 147 149 159 169 181 193 205 217

Enlarged scale pages **1:10,000** 6.3 inches to 1 mile

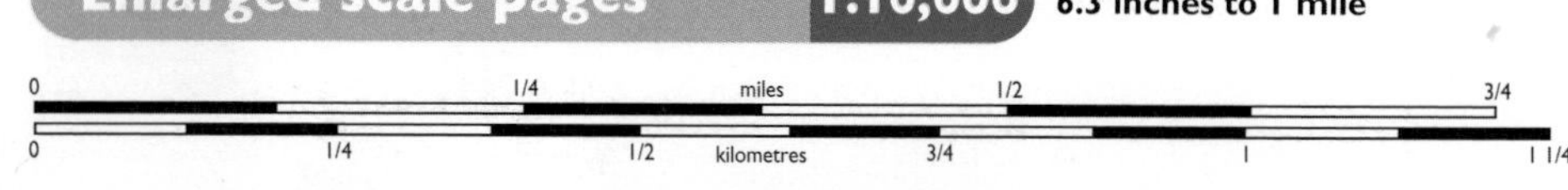

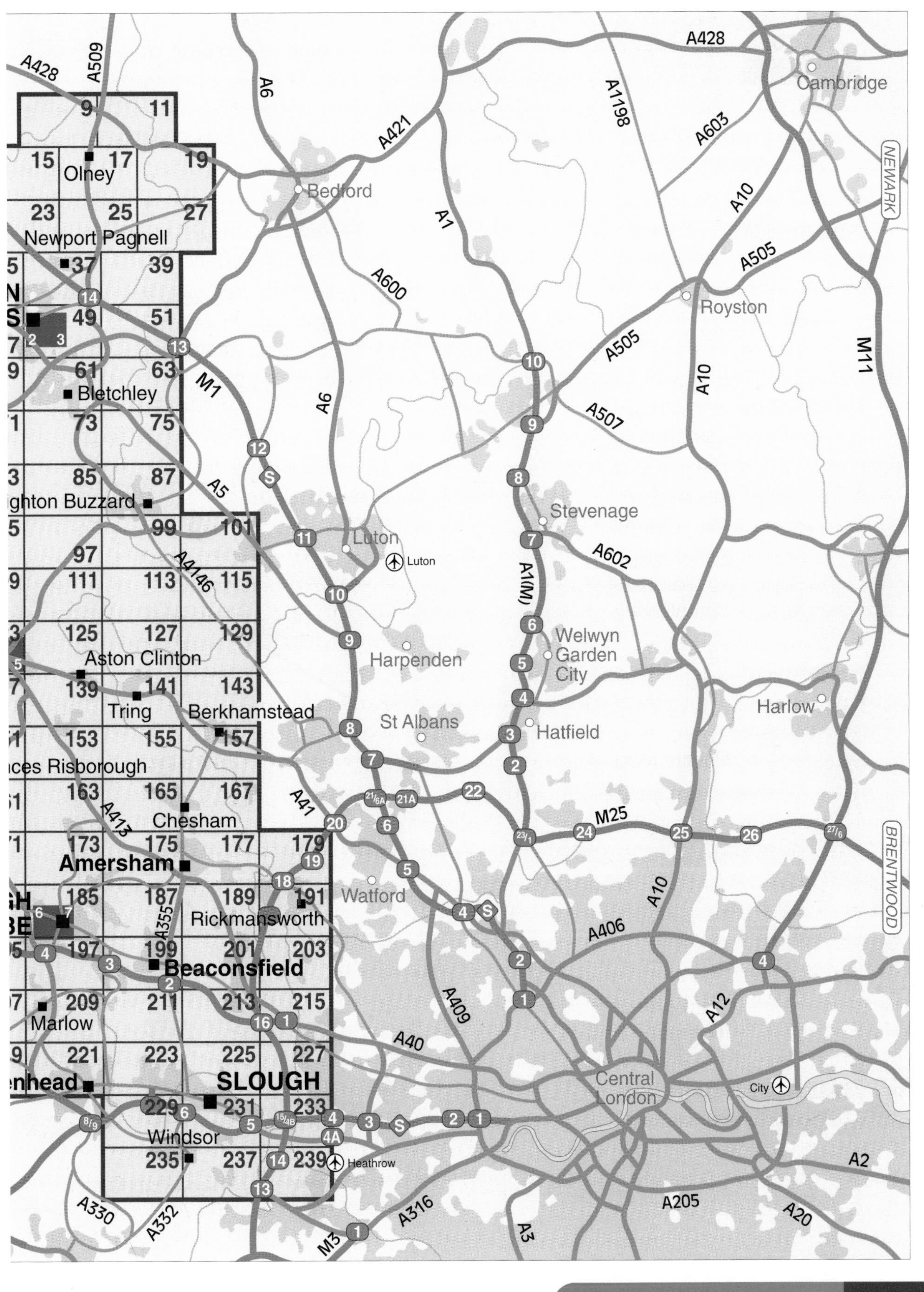


3.6 inches to 1 mile **Scale of main map pages 1:17,500**

0 1/2 miles 1

0 1/2 1 kilometres 1 1/2 2

Junction 9 Motorway & junction

Services Motorway service area

Primary road single/dual carriageway

Services Primary road service area

A road single/dual carriageway

B road single/dual carriageway

Other road single/dual carriageway

Restricted road

Private road

One way street

Pedestrian street

Track/ footpath

Road under construction

Road tunnel

P Parking

P+ Park & Ride

Bus/coach station

Railway & main railway station

Railway & minor railway station

Underground station

Light railway & station

Preserved private railway

LC Level crossing

Tramway

Ferry route

Airport runway

Boundaries- borough/ district

Mounds

93 Page continuation 1:17,500

7 Page continuation to enlarged scale 1:10,000

| Symbol | Meaning |
|---|---|
| | River/canal lake, pier |
| | Aqueduct lock, weir |
| 465 ▲ Winter Hill | Peak (with height in metres) |
| | Beach |
| | Coniferous woodland |
| | Broadleaved woodland |
| | Mixed woodland |
| | Park |
| | Cemetery |
| | Built-up area |
| | Featured building |
| | City wall |
| A&E | Accident & Emergency hospital |
| | Toilet |
| | Toilet with disabled facilities |
| | Petrol station |
| PH | Public house |
| PO | Post Office |
| | Public library |
| i | Tourist Information Centre |
| | Castle |
| | Historic house/ building |
| Wakehurst Place NT | National Trust property |
| M | Museum/ art gallery |
| ✝ | Church/chapel |
| | Country park |
| | Theatre/ performing arts |
| | Cinema |

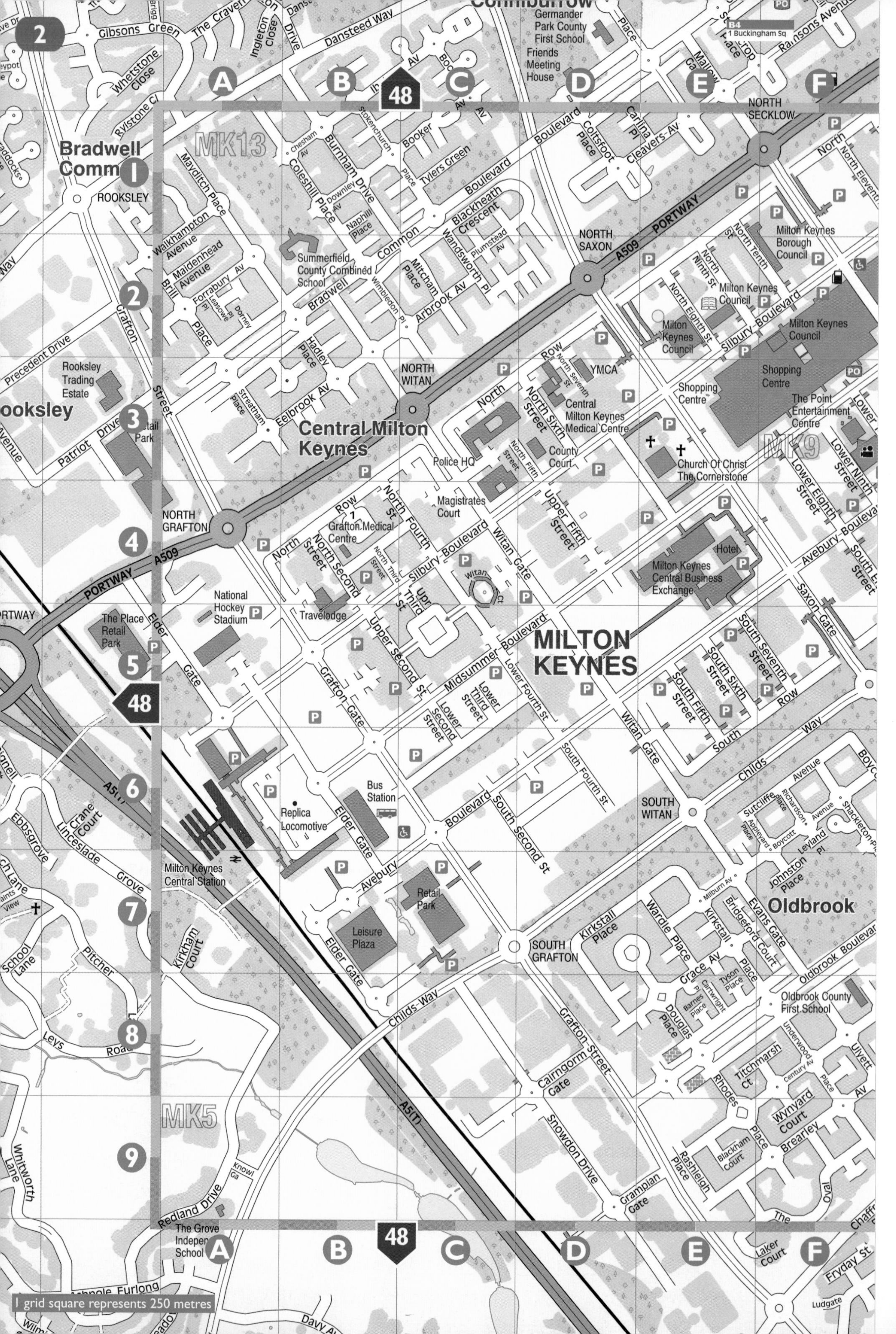


48

1 grid square represents 250 metres

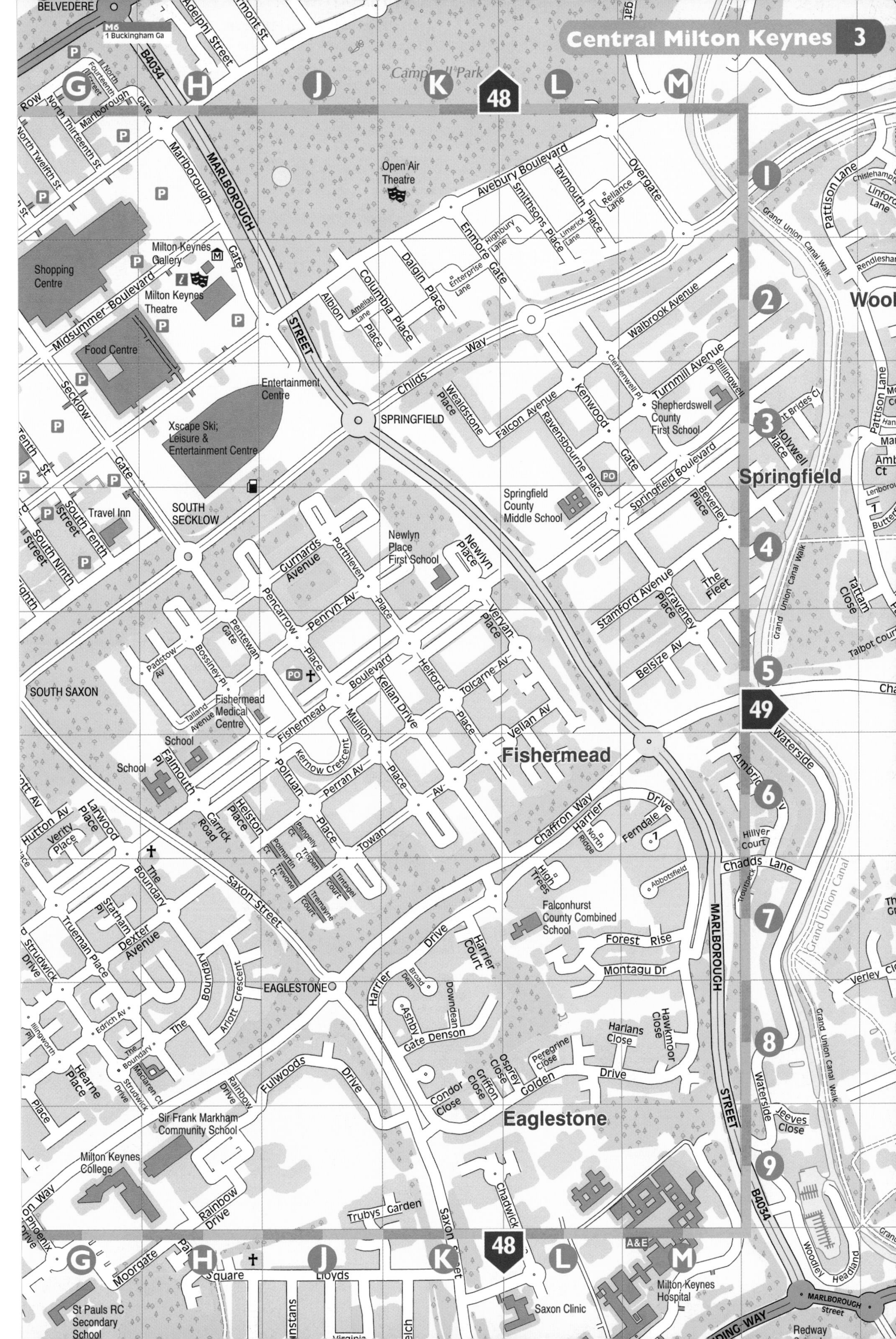
BELVEDERE
M6
1 Buckingham Ga
Campbell Park
48
G
H
J
K
L
M
B4034
Marlborough Gate
MARLBOROUGH STREET
North Fourteenth Street
North Thirteenth St
North Twelfth St
Row
Open Air Theatre
Avebury Boulevard
Smithsons Place
Taymouth Place
Overgate
Reliance Lane
Limerick Lane
Highbury Lane
Enmore Gate
Enterprise Lane
Dalgin Place
Columbia Place
Albion Place
Amelias Lane
Milton Keynes Gallery
Milton Keynes Theatre
Shopping Centre
Midsummer Boulevard
Food Centre
Secklow Gate
Entertainment Centre
Xscape Ski; Leisure & Entertainment Centre
SPRINGFIELD
Childs Way
Walbrook Avenue
Clerkenwell Pl
Turnmill Avenue
Billingwell Pl
Shepherdswell County First School
Wealdstone Place
Falcon Avenue
Kenwood Gate
Ravensbourne Place
Springfield Boulevard
Springfield County Middle School
Beverley Place
Springfield
Grand Union Canal Walk
Pattison Lane
Chislehampton
Linford Lane
Rendlesham
Wool
St Brides Cl
Holywell Place
Amb Ct
Lenborough
Butterfield
Tattam Close
Talbot Court
Travel Inn
SOUTH SECKLOW
South Tenth Street
South Ninth Street
Tenth St
Eighth
Newlyn Place First School
Newlyn Place
Gurnards Avenue
Porthleven Place
Pencarrow Place
Penryn Av
Stamford Avenue
Graveney Place
The Fleet
Belsize Av
Veryan Place
Pentewan Gate
Padstow Av
Bossiney Pl
Helford Place
Tolcarne Av
Kellan Drive
Boulevard
SOUTH SAXON
Talland Avenue
Fishermead Medical Centre
Fishermead Boulevard
Mullion Place
Vellan Av
Fishermead
Cha
49
Waterside
School
Falmouth Pl
Kernow Crescent
Perran Av
Polruan Place
Towan Av
Ambridge Way
Hillyer Court
Chadds Lane
Troutbeck
Chaffron Way
Harrier Drive
North Ridge
Ferndale
Abbotsfield
High Trees
Hutton Av
Larwood Place
Verity Place
Carrick Road
Helston Place
Pengelly Ct
Polmartin Ct
Trispen Ct
Trevone Ct
Tintagel Court
Tremayne Court
The Boundary
Saxon Street
Falconhurst County Combined School
Forest Rise
Montagu Dr
Grand Union Canal
The Gr
Verley Cl
Statham Pl
Dexter Avenue
Trueman Place
Strudwick Drive
Boundary
Arlott Crescent
EAGLESTONE
Harrier Court
Harrier Drive
Broad Dean
Downdean
Ashby
Gate Denson
Harlans Close
Hawkmoor Close
Edrich Av
Illingworth Pl
Hearne Place
Maclaren Ct
Osprey Close
Griffon Close
Peregrine Close
Condor Close
Golden Drive
Rainbow Drive
Fulwoods Drive
Eaglestone
Jeeves Close
Sir Frank Markham Community School
Milton Keynes College
Phoenix Drive
Way
Rainbow Drive
Trubys Garden
Chadwick
Saxon Street
Woodley
Headland
A&E
Moorgate
Square
Lloyds
Milton Keynes Hospital
Saxon Clinic
St Pauls RC Secondary School
Virginia
Redway
MARLBOROUGH Street
Grand

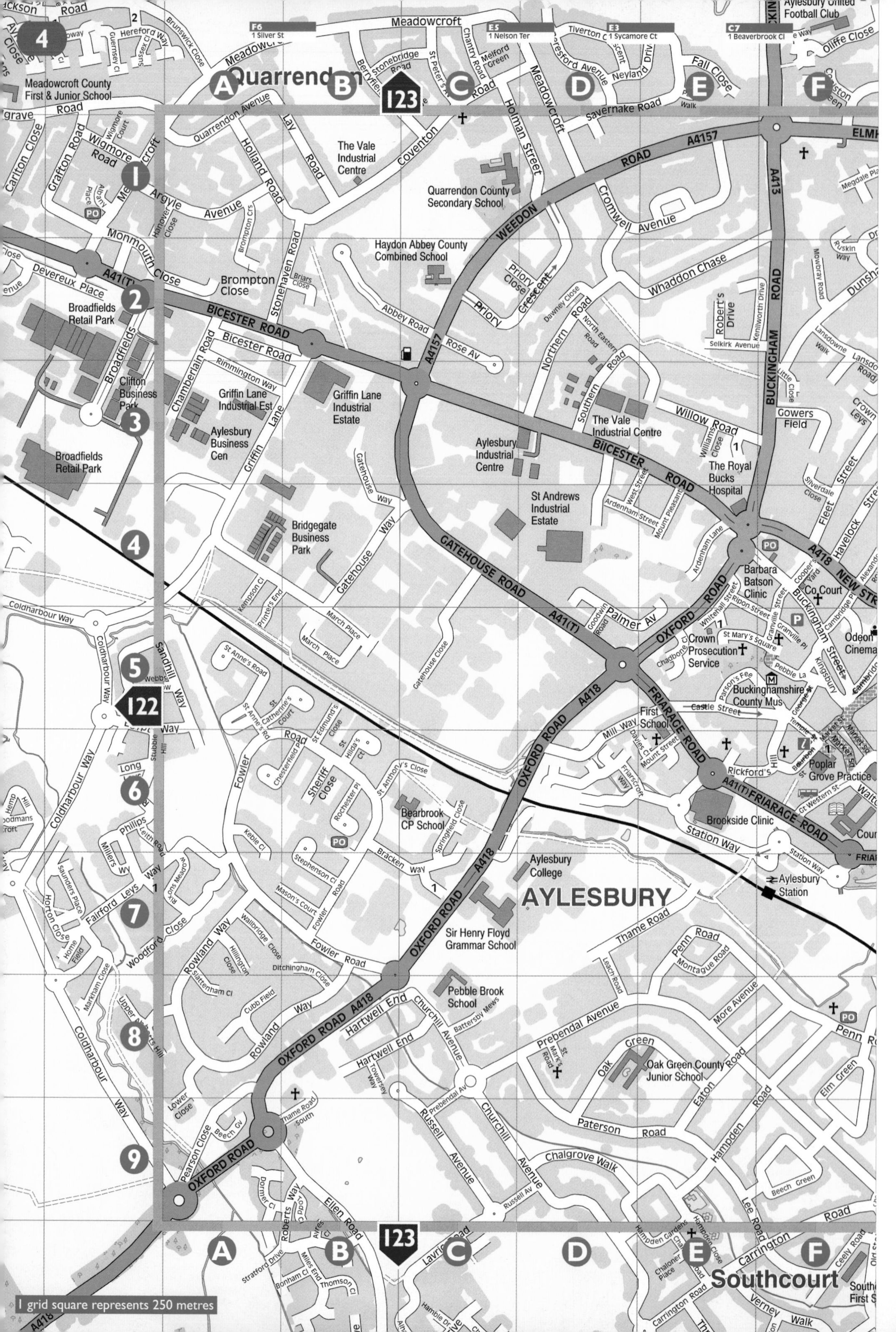
4
Quarrendon
Meadowcroft County
First & Junior School
F6
1 Silver St
E5
1 Nelson Ter
E3
1 Sycamore Ct
C7
1 Beaverbrook Cl
Aylesbury United
Football Club
Meadowcroft
123
The Vale
Industrial
Centre
Quarrendon County
Secondary School
Haydon Abbey County
Combined School
Brompton
Close
Broadfields
Retail Park
Clifton
Business
Park
Griffin Lane
Industrial Est
Aylesbury
Business
Cen
Griffin Lane
Industrial
Estate
Broadfields
Retail Park
The Vale
Industrial Centre
Aylesbury
Industrial
Centre
St Andrews
Industrial
Estate
The Royal
Bucks
Hospital
Bridgegate
Business
Park
Barbara
Batson
Clinic
Co Court
Odeon
Cinema
Crown
Prosecution
Service
Buckinghamshire
County Mus
First
School
Poplar
Grove Practice
Bearbrook
CP School
Brookside Clinic
Aylesbury
College
AYLESBURY
Aylesbury
Station
Sir Henry Floyd
Grammar School
Pebble Brook
School
Oak Green County
Junior School
122
Southcourt
BICESTER ROAD
WEEDON ROAD A4157
BUCKINGHAM ROAD
A413
GATEHOUSE ROAD
A41(T)
OXFORD ROAD A418
FRIARAGE ROAD
A418 NEW STREET
Savernake Road
Cromwell Avenue
Whaddon Chase
Coldharbour Way
Fowler Road
Prebendal Avenue
Paterson Road
Chalgrove Walk
Hampden Road
Thame Road
Penn Road
Station Way
Rowland Way
Churchill Avenue
Russell Avenue
Hartwell End
Carrington Road
A
B
C
D
E
F
1
2
3
4
5
6
7
8
9
1 grid square represents 250 metres

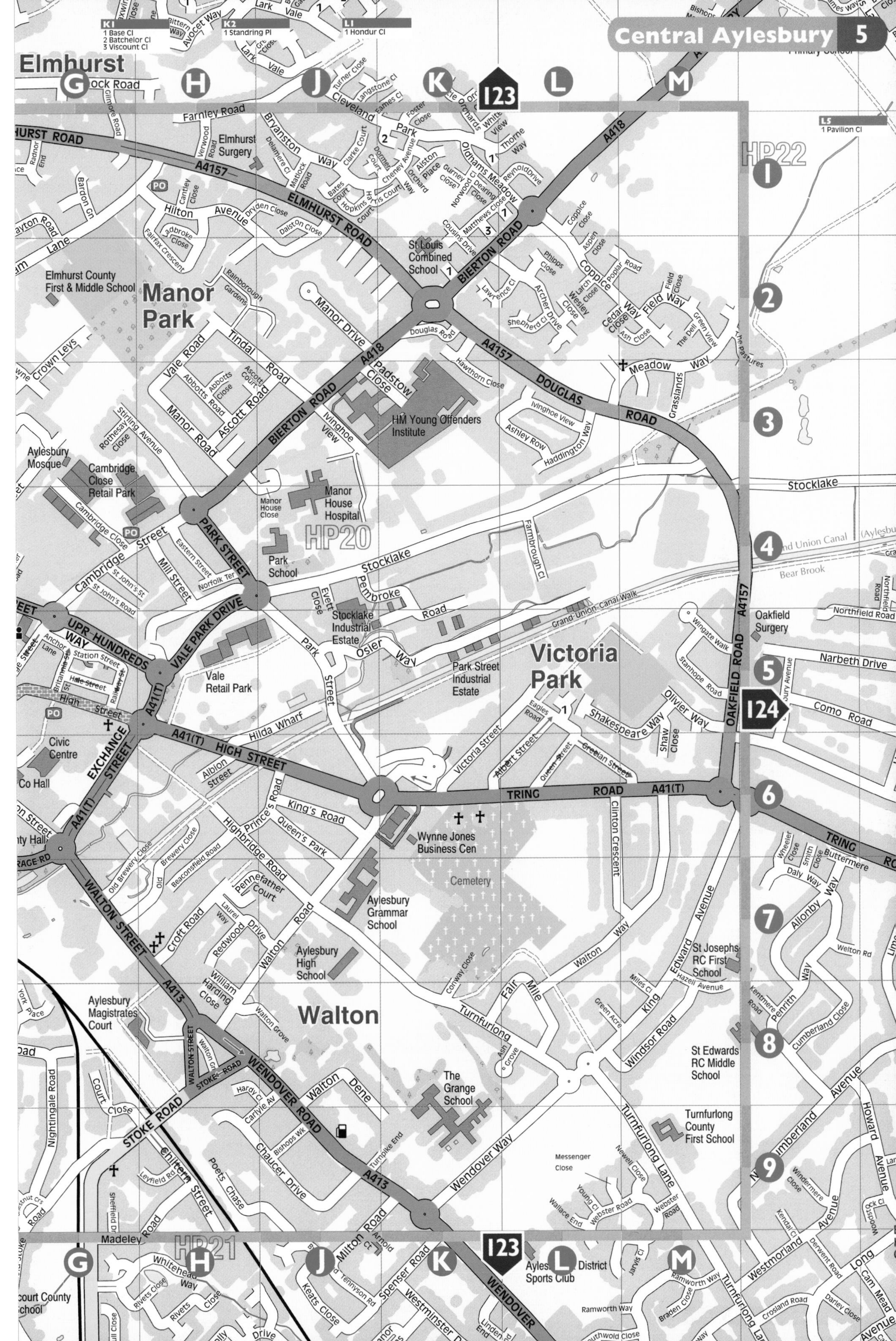
Elmhurst
Manor Park
Victoria Park
Walton
HP20
HP21
HP22
Elmhurst Surgery
Elmhurst County First & Middle School
St Louis Combined School
HM Young Offenders Institute
Manor House Hospital
Aylesbury Mosque
Cambridge Close Retail Park
Park School
Stocklake Industrial Estate
Park Street Industrial Estate
Vale Retail Park
Civic Centre
Wynne Jones Business Cen
Cemetery
Aylesbury Grammar School
Aylesbury High School
Aylesbury Magistrates Court
The Grange School
Oakfield Surgery
St Josephs RC First School
St Edwards RC Middle School
Turnfurlong County First School
Aylesbury District Sports Club
Grand Union Canal
Bear Brook
ELMHURST ROAD
BIERTON ROAD
DOUGLAS ROAD
OAKFIELD ROAD
TRING ROAD
HIGH STREET
PARK STREET
VALE PARK DRIVE
UPR HUNDREDS WAY
EXCHANGE STREET
WALTON STREET
WENDOVER ROAD
STOKE ROAD
Stocklake
Cambridge Street
K1 1 Base Cl 2 Batchelor Cl 3 Viscount Cl
K2 1 Standring Pl
L1 1 Hondur Cl
L5 1 Pavilion Cl
123
124

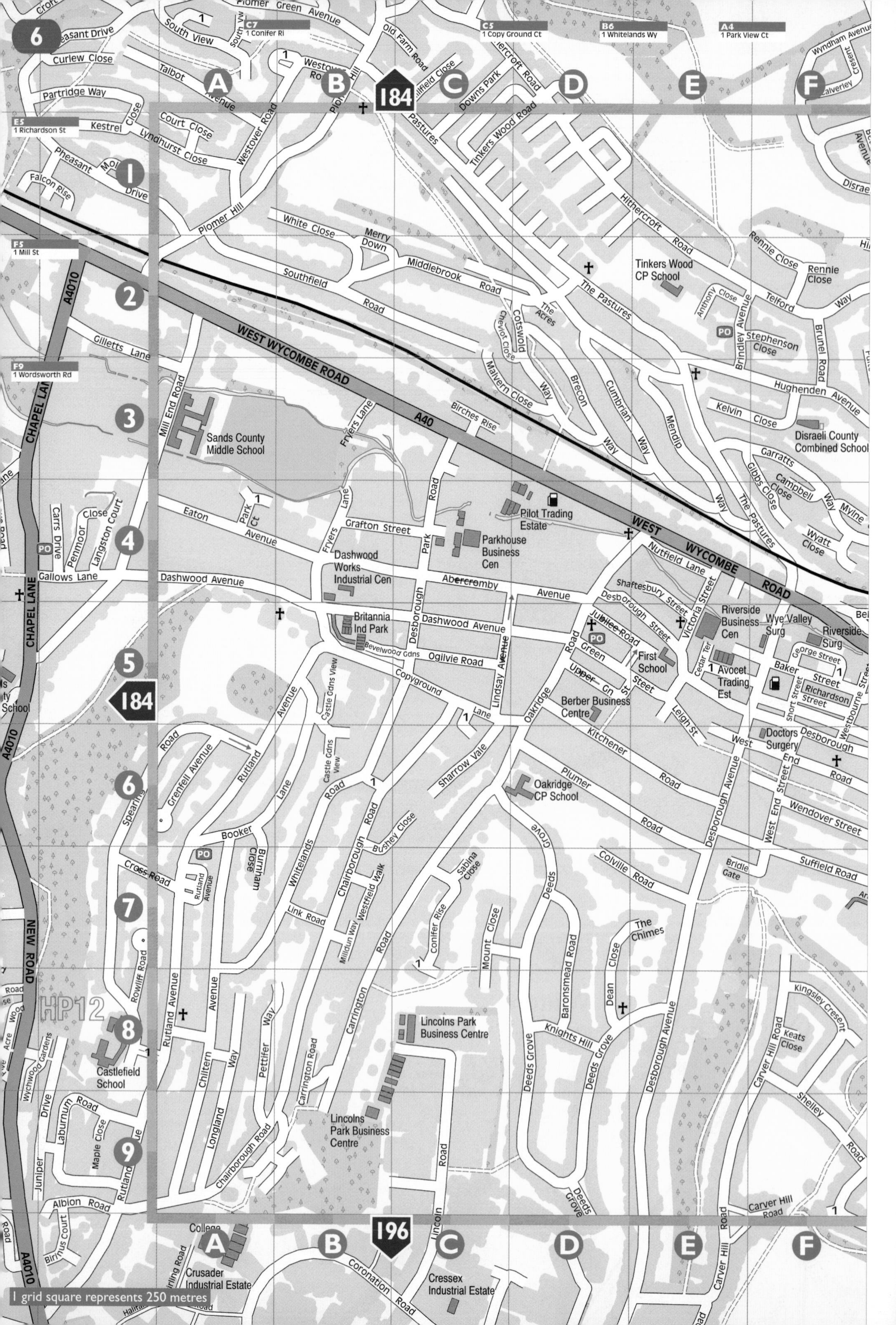
C7 1 Conifer Ri
C5 1 Copy Ground Ct
B6 1 Whitelands Wy
A4 1 Park View Ct
E5 1 Richardson St
F5 1 Mill St
F9 1 Wordsworth Rd
184
196
WEST WYCOMBE ROAD
A40
CHAPEL LANE
NEW ROAD
A4010
Sands County Middle School
Pilot Trading Estate
Parkhouse Business Cen
Dashwood Works Industrial Cen
Britannia Ind Park
Tinkers Wood CP School
Disraeli County Combined School
Riverside Business Cen
Wye Valley Surg
Riverside Surg
First School
Avocet Trading Est
Berber Business Centre
Doctors Surgery
Oakridge CP School
Lincolns Park Business Centre
Castlefield School
Crusader Industrial Estate
Cressex Industrial Estate
HP12
Dashwood Avenue
Desborough Avenue
Desborough Road
Plomer Hill
Hughenden Avenue
Copyground Lane
Chairborough Road
Carrington Road
Rutland Avenue
Deeds Grove
Carver Hill Road
Coronation Road
1 grid square represents 250 metres

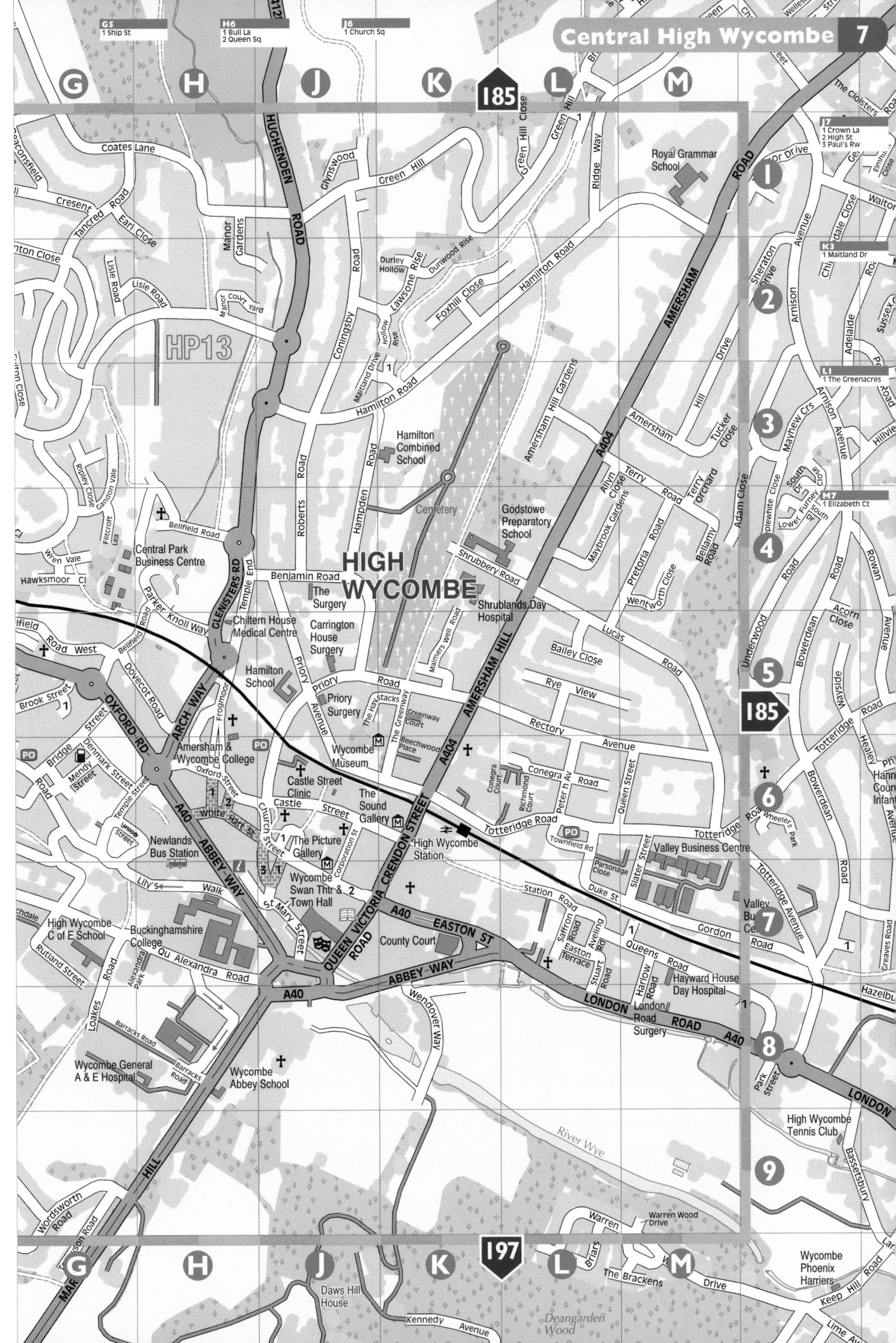
G5
1 Ship St
H6
1 Bull La
2 Queen Sq
J6
1 Church Sq
J7
1 Crown La
2 High St
3 Paul's Rw
K3
1 Maitland Dr
L1
1 The Greenacres
M7
1 Elizabeth Ct
185
197
HP13
HIGH WYCOMBE
Royal Grammar School
Hamilton Combined School
Godstowe Preparatory School
Cemetery
Central Park Business Centre
The Surgery
Chiltern House Medical Centre
Carrington House Surgery
Shrublands Day Hospital
Hamilton School
Priory Surgery
Wycombe Museum
Amersham & Wycombe College
Castle Street Clinic
The Sound Gallery
The Picture Gallery
High Wycombe Station
Newlands Bus Station
Wycombe Swan Thtr & Town Hall
Valley Business Centre
High Wycombe C of E School
Buckinghamshire College
County Court
Hayward House Day Hospital
London Road Surgery
Wycombe General A & E Hospital
Wycombe Abbey School
High Wycombe Tennis Club
River Wye
Warren Wood Drive
Wycombe Phoenix Harriers
Daws Hill House
Deangarden Wood
Coates Lane
Green Hill
Hughenden Road
Amersham Road
Amersham Hill
Hamilton Road
Queen Victoria Road
Crendon Street
Abbey Way
Oxford Rd
Arch Way
Easton St
London Road
Totteridge Road
Rectory Avenue
Lucas Road
Gordon Road
Queens Road
Priory Road
Castle Street
Benjamin Road
Marlow Hill
Alexandra Road
Wendover Way
Kennedy Avenue
The Brackens

Young
Dentonwood Lodge
Ausway
A
B
C
D
E
F
1
2
3
4
5
6
7
8
Denton Road
Chase Park Road
South Vale
Gees Farm
Blenley Lodge
New Hay Farm
Hops Copse
Chase Park
Yardley Chase
Howcut Lane
Chase Park Farm
The Wold
Arniss Copse
Sane Copse
Grimpsey Copse
Hay Copse
Church Slade
Milton Keynes Boundary Walk
Manor Farm
Cowpers Oak Lodge
Ravenstone Road Copse
Kilwick Wood
Northamptonshire County
Milton Keynes
Great Wood
15
Woodlands
1 grid square represents 500 metres

Hastings
High St
PO
Highfield Way
The Lodge
G
H
J
K
L
M
A428(T)
BEDFORD ROAD EAST
B5388
Long Furlong
Roundhay Farm
Old Pastures
Northamptons
Milton K
1
2
3
4
5
6
7
8
10
16
New Pastures Farm
The Pastures
Warrington Lodge
Old Pond Close
Milton Keynes Boundary Walk
Olney Lane End
Pastures Farm
Warrington
Olney Hyde
Olney Park Farm
Court Farm
Longland Farm
A509
Hungary Hall
YARDLEY ROAD
WARRINGTON ROAD
LAVENDON ROAD
Stilebrook Road
Kippel Hill
Lilly Hill
Ferne Furlong
B565
WELLINGBOROU

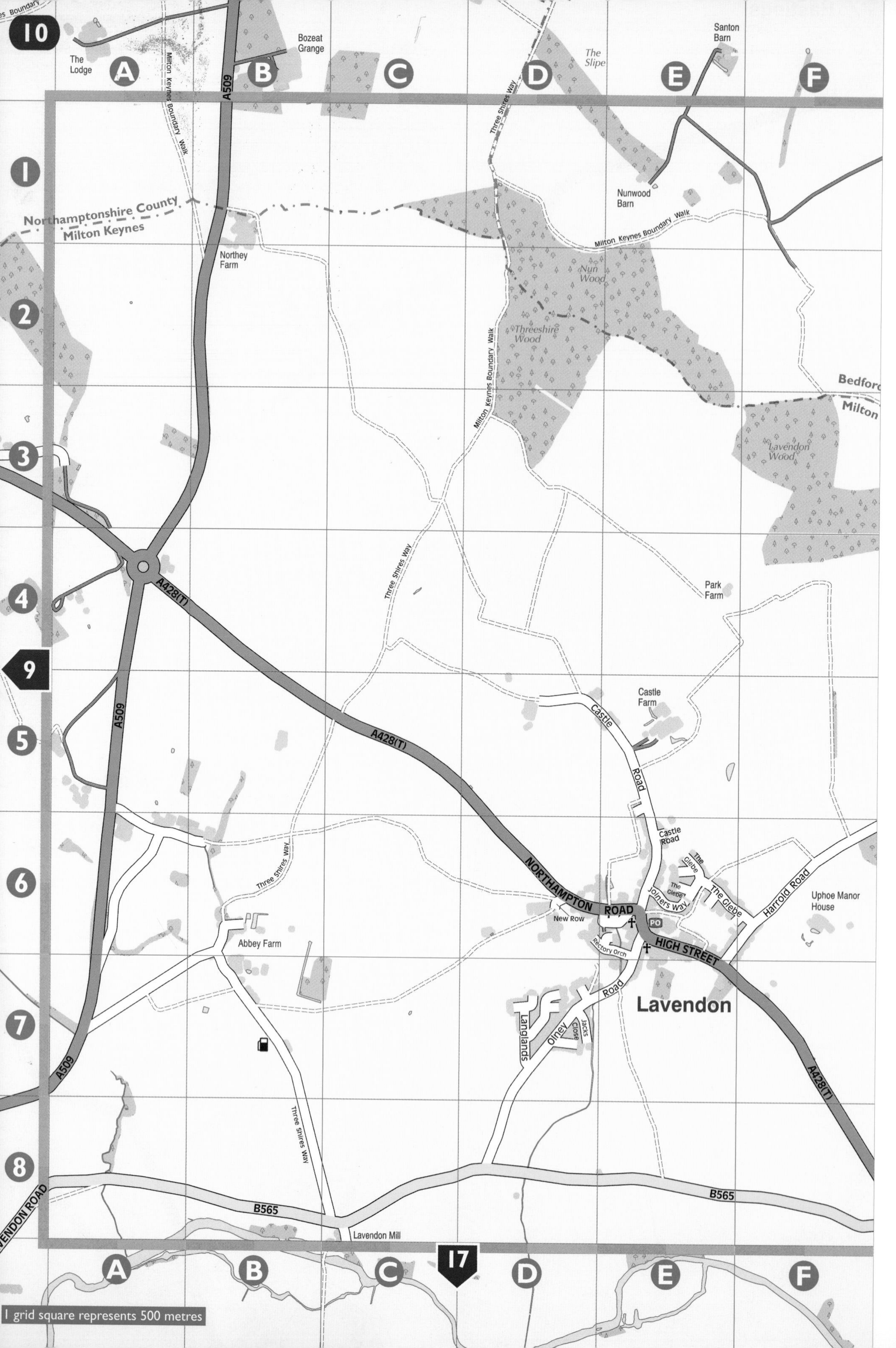
10
The Lodge
Bozeat Grange
The Slipe
Santon Barn
A509
Milton Keynes Boundary Walk
Three Shires Way
Northamptonshire County
Milton Keynes
Northey Farm
Nunwood Barn
Nun Wood
Threeshire Wood
Bedford
Milton
Lavendon Wood
Park Farm
A428(T)
9
Castle Farm
Castle Road
Northampton Road
New Row
PO
The Glebe
Joiners Way
Harrold Road
Uphoe Manor House
High Street
Rectory Orch
Abbey Farm
Olney Road
Langlands
Jacks Close
Lavendon
B565
Lavendon Mill
Lavendon Road
17
A B C D E F
1 2 3 4 5 6 7 8
1 grid square represents 500 metres

K8
1 Hawthorn Cl
2 Mordaunt Cl
3 The Pyghtle
M2
1 Rectory Cl
New Road
Priory Farm
High Street
Harrold Lower School
Mowhills
Hall Close
Mansion La
River Great Ouse
Middle Farm
Carlton Road
Chell
Moor
Causeway
Carlton Lower School
Rectory Close
The Marsh
High Street
Beeby Way
Marsh Farm
Manor Close
Harrold Lodge Farm
Milton Keynes Boundary Walk
Keynes
Spring Close Farm
Church Farm
Turvey Road
School Lane
Valley View Farm
Harrold Road
Snelson
Turvey Road
St Margarets School
Northey Farm
High Elms
Milton Keynes Boundary Walk
Snip Wood
Carlton Road
Milton Keynes
Bedfordshire County
Carlton Road
Turvey House
Turvey Lower School
Grove Rd
Norfolk Rd
Turvey
May Road
Grove Court
Bamfords Lane
Laws Cl
Elmwood
Cold Brayfield
BEDFORD ROAD
BRIDGE STREET
HIGH STREET
BEDFORD ROAD
Mill Lane
Newton
Tandys Cl
Jack's Lane
Turvey Abbey
G
H
J
K
L
M
1
2
3
4
5
6
7
8
18

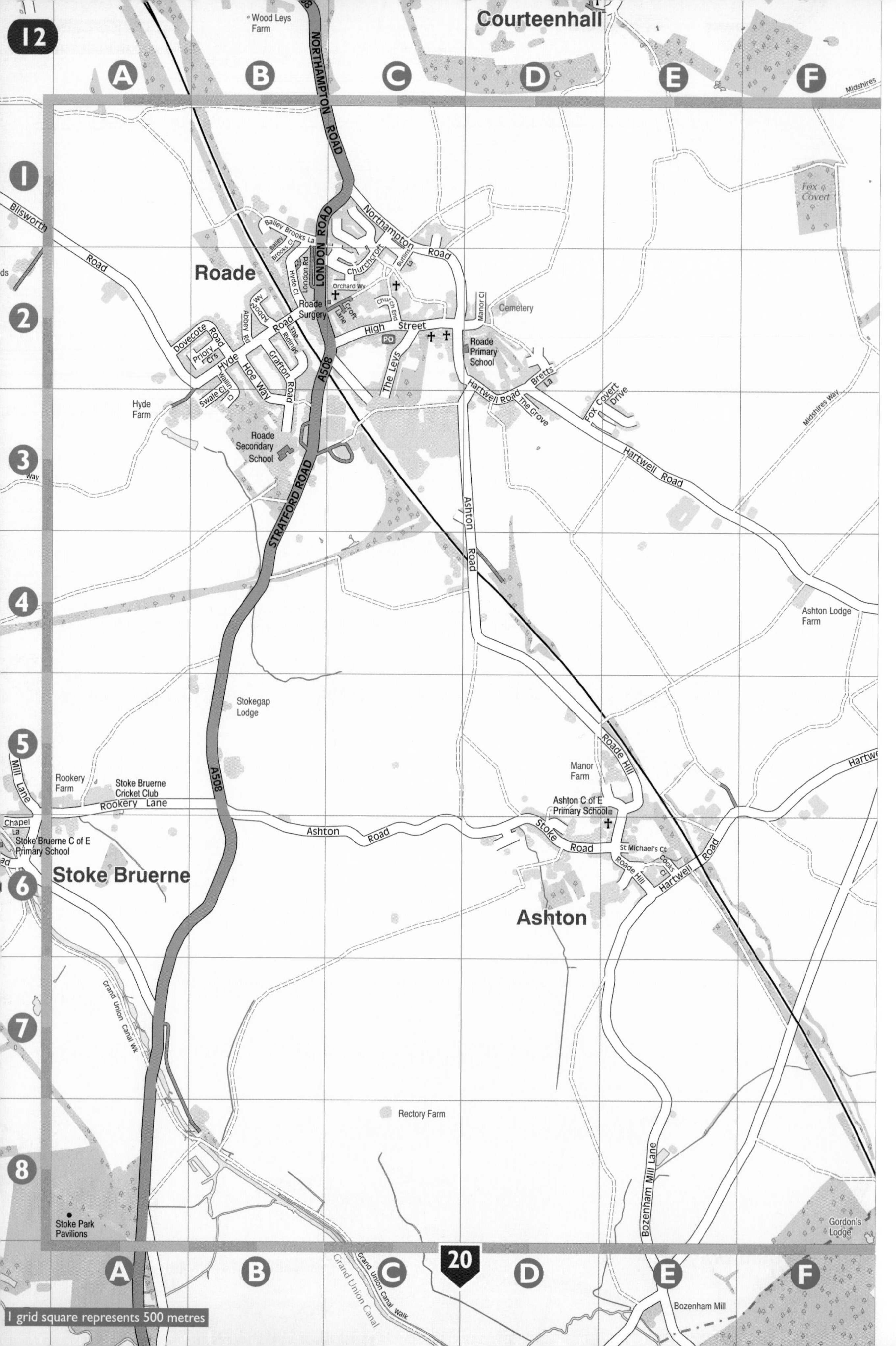
Courteenhall
Wood Leys Farm
NORTHAMPTON ROAD
A B C D E F
1 2 3 4 5 6 7 8
Midshires Way
Fox Covert
Bilsworth Road
Roade
Bailey Brooks La
Bailey Brooks Cl
Hyde Cl
London Rd
LONDON ROAD
Northampton Road
Churchcroft
Butlins La
Orchard Wy
Croft Lane
Church End
Manor Cl
Cemetery
Abbots Wy
Abbey Rd
Roade Surgery
Road
The Ridings
High Street
PO
Dovecote Road
Priory Crs
Hyde
Hoe Way
Grafton Road
The Leys
A508
Roade Primary School
Walling Cl
Swale Cl
Hartwell Road
The Grove
Bretts La
Fox Covert Drive
Hyde Farm
Roade Secondary School
Hartwell Road
STRATFORD ROAD
Ashton Road
Ashton Lodge Farm
Stokegap Lodge
Roade Hill
Manor Farm
Mill Lane
Rookery Farm
Stoke Bruerne Cricket Club
Rookery Lane
Ashton C of E Primary School
Hartwell
Chapel La
Stoke Bruerne C of E Primary School
Ashton Road
Stoke Road
St Michael's Ct
Cooks Cl
Roade Hill
Hartwell Road
Stoke Bruerne
Ashton
Grand Union Canal Wk
Rectory Farm
Bozenham Mill Lane
Stoke Park Pavilions
Gordon's Lodge
Grand Union Canal
Grand Union Canal Walk
Bozenham Mill
1 grid square represents 500 metres

20

H5
1 Amberley Rd
2 Stonehurst Cl
3 Swyncombe Gn
K4
1 Crabtree Cl
G
H
J
K
L
M
Salcey Forest
Midshires Way
1
Salcey Lawn
Salcey Forest
2
Ashwood Farm
Hartwell Clear Copse
3
M1
Rowley Wood
Forest Gld
Wood La
Forest Road
Meadslade
Oak Cl
Barley Cl
Stoney Way
Salcey Avenue
Hazel Cl
Rush Cl
Sandpit Copse
4
Forest Vw
Salcey Cl
Lime Cl
Rose Cl
Grafton Cl
Cemetery
Church Cl
Malting Wy
School La
Sch
PO
Stocking Cl
Hartwell
14
Ashton Road
Blacksmith's Way
Robins Cl
Road
Lower End
Park Road
Park La
Lower End
5
Park Farm
Folly Lane
Park Rd
Elms Farm
M1
6
Forest Far
Hartwell End House
Salcey Gre
7
Chapel Farm
Circular Ride
8
Hanslope Boundary Wk
Milton Keynes
Roselane Farm
21
Hartwell Road
Road

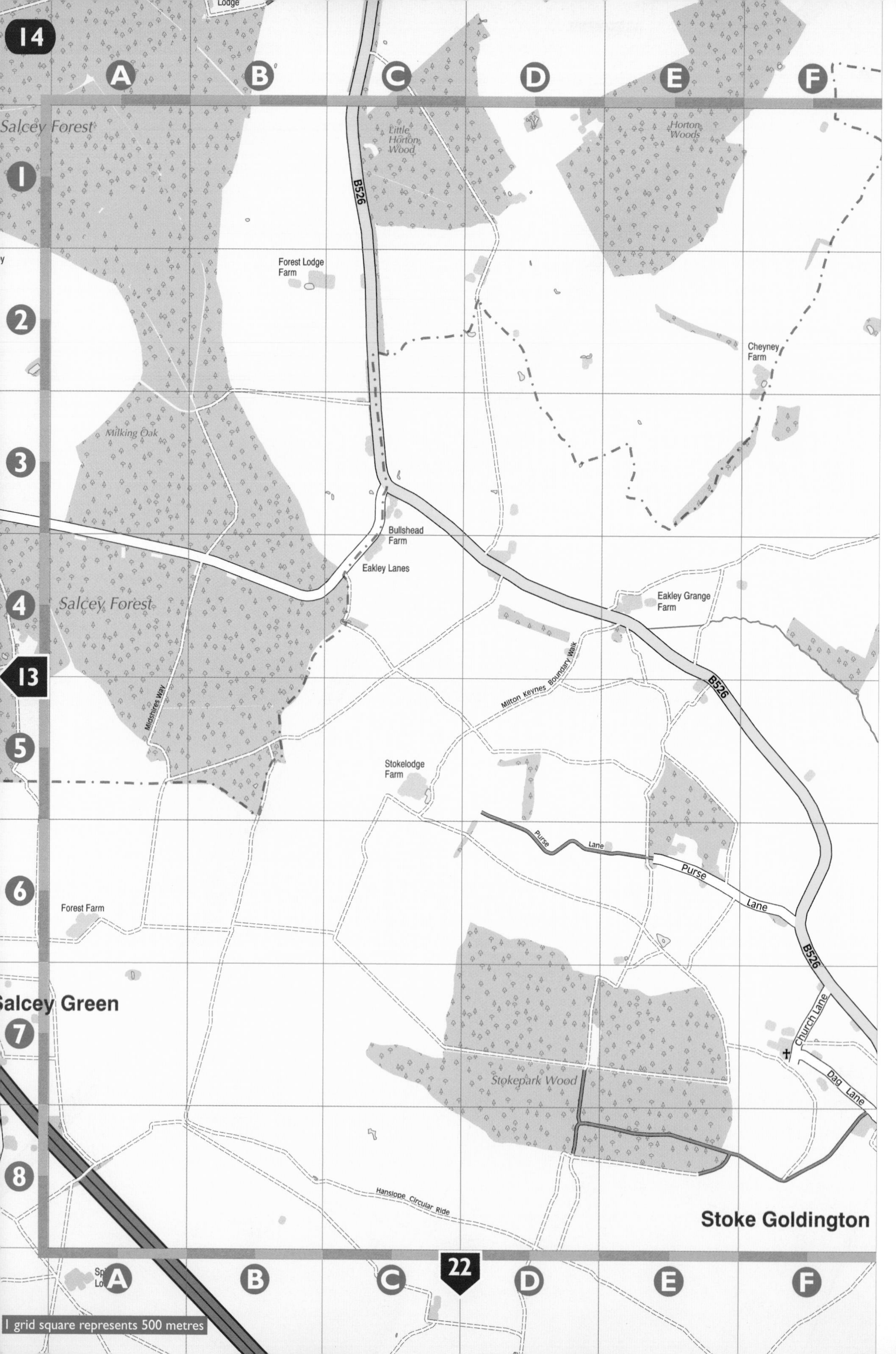
Lodge
A
B
C
D
E
F
Salcey Forest
Little Horton Wood
Horton Woods
1
B526
Forest Lodge Farm
2
Cheyney Farm
Milking Oak
3
Bullshead Farm
Eakley Lanes
Salcey Forest
4
Eakley Grange Farm
Milton Keynes Boundary Walk
13
B526
Midshires Way
5
Stokelodge Farm
Purse Lane
Purse Lane
6
Forest Farm
B526
Salcey Green
7
Church Lane
Stokepark Wood
Dag Lane
8
Hanslope Circular Ride
Stoke Goldington
22
A
B
C
D
E
F
1 grid square represents 500 metres

J4
1 Chaseport Cl
M5
1 Cowpers Orch
G
H
J
8
K
L
M
Hungary Hall
Milton Keynes Boundary Walk
Woodlands
Northend
Parkfield Farm
Milton Keynes Boundary Walk
Cemetery
Ravenstone
Milton Keynes Boundary Walk
Abbey Way
Common Street
Weston Road
Wood Lane
High Street
16
PO
High
Pevers Lane
The Close
Wes
Ravenstone Mill Road
Woolwich Barn
Springbank Court
Mount Pleasant
HIGH STREET
Orchard Wy
Malting Cl
Birds La
PO
Westside La
Leaside
Ram Aly
Baker's Cl
Ravenstone Mill
Town End Cres
23
1
2
3
4
5
6
7
8

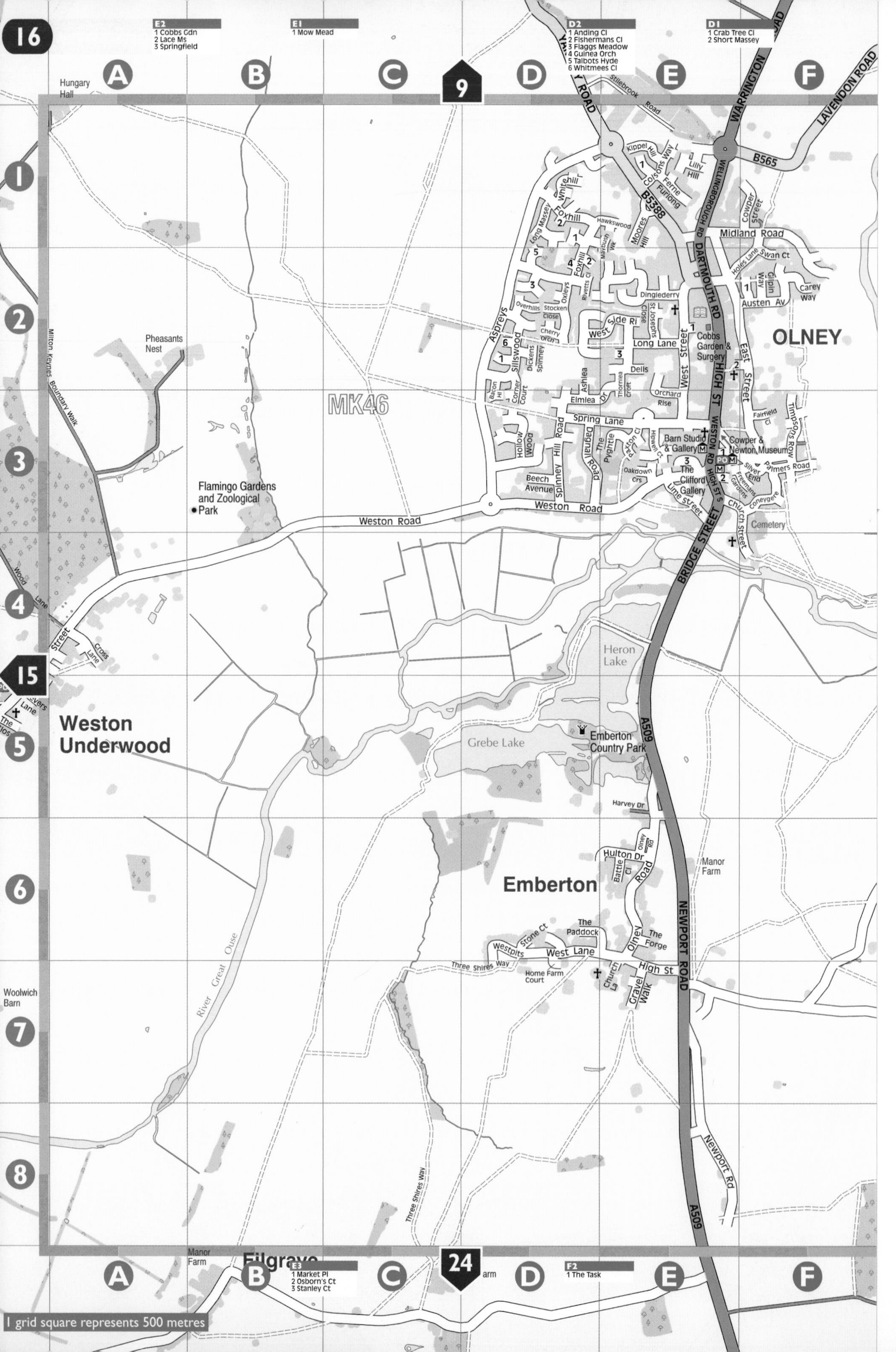
E2
1 Cobbs Gdn
2 Lace Ms
3 Springfield
E1
1 Mow Mead
D2
1 Anding Cl
2 Fishermans Cl
3 Flaggs Meadow
4 Guinea Orch
5 Talbots Hyde
6 Whitmees Cl
D1
1 Crab Tree Cl
2 Short Massey
A
B
C
9
D
E
F
Hungary Hall
1
2
3
4
5
6
7
8
Pheasants Nest
Milton Keynes Boundary Walk
MK46
Flamingo Gardens and Zoological Park
Weston Road
Wood Lane
Street
Cross Lane
15
Weston Underwood
Lane
The Clos
OLNEY
Stilebrook Road
Warrington Road
Lavendon Road
B565
Kippel Hill
Colsons Way
Lilly Hill
Ferne Furlong
Wellingborough Rd
B5388
Whitehill
Foxhill
Long Massey
Hawkswood
Maybush Wk
Moores Hill
Midland Road
Cowper Street
Holes Lane
Swan Ct
Gilpin Way
Carey Way
Austen Av
Dartmouth Rd
Dinglederry
Oxleys
Rivetts Cl
Overhills
Stocken Close
Cherry Orch
West Side Ri
St Josephs Close
Aspreys
Sillswood
Dickens Spinney
Long Lane
West Street
Cobbs Garden & Surgery
High St
East Street
Dells
Ashlea
Thornlea Croft
Orchard Rise
Baxton Hl
Corner Court
Elmlea Dr
Spring Lane
Fairfield Cl
Timpsons Row
Hollow Wood
Hill Road
Dagnall Road
The Pyghtle
Yaxton Cl
Hipwell Ct
Barn Studio & Gallery
Weston Rd
Cowper & Newton Museum
Palmers Road
Silver End
Oakdown Crs
The Clifford Gallery
Freemans Gardens
Coneygere
Beech Avenue
Spinney Hill Road
Lime Street
High St S
Church Street
Cemetery
Bridge Street
Heron Lake
Grebe Lake
Emberton Country Park
A509
Harvey Dr
Olney Rd
Hulton Dr
Battle Cl
Road
Manor Farm
Emberton
Newport Road
The Paddock
Stone Ct
Westpits
West Lane
Olney
The Forge
Three Shires Way
Home Farm Court
Church La
High St
Gravel Walk
Woolwich Barn
River Great Ouse
Newport Rd
Three Shires Way
Manor Farm
Filgrave
E3
1 Market Pl
2 Osborn's Ct
3 Stanley Ct
24
F2
1 The Task
1 grid square represents 500 metres

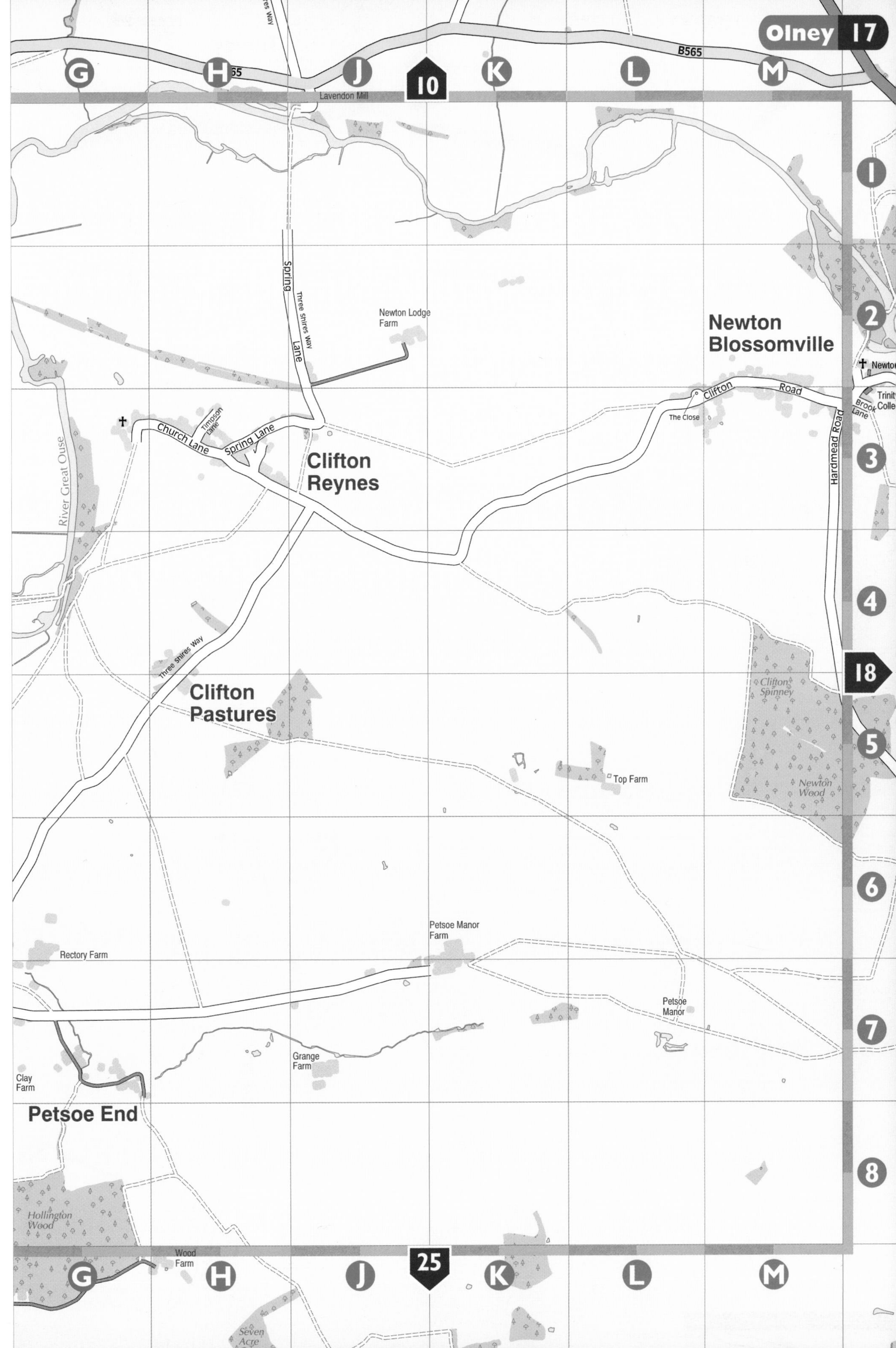
B565
Lavendon Mill
10
G
H
J
K
L
M
1
2
3
4
5
6
7
8
18
25
Spring Lane
Three Shires Way
Newton Lodge Farm
Newton Blossomville
Clifton Road
The Close
Brook Lane
Hardmead Road
Church Lane
Timoson Lane
Spring Lane
Clifton Reynes
River Great Ouse
Clifton Pastures
Clifton Spinney
Newton Wood
Top Farm
Petsoe Manor Farm
Rectory Farm
Petsoe Manor
Grange Farm
Clay Farm
Petsoe End
Hollington Wood
Wood Farm
Seven Acre

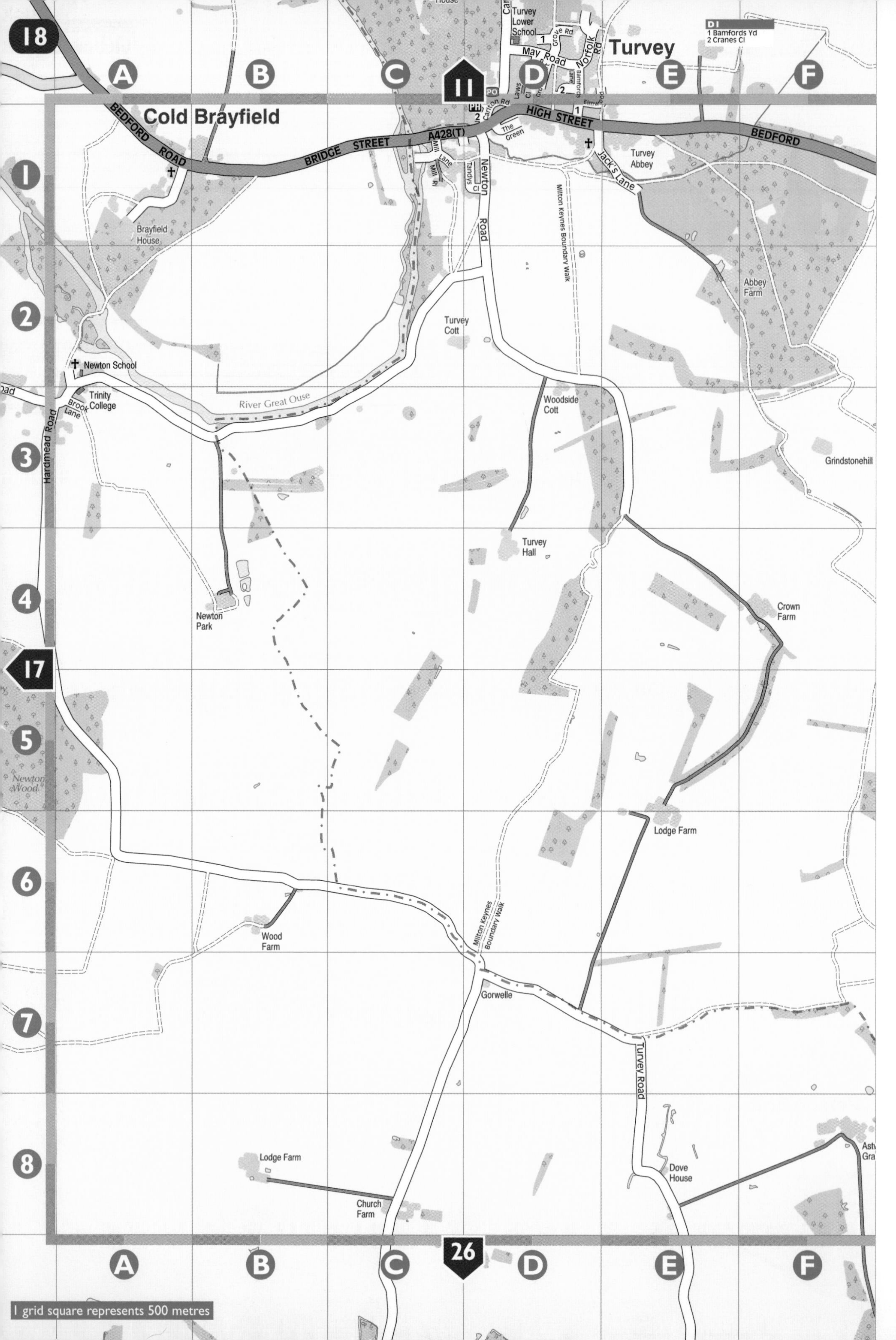

D1
1 Bamfords Yd
2 Cranes Cl
Turvey
Turvey Lower School
Grove Rd
May Road
Norfolk Rd
Bamfords Lane
Laws Cl
Elmwood
11
PO
PH
Carlton Rd
HIGH STREET
The Green
Cold Brayfield
BEDFORD ROAD
BRIDGE STREET
A428(T)
BEDFORD
Mill Lane
Mill Rd
Tandys Cl
Newton Road
Turvey Abbey
Jack's Lane
Milton Keynes Boundary Walk
Brayfield House
Abbey Farm
Turvey Cott
Newton School
Trinity College
Brook Lane
Hardmead Road
River Great Ouse
Woodside Cott
Grindstonehill
Turvey Hall
Newton Park
Crown Farm
17
Newton Wood
Lodge Farm
Wood Farm
Milton Keynes Boundary Walk
Gorwelle
Turvey Road
Lodge Farm
Dove House
Church Farm
26
A B C D E F
1 2 3 4 5 6 7 8
1 grid square represents 500 metres

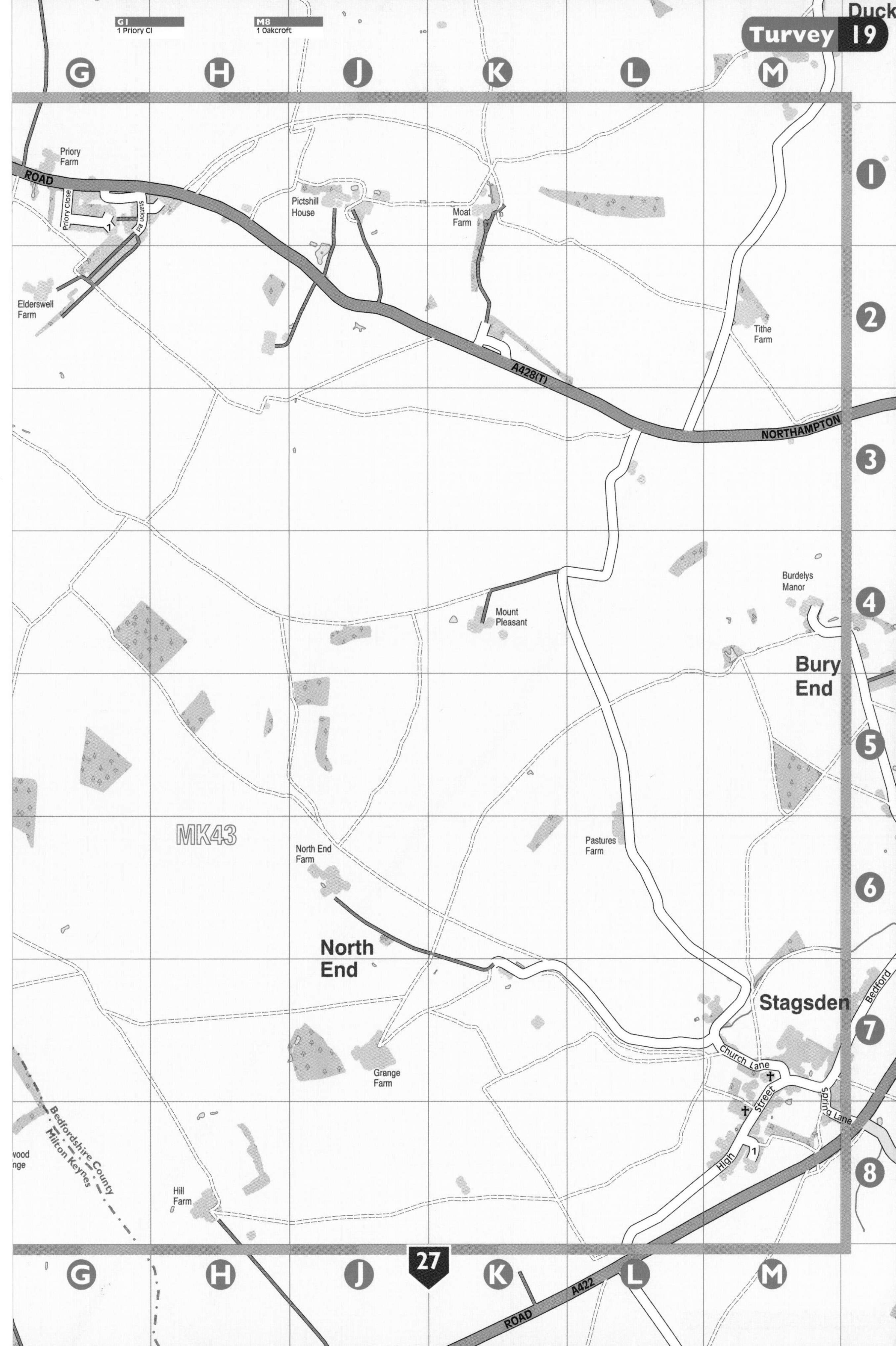
G1
1 Priory Cl
M8
1 Oakcroft
G H J K L M
1 2 3 4 5 6 7 8
Priory Farm
ROAD
Priory Close
Station Rd
Pictshill House
Moat Farm
Elderswell Farm
Tithe Farm
A428(T)
NORTHAMPTON
Burdelys Manor
Mount Pleasant
Bury End
MK43
Pastures Farm
North End Farm
North End
Stagsden
Bedford
Church Lane
Spring Lane
High Street
Grange Farm
Bedfordshire County
Milton Keynes
Hill Farm
ROAD
A422

27

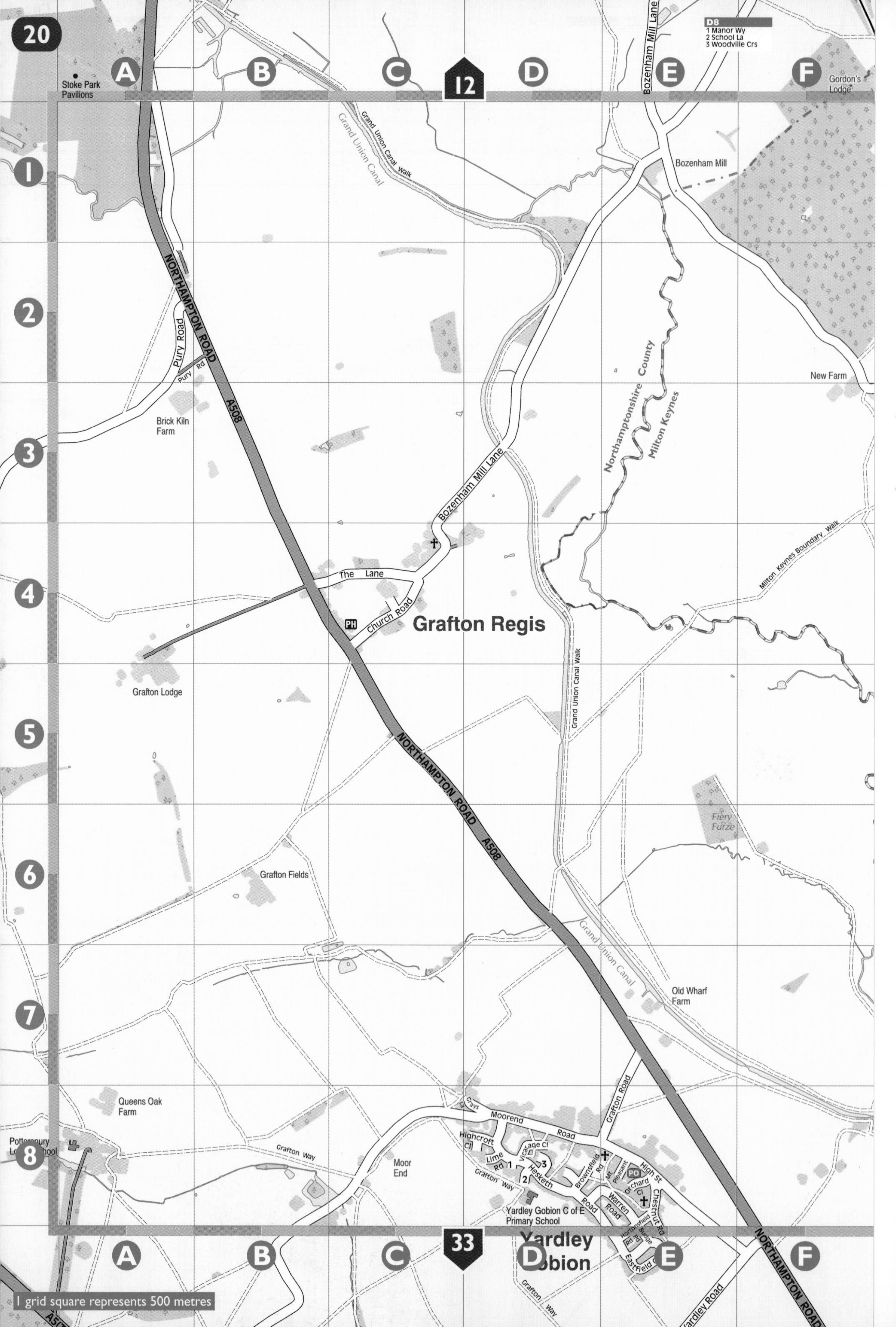

D8
1 Manor Wy
2 School La
3 Woodville Crs
12
33
A
B
C
D
E
F
1
2
3
4
5
6
7
8
Stoke Park Pavilions
Gordon's Lodge
Bozenham Mill Lane
Bozenham Mill
Grand Union Canal Walk
Grand Union Canal
NORTHAMPTON ROAD
A508
Pury Road
Pury Rd
Brick Kiln Farm
New Farm
Northamptonshire County
Milton Keynes
Milton Keynes Boundary Walk
The Lane
Church Road
PH
Grafton Regis
Grafton Lodge
Fiery Furze
Grafton Fields
Old Wharf Farm
Queens Oak Farm
Grafton Road
Grays
Moorend Road
Highcroft Cl
Vicarage Cl
Lime Rd
Hesketh Road
Brownsfield Rd
Mt Pleasant
High St
PO
Orchard Cl
Chestnut Rd
Warren Road
Hortonsfield Rd
Burdock Rd
Eastfield
Grafton Way
Moor End
Yardley Gobion C of E Primary School
Yardley Gobion
Yardley Road
1 grid square represents 500 metres

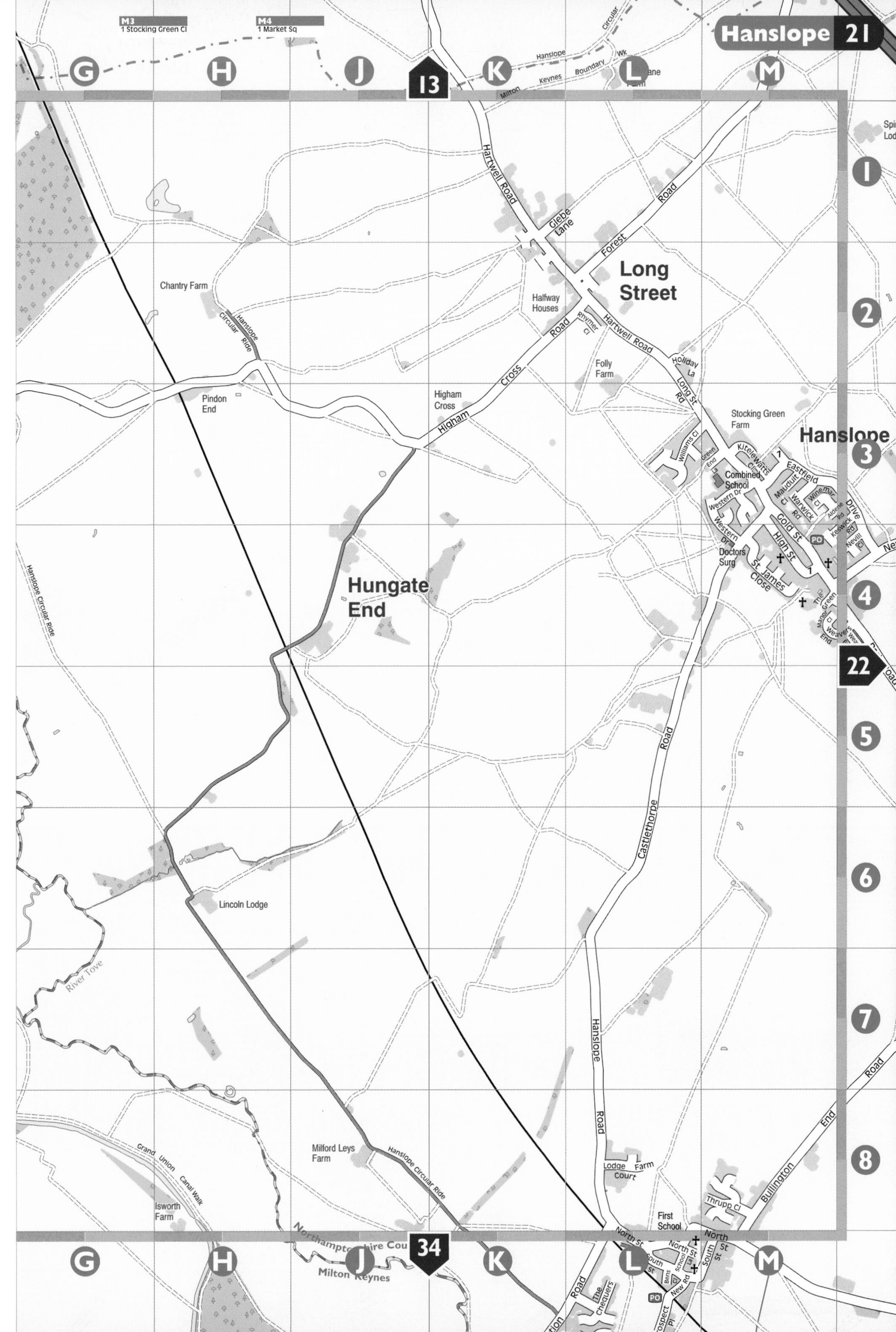
M3
1 Stocking Green Cl
M4
1 Market Sq
13
22
34
Long Street
Hanslope
Hungate End
Chantry Farm
Halfway Houses
Folly Farm
Pindon End
Higham Cross
Stocking Green Farm
Combined School
Doctors Surg
Lincoln Lodge
Milford Leys Farm
Isworth Farm
Lodge Farm
Lodge Court
First School
Hartwell Road
Glebe Lane
Forest Road
Higham Cross Road
Rhymer Cl
Holiday La
Long St Rd
Williams Cl
Green End
Kitelewatts Cl
Eastfield Drive
Mauduit Cl
Winemar Cl
Warwick Rd
Aldene Rd
Keswick Rd
Nevill Cl
Western Dr
Gold St
High St
St James Close
Manor Cl
Weavers End
Castlethorpe Road
Hanslope Road
Bullington End Road
Thrupp Cl
North St
South St
Bens Cl
School La
New Rd
Prospect Pl
The Chequers
Hanslope Circular Ride
Grand Union Canal Walk
River Tove
Milton Keynes Boundary Wk
Northamptonshire Cou
Milton Keynes
PO
G
H
J
K
L
M
1
2
3
4
5
6
7
8

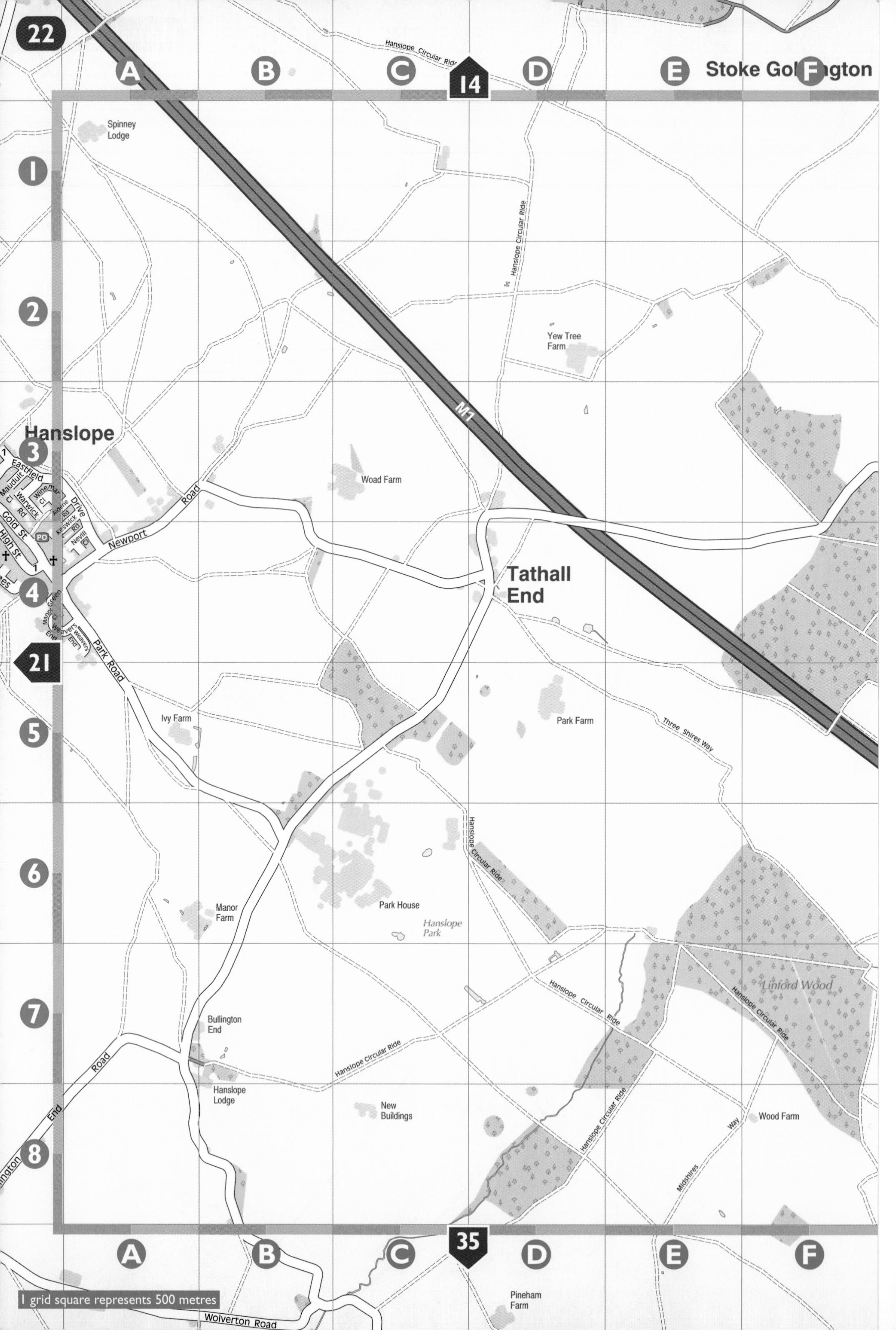
Stoke Goldington
Hanslope Circular Ride
14
Spinney Lodge
M1
Yew Tree Farm
Hanslope
Eastfield
Mauduit Cl
Warwick Rd
Winemar Cl
Aldene
Drive
Keswick Rd
Nevill Cl
Gold St
High St
PO
Newport Road
Woad Farm
Tathall End
Manor Green Cl
Weavers End
Park Road
21
Ivy Farm
Park Farm
Three Shires Way
Hanslope Circular Ride
Park House
Hanslope Park
Manor Farm
Linford Wood
Bullington End
Road
End
Hanslope Lodge
New Buildings
Wood Farm
Way
Midshires
35
Pineham Farm
Wolverton Road
A
B
C
D
E
F
1
2
3
4
5
6
7
8
1 grid square represents 500 metres

G
H
J
15
K
L
M
Ravenstone Mill
Birds La
Westst
PO
Leaside
Baker's Cl
Town End Crs
River Great Ouse
B526
Park Farm
Bunsty Farm
Tyringham
Back Dr
Tyringham Hall
Tyringham Health Clinic
Fences Lane
Three Shires Way
Gayhurst Wood
Gayhurst
24
Gayhurst House
Quarry Hall Farm
Dairy Farm
Three Shires Way
Hoo Wood
Mill Farm
River Great Ouse
Kickle's Farm
M1
Hanslope Circular Ride
Flora Thompson Drive
Larkin Cl
Heaney Cl
Little Linford
36
Elliot Cl
Westbury Lane
Shakespeare Cl
Carroll Cl
Sitwell Cl
Spark Wy
Christie Cl
Herriot Cl
Swift Cl
1
2
3
4
5
6
7
8

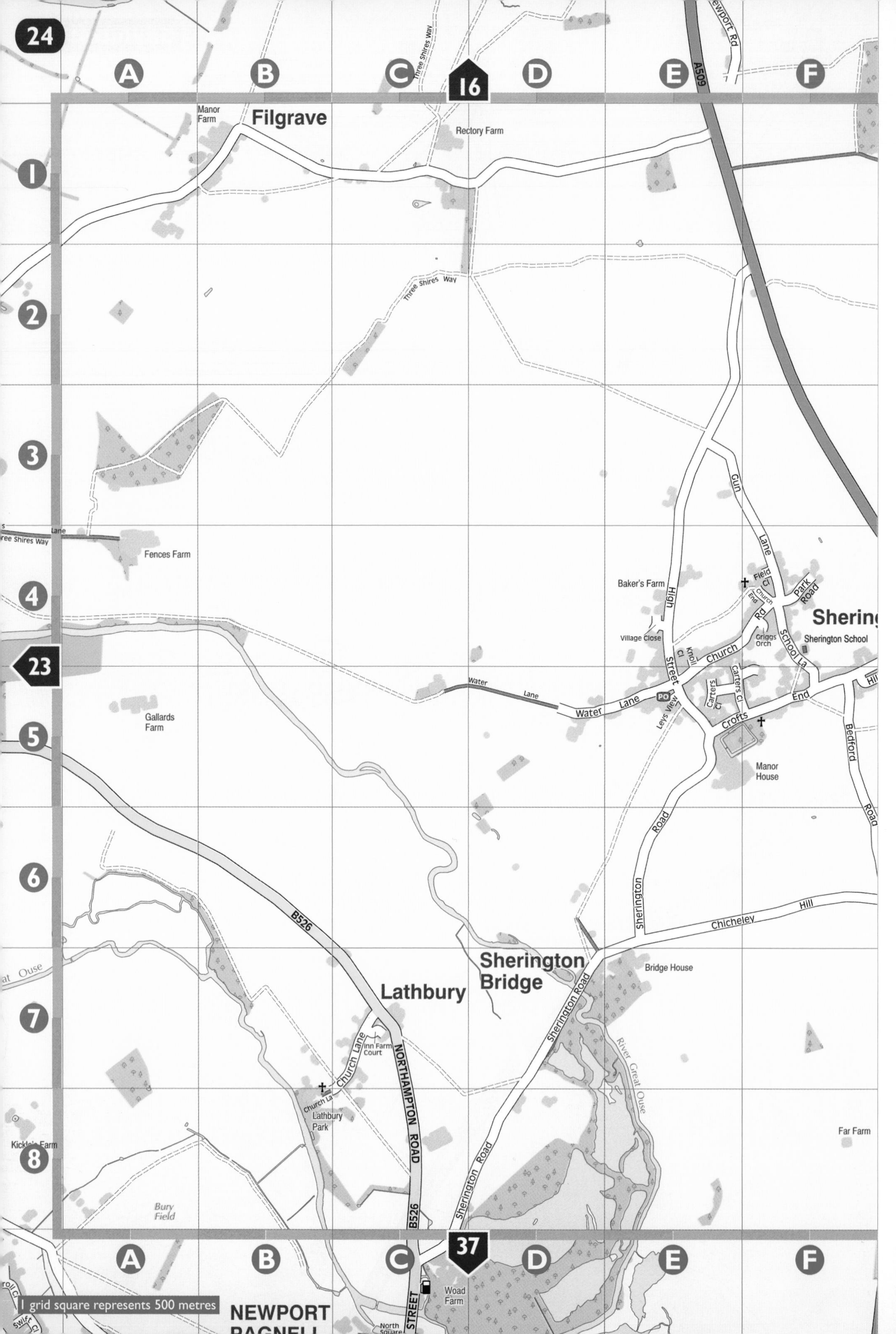
16
Filgrave
Manor Farm
Rectory Farm
Three Shires Way
A509
Newport Rd
Fences Farm
Baker's Farm
High Street
Gun Lane
Field Cl
Church End
Park Road
Sherin
Sherington School
Village Close
Knoll Cl
Church Rd
Griggs Orch
School La
Carters Cl
Water Lane
PO
Leys View
Crofts End
Bedford Road
Manor House
Gallards Farm
23
Sherington Road
Chicheley Hill
B526
Sherington Bridge
Lathbury
Bridge House
River Great Ouse
Church Lane
Inn Farm Court
NORTHAMPTON ROAD
Church La
Lathbury Park
Kickle's Farm
Far Farm
Bury Field
37
Woad Farm
NEWPORT PAGNELL
STREET
North Square
1 grid square represents 500 metres

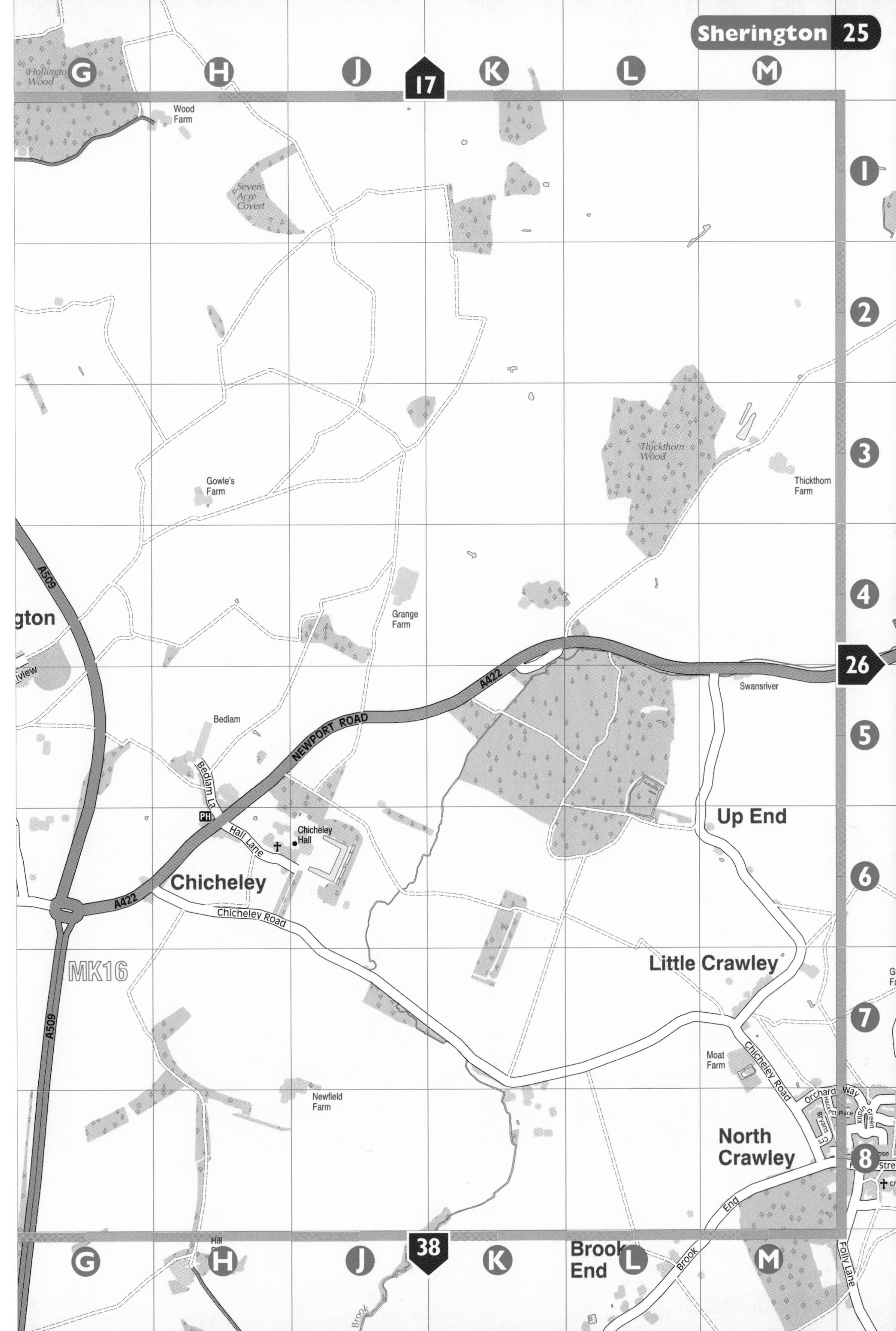

G
H
J
17
K
L
M
Hollington Wood
Wood Farm
Seven Acre Covert
1
2
3
4
5
6
7
8
Thickthorn Wood
Thickthorn Farm
Gowle's Farm
A509
Grange Farm
gton
lview
26
A422
NEWPORT ROAD
Swansriver
Bedlam
Bedlam La
PH
Hall Lane
Chicheley Hall
Up End
Chicheley
A422
Chicheley Road
MK16
Little Crawley
A509
Moat Farm
Chicheley Road
Orchard Way
Hackett Place
Bryans Cl
Kilpin Green
North Crawley
Newfield Farm
Hill
38
Brook End
Brook End
Folly Lane
Brook

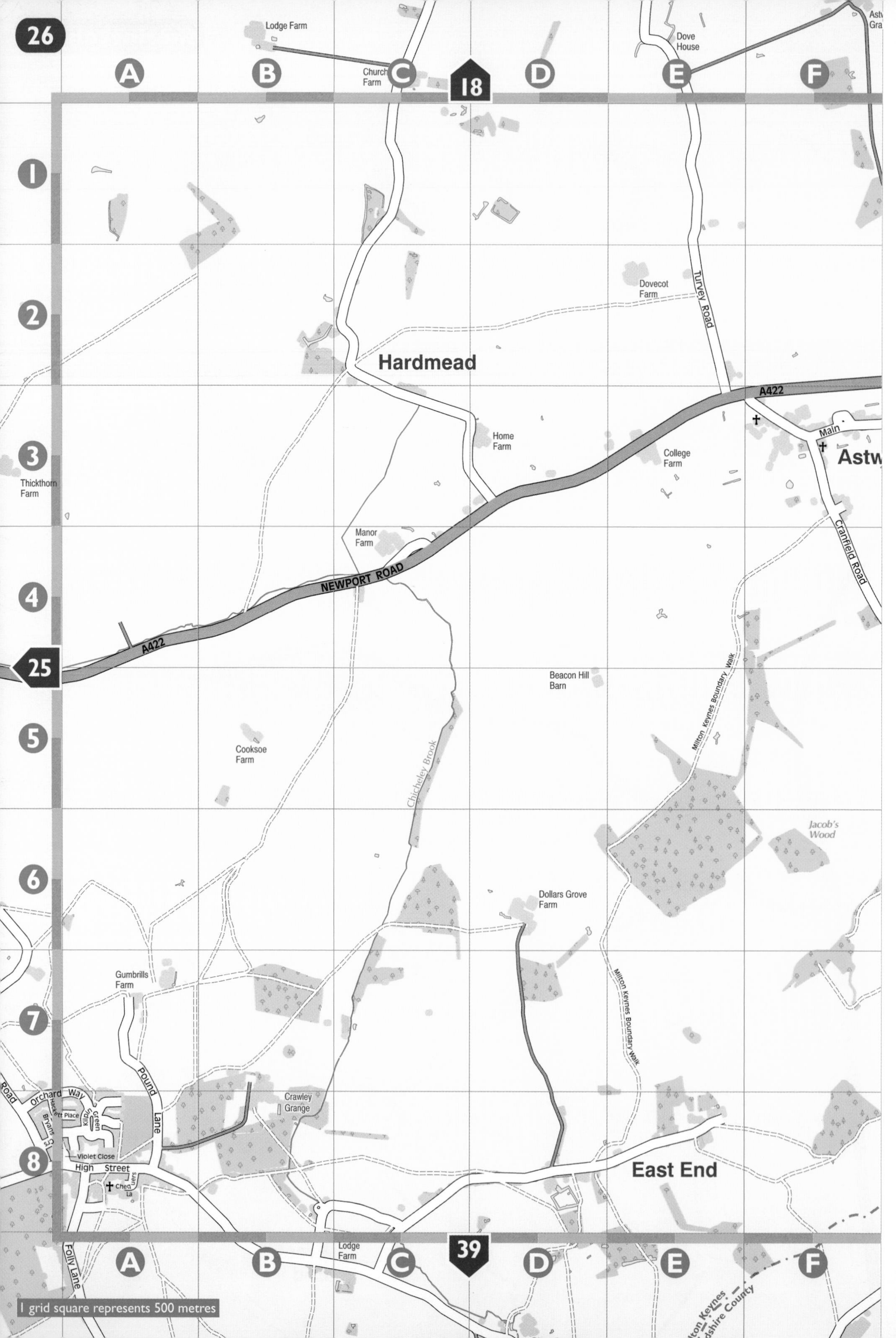


1 grid square represents 500 metres

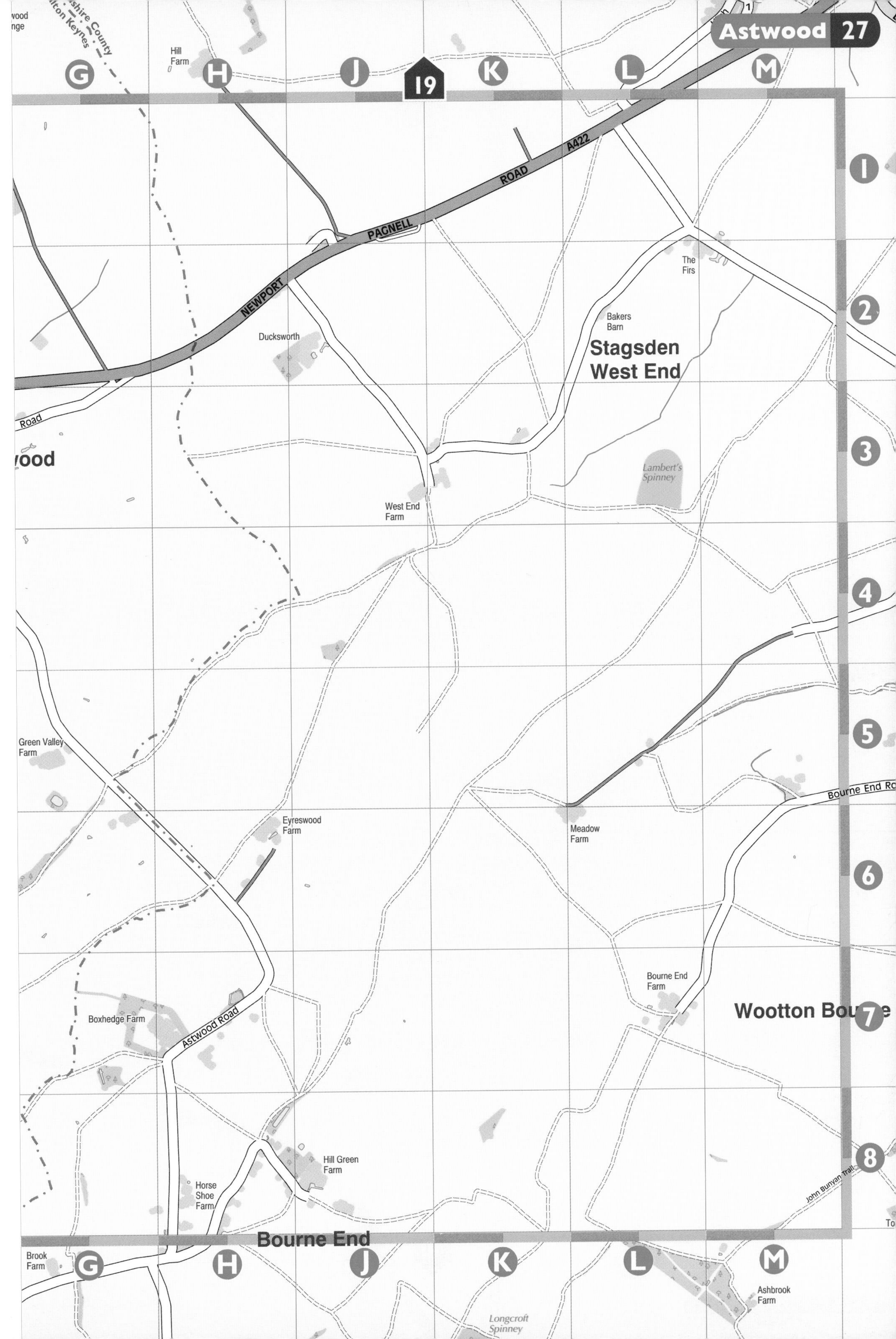

19
G
H
J
K
L
M
1
2
3
4
5
6
7
8
Hill Farm
A422
ROAD
PAGNELL
NEWPORT
Road
Duckswort
The Firs
Bakers Barn
Stagsden West End
Lambert's Spinney
West End Farm
Green Valley Farm
Eyreswood Farm
Meadow Farm
Bourne End Road
Bourne End Farm
Wootton Bourne
Boxhedge Farm
Astwood Road
Hill Green Farm
Horse Shoe Farm
John Bunyan Trail
Bourne End
Brook Farm
Ashbrook Farm
Longcroft Spinney

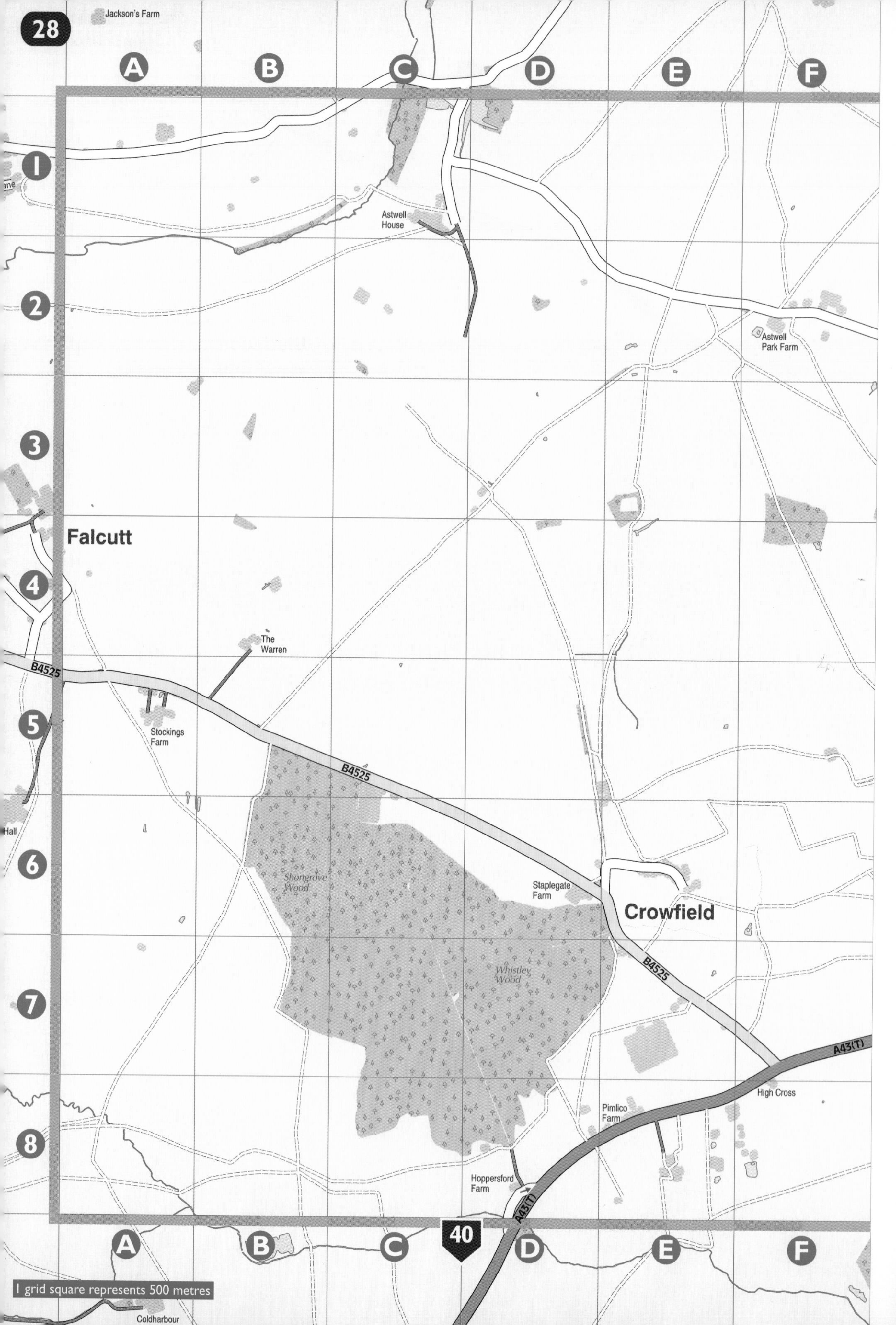
Jackson's Farm
A
B
C
D
E
F
1
2
3
4
5
6
7
8
Astwell House
Astwell Park Farm
Falcutt
The Warren
B4525
Stockings Farm
B4525
Hall
Shortgrove Wood
Staplegate Farm
Crowfield
B4525
Whistley Wood
A43(T)
High Cross
Pimlico Farm
Hoppersford Farm
A43(T)
A
B
C
40
D
E
F
1 grid square represents 500 metres
Coldharbour

G
H
J
K
L
M
1
2
3
4
5
6
7
8
30
41
Wappenham Lodge Farm
Monk's Wood
Blackmire's Farm
Priesthaywood Farm
Hazelborough Wood
Wild House Farm
Wappenham Road
Old Park Farm
A43(T)
Primrose Hill Farm
Burnham Place
Church End
The Hill
Syresham
Kingshill Farm
Brackley Hatch
Broad St
Bell Lane
Magdalen Cl
Malt La
High St
The Pound
PO
Syresham C of E Primary School
Abbey Road
Blenheim Place
MAIN ROAD
Abbey Way House
Earl's Wood
Buttockspire Wood
Northamptonshire County
Buckinghamshire County
Westbury

29

42

1 grid square represents 500 metres

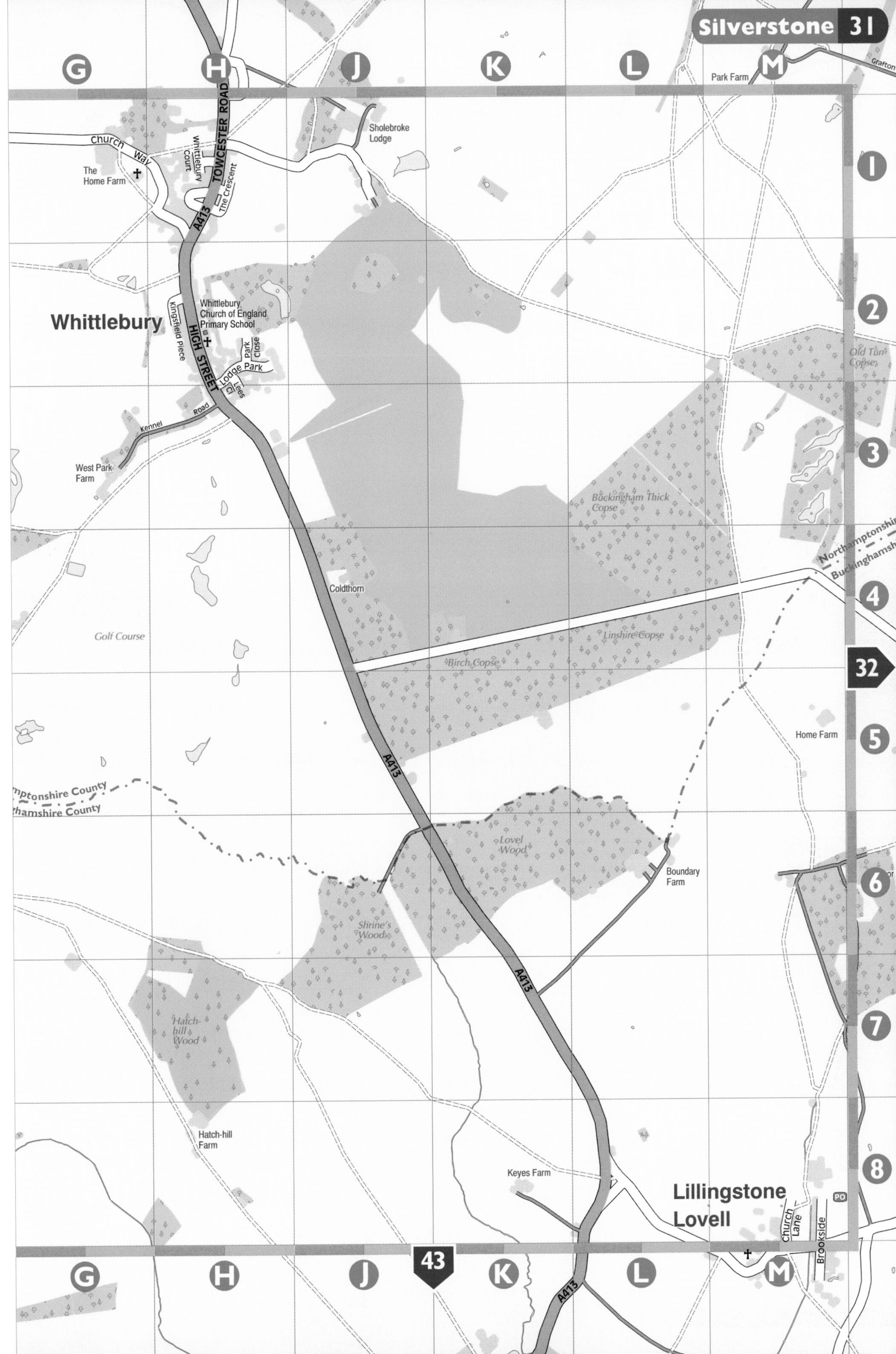

G
H
J
K
L
M
Grafton W
Park Farm
TOWCESTER ROAD
Sholebroke Lodge
Church Way
Whittlebury Court
The Crescent
The Home Farm
A413
1
Whittlebury
Whittlebury Church of England Primary School
Kingsfield Piece
HIGH STREET
Park Close
Lodge Park
Lees Cl
2
Old Tun Copse
Kennel Road
West Park Farm
3
Buckingham Thick Copse
Northamptonshire
Buckinghamshire
Coldthorn
4
Golf Course
Linshire Copse
Birch Copse
32
Home Farm
5
mptonshire County
hamshire County
Lovel Wood
Boundary Farm
6
Shrine's Wood
7
Hatch-bill Wood
Hatch-hill Farm
8
Keyes Farm
Lillingstone Lovell
PO
Church Lane
Brookside
43

32
Potterspury Lodge School
Grafton Way
Bradlem Pond
King's Copse
Bear's Copse
Lady Copse
Waterslade Copse
Old Tun Copse
Say's Copse
Whittlewood Forest
Kennels Drive
Wakefield Farm
Northamptonshire County
Buckinghamshire County
Main Drive
Wakefield Lodge
31
Wakefield Lawn
Briary Wood
Redmoor Copse
Manor House
Briary Wood Farm
Deanshanger Drive
East Ashalls Copse
Forest Farm
Bradley Fields Farm
Wicken Wood
Hurst Farm
PO
Brookside
44
Leckhampstead Wood
1 grid square represents 500 metres

J3
1 Brownswood Dr
2 Elmfield Cl
Grafton Way
Moor End
20
Highcroft Cl
Lime Rd
Vicarage Cl
Hesketh
Brownsfield Rd
Mt Pleasant
High St
Orchard Cl
Warren Road
Chestnut Rd
Hortonsfield Rd
Budge Rd
Eastfield Crs
Yardley Gobion C of E Primary School
Yardley Gobion
Grafton Way
Yardley Road
NORTHAMPTON ROAD A508
Yardley Road
Beech House Farm
Beech House Drive
Cheley Well
Assart Farm
Towcester Drive
Blackwell End
The Orch
Sanders Lane
Meadow View
Woods Lane
Church Lane
High Street
Mays Way
John Hellins Primary School
Homestead Wy
North Wy
Chettle Pl
Church End
Poundfield Road
Furtho La
Grafton Close
Grafton Way
Manor Farm
Main Drive
Potterspury
Potterspury House
A5(T)
34
Cherrytree Lodge
Knotwo Farm
Green Farm
Grange Farm
Shrobb Lodge Farm
Puxley
A422
Old Stratford
Hanger Lodge
County Primary School
Dickens Drive
Folly Fields Farm
45
Glebe
Road
Hayes Road
Chantry Farm
G
H
J
K
L
M
1
2
3
4
5
6
7
8

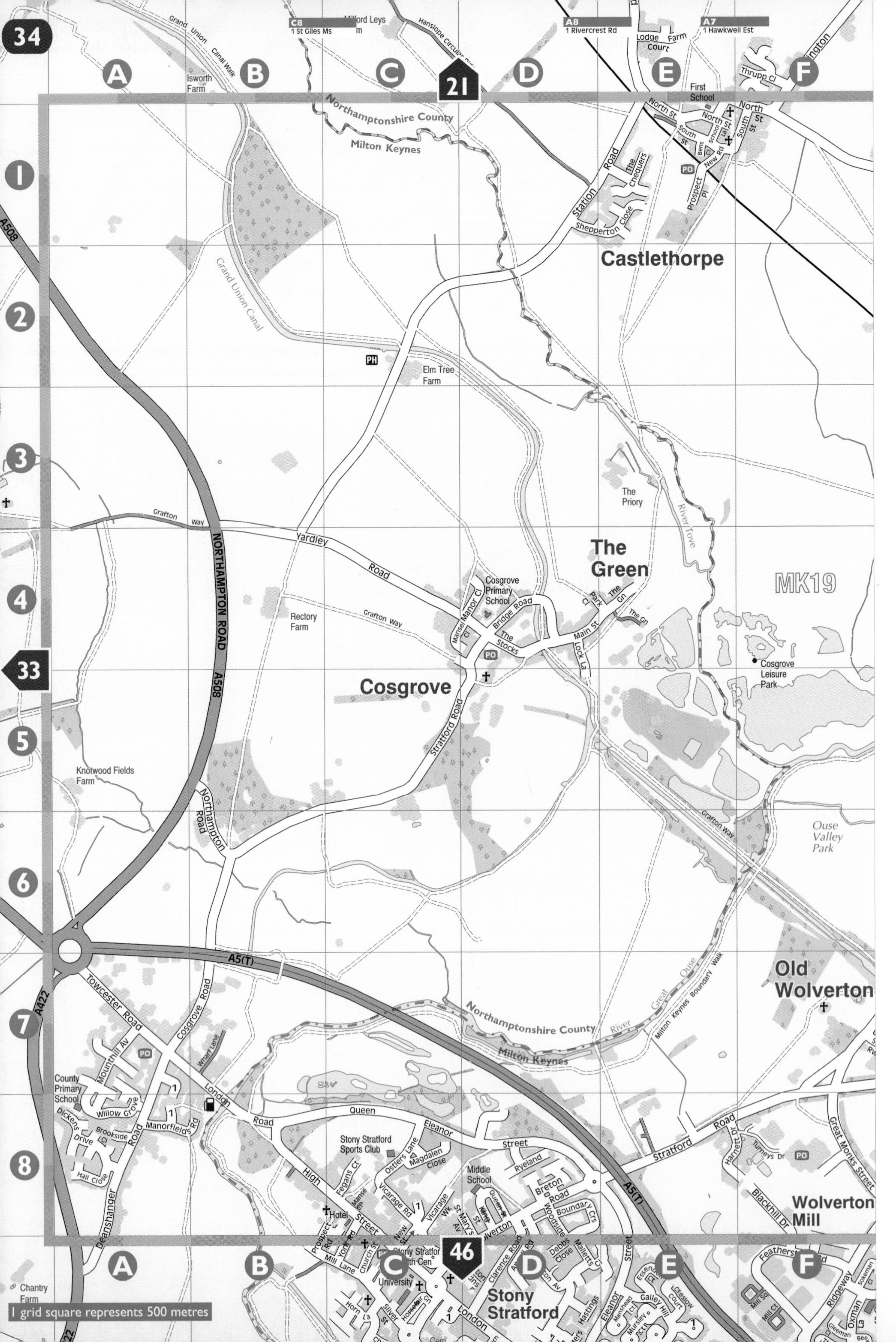
C8 1 St Giles Ms
A8 1 Rivercrest Rd
A7 1 Hawkwell Est
21
33
46
Castlethorpe
The Green
Cosgrove
MK19
Old Wolverton
Wolverton Mill
Stony Stratford
Northamptonshire County
Milton Keynes
Grand Union Canal
Isworth Farm
Elm Tree Farm
The Priory
River Tove
Cosgrove Primary School
Rectory Farm
Cosgrove Leisure Park
Ouse Valley Park
Knotwood Fields Farm
NORTHAMPTON ROAD A508
Grafton Way
Yardley Road
Station Road
Stratford Road
A5(T)
Towcester Road
Cosgrove Road
London Road
Queen Eleanor Street
High Street
Stony Stratford Sports Club
Middle School
County Primary School
Milton Keynes Boundary Walk
River Great Ouse
Chantry Farm
1 grid square represents 500 metres

J7
1 Radcliffe St
L7
1 Gerard Cl
2 Glyn St
3 School St
L8
1 Van Der Bilt Ct
22
36
47
M8
1 Chancery Cl
M7
1 Evelyn Pl
2 Heydon Ct
3 North St
M6
1 Earls Willow
2 Thompson St
Wolverton Road
Pineham Farm
Hansiope Circular Ride
Pike's Farm
Field House
Lodge Farm Industrial Estate
Lodge Farm
High Street
Haversham
Haversham Manor
Chalmers Av
Rowan Dr
Keppel Avenue
Brookfield Road
Manor Dr
The Crescent
Haversham Road
River Great Ouse
Manor Farm
Colts Holm Road
Dickens Rd
Old Wolverton Road
Bridgeturn Avenue
Grafton St
New Bradwell
Newport Road
Canons Road
Dean's Road
Grand Union Canal Walk
Wolverton Station
Grafton Street
Stonebridge
Newport Rd
Caledonian Rd
Wallace St
Wood St
Qu Anne St
Bounty St
School House
Combined Sch
Church St
High St
Permayne
New Bradwell Mosque
Bridgeway
Harwood St
Chipperfield Rd
Pepper Hill County First School
Midshires Way
Longville
Trinity Rd
Carlton Rd
The Meacham Clinic
N Buckinghamshire Wy
Stratford Road
Cambridge St
Church St
Creed St
St Georges Wy
McConnell Drive
Buckingham St
Radcliffe St
Aylesbury St
MK12
Radcliffe School
Anson Road
Jersey Road
Peel Rd
Windsor Street
Oxford St
Green Lane
Moon St
Victoria Street
Stacey Av
Bushfield County Middle School
Wyvern County First School
Eton Crs
Western Road
Woburn Av
Furze Wy
Cemetery
Wolverton
Osbourne St
Wolverton Sports Club
Marina Drive
Nightingale Crs
Mill La
Windmill
Bradwell Road
Bradville
Kingsfold
Althorpe Crescent
Stanton Av
Fingle Dr
Grand Union Canal WK
Blue Bridge
Blackwood Crs
Culbertson Lane
Mortons Fk
Gardner Ct
Vienna Gv
Wheelers Lane
Chalfont Cl
Amos Ct
Parker Cl
Sunbury Cl
Mathiesen Rd
Abbey Way
Haltonchesters
Bishopstone
Withington
Harvester
Monks Way
Ardwell Lane
Field La
Combined School
Frank Atter Croft
Middle School
Wolverton Hlth Centre & Day Hosp
Gloucester Rd
Southern Way
St John's Crs
Myrtle Bank
Bancroft Park
Bancroft
Spoonley Wd
Willowford
MK13
A422
Lundholme
Hill
Hansiope Ct

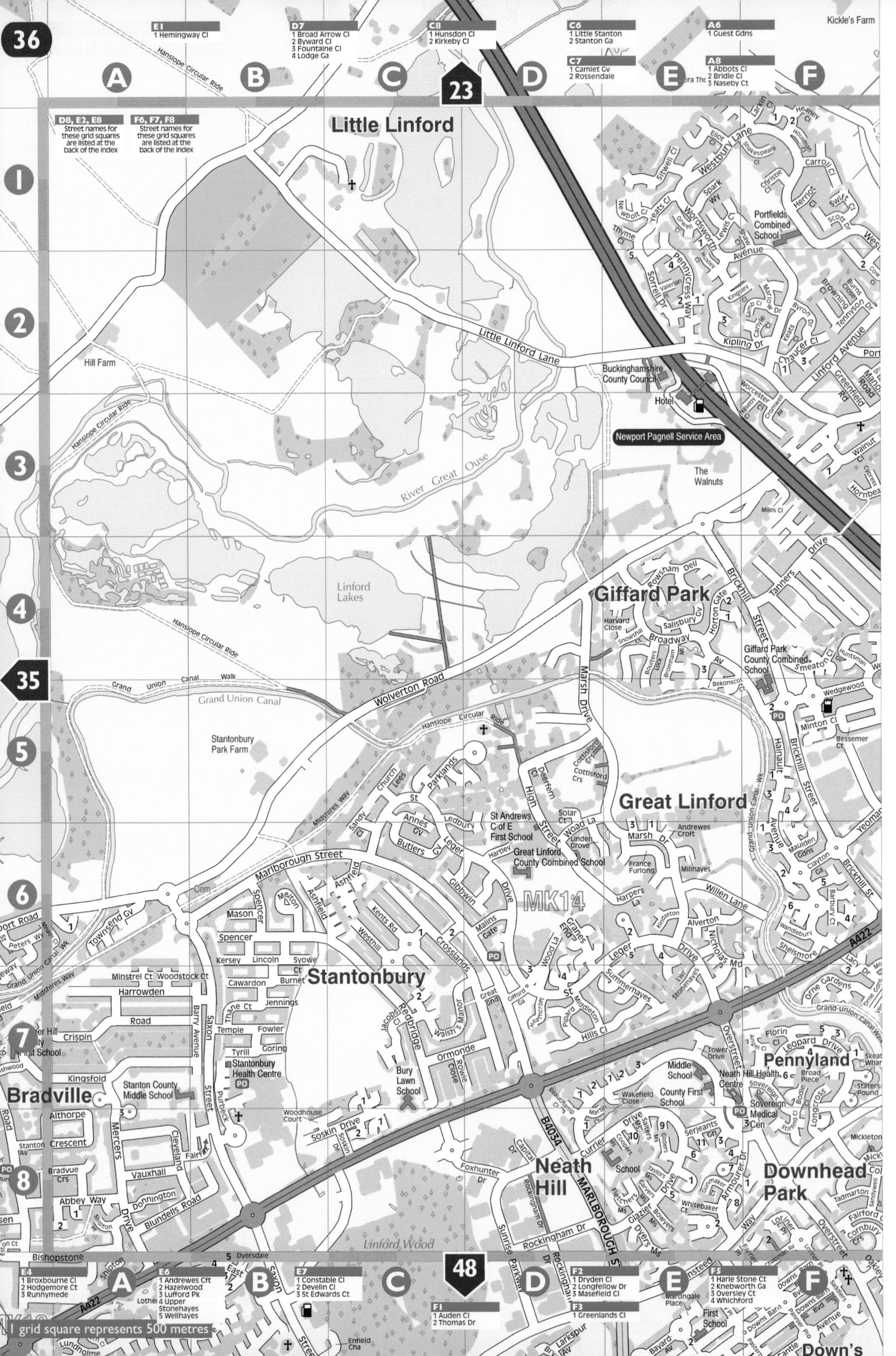
E1
1 Hemingway Cl
D7
1 Broad Arrow Cl
2 Byward Cl
3 Fountaine Cl
4 Lodge Ga
C8
1 Hunsdon Cl
2 Kirkeby Cl
C6
1 Little Stanton
2 Stanton Ga
C7
1 Camlet Gv
2 Rossendale
A6
1 Guest Gdns
A8
1 Abbots Cl
2 Bridle Cl
3 Naseby Ct
Kickle's Farm
23
D8, E2, E8
Street names for these grid squares are listed at the back of the index
F6, F7, F8
Street names for these grid squares are listed at the back of the index
Little Linford
Little Linford Lane
Hill Farm
Hanslope Circular Ride
River Great Ouse
Linford Lakes
Buckinghamshire County Council
Hotel
Newport Pagnell Service Area
The Walnuts
Portfields Combined School
Giffard Park
Giffard Park County Combined School
35
Grand Union Canal
Grand Union Canal Walk
Wolverton Road
Stantonbury Park Farm
Great Linford
St Andrews C of E First School
Great Linford County Combined School
MK14
Marlborough Street
Stantonbury
Stantonbury Health Centre
Stanton County Middle School
Bury Lawn School
Bradville
Middle School
County First School
Neath Hill Health Centre
Pennyland
Sovereign Medical Cen
Neath Hill
Downhead Park
Linford Wood
B4034
MARLBOROUGH ST
A422
48
E4
1 Broxbourne Cl
2 Hodgemore Ct
3 Runnymede
E6
1 Andrewes Cft
2 Hazelwood
3 Lufford Pk
4 Upper Stonehayes
5 Wellhayes
E7
1 Constable Cl
2 Develin Cl
3 St Edwards Ct
F1
1 Auden Cl
2 Thomas Dr
F2
1 Dryden Cl
2 Longfellow Dr
3 Masefield Cl
F3
1 Greenlands Cl
F5
1 Harle Stone Ct
2 Knebworth Ga
3 Oversley Ct
4 Whichford
1 grid square represents 500 metres

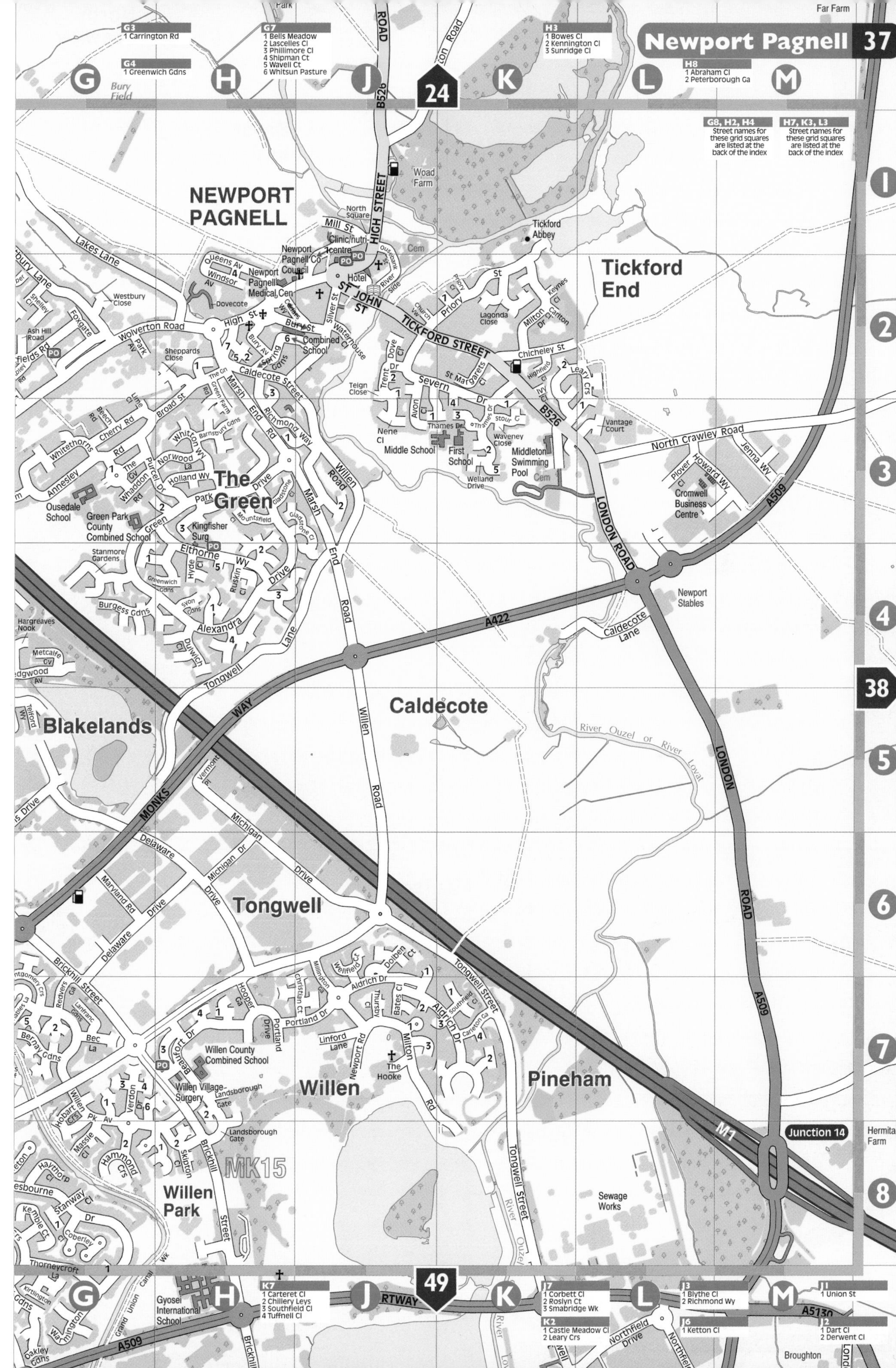
G3
1 Carrington Rd
G4
1 Greenwich Gdns
G7
1 Bells Meadow
2 Lascelles Cl
3 Phillimore Cl
4 Shipman Ct
5 Wavell Ct
6 Whitsun Pasture
H3
1 Bowes Cl
2 Kennington Cl
3 Sunridge Cl
H8
1 Abraham Cl
2 Peterborough Ga
G8, H2, H4
Street names for these grid squares are listed at the back of the index
H7, K3, L3
Street names for these grid squares are listed at the back of the index
Far Farm
24
38
49
G
H
J
K
L
M
1
2
3
4
5
6
7
8
NEWPORT PAGNELL
Tickford End
The Green
Blakelands
Caldecote
Tongwell
Willen
Pineham
Willen Park
MK15
Bury Field
Woad Farm
Tickford Abbey
North Square
Mill St
High Street
B526
Newport Pagnell Co Council
Newport Pagnell Medical Cen
Clinic/nutri-centre
Hotel
St John St
Tickford Street
Wolverton Road
Lakes Lane
Westbury Close
Dovecote
Queens Av
Windsor Av
Sheppards Close
Caldecote Street
Combined School
Waterhouse Cl
Silver St
Bury St
Bury Av
Spring Gdns
Marsh End Rd
Richmond Way
Willen Road
Marsh End Road
Broad St
Lime Cl
Beech Rd
Cherry Rd
Whitethorns
Annesley Rd
Ousedale School
Green Park County Combined School
Kingfisher Surg
Elthorne Wy
Hyde Cl
Ruskin Cl
Gladstone Cl
Mountsfield Cl
Stanmore Gardens
Greenwich Gdns
Burgess Gdns
Syon Gdns
Alexandra Drive
Dulwich Cl
Tongwell Lane
Hargreaves Nook
Metcalfe Gv
Edgwood Av
Telford Wy
Ash Hill Road
Foxgate
Shelley Cl
Park Av
Teign Close
Trent Dr
Dove Cl
Severn Dr
St Margarets Cl
Avon Cl
Thames Dr
Nene Cl
Middle School
First School
Waveney Close
Stour Cl
Welland Drive
Middleton Swimming Pool
Cem
Church Vw
Priory St
Lagonda Close
Milton Dr
Carlton Cl
Keynes Cl
Chicheley St
Highfield
Leary Crs
Ivy Cl
Vantage Court
North Crawley Road
Jenna Wy
Howard Wy
Plover Cl
Cromwell Business Centre
A509
London Road
Newport Stables
Caldecote Lane
A422
Monks Way
River Ouzel or River Lovat
Vermont Pl
Michigan Drive
Michigan Dr
Delaware Drive
Maryland Rd
Brickhill Street
Tongwell Street
Dolben Ct
Wellfield Ct
Aldrich Dr
Millington Ga
Christian Ct
Hooper Ga
Portland Drive
Portland Dr
Thursby Cl
Bates Cl
Southfield Cl
Carleton Ga
Linford Lane
Newport Rd
Milton Rd
The Hooke
Beaufort Dr
Willen County Combined School
Willen Village Surgery
Landsborough Gate
Bec La
Redvers Ga
Lanfranc Gdns
Bernay Gdns
Willen Pk Av
Hobart Crs
Verdon Dr
Massie Cl
Hammond Crs
Skipton Cl
Haythorp Cl
Stanway Cl
Kemble Ct
Coberley Cl
Thorneycroft La
Kirtlington
Warmington Gdns
Oakley Gdns
Grand Union Canal Wk
Gyosei International School
A509
Brickhill
Sewage Works
River Ouzel
Junction 14
M1
Hermitage Farm
K7
1 Carteret Cl
2 Chillery Leys
3 Southfield Cl
4 Tuffnell Cl
J7
1 Corbett Cl
2 Roslyn Ct
3 Smabridge Wk
K2
1 Castle Meadow Cl
2 Leary Crs
J3
1 Blythe Cl
2 Richmond Wy
J6
1 Ketton Cl
J1
1 Union St
J2
1 Dart Cl
2 Derwent Cl
A5130
Northfield Drive
Broughton

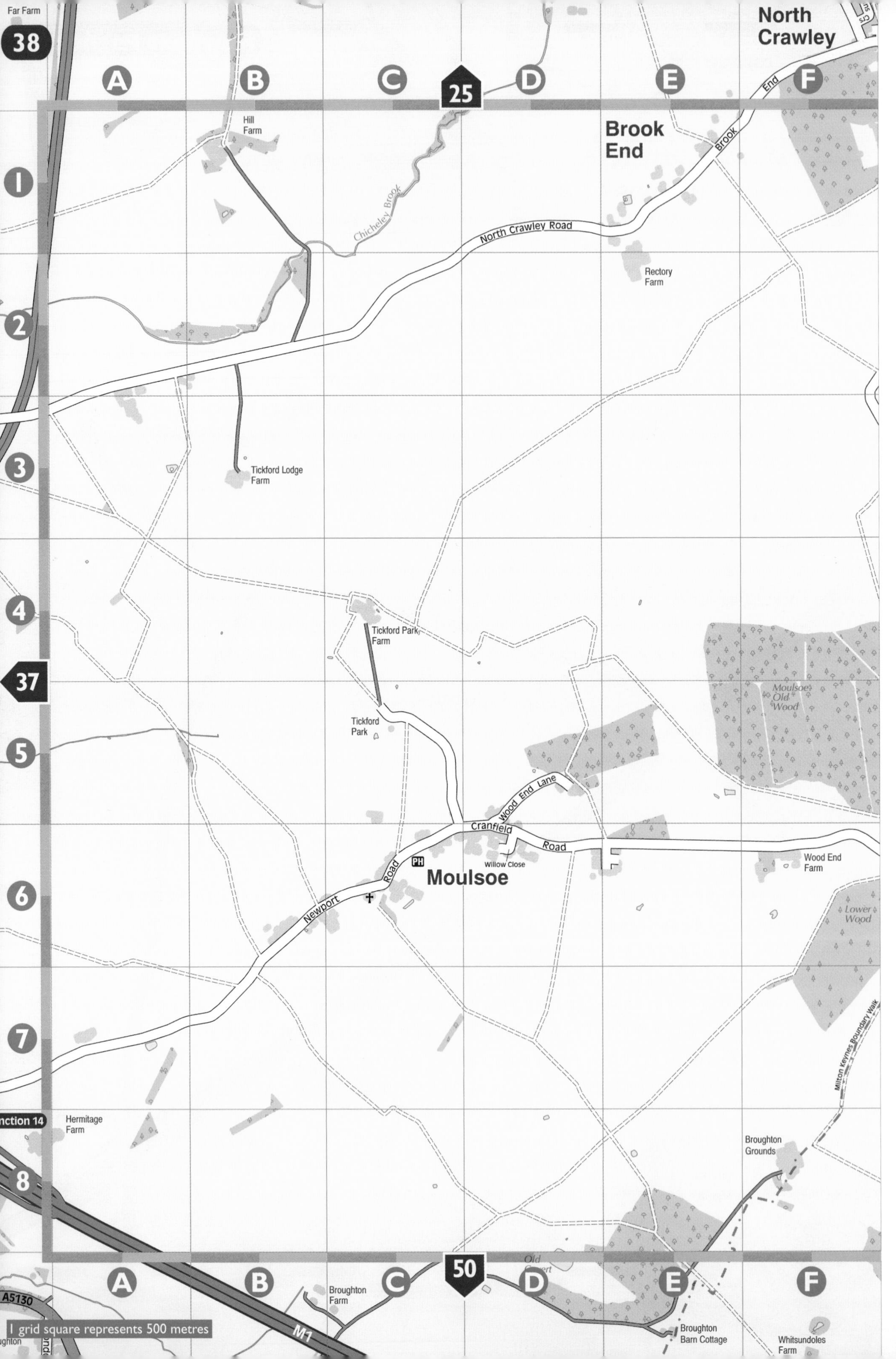

Far Farm
38
North Crawley
A
B
C
25
D
E
F
Brook End
Hill Farm
Brook End
Chicheley Brook
North Crawley Road
Rectory Farm
Tickford Lodge Farm
Tickford Park Farm
37
Tickford Park
Moulsoe Old Wood
Wood End Lane
Cranfield Road
Willow Close
Newport Road
PH
Moulsoe
Wood End Farm
Lower Wood
Milton Keynes Boundary Walk
Junction 14
Hermitage Farm
Broughton Grounds
50
Broughton Farm
A5130
M1
Broughton Barn Cottage
Whitsundoles Farm
1 grid square represents 500 metres
1
2
3
4
5
6
7
8

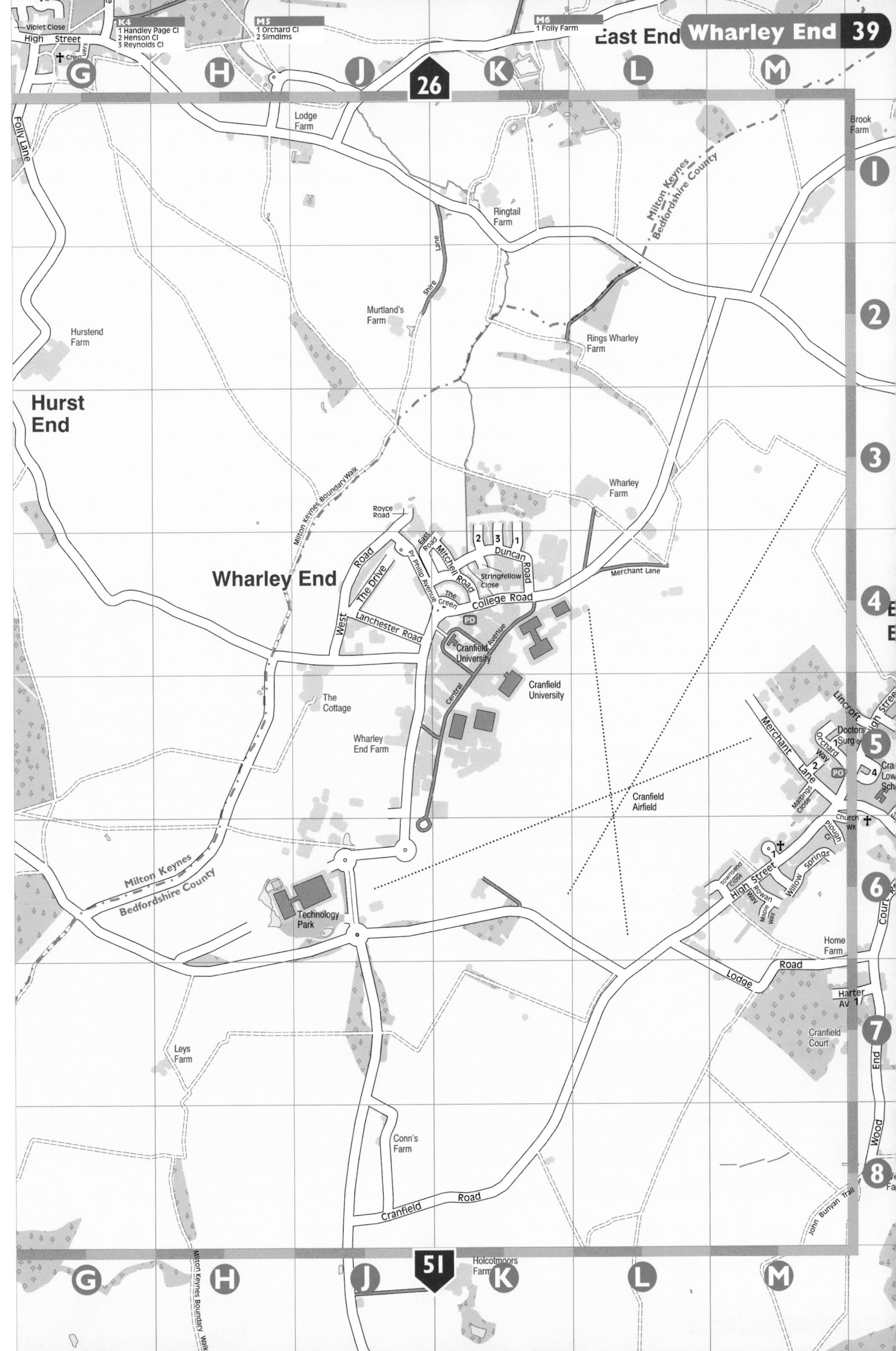

East End
K4
1 Handley Page Cl
2 Henson Cl
3 Reynolds Cl
M5
1 Orchard Cl
2 Simdims
M6
1 Folly Farm
Violet Close
High Street
26
51
Folly Lane
Lodge Farm
Brook Farm
Milton Keynes Bedfordshire County
Ringtail Farm
Shire Lane
Murtland's Farm
Hurstend Farm
Rings Whharley Farm
Hurst End
Wharley Farm
Milton Keynes Boundary Walk
Royce Road
Wharley End
East Road
Mitchell Road
Duncan Road
Stringfellow Close
Merchant Lane
West Road
The Drive
Pr Philip Avenue
The Green
College Road
Lanchester Road
PO
Cranfield University
Avenue
Central
The Cottage
Wharley End Farm
Cranfield Airfield
Merchant Lane
Orchard Way
Maltings Close
Lincroft
Doctors Surg
Church Wk
Plough Cl
Townsend Close
High Street
Rowan Way
Maple Way
Willow Springs
Milton Keynes Bedfordshire County
Technology Park
Home Farm
Lodge Road
Harter Av
Cranfield Court
Leys Farm
Conn's Farm
Cranfield Road
End
Wood
John Bunyan Trail
Holcotmoors Farm
Milton Keynes Boundary Walk

28
A
B
C
D
E
F
1
2
3
4
5
6
7
8
Farm
Hoppersford Farm
Coldharbour Farm
A43(T)
The Avenue
Farrer Close
PO
Chapel Lane
Mill
Road
Whitfield
Dropshort Farm
Northamptonshire County
Buckinghamshire County
Turweston Airfield
Road
Turweston
Oatleys Hall
Westbury Circular Ride
Main Street
Chapel La
Westbury Circular Ride
Oatleys Farm
Mill La
A422
52
Grovehill Farm
Road
1 grid square represents 500 metres

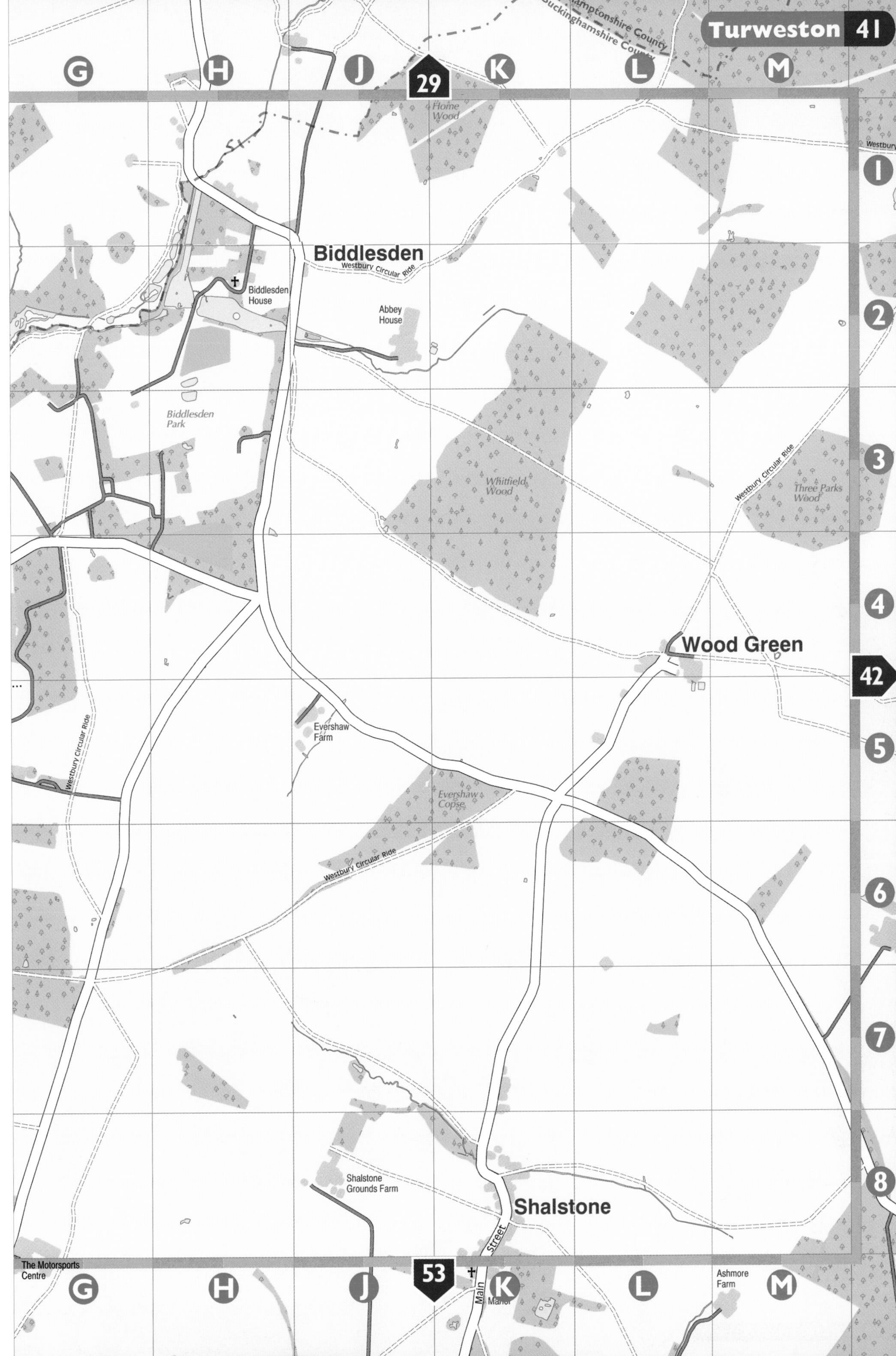

G
H
J
29
K
L
M
Northamptonshire County
Buckinghamshire County
Home Wood
Westbury
1
Biddlesden
Westbury Circular Ride
Biddlesden House
Abbey House
2
Biddlesden Park
3
Whitfield Wood
Westbury Circular Ride
Three Parks Wood
4
Wood Green
42
5
Evershaw Farm
Westbury Circular Ride
Evershaw Copse
Westbury Circular Ride
6
7
8
Shalstone Grounds Farm
Shalstone
Main Street
The Motorsports Centre
53
Main
Manor
Ashmore Farm

Silverstone
Golf Club
Red Ditches
Farm
A
B
C
30
D
E
F
Westbury Circular Ride
Point
Copse
Sawpit
Wood
Home
Wood
Thatcham
Ponds Farm
Blackpit
Farm
Parkfields
Woodlands
Farm
Stowe
Woods
Tilehouse
Wood
1
2
3
Three Parks
Wood
4
41
Gorrell
Farm
Dadford
5
Bourbon
Tower
6
Boycott Manor
Farm
Home
Farm
Oxford Water
Stowe
School
Riding
School
7
Boycott
Manor
Stowe
Park
Palladian
Bridge
Stowe Landscape
Gardens (NT)
The Lake
8
Welsh Lane
54
New Inn
Farm
Corinthian
Arch
Boycott
Farm
1 grid square represents 500 metres

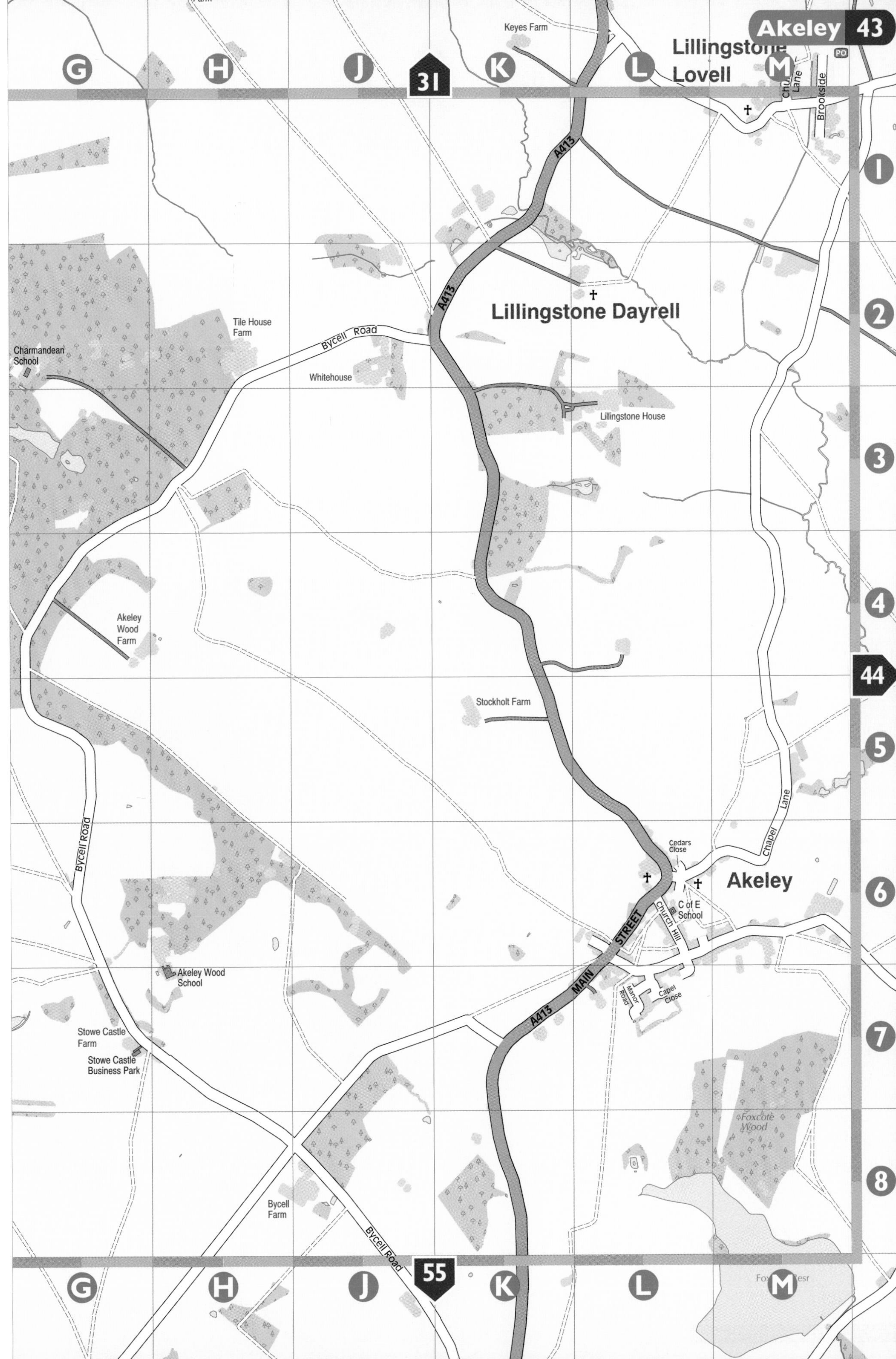
Farm
Keyes Farm
Lillingstone Lovell
PO
Church Lane
Brookside
G
H
J
K
L
M
31
1
2
3
4
5
6
7
8
44
55
A413
Lillingstone Dayrell
Tile House Farm
Charmandean School
Bycell Road
Whitehouse
Lillingstone House
Akeley Wood Farm
Stockholt Farm
Cedars Close
Chapel Lane
Akeley
C of E School
Church Hill
MAIN STREET
Manor Road
Capel Close
Akeley Wood School
Stowe Castle Farm
Stowe Castle Business Park
Foxcote Wood
Bycell Farm
Bycell Road

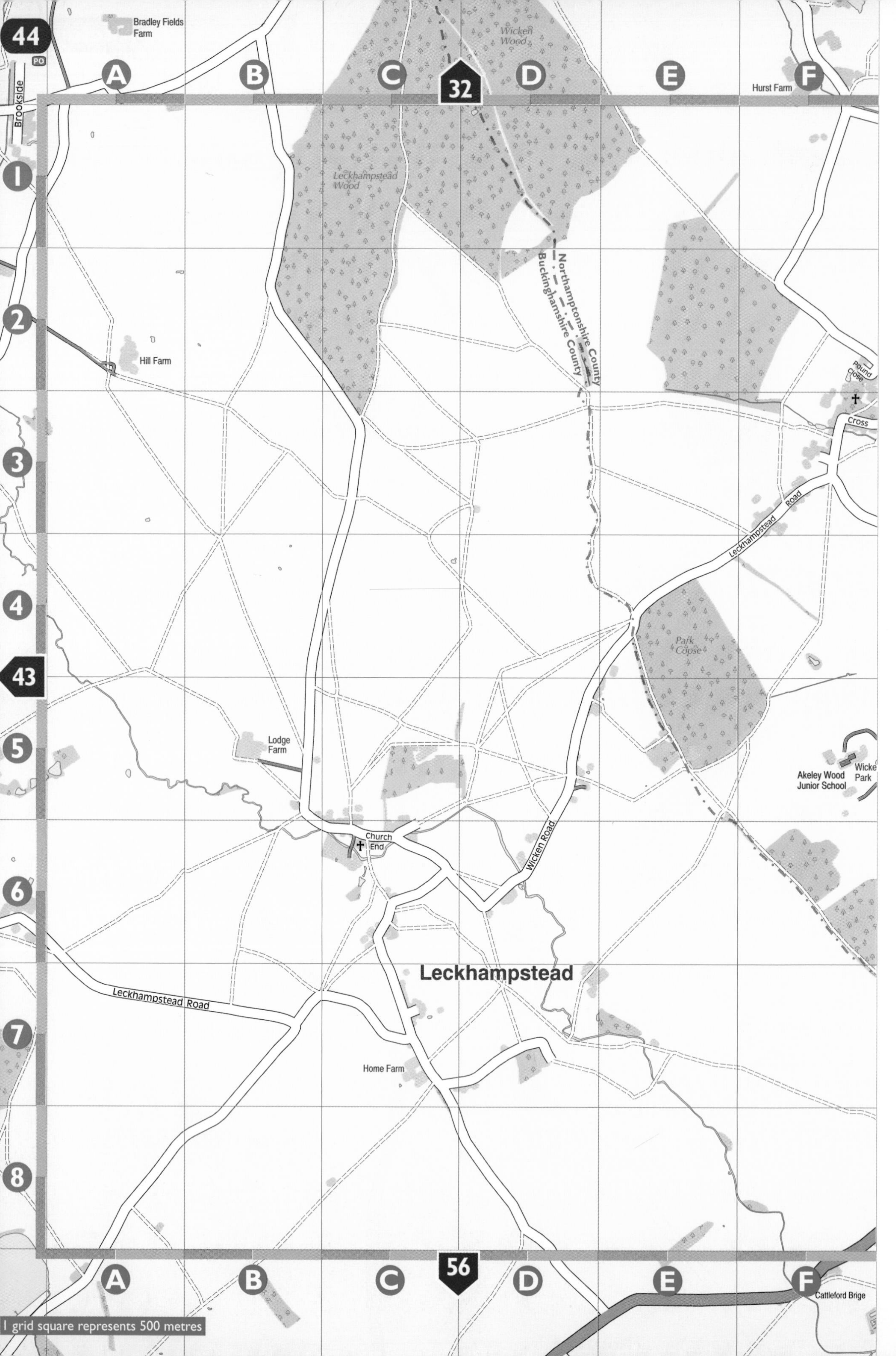
44
Bradley Fields Farm
PO
Lane
Brookside
A
B
C
32
D
E
F
Wicken Wood
Hurst Farm
1
Leckhampstead Wood
Northamptonshire County
Buckinghamshire County
2
Hill Farm
Pound Close
Cross
3
Leckhampstead Road
4
Park Copse
43
5
Lodge Farm
Akeley Wood Junior School
Wicke Park
Church End
Wicken Road
6
Leckhampstead
Leckhampstead Road
7
Home Farm
8
A
B
C
56
D
E
F
Cattleford Brige
1 grid square represents 500 metres

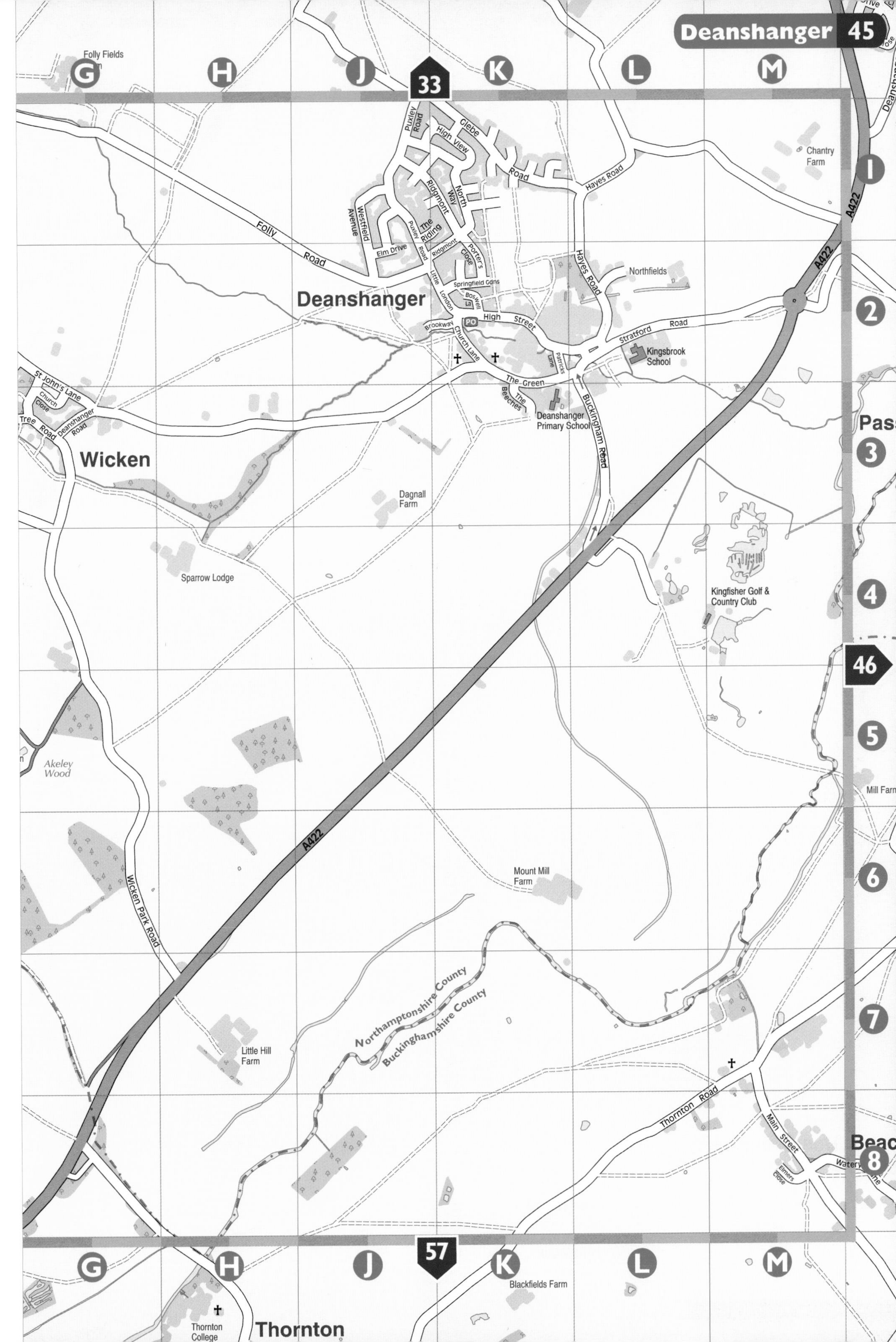

Folly Fields
G
H
J
33
K
L
M
Puxley Road
Glebe
High View
Road
Hayes Road
Chantry Farm
1
A422
Ridgmont
North Way
Westfield Avenue
The Riding
Puxley Road
Elm Drive
Folly
Road
Ridgmont
Porter's Close
Hayes Road
Northfields
Little London
Springfield Gdns
Boswell La
Deanshanger
High Street
Stratford Road
2
Brookway
Church Lane
Kingsbrook School
Patricks Lane
The Green
St John's Lane
Church Close
Tree Road
Deanshanger Road
The Beeches
Deanshanger Primary School
Buckingham Road
Pass
3
Wicken
Dagnall Farm
Sparrow Lodge
Kingfisher Golf & Country Club
4
46
5
Akeley Wood
Mill Farm
A422
Wicken Park Road
Mount Mill Farm
6
Northamptonshire County
Buckinghamshire County
7
Little Hill Farm
Thornton Road
Main Street
Beac
Elmers Close
Watery Lane
8
G
H
57
J
K
L
M
Blackfields Farm
Thornton College
Thornton

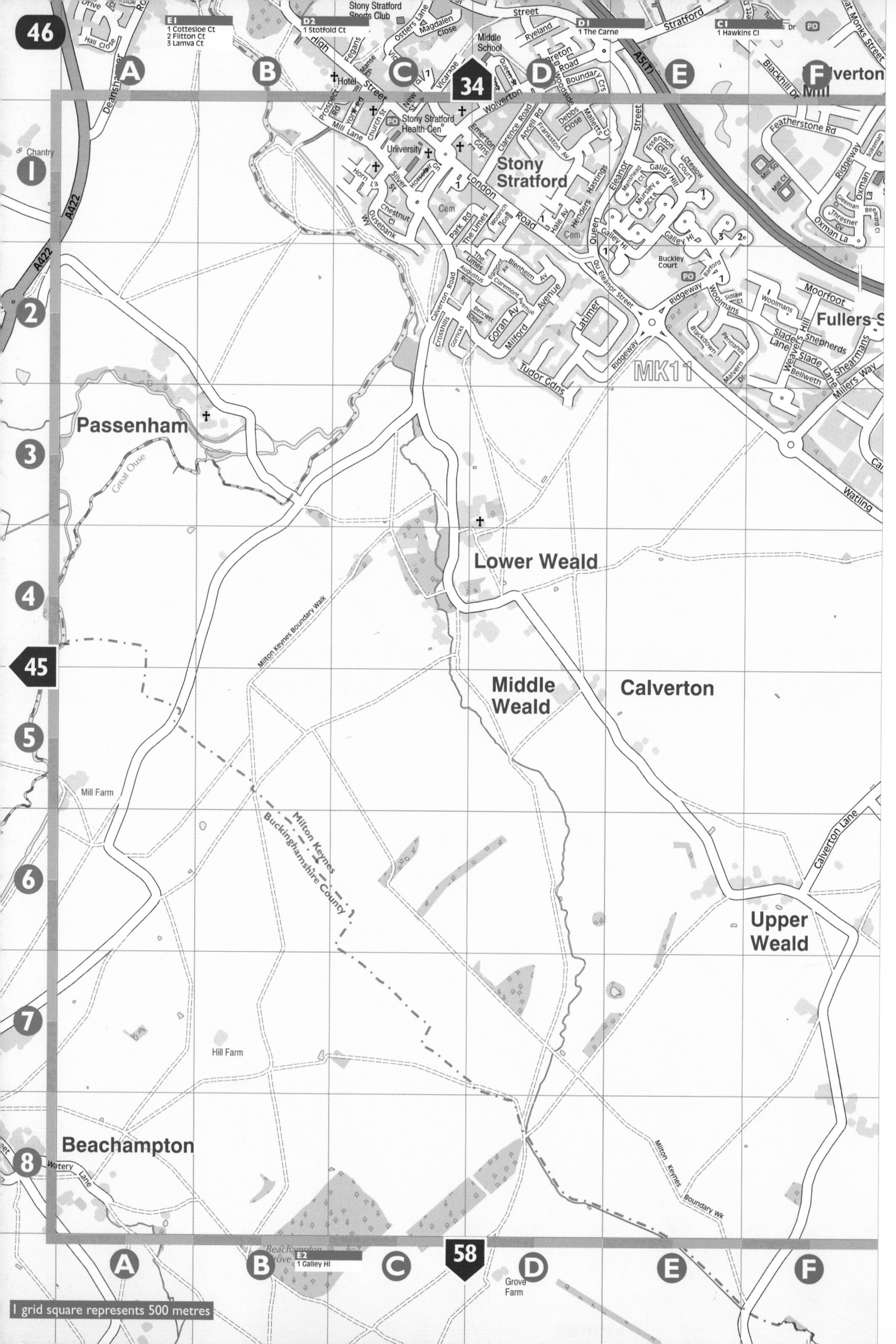
E1
1 Cottesloe Ct
2 Flitton Ct
3 Lamva Ct
D2
1 Stotfold Ct
D1
1 The Carne
C1
1 Hawkins Cl
Stony Stratford
Passenham
Lower Weald
Middle Weald
Calverton
Upper Weald
Beachampton
Mill Farm
Hill Farm
Grove Farm
MK11
Great Ouse
Milton Keynes Boundary Walk
Milton Keynes
Buckinghamshire County
Milton Keynes Boundary Wk
Calverton Road
Calverton Lane
Watery Lane
Ridgeway
Watling
A422
A5(T)
Wolverton Mill
Fullers Slade
E2
1 Galley Hl
Beachampton Grove
1 grid square represents 500 metres

34
45
58

G1
1 Akerman Cl
2 Buckman Cl
3 Catchpole Cl
4 Cotman Cl
5 Freeman Cl
6 Herdman Cl
J2
1 Broomfield
J4
1 Sedgemere
J5
1 Littlemere
2 Tadmere
K1
1 Fernan Dell
K2
1 Lingfield
K4
1 Medhurst
2 Norrington
35
Wolverton
Blue Bridge
Milton Keynes Museum of Industry & Rural Life
Greenleys
Milton Keynes Rugby Club
Bancroft
Bancroft Park
MK13
Bradwell
Bradwell Priory (remains)
Golf Course
Kiln Farm Industrial Estate
Two Mile Ash
Two Mile Ash Middle School
Wymbush
Rooksley
Kart Circuit
National Badminton Centre
48
Great Holm
Cemetery
MK8
Crowhill
Shenley Church End
Shenley Leisure Centre
Denbigh School
Watling Vale Medical Cen
Loughton Manor First School
Common Farm
Shenley Hill Farm
Whitehouse Farm
Grange Farm
North Buckinghamshire Way
Watling Street
Monks Way
A5(T)
A422
Dansteed Way
Portway
M3, M7, M8
Street names for these grid squares are listed at the back of the index
59
M5
1 Badminton Vw
M6
1 Greenhill Cl
2 Hutchings Cl
3 Lamport Ct
M2
1 Atterbrook
2 Rickyard Cl
3 St Lawrence Vw
4 Vicarage Gdns
L7
1 Blatherwick Ct
H4, K3, L5, L6
Street names for these grid squares are listed at the back of the index
K7
1 Beckinsale Gv
2 Cogan Ct
3 Wilson Ct
L1
1 Benwell Cl
2 Constantine Wy
3 Rudchesters
K5
1 Farnham Ct
2 Lydiard
K6
1 Gallagher Cl
2 Hathaway Ct

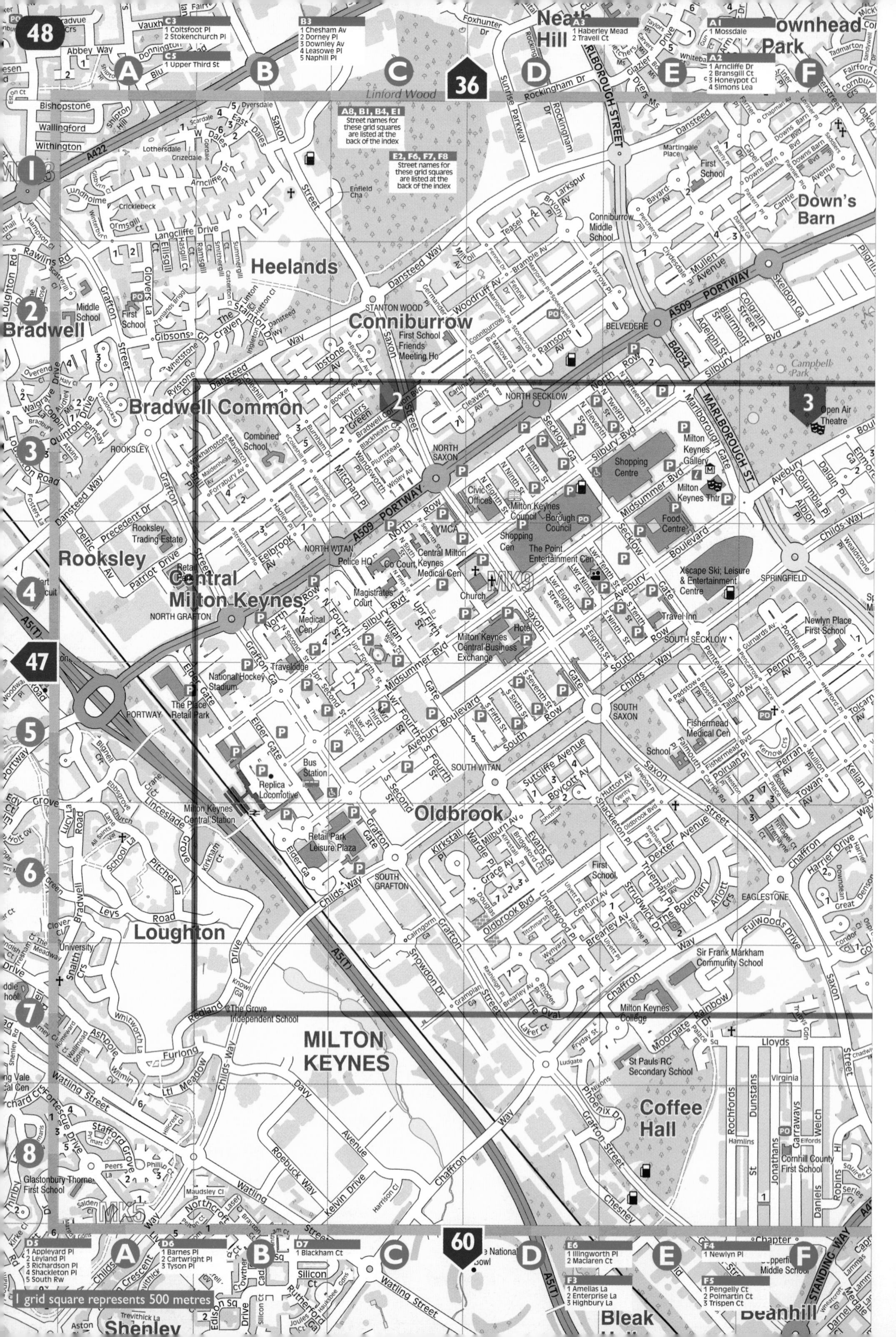

48
C3
1 Coltsfoot Pl
2 Stokenchurch Pl
C5
1 Upper Third St
B3
1 Chesham Av
2 Dorney Pl
3 Downley Av
4 Leasowe Pl
5 Naphill Pl
A3
1 Haberley Mead
2 Travell Ct
A1
1 Mossdale
A2
1 Arncliffe Dr
2 Bransgill Ct
3 Honeypot Cl
4 Simons Lea
36
A8, B1, B4, E1
Street names for these grid squares are listed at the back of the index
E2, F6, F7, F8
Street names for these grid squares are listed at the back of the index
Linford Wood
Neath Hill
Downhead Park
Heelands
Conniburrow
Down's Barn
Bradwell
Bradwell Common
Rooksley
Central Milton Keynes
Oldbrook
Loughton
MILTON KEYNES
Coffee Hall
Shenley
Bleak
Beanhill
MK9
MK5
A509 PORTWAY
MARLBOROUGH STREET
2
3
47
60
Open Air Theatre
Shopping Centre
Milton Keynes Gallery
Milton Keynes Thtr
Civic Offices
Milton Keynes Council
Borough Council
Shopping Cen
The Point Entertainment Cen
Xscape Ski; Leisure & Entertainment Centre
Food Centre
Central Milton Keynes Medical Cen
Police HQ
Co Court
Magistrates Court
Milton Keynes Central Business Exchange
National Hockey Stadium
The Place Retail Park
Bus Station
Replica Locomotive
Milton Keynes Central Station
Retail Park Leisure Plaza
Rooksley Trading Estate
Combined School
Newlyn Place First School
Fishermead Medical Cen
Sir Frank Markham Community School
Milton Keynes College
St Pauls RC Secondary School
The Grove Independent School
Cornhill County First School
Glastonbury Thorne First School
Conniburrow Middle School
First School Friends Meeting Ho
D5
1 Appleyard Pl
2 Leyland Pl
3 Richardson Pl
4 Shackleton Pl
5 South Rw
D6
1 Barnes Pl
2 Cartwright Pl
3 Tyson Pl
D7
1 Blackham Ct
E6
1 Illingworth Pl
2 Maclaren Ct
F3
1 Amelias La
2 Enterprise La
3 Highbury La
F4
1 Newlyn Pl
F5
1 Pengelly Ct
2 Polmartin Ct
3 Trispen Ct
1 grid square represents 500 metres

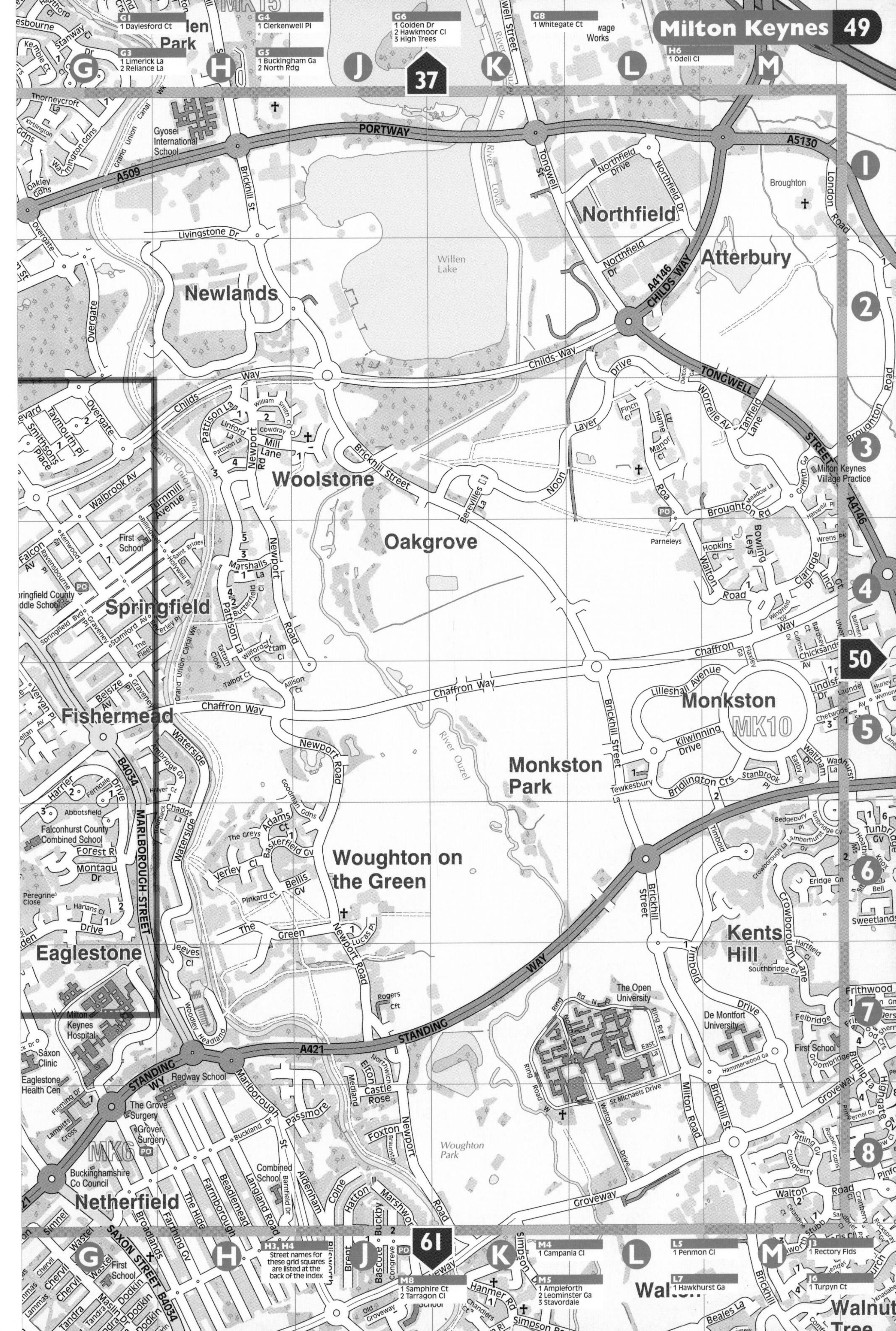
G1 1 Daylesford Ct
G3 1 Limerick La 2 Reliance La
G4 1 Clerkenwell Pl
G5 1 Buckingham Ga 2 North Rdg
G6 1 Golden Dr 2 Hawkmoor Cl 3 High Trees
G8 1 Whitegate Ct
H6 1 Odell Cl
37
Gyosei International School
PORTWAY
A509
A5130
Broughton
Northfield
Atterbury
Willen Lake
Newlands
Woolstone
Oakgrove
Springfield
Fishermead
Monkston
MK10
Monkston Park
Woughton on the Green
Kents Hill
Eaglestone
Netherfield
MK6
CHILDS WAY
A4146
TONGWELL STREET
Chaffron Way
Brickhill Street
Newport Road
River Ouzel
Grand Union Canal
MARLBOROUGH STREET
B4034
A421
STANDING WAY
The Open University
De Montfort University
Milton Keynes Village Practice
Milton Keynes Hospital
Saxon Clinic
Eaglestone Health Cen
Redway School
The Grove Surgery
Grove Surgery
Buckinghamshire Co Council
Falconhurst County Combined School
Combined School
Woughton Park
Groveway
50
61
H3, H4 Street names for these grid squares are listed at the back of the index
M4 1 Campania Cl
M5 1 Ampleforth 2 Leominster Ga 3 Stavordale
M8 1 Samphire Ct 2 Tarragon Cl
L5 1 Penmon Cl
L7 1 Hawkhurst Ga
J3 1 Rectory Flds
J6 1 Turpyn Ct
Walton
Walnut Tree

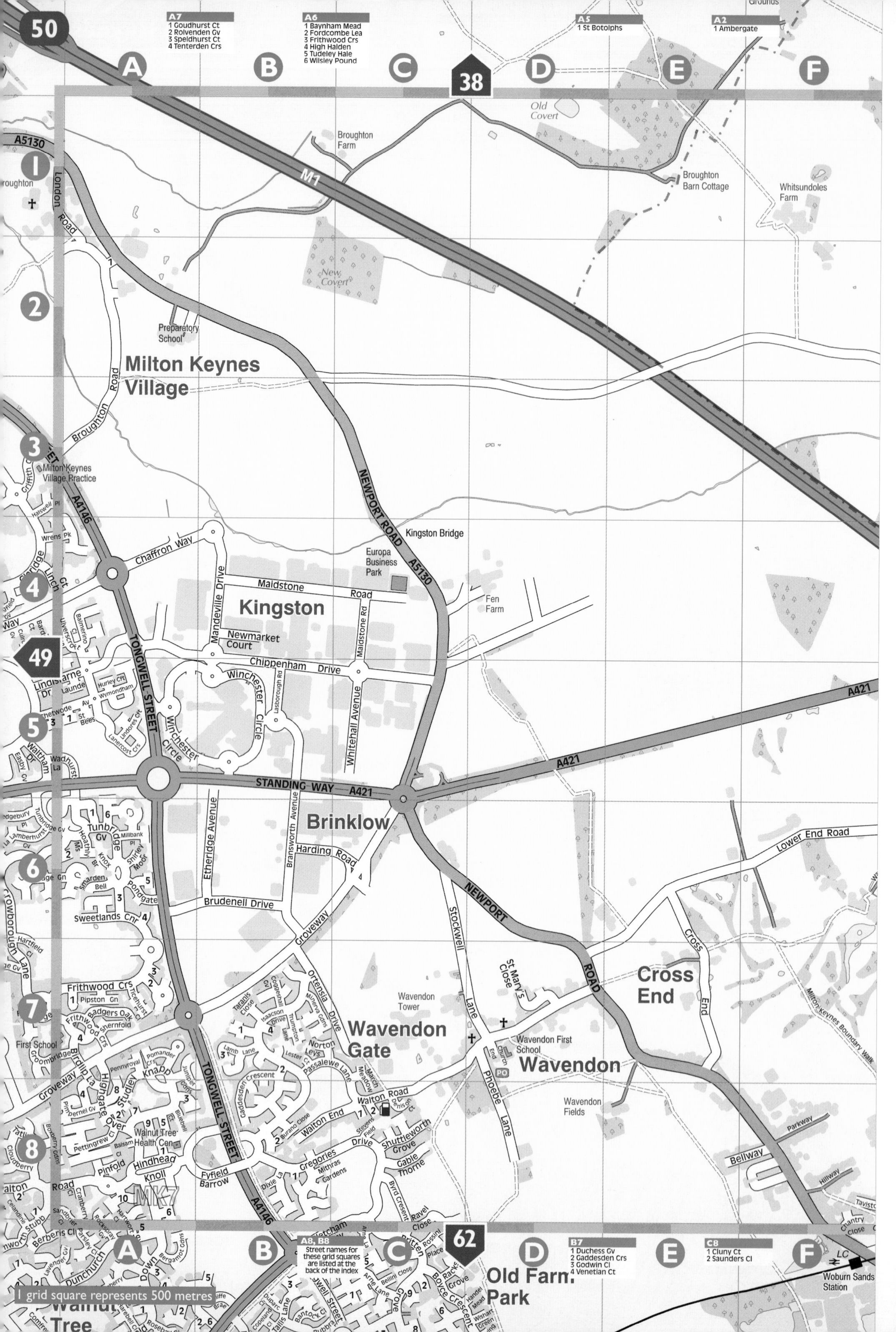
A7
1 Goudhurst Ct
2 Rolvenden Gv
3 Speldhurst Ct
4 Tenterden Crs
A6
1 Baynham Mead
2 Fordcombe Lea
3 Frithwood Crs
4 High Halden
5 Tudeley Hale
6 Wilsley Pound
A5
1 St Botolphs
A2
1 Ambergate
38
Old Covert
Broughton Farm
M1
Broughton Barn Cottage
Whitsundoles Farm
New Covert
A5130
London Road
Preparatory School
Milton Keynes Village
Broughton Road
Milton Keynes Village Practice
A4146
NEWPORT ROAD
Kingston Bridge
Europa Business Park
Chaffron Way
Maidstone Road
Kingston
Mandeville Drive
Maidstone Rd
Fen Farm
Newmarket Court
Chippenham Drive
Winchester Circle
Whitehall Avenue
Lasborough Rd
TONGWELL STREET
49
A421
STANDING WAY
Brinklow
Etheridge Avenue
Bransworth Avenue
Harding Road
Lower End Road
Brudenell Drive
Groveway
Stockwell Lane
NEWPORT ROAD
St Mary's Close
Cross End
Wavendon Tower
Wavendon Gate
Wavendon First School
Wavendon
Phoebe Lane
Wavendon Fields
Milton Keynes Boundary Walk
Frithwood Crs
Pipston Gn
Badgers Oak
Sheernfold
First School
Groveway
Walnut Tree Health Cen
Hindhead Knoll
Fyfield Barrow
Gaddesden Crescent
Walton Road
Walton End
Gregories Drive
Shuttleworth Grove
Gable Thorne
Mithras Gardens
Byrd Crescent
Bellway
Parkway
Hillway
MK7
Road
62
B7
1 Duchess Gv
2 Gaddesden Crs
3 Godwin Cl
4 Venetian Ct
C8
1 Cluny Ct
2 Saunders Cl
A8, B8
Street names for these grid squares are listed at the back of the index
Old Farm Park
Woburn Sands Station
Walnut Tree
1 grid square represents 500 metres

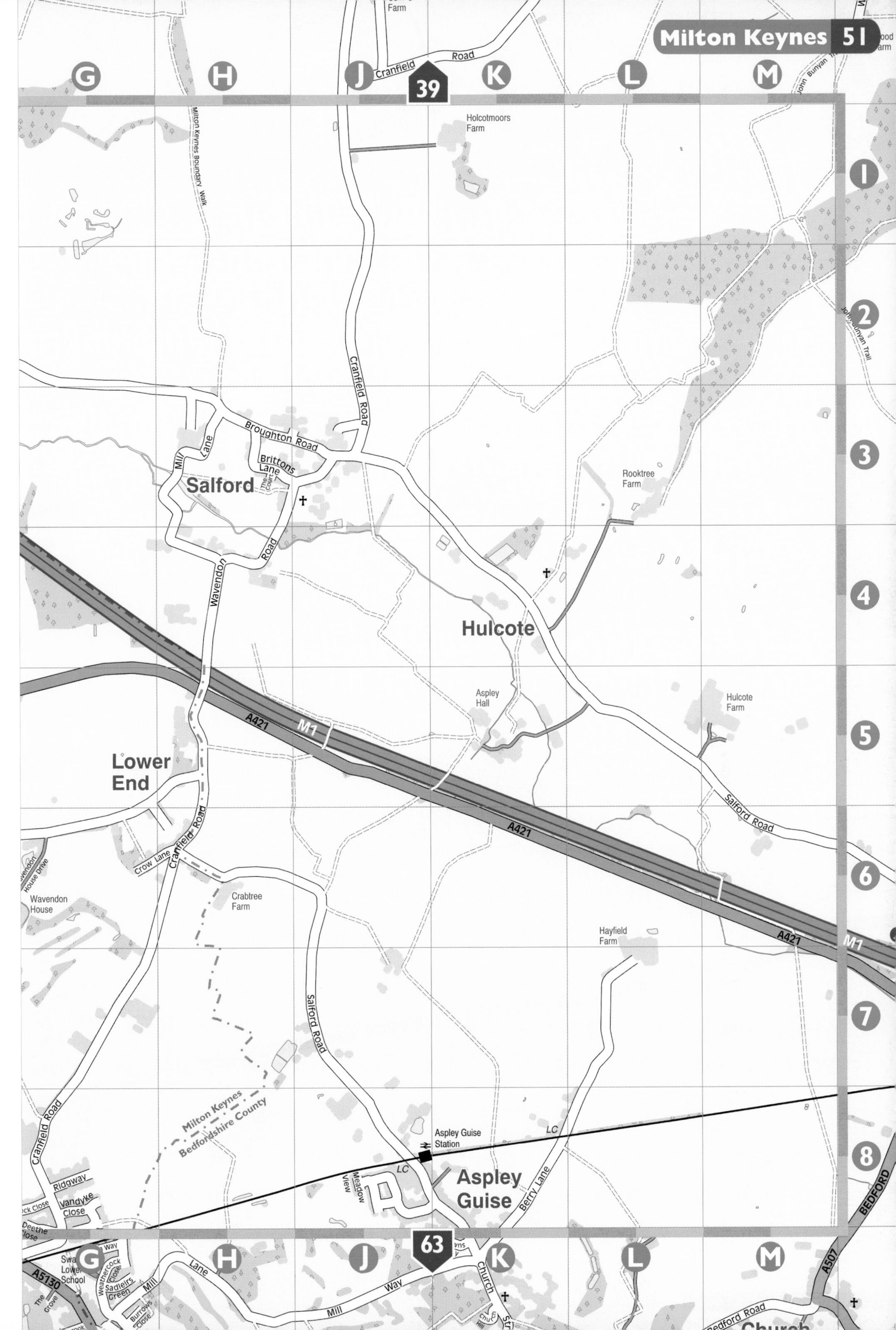

Milton Keynes 51
39
63
G
H
J
K
L
M
1
2
3
4
5
6
7
8
Farm
Cranfield Road
Holcotmoors Farm
Milton Keynes Boundary Walk
John Bunyan Trail
Cranfield Road
Broughton Road
Brittons Lane
The Court
Mill Lane
Salford
Wavendon Road
Rooktree Farm
Hulcote
Aspley Hall
Hulcote Farm
A421
M1
Lower End
Salford Road
Crow Lane
Cranfield Road
Wavendon House Drive
Wavendon House
Crabtree Farm
Hayfield Farm
Salford Road
Milton Keynes
Bedfordshire County
Cranfield Road
Aspley Guise Station
LC
Meadow View
Aspley Guise
Berry Lane
Ridgway
Vandyke Close
Deethe Close
Way
Lower School
A5130
The Grove
Wethercock Close
Sadleirs Green
Burrows Close
Mill
Lane
Mill
Way
Church
Church Hill
BEDFORD
A507
Bedford Road

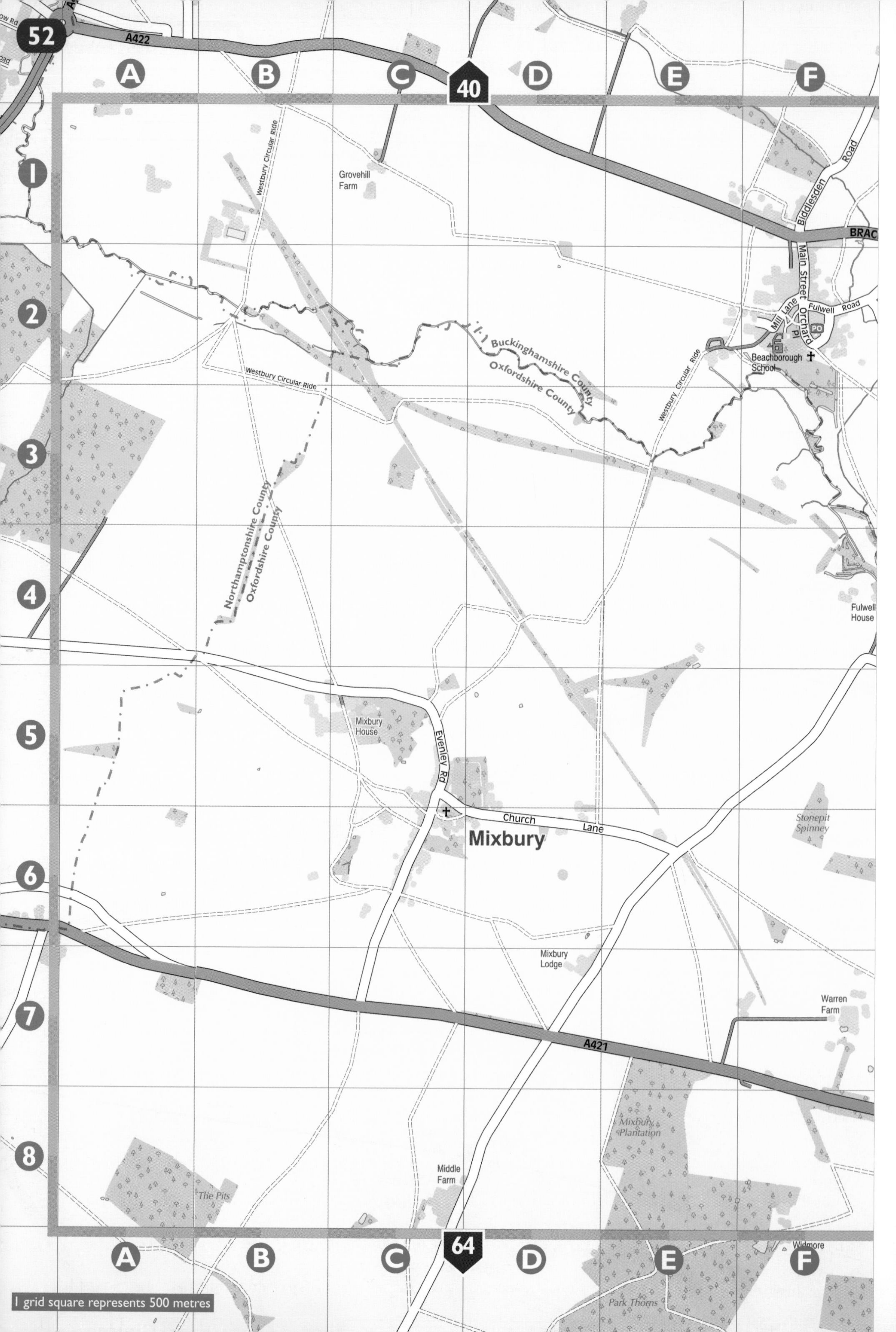

52
40
64
A
B
C
D
E
F
1
2
3
4
5
6
7
8
A422
A421
Westbury Circular Ride
Grovehill Farm
Biddlesden Road
BRAC
Main Street
Mill Lane
Orchard Pl
Fulwell Road
PO
Beachborough School
Buckinghamshire County
Oxfordshire County
Northamptonshire County
Fulwell House
Mixbury House
Evenley Rd
Church Lane
Mixbury
Stonepit Spinney
Mixbury Lodge
Warren Farm
Mixbury Plantation
Middle Farm
The Pits
Widmore
Park Thorns
1 grid square represents 500 metres

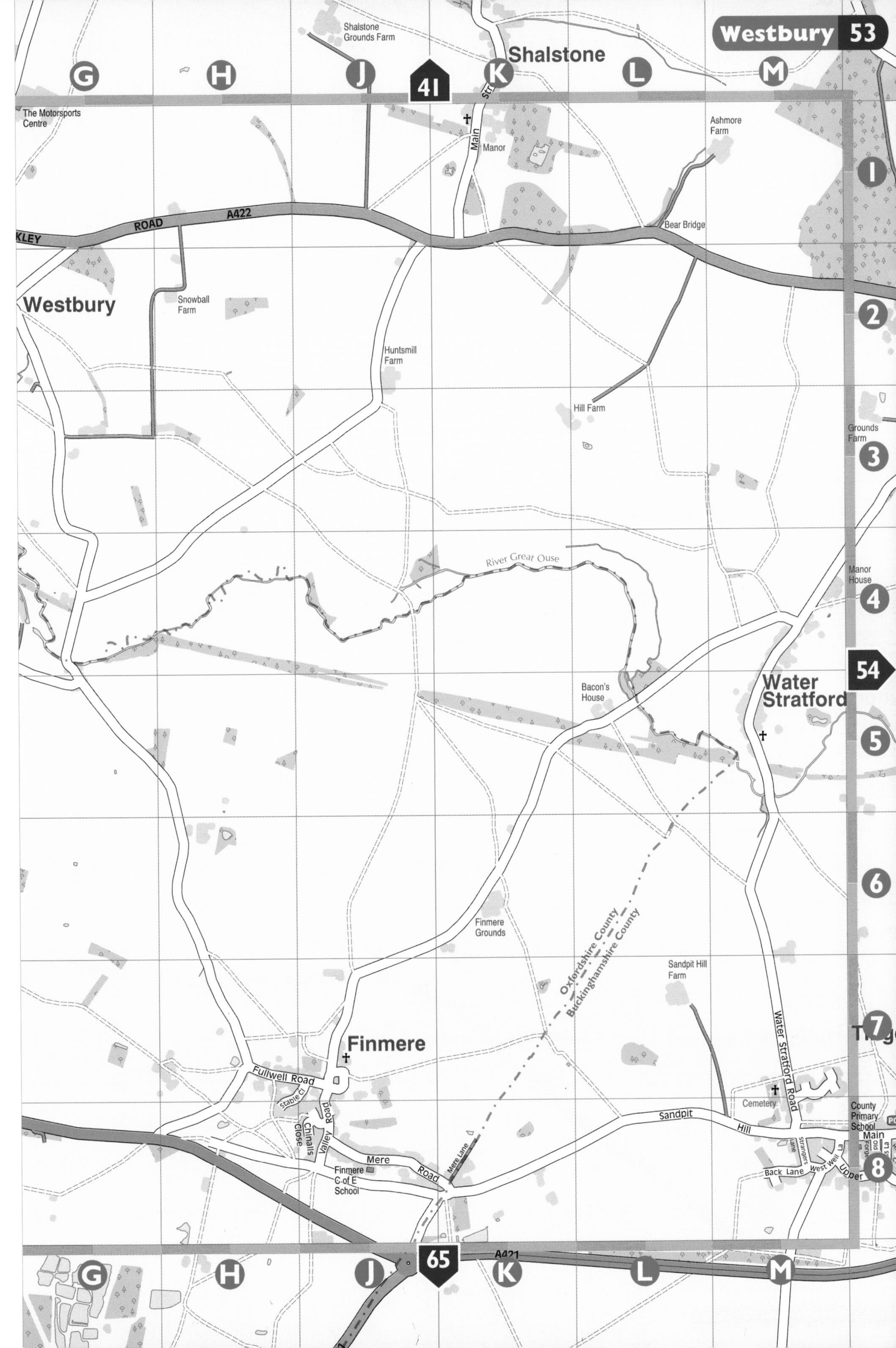
Shalstone
Shalstone Grounds Farm
G
H
J
41
K
L
M
The Motorsports Centre
Main Str
Manor
Ashmore Farm
I
ROAD
A422
KLEY
Bear Bridge
Westbury
Snowball Farm
2
Huntsmill Farm
Hill Farm
Grounds Farm
3
River Great Ouse
Manor House
4
54
Water Stratford
Bacon's House
5
6
Finmere Grounds
Oxfordshire County
Buckinghamshire County
Sandpit Hill Farm
Water Stratford Road
7
Finmere
Fullwell Road
Stable Cl
Valley Road
Chinalls Close
Mere
Road
Mere Lane
Finmere C of E School
Sandpit
Hill
Cemetery
County Primary School
Main
Back Lane
West Well
Upper
8
65
A421
G
H
J
K
L
M

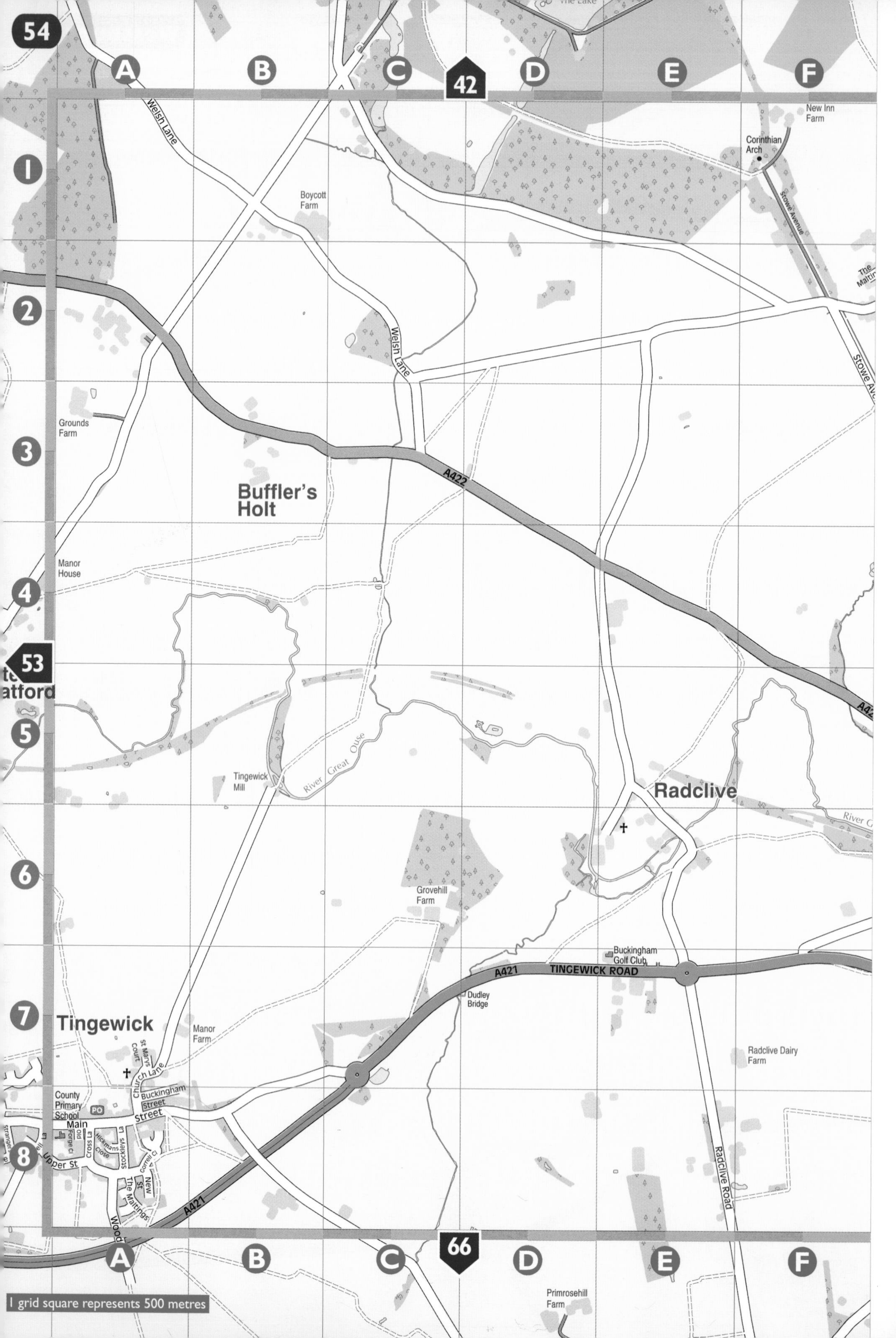

54
A
B
C
42
D
E
F
1
2
3
4
5
6
7
8
53
66
Welsh Lane
Boycott Farm
New Inn Farm
Corinthian Arch
Stowe Avenue
The Maltings
Grounds Farm
A422
Buffler's Holt
Manor House
Tingewick Mill
River Great Ouse
Radclive
River G
Grovehill Farm
Buckingham Golf Club
A421
TINGEWICK ROAD
Dudley Bridge
Tingewick
Manor Farm
Radclive Dairy Farm
St Marys Court
Church Lane
Buckingham Street
County Primary School
PO
Main Street
Old Forge Cl
Cross La
Hickmans Close
Stocks La
Upper St
Correll Cl
The Maltings
New St
Wood
Radclive Road
Primrosehill Farm
1 grid square represents 500 metres

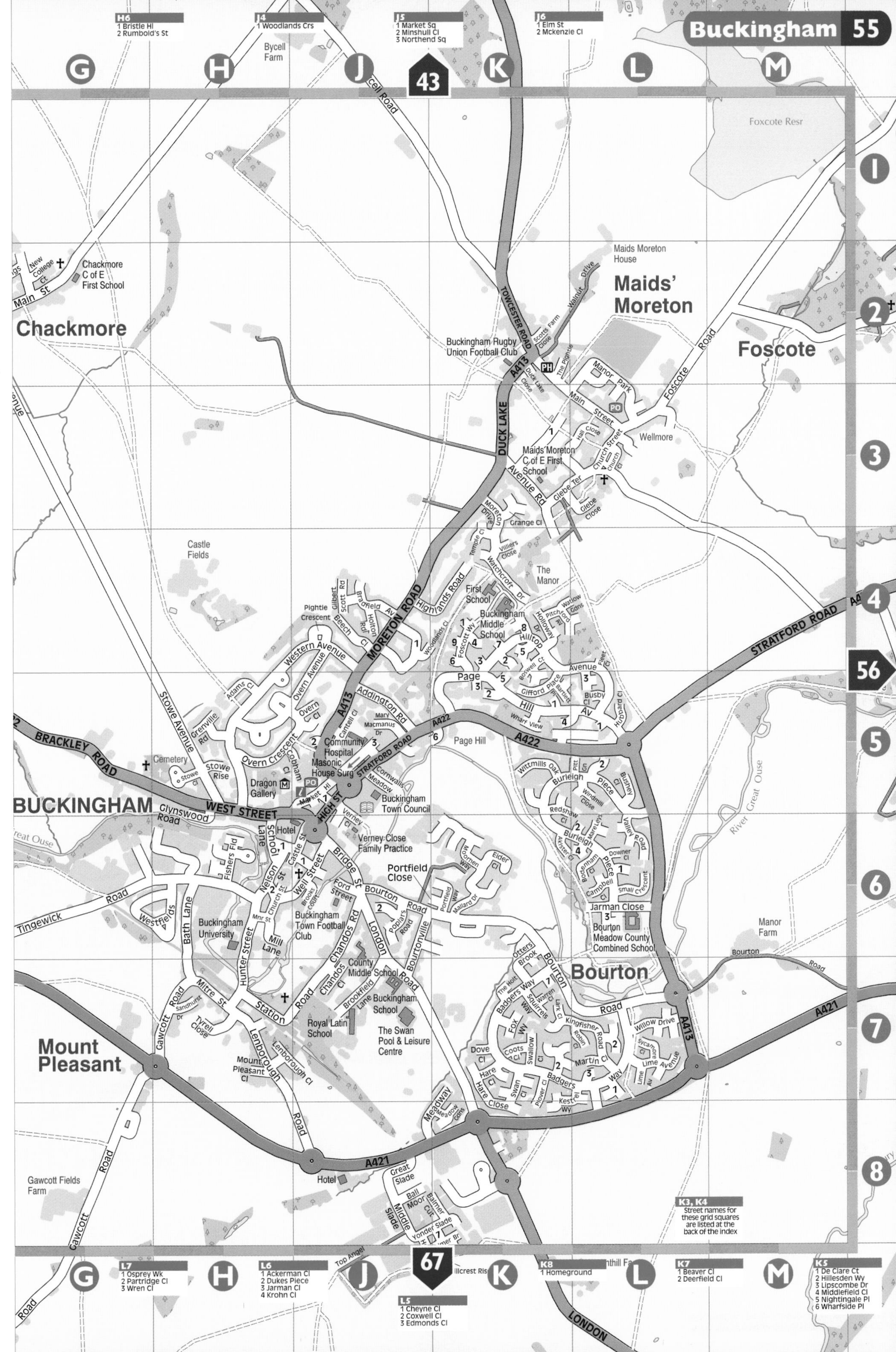
H6
1 Bristle Hl
2 Rumbold's St
J4
1 Woodlands Crs
J5
1 Market Sq
2 Minshull Cl
3 Northend Sq
J6
1 Elm St
2 Mckenzie Cl
Bycell Farm
Foxcote Resr
Maids Moreton House
Maids' Moreton
Chackmore
Chackmore C of E First School
Foscote
Buckingham Rugby Union Football Club
Maids Moreton C of E First School
Wellmore
Castle Fields
The Manor
First School
Buckingham Middle School
Community Hospital
Masonic House Surg
Dragon Gallery
Buckingham Town Council
BUCKINGHAM
Verney Close Family Practice
Portfield Close
Page Hill
Buckingham University
Buckingham Town Football Club
County Middle School
Buckingham School
Royal Latin School
The Swan Pool & Leisure Centre
Jarman Close
Bourton Meadow County Combined School
Bourton
Manor Farm
Mount Pleasant
Gawcott Fields Farm
Hotel
STRATFORD ROAD
WEST STREET
BRACKLEY ROAD
MORETON ROAD
TOWCESTER ROAD
DUCK LAKE
A413
A422
A421
River Great Ouse
K3, K4
Street names for these grid squares are listed at the back of the index
L7
1 Osprey Wk
2 Partridge Cl
3 Wren Cl
L6
1 Ackerman Cl
2 Dukes Piece
3 Jarman Cl
4 Krohn Cl
L5
1 Cheyne Cl
2 Coxwell Cl
3 Edmonds Cl
K8
1 Homeground
K7
1 Beaver Cl
2 Deerfield Cl
K5
1 De Clare Ct
2 Hillesden Wy
3 Lipscombe Dr
4 Middlefield Cl
5 Nightingale Pl
6 Wharfside Pl

43
56
67

A
B
C
44
D
E
F
Cattleford Brige
1
2
Hydelane Farm
Thornborough Mill
Nature Reserve
Reservoir
3
Home Farm
4
ORD ROAD A422
55
Old Mill House
5
Lower End
White House Farm
Hatchet Leys La
Back Street
Lower End
High Street
Palmers Moor
Thornborough First School
Church Lane
The Gn
6
Western Green Farm
Road
A421
7
PH
Bourton Grounds
The Folly
Bridge
Priory Farm
8
Padbury Brook (The Twins)
Coombs
A
B
C
68
D
E
F
1 grid square represents 500 metres

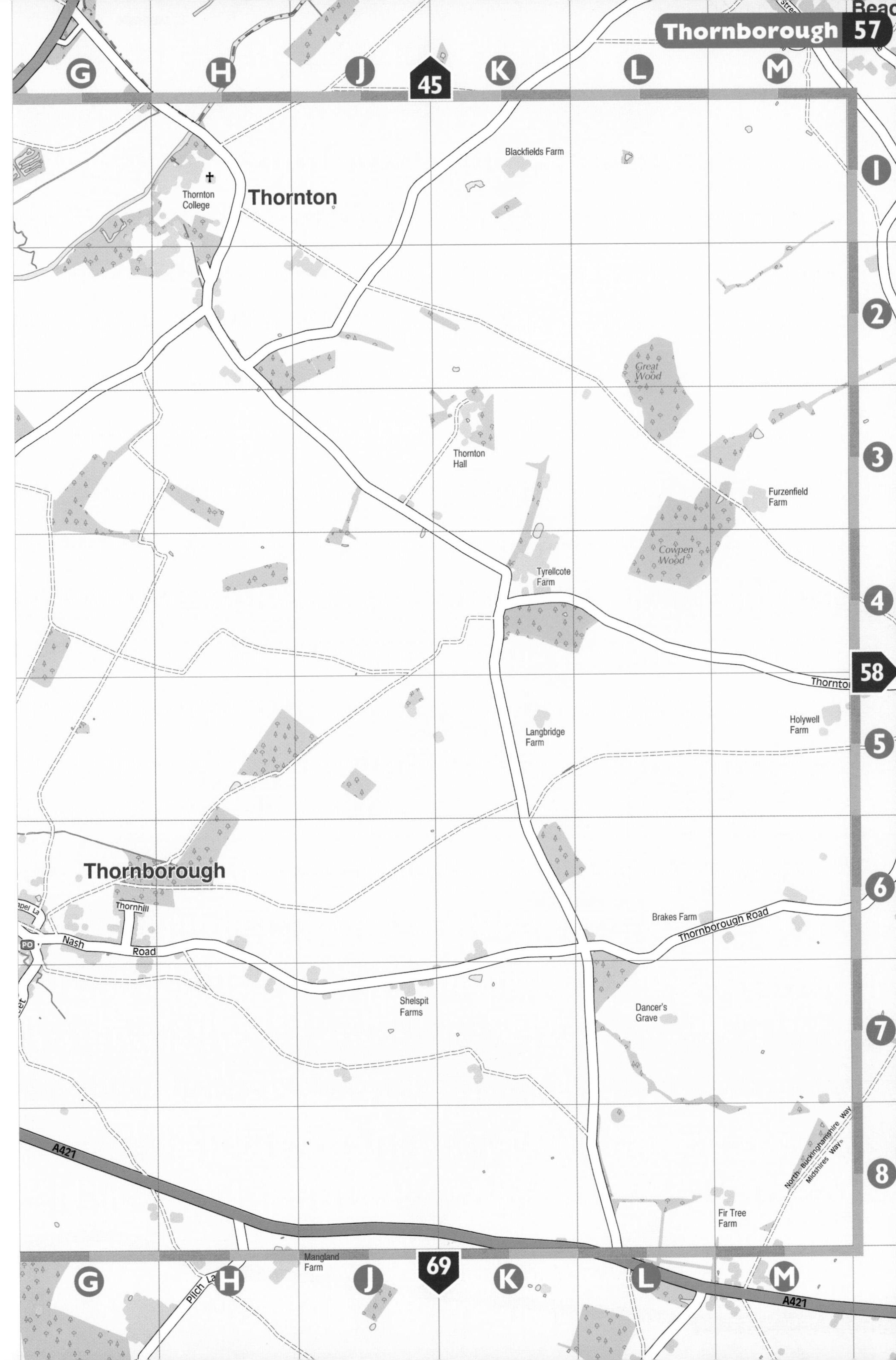
G
H
J
45
K
L
M
Beac
Thornton
Thornton College
Blackfields Farm
Great Wood
Thornton Hall
Furzenfield Farm
Cowpen Wood
Tyrellcote Farm
Thornton
58
Holywell Farm
Langbridge Farm
Thornborough
Thornhill
PO
Nash Road
Brakes Farm
Thornborough Road
Shelspit Farms
Dancer's Grave
A421
North Buckinghamshire Way
Midshires Way
Fir Tree Farm
Mangland Farm
69
Pilch La
1
2
3
4
5
6
7
8

Beachampton
58
46
57
70
A
B
C
D
E
F
1
2
3
4
5
6
7
8
B5
1 Old English Cl
Milton Keynes
Boundary Wk
Beachampton Grove
Grove Farm
Milton Keynes Boundary Wk
Potash Farm
The Oaks
Stratford Road
Whaddon Road
Nash Road
Midshires Way
Nash
High Street
Stratford Road
Barnhill Farm
Wood End
Wood End
Roundhill Farm
Winslow Road
College Wood
Buckinghamshire Way
Fincorrie Farm
Whaddon
Parkhill Farm
Chase
Cross Roads Farm
Briarsbank Farm
A421
Warren Road
Warren Farm
1 grid square represents 500 metres

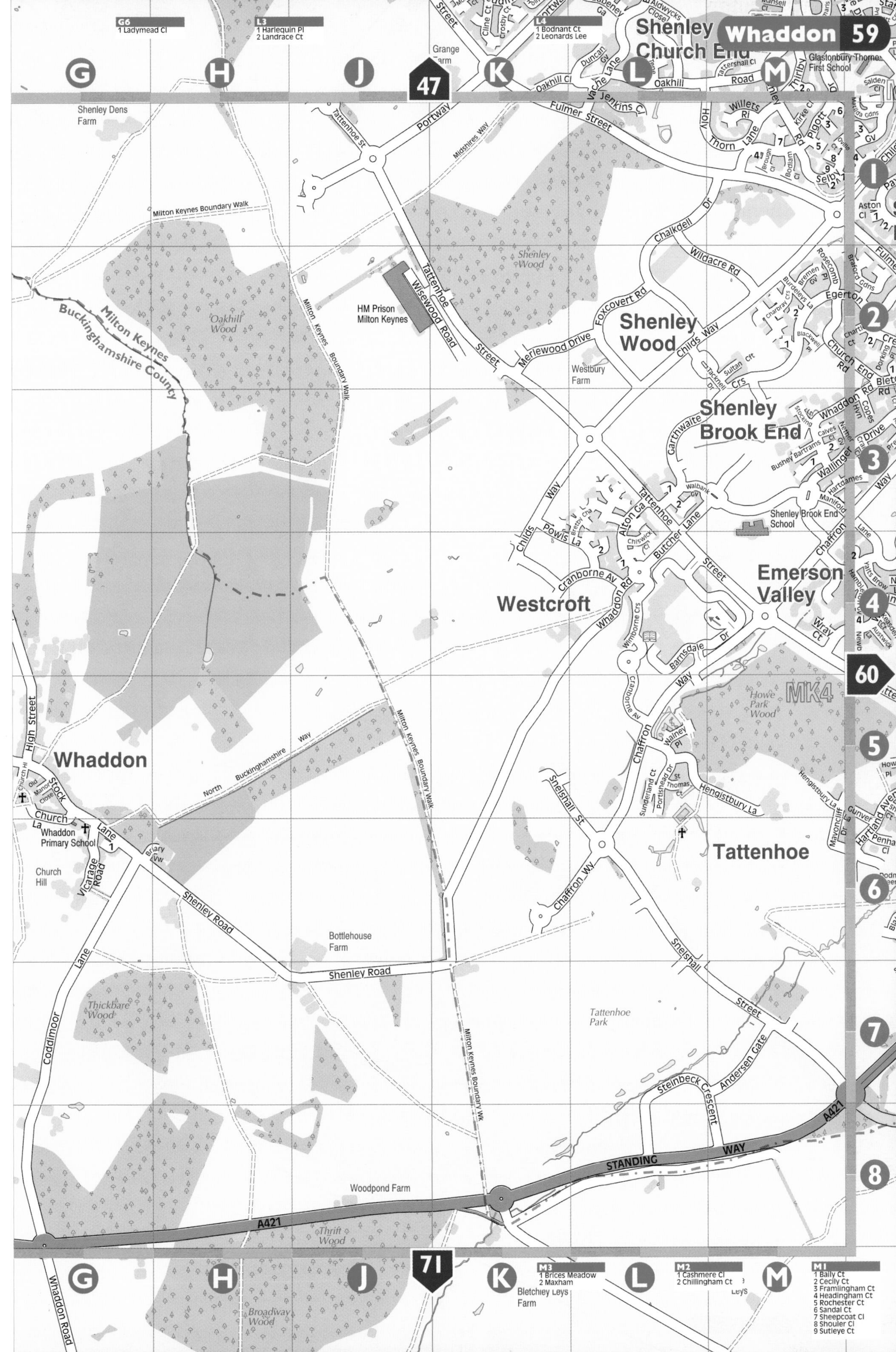
G6
1 Ladymead Cl
L3
1 Harlequin Pl
2 Landrace Ct
L4
1 Bodnant Ct
2 Leonards Lee
G
H
J
47
K
L
M
Shenley Church End
Grange Farm
Oakhill Cl
Vache Lane
Oakhill Road
Tattershall Cl
Glastonbury Thorne First School
Shenley Dens Farm
Fulmer Street
Jenkins Cl
Willets Ri
Holy Thorn Lane
Kirke Cl
Pigott
Bodiam Cl
Selby
Brougham Cl
Tattenhoe St
Portway
Midshires Way
Milton Keynes Boundary Walk
Chalkdell Dr
Wildacre Rd
Rosecomb Pl
Bremen Gv
Burdeleys La
Egerton
Shenley Wood
Oakhill Wood
HM Prison Milton Keynes
Wisewood Road
Tattenhoe Street
Foxcovert Rd
Merlewood Drive
Childs Way
Charbray Crs
Blackwell Pl
Church End Rd
Sultan Cft
Tackney Dr
Westbury Farm
Milton Keynes
Buckinghamshire County
Shenley Brook End
Garthwaite Crs
Whaddon Rd
Stocking Gn
Calves Cl
Bushey Bartrams
Wallinger Drive
Hartdames
Manifold
Walbank Gv
Shenley Brook End School
Chaffron Way
Alton Ga
Chiswick Cl
Butcher Lane
Powis La
Bretby Cha
Tattenhoe Street
Emerson Valley
Wray Ct
Westcroft
Cranborne Av
Whaddon Rd
Wimborne Crs
Barnsdale Dr
60
Howe Park Wood
MK4
Walney Pl
Sunderland Ct
Portishead Dr
St Thomas Ct
Hengistbury La
Gunver La
Mavoncliff Dr
Hartland Avenue
Penhale Cl
Snelshall St
High Street
Whaddon
Church Hl
Old Manor Close
Stock Lane
Church La
Whaddon Primary School
North Buckinghamshire Way
Briary Vw
Church Hill
Vicarage Road
Tattenhoe
Shenley Road
Chaffron Wy
Bottlehouse Farm
Shenley Road
Snelshall Street
Coddimoor Lane
Thickbare Wood
Tattenhoe Park
Andersen Gate
Steinbeck Crescent
A421
Standing Way
Woodpond Farm
Thrift Wood
71
Whaddon Road
Broadway Wood
Bletchley Leys Farm
M3
1 Brices Meadow
2 Maxham
M2
1 Cashmere Cl
2 Chillingham Ct
M1
1 Bally Ct
2 Cecily Ct
3 Framlingham Ct
4 Headingham Ct
5 Rochester Ct
6 Sandal Ct
7 Sheepcoat Cl
8 Shouler Cl
9 Sutleye Ct
1
2
3
4
5
6
7
8

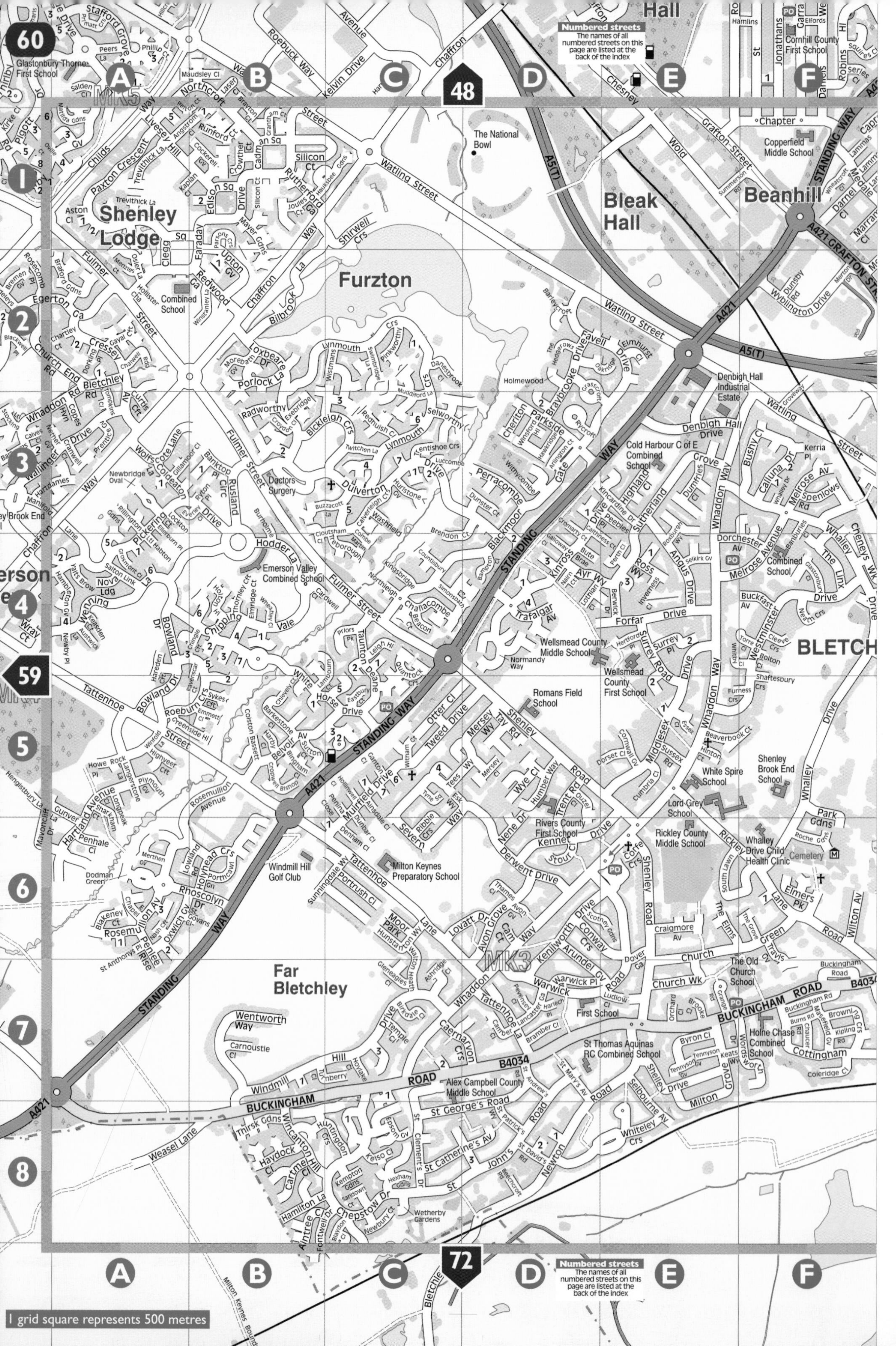
60
48
59
72
A
B
C
D
E
F
1
2
3
4
5
6
7
8
Numbered streets
The names of all numbered streets on this page are listed at the back of the index
Shenley Lodge
Furzton
Bleak Hall
Beanhill
Far Bletchley
BLETCH
Glastonbury Thorne First School
Combined School
The National Bowl
Copperfield Middle School
Cornhill County First School
Denbigh Hall Industrial Estate
Cold Harbour C of E Combined School
Doctors Surgery
Emerson Valley Combined School
Wellsmead County Middle School
Wellsmead County First School
Romans Field School
White Spire School
Shenley Brook End School
Lord Grey School
Rickley County Middle School
Rivers County First School
Whalley Drive Child Health Clinic
Cemetery
Windmill Hill Golf Club
Milton Keynes Preparatory School
The Old Church School
First School
St Thomas Aquinas RC Combined School
Holne Chase Combined School
Alex Campbell County Middle School
Wetherby Gardens
Newbridge Oval
Holmewood
Dodman Green
Watling Street
Standing Way
A421
A5(T)
Buckingham Road
B4034
Fulmer Street
Chaffron Way
Tattenhoe Street
Whaddon Way
Shenley Road
MK3
MK5
1 grid square represents 500 metres

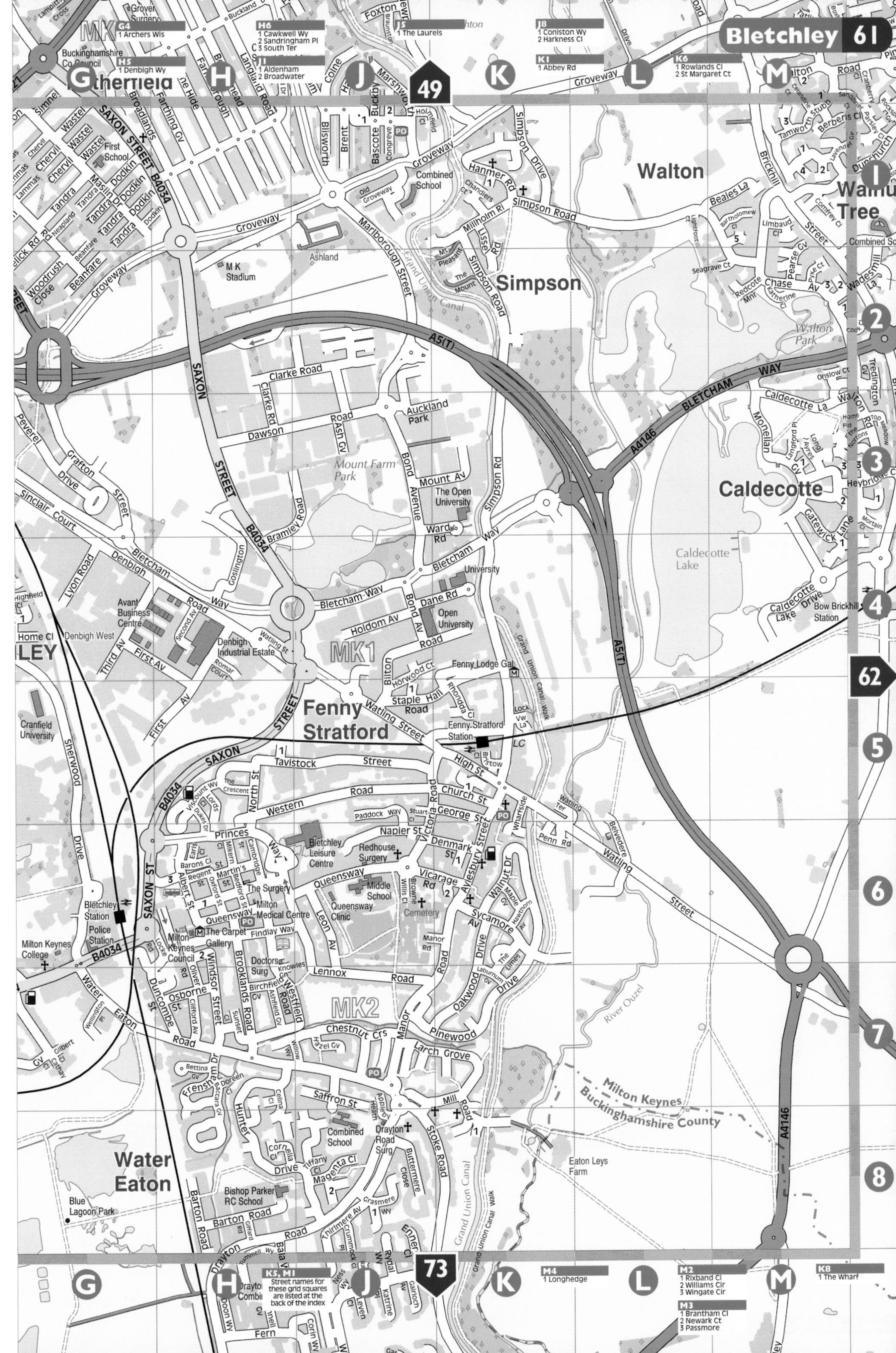
G4
1 Archers Wls
H5
1 Denbigh Wy
H6
1 Cawkwell Wy
2 Sandringham Pl
3 South Ter
J1
1 Aldenham
2 Broadwater
J5
1 The Laurels
J8
1 Coniston Wy
2 Harkness Cl
K1
1 Abbey Rd
K6
1 Rowlands Cl
2 St Margaret Ct
49
Buckinghamshire Co Council
Walton
Walnut Tree
Simpson
Caldecotte
Caldecotte Lake
Walton Park
Bow Brickhill Station
Combined School
Ashland
M K Stadium
Grand Union Canal
A5(T)
BLETCHAM WAY
A4146
Groveway
Simpson Road
Simpson Drive
Marlborough Street
SAXON STREET
B4034
Clarke Road
Dawson Road
Auckland Park
Mount Farm Park
Bond Avenue
Mount Av
The Open University
Bramley Road
Bletcham Way
Denbigh Road
Avant Business Centre
Denbigh West
Denbigh Industrial Estate
Watling St
MK1
Holdom Av
Dane Rd
Open University
Fenny Lodge Gal
Sinclair Court
Grafton Street
Lyon Road
Cranfield University
Sherwood Drive
Fenny Stratford
Fenny Stratford Station
Watling Street
Tavistock Street
Western Road
High St
Church St
George St
Napier St
Princes Way
Bletchley Leisure Centre
Redhouse Surgery
Queensway
Middle School
Queensway Clinic
Cemetery
Aylesbury Street
Victoria Road
Walnut Dr
Sycamore Av
Bletchley Station
Police Station
Milton Keynes College
Milton Keynes Council
The Carpet Gallery
Milton Medical Centre
The Surgery
Doctors Surg
Lennox Road
Brooklands Road
Windsor Street
Osborne St
Duncombe St
Water Eaton Road
MK2
Chestnut Crs
Pinewood Dr
Larch Grove
Oakwood Drive
Mill Road
Stoke Road
Saffron St
Combined School
Drayton Road Surg
Water Eaton
Blue Lagoon Park
Bishop Parker RC School
Barton Road
Drayton Road
River Ouzel
Milton Keynes
Buckinghamshire County
Eaton Leys Farm
62
73
K5, M1
Street names for these grid squares are listed at the back of the index
M4
1 Longhedge
M2
1 Rixband Cl
2 Williams Cir
3 Wingate Cir
M3
1 Brantham Cl
2 Newark Ct
3 Passmore
K8
1 The Wharf

62
B2
1 Gershwin Ct
2 Schumann Cl
B1
1 Bowen Cl
2 Camomile Ct
3 Gabriel Cl
4 Mahler Cl
5 Spearmint Cl
6 Twyford La
A3
1 Berrystead
2 Hele Ct
3 Mapledurham
A1
1 Coriander Ct
2 Meadowsweet
3 Nutmeg Cl
4 Paprika Ct
5 Silverweed Ct
50
Old Farm Park
Walnut Tree
Woburn Sands
Woburn Sands Station
Woodley's Farm
Browns Wood
Combined School
Caraway Close
Bletcham Way
Tongwell Street
Brickhill Street
Sherbourne Dr
Bradbourne Drive
Morley Crescent
Rodwell Gardens
Boyce Crescent
Beethoven Cl
Curzon Place
Heybridge Crs
Gatewick Lane
Station Road
Greenways
Downs View
Rushmere Close
Parkway
Church Road
London End Lane
Bow Brickhill
Bow Brickhill Road
Woburn Sands Road
Wavendon Wood
Milton Keynes Boundary Walk
Milton Keynes
Bedfordshire County
61
Back Wood
Bell's Copse
Woburn Golf & Country Club
Glebe Farm
Little Brickhill Copse
A5(T)
Woburn Road
74
C1
Street names for this grid square are listed at the back of the index
C2
1 Ireland Cl
C4
1 Edwin Cl
2 Grovesbrook
3 Haynes Cl
C5
1 Drakewell Rd
D1
1 Davenport Lea
Little Brickhill
Wyness Avenue
1 grid square represents 500 metres

Aspley Guise Station
H2 1 Concra Pk
H3 1 Church Rd
L2 1 Guise Ct
Aspley Guise
51
Ridgway
Berry Lane
BEDFORD
Swallowfield Lower School
Fulbrook Secondary School
Mill Lane
Mill Way
Church Street
Browns Way
Bedford Road
Church End
A507
Crow Lane
Crawley Park
Aspley Guise Golf Club & Shop
The Mount
West Hill
Hotel
Spinney Lane
Aspley Guise Primary School
Mount Pleasant
San Remo Road
Elm Grove
Theydon Avenue
Wood Street
The Leys
Asplands Medical Centre
STATION ROAD
HIGH STREET
Weathercock Lane
Russell Street
Vicarage Street
St Vincents
Aspley Hill
Downham Road
Chapel Street
Sheldon Court
Hardwick Road
Dene Close
Duke Street
Mentone Av
Woodside
Wood Lane
Green Lane
Woburn Lane
Peers Drive
Horsepool Lane
A5130
Aspley Heath
Bishops Wk
Hardwick Mews
Narrow Path
Church Road
Sandy Lane
Holly Walk
Fernwood School
WOBURN ROAD
Aspley Wood
Old Wavendon Heath
Birchmoor Farm
Aspley Lane
CRAWLEY ROAD
The Evergreens
New Wavendon Heath
A5130
Birchmoor Green
Dolton's Farm
Hundreds Farm
Drakeloe Close
Eleanor Close
The Surgery
BEDFORD STREET
Marquis Court
Lower School
HIGH STREET
Park Street
Woburn
Timber Lane
Duck Lane
London End
Maryland College
Leighton Street
GEORGE STREET
Greensand Ridge Walk
A4012
Charle Wood
Lowe's Wood
Pinfoldpond
75
Job's Farm
L8 1 Bloomsbury Cl
L7 1 Howland Pl
Speedwell Farm
Utcoate Grange
G H J K L M
1 2 3 4 5 6 7 8

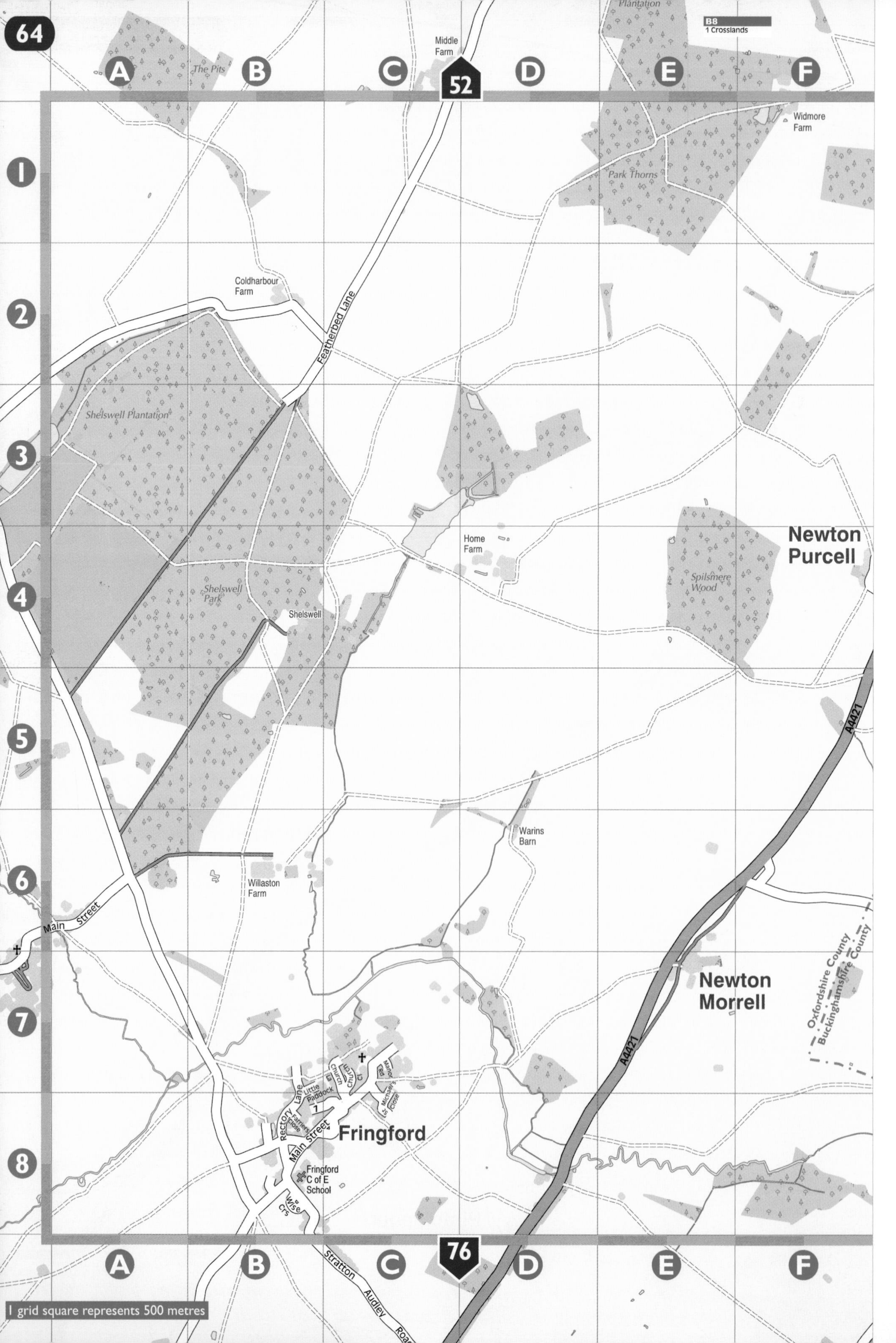
The Pits
Plantation
B8
1 Crosslands
Middle Farm
52
Widmore Farm
Park Thorns
Coldharbour Farm
Featherbed Lane
Shelswell Plantation
Home Farm
Newton Purcell
Spilsmere Wood
Shelswell Park
Shelswell
A4421
Warins Barn
Willaston Farm
Main Street
Newton Morrell
Oxfordshire County
Buckinghamshire County
Rectory Lane
Little Paddock
Church Cl
Manor Rd
St Michaels Close
Farmers Close
Main Street
Fringford
Fringford C of E School
Wise Crs
76
Stratton Audley Road
A B C D E F
1 2 3 4 5 6 7 8
1 grid square represents 500 metres

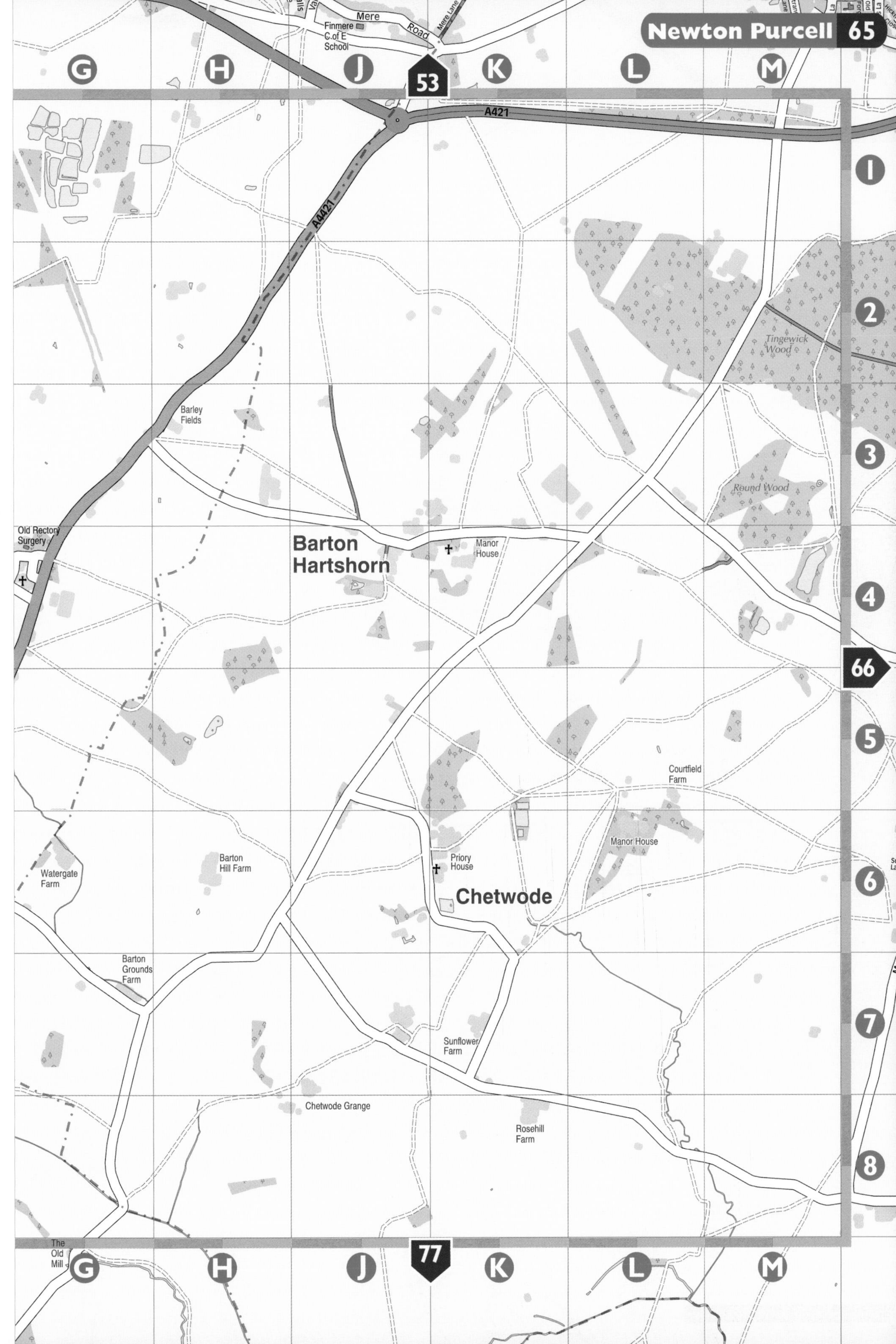

Mere
Road
Mere Lane
Finmere C of E School
53
G
H
J
K
L
M
A421
A4421
Tingewick Wood
Round Wood
Barley Fields
Old Rectory Surgery
Barton Hartshorn
Manor House
66
Courtfield Farm
Manor House
Barton Hill Farm
Priory House
Chetwode
Watergate Farm
Barton Grounds Farm
Sunflower Farm
Chetwode Grange
Rosehill Farm
The Old Mill
77
1
2
3
4
5
6
7
8

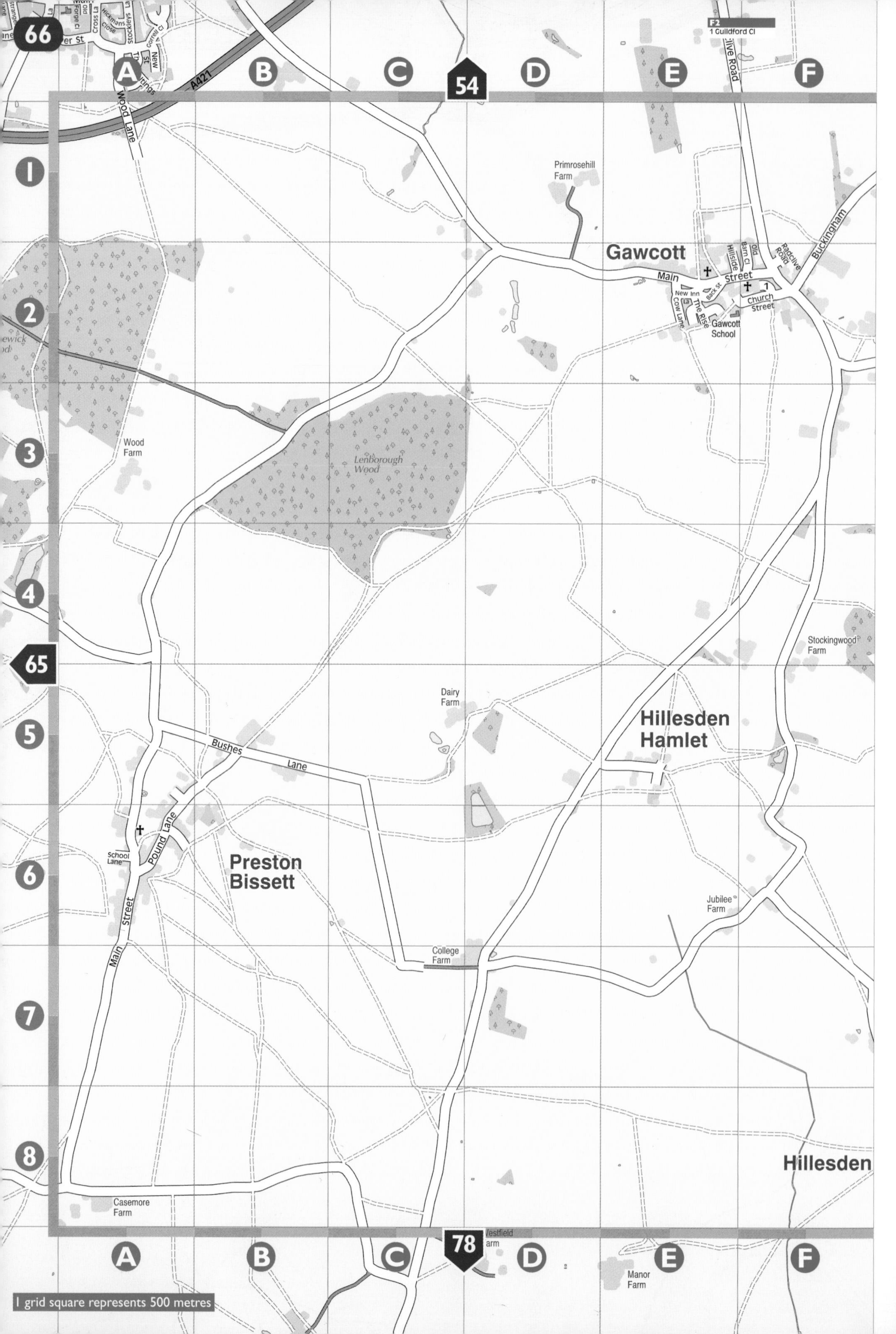
66
54
65
78
A
B
C
D
E
F
1
2
3
4
5
6
7
8
F2
1 Guildford Cl
A421
Wood Lane
Primrosehill Farm
Gawcott
Main Street
New Inn
Cow Lane
The Rise
Back St
Hillside
Barn Cl
Old Road
Radclive Road
Buckingham
Church Street
Gawcott School
Wood Farm
Lenborough Wood
Stockingwood Farm
Dairy Farm
Hillesden Hamlet
Bushes Lane
Pound Lane
School Lane
Preston Bissett
Main Street
Jubilee Farm
College Farm
Hillesden
Casemore Farm
Manor Farm
1 grid square represents 500 metres

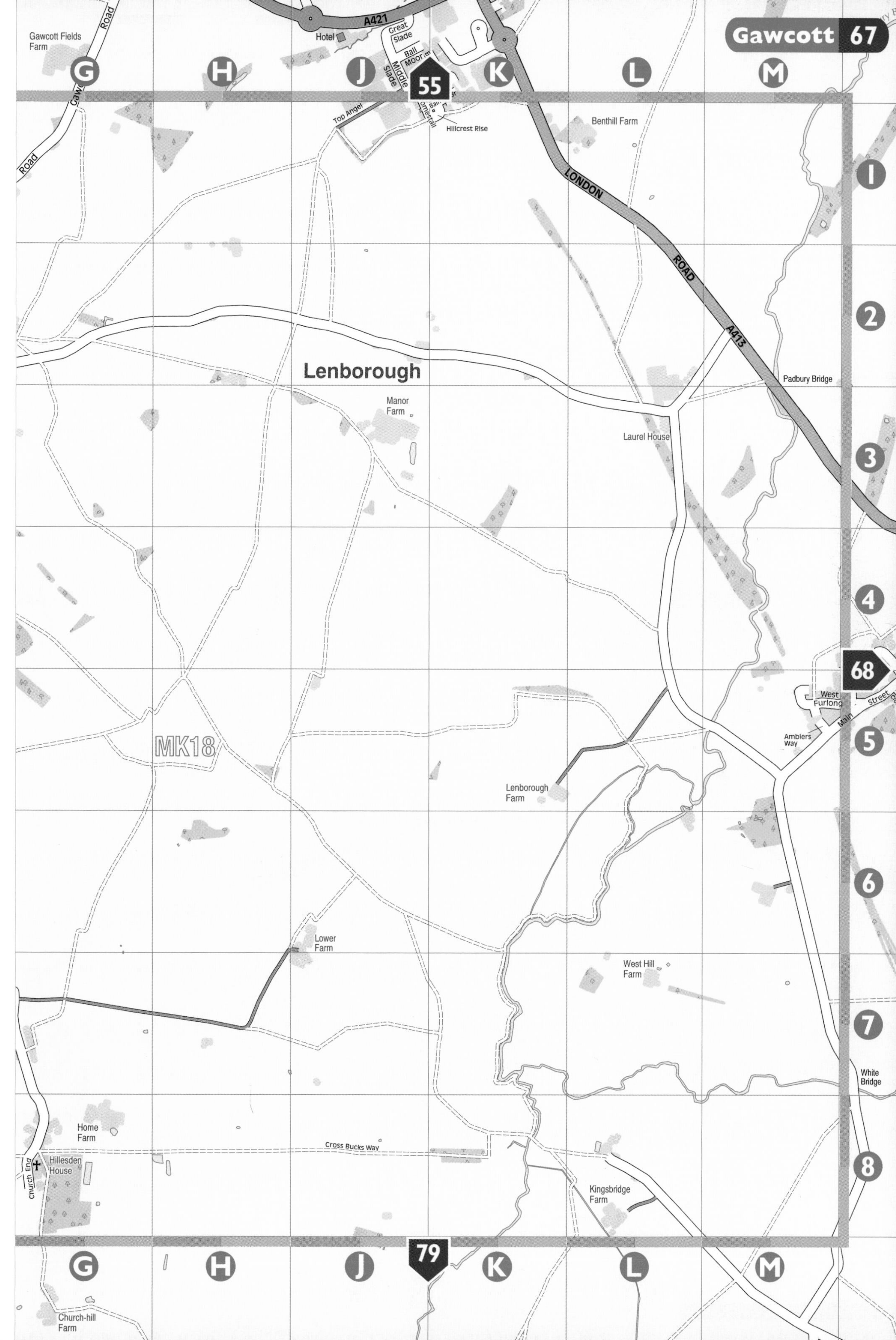
A421
Hotel
Great Slade
Ball Moor
Middle Slade
55
Top Angel
Hillcrest Rise
Gawcott Fields Farm
Gawcott Road
Benthill Farm
LONDON ROAD
A413
Padbury Bridge
Lenborough
Manor Farm
Laurel House
68
West Furlong
Main Street
Amblers Way
MK18
Lenborough Farm
Lower Farm
West Hill Farm
White Bridge
Home Farm
Cross Bucks Way
Hillesden House
Church End
Kingsbridge Farm
79
Church-hill Farm
G
H
J
K
L
M
1
2
3
4
5
6
7
8

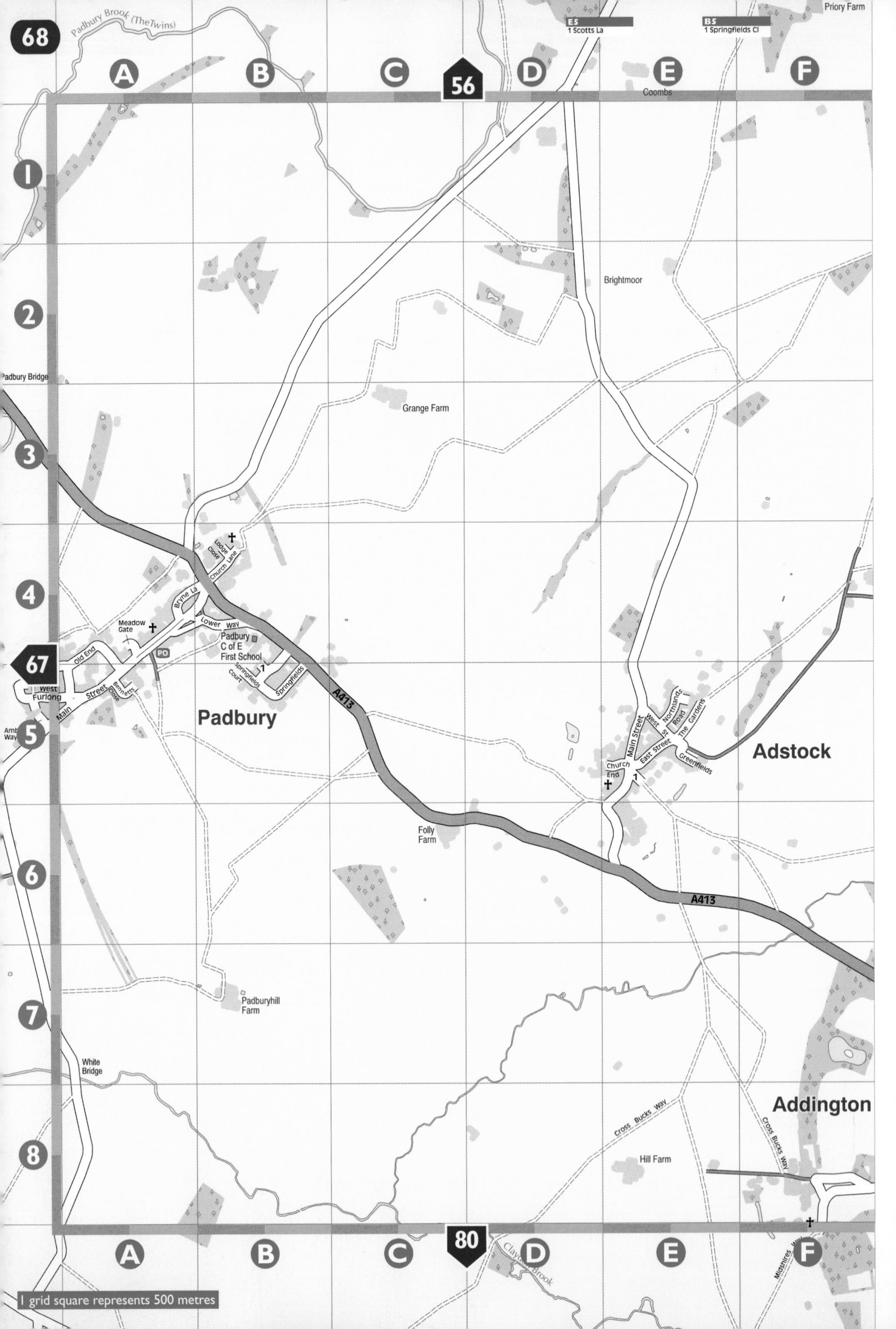

Padbury Brook (The Twins)
E5 1 Scotts La
B5 1 Springfields Cl
Priory Farm
56
Coombs
Brightmoor
Padbury Bridge
Grange Farm
Lodge Close
Church Lane
Bryne La
Lower Way
Meadow Gate
Padbury C of E First School
PO
Old End
West Furlong
Main Street
Bennetts Close
Springfields Court
Springfields
A413
Padbury
Amb Way
67
Folly Farm
Main Street
West St
Northlands Road
The Gardens
East Street
Greenfields
Church End
Adstock
Padburyhill Farm
White Bridge
Addington
Cross Bucks Way
Hill Farm
Midshires Way
Claydon Brook
80
1 grid square represents 500 metres

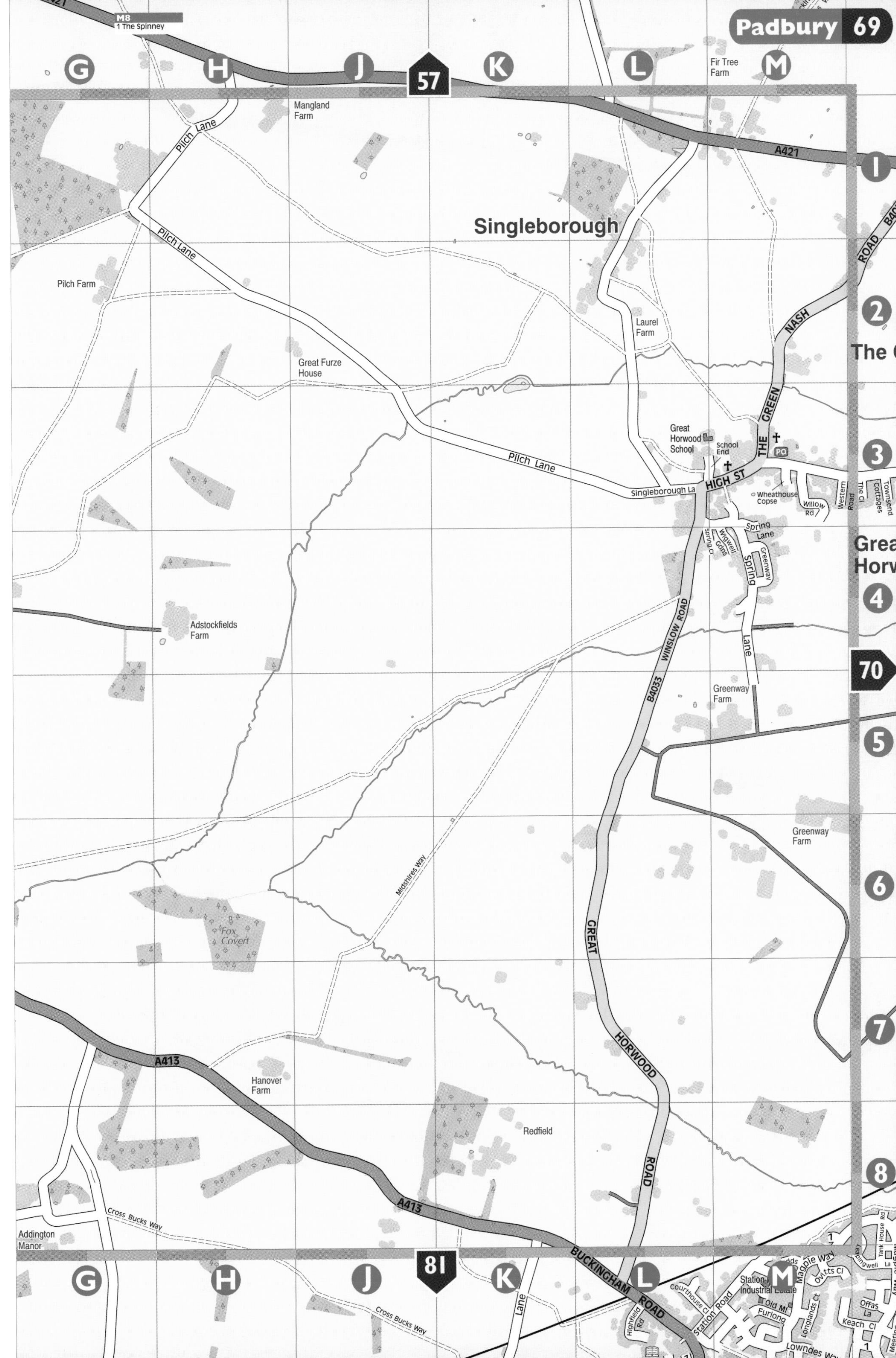
A421
M8
1 The Spinney
G
H
J
57
K
L
Fir Tree Farm
M
Mangland Farm
Pilch Lane
A421
1
Singleborough
Pilch Lane
B4033
ROAD
Pilch Farm
NASH
2
Laurel Farm
The C
Great Furze House
THE GREEN
Great Horwood School
School End
PO
3
Pilch Lane
Singleborough La
HIGH ST
Wheathouse Copse
Willow Rd
Western Road
The Cl
Townsend Cottages
Spring Lane
Spring Cl
Winwell Gdns
Spring
Greenway
Grea
Horw
WINSLOW ROAD
4
Adstockfields Farm
Lane
70
B4033
Greenway Farm
5
Greenway Farm
Midshires Way
6
Fox Covert
GREAT
7
A413
HORWOOD
Hanover Farm
Redfield
ROAD
8
A413
Cross Bucks Way
Addington Manor
BUCKINGHAM
G
H
J
81
K
L
M
ROAD
Magpie Way
Station Industrial Estate
Courthouse Cl
Station Road
Old Ml Furlong
Longlands Ct
Ovitts Cl
Offas La
Keach Cl
Cross Bucks Way
Lane
Highfield Rd
Lowndes Way
Magpie Way
Meeting

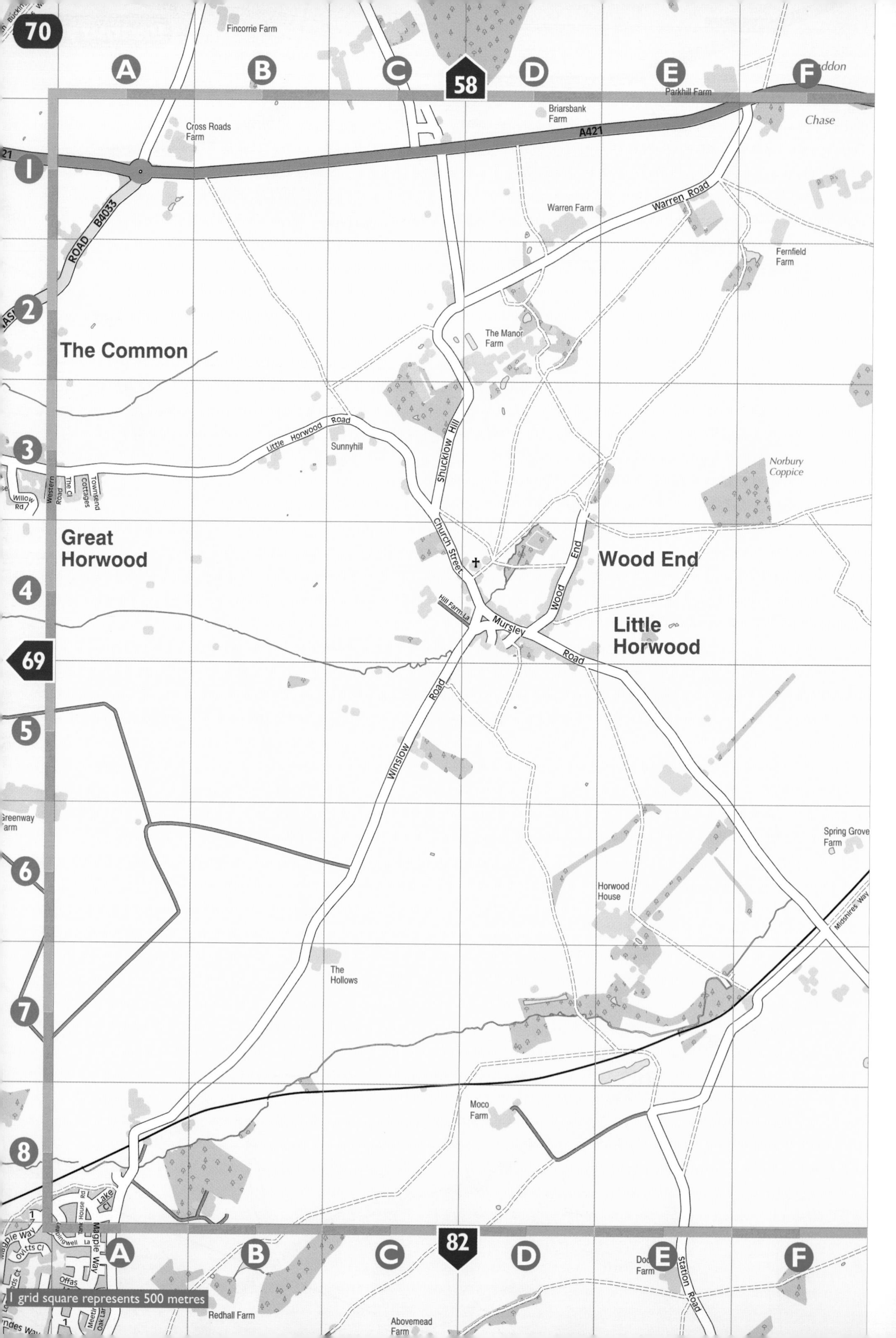

Fincorrie Farm
58
Parkhill Farm
Chase
Briarsbank Farm
Cross Roads Farm
A421
ROAD B4033
Warren Farm
Warren Road
Fernfield Farm
The Common
The Manor Farm
Little Horwood Road
Sunnyhill
Shucklow Hill
Norbury Coppice
Western Road
The Cl
Cottages
Townsend
Willow Rd
Great Horwood
Church Street
Wood End
Wood End
Hill Farm La
Mursley Road
Little Horwood
69
Winslow Road
Greenway Farm
Spring Grove Farm
Horwood House
Midshires Way
The Hollows
Moco Farm
Lake Cl
Magpie Way
Ovitts Cl
Offas
82
Station Road
Redhall Farm
Abovemead Farm
1 grid square represents 500 metres

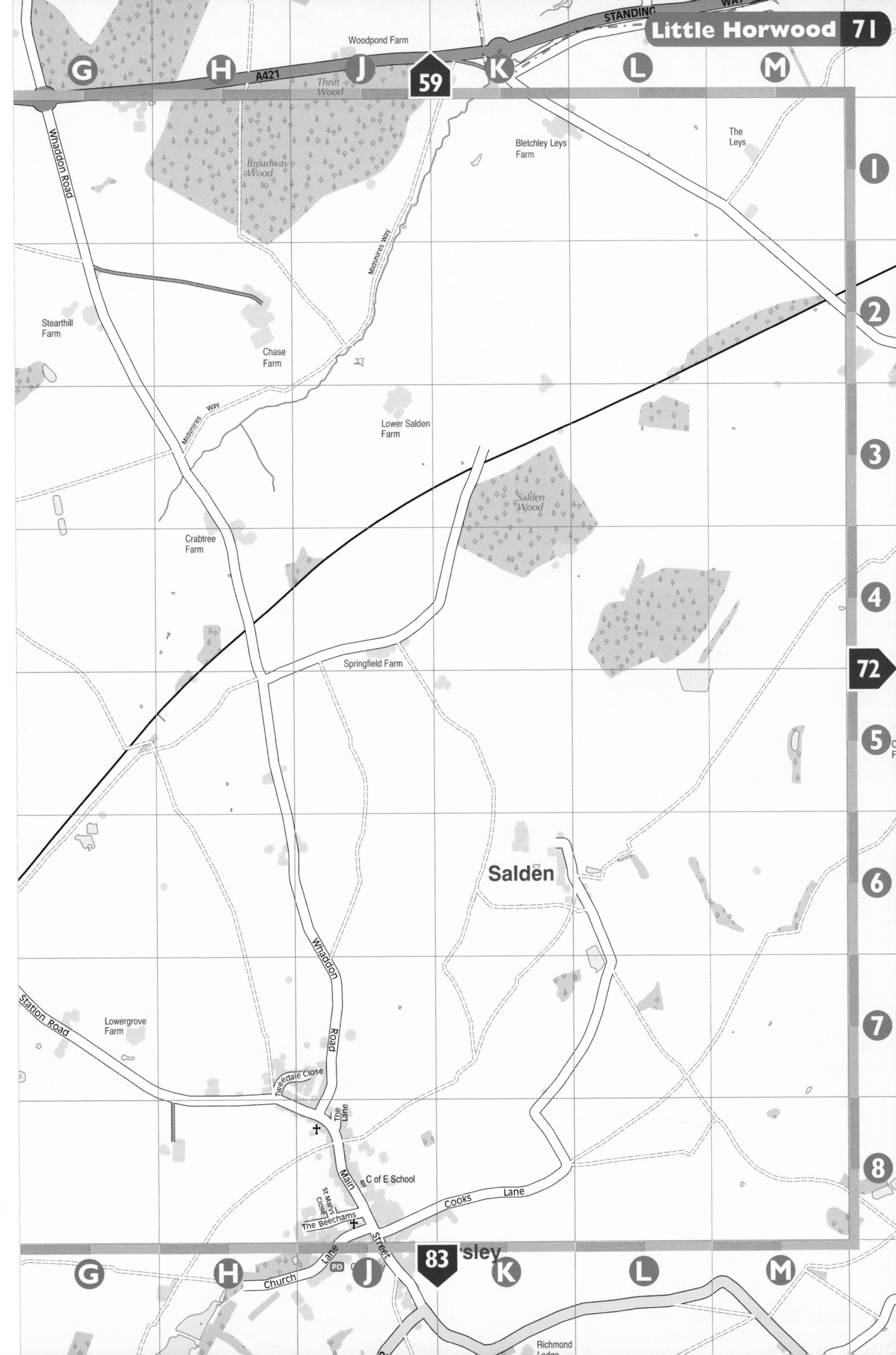
STANDING
WAY
Woodpond Farm
A421
Thrift Wood
59
G
H
J
K
L
M
Bletchley Leys Farm
The Leys
Broadway Wood
Whaddon Road
Midshires Way
I
2
3
4
5
6
7
8
Stearthill Farm
Chase Farm
Lower Salden Farm
Salden Wood
Crabtree Farm
Springfield Farm
72
Salden
Whaddon Road
Station Road
Lowergrove Farm
Tweedale Close
The Lane
Main Street
C of E School
St Mary's Close
The Beechams
Cooks Lane
83
Church Lane
PO
Richmond

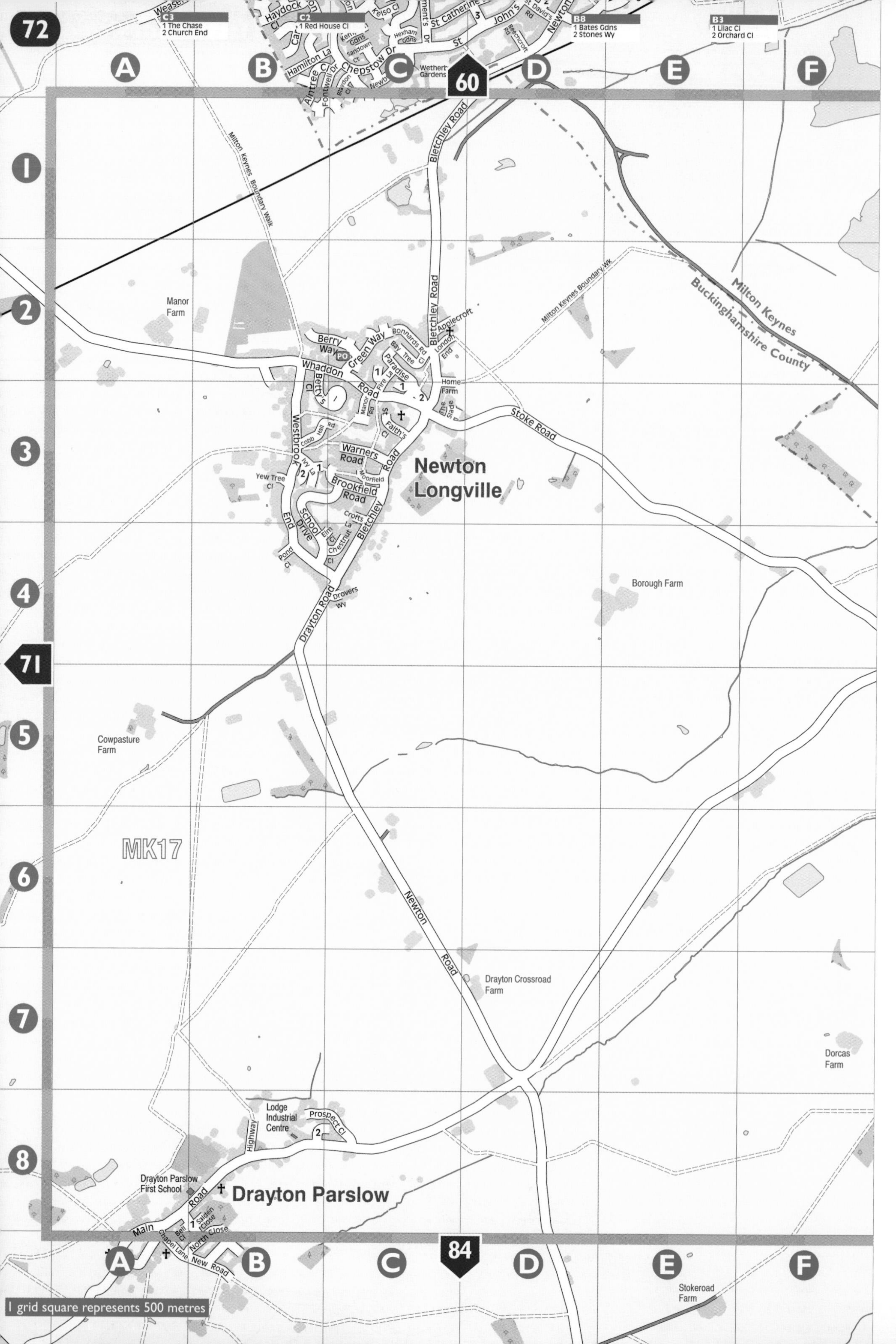
C3
1 The Chase
2 Church End
C2
1 Red House Cl
B8
1 Bates Gdns
2 Stones Wy
B3
1 Lilac Cl
2 Orchard Cl
A
B
C
D
E
F
60
1
2
3
4
5
6
7
8
71
84
Haydock Cl
Hamilton La
Aintree Cl
Fontwell Dr
Chepstow Dr
Sandown Ct
Kelso Cl
Hexham Gdns
Wetherby Gardens
St Catherine's
St John's
St David's Rd
Beechcroft Rd
Newton
Bletchley Road
Milton Keynes Boundary Walk
Milton Keynes Boundary Wk
Milton Keynes
Buckinghamshire County
Manor Farm
Berry Way
PO
Green Way
Bonnards Rd
Bay Tree Cl
Paradise
Applecroft
London End
Home Farm
The Slade
Whaddon Road
Betty's Cl
Manor Rd
St Faith's Cl
Stoke Road
Westbrook End
Cobb Hall Rd
Warners Road
Yew Tree Cl
Moorfield
Brookfield Road
School Drive
Crofts La
Elm Cl
Chestnut Cl
Pond Cl
Newton Longville
Borough Farm
Drayton Road
Drovers Wy
Cowpasture Farm
MK17
Newton Road
Drayton Crossroad Farm
Dorcas Farm
Lodge Industrial Centre
Prospect Cl
Highway
Drayton Parslow First School
Drayton Parslow
Main Road
Salden Close
North Close
Chapel Lane
New Road
Stokeroad Farm
1 grid square represents 500 metres

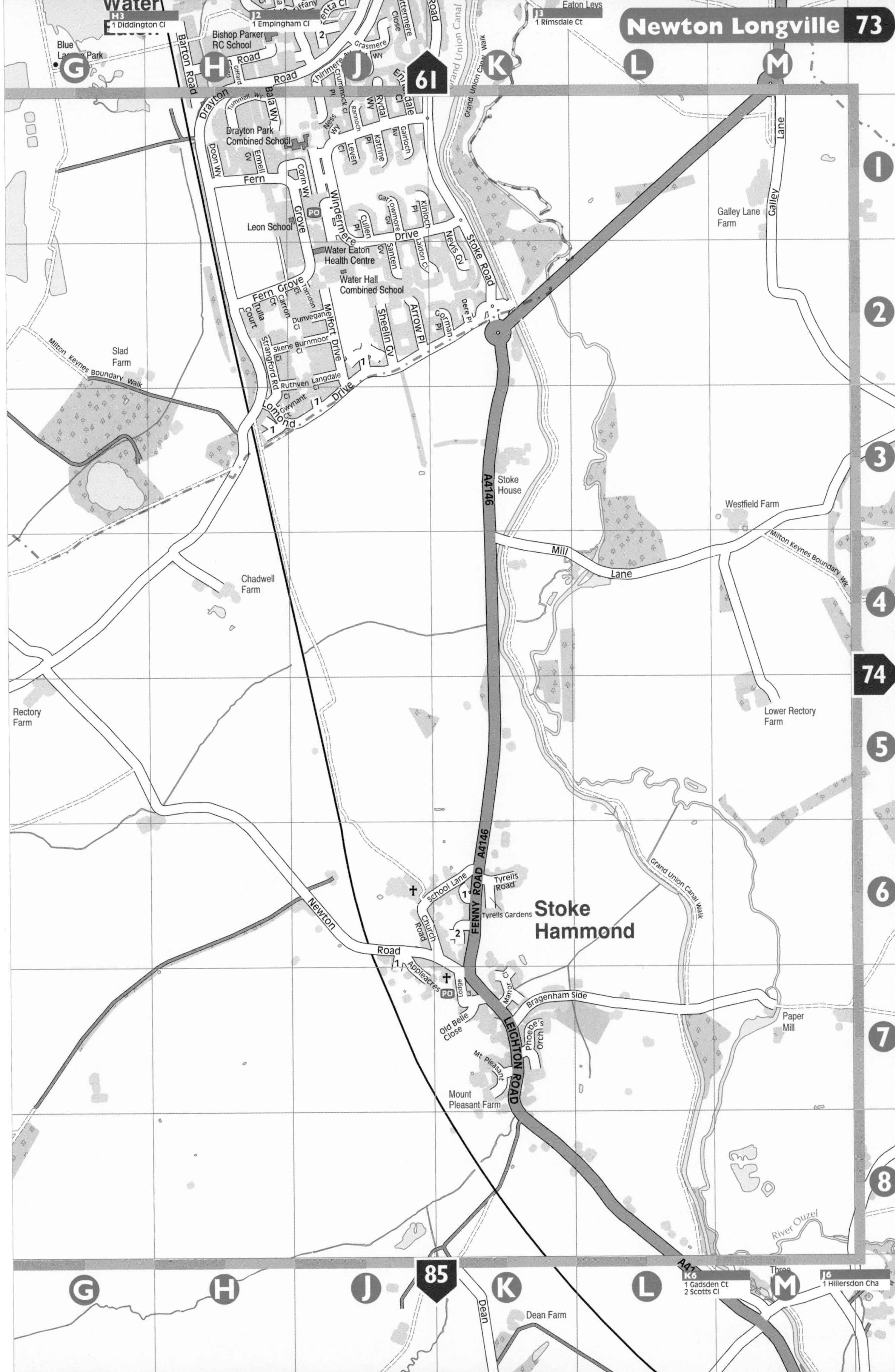
Water Eaton
H3 1 Diddington Cl
J2 1 Empingham Cl
J3 1 Rimsdale Ct
Eaton Leys
Blue Lagoon Park
Bishop Parker RC School
Drayton Park Combined School
Leon School
Water Eaton Health Centre
Water Hall Combined School
Grand Union Canal
Grand Union Canal Walk
Galley Lane Farm
Galley Lane
Slad Farm
Milton Keynes Boundary Walk
Stoke House
Westfield Farm
Mill Lane
Chadwell Farm
Rectory Farm
Lower Rectory Farm
Stoke Road
Fenny Road
A4146
Stoke Hammond
School Lane
Tyrells Road
Tyrells Gardens
Church Road
Newton Road
Appleacres
Bragenham Side
Paper Mill
Old Belle Close
Phoebe's Orch
Mt Pleasant
Leighton Road
Mount Pleasant Farm
River Ouzel
K6 1 Gadsden Ct 2 Scotts Cl
J6 1 Hillersdon Cha
Dean Farm
Three
61
74
85
G H J K L M
1 2 3 4 5 6 7 8

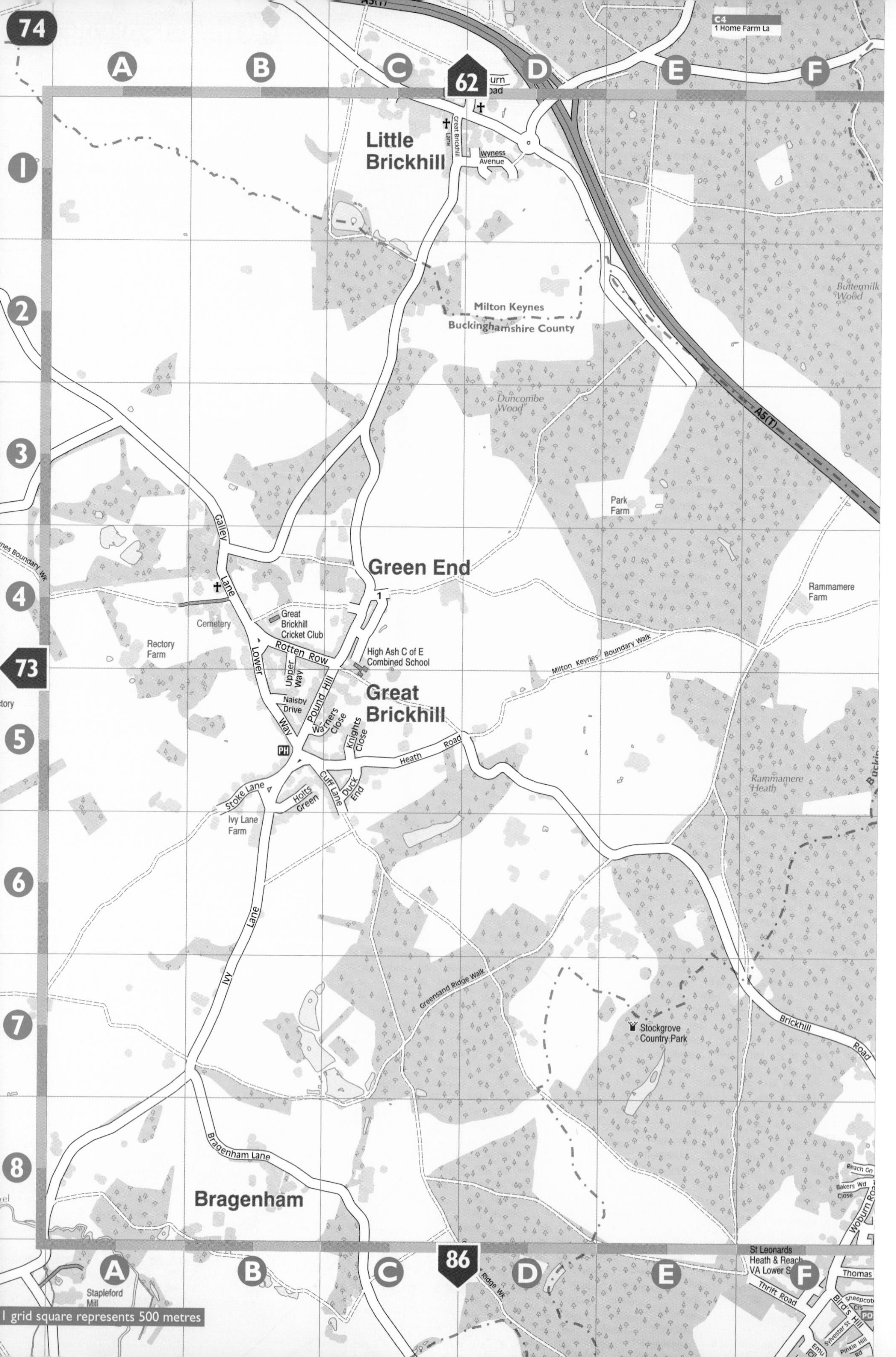


1 grid square represents 500 metres

63
87
G
H
J
K
L
M
1
2
3
4
5
6
7
8
Leighton
Greensand Ridge Walk
Greensand Ridge Walk
Lowe's Wood
Coldpond
Job's Farm
A4012
LONDON ROAD
Speedwell Farm
Utcoate Grange
Greensand Ridge Walk
Milton Keynes Boundary Walk
Apesfield Farm
Old Farm
Sheeplane
Bushycommon Wood
Hill Farm
A5(T)
Buckinghamshire County
Bedfordshire County
Kings Wood
King's Wood
Manor Farm
Potsgrove
Woburn Road
A5(T)
Home Wood
Woburn Road
Bat Par
Fox Corner
Overendgreen Farm
Overend
Green
Lane
Eastern Way
Grange Gdns
Lane
St
Reach
Heath and Reach
The Dell
Gig
Lane
Kingsway Farm
Fourne Hill Farm
A5(T)

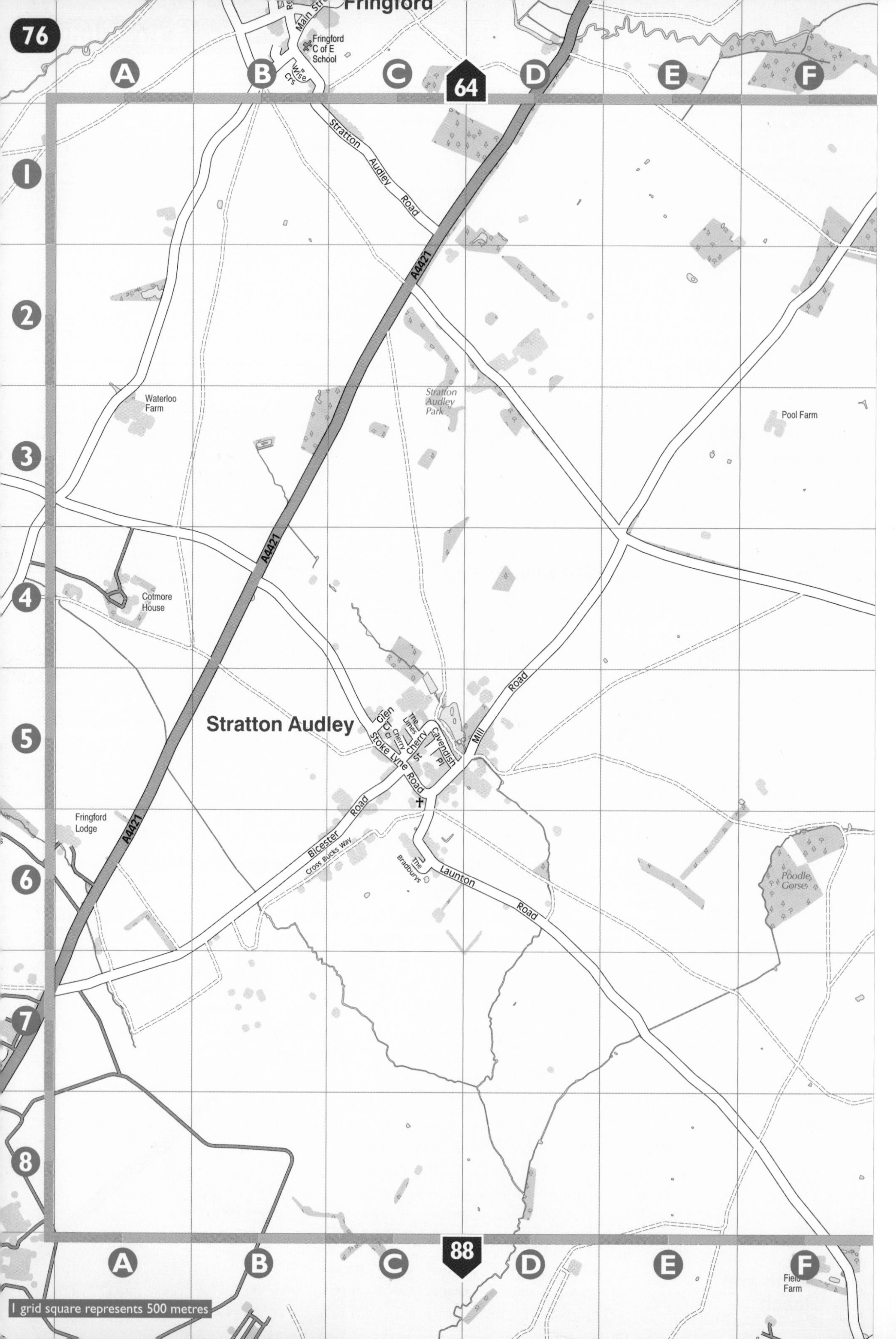
Fringford
Main St
Fringford C of E School
Wise Crs
A
B
C
64
D
E
F
Stratton Audley Road
A4421
1
2
3
4
5
6
7
8
Waterloo Farm
Stratton Audley Park
Pool Farm
Cotmore House
Stratton Audley
Glen Cl
The Limes
Cherry Cl
Cherry St
Cavendish Pl
Mill Road
Stoke Lyne Road
Fringford Lodge
Bicester Road
Cross Bucks Way
The Bradburys
Launton Road
Poodle Gorse
88
Field Farm
1 grid square represents 500 metres

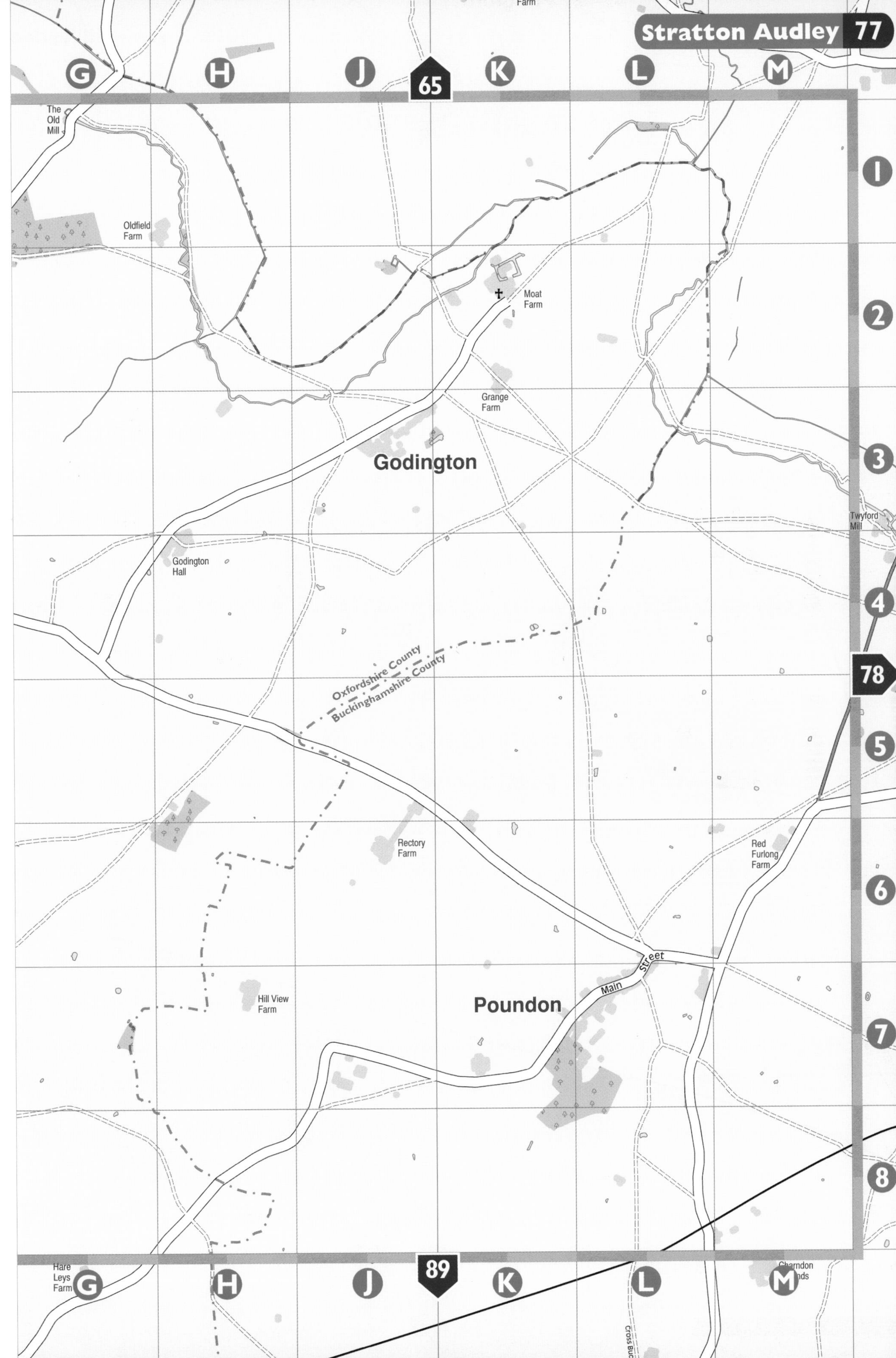

Farm
G
H
J
65
K
L
M
The Old Mill
Oldfield Farm
Moat Farm
Grange Farm
Godington
Twyford Mill
Godington Hall
Oxfordshire County
Buckinghamshire County
78
Rectory Farm
Red Furlong Farm
Main Street
Poundon
Hill View Farm
Hare Leys Farm
89
Charndon
1
2
3
4
5
6
7
8

78
66
77
90
Hillesden
Westfield Farm
Manor Farm
Cowley Farm
Cross Bucks Way
Cowley Lodge
Twyford Mill
Three Bridge Mill
Briarhill
Twyford C of E First School
Church Street
Grange
School Lane
Mill Lane
Main St
Twyford
PO
Bicester Road
Portway Road
Rose Hl Crs
Portway Farm
Twyford Lodge
Nature Reserve (Calvert Jubilee)
Grebe Lake
Barclay Close
School Hill
Charndon
Main Street
1 grid square represents 500 metres

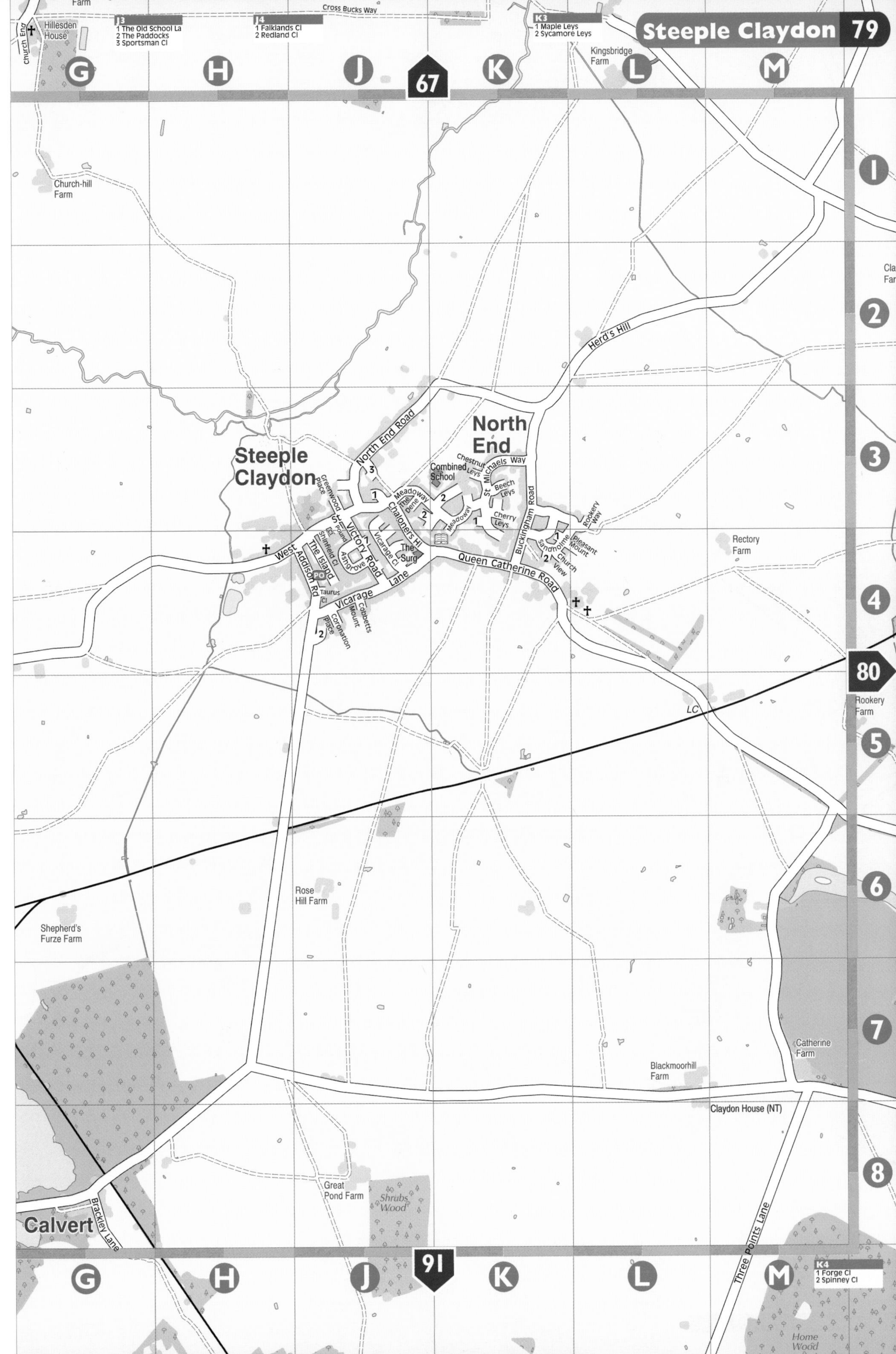

Farm
Cross Bucks Way
J3
1 The Old School La
2 The Paddocks
3 Sportsman Cl
J4
1 Falklands Cl
2 Redland Cl
K3
1 Maple Leys
2 Sycamore Leys
Church End
Hillesden House
Kingsbridge Farm
67
Church-hill Farm
Clay Farm
Herd's Hill
North End Road
North End
Steeple Claydon
Chestnut Leys
St Michaels Way
Combined School
Greenwood Place
Meadoway
The Dene
Beech Leys
St Michaels Way
Cherry Leys
Buckingham Road
Rookery Way
Chaloners Hl
Victory Road
Vicarage Cl
The Surg
St Pound
Shirefield Cl
The Island
Ashgrove
West
Addison Rd
PO
Taurus Cl
Sandholme
Pleasant Mount
Church View
Queen Catherine Road
Lane
Vicarage
Cobbetts Mount
Coronation Place
Rectory Farm
80
Rookery Farm
LC
Rose Hill Farm
Shepherd's Furze Farm
Catherine Farm
Blackmoorhill Farm
Claydon House (NT)
Great Pond Farm
Shrubs Wood
Calvert
Brackley Lane
Three Points Lane
91
K4
1 Forge Cl
2 Spinney Cl
Home Wood
G H J K L M
1 2 3 4 5 6 7 8

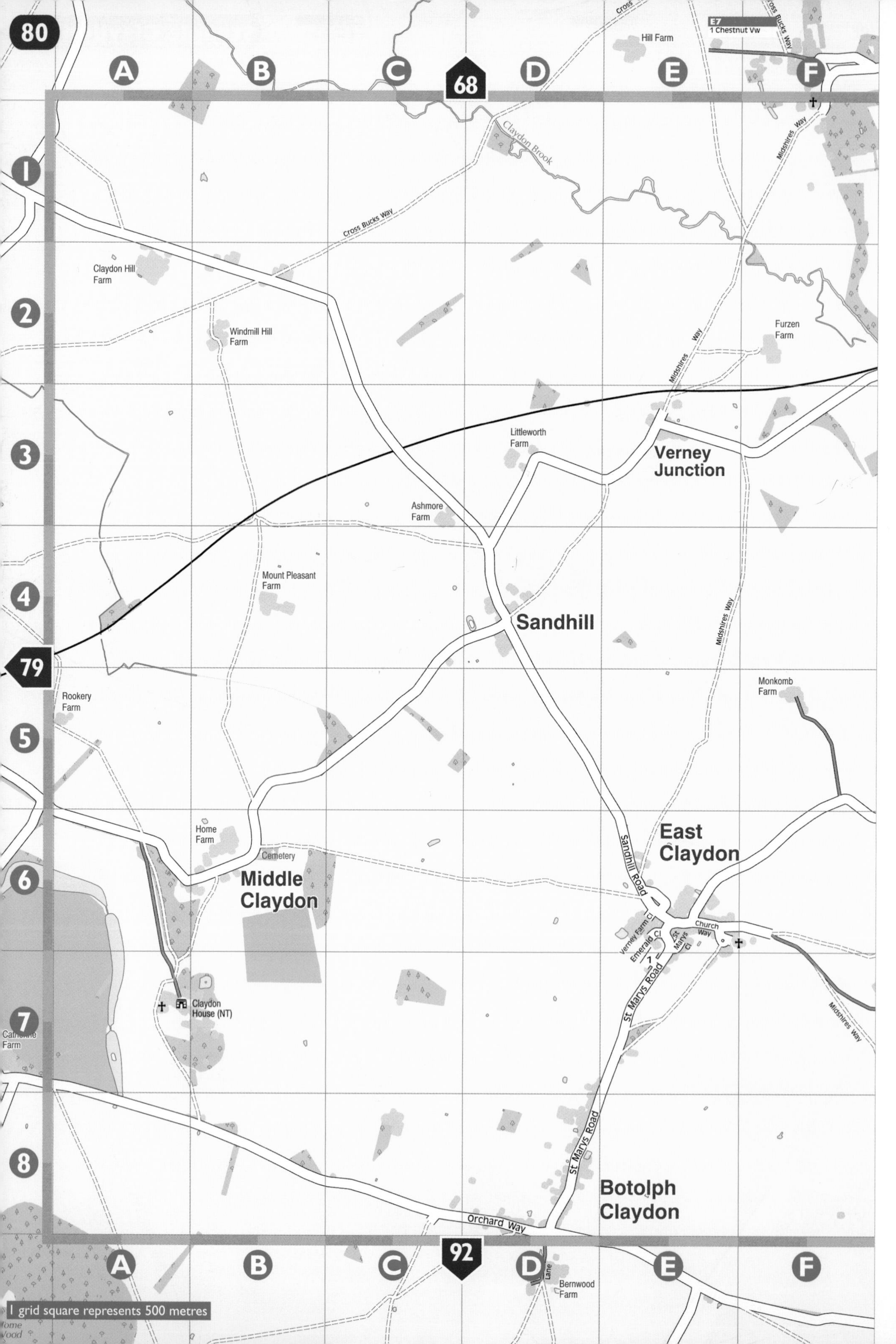
68
79
92
A
B
C
D
E
F
1
2
3
4
5
6
7
8
E7
1 Chestnut Vw
Cross Bucks Way
Hill Farm
Claydon Brook
Midshires Way
Cross Bucks Way
Claydon Hill Farm
Windmill Hill Farm
Furzen Farm
Midshires Way
Littleworth Farm
Verney Junction
Ashmore Farm
Mount Pleasant Farm
Sandhill
Midshires Way
Rookery Farm
Monkomb Farm
Home Farm
Cemetery
Middle Claydon
East Claydon
Sandhill Road
Verney Farm Cl
Emerald Cl
St Marys Cl
Church Way
St Marys Road
Midshires Way
Claydon House (NT)
Catherine Farm
St Marys Road
Botolph Claydon
Orchard Way
Lane
Bernwood Farm
1 grid square represents 500 metres

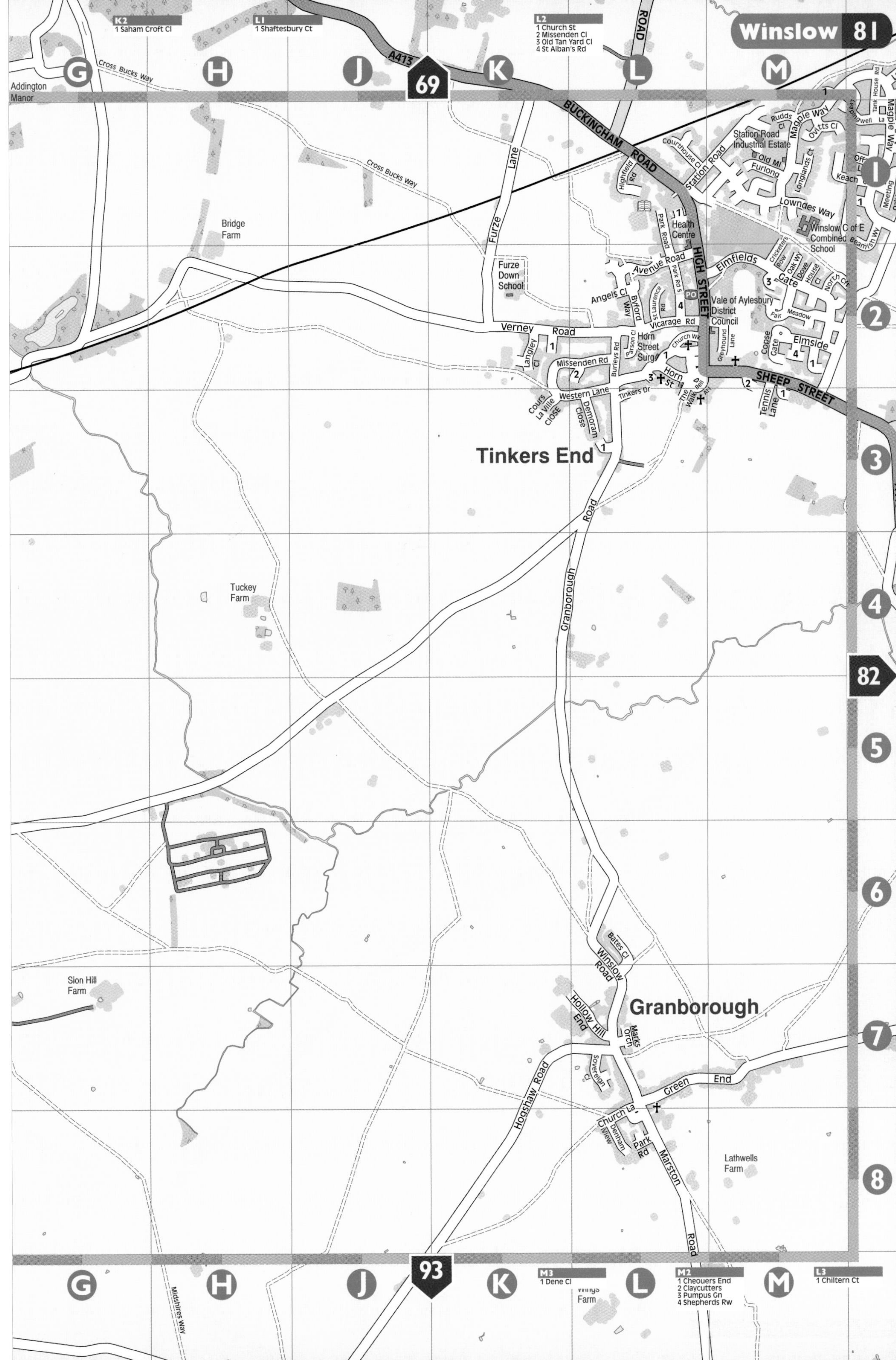
K2
1 Saham Croft Cl
L1
1 Shaftesbury Ct
L2
1 Church St
2 Missenden Cl
3 Old Tan Yard Cl
4 St Alban's Rd
G
H
J
K
L
M
69
A413
ROAD
Addington Manor
Cross Bucks Way
Cross Bucks Way
BUCKINGHAM ROAD
Furze Lane
Bridge Farm
Station Road
Station Road Industrial Estate
Courthouse Cl
Highfield Rd
Rudds Cl
Magpie Way
Ovitts Cl
Old Ml
Furlong
Longlands Ct
Tank House Rd
Magpie Way
Keach
Meeting Oak Lane
Lowndes Way
Winslow C of E Combined School
Beamish Wy
Park Road
Health Centre
HIGH STREET
Avenue Road
Park Rd S
Elmfields
Cricketers Row
Oak Wy
Dove House Cl
North Cft
Gate
Meadow
Furze Down School
Angels Cl
Byford Way
St Laurence Rd
PO
Vale of Aylesbury District Council
Vicarage Rd
Verney Road
Langley Cl
Horn Street Surg
Church Wk
Greyhound Lane
Copse Gate
Elmside
Missenden Rd
Burleys Rd
Parson Cl
Horn St
The Walk
Bell Aly
SHEEP STREET
Tennis Lane
Western Lane
Tinkers Dr
Cours La Ville CLOSE
Demoram Close
Tinkers End
Road
Granborough
Tuckey Farm
82
1
2
3
4
5
6
7
8
A413
Bates Cl
Winslow Road
Granborough
Hollow Hill End
Marks Orch
Sion Hill Farm
Sovereign Cl
Hogshaw Road
Green End
Church La
Denham View
Park Rd
Marston Road
Lathwells Farm
93
M3
1 Dene Cl
M2
1 Chequers End
2 Claycutters
3 Pumpus Gn
4 Shepherds Rw
L3
1 Chiltern Ct
Wings Farm
Midshires Way

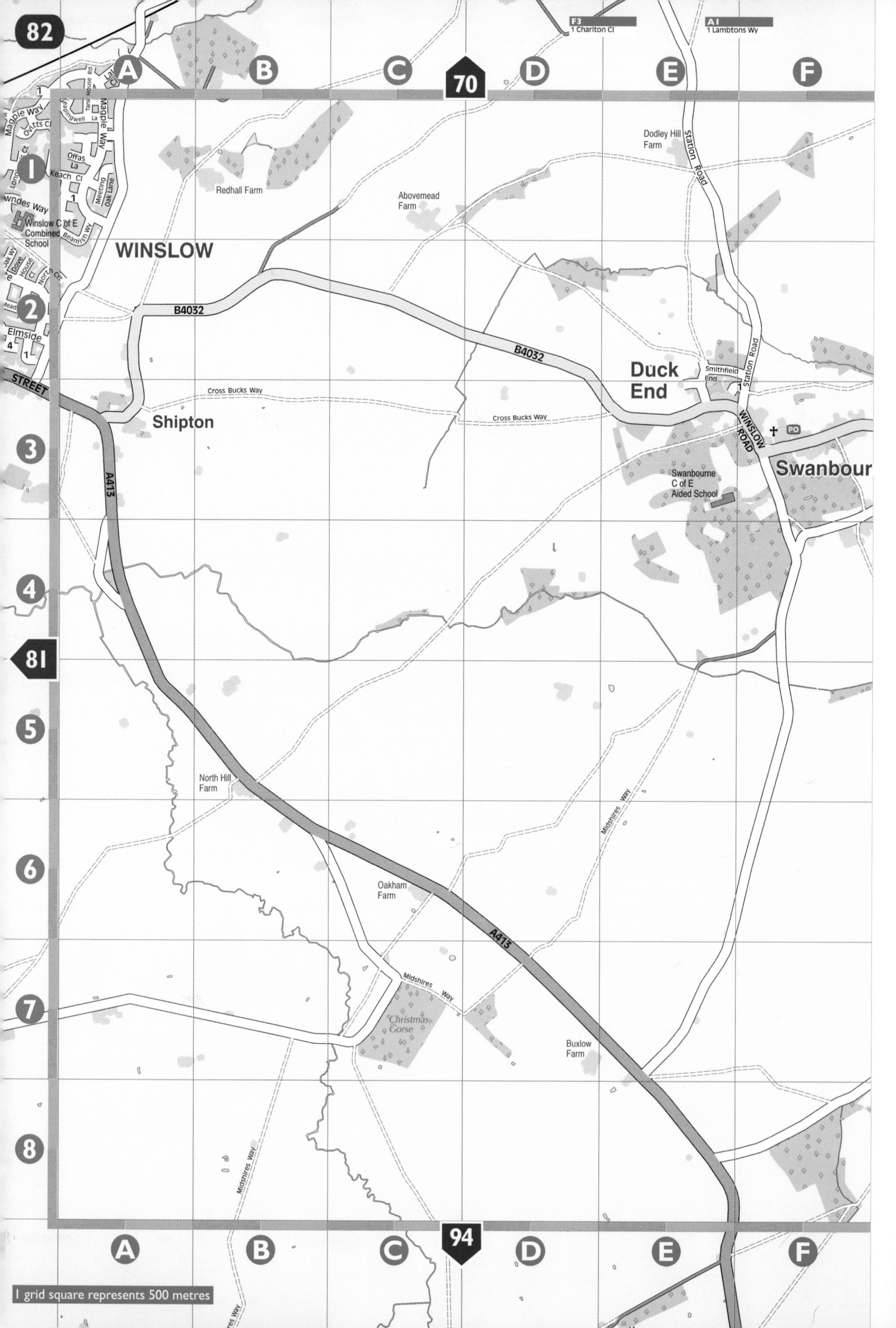

82
70
81
94
A
B
C
D
E
F
1
2
3
4
5
6
7
8
F3 1 Charlton Cl
A1 1 Lambtons Wy
WINSLOW
Redhall Farm
Abovemead Farm
Dodley Hill Farm
Station Road
B4032
Duck End
Smithfield End
Cross Bucks Way
Shipton
WINSLOW ROAD
Swanbour
Swanbourne C of E Aided School
A413
North Hill Farm
Midshires Way
Oakham Farm
Christmas Gorse
Buxlow Farm
Winslow C of E Combined School
Magpie Way
Offas La
Keach Cl
Meeting Oak Lane
Elmside
STREET
1 grid square represents 500 metres

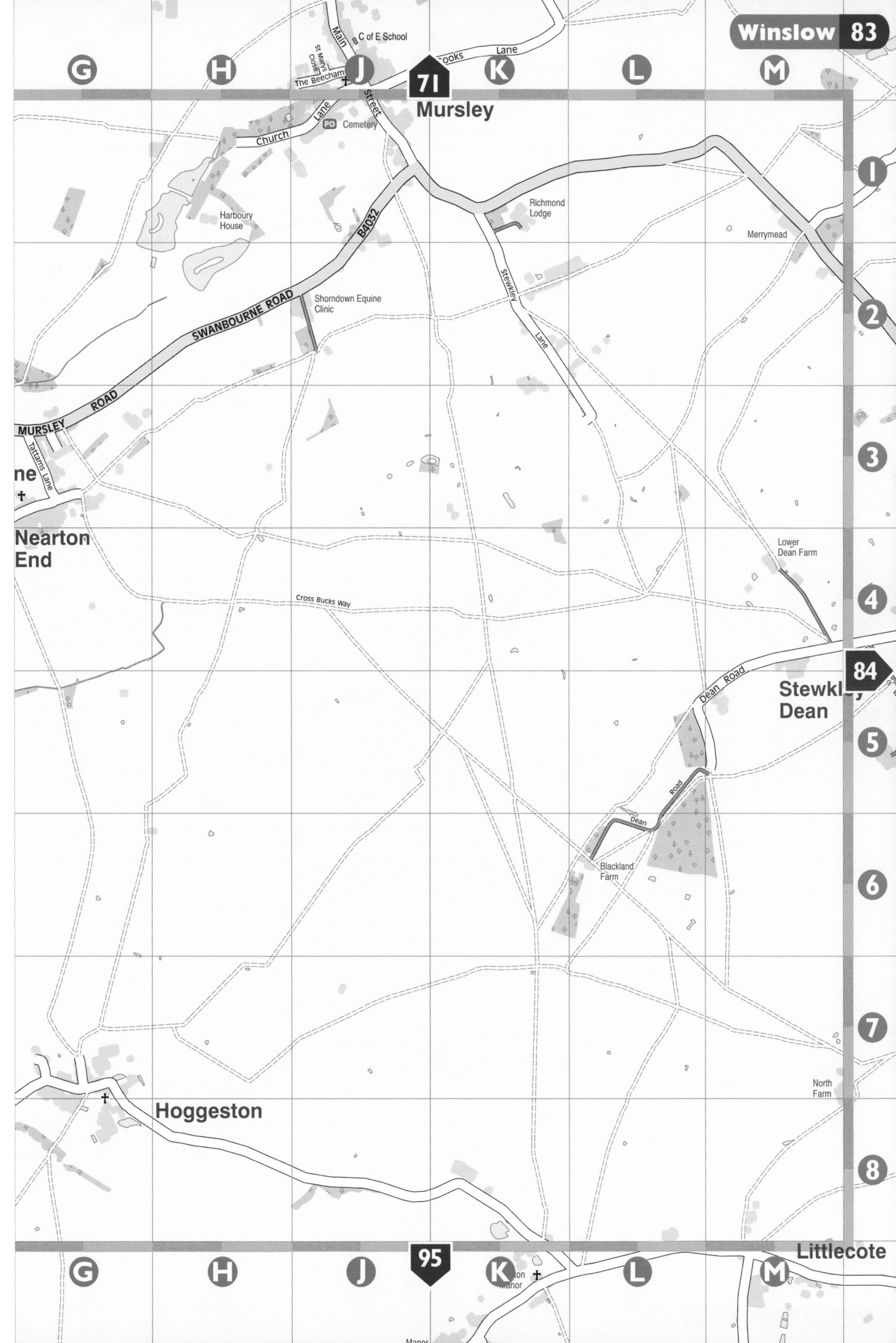
G
H
J
K
L
M
71
Mursley
Main
C of E School
St Mary's Close
The Beechams
Cooks
Lane
Church
Lane
Street
PO
Cemetery
Harboury House
Richmond Lodge
B4032
Merrymead
Stewkley
Lane
Shorndown Equine Clinic
SWANBOURNE ROAD
MURSLEY
ROAD
Tattams Lane
Nearton End
Cross Bucks Way
Lower Dean Farm
84
Dean Road
Stewkley Dean
Road
Dean
Blackland Farm
North Farm
Hoggeston
95
Littlecote
Manor
1
2
3
4
5
6
7
8

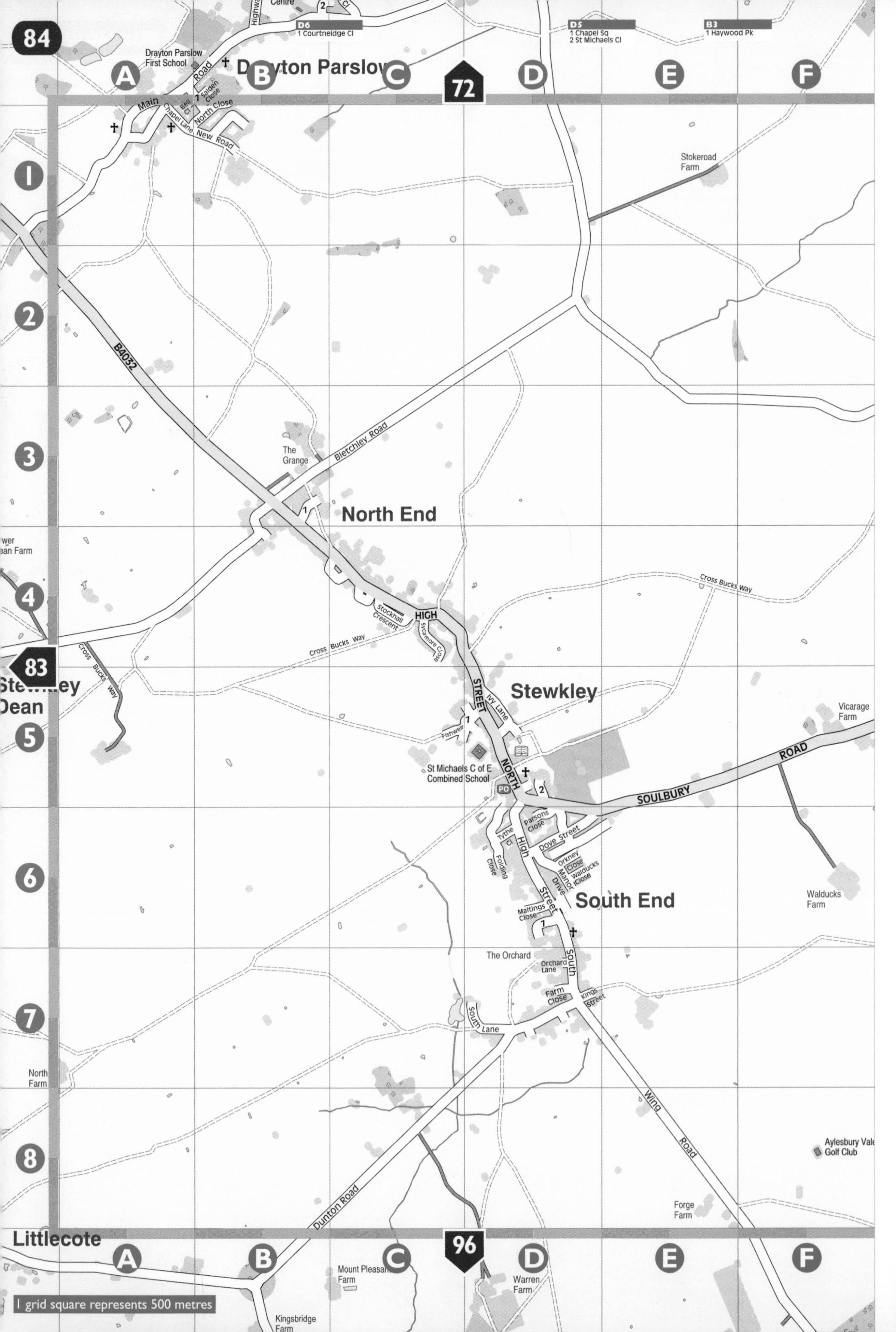
D6
1 Courtneidge Cl
D5
1 Chapel Sq
2 St Michaels Cl
B3
1 Haywood Pk
Drayton Parslow First School
Drayton Parslow
72
Main
Road
Bell Cl
Salden Close
North Close
Chapel Lane
New Road
Stokeroad Farm
B4032
Bletchley Road
The Grange
North End
Cross Bucks Way
Stockhall Crescent
HIGH
Sycamore Close
STREET
Ivy Lane
Stewkley
Fishweir
St Michaels C of E Combined School
NORTH
PO
SOULBURY
ROAD
Vicarage Farm
Parsons Close
Tythe Cl
Dove Street
High
Folding Close
Orkney Close
Manor Drive
Walducks Close
Street
South End
Walducks Farm
Maltings Close
The Orchard
Orchard Lane
South
Farm Close
Kings Street
South Lane
Wing
Road
Aylesbury Vale Golf Club
Dunton Road
Forge Farm
North Farm
Stewkley Dean
83
Littlecote
96
Mount Pleasant Farm
Warren Farm
Kingsbridge Farm
A
B
C
D
E
F
1
2
3
4
5
6
7
8
1 grid square represents 500 metres

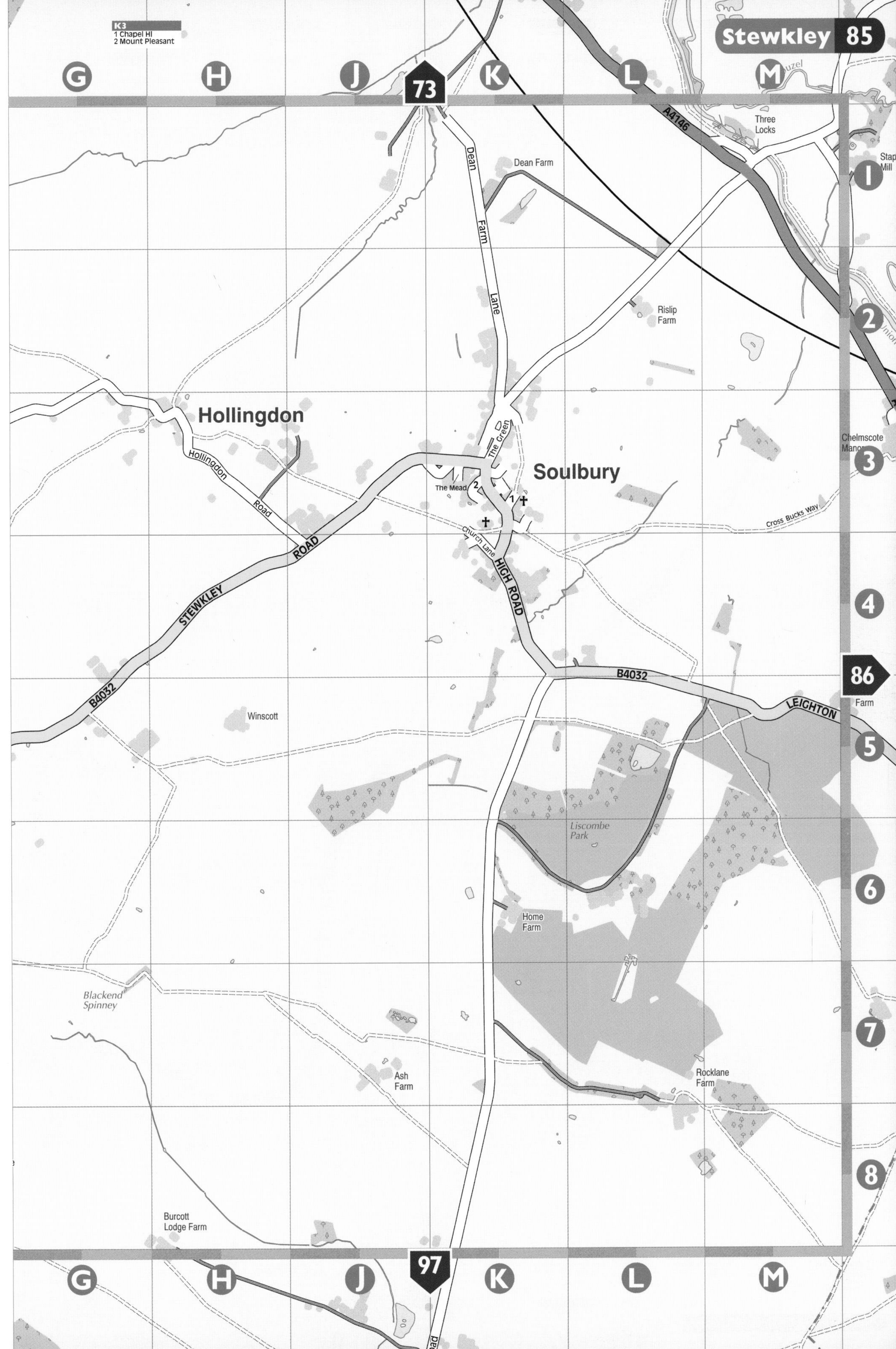
K3
1 Chapel Hl
2 Mount Pleasant
G
H
J
73
K
L
M
A4146
Three Locks
Dean Farm
Dean Farm Lane
Rislip Farm
Hollingdon
Hollingdon Road
The Green
Soulbury
The Mead
Church Lane
HIGH ROAD
STEWKLEY ROAD
Cross Bucks Way
Chelmscote Manor
B4032
LEIGHTON
Farm
Winscott
Liscombe Park
Home Farm
Blackend Spinney
Ash Farm
Rocklane Farm
Burcott Lodge Farm
86
97
1
2
3
4
5
6
7
8

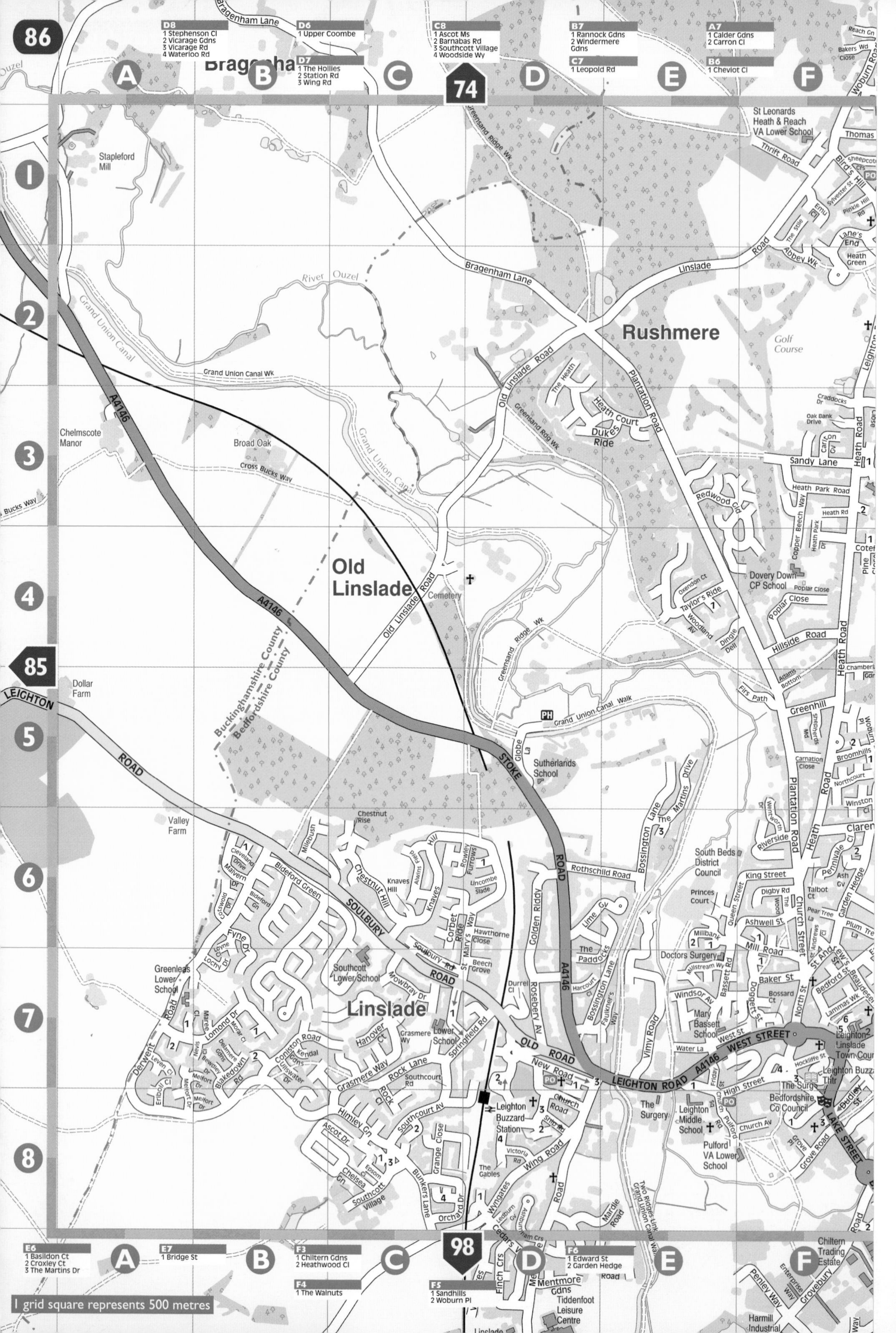

86
D8
1 Stephenson Cl
2 Vicarage Gdns
3 Vicarage Rd
4 Waterloo Rd
D6
1 Upper Coombe
D7
1 The Hollies
2 Station Rd
3 Wing Rd
C8
1 Ascot Ms
2 Barnabas Rd
3 Southcott Village
4 Woodside Wy
B7
1 Rannock Gdns
2 Windermere Gdns
C7
1 Leopold Rd
A7
1 Calder Gdns
2 Carron Cl
B6
1 Cheviot Cl
74
Bragenham Lane
Stapleford Mill
St Leonards Heath & Reach VA Lower School
Thrift Road
Bragenham Lane
River Ouzel
Linslade Road
Rushmere
Golf Course
Grand Union Canal
Grand Union Canal Wk
Old Linslade Road
Plantation Road
Heath Court
Dukes Ride
Greensand Rdg Wk
Chelmscote Manor
Broad Oak
Cross Bucks Way
A4146
Sandy Lane
Heath Park Road
Redwood Gld
Old Linslade
Cemetery
Dovery Down CP School
Taylor's Ride
Hillside Road
Heath Road
85
Dollar Farm
LEIGHTON ROAD
Buckinghamshire County
Bedfordshire County
Grand Union Canal Walk
Globe La
Sutherlands School
STOKE ROAD
Valley Farm
Chestnut Rise
Knaves Hill
Rothschild Road
Bossington Lane
The Martins Drive
South Beds District Council
King Street
SOULBURY ROAD
Greenleas Lower School
Southcott Lower School
Linslade
Mowbray Dr
Rosebery Av
Doctors Surgery
Mill Road
Church Street
Mary Bassett School
Leighton Linslade Town Council
OLD ROAD
Coniston Road
Grasmere Way
Rock Lane
Lower School
Springfield Rd
New Road
LEIGHTON ROAD
WEST STREET
High Street
The Surgery
Leighton Middle School
Pulford VA Lower School
Bedfordshire Co Council
LAKE STREET
Leighton Buzzard Station
Wing Road
Himley Gn
Ascot Dr
Chelsea Gn
Southcott Village
Bunkers Lane
Grange Close
Orchard Dr
The Gables
Two Ridges Link
98
E6
1 Basildon Ct
2 Croxley Ct
3 The Martins Dr
E7
1 Bridge St
F3
1 Chiltern Gdns
2 Heathwood Cl
F4
1 The Walnuts
F5
1 Sandhills
2 Woburn Pl
F6
1 Edward St
2 Garden Hedge
Mentmore Gdns
Tiddenfoot Leisure Centre
Chiltern Trading Estate
Harmill Industrial
1 grid square represents 500 metres

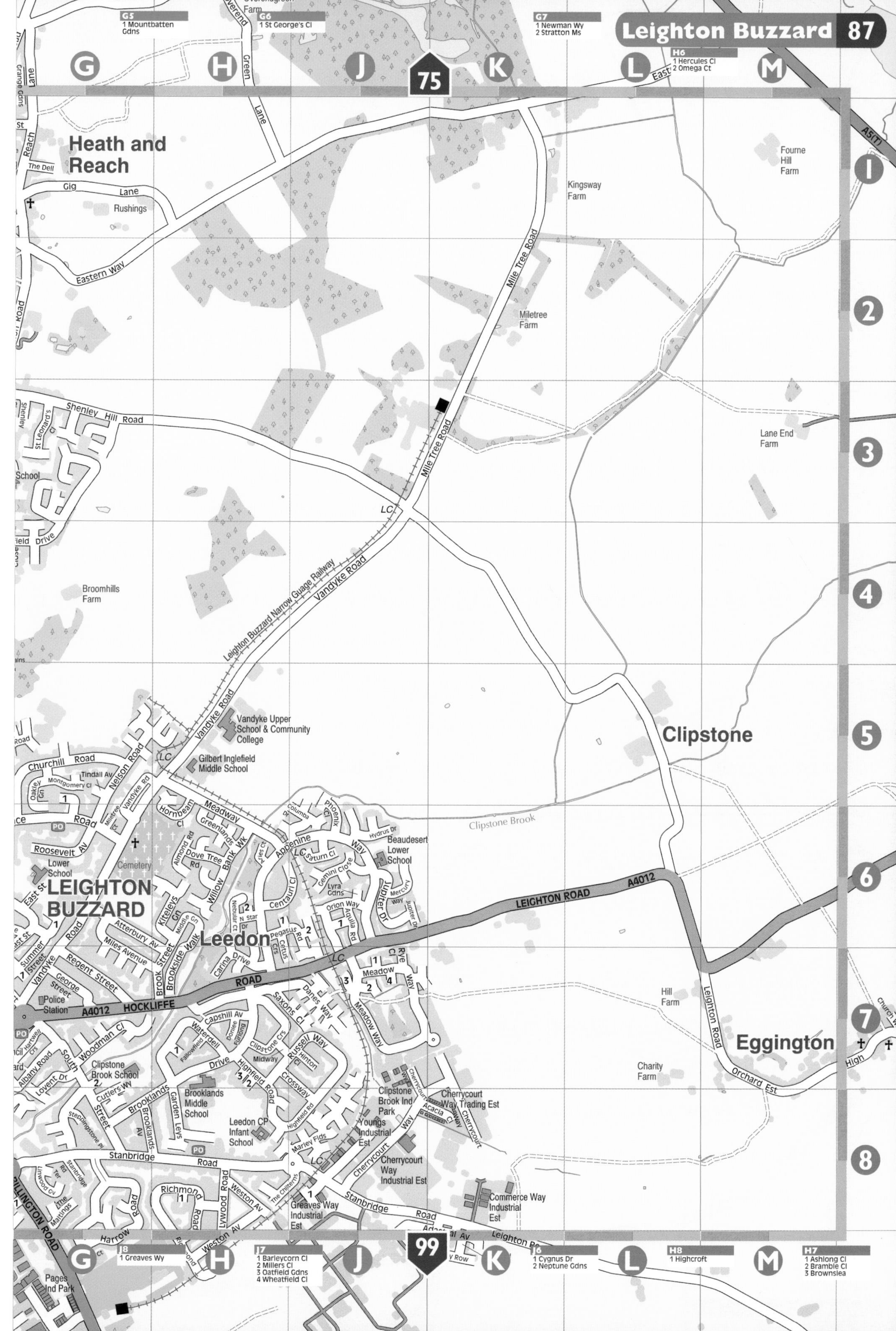
G5 1 Mountbatten Gdns
G6 1 St George's Cl
G7 1 Newman Wy 2 Stratton Ms
H6 1 Hercules Cl 2 Omega Ct
Overendgreen Farm
75
Heath and Reach
Gig Lane
Rushings
Eastern Way
Kingsway Farm
Fourne Hill Farm
Mile Tree Road
Miletree Farm
Shenley Hill Road
Lane End Farm
Broomhills Farm
Leighton Buzzard Narrow Guage Railway
Vandyke Road
Vandyke Upper School & Community College
Gilbert Inglefield Middle School
Clipstone
Clipstone Brook
Beaudesert Lower School
LEIGHTON BUZZARD
Leedon
LEIGHTON ROAD
A4012
HOCKLIFFE ROAD
Hill Farm
Leighton Road
Eggington
Charity Farm
Orchard Est
Clipstone Brook School
Brooklands Middle School
Leedon CP Infant School
Clipstone Brook Ind Park
Youngs Industrial Est
Cherrycourt Way Trading Est
Cherrycourt Way Industrial Est
Commerce Way Industrial Est
Greaves Way Industrial Est
Stanbridge Road
BILLINGTON ROAD
Pages Ind Park
99
J8 1 Greaves Wy
J7 1 Barleycorn Cl 2 Millers Cl 3 Oatfield Gdns 4 Wheatfield Cl
J6 1 Cygnus Dr 2 Neptune Gdns
H8 1 Highcroft
H7 1 Ashlong Cl 2 Bramble Cl 3 Brownslea

A5 1 Heron Ct
A2 1 Fulmar Ct
76
A
B
C
D
E
F
1
2
3
4
5
6
7
8
Field Farm
Skimmingdish Lane
Sunderland Drive
Duxford Close
Lerwick Croft
Hart Cl
Boston Rd
Tangmere Cl
Benson Cl
Lyneham Rd
Manston Cl
Scampton Cl
Telford Rd
Launton Road
Jarvis' Lane
Granville Way
Launton Business Centre
LC
Station Road
Grange Farm
Blenheim Dr
Manor Farm
Bicester Road
The Glades
Sycamore Rd
Ancil Av
Lane End
The Spinney
Sherwood Close
Skinner Road
The Poplars
The Green
Launton
Blackthorn Road
West End
West End Close
Chestnut Cl
Charbridge Lane
Cavray Drive
Heron Drive
Falcon Mead
Osprey Close
Merganser Drive
Partridge
Langford Medical
Peregrine Way
Shearwater Dr
Merlin Way
Swallow Close
Avocet Way
Primary School
Ravencroft
Wretchwick Way
Little Wretchwick Farm
A41(T)
Pioneer Road
Wretchwick Farm
Mill House
102
Hill Farm
B4011
1 grid square represents 500 metres

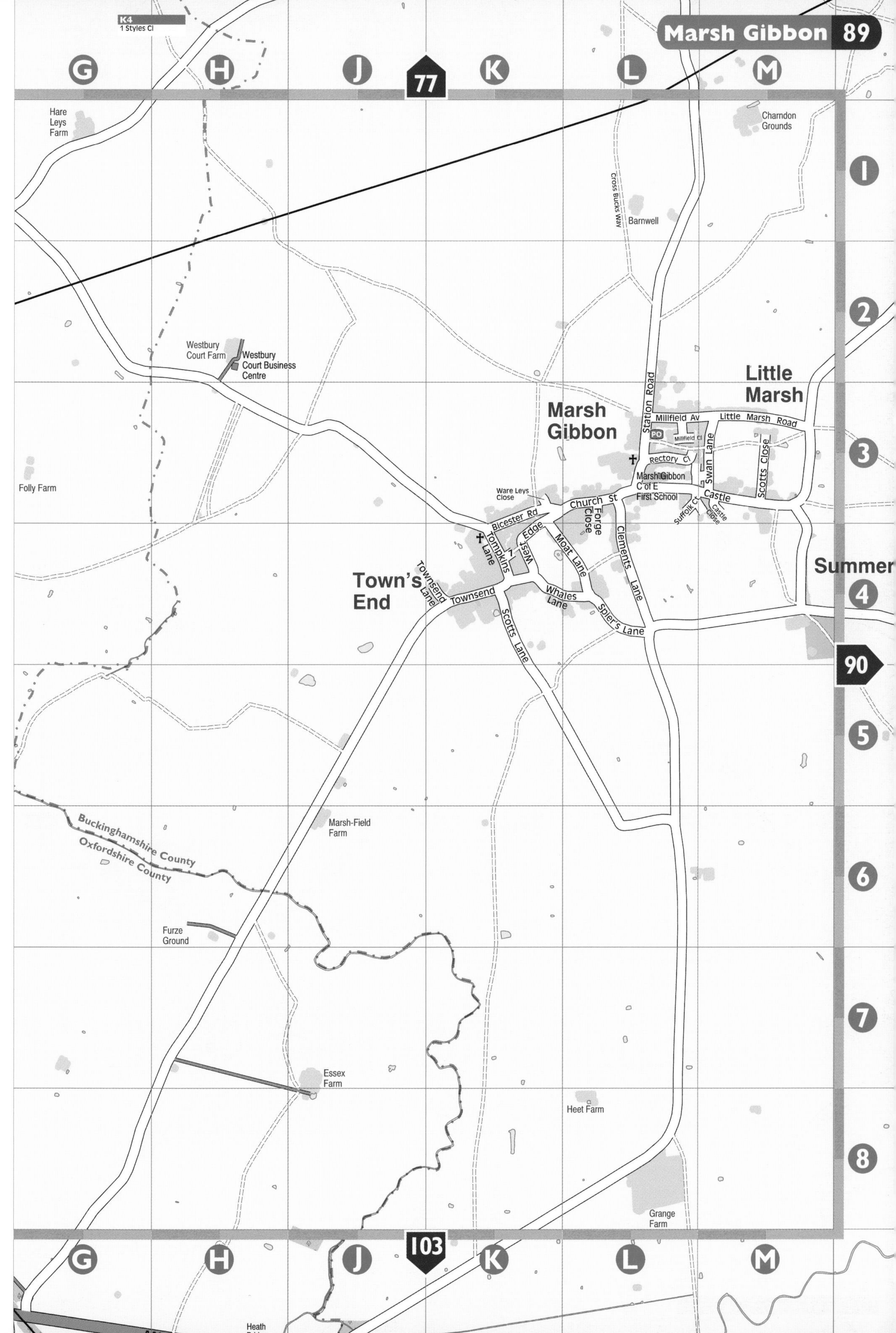
K4
1 Styles Cl
G
H
J
77
K
L
M
Hare Leys Farm
Charndon Grounds
Cross Bucks Way
Barnwell
Westbury Court Farm
Westbury Court Business Centre
Little Marsh
Marsh Gibbon
Station Road
Millfield Av
Little Marsh Road
PO
Millfield Cl
Swan Lane
Scotts Close
Rectory Cl
Marsh Gibbon C of E First School
Ware Leys Close
Church St
Castle
Suffolk Ct
Castle Close
Folly Farm
Bicester Rd
Forge Close
Tompkins Lane
West Edge
Moat Lane
Clements Lane
Summer
Town's End
Townsend Lane
Townsend
Whales Lane
Spier's Lane
Scotts Lane
Marsh-Field Farm
Buckinghamshire County
Oxfordshire County
Furze Ground
Essex Farm
Heet Farm
Grange Farm
Heath
103
90
1
2
3
4
5
6
7
8

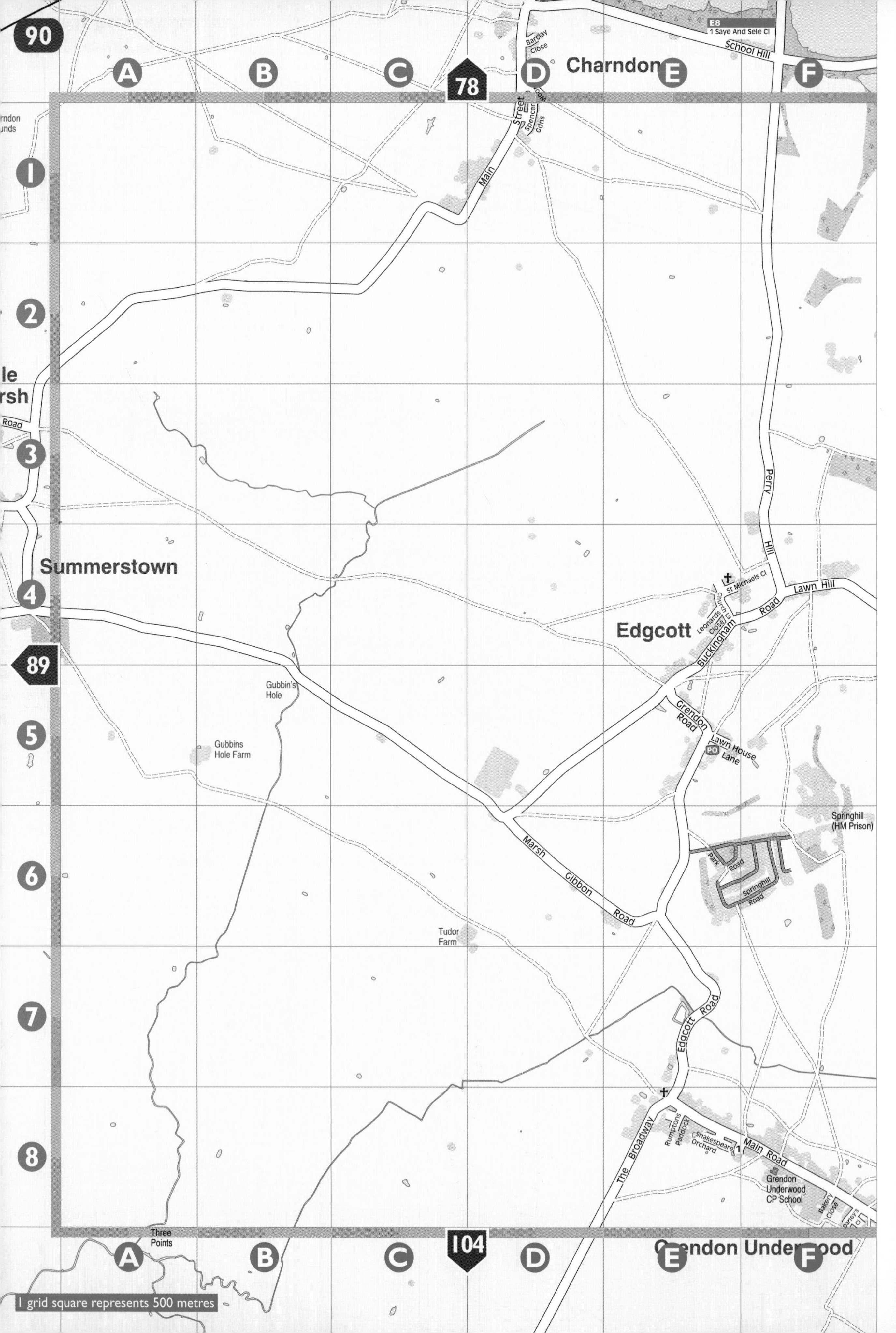

78
Charndon
E8
1 Saye And Sele Cl
School Hill
Barclay Close
Main Street
Spencer Gdns
Summerstown
89
Gubbin's Hole
Gubbins Hole Farm
Edgcott
St Michaels Cl
Church La
Leonards Close
Lawn Hill
Buckingham Road
Perry Hill
Grendon Road
Lawn House Lane
PO
Springhill (HM Prison)
Park Road
Springhill Road
Marsh Gibbon Road
Tudor Farm
Edgcott Road
The Broadway
Rumptons Paddock
Shakespeare Orchard
Main Road
Grendon Underwood CP School
Bakery Close
Three Points
104
Grendon Underwood
1 grid square represents 500 metres

Calve
Bradley Lane
Great Pond Farm
Shrubs Wood
79
G
H
J
K
L
M
Three Points Lane
1
2
3
4
5
6
7
8
Home Wood
Decoypond Wood
Knowlhill Farm
Sheephouse Wood
Romer Wood
92
Finemerehi House
Rosall Farm
Greatmoor
Woodlands Farm
Grendon Wood
North Farm
Doddershall Wood
PO
105
Main Road

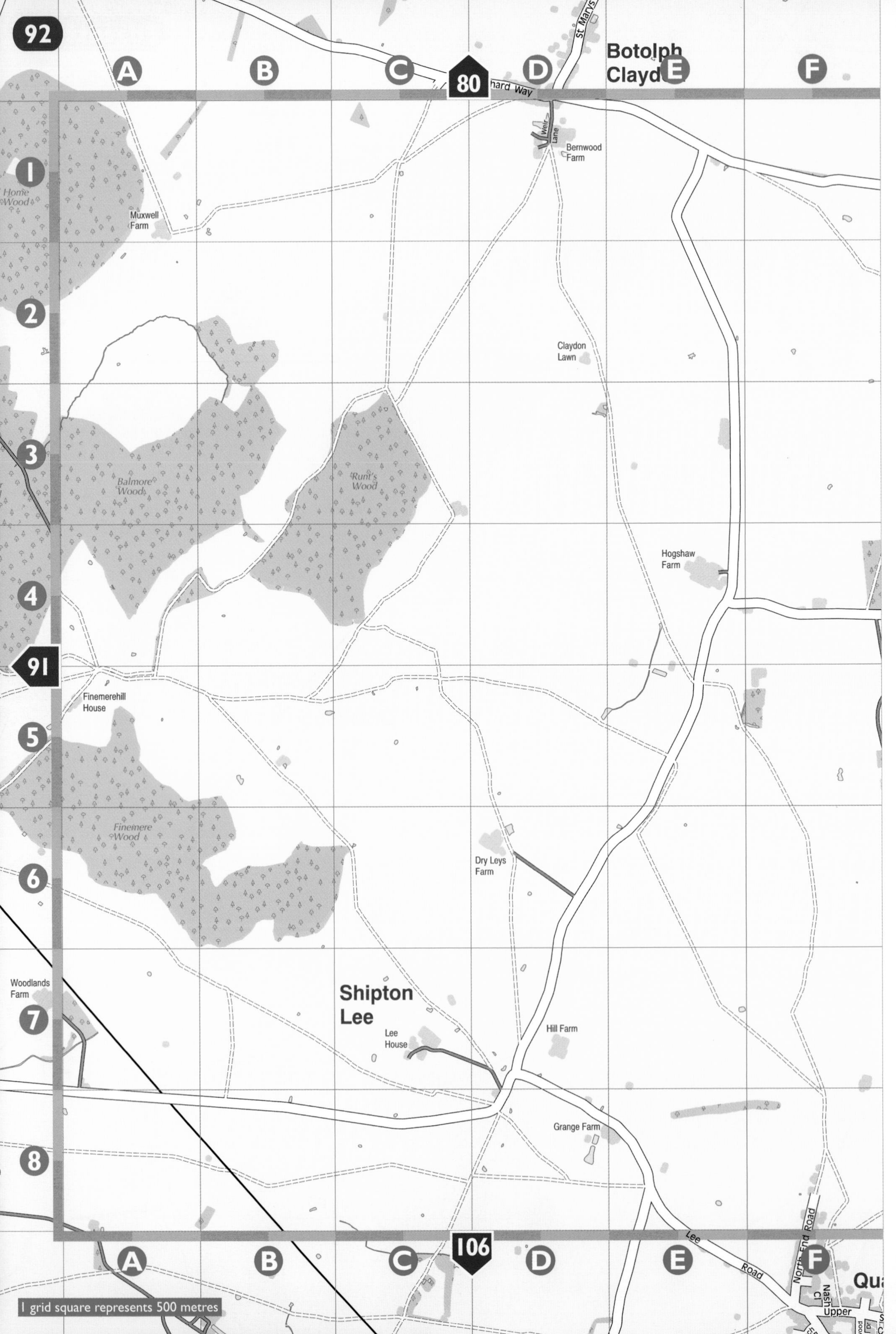


1 grid square represents 500 metres

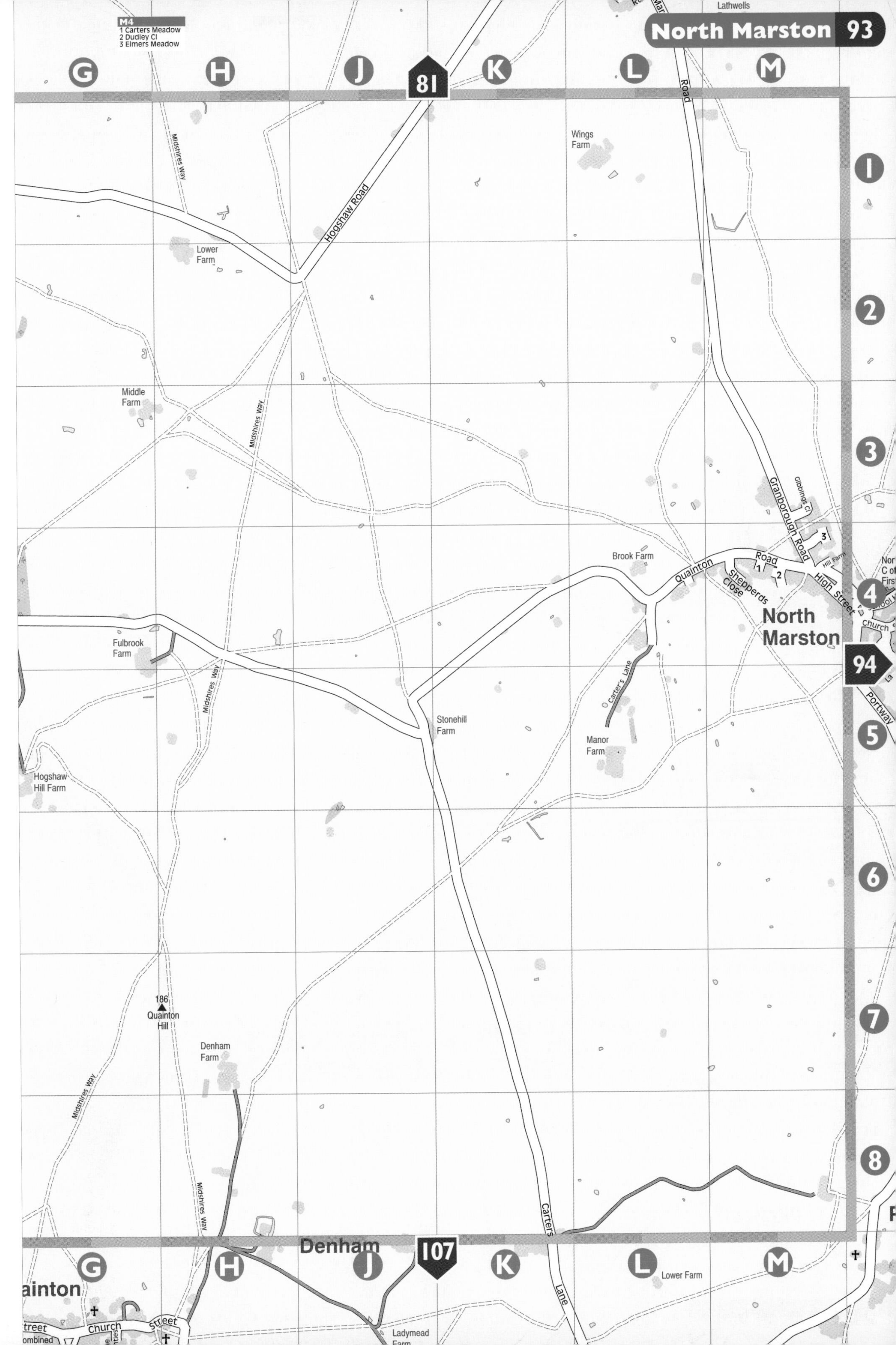
M4
1 Carters Meadow
2 Dudley Cl
3 Elmers Meadow
G
H
J
81
K
L
M
Lathwells
Road
Wings Farm
Midshires Way
Hogshaw Road
Lower Farm
Middle Farm
Midshires Way
Gibbings Cl
Granborough Road
Brook Farm
Quainton
Road
Shepperds Close
High Street
Hill Farm
North Marston
Church
Fulbrook Farm
Midshires Way
Carter's Lane
Stonehill Farm
Manor Farm
Portway
Hogshaw Hill Farm
186
Quainton Hill
Denham Farm
Midshires Way
Midshires Way
Carters
Denham
107
Lower Farm
Lane
ainton
Church
Street
Ladymead Farm
94
1
2
3
4
5
6
7
8

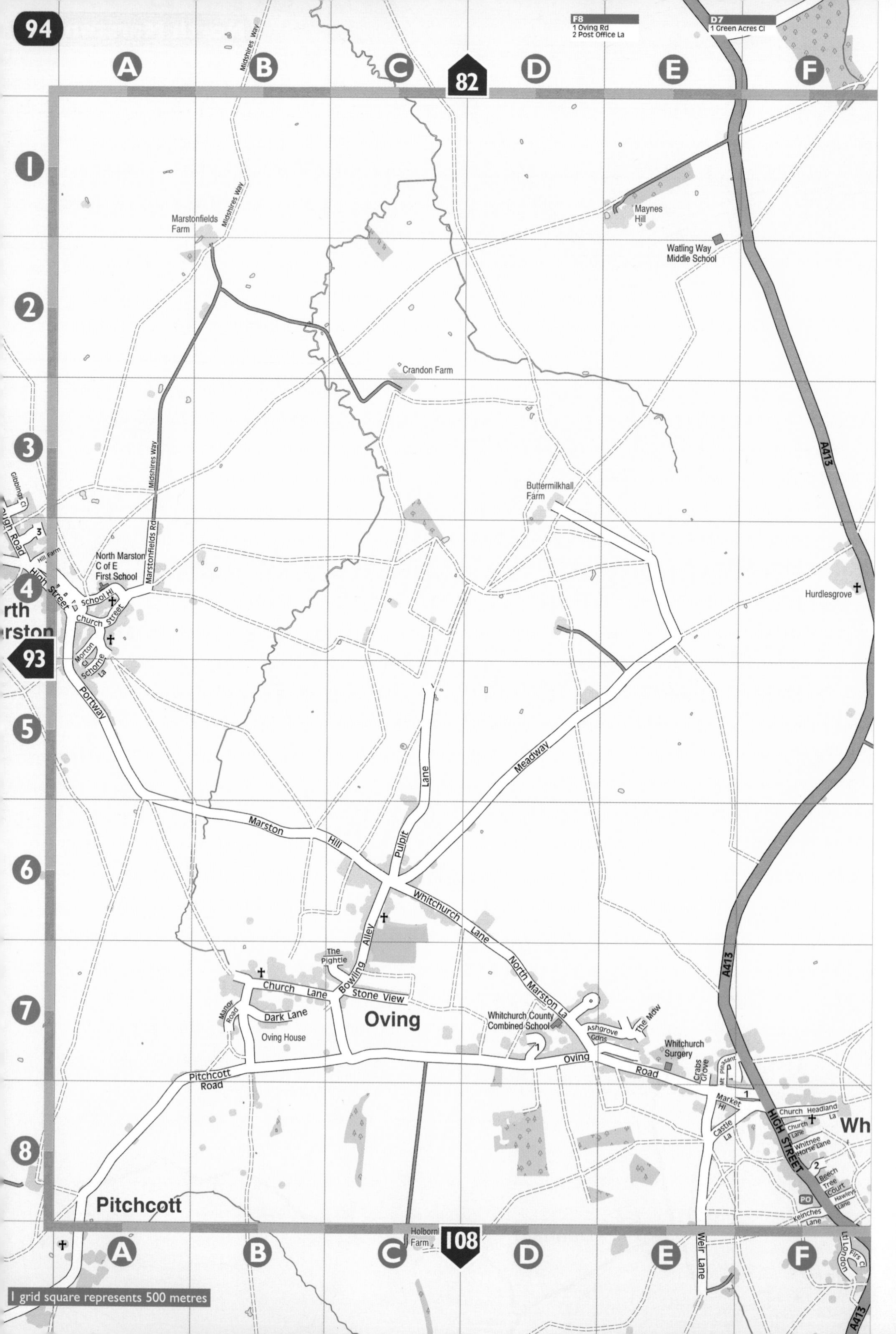
F8
1 Oving Rd
2 Post Office La
D7
1 Green Acres Cl
82
108
93
Midshires Way
Marstonfields Farm
Maynes Hill
Watling Way Middle School
Crandon Farm
Buttermilkhall Farm
North Marston C of E First School
Marstonfields Rd
School Hl
Church Street
High Street
Morton Cl
Schorne La
Portway
Gibbings Cl
Hill Farm
Hurdlesgrove
A413
Meadway
Pulpit Lane
Marston Hill
Whitchurch Lane
North Marston La
Bowling Alley
The Pightle
Church Lane
Stone View
Manor Road
Dark Lane
Oving House
Oving
Whitchurch County Combined School
Ashgrove Gdns
The Mdw
Whitchurch Surgery
Crabs Grove
Mt Pleasant
Oving Road
Market Hl
Castle La
Pitchcott Road
Pitchcott
HIGH STREET
Church Headland La
Church Lane
Whitnee
Horse Lane
Beech Tree Court
Hawleys Lane
Kelnches Lane
PO
Holborn Farm
Weir Lane
Lt London
Firs Cl
rth
rston
Wh
1 grid square represents 500 metres

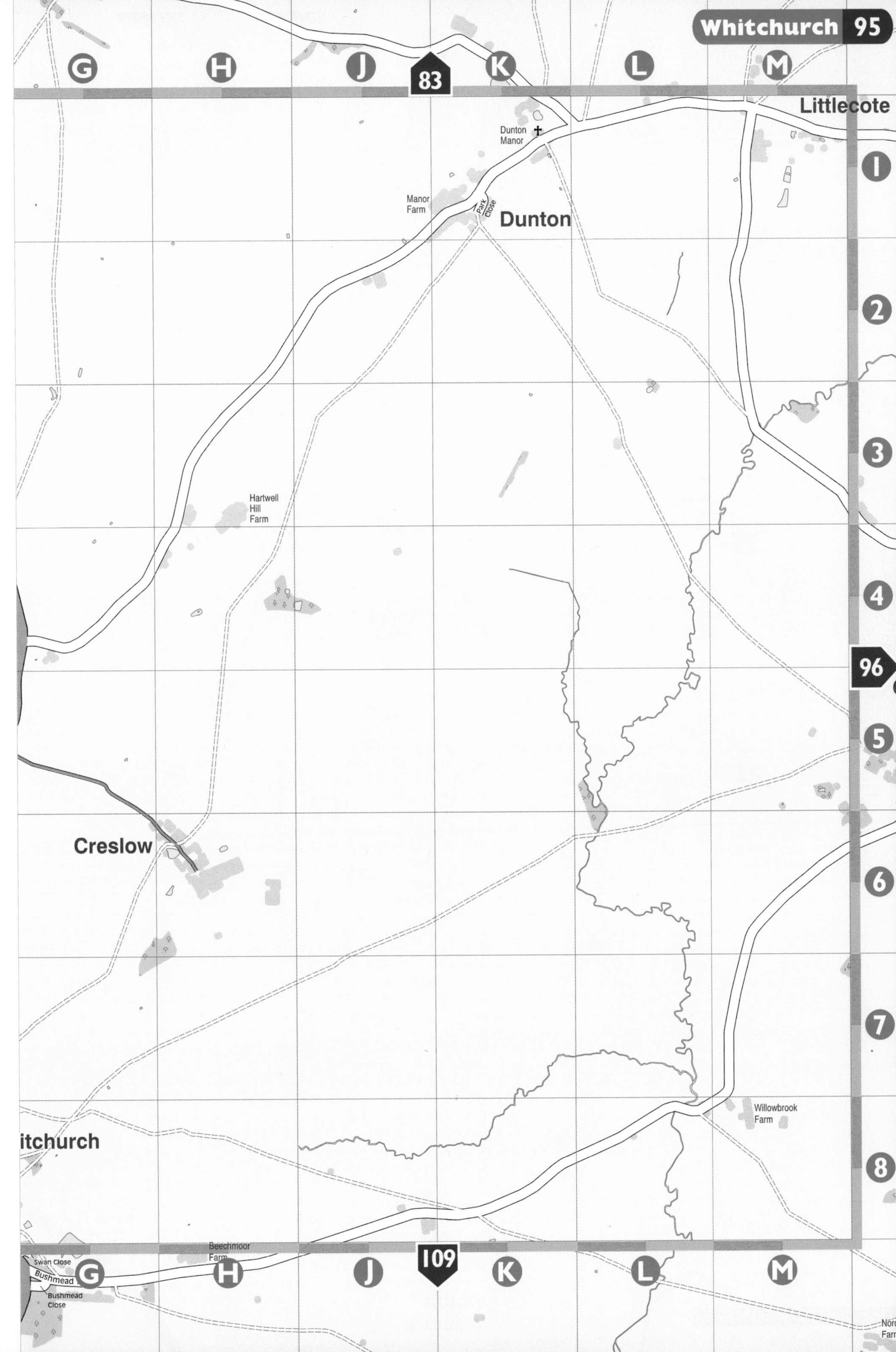
G
H
J
83
K
L
M
Littlecote
Dunton Manor
Manor Farm
Park Close
Dunton
Hartwell Hill Farm
96
Creslow
Willowbrook Farm
itchurch
Beechmoor Farm
109
Swan Close
Bushmead
Bushmead Close
1
2
3
4
5
6
7
8

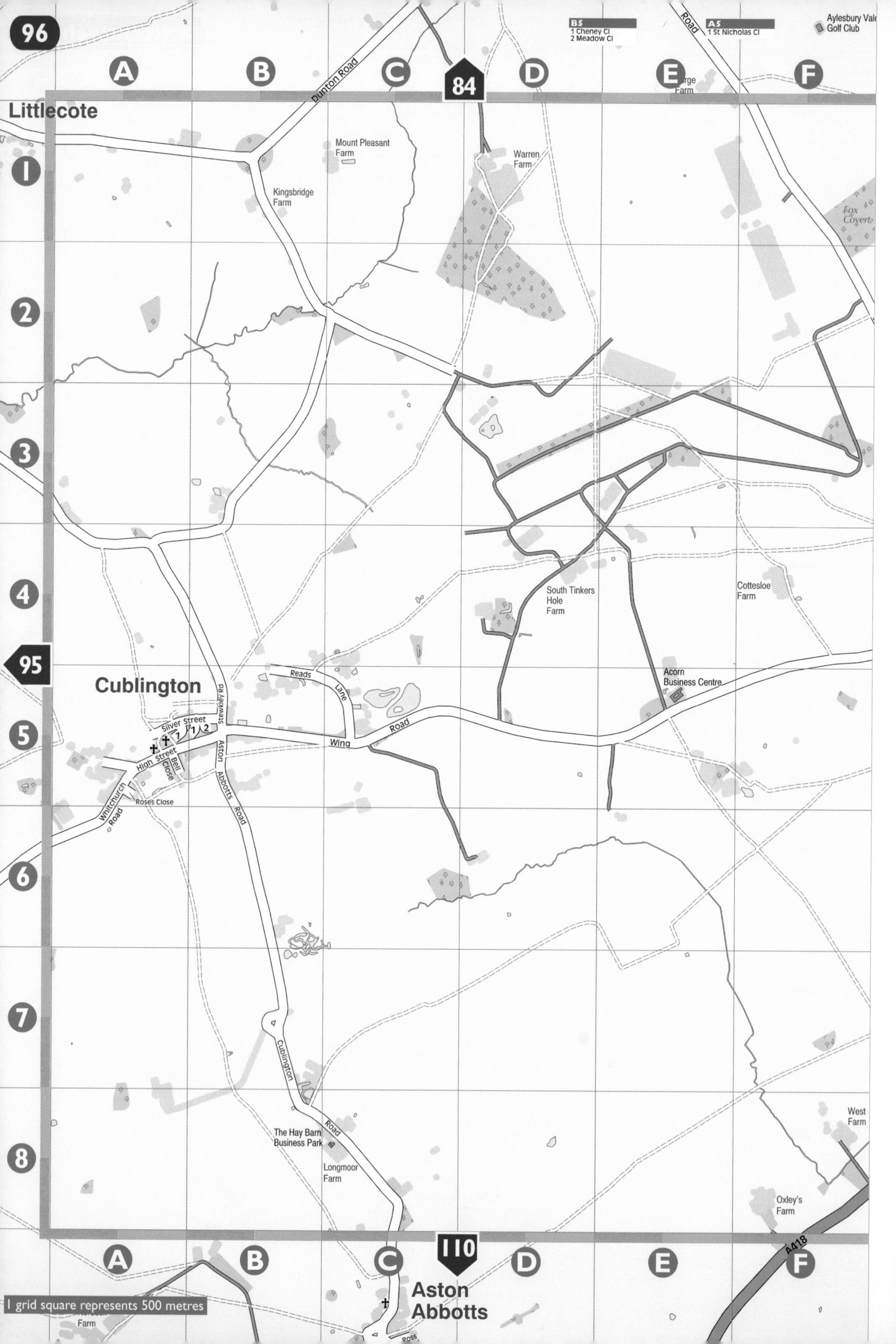

B5
1 Cheney Cl
2 Meadow Cl
A5
1 St Nicholas Cl
Aylesbury Vale Golf Club
84
Littlecote
Dunton Road
Mount Pleasant Farm
Warren Farm
Kingsbridge Farm
Fox Covert
South Tinkers Hole Farm
Cottesloe Farm
95
Cublington
Reads Lane
Stewkley Rd
Acorn Business Centre
Silver Street
Wing Road
High Street
Bell Close
Aston Abbotts Road
Whitchurch Road
Roses Close
Cublington Road
The Hay Barn Business Park
Longmoor Farm
West Farm
Oxley's Farm
110
A418
Aston Abbotts
1 grid square represents 500 metres
Farm

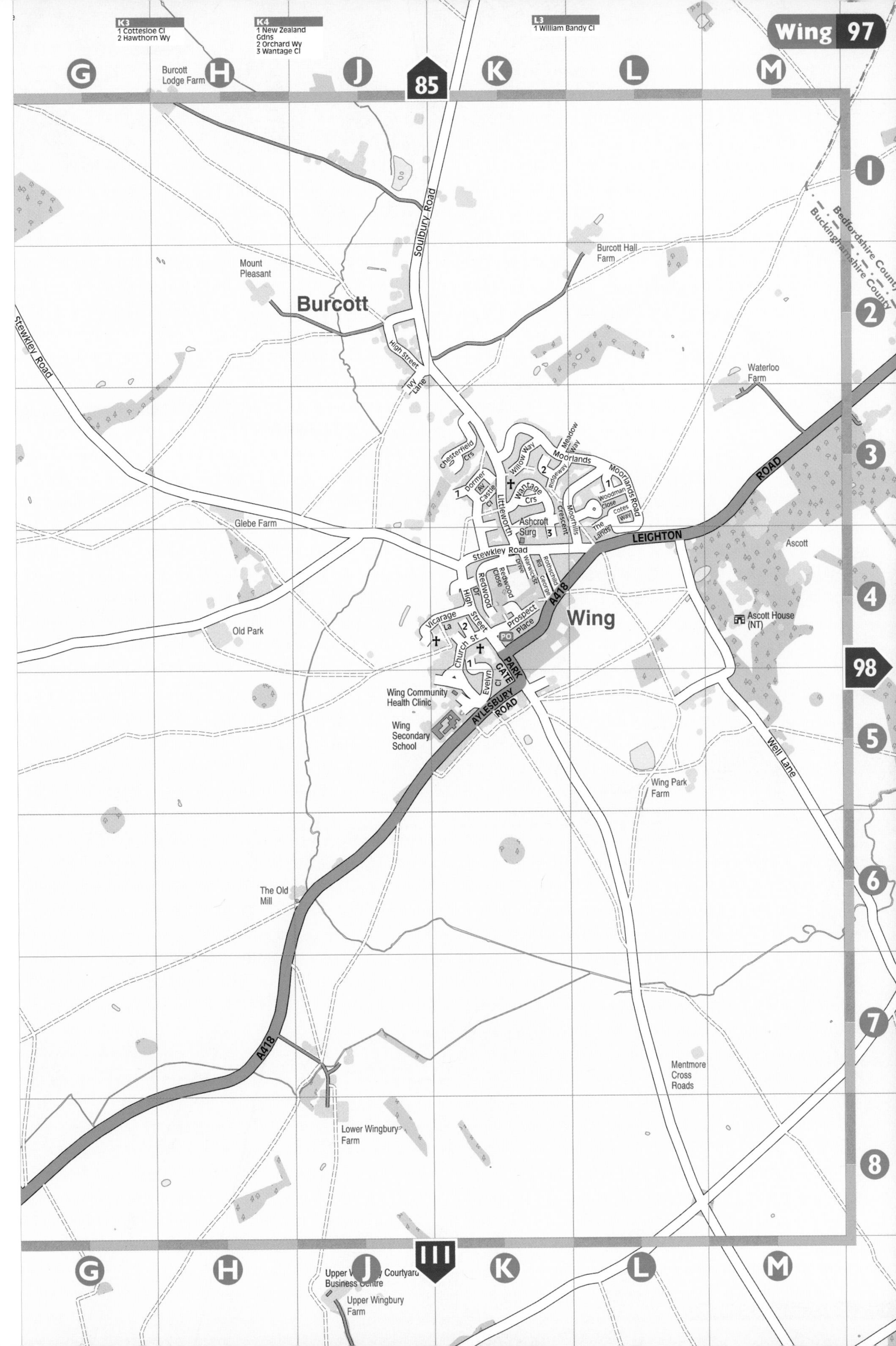
K3
1 Cottesloe Cl
2 Hawthorn Wy
K4
1 New Zealand Gdns
2 Orchard Wy
3 Wantage Cl
L3
1 William Bandy Cl
85
98
111
Burcott Lodge Farm
Burcott
Mount Pleasant
Soulbury Road
Burcott Hall Farm
Stewkley Road
High Street
Ivy Lane
Waterloo Farm
Bedfordshire County
Buckinghamshire County
Chesterfield Crs
Dormer Av
Castle Cl
Littleworth
Willow Way
Wantage Crs
Meadow Way
Moorlands
Ridgeway
Crescent
Moorhills
Moorlands Road
Woodman Close
Cotes Way
The Lands
Ashcroft Surg
Glebe Farm
LEIGHTON ROAD
Stewkley Road
Redwood Drive
Redwood Close
Warwick St
George Rd
Rothschild
High Street
Vicarage La
Church St
Prospect Place
Wing
Old Park
PARK GATE
Evelyn Cl
Ascott
Ascott House (NT)
Wing Community Health Clinic
Wing Secondary School
AYLESBURY ROAD
Well Lane
Wing Park Farm
The Old Mill
A418
Mentmore Cross Roads
Lower Wingbury Farm
Upper Wingbury Farm
Business Centre

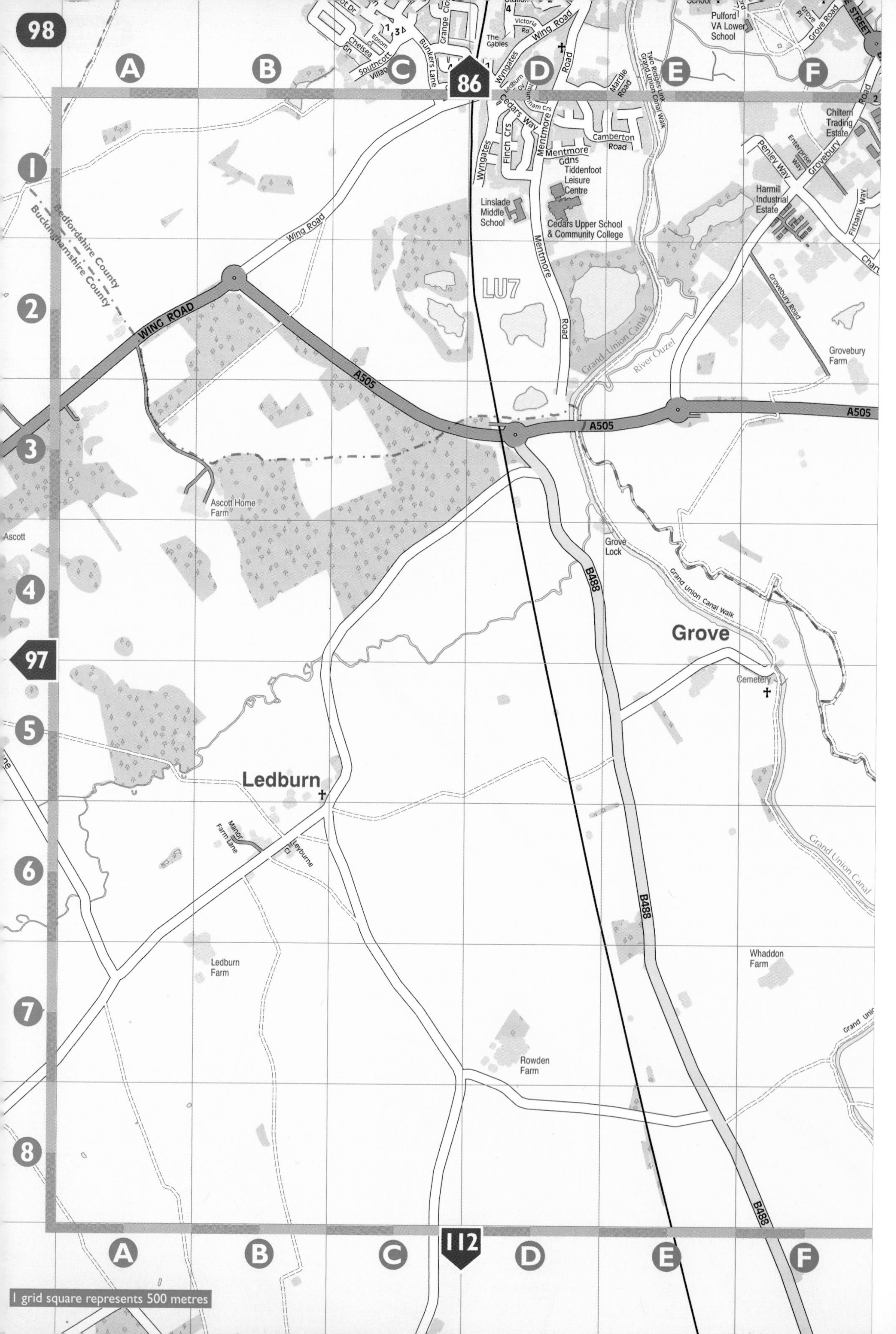
A
B
C
D
E
F
86
1
2
3
4
5
6
7
8
97
112
Wing Road
WING ROAD
A505
B488
Bedfordshire County
Buckinghamshire County
Southcott Village
Chelsea Gn
Epsom Cl
Bunkers Lane
Grange Cl
The Gables
Victoria Rd
Wyngates
Ledburn Gv
Cedars Way
Finch Crs
Mentmore Gdns
Mentmore Road
Camberton Road
Mardle Road
Two Ridges Link
Grand Union Canal Walk
Pulford VA Lower School
Grove Road
Grove Pl
STREET
Chiltern Trading Estate
Penley Way
Enterprise Way
Grovebury Road
Harmill Industrial Estate
Firbank Way
Tiddenfoot Leisure Centre
Linslade Middle School
Cedars Upper School & Community College
LU7
Grand Union Canal
River Ouzel
Grovebury Farm
Ascott Home Farm
Ascott
Grove Lock
Grove
Cemetery
Ledburn
Manor Farm Lane
Leyburne Cl
Ledburn Farm
Whaddon Farm
Rowden Farm
1 grid square represents 500 metres

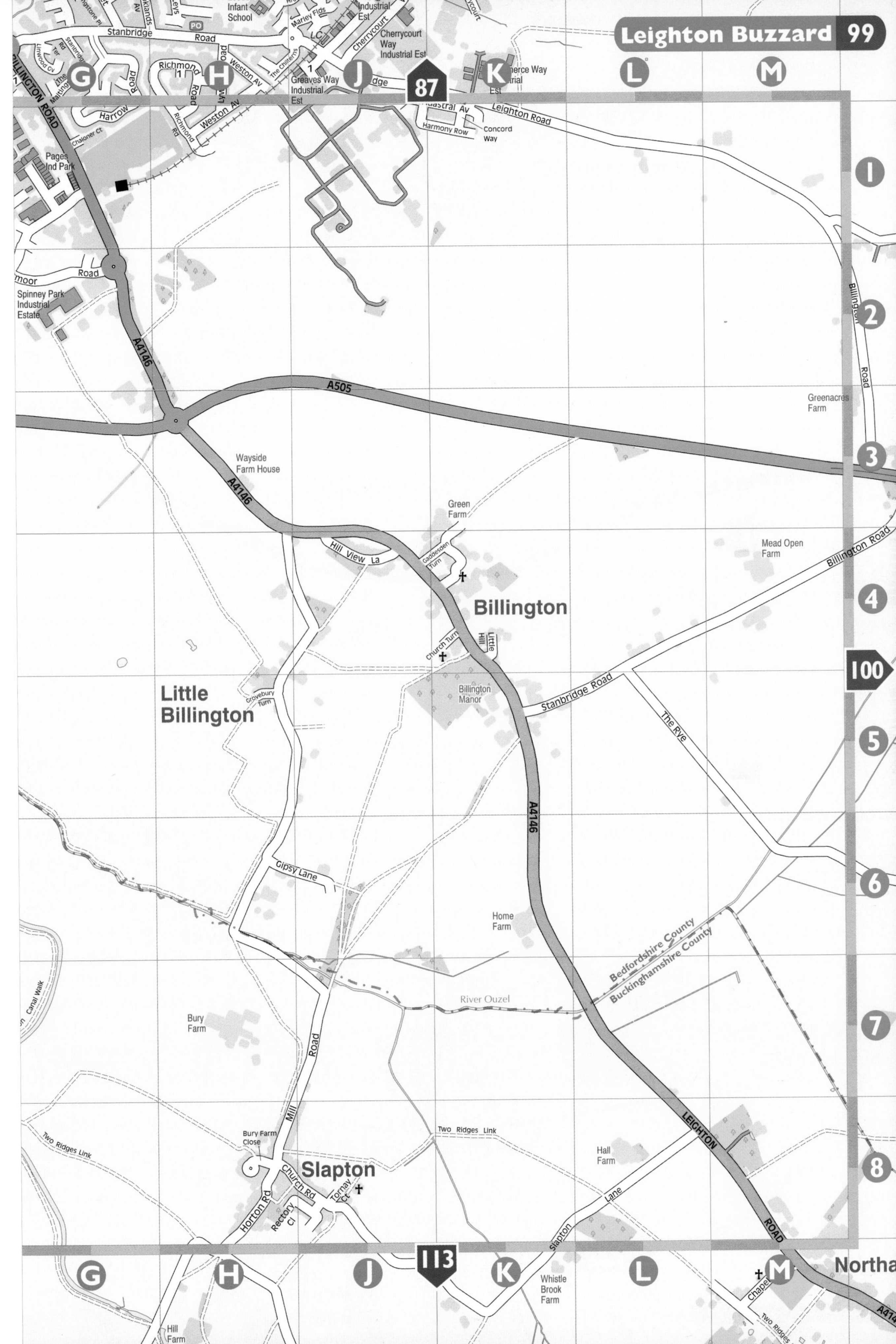

Stanbridge Road
Richmond Road
Weston Av
Harrow Road
Chaloner Ct
Pages Ind Park
BILLINGTON ROAD
Spinney Park Industrial Estate
Greaves Way Industrial Est
Cherrycourt Way Industrial Est
Harmony Row
Concord Way
Leighton Road
Billington Road
A4146
A505
Greenacres Farm
Wayside Farm House
Green Farm
Hill View La
Gaddesden Turn
Billington
Little Hill
Church Turn
Billington Manor
Stanbridge Road
Mead Open Farm
Billington Road
Little Billington
Grovebury Turn
The Rye
Gipsy Lane
Home Farm
Bedfordshire County
Buckinghamshire County
River Ouzel
Canal Walk
Bury Farm
Mill Road
Two Ridges Link
Bury Farm Close
Slapton
Church Rd
Tornay Ct
Horton Rd
Rectory Cl
Hall Farm
Slapton Lane
LEIGHTON ROAD
Whistle Brook Farm
Hill Farm
Chapel
Two Ridges
G H J K L M
1 2 3 4 5 6 7 8
87
100
113

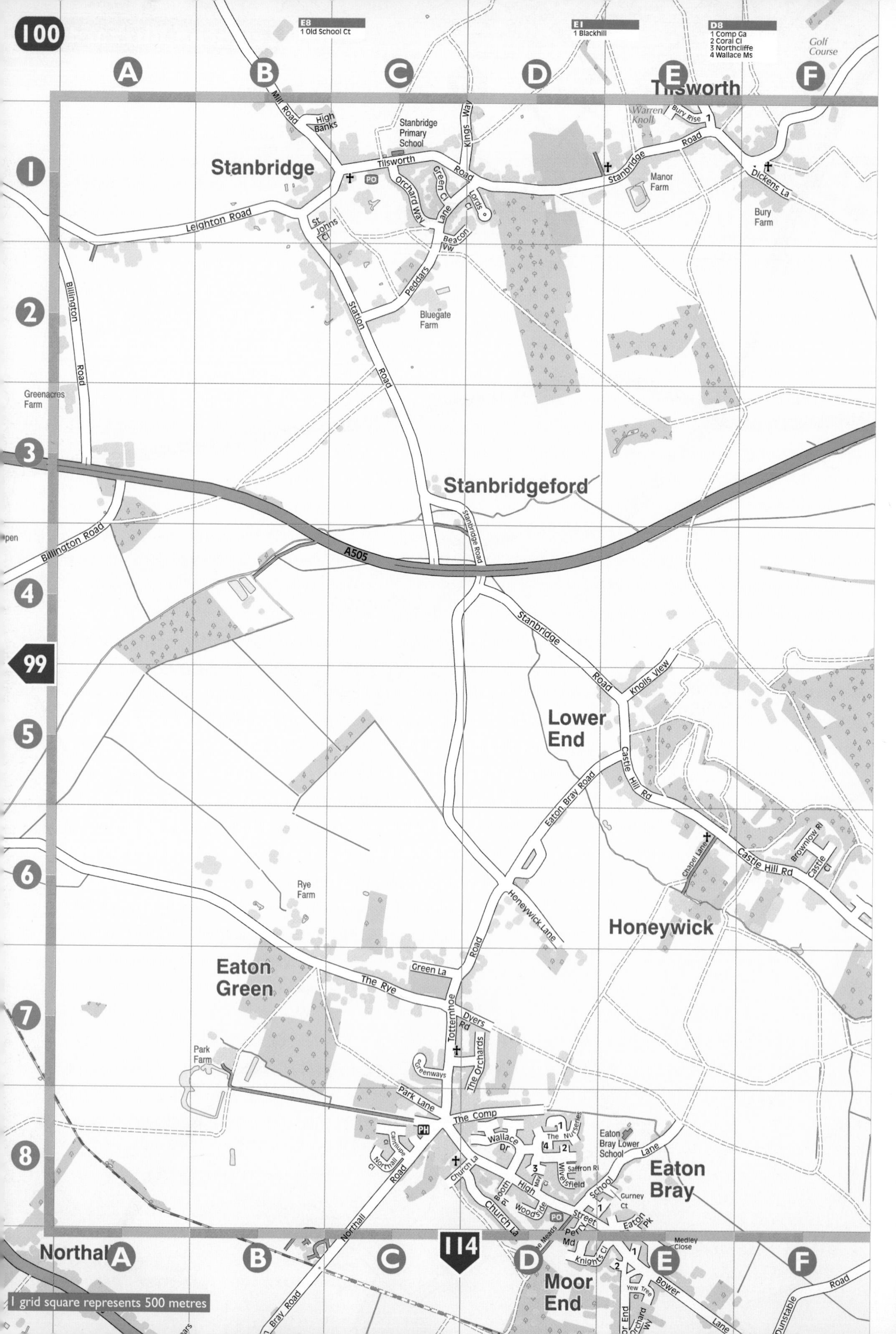
E8
1 Old School Ct
E1
1 Blackhill
D8
1 Comp Ga
2 Coral Cl
3 Northcliffe
4 Wallace Ms
Golf Course
Tilsworth
Warren Knoll
Bury Rise
Stanbridge
Stanbridge Primary School
High Banks
Mill Road
Kings Way
Tilsworth Road
Orchard Way
Green Cl
Lane
Lords Cl
Beacon Vw
St Johns Cl
Leighton Road
Manor Farm
Dickens La
Bury Farm
Peddars
Station Road
Bluegate Farm
Billington Road
Greenacres Farm
Stanbridgeford
Stanbridge Road
A505
Billington Road
Stanbridge Road
Knolls View
Lower End
Castle Hill Rd
Eaton Bray Road
Chapel Lane
Castle Hill Rd
Brownlow Ri
Castle Cl
Honeywick Lane
Honeywick
Rye Farm
Eaton Green
Green La
The Rye
Road
Totternhoe
Dyers Rd
The Orchards
Greenways
Park Farm
Park Lane
The Comp
Wallace Dr
The Nurseries
Eaton Bray Lower School
Lane
Eaton Bray
Northall Cl
Northall Road
Church La
Saffron Ri
Wivesfield
High St
Booth Pl
Woodside
School Street
Gurney Ct
Eaton Pk
Church La
The Meads
Perry Md
Knights Cl
Medley Close
Moor End
Yew Tree Cl
Bower Lane
Dunstable Road
Northall
Eaton Bray Road
1 grid square represents 500 metres
99
114
A B C D E F
1 2 3 4 5 6 7 8

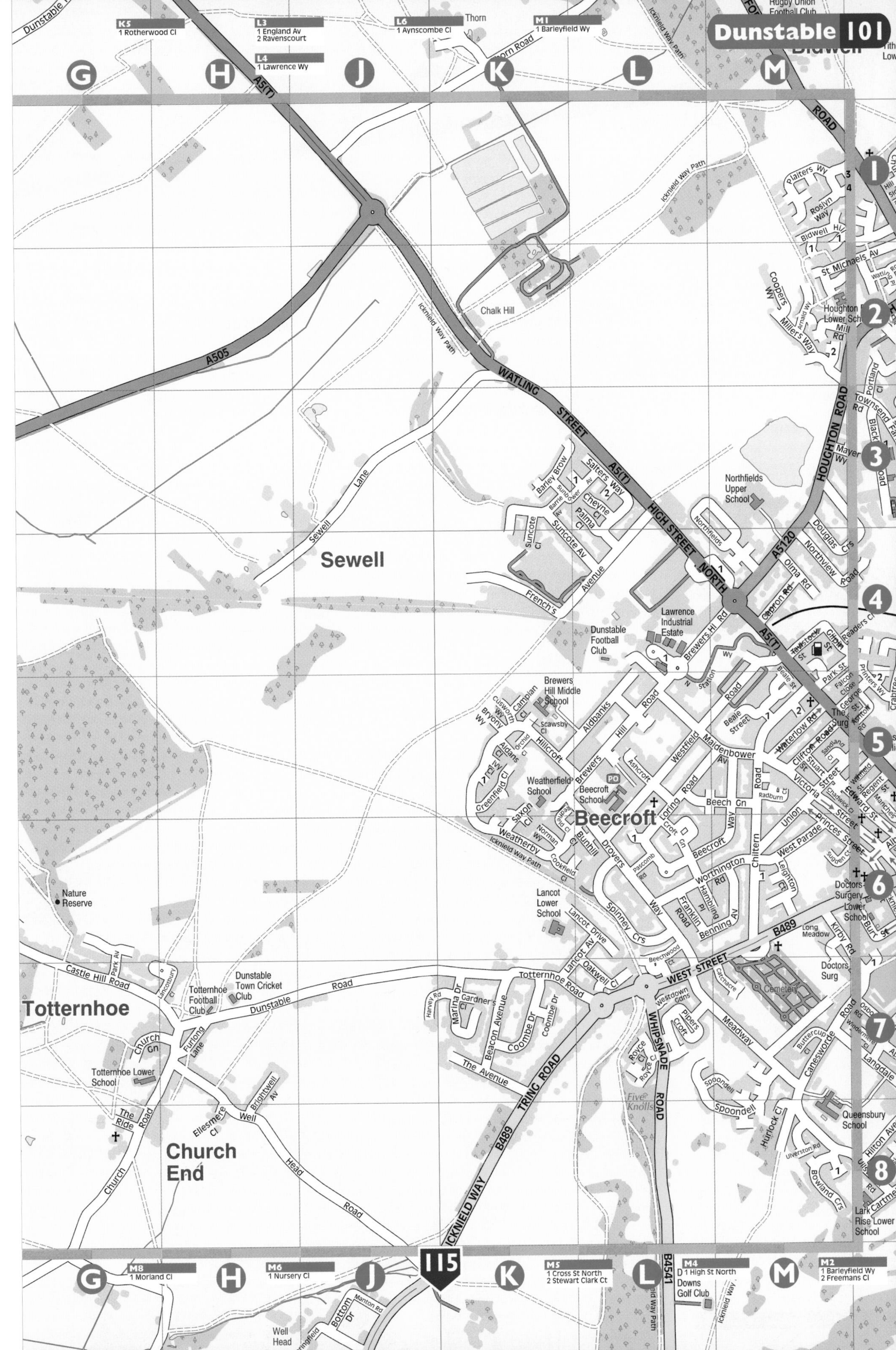
K5
1 Rotherwood Cl
L3
1 England Av
2 Ravenscourt
L4
1 Lawrence Wy
L6
1 Aynscombe Cl
M1
1 Barleyfield Wy
Sewell
Beecroft
Totternhoe
Church End
Chalk Hill
Lawrence Industrial Estate
Dunstable Football Club
Northfields Upper School
Brewers Hill Middle School
Weatherfield School
Beecroft School
Lancot Lower School
Dunstable Town Cricket Club
Totternhoe Football Club
Totternhoe Lower School
Nature Reserve
Queensbury School
Lark Rise Lower School
Five Knolls
Cemetery
WATLING STREET
HIGH STREET NORTH
HOUGHTON ROAD
WEST STREET
TRING ROAD
WHIPSNADE ROAD
ICKNIELD WAY
A505
A5(T)
A5120
B489
B4541
M8
1 Morland Cl
M6
1 Nursery Cl
115
M5
1 Cross St North
2 Stewart Clark Ct
M4
1 High St North
M2
1 Barleyfield Wy
2 Freemans Cl
Downs Golf Club
Well Head

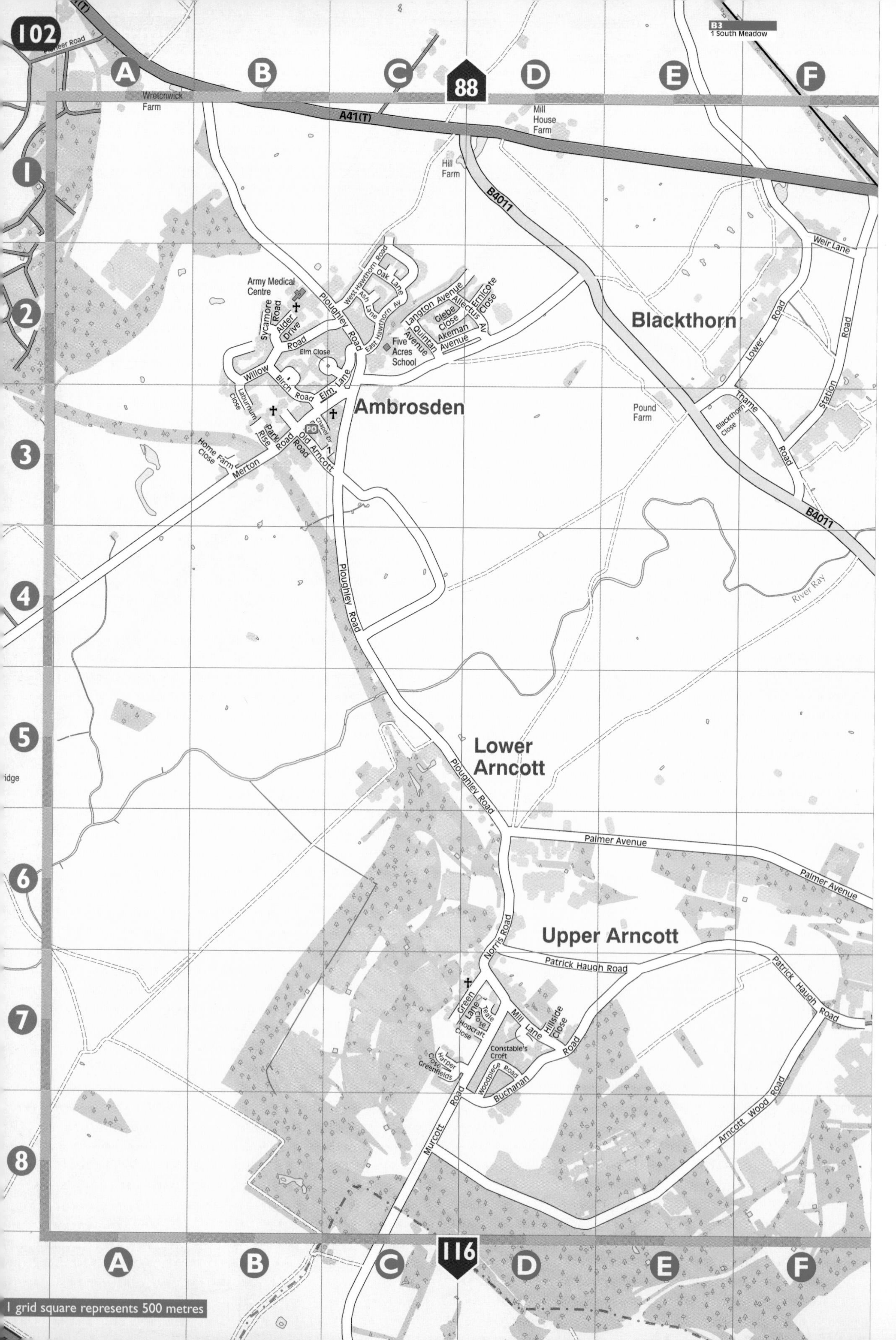
B3
1 South Meadow
A
B
C
88
D
E
F
Wretchwick Farm
A41(T)
Mill House Farm
Hill Farm
B4011
Blackthorn
Weir Lane
Lower Road
Station Road
Thame Road
Blackthorn Close
Pound Farm
Army Medical Centre
Sycamore Road
Alder Drive
Ploughley Road
West Hawthorn Road
Oak Lane
Ash Lane
East Hawthorn Av
Langton Avenue
Allectus Av
Ernicote Close
Glebe Close
Akeman Avenue
Quintan Avenue
Five Acres School
Elm Close
Willow Road
Birch Road
Elm Lane
Laburnum Close
Ambrosden
Park Rise
Road
Old Arncott Road
Chapel Dr
PO
Home Farm Close
Merton
River Ray
Lower Arncott
Palmer Avenue
Upper Arncott
Norris Road
Patrick Haugh Road
Green Lane
Teale Close
Hopcraft Close
Mill Lane
Hillside Close
Constable's Croft
Harper Close
Greenfields
Woodpiece Road
Buchanan Road
Murcott Road
Arncott Wood Road
1
2
3
4
5
6
7
8
116
1 grid square represents 500 metres

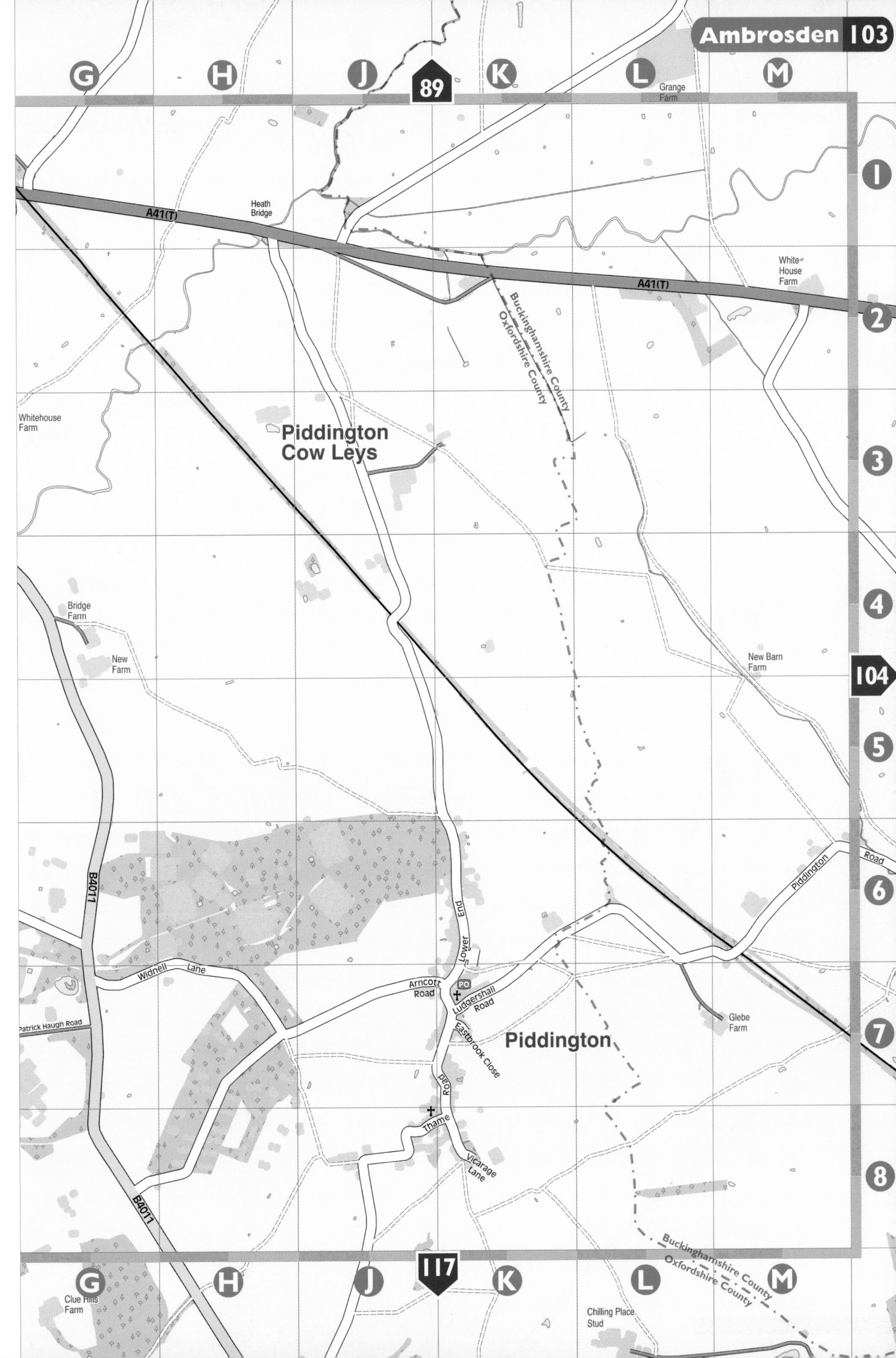
G
H
J
89
K
L
M
Grange Farm
Heath Bridge
A41(T)
A41(T)
White House Farm
Buckinghamshire County
Oxfordshire County
Whitehouse Farm
Piddington Cow Leys
Bridge Farm
New Farm
New Barn Farm
104
Piddington Road
B4011
Lower End
Widnell Lane
Arncott Road
PO
Ludgershall Road
Patrick Haugh Road
Eastbrook Close
Piddington
Glebe Farm
Thame Road
Vicarage Lane
B4011
Buckinghamshire County
Oxfordshire County
117
Clue Hills Farm
Chilling Place Stud
1
2
3
4
5
6
7
8

90
118
103
A
B
C
D
E
F
1
2
3
4
5
6
7
8
Grendon Underwood
Grendon Underwood CP School
Bakery Close
1 Solters Cl
The Broadway
Three Points
A41(T)
Rookery Farm
Tetchwick
Tetchwick Brook
Tittershall Wood
Bicester Road
Road
High Street
PO
Duck Lane
White Hart Close
Salters Lane
Brook Close
Ludgershall
Church Lane
Wotton End
Brill Road
Kingswood Lane
Clearfields Farm
The Lake
Wotton House
1 grid square represents 500 metres

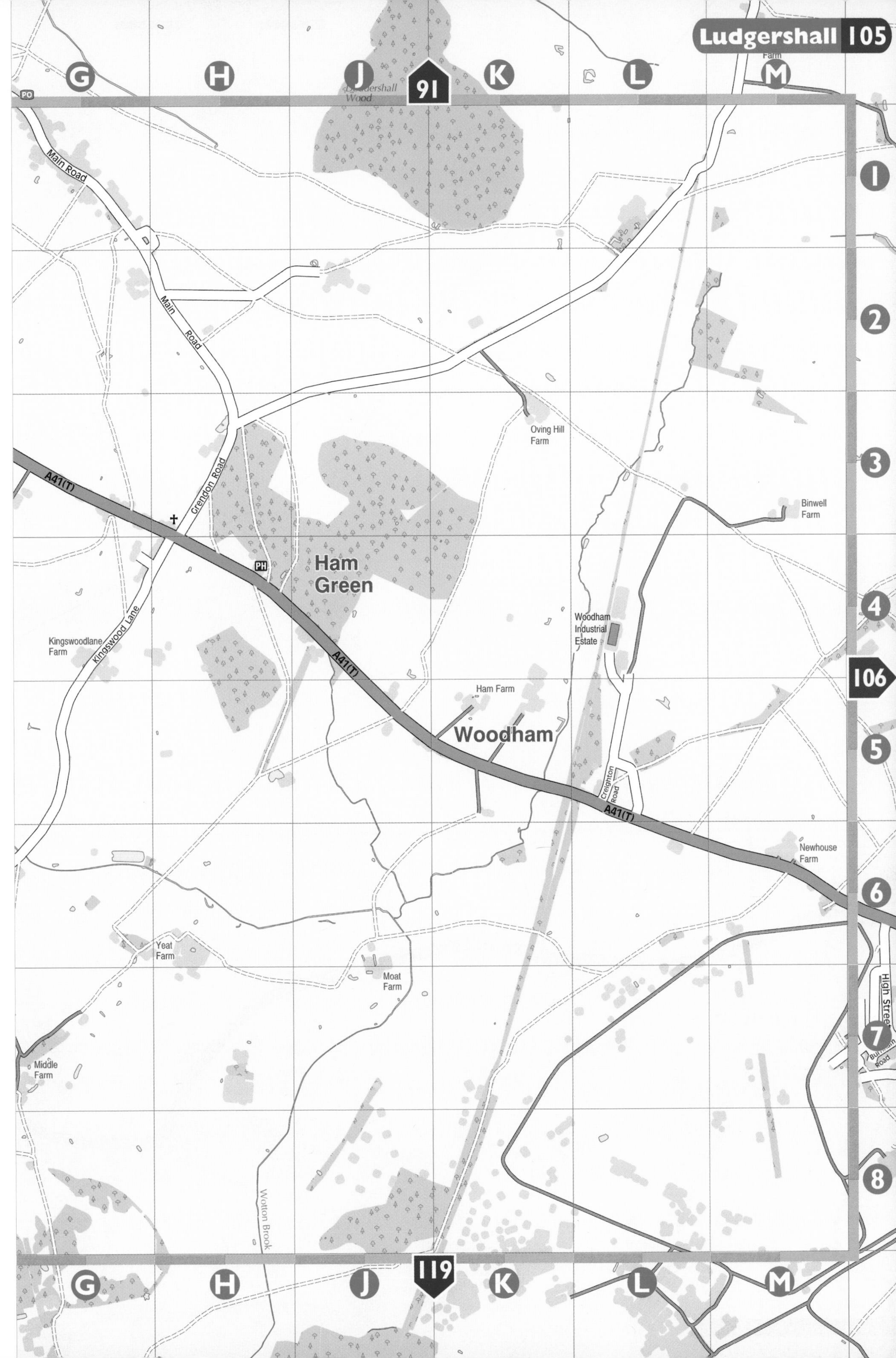
G
H
J
K
L
M
91
Farm
Ludgershall Wood
PO
Main Road
Main Road
1
2
3
4
5
6
7
8
A41(T)
Grendon Road
Oving Hill Farm
Binwell Farm
Ham Green
PH
Kingswood Lane
Kingswoodlane Farm
Woodham Industrial Estate
106
Ham Farm
Woodham
A41(T)
Creighton Road
A41(T)
Newhouse Farm
Yeat Farm
Moat Farm
High Street
Middle Farm
Wotton Brook
119
G
H
J
K
L
M

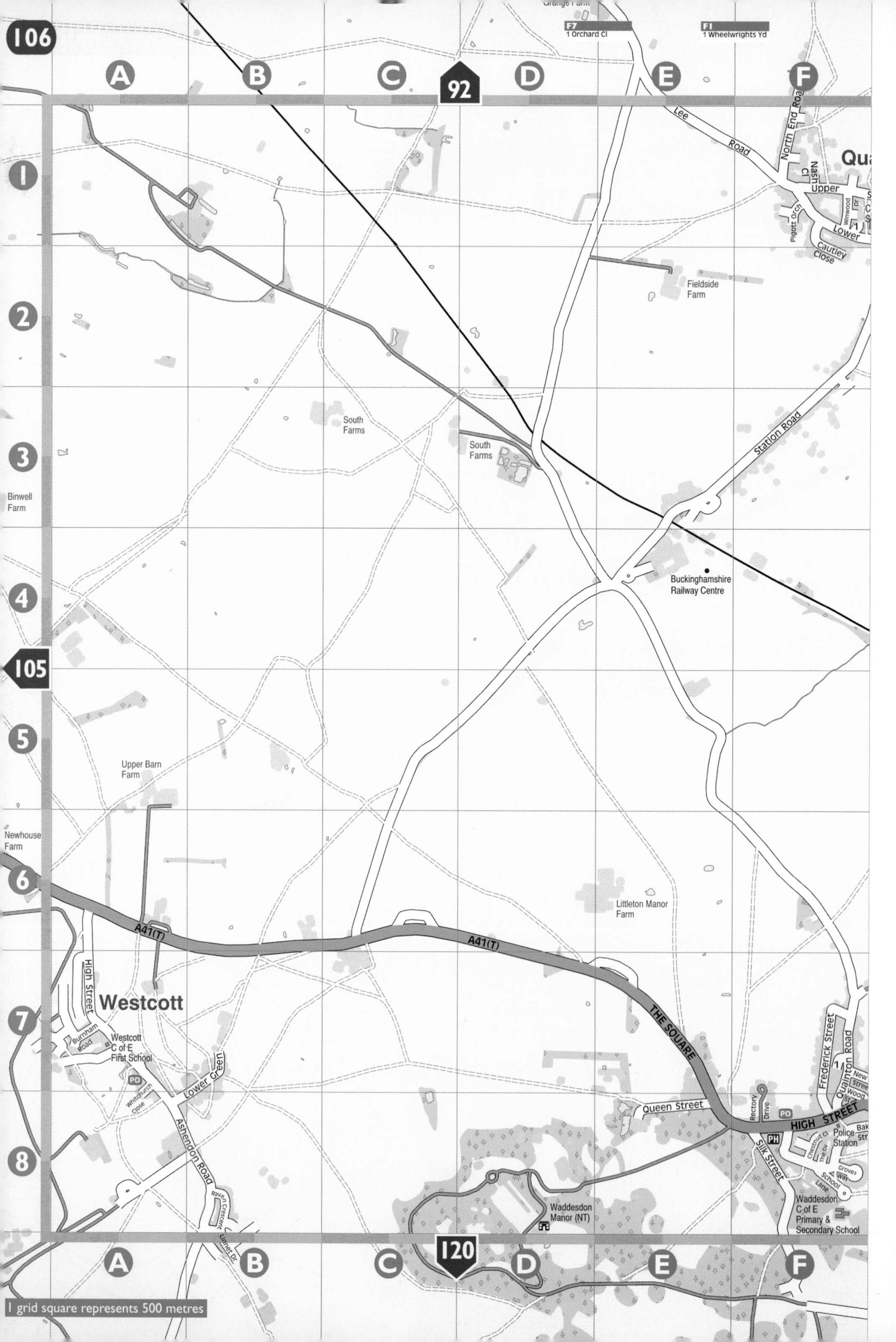
F7
1 Orchard Cl
F1
1 Wheelwrights Yd
A
B
C
92
D
E
F
1
2
3
4
105
5
6
7
8
Lee Road
North End Road
Nash Cl
Upper
Pigott Orch
Winwood
Lower
Cautley Close
Fieldside Farm
South Farms
South Farms
Station Road
Binwell Farm
Buckinghamshire Railway Centre
Upper Barn Farm
Newhouse Farm
Littleton Manor Farm
A41(T)
A41(T)
High Street
Westcott
Burnham Road
Westcott C of E First School
PO
Whitchurch Close
Lower Green
Ashendon Road
Raven Crescent
Linnet Dr
THE SQUARE
Queen Street
Rectory Drive
PO
HIGH STREET
PH
Silk Street
Frederick Street
Quainton Road
Police Station
Chestnut Cl
The Ov
School Lane
Groves Way
Waddesdon Manor (NT)
Waddesdon C of E Primary & Secondary School
120
A
B
C
D
E
F

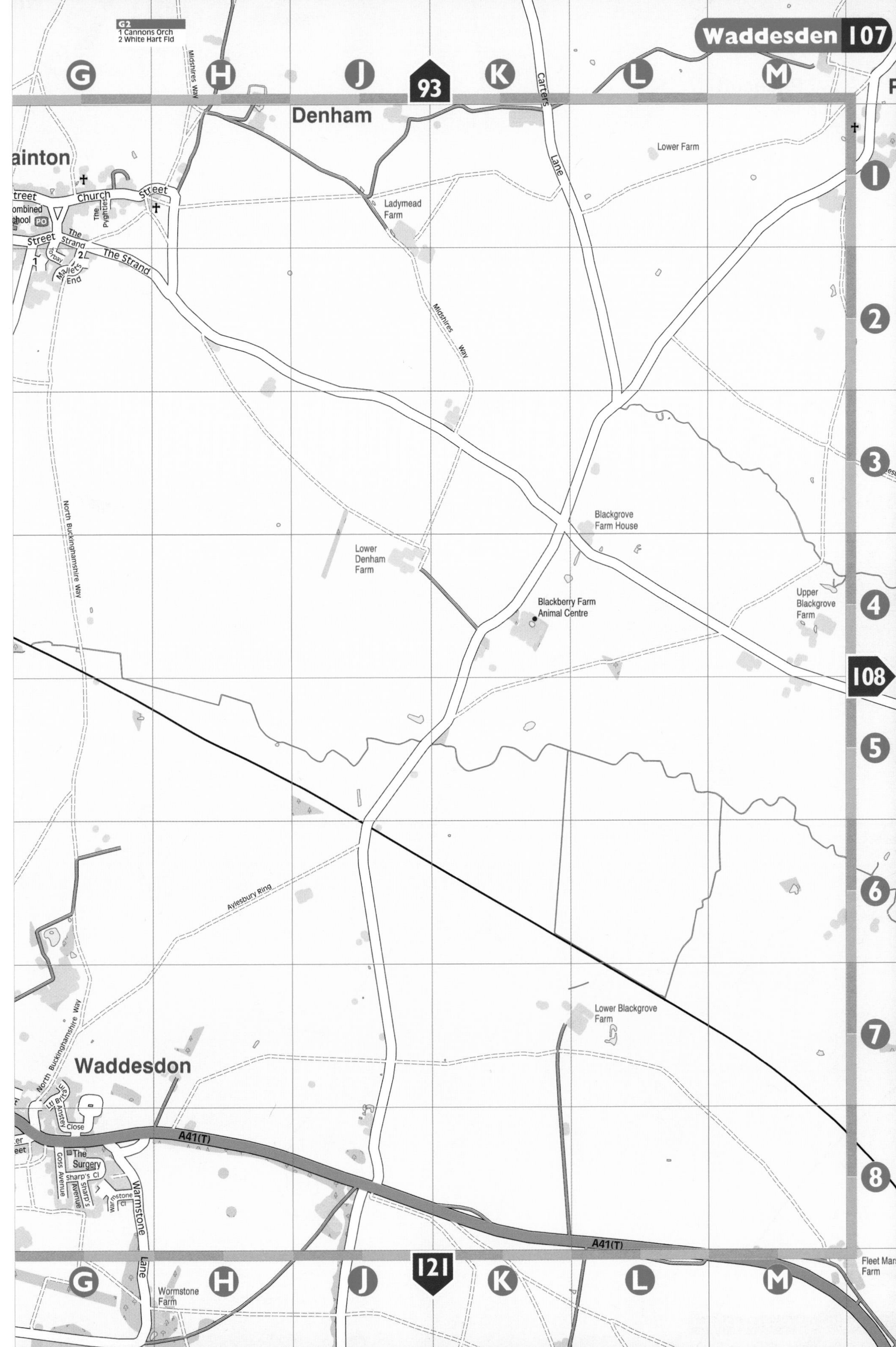
G2
1 Cannons Orch
2 White Hart Fld
G
H
J
K
L
M
93
Denham
Midshires Way
Carters Lane
Lower Farm
ainton
Church Street
Street
Combined School
PO
The Pyghtles
The Strand
Torbay
Mallets End
Ladymead Farm
Midshires Way
North Buckinghamshire Way
Blackgrove Farm House
Lower Denham Farm
Blackberry Farm Animal Centre
Upper Blackgrove Farm
108
Aylesbury Ring
Lower Blackgrove Farm
North Buckinghamshire Way
Waddesdon
Anstey Close
The Surgery
Goss Avenue
Sharp's Cl
Sharp's Avenue
Warmstone Cl
Warmstone Lane
A41(T)
A41(T)
121
Wormstone Farm
Fleet Marsh Farm
1
2
3
4
5
6
7
8

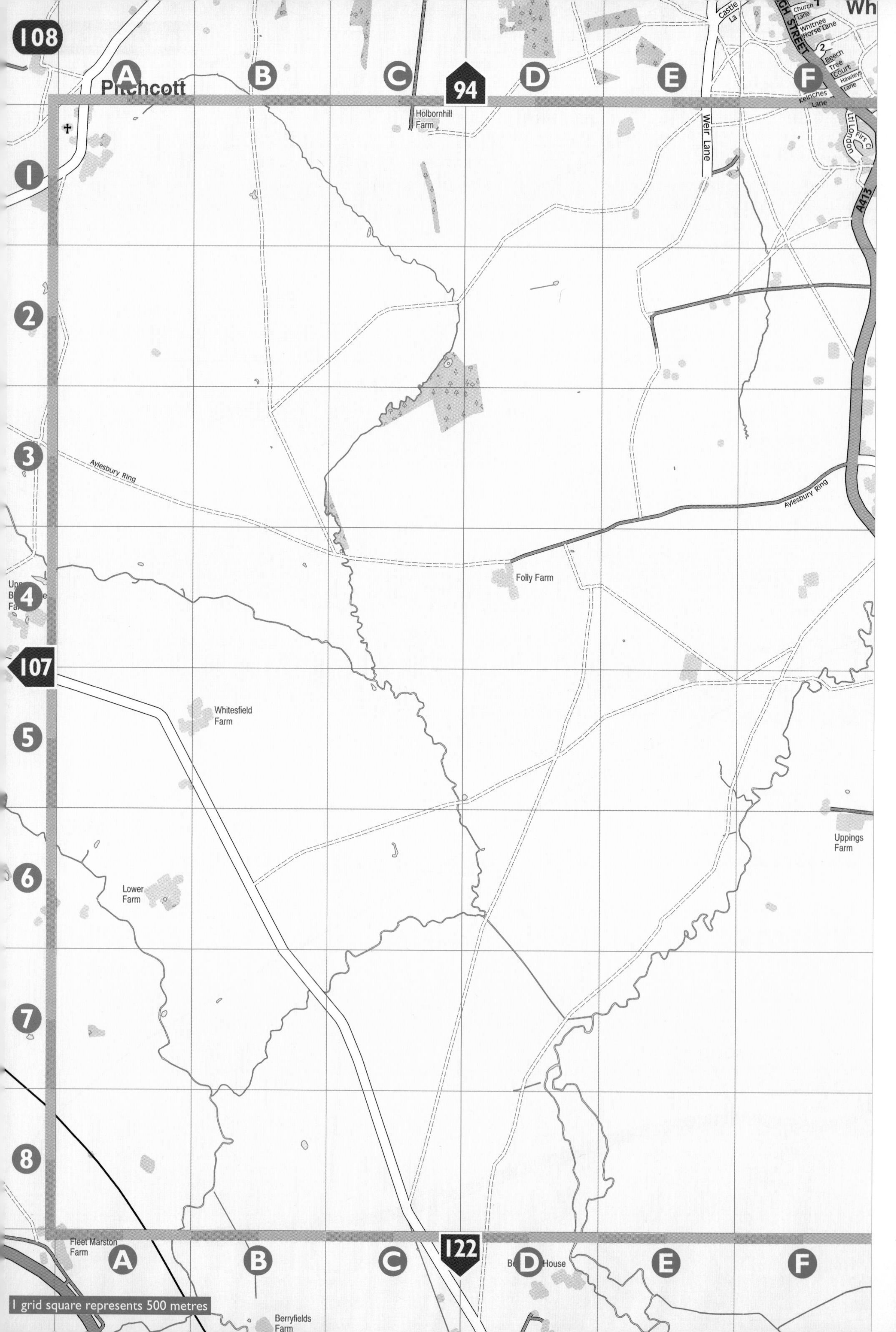


1 grid square represents 500 metres

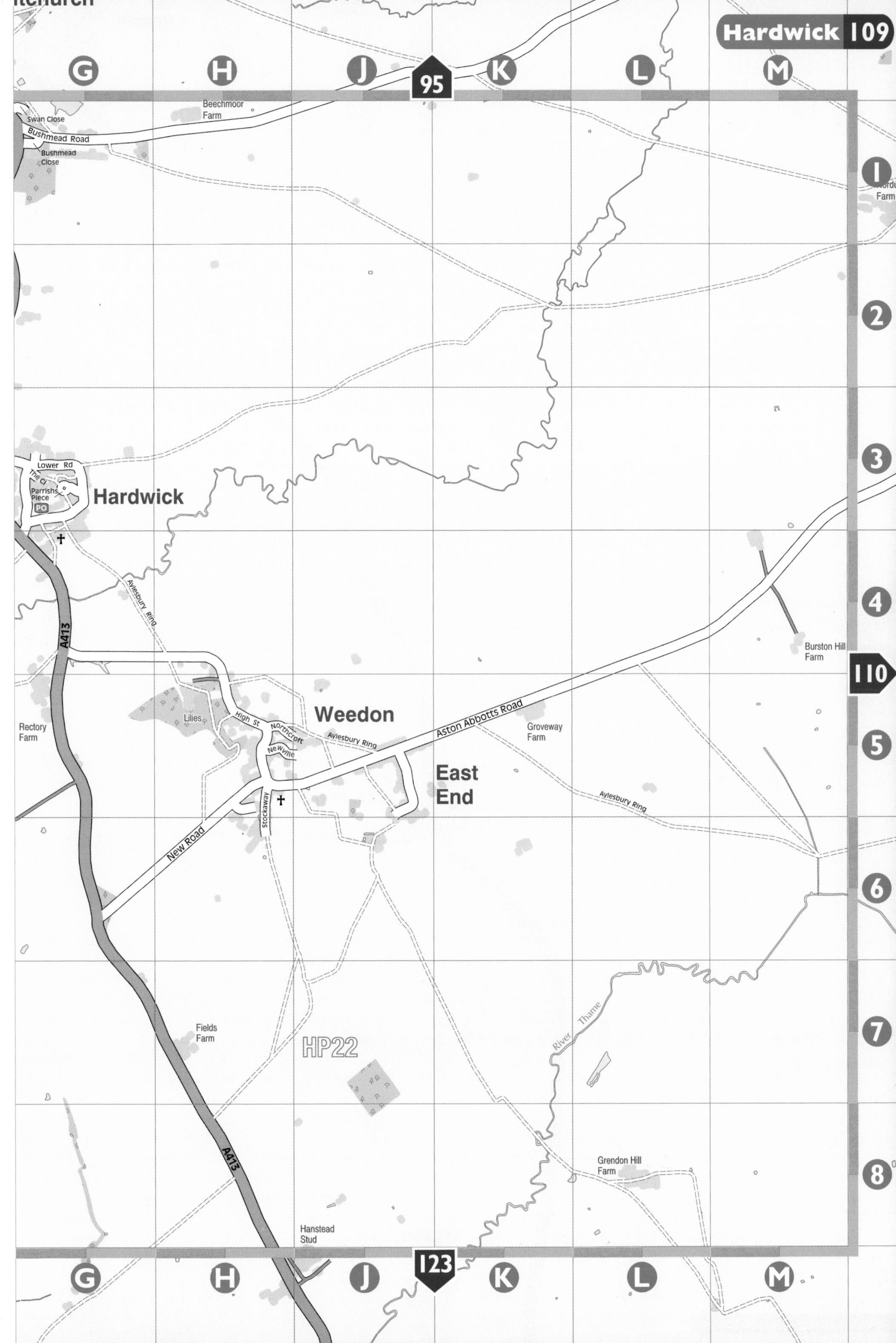
itchurch
G
H
J
95
K
L
M
Beechmoor
Farm
Swan Close
Bushmead Road
Bushmead
Close
1
Farm
2
3
Lower Rd
The Cl
Parrishs
Piece
PO
Hardwick
4
Aylesbury Ring
A413
Burston Hill
Farm
110
Rectory
Farm
Lilies
High St
Northcroft
Newville
Weedon
Aylesbury Ring
Aston Abbotts Road
Groveway
Farm
5
East
End
Aylesbury Ring
Stockaway
New Road
6
River Thame
Fields
Farm
HP22
7
A413
Grendon Hill
Farm
8
Hanstead
Stud
G
H
J
123
K
L
M

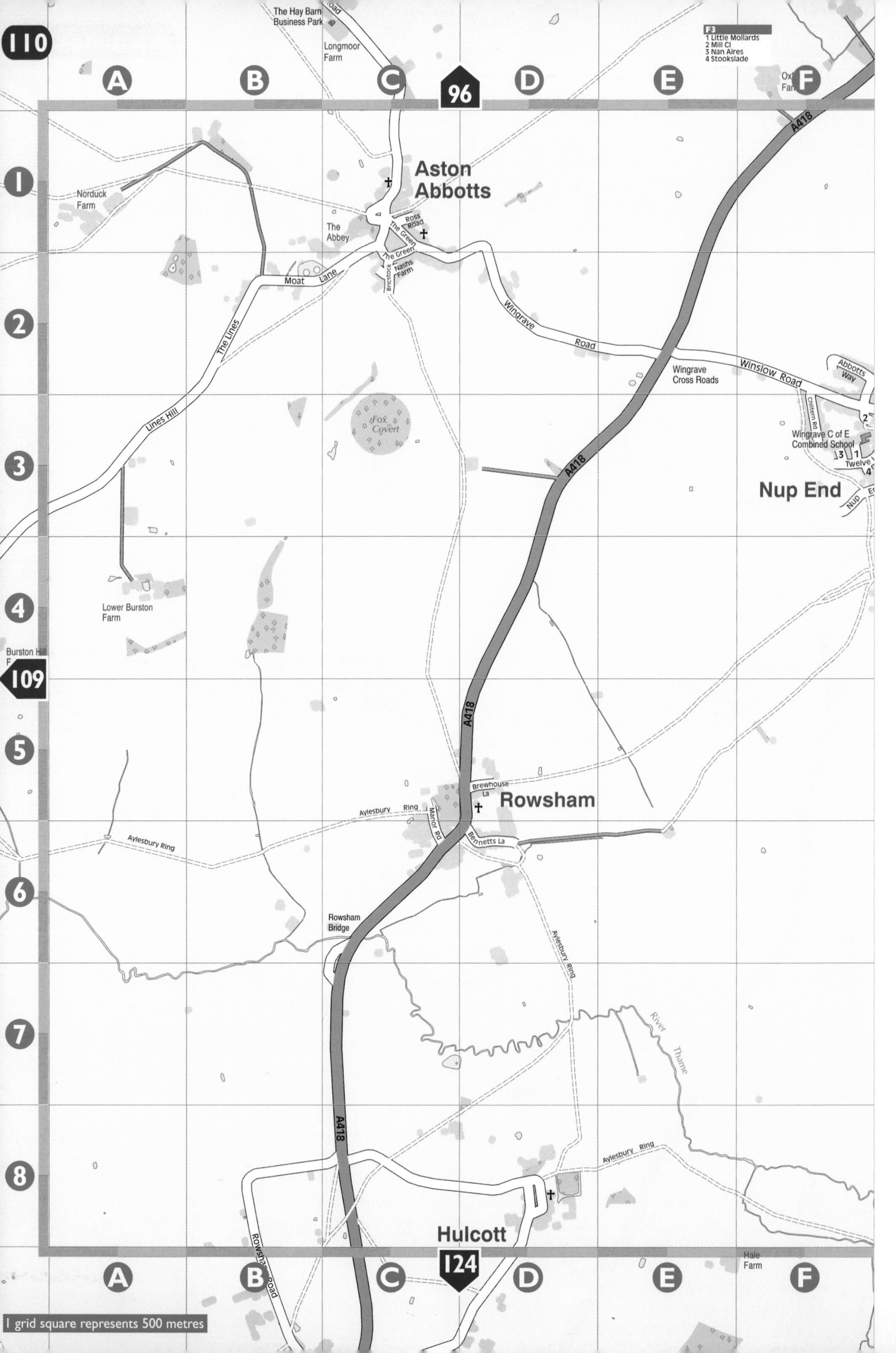

The Hay Barn Business Park
Longmoor Farm
F3
1 Little Mollards
2 Mill Cl
3 Nan Aires
4 Stookslade
A
B
C
D
E
F
96
1
2
3
4
5
6
7
8
Norduck Farm
Aston Abbotts
The Abbey
Ross Road
The Green
Nashs Farm
Bricstock
Moat Lane
The Lines
Wingrave Road
Winslow Road
Wingrave Cross Roads
Abbotts Way
Chiltern Rd
Wingrave C of E Combined School
Twelve
Nup End
A418
Lines Hill
Fox Covert
Lower Burston Farm
Burston Hill F
109
Brewhouse La
Rowsham
Aylesbury Ring
Manor Rd
Bennetts La
Rowsham Bridge
River Thame
Hulcott
Rowsham Road
124
Hale Farm

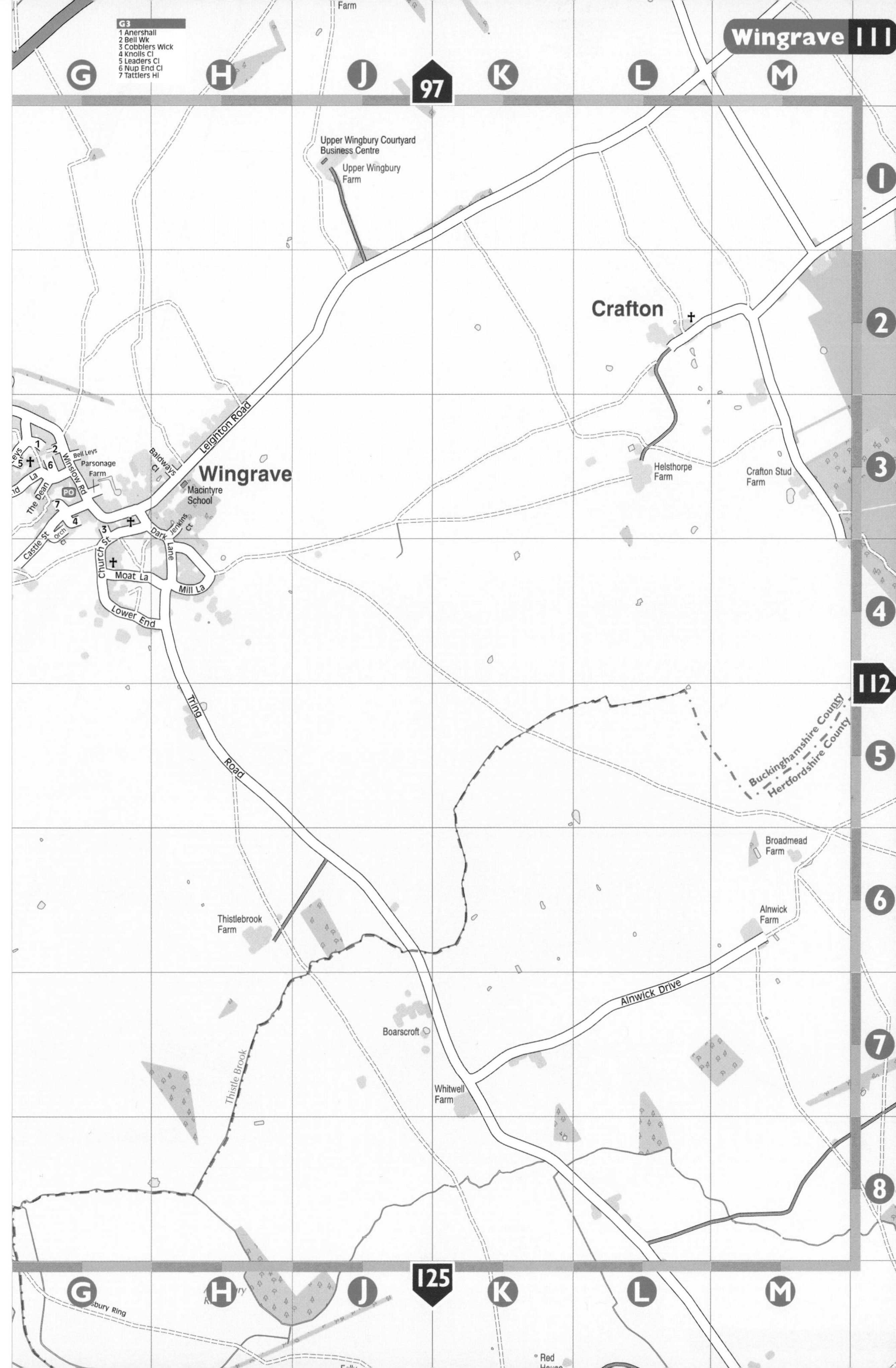
G3
1 Anershall
2 Bell Wk
3 Cobblers Wick
4 Knolls Cl
5 Leaders Cl
6 Nup End Cl
7 Tattlers Hl
Farm
G
H
J
97
K
L
M
Upper Wingbury Courtyard Business Centre
Upper Wingbury Farm
Crafton
Leighton Road
Wingrave
Bell Leys
Parsonage Farm
Winslow Rd
The Dean
Baldways Cl
Macintyre School
Helsthorpe Farm
Crafton Stud Farm
Castle St
Orch Cl
Church St
Dark Lane
Jenkins Ct
Moat La
Mill La
Lower End
Tring Road
Buckinghamshire County
Hertfordshire County
Broadmead Farm
Thistlebrook Farm
Alnwick Farm
Alnwick Drive
Boarscroft
Whitwell Farm
Thistle Brook
1
2
3
4
112
5
6
7
8
125
Red

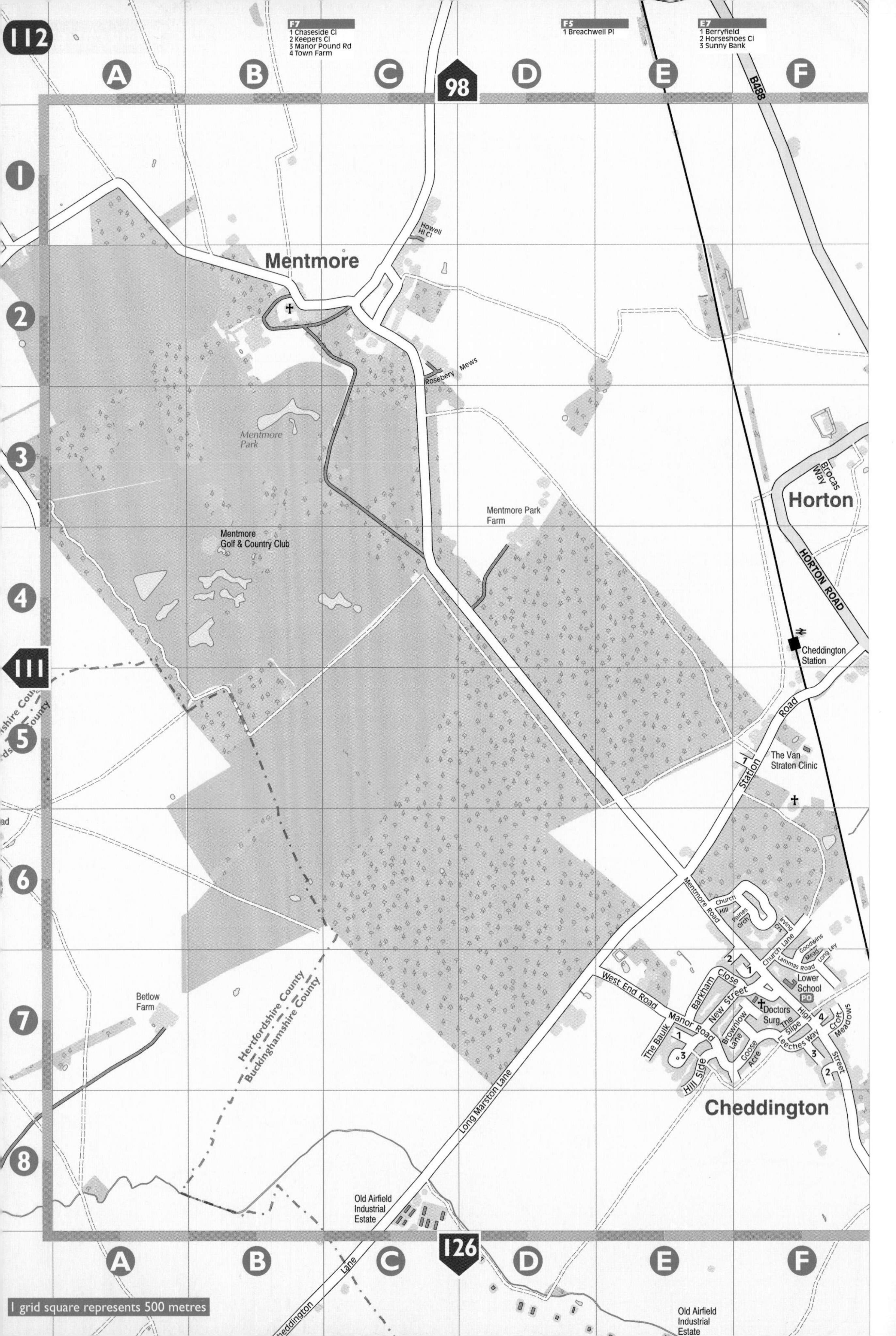
F7
1 Chaseside Cl
2 Keepers Cl
3 Manor Pound Rd
4 Town Farm
F5
1 Breachwell Pl
E7
1 Berryfield
2 Horseshoes Cl
3 Sunny Bank
A
B
C
98
D
E
F
B488
Mentmore
Howell Hl Cl
Rosebery Mews
Mentmore Park
Mentmore Park Farm
Mentmore Golf & Country Club
Horton
Brocas Way
HORTON ROAD
Cheddington Station
111
Station Road
The Van Straten Clinic
Mentmore Road
Church Hill
Paines Orch
Irving Cres
Church Lane
Goodwins Mead
Lammas Road
Long Ley
Lower School
PO
West End Road
Barkham Close
New Street
Doctors Surg
High Street
Croft Meadows
Manor Road
The Baulk
Hill Side
Brownlow Lane
Goose Acre
The Slipe
Leeches Way
Cheddington
Betlow Farm
Hertfordshire County
Buckinghamshire County
Long Marston Lane
Old Airfield Industrial Estate
126
Cheddington Lane
1 grid square represents 500 metres

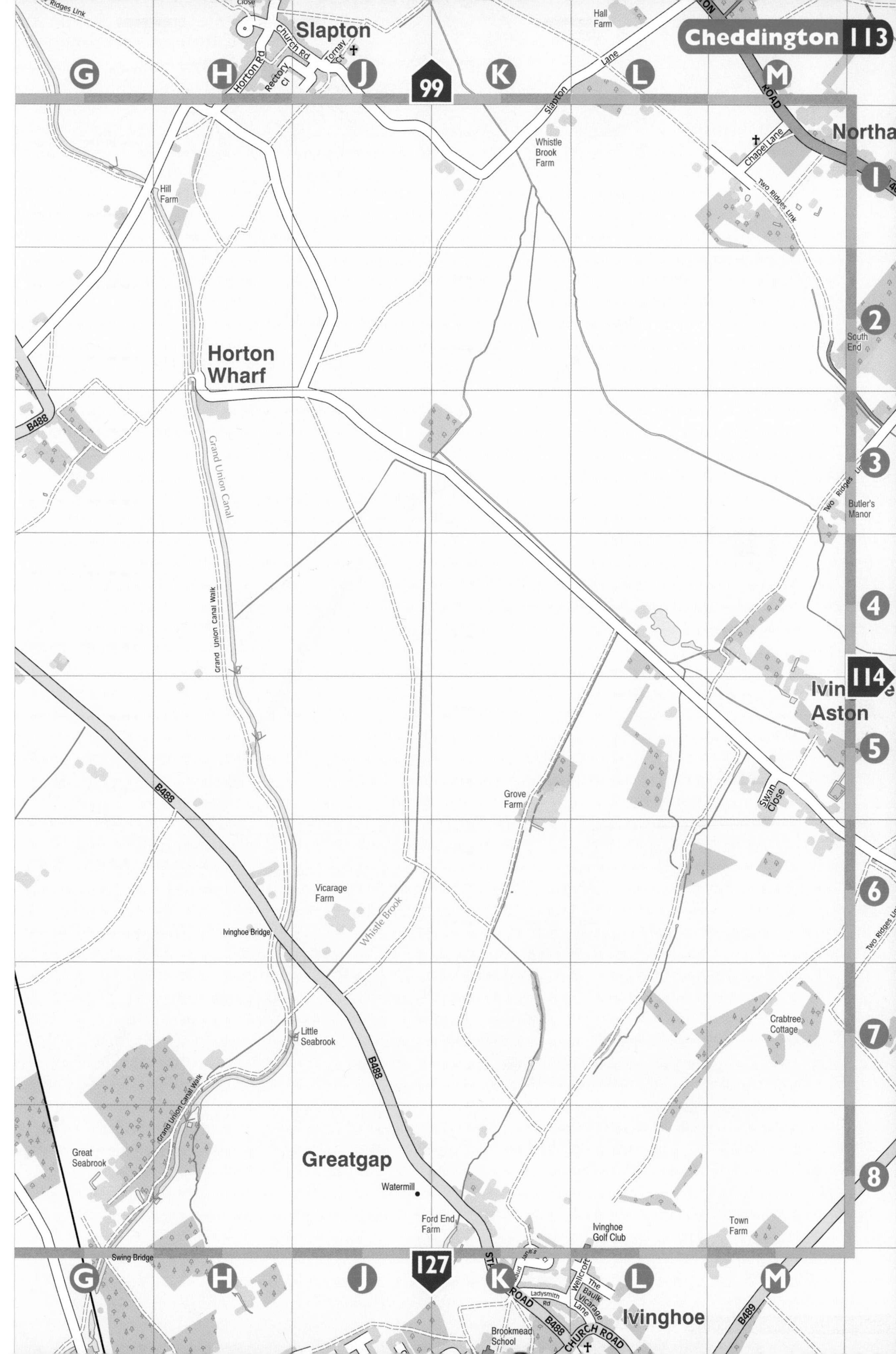
Slapton
Church Rd
Horton Rd
Rectory Cl
Tornay Ct
Hall Farm
Slapton Lane
Whistle Brook Farm
Northa
Chapel Lane
Two Ridges Link
Hill Farm
Horton Wharf
Grand Union Canal
Grand Union Canal Walk
B488
South End
Butler's Manor
Ivinghoe Aston
Swan Close
Grove Farm
Vicarage Farm
Whistle Brook
Ivinghoe Bridge
Little Seabrook
Crabtree Cottage
Great Seabrook
Greatgap
Watermill
Ford End Farm
Ivinghoe Golf Club
Town Farm
Swing Bridge
Ladysmith Rd
Wellcroft
The Baulk
Vicarage Lane
Church Road
Ivinghoe
Brookmead School
B489
G
H
J
K
L
M
1
2
3
4
5
6
7
8

99
114
127

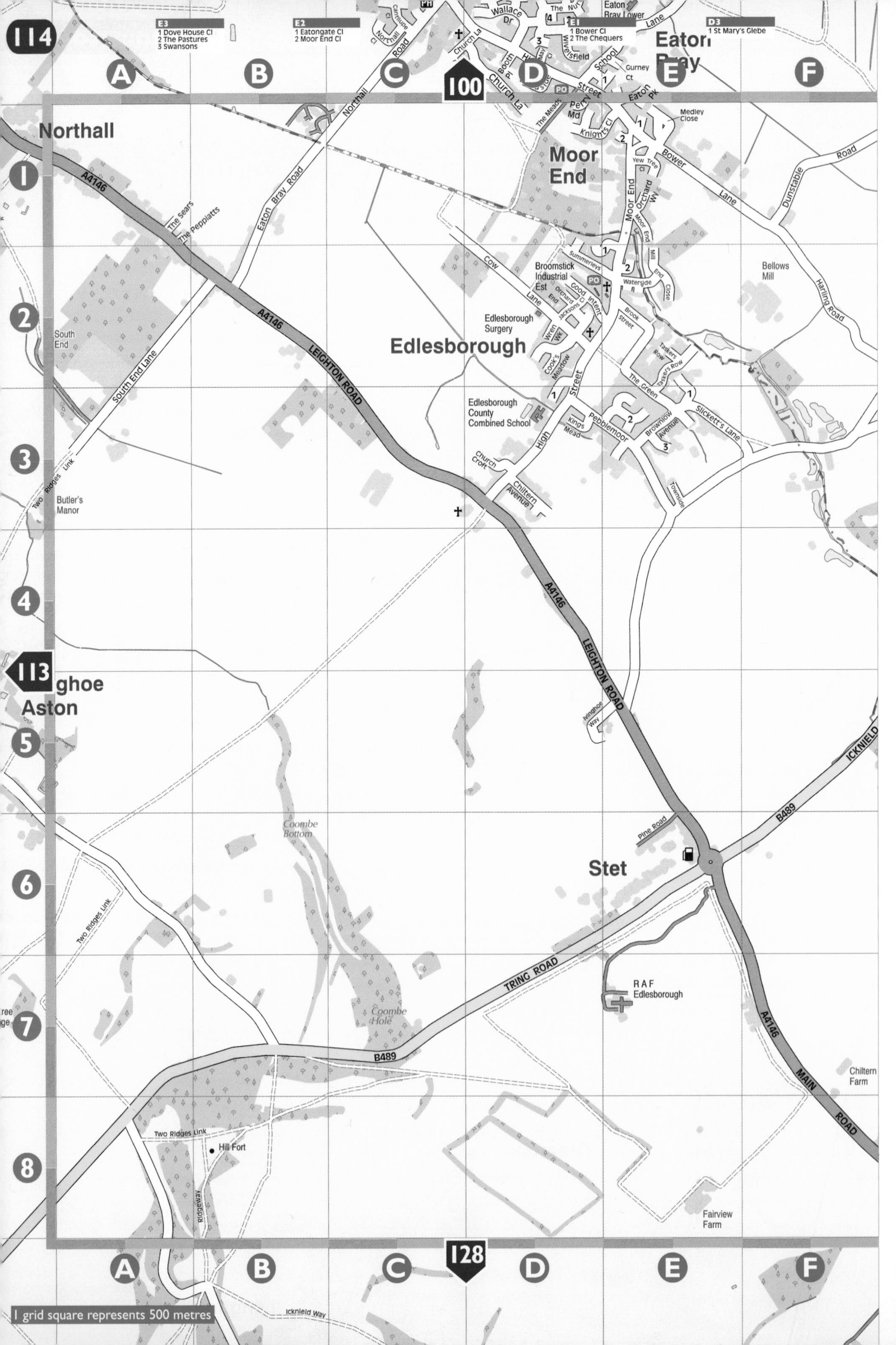
E3
1 Dove House Cl
2 The Pastures
3 Swansons
E2
1 Eatongate Cl
2 Moor End Cl
E1
1 Bower Cl
2 The Chequers
D3
1 St Mary's Glebe
100
Northall
Eaton Bray
Moor End
Edlesborough
Broomstick Industrial Est
Edlesborough Surgery
Edlesborough County Combined School
Bellows Mill
South End
Butler's Manor
Aston
Coombe Bottom
Coombe Hole
Stet
RAF Edlesborough
Hill Fort
Chiltern Farm
Fairview Farm
A4146
LEIGHTON ROAD
MAIN ROAD
TRING ROAD
B489
ICKNIELD
Eaton Bray Road
South End Lane
Two Ridges Link
Ridgeway
Icknield Way
Cow Lane
High Street
Moor End
Bower Lane
Dunstable Road
Harling Road
Slickett's Lane
Pebblemoor
Brownlow Avenue
Townside
Chiltern Avenue
Church Croft
Kings Mead
The Green
Taskers Row
Brook Street
Good Intent
Wren Wk
Cook's Meadow
Summerleys
Waterside
Orchard Wy
Yew Tree Cl
Knights Cl
Medley Close
Pine Road
Iwinghoe Way
The Sears
The Pepplatts
Northall Road
Church La
School
Gurney Ct
Wallace Dr
Eaton Pk
128
113
1 grid square represents 500 metres

Church End
Dunstable Downs Golf Club
Well Head
Doolittle Mill
Bottom Dr
Manton Rd
Springfield Rd
B489
B4541
Icknield Way Path
Dunstable Downs Country Park
Dunstable Downs
TRING ROAD
Icknield Way Farm
Harling Road
Icknield Way
LU6
Chute Farm
DAGNALL ROAD
B4540
Valance-end Farm
WAY
Sallowsprings
Tree Cathedral
Icknield Way
B4506
Willow Farm
Bedfordshire County
Buckinghamshire County
Dukes Avenue
Escarpment Avenue
Whipsnade
The Green
Studham Lane
Central Av
White Lion
Miss Joans Ride
Cut Throat Avenue
Whipsnade Park Zoo
Humphrey Talbot Avenue
Valley Close
Sir Peter's Wy
Collyers
DUNSTABLE ROAD
NORTH
Dagnall
Deans Meadow
Dagnall CP School
MAIN
Isle of Wight Lane
Lark Rise Lower School
Ulverston Rd
Cartmel

101
129

A
B
C
D
E
F
102
1
2
3
4
5
6
7
8
New Park Farm
Red House Farm
Oldhouse Spinney
Oxfordshire County
Buckinghamshire County
Four Winds Farm
Buckinghamshire County
Oxfordshire County
Whitecross Green
Panshill Fms
Panshill Fms
M40
Decoy Pond
Boarstall Decoy (NT)
Whitecross Green Wood
Old Arngrove
Warren Farm
New Arngrove Farm
Gardner's Barn
Honeyburge
M40
Danes Brook
Pasture Farm
Brill Road
Mill Lane
The Green
130
New Farm
PO
Golf Club
Buckinghamshire
Oxfordshire
1 grid square represents 500 metres

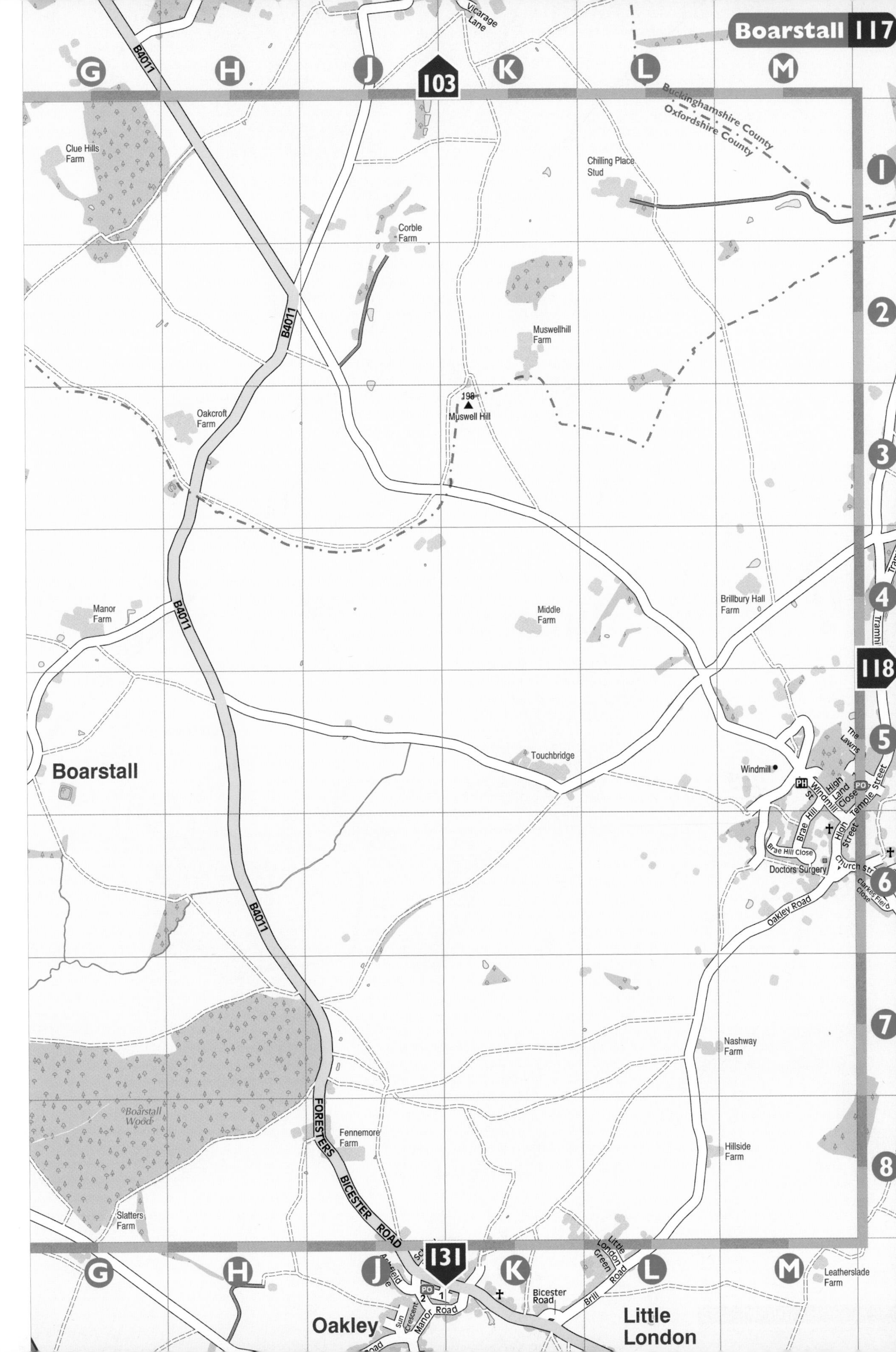
Vicarage Lane
G
H
J
103
K
L
M
B4011
Buckinghamshire County
Oxfordshire County
Clue Hills Farm
Chilling Place Stud
1
Corble Farm
2
B4011
Muswellhill Farm
198
Muswell Hill
Oakcroft Farm
3
Manor Farm
B4011
Middle Farm
Brillbury Hall Farm
4
118
5
The Lawns
Touchbridge
Boarstall
Windmill
PH
High St
Windmill
High Land Close
PO
Temple Street
Brae Hill
High Street
Brae Hill Close
Church St
Doctors Surgery
6
Clarkes Field Close
Oakley Road
B4011
7
Nashway Farm
FORESTERS
Boarstall Wood
Fennemore Farm
BICESTER ROAD
Hillside Farm
8
Slatters Farm
Little London Green Road
131
G
H
J
K
L
M
Leatherslade Farm
PO
Bicester Road
Oakley
Sun Crescent
Manor Road
Brill Road
Little London

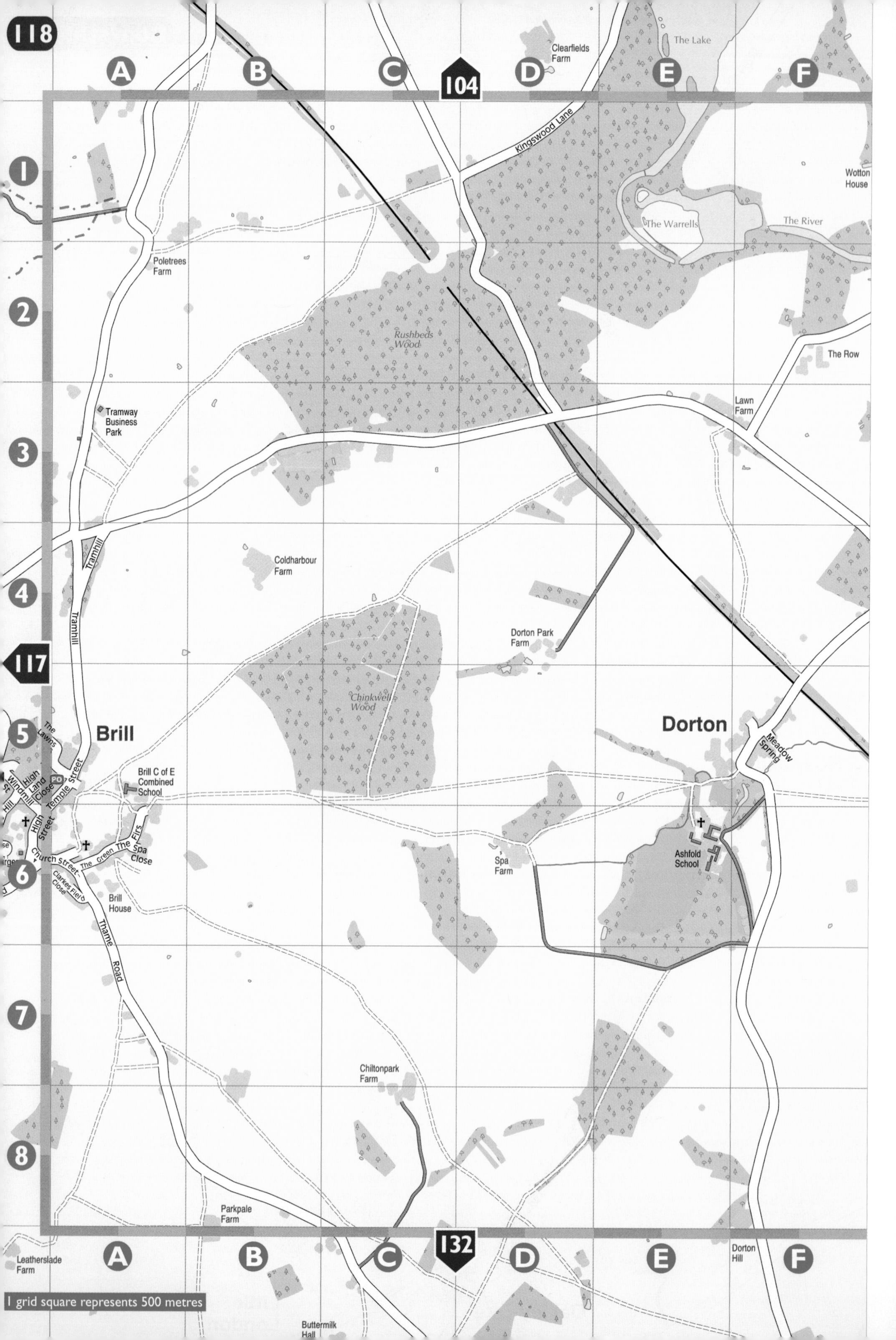
A
B
C
104
D
E
F
Clearfields Farm
The Lake
Kingswood Lane
Wotton House
The Warrells
The River
Poletrees Farm
Rushbeds Wood
The Row
Lawn Farm
Tramway Business Park
Tramhill
Coldharbour Farm
Dorton Park Farm
117
Chinkwell Wood
Brill
Dorton
The Lawns
Meadow Spring
Brill C of E Combined School
High Street
Windmill
Temple Street
Church Street
The Green
The Firs
Spa Close
Clarkes Field Close
Spa Farm
Ashfold School
Brill House
Thame Road
Chiltonpark Farm
Parkpale Farm
132
Leatherslade Farm
Dorton Hill
Buttermilk Hall
1
2
3
4
5
6
7
8

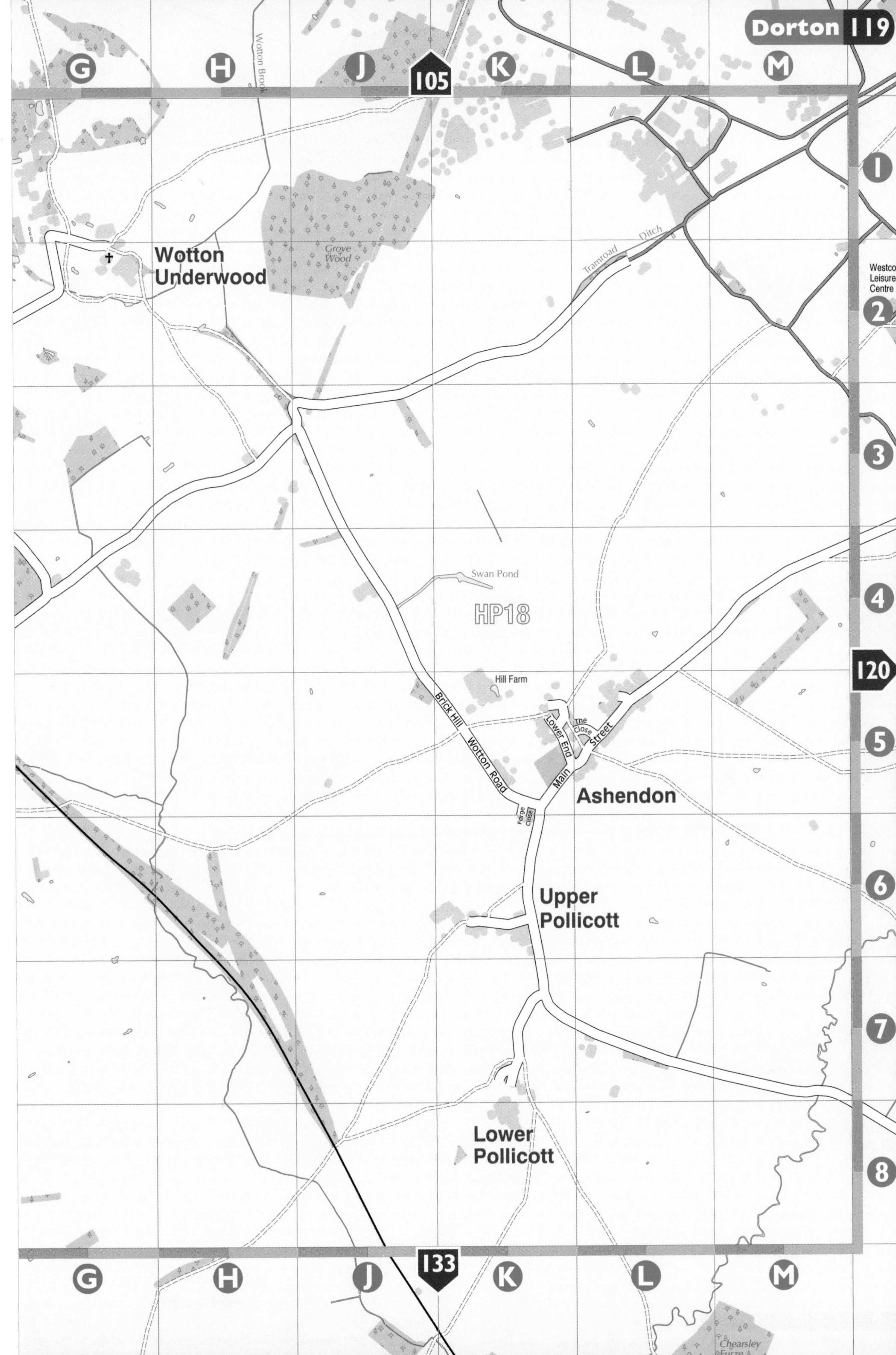
G
H
J
105
K
L
M
Wotton Brook
Wotton
Underwood
Grove
Wood
Tramroad
Ditch
Westcott
Leisure
Centre
1
2
3
4
5
6
7
8
Swan Pond
HP18
Hill Farm
120
Brick Hill
Wotton Road
Lower End
The
Close
Street
Main
Forge
Close
Ashendon
Upper
Pollicott
Lower
Pollicott
133
Chearsley
Furze
G
H
J
K
L
M

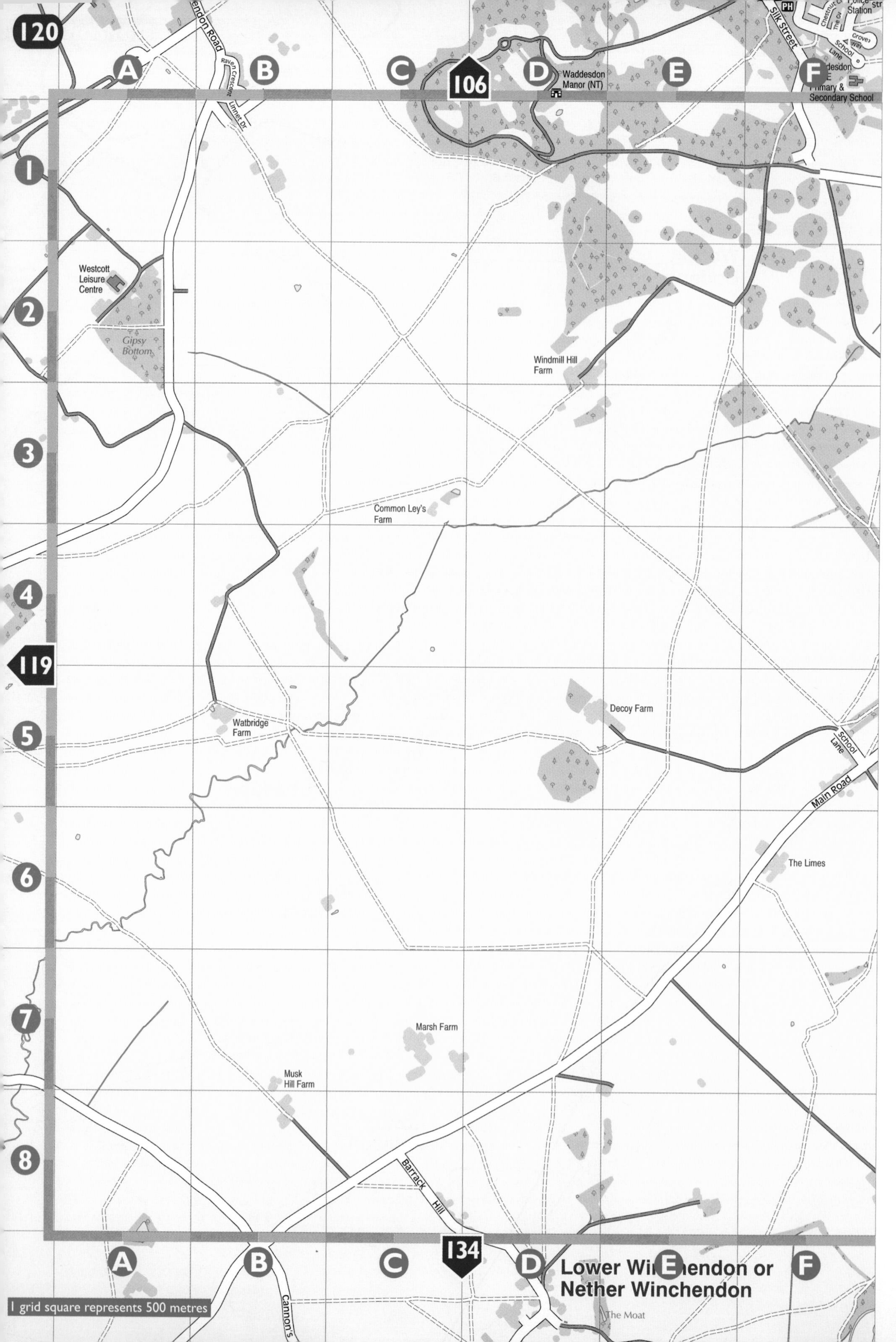
A
B
C
D
E
F
106
Waddesdon Manor (NT)
Silk Street
Police Station
Chestnut Cl
Grove Way
School Lane
Waddesdon CE Primary & Secondary School
PH
Raven Crescent
Linnet Dr
Westcott Leisure Centre
Gipsy Bottom
Windmill Hill Farm
Common Ley's Farm
Watbridge Farm
Decoy Farm
School Lane
Main Road
The Limes
Marsh Farm
Musk Hill Farm
Barrack Hill
Cannon's
134
119
1
2
3
4
5
6
7
8
Lower Winchendon or Nether Winchendon
The Moat
1 grid square represents 500 metres

The Surgery
Goss Avenue
Sharp's Cl
Sharp's Avenue
Warmstone Cl
Warmstone Lane
G
H
J
K
L
M
107
A41(T)
Fleet Marsh Farm
Wormstone Farm
1
North Buckinghamshire Way
Cranwell Farms
2
Midshires Way
Cranwell Farms
Waddesdon Hill
3
Coney Hill Farm
Aylesbury Ring
4
Sheepcot Hill
Eythrope Park Farm
122
Church Lane
Upper Winchendon
Midshires Way
Eythrope Park
5
Eythrope
Model Farm
Eythrope Road
6
The Pavilion
Beachendon Farm
7
Thame Valley Walk
River Thame
Eythrope
8
Mainshill Farm
Starveall
135

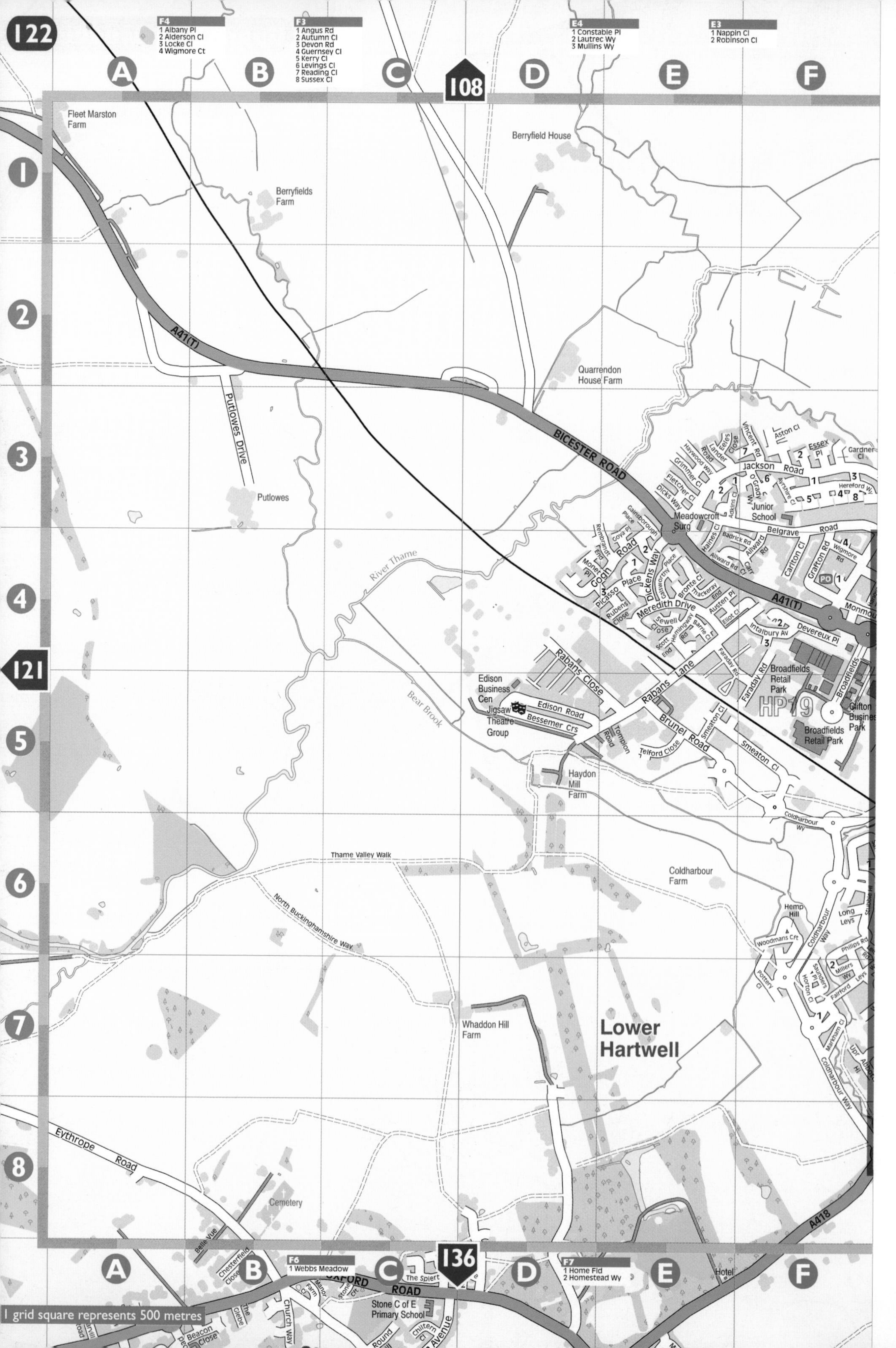
F4
1 Albany Pl
2 Alderson Cl
3 Locke Cl
4 Wigmore Ct
F3
1 Angus Rd
2 Autumn Cl
3 Devon Rd
4 Guernsey Cl
5 Kerry Cl
6 Levings Cl
7 Reading Cl
8 Sussex Cl
E4
1 Constable Pl
2 Lautrec Wy
3 Mullins Wy
E3
1 Nappin Cl
2 Robinson Cl
A
B
C
108
D
E
F
1
2
3
4
121
5
6
7
8
Fleet Marston Farm
Berryfield House
Berryfields Farm
A41(T)
Quarrendon House Farm
Putlowes Drive
Putlowes
BICESTER ROAD
River Thame
Bear Brook
Edison Business Cen
Jigsaw Theatre Group
Edison Road
Bessemer Crs
Rabans Close
Rabans Lane
Tompion Road
Brunel Road
Telford Close
Smeaton Cl
Haydon Mill Farm
Meadowcroft Surg
Junior School
Jackson Road
Belgrave Road
Meredith Drive
Dickens Way
Picasso Place
Gogh Road
Rubens Close
Broadfields Retail Park
Broadfields
HP19
Clifton Business Park
Devereux Pl
Faraday Rd
Coldharbour Way
Coldharbour Farm
Thame Valley Walk
North Buckinghamshire Way
Hemp Hill
Woodmans Cft
Pottery Cl
Long Leys
Whaddon Hill Farm
Lower Hartwell
Eythrope Road
Cemetery
A418
A
B
F6
1 Webbs Meadow
C
136
D
F7
1 Home Fld
2 Homestead Wy
E
Hotel
F
OXFORD ROAD
The Spiert
Stone C of E Primary School
Church Way
Beacon Close
Chesterfield Close
Belle Vue
The Glebe

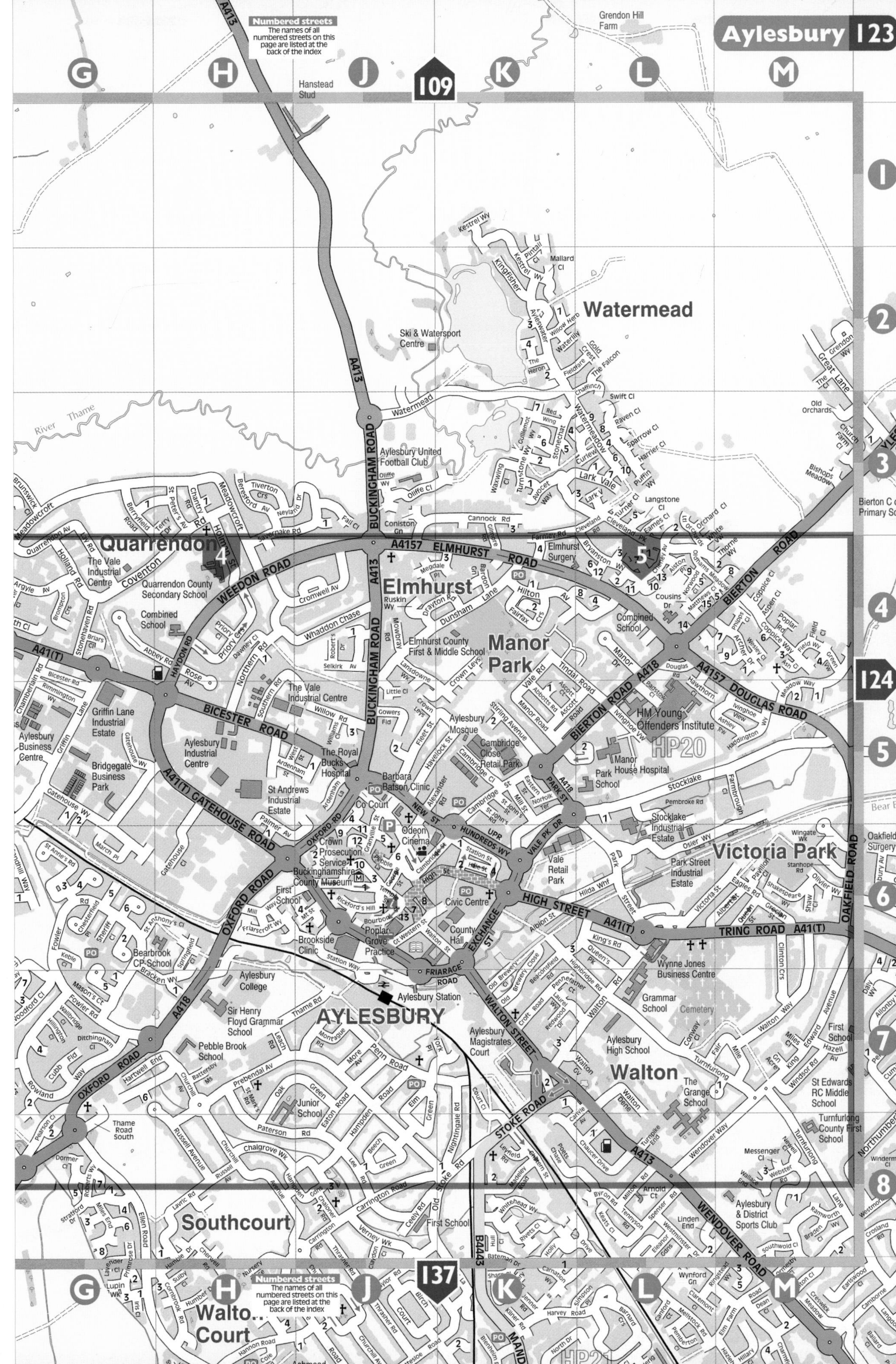
Numbered streets
The names of all numbered streets on this page are listed at the back of the index
G
H
J
K
L
M
109
124
137
Grendon Hill Farm
Hanstead Stud
Watermead
Ski & Watersport Centre
Aylesbury United Football Club
River Thame
Quarrendon
Elmhurst
Manor Park
Victoria Park
Walton
AYLESBURY
Southcourt
Walton Court
HP20
A413
A4157 ELMHURST ROAD
A41(T)
A418
A4157 DOUGLAS ROAD
BUCKINGHAM ROAD
WEEDON ROAD
BICESTER ROAD
A41(T) GATEHOUSE ROAD
OXFORD ROAD
BIERTON ROAD
HIGH STREET
TRING ROAD A41(T)
OAKFIELD ROAD
WALTON STREET
STOKE ROAD
WENDOVER ROAD
FRIARAGE ROAD
EXCHANGE ST
B4443
The Vale Industrial Centre
Quarrendon County Secondary School
Combined School
Griffin Lane Industrial Estate
Aylesbury Business Centre
Bridgegate Business Park
Aylesbury Industrial Centre
St Andrews Industrial Estate
The Royal Bucks Hospital
Barbara Batson Clinic
Elmhurst County First & Middle School
Aylesbury Mosque
Cambridge Close Retail Park
HM Young Offenders Institute
Manor House Hospital
Park School
Stocklake Industrial Estate
Park Street Industrial Estate
Vale Retail Park
Civic Centre
County Hall
Odeon Cinema
Crown Prosecution Service
Buckinghamshire County Museum
Co Court
First School
Brookside Clinic
Poplar Grove Practice
Bearbrook CP School
Aylesbury College
Aylesbury Station
Sir Henry Floyd Grammar School
Pebble Brook School
Aylesbury Magistrates Court
Wynne Jones Business Centre
Grammar School
Cemetery
Aylesbury High School
The Grange School
Junior School
St Edwards RC Middle School
Turnfurlong County First School
Aylesbury & District Sports Club
Elmhurst Surgery
Oakfield Surgery
Bierton C of E Primary School
Thame Road South
Old Orchards
Bishops Meadow
Linden End
First School

1 grid square represents 500 metres

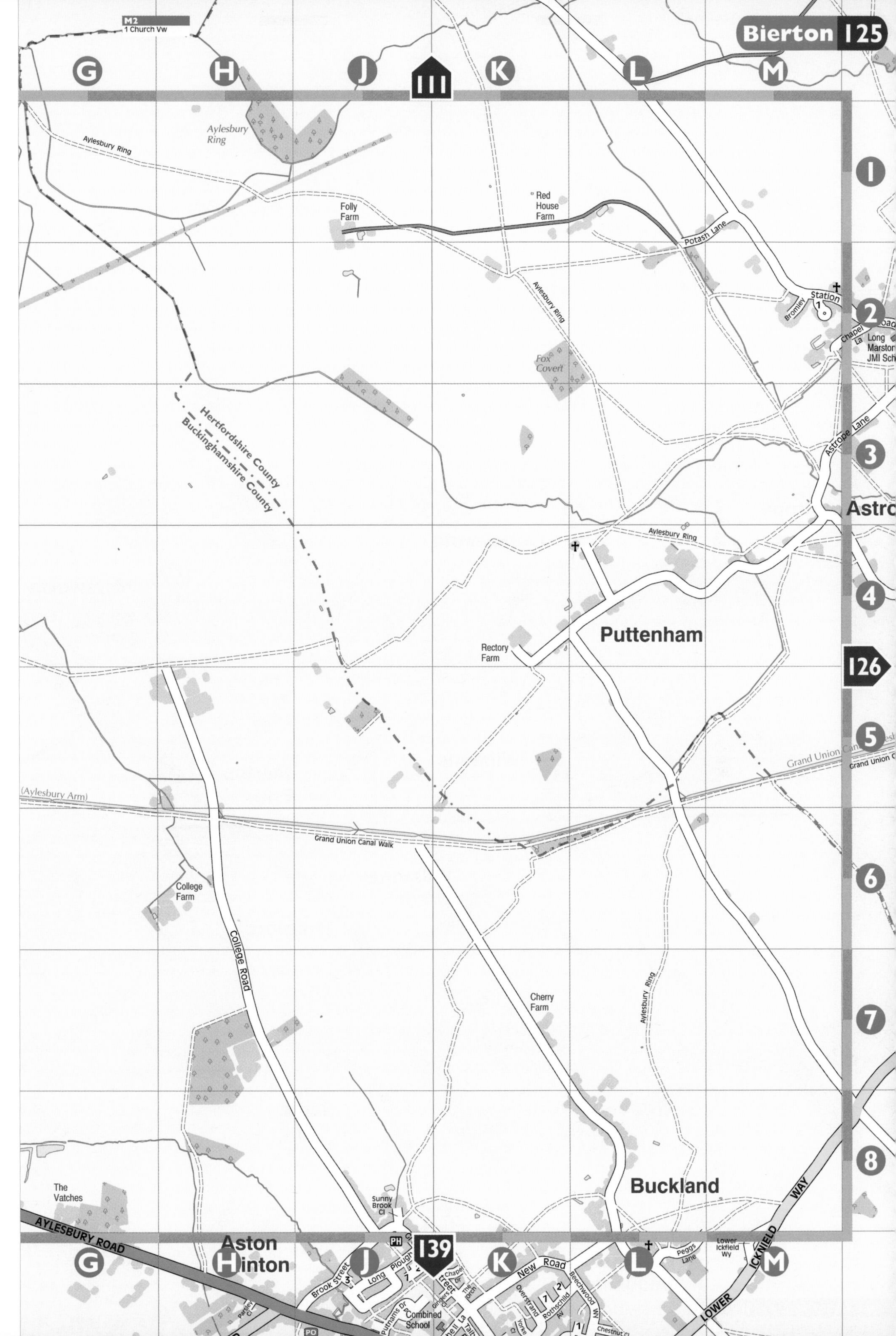
M2
1 Church Vw
G
H
J
111
K
L
M
Aylesbury Ring
Aylesbury Ring
Folly Farm
Red House Farm
Potash Lane
Aylesbury Ring
Station
Bromley
Chapel La
Long Marston JMI Sch
Fox Covert
Hertfordshire County
Buckinghamshire County
Astrope Lane
Astro
Aylesbury Ring
Puttenham
Rectory Farm
126
Grand Union Canal
Grand Union Ca
(Aylesbury Arm)
Grand Union Canal Walk
College Farm
College Road
Cherry Farm
Aylesbury Ring
Buckland
The Vatches
Sunny Brook Cl
AYLESBURY ROAD
Aston Hinton
PH
139
Brook Street
Long
Plough
Chapel Dr
New Road
Peggs Lane
Lower Ickfield Wy
LOWER ICKNIELD WAY
Puttnams Dr
Combined School
Overstrand
Rothschild Av
Beechwood Wy
Yorke
Chestnut Cl
PO
1
2
3
4
5
6
7
8

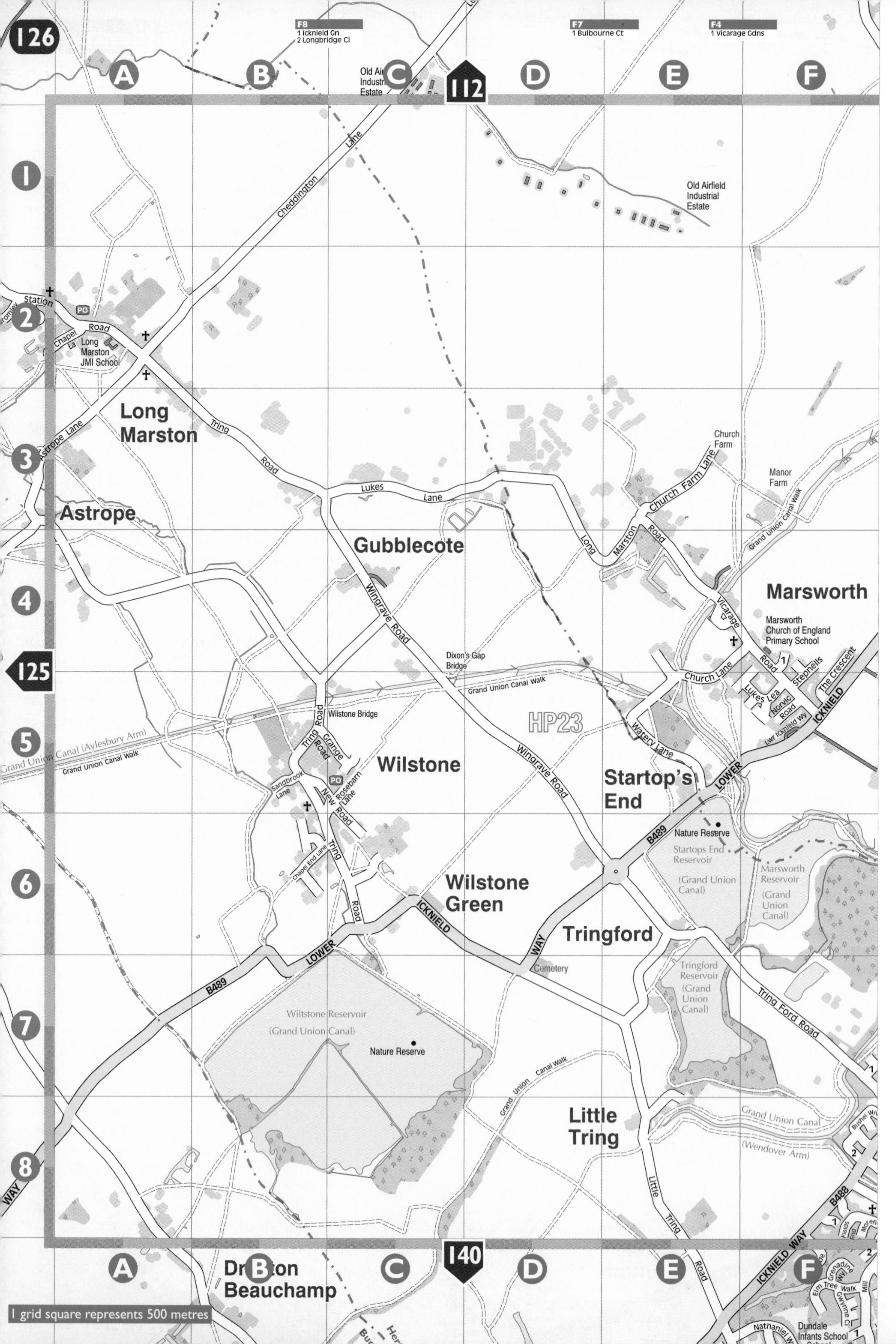
126
F8
1 Icknield Gn
2 Longbridge Cl
F7
1 Bulbourne Ct
F4
1 Vicarage Gdns
112
Old Airfield Industrial Estate
Cheddington Lane
Long Marston
Station Road
Chapel La
Long Marston JMI School
Astrope Lane
Tring Road
Astrope
Lukes Lane
Gubblecote
Church Farm
Manor Farm
Church Farm Lane
Long Marston Road
Grand Union Canal Walk
Marsworth
Vicarage Road
Marsworth Church of England Primary School
Wingrave Road
Dixon's Gap Bridge
Church Lane
Stepnells
The Crescent
Lukes Lea
Norvic Road
Lwr Icknield Wy
ICKNIELD
125
HP23
Wilstone Bridge
Tring Road
Grange Road
Grand Union Canal (Aylesbury Arm)
Wilstone
Watery Lane
Startop's End
Sandbrook Lane
Rosebarn Lane
New Road
LOWER
B489
Nature Reserve
Startops End Reservoir
Marsworth Reservoir (Grand Union Canal)
Chapel End Lane
Wilstone Green
ICKNIELD WAY
Tringford
Cemetery
Tringford Reservoir (Grand Union Canal)
Tring Ford Road
Wiltstone Reservoir (Grand Union Canal)
Nature Reserve
Grand Union Canal Walk
Little Tring
Grand Union Canal (Wendover Arm)
Little Tring Road
B488
140
Drayton Beauchamp
Dundale Infants School
Elm Tree Walk
Grenadine Way
Gwynne Cl
Nathaniel Wk
Bushel Wharf
1 grid square represents 500 metres

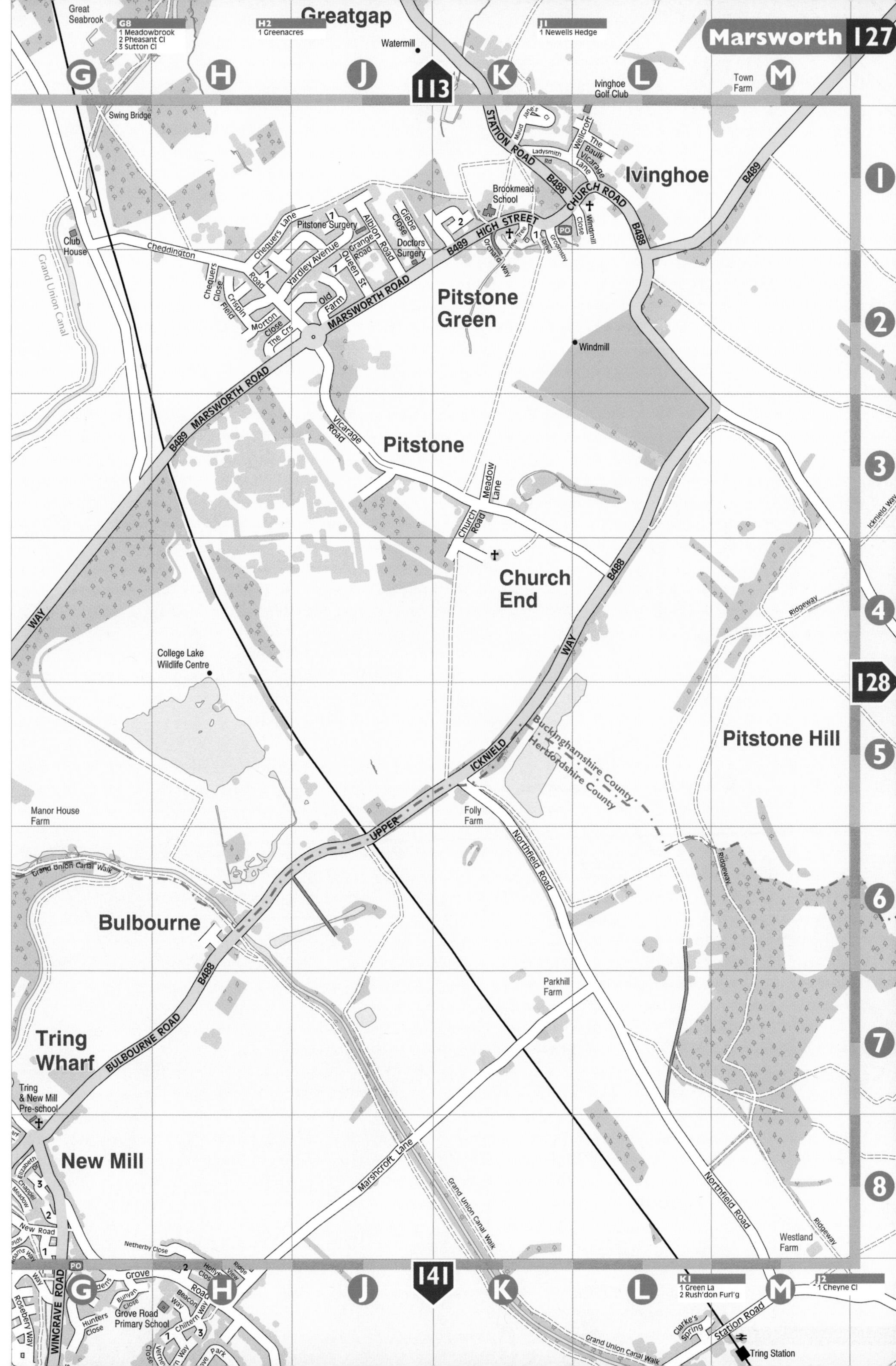
Greatgap
Great Seabrook
G8
1 Meadowbrook
2 Pheasant Cl
3 Sutton Cl
H2
1 Greenacres
J1
1 Newells Hedge
Watermill
113
Ivinghoe Golf Club
Town Farm
Swing Bridge
Station Road
Maud Janes Cl
Wellcroft
The Baulk
Vicarage Lane
Ladysmith Rd
Ivinghoe
B489
B488
Church Road
Brookmead School
Windmill Close
Pistone Surgery
Chequers Lane
Albion Road
Glebe Close
Doctors Surgery
Grange Road
Queen St
Yardley Avenue
High Street
Orchard Way
Yew Tree
Gromsby Drive
Club House
Cheddington
Grand Union Canal
Chequers Close
Crispin Field
Morton Close
The Crs
Old Farm
Marsworth Road
Pitstone Green
Windmill
Vicarage Road
Pitstone
Meadow Lane
Church Road
Church End
Icknield Way
Ridgeway
Way
College Lake Wildlife Centre
Upper Icknield Way
Buckinghamshire County
Hertfordshire County
128
Pitstone Hill
Manor House Farm
Folly Farm
Northfield Road
Grand Union Canal Walk
Bulbourne
B488
Parkhill Farm
Tring Wharf
Bulbourne Road
Tring & New Mill Pre-school
New Mill
Elizabeth
Chapel Meadow
New Road
Marshcroft Lane
Grand Union Canal Walk
Northfield Road
Ridgeway
Westland Farm
Netherby Close
Hollyfield Close
Ridge View
PO
Grove
Bunyan Close
Hunters Close
Grove Road Primary School
Beacon Way
Chiltern Way
Park
Wingrave Road
Rosebery Way
141
K1
1 Green La
2 Rush'don Furl'g
J2
1 Cheyne Cl
Clarke's Spring
Station Road
Tring Station
G H J K L M
1 2 3 4 5 6 7 8

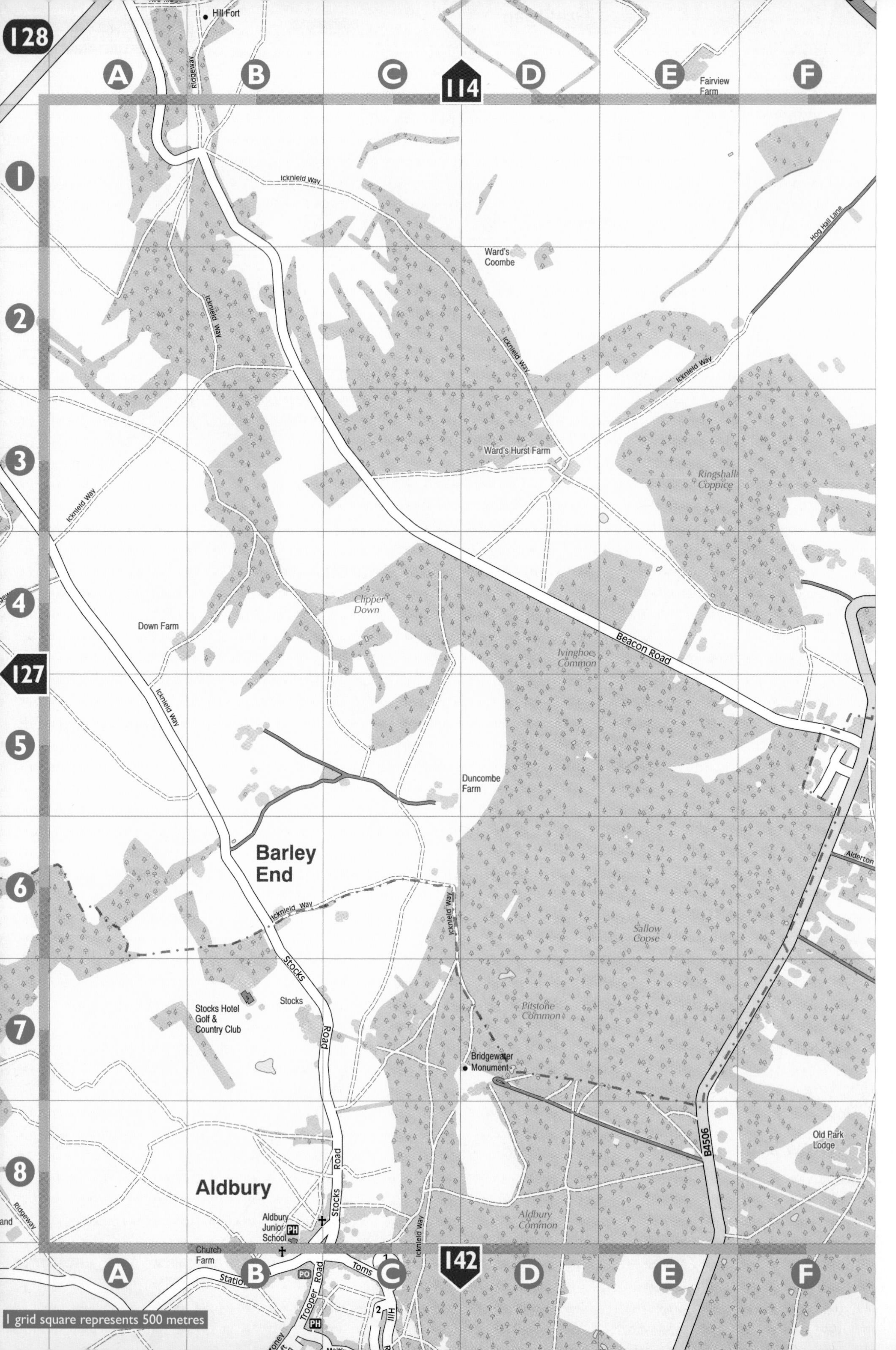
128
114
127
142
A
B
C
D
E
F
1
2
3
4
5
6
7
8
Hill Fort
Ridgeway
Fairview Farm
Icknield Way
Ward's Coombe
Hog Hall Lane
Ward's Hurst Farm
Ringshall Coppice
Clipper Down
Down Farm
Beacon Road
Ivinghoe Common
Duncombe Farm
Barley End
Alderton
Sallow Copse
Stocks Road
Stocks
Stocks Hotel Golf & Country Club
Pitstone Common
Bridgewater Monument
B4506
Old Park Lodge
Aldbury
Aldbury Common
Aldbury Junior School
PH
PO
Church Farm
Station
Trooper Road
Toms
Hill
1 grid square represents 500 metres

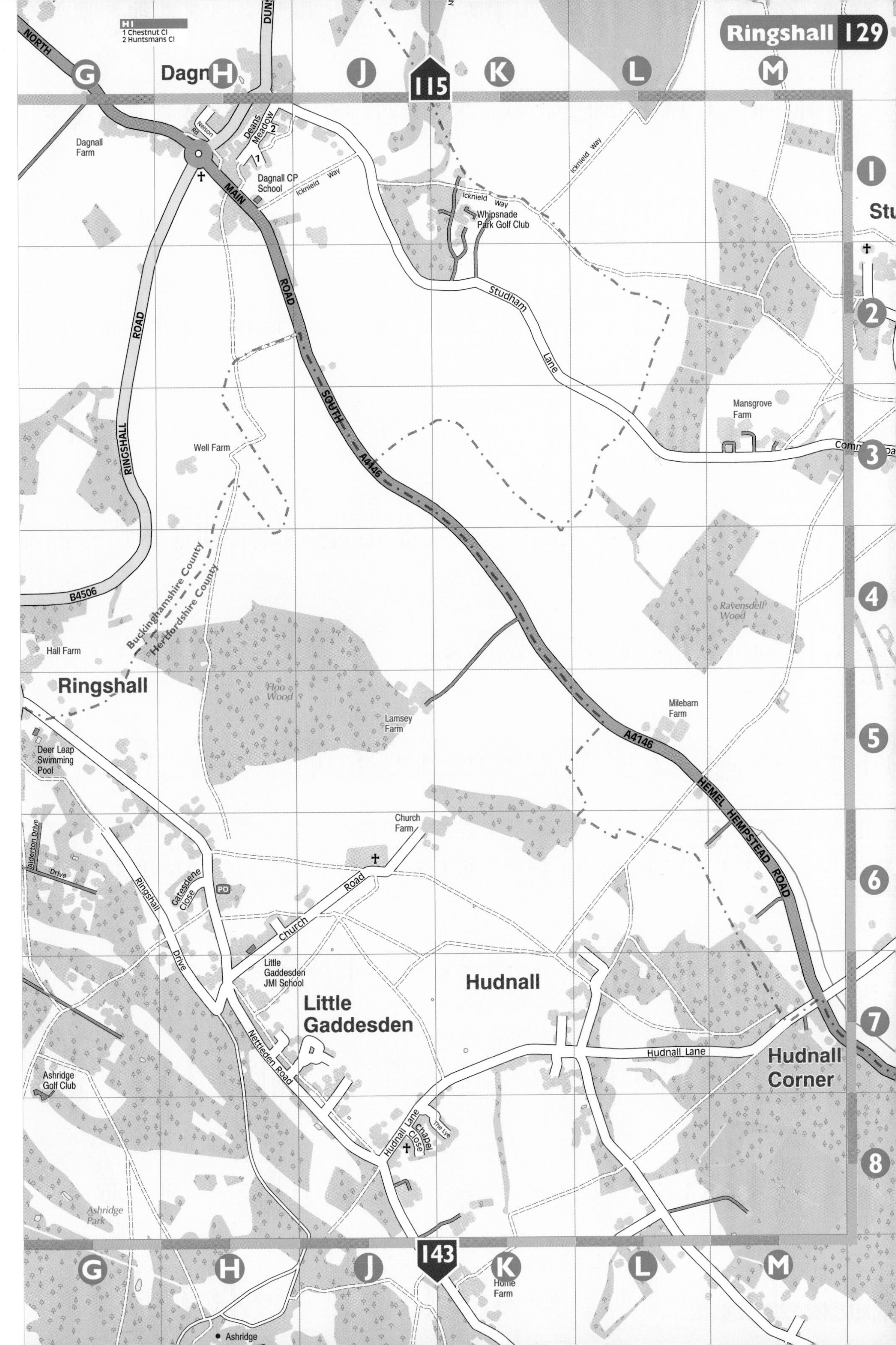
H1
1 Chestnut Cl
2 Huntsmans Cl
115
G
H
J
K
L
M
Dagn
Dagnall Farm
Nelson Rd
Deans Meadow
Dagnall CP School
Icknield Way
Whipsnade Park Golf Club
Studham Lane
MAIN ROAD SOUTH
A4146
RINGSHALL ROAD
B4506
Well Farm
Mansgrove Farm
Buckinghamshire County
Hertfordshire County
Hall Farm
Ringshall
Hoo Wood
Lamsey Farm
Ravensdell Wood
Milebarn Farm
Deer Leap Swimming Pool
HEMEL HEMPSTEAD ROAD
Church Farm
Alderton Drive
Ringshall Drive
Gatesdene Close
PO
Church Road
Little Gaddesden JMI School
Little Gaddesden
Hudnall
Hudnall Lane
Hudnall Corner
Nettleden Road
Ashridge Golf Club
Chapel Close
The Lye
Ashridge Park
143
Home Farm
Ashridge
1
2
3
4
5
6
7
8

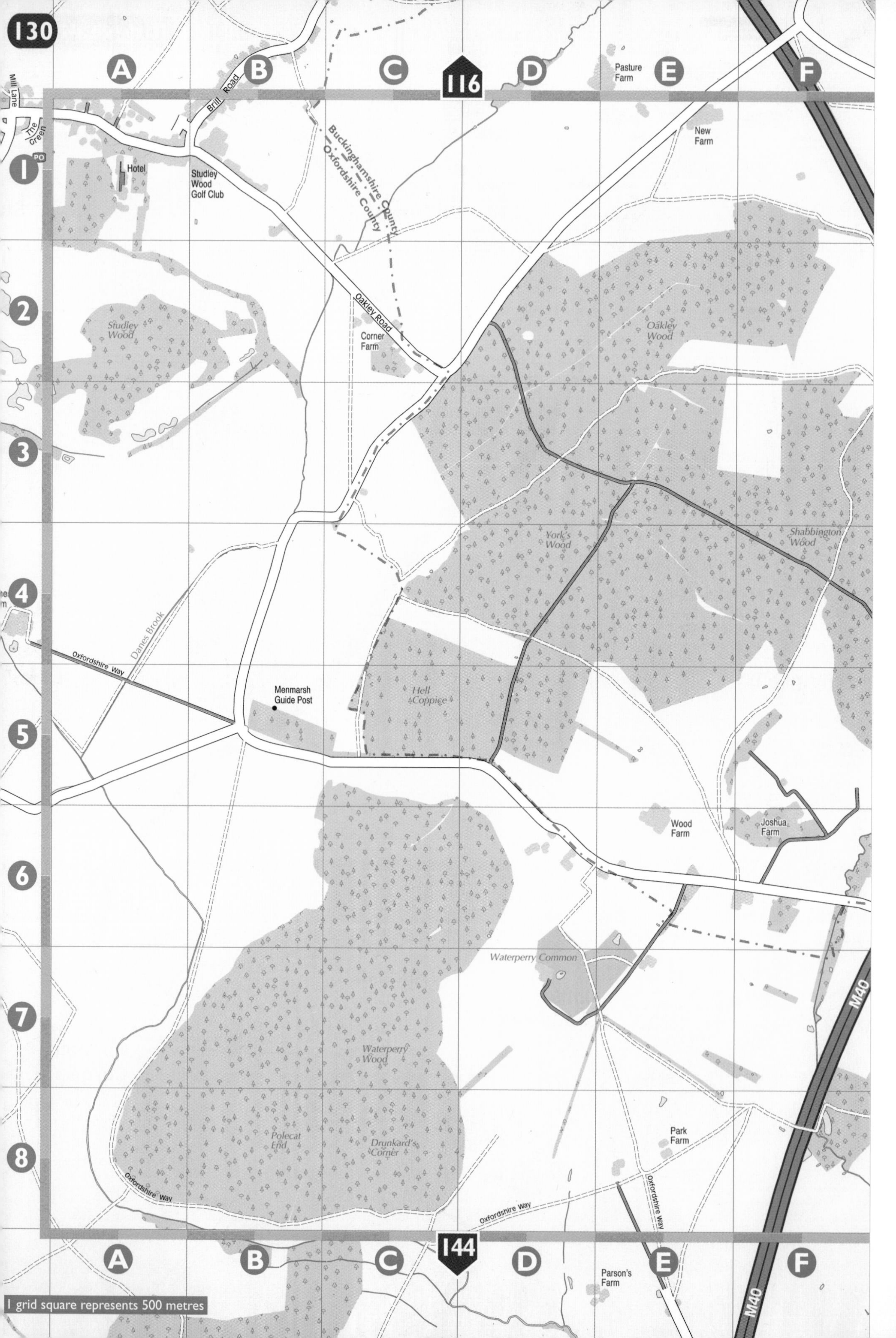
116
A
B
C
D
E
F
1
2
3
4
5
6
7
8
Mill Lane
The Green
PO
Hotel
Brill Road
Studley Wood Golf Club
Buckinghamshire County
Oxfordshire County
Pasture Farm
New Farm
Oakley Road
Corner Farm
Studley Wood
Oakley Wood
Shabbington Wood
York's Wood
Danes Brook
Oxfordshire Way
Menmarsh Guide Post
Hell Coppice
Wood Farm
Joshua Farm
Waterperry Common
M40
Waterperry Wood
Polecat End
Drunkard's Corner
Park Farm
Oxfordshire Way
Oxfordshire Way
Oxfordshire Way
144
A
B
C
D
E
F
Parson's Farm
M40
1 grid square represents 500 metres

1 Brookside
2 The Turnpike
117
132
145
Oakley
Little London
Worminghall
Slatters Farm
Hillside Farm
Leatherslade Farm
Jericho Farm
Woodground Farm
Waterslade Farm
Catsbrain Farm
Field Farm
Thomley Hall Farm
Ixhill
Bicester Road
Oxford Road
Manor Road
School Lane
Hill View
Ashfield Rise
Sun Crescent
Little London Green
Brill Road
B4011
Elmwood Close
Bradley Close
Oakley Combined School
Meadow Close
Fennemore Close
Mill Road
Orchard Close
Worminghall Road
Forge Close
College Crescent
M40
Menmarsh Road
Ickford Road
Waterperry Rd
Kings Cl

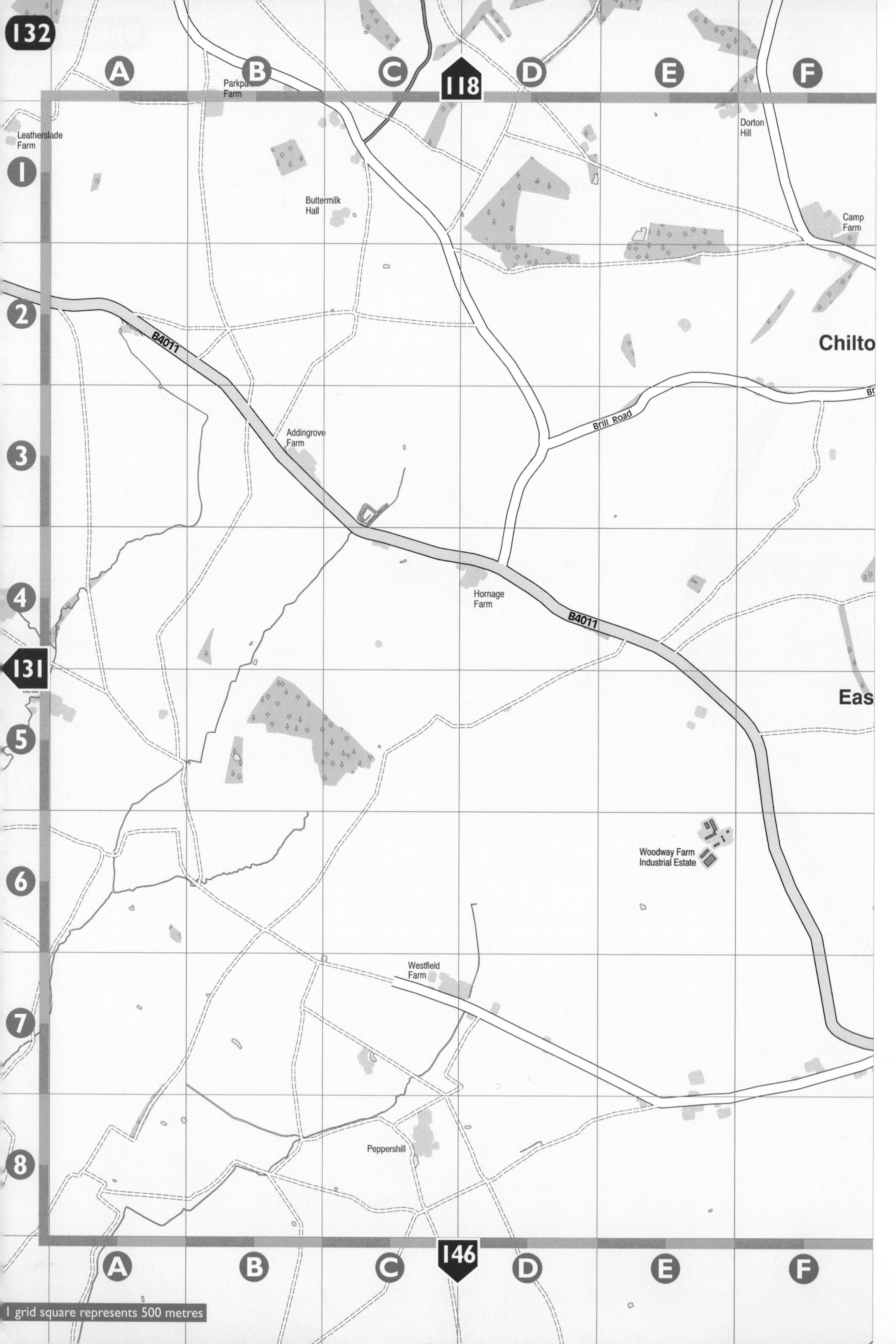

118
A
B
C
D
E
F
Parkpa
Farm
Leatherslade
Farm
Dorton
Hill
Buttermilk
Hall
Camp
Farm
1
2
B4011
Chilto
Brill Road
Addingrove
Farm
3
Hornage
Farm
4
B4011
131
Eas
5
Woodway Farm
Industrial Estate
6
Westfield
Farm
7
Peppershill
8
146
1 grid square represents 500 metres

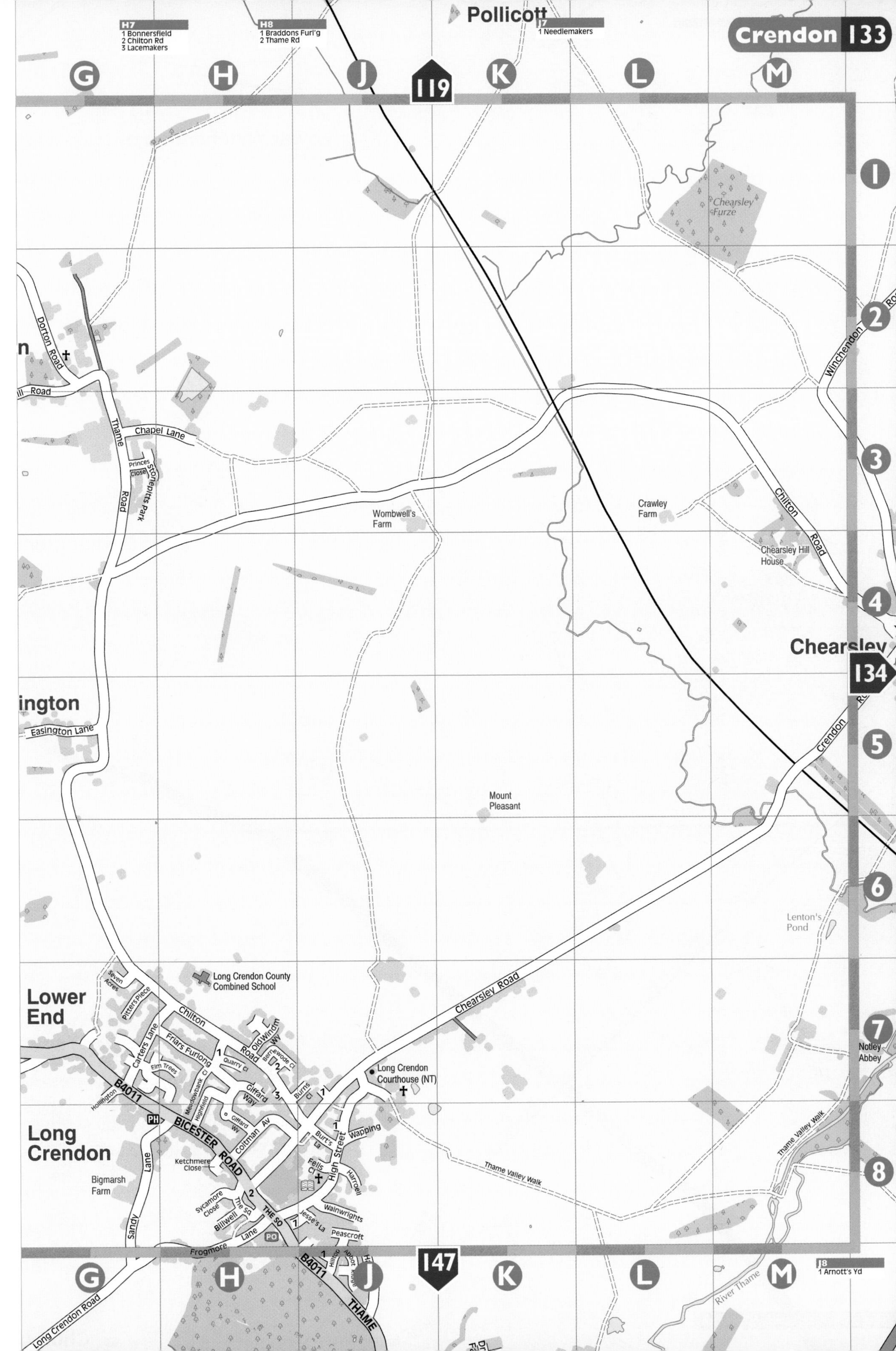
Pollicott
H7
1 Bonnersfield
2 Chilton Rd
3 Lacemakers
H8
1 Braddons Furl'g
2 Thame Rd
J7
1 Needlemakers
119
Chearsley Furze
Winchendon Road
Dorton Road
Thame Road
Chapel Lane
Princes Close
Stonepitts Park
Wombwell's Farm
Crawley Farm
Chilton Road
Chearsley Hill House
Chearsley
134
Crendon Road
Easington Lane
Mount Pleasant
Lenton's Pond
Long Crendon County Combined School
Lower End
Seven Acres
Pitters Piece
Chilton Road
Carters Lane
Friars Furlong
Old Windmill Way
Quarry Cl
Elm Trees
Meadowbank Cl
Giffard Way
Burns Cl
Chearsley Road
Long Crendon Courthouse (NT)
Notley Abbey
Hollington
B4011
BICESTER ROAD
Long Crendon
Coltman Av
Burt's La
Wapping
High Street
Thame Valley Walk
Ketchmere Close
Bigmarsh Farm
Fells Cl
Harroell
Sycamore Close
The Sq
Billwell
Wainwrights
Jesse's La
Peascroft
Sandy Lane
Frogmore Lane
THE SQ
147
J8
1 Arnott's Yd
River Thame
Long Crendon Road
THAME

F7
1 Cottland Clay
2 Mallard Cft

E8
1 Hordern Cl

E3
1 Church Cl

A4
1 Bernard's Cl
2 Church Piece
3 Evans Cl

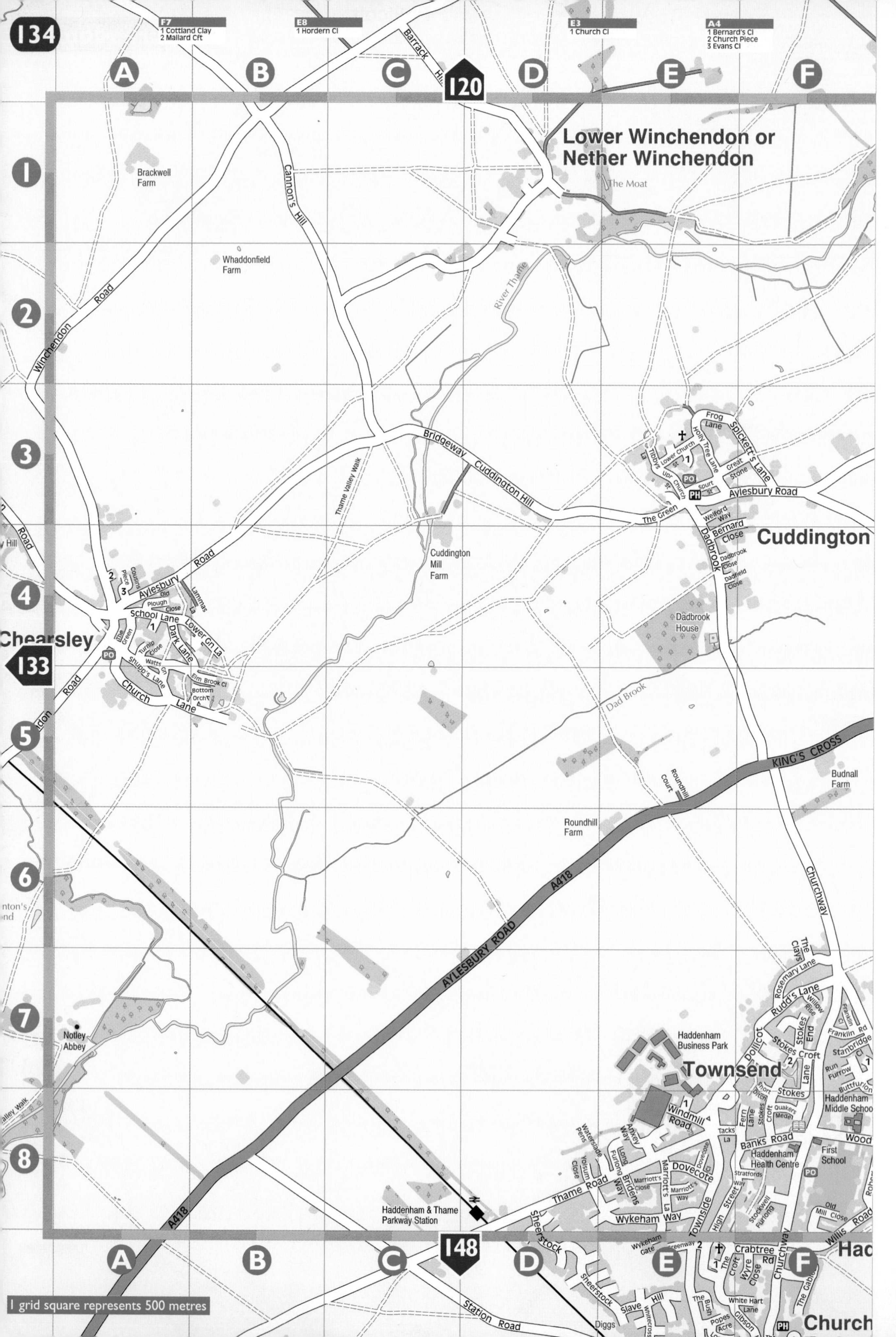

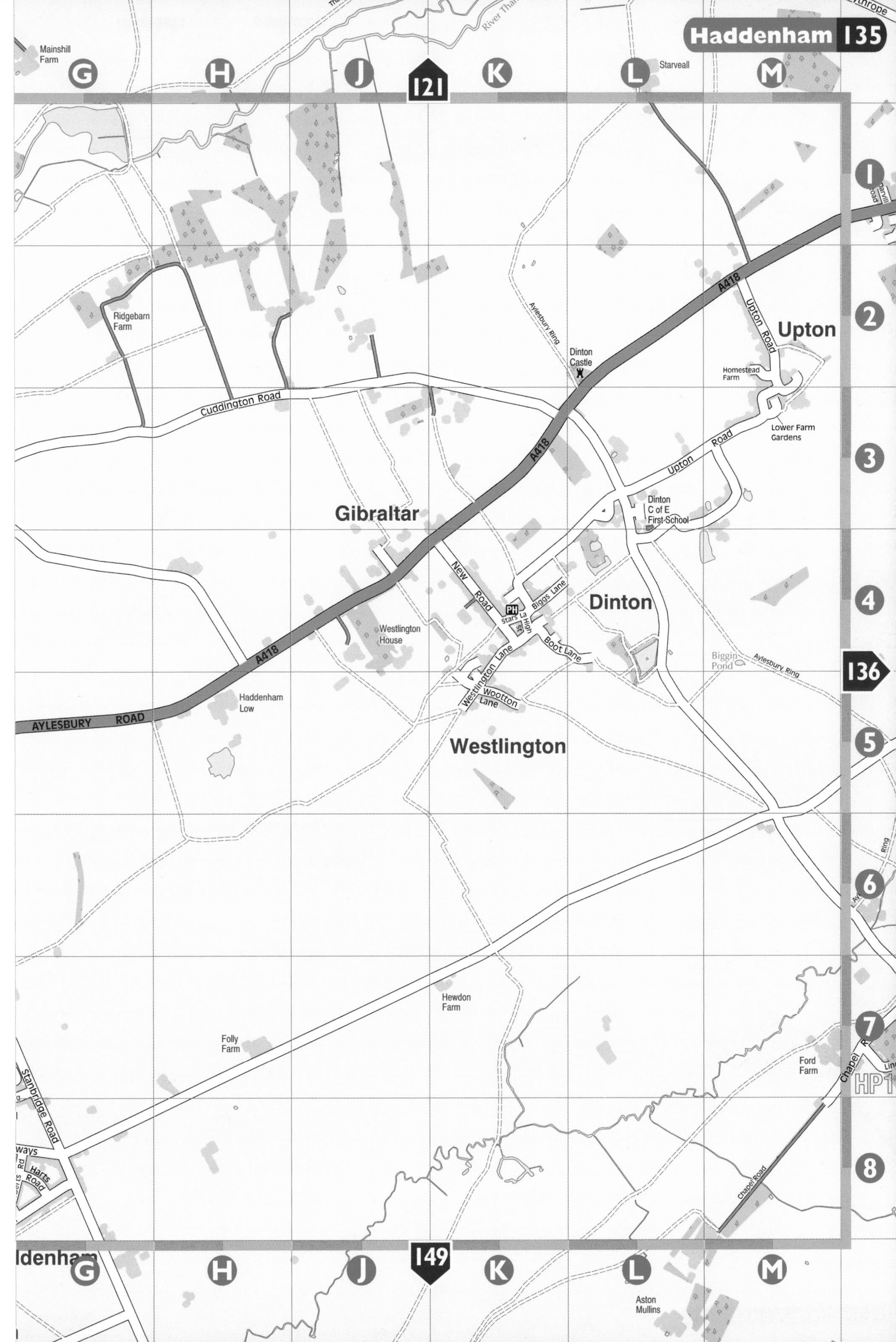

G
H
J
121
K
L
M
Mainshill Farm
Starveall
River Thame
Ridgebarn Farm
Cuddington Road
A418
Aylesbury Ring
Dinton Castle
Upton Road
Upton
Homestead Farm
Lower Farm Gardens
Gibraltar
Dinton C of E First School
New Road
Biggs Lane
PH
Stars La
High St
Dinton
Westlington House
Boot Lane
Westlington Lane
Wootton Lane
Biggin Pond
Aylesbury Ring
AYLESBURY ROAD
Haddenham Low
Westlington
Hewdon Farm
Folly Farm
Ford Farm
Chapel Road
Stanbridge Road
Harts Road
ldenham
HP17
1
2
3
4
136
5
6
7
8
149
G
H
J
K
L
M
Aston Mullins

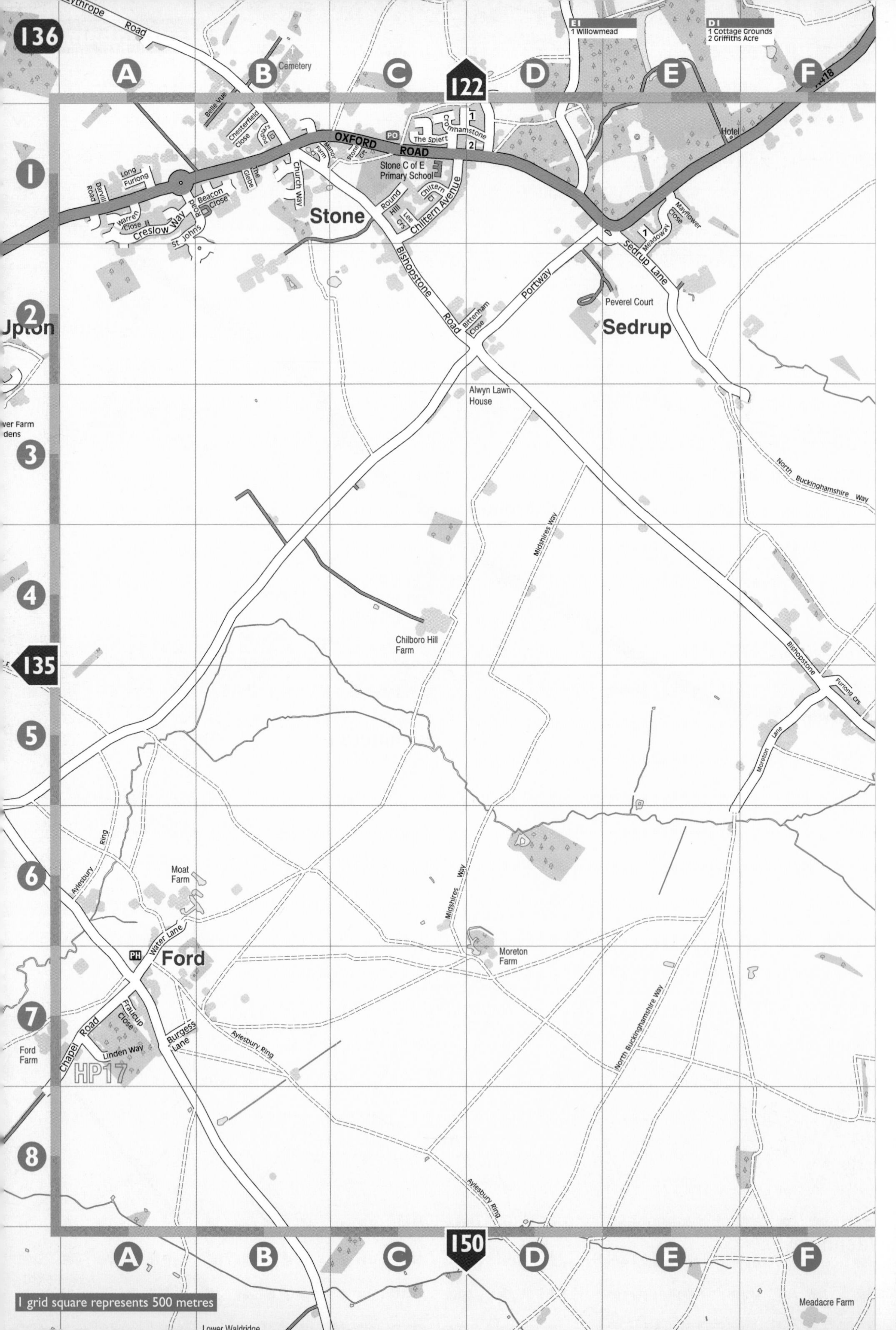

E1
1 Willowmead
D1
1 Cottage Grounds
2 Griffiths Acre
A
B
C
D
E
F
122
Cemetery
Road
Belle Vue
Chesterfield Close
Poplars
Oxford Road
PO
The Spiert
Cromhamstone
Hotel
A418
Long Furlong
Darvill Road
The Glebe
Church Way
Manor Farm
Stone Cft
Stone C of E Primary School
Warren Close
Creslow Way
Beacon Close
St Johns Road
Stone
Round Hill
Lee Crs
Chiltern Cl
Chiltern Avenue
Mayflower Close
Meadoway
Sedrup Lane
Bishopstone Road
Bittenham Close
Portway
Peverel Court
Sedrup
Upton
Alwyn Lawn House
North Buckinghamshire Way
Midshires Way
Chilboro Hill Farm
135
Bishopstone
Furlong Crs
Moreton Lane
Aylesbury Ring
Moat Farm
Water Lane
Ford
Moreton Farm
Fraucup Close
Chapel Road
Linden Way
Burgess Lane
Ford Farm
HP17
150
Meadacre Farm
Lower Waldridge
1
2
3
4
5
6
7
8
1 grid square represents 500 metres

G1
1 Crocus Dr
2 Cyclamen Pl
3 Foxglove
H2
1 Harbourne Cl
2 Kennet Cl
3 Tamar Cl
J1
1 Blythe Cl
2 Vicarage Rd
H1, J3, K2
Street names for these grid squares are listed at the back of the index
Southcourt
Walton Court
123
Ashmead County Combined School
The Mandeville Surgery
Mandeville School
Churchill Avenue
Bowler Road
MANDEVILLE ROAD
B4443
HP21
Stoke Mandeville Sports Stadium
Stoke Mandeville Hospital
Aylesbury & District Sports Club
WENDOVER ROAD
Kingsland Road
LOWER ROAD
Westfield
Hall End
Weston Way Industrial Estate
Stoke Mandeville Combined School
Moat Farm
138
Bishopstone
Standal's Farm
Marsh Lane
Whitehorn Farm
A4010
Risborough Rd
Goat Centre
North Lee Lane
Marsh
Marsh Mill Farm
Marsh Hill Farm
Aspley Manor Farm
North Lee
151
Kimblewick Road
High Holborn Farm
M4
1 Weston Wy
M2
1 Diane Wk
2 Lowbrook Cl
3 Marsham Cl
4 Thorpe Cl
M1
1 Ashford Cl
2 Coppidwell Dr
3 Glenfield Cl
4 Haven Shaw Cl
5 Lynwood Rd
6 Redland Wy
L1
1 Mellstock Rd
K1
1 Carnation Wy
2 Melbourne Cl
K3
1 Batt Furlong
2 Otway Cl
3 Rake Wy
4 Shaw Ct
5 Stoke Farm La

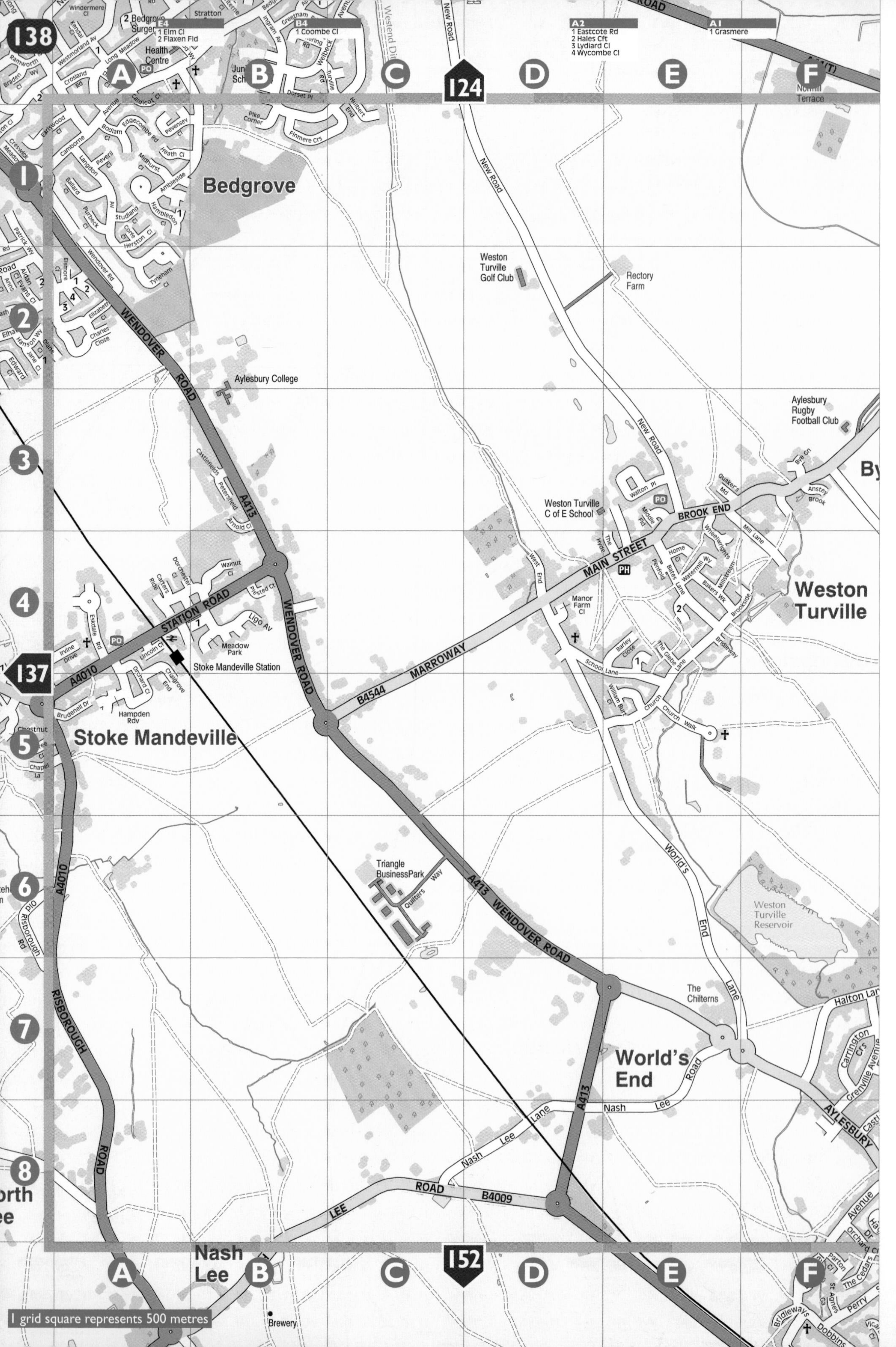

138
124
137
152
E4
1 Elm Cl
2 Flaxen Fld
B4
1 Coombe Cl
A2
1 Eastcote Rd
2 Hales Cft
3 Lydiard Cl
4 Wycombe Cl
A1
1 Grasmere
Bedgrove
Weston Turville Golf Club
Rectory Farm
Aylesbury College
Aylesbury Rugby Football Club
Weston Turville C of E School
Weston Turville
Stoke Mandeville
Stoke Mandeville Station
Triangle BusinessPark
Weston Turville Reservoir
The Chilterns
World's End
Nash Lee
Brewery
WENDOVER ROAD
A413
STATION ROAD
A4010
B4544
MARROWAY
MAIN STREET
BROOK END
New Road
World's End Lane
RISBOROUGH ROAD
LEE ROAD
B4009
Nash Lee Lane
Nash Lee Road
AYLESBURY
Halton Lane
1 grid square represents 500 metres

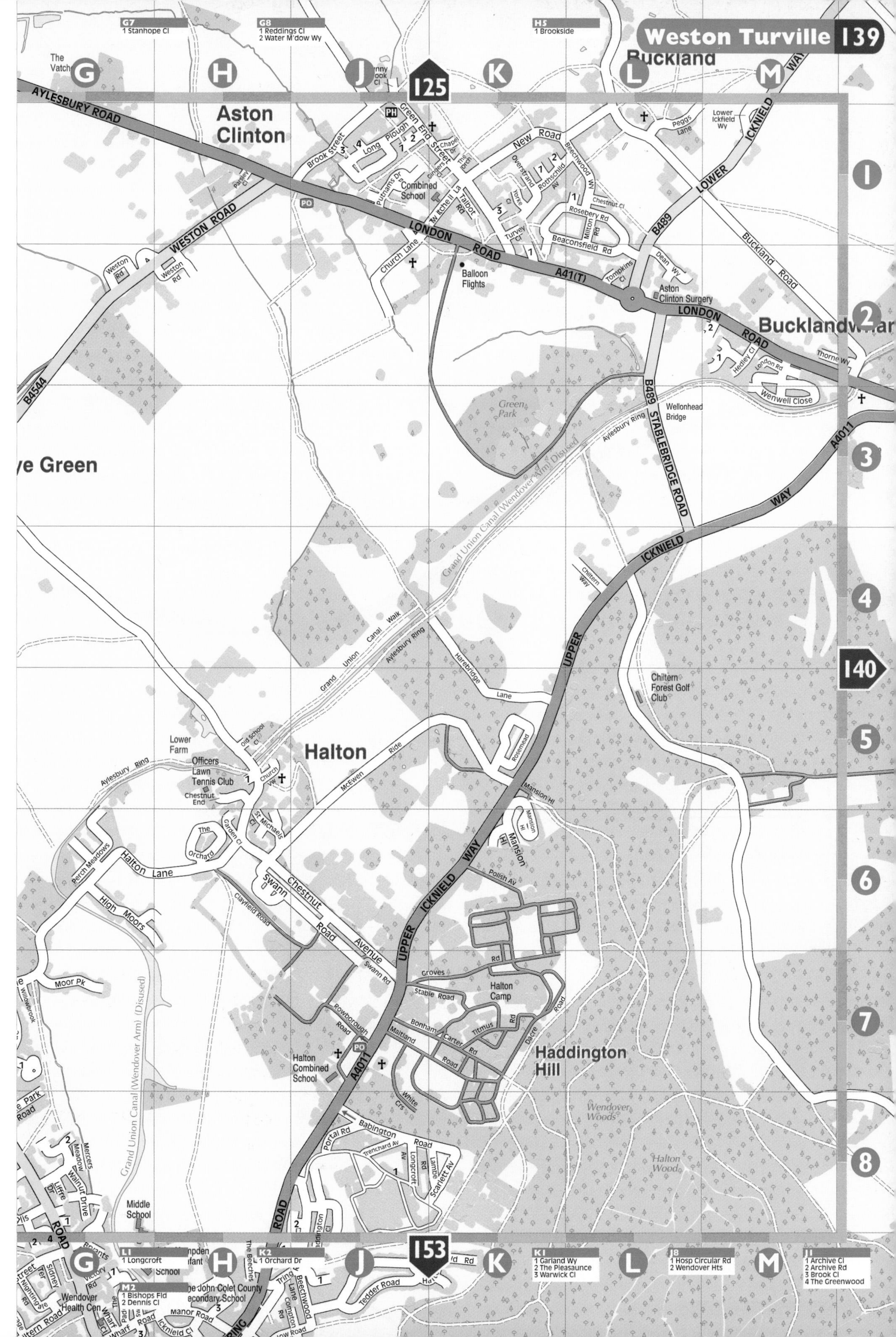
G7
1 Stanhope Cl
G8
1 Reddings Cl
2 Water M'dow Wy
H5
1 Brookside
Buckland
Aston Clinton
Halton
Haddington Hill
Bucklandwharf
AYLESBURY ROAD
WESTON ROAD
LONDON ROAD
A41(T)
LOWER ICKNIELD WAY
B489
STABLEBRIDGE ROAD
UPPER ICKNIELD WAY
A4011
Grand Union Canal (Wendover Arm) Disused
Aylesbury Ring
Combined School
Balloon Flights
Aston Clinton Surgery
Green Park
Wellonhead Bridge
Chiltern Forest Golf Club
Officers Lawn Tennis Club
Lower Farm
Halton Camp
Halton Combined School
Wendover Woods
Halton Wood
Middle School
Halton Lane
Chestnut Avenue
Swann Road
McEwen Ride
Harebridge Lane
Babington Road
Wenwell Close
New Road
Beaconsfield Rd
Rosebery Rd
125
140
153
K1
1 Garland Wy
2 The Pleasaunce
3 Warwick Cl
J8
1 Hosp Circular Rd
2 Wendover Hts
J1
1 Archive Cl
2 Archive Rd
3 Brook Cl
4 The Greenwood
L1
1 Longcroft
M2
1 Bishops Fld
2 Dennis Cl
K2
1 Orchard Dr

1 grid square represents 500 metres

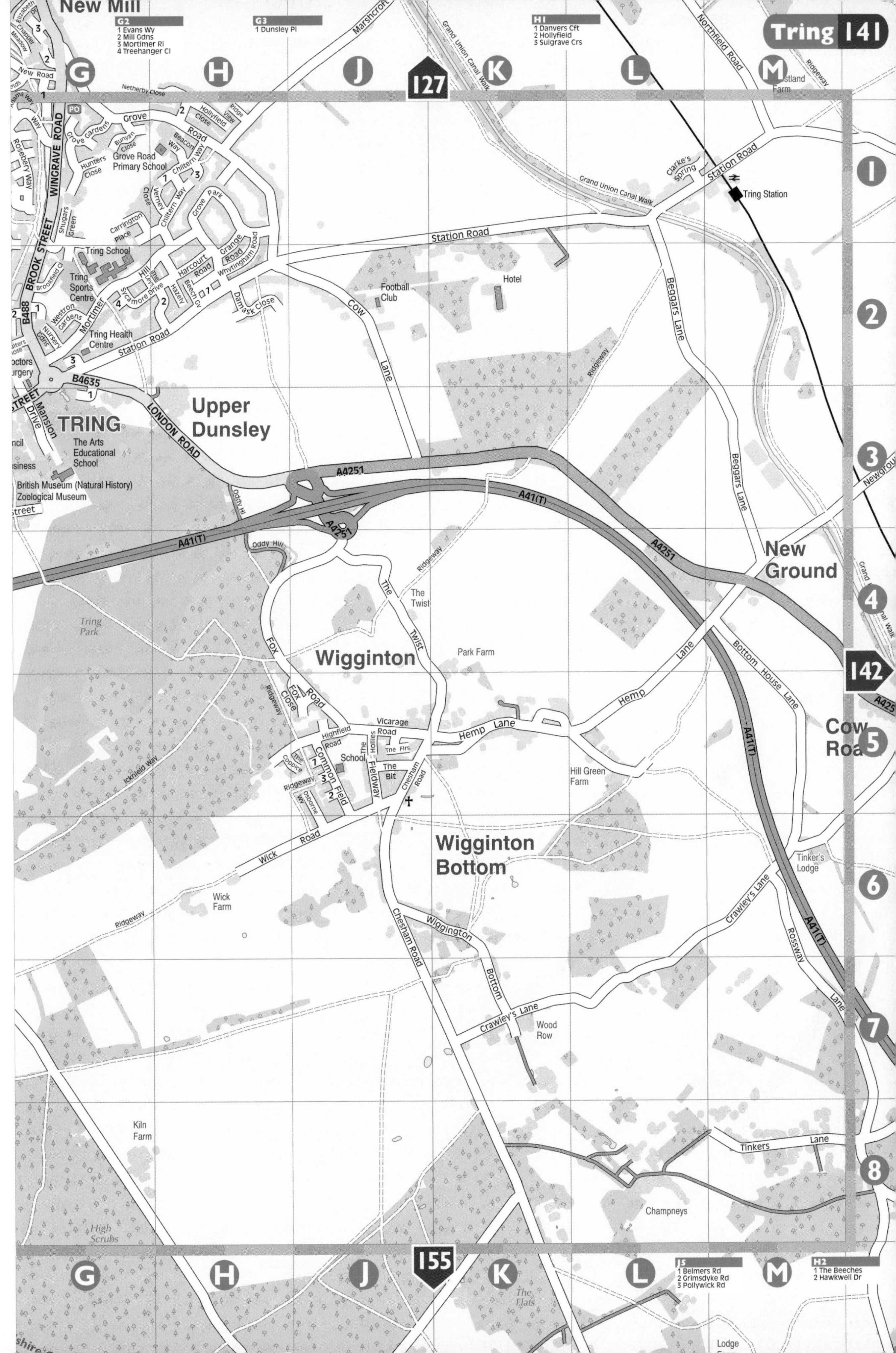
New Mill
G2
1 Evans Wy
2 Mill Gdns
3 Mortimer Rl
4 Treehanger Cl
G3
1 Dunsley Pl
H1
1 Danvers Cft
2 Hollyfield
3 Sulgrave Crs
127
142
155
J5
1 Belmers Rd
2 Grimsdyke Rd
3 Pollywick Rd
H2
1 The Beeches
2 Hawkwell Dr
TRING
Upper Dunsley
Wigginton
Wigginton Bottom
New Ground
Tring Station
Station Road
Grand Union Canal Walk
Northfield Road
Marshcroft
Netherby Close
Grove Road
Hollyfield Close
Ridge View
Beacon Way
Chiltern Way
Grove Road Primary School
Hunters Close
Bunyan Close
Grove Gardens
Wingrave Road
Rosebery Way
Brook Street
Shugars Green
Carrington Place
Grove Park
Grange Road
Whytingham Road
Tring School
Tring Sports Centre
Harcourt Road
Sycamore Drive
Hazely
Beech Gv
Damask Close
Westron Gardens
Mortimer
Nursery Gdns
Tring Health Centre
B488
B4635
London Road
Mansion Drive
The Arts Educational School
British Museum (Natural History) Zoological Museum
Cow Lane
Football Club
Hotel
Beggars Lane
Ridgeway
A4251
A41(T)
Oddy Hill
The Twist
Tring Park
Fox Road
Fox Close
Park Farm
Hemp Lane
Bottom House Lane
Vicarage Road
Highfield Road
The Hollies
The Firs
The Bit
School
The Coppice
Common Field
Fieldway
Chesham Road
Osborne Wy
Icknield Way
Hill Green Farm
Wick Road
Wick Farm
Tinker's Lodge
Crawley's Lane
Rossway Lane
Wigginton Bottom
Wood Row
Kiln Farm
Tinkers Lane
Champneys
High Scrubs
The Flats
Lodge
Cow Roa
Clarke's Spring
Westland Farm

D8
1 Applecroft
2 Duncombe Rd
D7
1 Emerton Ct
C7
1 Dell Rd
2 Home Farm Rd
3 Meadowcroft
C1
1 Beechwood Dr
2 Toms Hill Cl
Aldbury
128
Church Farm
Station Road
Trooper Road
Toms Hill Road
Stoney Croft
Malting Lane
Icknield Way
B4506
Newground Road
Grand Union Canal Walk
141
Norcott Hall Farm
Northchurch Common
Hill Farm
A4251
Cow Roast
Wharf La
Tinker's Lodge
Northchurch Farm
Grand Union Canal
A41(T)
Dudswell
Boswick La
Dudswell Lane
Hamberlins Farm
TRING ROAD
Northchurch Cricket Club
River Bulbourne
NEW ROAD
Hamberlins Lane
Pea Lane
Lyme Av
Birch Rd
Ashby Road
Covert Close
High Street
Peter's Place
Park Rise
St Mary's Av
Mandelyns
Kite Field
Cemetery
First School
HIGH STREET
Seymour Road
Alma Road
Northchurch
Shootersway
Westfield
Loxley Road
Valley Road
The Mead
North Bridge Road
Billet Lane
Bridle Way
Long View
Haynes Mead
Field
Spring Way
156
E7
1 Bridgewater Hl
2 Connaught Gdns
3 Dorrien's Cft
E8
1 Bulbourne Cl
2 Midcot Wy
3 Peacocks Cl
4 Salter's Cl
5 Stoney Cl
F8
1 Beckets Sq
2 Delifield
3 Dukes Wy
4 Montgomerie Cl
5 Pages Cft
Shootersway
The Larches
Health Centre
1 grid square represents 500 metres

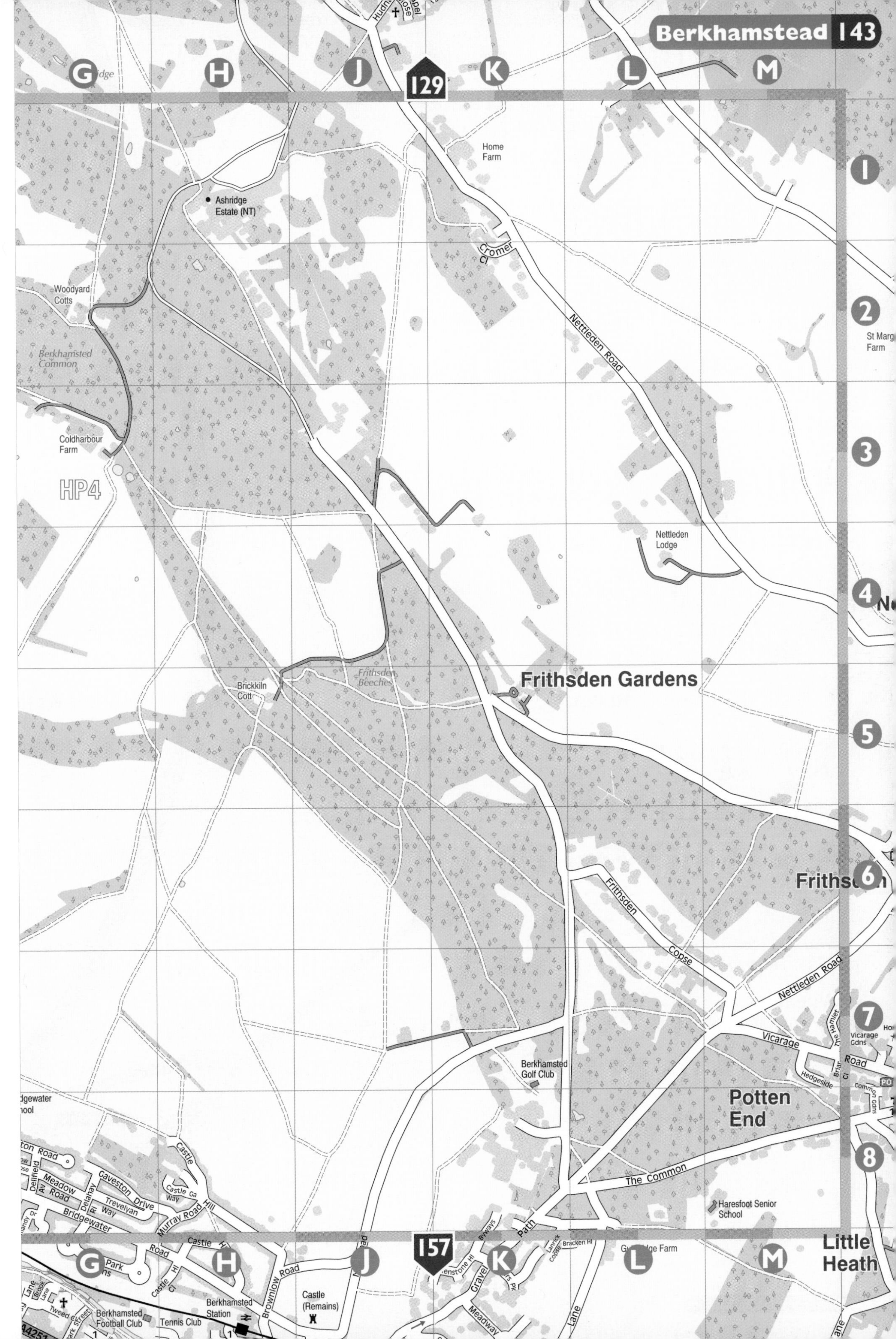
129
Home Farm
Ashridge Estate (NT)
Cromer Cl
Woodyard Cotts
Berkhamsted Common
Nettleden Road
St Marg Farm
Coldharbour Farm
HP4
Nettleden Lodge
Frithsden Gardens
Frithsden Beeches
Brickkiln Cott
Frithsden Copse
Nettleden Road
Vicarage Road
The Hamlet
Vicarage Gdns
Briar Cl
Hedgeside
Common Gdns
PO
Berkhamsted Golf Club
Potten End
The Common
Haresfoot Senior School
Castle Hill
Caveston Drive
Meadow Road
Delahay Rise
Trevelyan Way
Bridgewater Road
Castle Gate Way
Murray Road
Brownlow Road
Castle (Remains)
Berkhamsted Station
Berkhamsted Football Club
Tennis Club
Tweed
Park Street
Brook Lane
Meadway
Gravel Path
Byways
Bracken Hl
Little Heath
157
A4251
Lane

B6
1 Biscoe Ct
2 Sunnyside
3 Tyndale Pl
A6
1 Hathaways
2 Morland Cl
3 Mulberry Dr
4 St Mary's Cl
Polecat End
Drunkard's Corner
Park Farm
Oxfordshire Way
130
A
B
C
D
E
F
1
2
3
4
5
6
7
8
Parson's Farm
M40
Holton Wood
OX33
Warren Farm
Old Park Farm
Townsend Farm
Holton Brook
Wheatley Rugby Club
Wheatley Park School
The Park Sports Centre
Holton
Wate
College Close
Oxford Brookes University
Park Hl
A40(T)
London Rd
Holloway Road
Morland
Ho Surg
The Glebe
Wheatley Business Centre
Holton Mill
Church
Road
Old
London Road
Street
Wren
Close
Farm Cl
Crown Road
Arson Cl
Ambrose Ri
Leyshon Rd
Cullum Rd
Miller Rd
The Av
Station Rd
Farm Rd
Wheatley Parish Council
Beech
Road
Kelham Hall Dr
Orchard Cl
Jackies La
Elm Cl
Hillary Wy
Roman
Elton Crs
Road
Wheatley
Hill
Ladder
Wheatley Bridge
Oxford Service Area
Coombe House
Sworford Lane
Coombe Wood
River Thame
1 grid square represents 500 metres

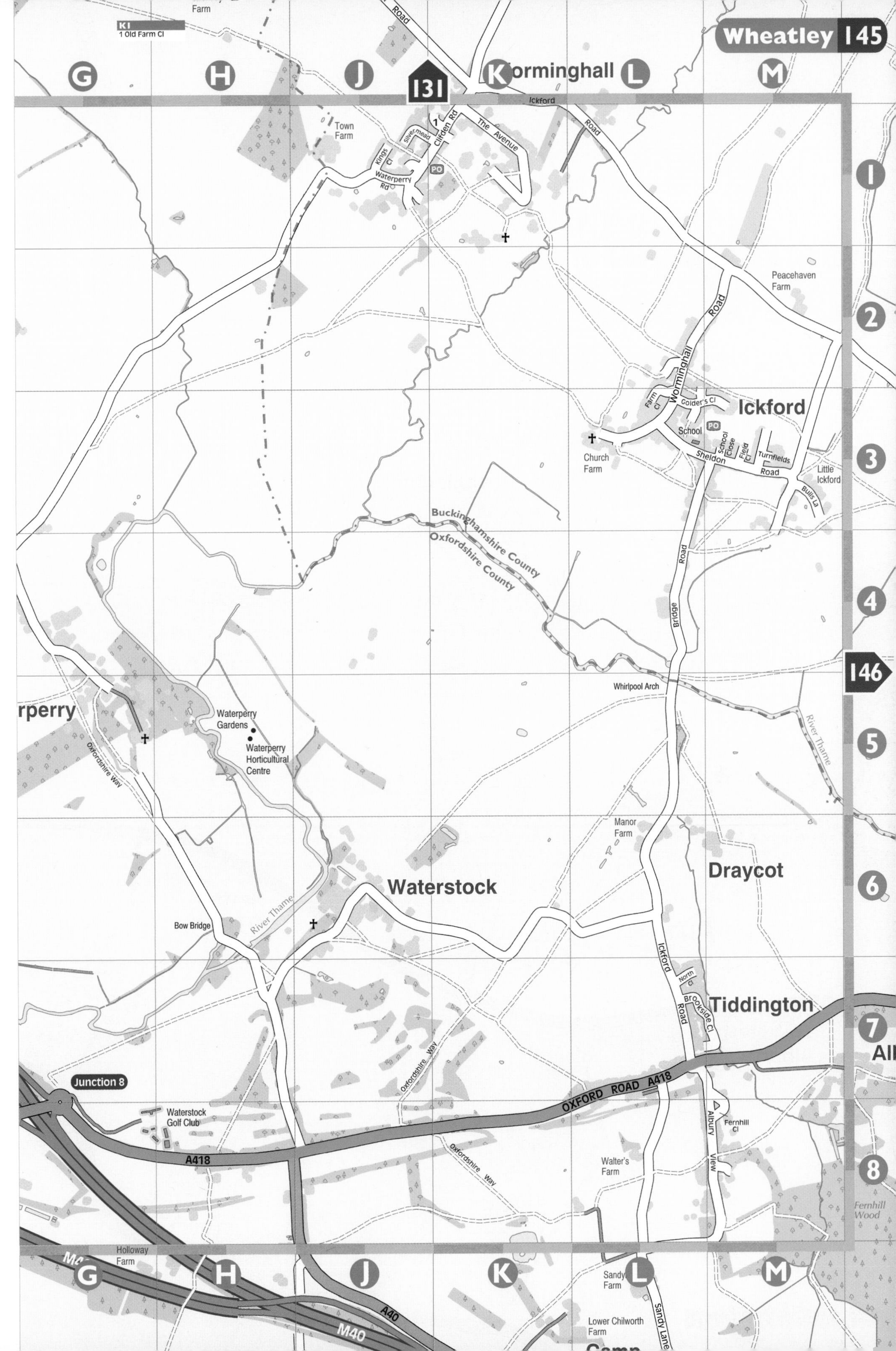
K1
1 Old Farm Cl
Farm
Worminghall
131
Ickford
Road
Town Farm
Silvermead
Clifden Rd
The Avenue
Kings Cl
Waterperry Rd
PO
Peacehaven Farm
Worminghall Road
Farm Cl
Golder's Cl
Ickford
School
PO
Church Farm
School Close
Field Cl
Turnfields
Sheldon Road
Little Ickford
Bulls La
Buckinghamshire County
Oxfordshire County
Bridge Road
146
Whirlpool Arch
River Thame
rperry
Waterperry Gardens
Waterperry Horticultural Centre
Oxfordshire Way
Manor Farm
Draycot
Waterstock
Bow Bridge
River Thame
Ickford Road
North Cl
Brookside Cl
Tiddington
Oxfordshire Way
Junction 8
OXFORD ROAD A418
Waterstock Golf Club
A418
Albury View
Fernhill Cl
Oxfordshire Way
Walter's Farm
Fernhill Wood
Holloway Farm
M40
Sandy Farm
Sandy Lane
A40
M40
Lower Chilworth Farm
G H J K L M
1 2 3 4 5 6 7 8

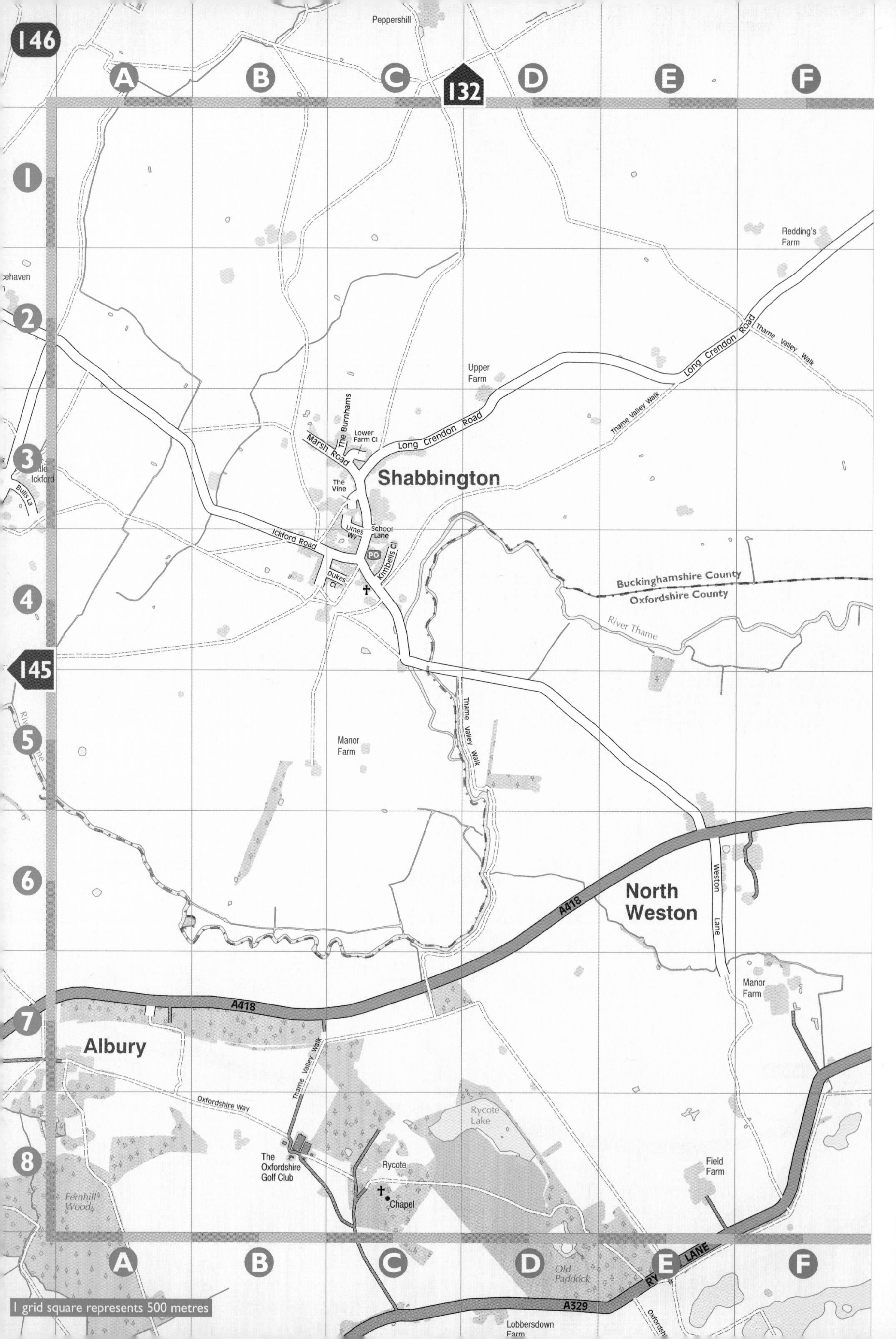

Peppershill
A
B
C
132
D
E
F
1
2
3
4
5
6
7
8
Redding's Farm
Upper Farm
Long Crendon Road
Thame Valley Walk
The Burnhams
Lower Farm Cl
Marsh Road
Shabbington
The Vine
Ickford Road
Limes Wy
School Lane
PO
Kimbells Cl
Dukes Cl
Buckinghamshire County
Oxfordshire County
River Thame
Little Ickford
Bulls La
145
Manor Farm
North Weston
A418
Weston Lane
Manor Farm
Albury
Oxfordshire Way
Rycote Lake
The Oxfordshire Golf Club
Rycote
Chapel
Field Farm
Fernhill Wood
Old Paddock
RYCOTE LANE
A329
Lobbersdown Farm
1 grid square represents 500 metres

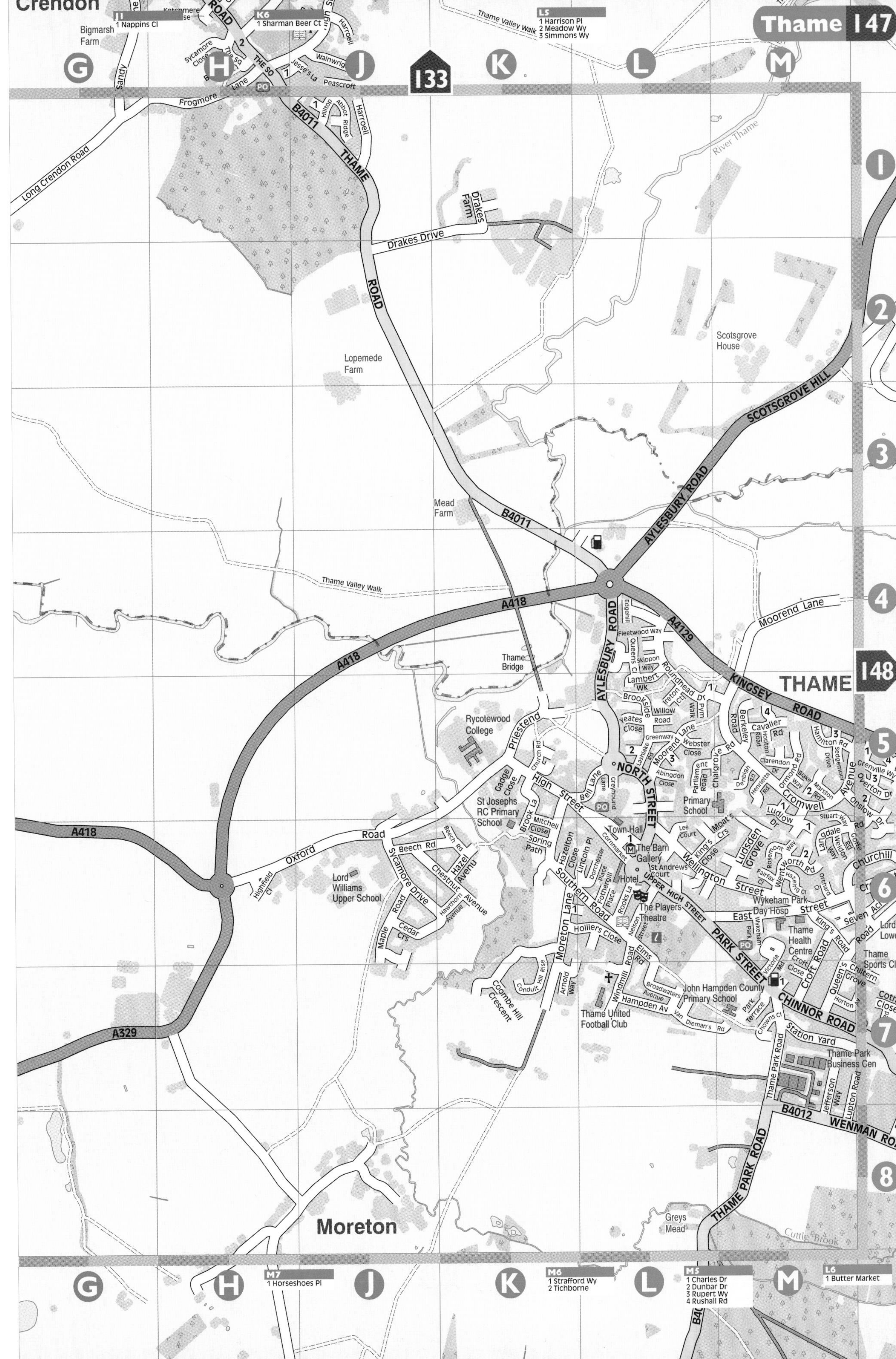

Crendon
J1
1 Nappins Cl
K6
1 Sharman Beer Ct
L5
1 Harrison Pl
2 Meadow Wy
3 Simmons Wy
Bigmarsh Farm
Sycamore Close
The Sq
THE SQ
Jesse's La
Wainwright
Peascroft
Harroell
Frogmore
Lane
Sandy
ROAD
133
Thame Valley Walk
Hilltop
Abbot Ridge
B4011
THAME
Long Crendon Road
River Thame
Drakes Farm
Drakes Drive
ROAD
Lopemede Farm
Scotsgrove House
SCOTSGROVE HILL
Mead Farm
B4011
AYLESBURY ROAD
Thame Valley Walk
A418
A418
A4129
Moorend Lane
Thame Bridge
Fleetwood Way
Queens Cl
Skippon Way
Lambert Wk
Roundhead Dr
Ireton Ct
Pym Walk
KINGSEY ROAD
THAME
148
Brookside
Willow Road
Yeates Close
Greenway
Moorend Lane
Webster Close
Rycotewood College
Priestend
Church Rd
AYLESBURY ROAD
Berkeley Road
Cavalier Rd
Hampden Rd
Hamilton Rd
Sedgemoor Drive
Grenville Wy
Overton Dr
Clarendon Dr
Ormond Rd
Blake Way
Marston Rd
Cromwell
Avenue
Onslow Dr
Gadge Close
High Street
Bell Lane
Greyhound Lane
NORTH STREET
Abingdon Close
Parliament Road
Chalgrove Rd
Denbigh Rd
Henrietta Rd
Primary School
Ludlow Dr
Stuart Way
Langdale
Weldon Rd
Coffe
St Josephs RC Primary School
Brook La
Mitchell Close
Spring Path
Town Hall
The Barn Gallery
Lee Court
Moat's Crs
King's Close
Wellington
Ludsden Grove
Rosemont
Wentworth Rd
Orchard Cl
Churchill
A418
Oxford
Road
Beech Rd
Hazel Avenue
Chestnut Avenue
Sycamore Drive
Highfield Cl
Lord Williams Upper School
Hazelton Close
Lincoln Pl
Dorchester Place
Fothergill Place
Rooks La
St Andrews Court
Hotel
UPPER HIGH STREET
Street
Wykeham Park Day Hosp
East Street
Seven Acres
Road
Lord Williams Lower School
Maple Road
Cedar Crs
Hawthorn Avenue
Moreton Lane
Southern Road
The Players Theatre
Nelson Street
Holliers Close
Elms Rd
PARK STREET
Park
Wykeham
Thame Health Centre
Croft Close
Croft Road
King's Road
Queen's Grove
Chiltern Grove
Thame Sports Club
Horton
Cotmore Close
Conduit Hill Rise
Arnold Way
Windmill Road
Broadwaters Avenue
Hampden Av
John Hampden County Primary School
Victoria Mead
Park Terrace
Van Dieman's Rd
Chowns Cl
CHINNOR ROAD
Coombe Hill Crescent
Thame United Football Club
Station Yard
Thame Park Business Cen
A329
Thame Park Road
Jefferson Way
Lupton Road
B4012
WENMAN ROAD
THAME PARK ROAD
Moreton
Greys Mead
Cuttle Brook
M7
1 Horseshoes Pl
M6
1 Strafford Wy
2 Tichborne
M5
1 Charles Dr
2 Dunbar Dr
3 Rupert Wy
4 Rushall Rd
L6
1 Butter Market
G
H
J
K
L
M
1
2
3
4
5
6
7
8

148
134
147
158
A
B
C
D
E
F
1
2
3
4
5
6
7
8
E1
1 Ctyd Cft
2 South End
A7
1 Lacey Dr
A5
1 Cavandish Wk
2 Digby Cl
3 Overton Dr
4 Pennington Pl
Banks Road
First School
Thame Road
Wykeham Way
Townside
High Street
Crabtree Rd
Churchway
Old Mill Close
Willis Road
The Gables
Sheerstock
Slave Hill
Whitecross Rd
Diggs
Station Road
Popes Acre
Long Wall
Gibson La
Flint Street
The Paddocks
Church End
Aston Rd
Haddenham First School
A418
Thame Road
Grove End Farm
Mill Lane
Decoy Pond
Tythrop House
Haddenham Road
A4129
KINGSEY ROAD
Chinnor Rugby Football Club
Kingsey Road
Churchill Crescent
Seven Acres
Towersey Road
Lord Williams Lower School
Thame Sports Club
Chiltern Grove
Towersey Drive
Cotmore Close
Cotmore Gardens
Thame Park Business Cen
WENMAN ROAD
HOWLAND ROAD
B4012
B4445
Windmill Road
Windmill Close
Thame Road
Court Cl
Towersey
Church La
Manor Road
Chinnor Road
Grange Farm
Blackditch Farm
CHINNOR ROAD
Grovehill
1 grid square represents 500 metres

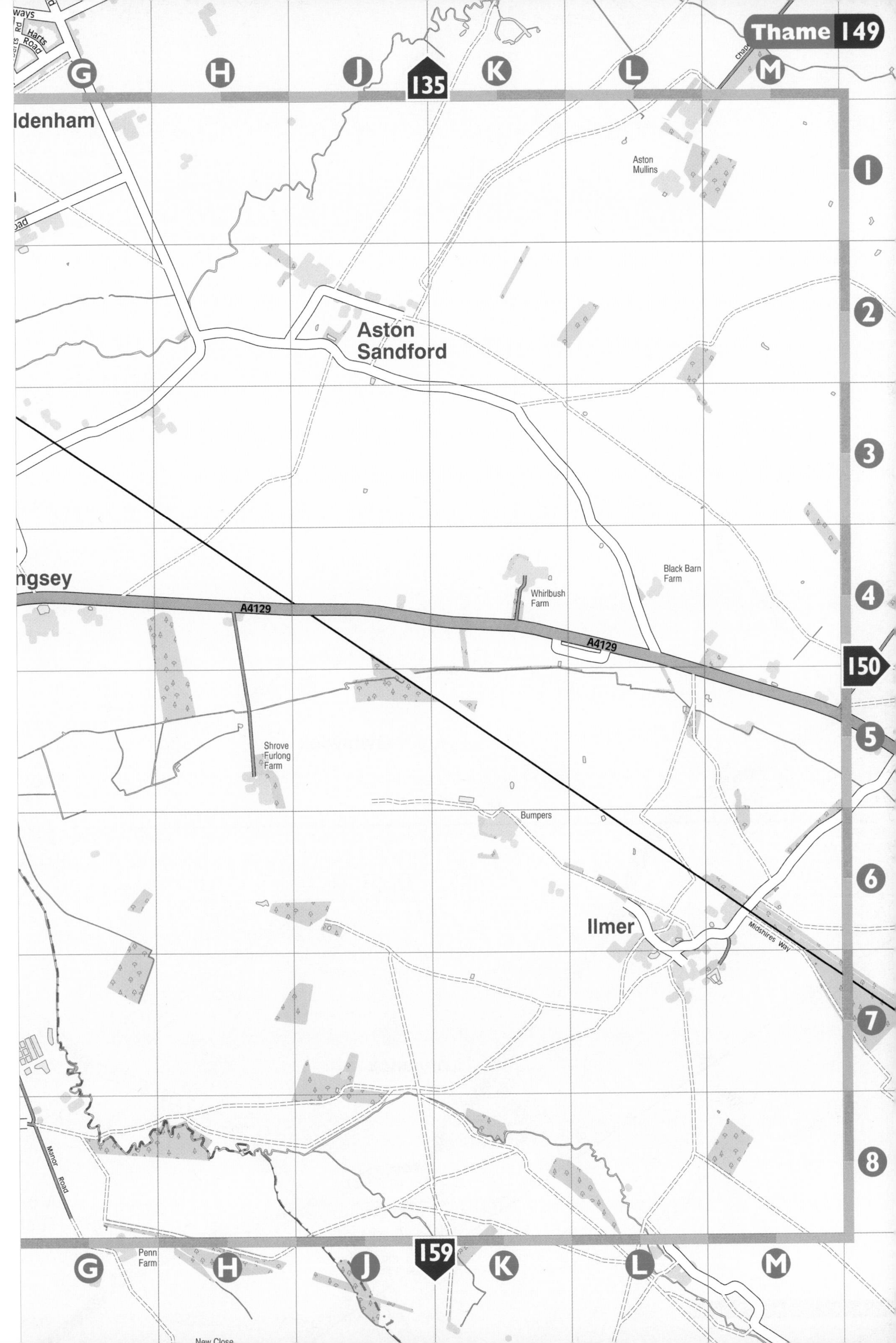
G
H
J
135
K
L
M
ldenham
Aston
Mullins
1
2
Aston
Sandford
3
Black Barn
Farm
Whirlbush
Farm
ngsey
A4129
A4129
4
150
5
Shrove
Furlong
Farm
Bumpers
6
Ilmer
Midshires Way
7
Manor Road
8
159
Penn
Farm
New Close

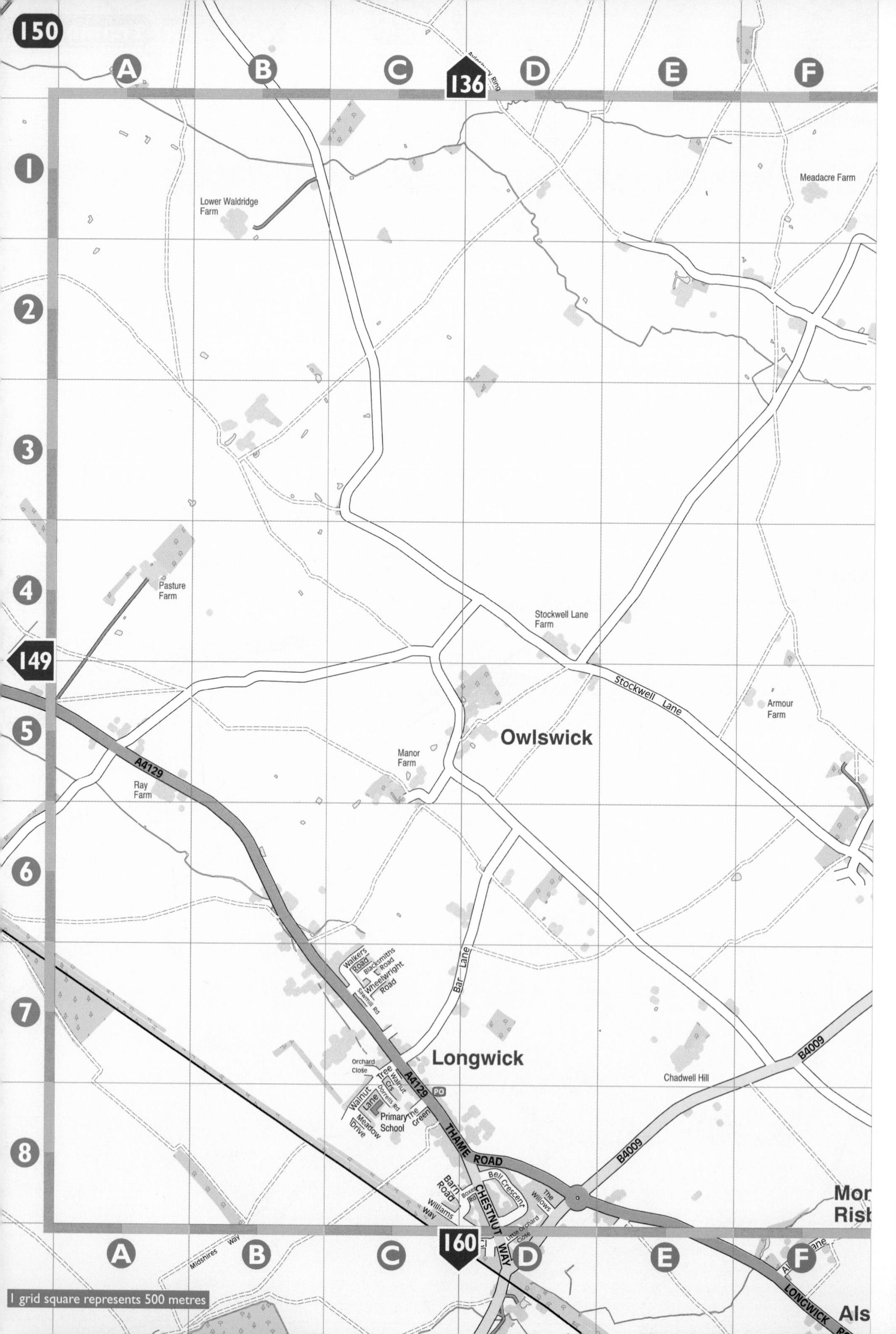
A
B
C
136
D
E
F
Aylesbury Ring
1
Lower Waldridge Farm
Meadacre Farm
2
3
4
Pasture Farm
Stockwell Lane Farm
149
Stockwell Lane
Armour Farm
5
Owlswick
Manor Farm
A4129
Ray Farm
6
Walkers Road
Blacksmiths Road
Wheelwright Road
Sawmill Rd
Bar Lane
7
Longwick
Orchard Close
Tree Crs
Walnut Crs
A4129
PO
Walnut Lane
Dorrells Rd
Primary School
The Green
Meadow Drive
THAME ROAD
B4009
Chadwell Hill
B4009
8
Barn Road
Boxer Rd
CHESTNUT WAY
Bell Crescent
The Willows
Williams Way
Little Orchard Close
Mon
Risb
A
Midshires Way
B
C
160
D
E
F
Lane
LONGWICK
Als
1 grid square represents 500 metres

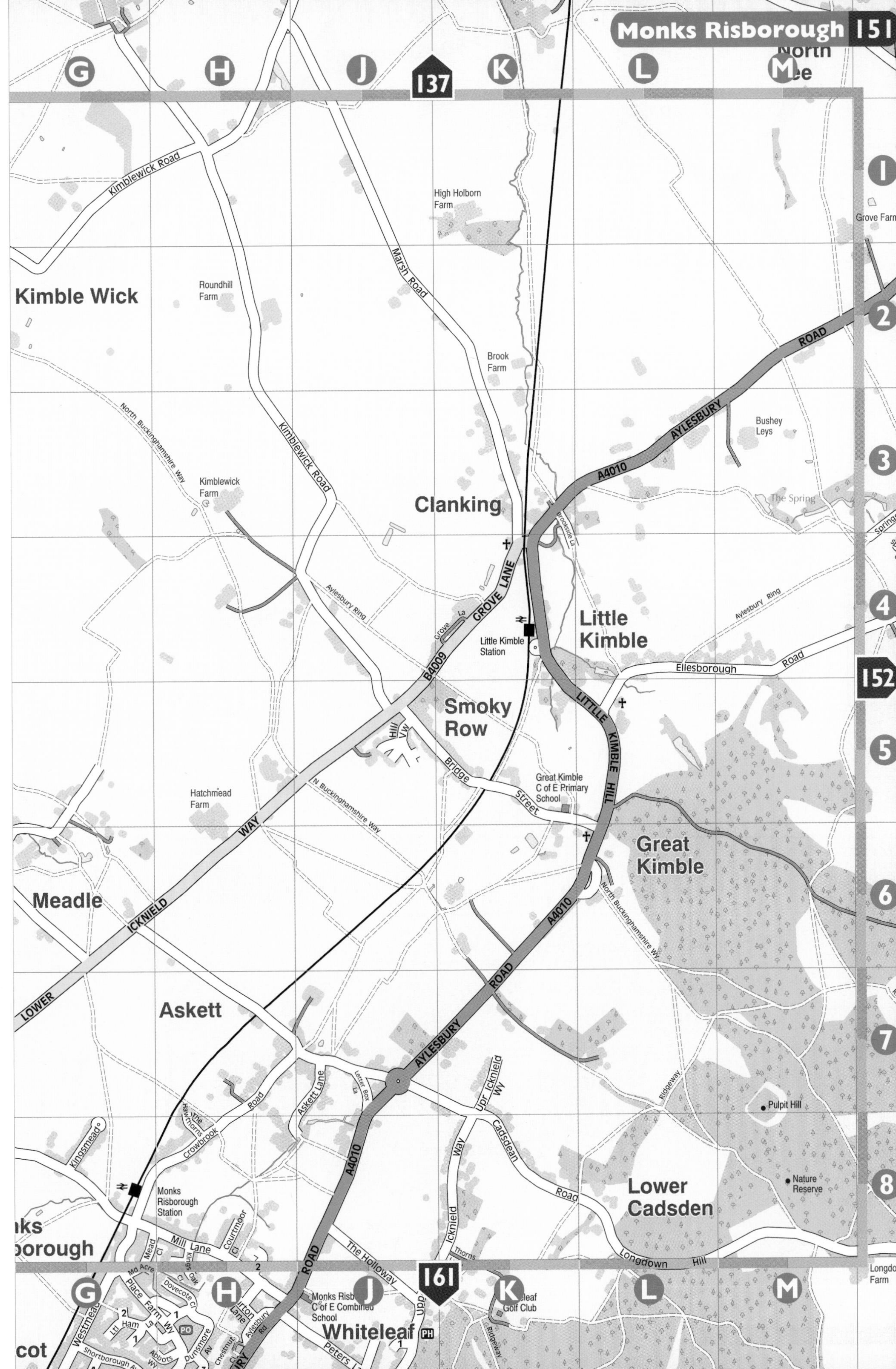
137
161
152
Kimble Wick
Kimblewick Road
Roundhill Farm
High Holborn Farm
Marsh Road
Brook Farm
Grove Farm
Bushey Leys
The Spring
North Buckinghamshire Way
Kimblewick Farm
Clanking
Aylesbury Ring
Grove La
GROVE LANE
B4009
Little Kimble Station
Little Kimble
Ellesborough Road
AYLESBURY ROAD
A4010
Brookside La
Smoky Row
Hill Vw
Bridge Street
Great Kimble C of E Primary School
LITTLE KIMBLE HILL
Hatchmead Farm
N Buckinghamshire Way
Great Kimble
Meadle
LOWER ICKNIELD WAY
Askett
Askett Lane
Letter Box La
Upr Icknield Wy
Cadsdean Road
Ridgeway
Pulpit Hill
Nature Reserve
Lower Cadsden
Longdown Hill
Longdown Farm
Kingsmead
The Hawthorns
Crowbrook Road
Monks Risborough Station
Mill Lane
Mead Cl
Kings Oak
Courtmoor Cl
Icknield Way
Thorns
The Holloway
Monks Risborough C of E Combined School
Whiteleaf
Golf Club
Place Farm Wy
Dovecote Cl
Ltl Ham La
Dunsmore Av
Abbots Wy
Chestnut
Aylesbury Rd
Peters La
Shortborough Av
Westmead

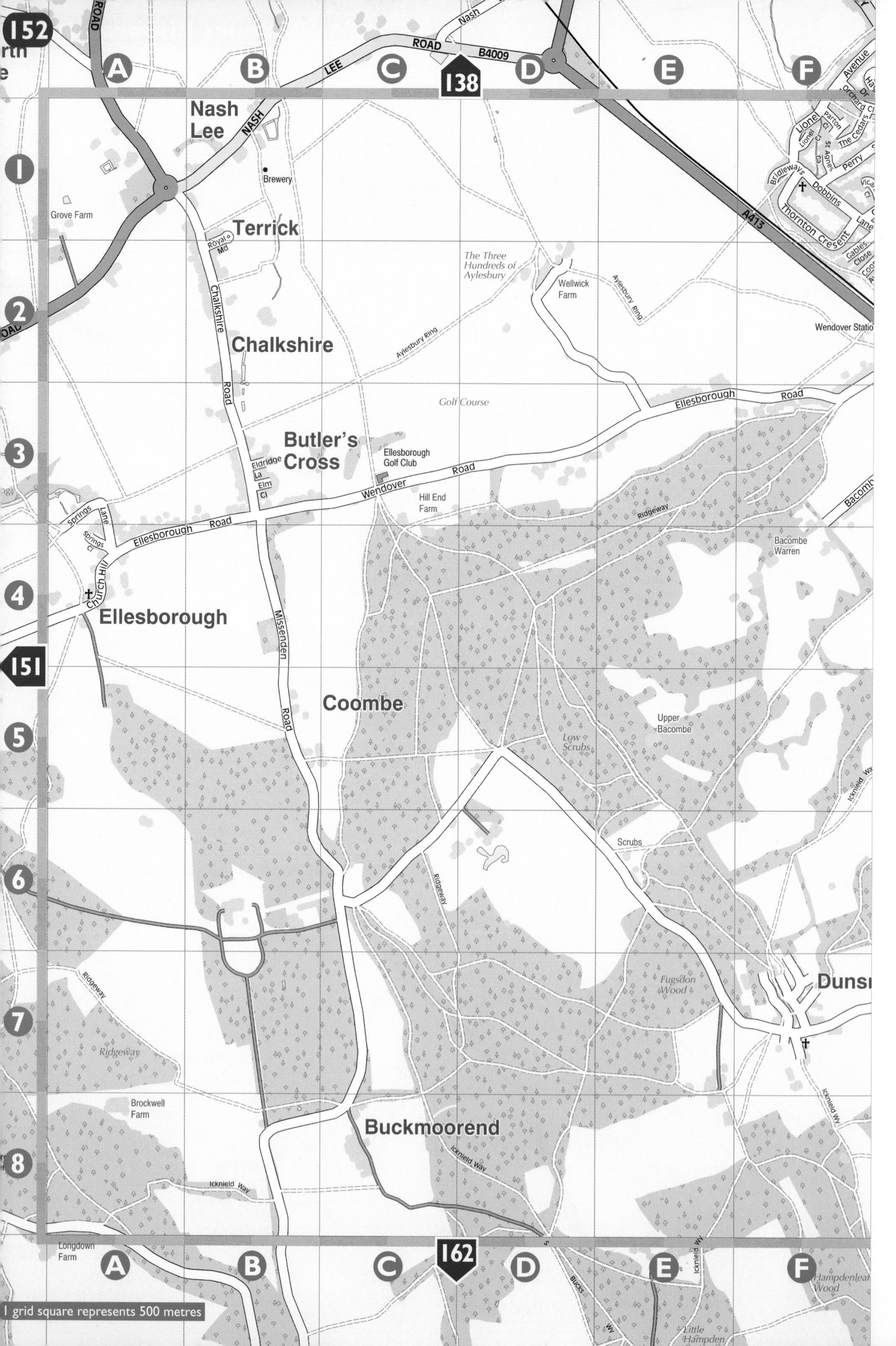

152
138
151
162
A
B
C
D
E
F
1
2
3
4
5
6
7
8
Nash Lee
NASH
LEE
ROAD
B4009
Nash
Brewery
Grove Farm
Terrick
Royal Md
Chalkshire
Chalkshire Road
The Three Hundreds of Aylesbury
Wellwick Farm
Aylesbury Ring
A413
Wendover Station
Lionel
Lionel Cl
Parton
The Cedars
Orchard Cl
Avenue
St Agnes Ga
Perry
Bridleways
Dobbins
Thornton Crescent
Gables Close
Vicarage Cl
Lane
Golf Course
Ellesborough Road
Butler's Cross
Eldridge La
Elm Cl
Ellesborough Golf Club
Wendover Road
Hill End Farm
Ridgeway
Bacombe Warren
Bacombe
Springs Lane
Springs Cl
Church Hill
Ellesborough
Missenden Road
Coombe
Upper Bacombe
Low Scrubs
Scrubs
Icknield Way
Fugsdon Wood
Dunsi
Ridgeway
Brockwell Farm
Buckmoorend
Icknield Way
Longdown Farm
Bucks
Icknield Wy
Hampdenleaf Wood
Little Hampden
1 grid square represents 500 metres

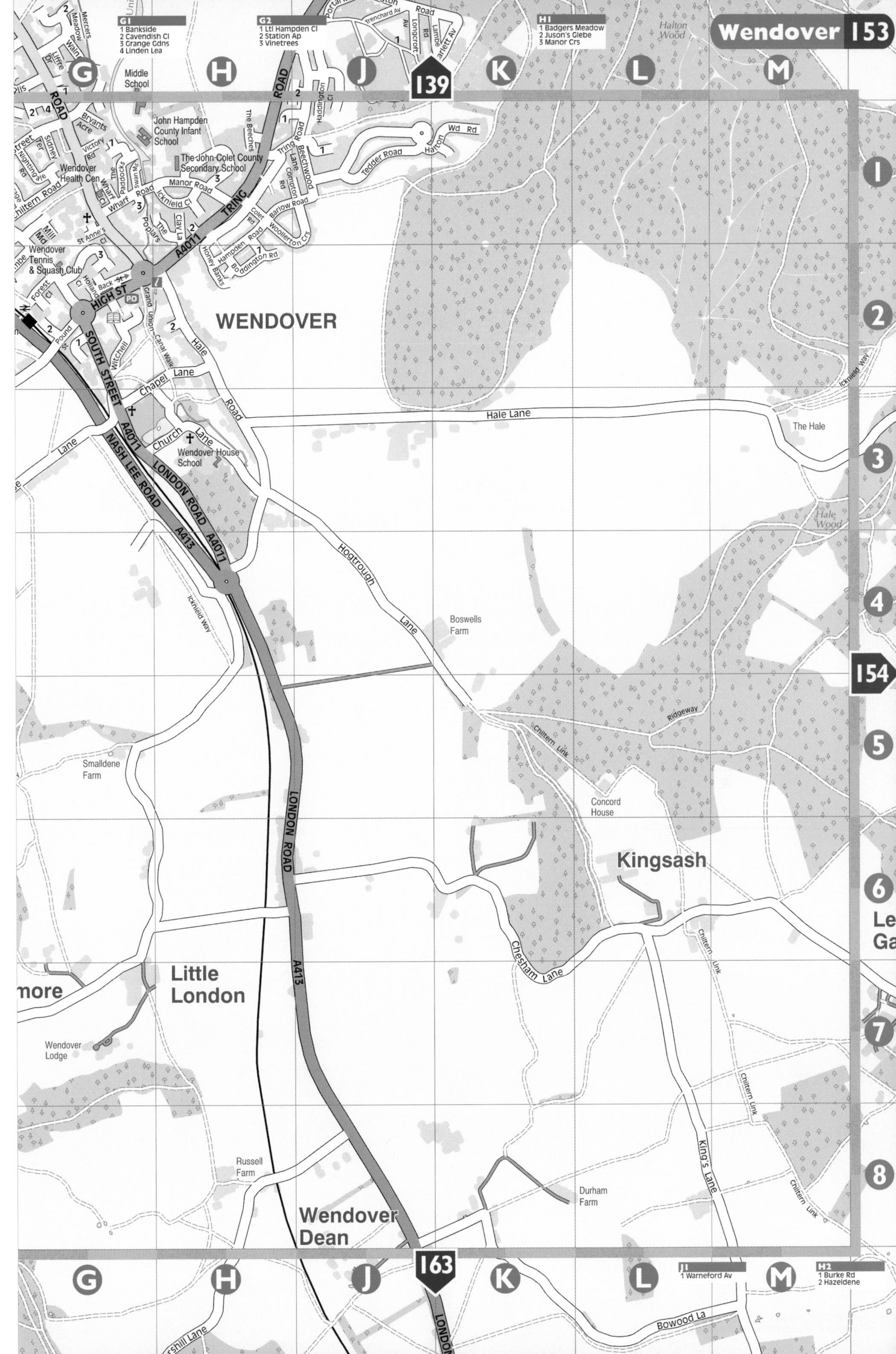
G1
1 Bankside
2 Cavendish Cl
3 Grange Gdns
4 Linden Lea
G2
1 Ltl Hampden Cl
2 Station Ap
3 Vinetrees
H1
1 Badgers Meadow
2 Juson's Glebe
3 Manor Crs
139
154
163
J1
1 Warneford Av
H2
1 Burke Rd
2 Hazeldene
G
H
J
K
L
M
1
2
3
4
5
6
7
8
Halton Wood
Middle School
John Hampden County Infant School
The John Colet County Secondary School
Wendover Health Cen
Wendover Tennis & Squash Club
WENDOVER
HIGH ST
SOUTH STREET
TRING ROAD
A4011
Tedder Road
Halton Wd Rd
Manor Road
Barlow Road
Woollerton Crs
Hampden Road
Boddington Rd
Chiltern Road
Chapel Lane
Church Lane
Hale Road
Hale Lane
The Hale
Hale Wood
Icknield Way
Wendover House School
NASH LEE ROAD
LONDON ROAD
A413
Hogtrough Lane
Boswells Farm
Ridgeway
Chiltern Link
Concord House
Kingsash
Smalldene Farm
Chesham Lane
Little London
Wendover Lodge
Russell Farm
Durham Farm
King's Lane
Wendover Dean
Bowood La
Grand Union Canal Walk

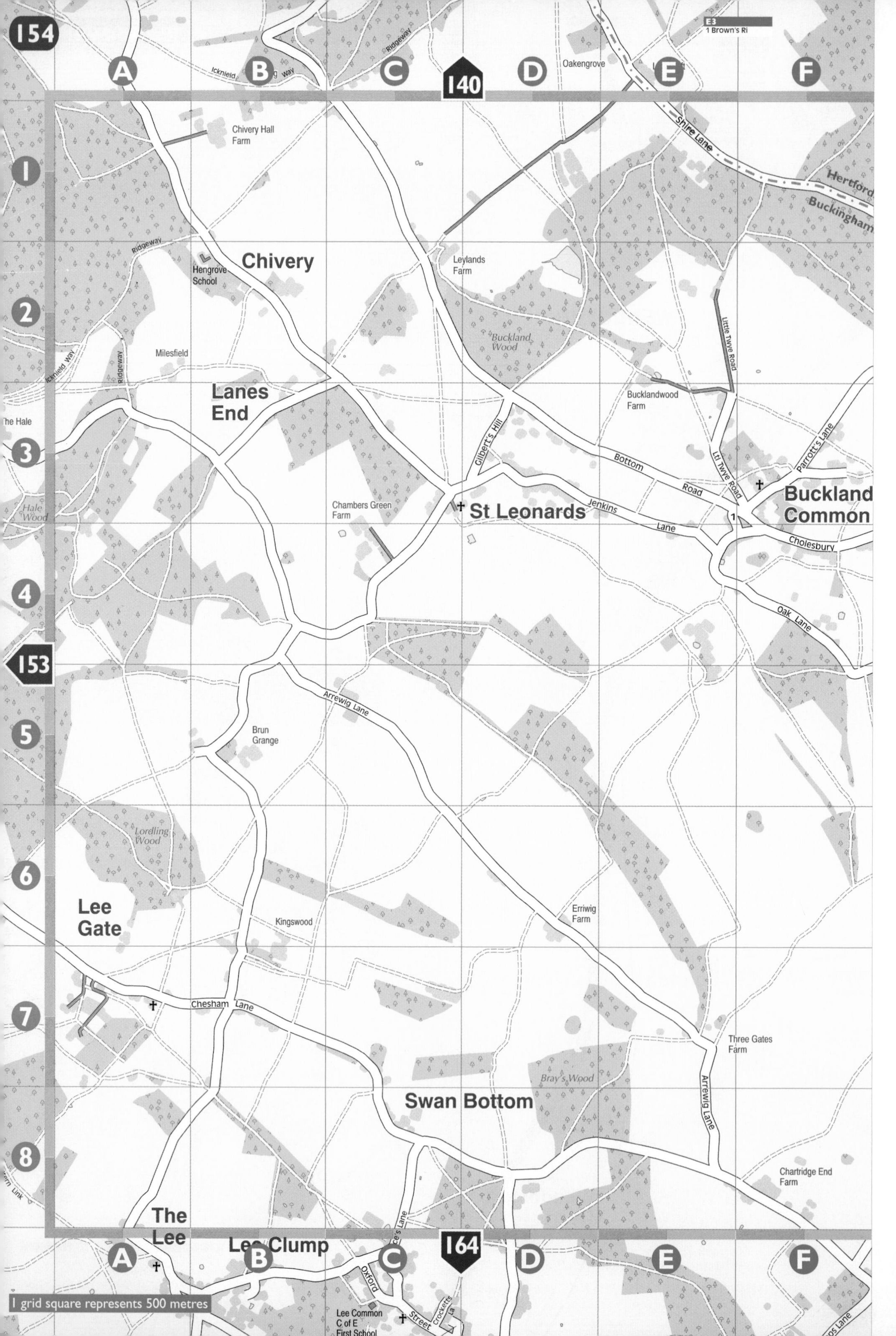


1 grid square represents 500 metres

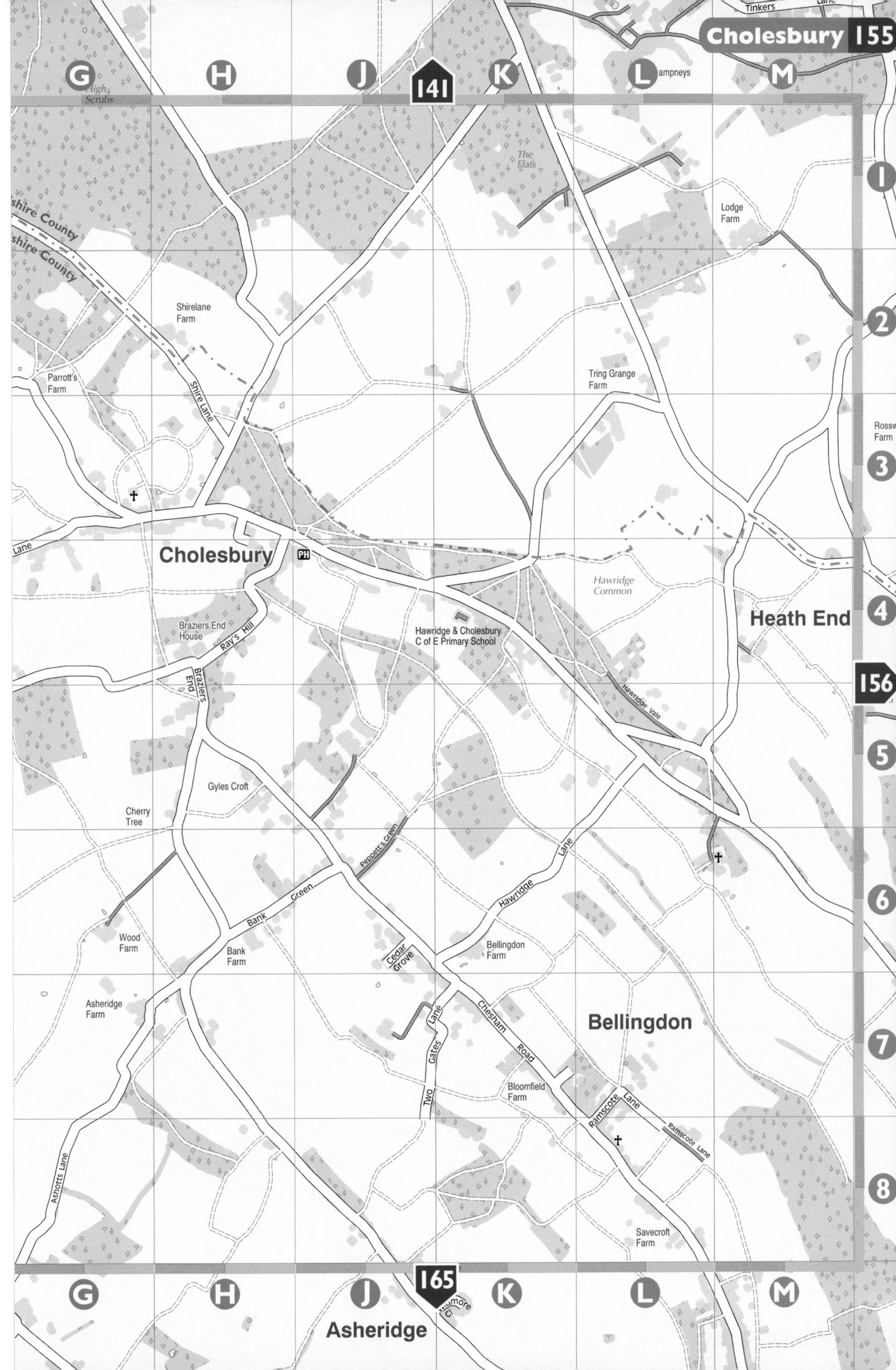
G
H
J
141
K
L
M
Tinkers
ampneys
High Scrubs
The Flats
shire County
shire County
Shirelane Farm
Lodge Farm
Parrott's Farm
Shire Lane
Tring Grange Farm
Rossw Farm
Lane
Cholesbury
PH
Hawridge Common
Heath End
Braziers End House
Ray's Hill
Hawridge & Cholesbury C of E Primary School
Braziers End
Hawridge Vale
156
Gyles Croft
Cherry Tree
Peppett's Green
Hawridge Lane
Bank Green
Wood Farm
Bank Farm
Bellingdon Farm
Cedar Grove
Asheridge Farm
Chesham Road
Two Gates Lane
Bellingdon
Bloomfield Farm
Ramscote Lane
Ramscote Lane
Ashotts Lane
Savecroft Farm
165
Asheridge
1
2
3
4
5
6
7
8

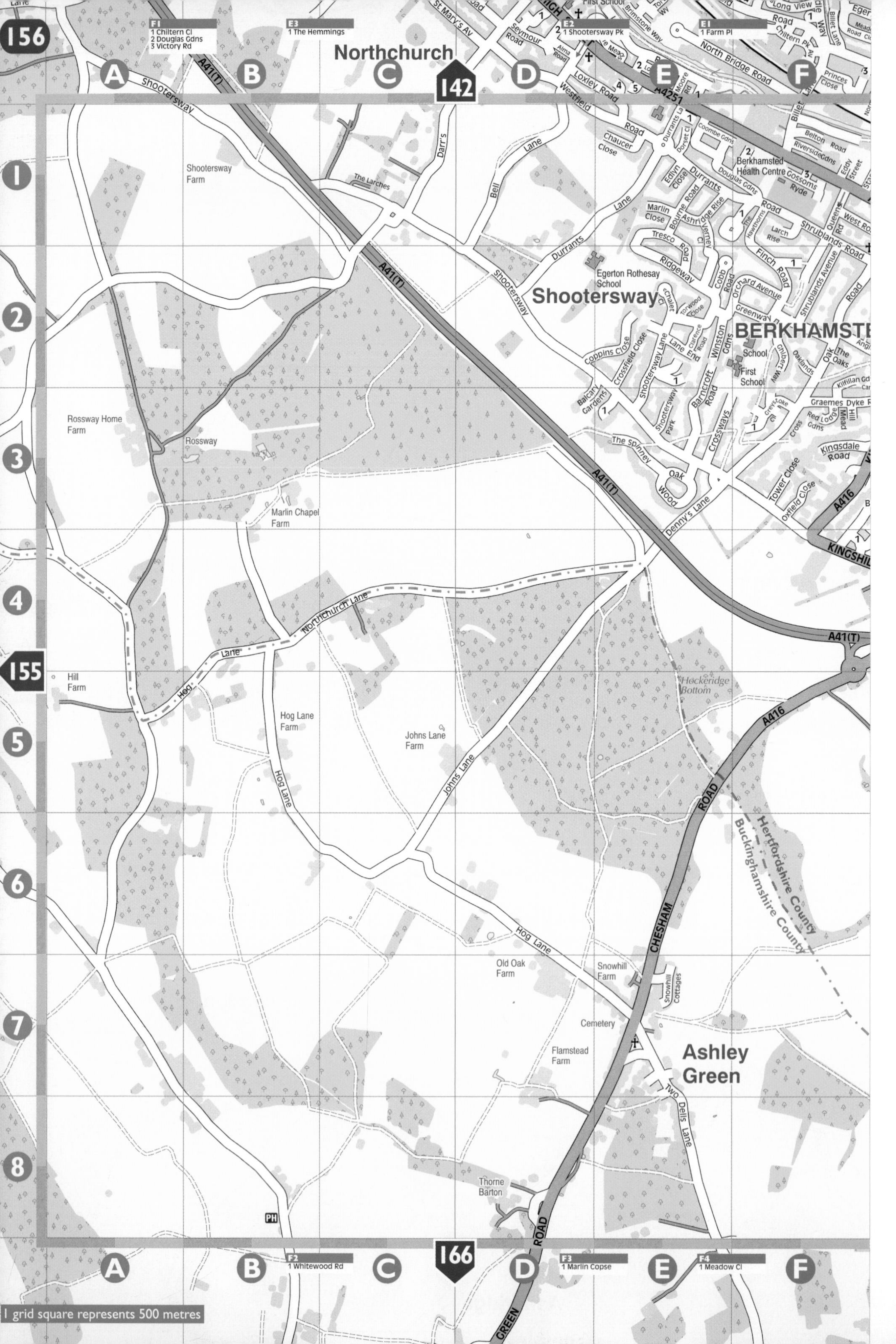


F2
1 Whitewood Rd
F3
1 Marlin Copse
F4
1 Meadow Cl

1 grid square represents 500 metres

G1
1 St John's Well Ct
G2
1 Boxwell Rd
2 Hamilton Rd
3 Park View Rd
4 Rosehill
H1
1 Greenes Ct
143
G
H
J
K
L
M
Little Heath
1
2
3
4
5
6
7
8
Meadow Road
Gaveston Drive
Trevelyan Way
Bridgewater Road
Murray Road
Castle Hill Av
South Park Gardens
Castle Hl
Brownlow Road
New Road
Castle (Remains)
Berkhamsted Station
Berkhamsted Football Club
Tennis Club
Broadwater
Lower Kings Road
Station Road
Whitehill
Gravel Path
Millfield
Meadway
Gilpin's Ride
House Lane
Ivy
Shenstone Hl
Hunters Pk
Bracken Hl
Gutteridge Farm
Haresfoot School
The Comm
Bulbeggars Lane
A4251
Park Street
Tweed
Boxwell Road Surg
Montessore School
Berkley Gallery
Service Practice
HIGH STREET
Mill Street
Berkhamsted Sch
Sch Ho
Castle Street
Chapel St
Bridge Street
School
Ellesmere Road
George Street
Manor Street Surg
Charles Street
Kitsbury Rd
North Road
Montague Road
Milton House Surg
Torrington Rd
Elm Gv
Church La
Water Lane
Victoria C of E Primary School
Berkhamsted School for Girls
Doctor's Commons Road
Pine Cl
Rectory Lane
Three Close La
Victoria Road
Highfield Road
Cloister Garth
Priory Gdns
LONDON ROAD
Old Mill Gdns
George St
Bank Mill
Bank Mill Lane
Curtis Way
Holly Dr
Swing Ga Lane
Greene Walk
Captains Wk
Lombardy Drive
Hillside Gdns
Cedar Road
Hall Park
Hall Park Hill
Hall Park Gate
London Rd
Fieldway
Garden Fld La
Upper Hall Park
Bankmill Bridge
River Bulbourne
Chesham Road
Beechcroft
Kestrel Cl
Robin Hill
Curlew Cl
Falcon Rdg
Loring Rd
Beech Drive
Woodlands Av
Oak Dr
Sycamore Rl
Hazel Rd
St Margaret's Close
Chestnut Drive
Briar Way
Coram Close
Hilltop
Alderley Court
Acacia Gv
Ashlyns Road
Upr Ashlyns Rd
Ashlyns School
The Thomas Coram Middle School
Ashlyns Hall
Cemetery
A41(T)
Long Green
Sandpit Green
Swing Gate Lane
Broadway Farm
Haresfoot Farm
Haresfoot Preparatory School
Bottom Farm
Lower Farm
Bourne Gutter
Vale Farm
Harriott's End Farm
White Hill
Bourne End La
Spencer's Farm
Hemming's Farm
167
G3, H2, H3
Street names for these grid squares are listed at the back of the index
K2
1 Paxton Rd
Grove Lane
Grove Farm
J3
1 Cedar Wy
J2
1 Cambridge Ter
2 Ivy House La
3 Little Bridge Rd
4 Manor St
J1
1 Hill Ct
Duckhall Farm
Whelpley

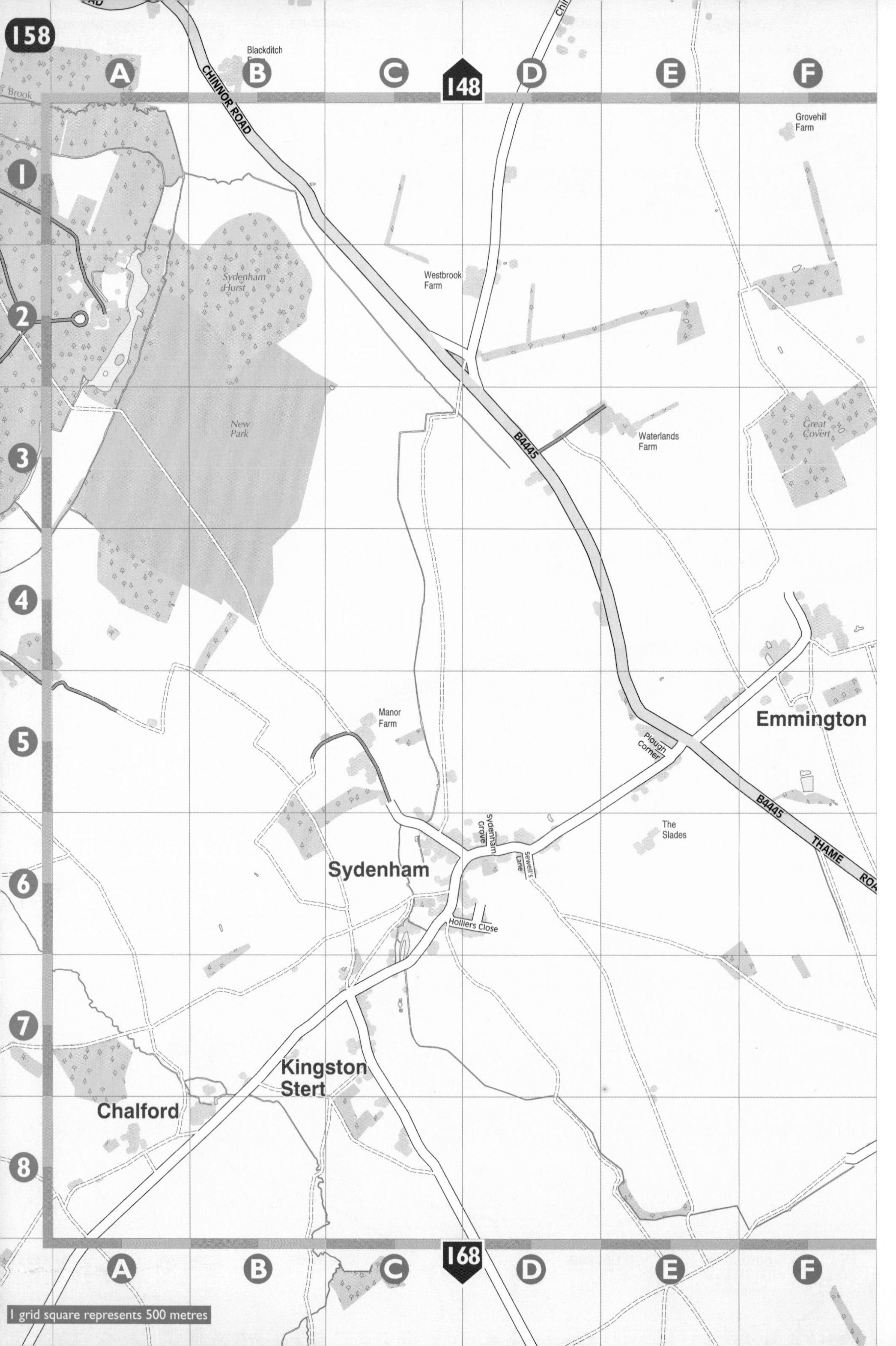

148
A
B
C
D
E
F
1
2
3
4
5
6
7
8
Blackditch
Brook
CHINNOR ROAD
Grovehill
Farm
Westbrook
Farm
Sydenham
Hurst
New
Park
B4445
Waterlands
Farm
Great
Covert
Emmington
Manor
Farm
Plough
Corner
Sydenham
Grove
Sewell's
Lane
The
Slades
B4445
THAME
Sydenham
Holliers Close
Kingston
Stert
Chalford
168
1 grid square represents 500 metres

G8
1 Ashridge
2 Hailey Cft
3 Robins Platt
H8
1 Lacemakers
2 Wheelers End
J6
1 Holland Cl
149
160
169
J7
1 Lwr Icknield Wy
Manor Road
Penn Farm
New Close Farm
Cuttle Brook
North Mill Road
The Ford
Forty Green
Holly Green
Holly Green Lane
Skittle Green
Home Farm
Henton
Old Orchard
Allnutt's Farm
Upper Farm
CHINNOR ROAD
West Lane
Bledlow Cricket Club
PH
B4009
LOWER ICKNIELD WAY
Oxfordshire County
Buckinghamshire County
Hempton Wainhill
Midshires Way
Lower Wainhill
LC
Chinnor & Princes Risborough Railway
The Cop
Bledlow Cross
Ridgeway
Elderdene
Leyburne Gdns
Springfield Gdns
Malyns Close
LOWER ROAD
Doveleat
Benton Drive
High Street
Grafton Orchard
Rectory Meadow
St Andrews C of E School
Mill Lane County Primary School
Van Diemens Close
Wellington House Practice
Duck Square
STATION ROAD
Musgrave Rd
Lime Gv
Church Road
PO
The Surgery
The Avenue
Hill Farm Court
Keens Lane
Mill Lane
Cherry Tree Road
Willow Road
Beech Road
Hedgerley
Foresters
Estover Way
Middle Way
Cleavers
Millers Turn
Conigre
Cowleaze
Oakley Lane
Rannal Drive
Benwells
Riders Way
Hillyers
Hunters Point
Fox Cover
Penley Cl
Flint Hollow
OAKLEY ROAD
B4009
Station Road
Church Lane
CHINNOR
Glynswood
Ravensmead
Meadow Road
Timber Way
Druids Walk
Greenwood
Oak End Way
Woodville
Wykeham Rise
Golden Hill
Hill Road
Meadow
Orchard Way
Glimbers Grove
St Andrew's Road
Elm Drive
Greenwood Avenue
Oakley
CROWELL ROAD
Tumulus
Bledlow Great Wood
G H J K L M
1 2 3 4 5 6 7 8

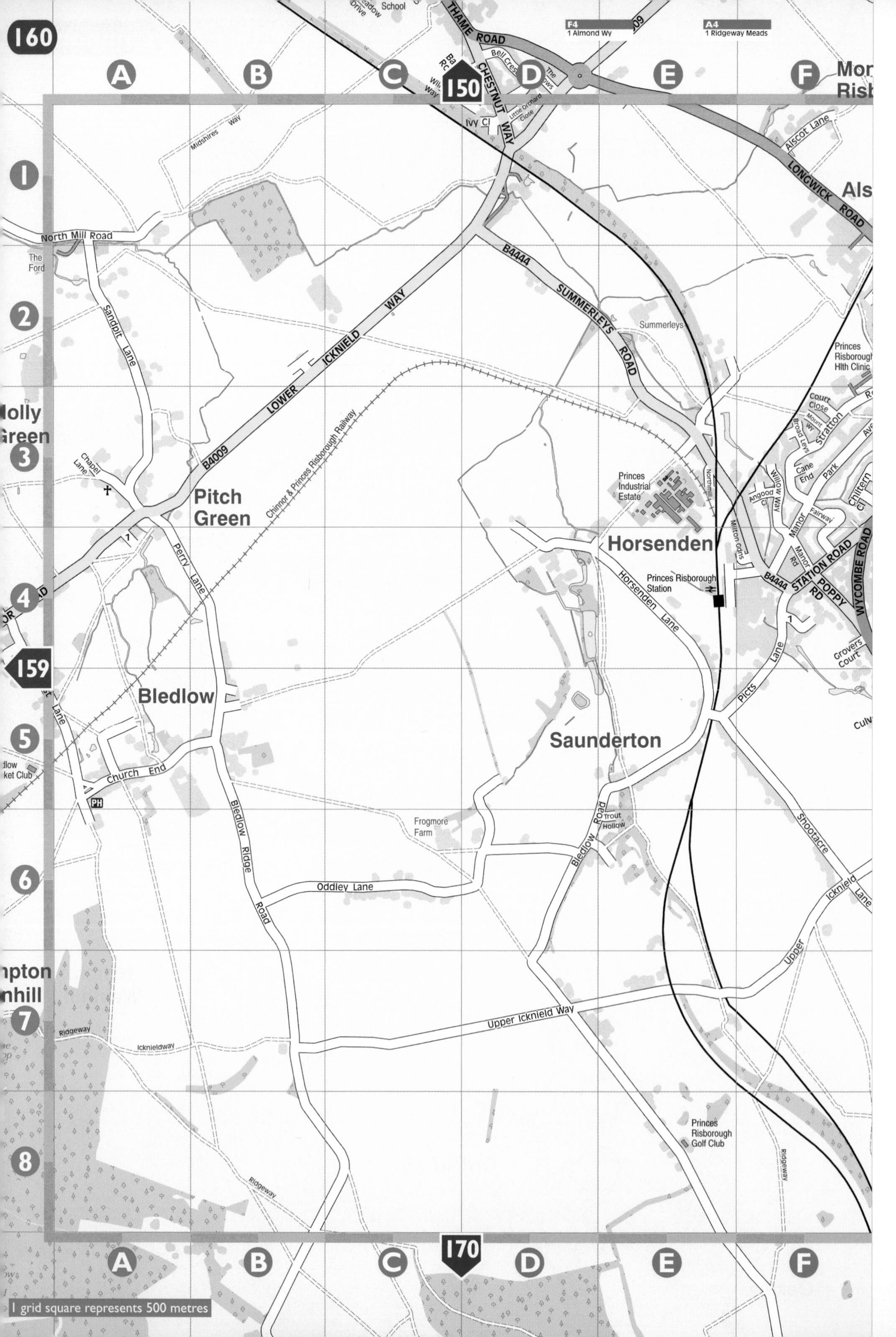
F4
1 Almond Wy
A4
1 Ridgeway Meads
A
B
C
D
E
F
150
170
159
School
THAME ROAD
Bell Cres
CHESTNUT WAY
Ivy Cl
Little Orchard Close
Midshires Way
LONGWICK ROAD
Alscot Lane
North Mill Road
The Ford
B4444
SUMMERLEYS ROAD
Summerleys
LOWER ICKNIELD WAY
B4009
Sandpit Lane
Chapel Lane
Pitch Green
Chinnor & Princes Risborough Railway
Princes Risborough Hlth Clinic
Court Close
Mount Wy
Broad Leys
Stratton
Cane End
Park
Willow Way
Angood Cl
Chiltern Cl
Fairway
Manor Rd
Princes Industrial Estate
Northmill
Milton Gdns
Horsenden
Horsenden Lane
Princes Risborough Station
STATION ROAD
POPPY RD
WYCOMBE ROAD
Grovers Court
Perry Lane
Bledlow
Lane
Church End
PH
Saunderton
Picts Lane
Bledlow Road
Trout Hollow
Frogmore Farm
Bledlow Ridge Road
Oddley Lane
Shootacre Lane
Upper Icknield Lane
Upper Icknield Way
Ridgeway
Icknieldway
Princes Risborough Golf Club
Pitch Green
Holly Green
1
2
3
4
5
6
7
8

G1
1 Canterbury Cl
2 Pilgrims Cl
3 Purssell Pl
4 Pymcombe Cl
G2
1 Malthouse Sq
151
Whiteleaf
PRINCES RISBOROUGH
Whiteleaf Golf Club
Longdown Farm
Monks Risborough C of E Combined School
Icknield County Middle School
Paddocks Hospital
Wellington House Surgery
St Teresas Catholic School
First School
Aldus Fine Art Gallery
Old Cross Keys Surg
Upper School
HP27
Green Hailey
Brimmers Farm
The Old House
Hillock Wood
Redland End
Pink Road
Pink Hill
Parslow's Hillock
Wardrobes
Wardrobes Lane
Woodway
Coppice House
Lily Farm
Lily Bottom Lane
Loosley Row
Loosley Hill
Pink Road
Foundry Lane
Cemetery
WYCOMBE ROAD
A4010
AYLESBURY ROAD
A4129
Kop Hill Rd
Icknield Way
Upper Icknield Way
Brimmers Road
Peters Lane
Longdown Hill
Ridgeway
Pyrtle Spring
162
171
J1
1 Whiteleaf Wy
H2
1 Bardolphs Cl
H1
1 Dunsmore Ride
2 Long Meadow Cl
3 Stopps Orch
G3
1 Bell La
2 Elmdale Gdns
3 Elm Rd
4 Princes Gdns
5 Pymcombe Cl

162
152
161
172
A
B
C
D
E
F
1
2
3
4
5
6
7
8
Icknield Way
Longdown Farm
Bucks Way
Hampdenlea Wood
Little Hampden Common
PH
Dirtywood Farm
South Bucks Way
Little Hampden
Solinger Farm
Hampden Bottom Farm
Court Field House
Cobblershill
Honor End Farm
Honor End Lane
Ferns Farm
Coppice House
Great Hampden
Monkton Wood
Hampden Common
Sports Centre
PO
Hampden Road
Hangings Lane
Monkton Farm
Highwood
Grubbins
Coppice
Bryants Bottom Road
Coleheath
Spring
Moses Plat Lane
Cornerways
1 grid square represents 500 metres

G7
1 John H'pden Wy
2 Parliament Cl
H7
1 Lyndon Cl
H8
1 Peter's Cl
2 Rosetree Cl
Russell Farm
Wendover Dean
Durnam Farm
153
164
173
Bowood La
Cobblershill Lane
Cockshoots Wood
LONDON ROAD
A413
Dutchlands Farm
Hunt's Green
Woodlands Park
King's Lane
South Bucks Way
Leather Lane
Hammond Farm
AYLESBURY ROAD
Road Farm
Havenfields
South Bucks Way
HP16
Rignall Farm
Mapridge Green Lane
Rignall Road
Aylesbury Road
Mobwell
Hotley Bottom
Hotley Bottom Lane
Gateway School
Winslow Field
The Garth
Elm Tree Gn
Walnut Cl
LINK ROAD
Lodge Wood
Broombarn Lane
Hill
Wibner Pond
Moat Farm
Grimms Hill
Upr Hollis
Little Hollis
Broomfield
Broomfield Cl
Firs Rise
STATION AP
A4128
MARTINSEND LANE
Great Missenden Station
Chiltern Mnr Pk
Bernards Cl
Trafford Road
Future School
High Street
Church Street
Back La
Doctors S
GREAT MISSENDEN
Greenlands Lane
Over Hampden
Potters Rd
Mandeville Rd
Beech La
Kiln Close
Prestwood County First School
Moat Lane
Moat Dr
Pankridge Farm
The Glebe
Laurel Cl
Chequers La
Pankridge Dr
Moat Close
Honor End Lane
Honorwood Cl
Chequers Dr
Prestwood Surgery
Flint Wy
Whitefield Lane
Hobbshill Rd
Misbourne Dr
Clarendon Rd
High St
A4128 HIGH STREET
Andlows Farm
John Hampden Surg
Junior School
Blacksmith La
Orchard Lane
Salmons La
New Rd
Green Park
Pepys Dr
Clare Road
Honor Road
Prestwood
Greame Av
Sixty Acres Road
Grims Dyke
Nairdwood Lane
Chern Close
Lane
Masons Ct
Hazell Rd
Acres
Peppard Meadow
Stevens Cl
Stocklands Wy
Groom Rd
Wright's Lane
Wren Rd
Wardes
Lane
Prestwood Lodge
Atkins Farm
A4128
M6
1 Headland Cl
2 Pump Meadow
J8
1 Coulson Ct

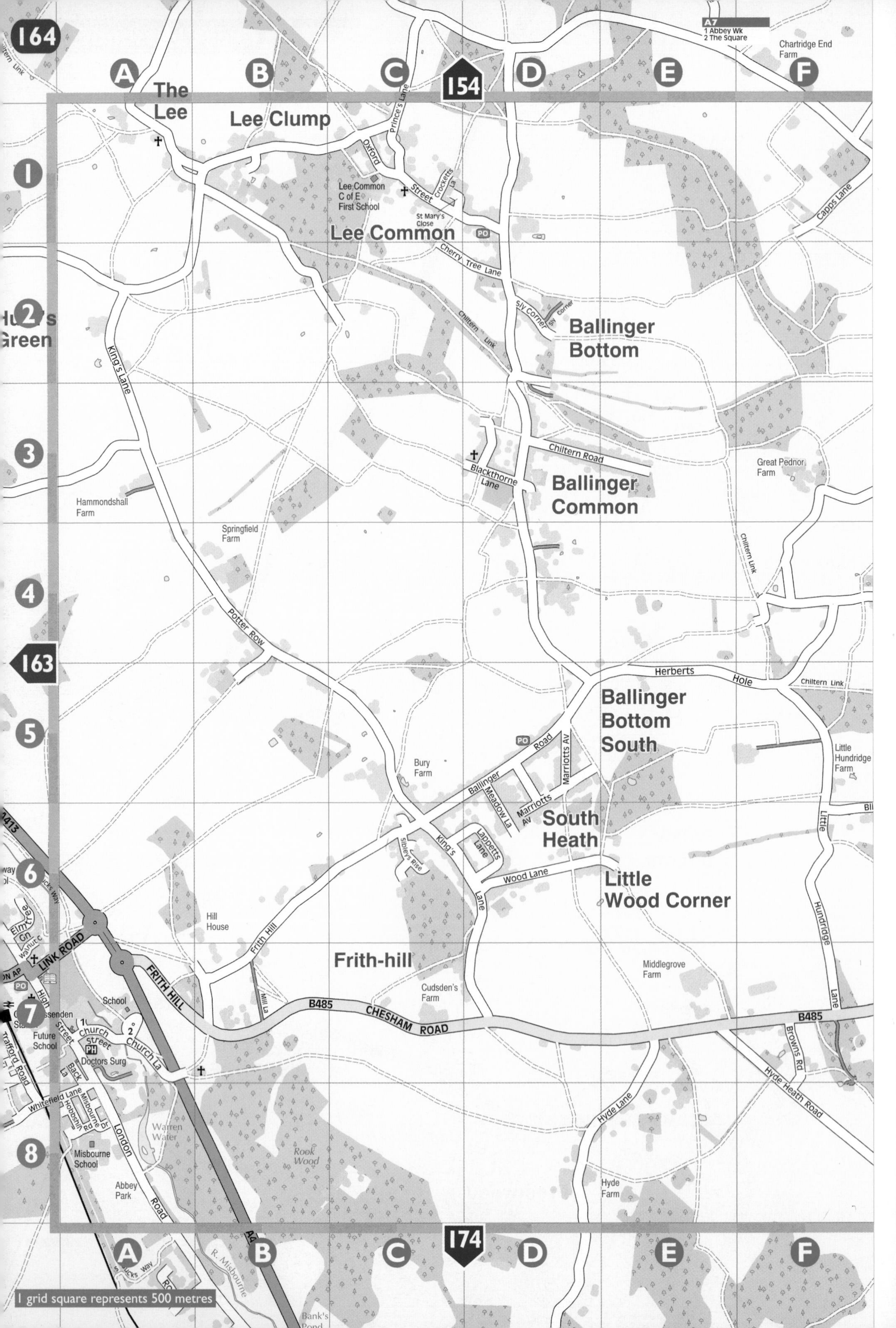
164
154
163
174
A
B
C
D
E
F
1
2
3
4
5
6
7
8
A7
1 Abbey Wk
2 The Square
Chartridge End Farm
The Lee
Lee Clump
Prince's Lane
Oxford
Street
Crocketts La
Lee Common C of E First School
St Mary's Close
Lee Common
PO
Cherry Tree Lane
Chiltern Link
Sly Corner
Ballinger Bottom
Capps Lane
King's Lane
Chiltern Road
Blackthorne Lane
Ballinger Common
Great Pednor Farm
Hammondshall Farm
Springfield Farm
Chiltern Link
Potter Row
Herberts Hole
Chiltern Link
Ballinger Bottom South
Ballinger Road
Marriotts Av
Bury Farm
Meadow La
Marriotts Av
Little Hundridge Farm
South Heath
Lappetts Lane
King's Lane
Siblevs Rise
Wood Lane
Little Wood Corner
Hundridge Lane
Hill House
Frith Hill
Frith-hill
LINK ROAD
FRITH HILL
Middlegrove Farm
Cudsden's Farm
School
Mill La
B485
CHESHAM ROAD
B485
Browns Rd
Hyde Heath Road
Future School
Church Street
PH
Church La
Doctors Surg
High Street
Back La
Whitefield Lane
Hobshill Rd
Misbourne Dr
London Road
Trafford Road
Warren Water
Rook Wood
Hyde Lane
Misbourne School
Abbey Park
Hyde Farm
R. Misbourne
A413
Bank's Pond
1 grid square represents 500 metres

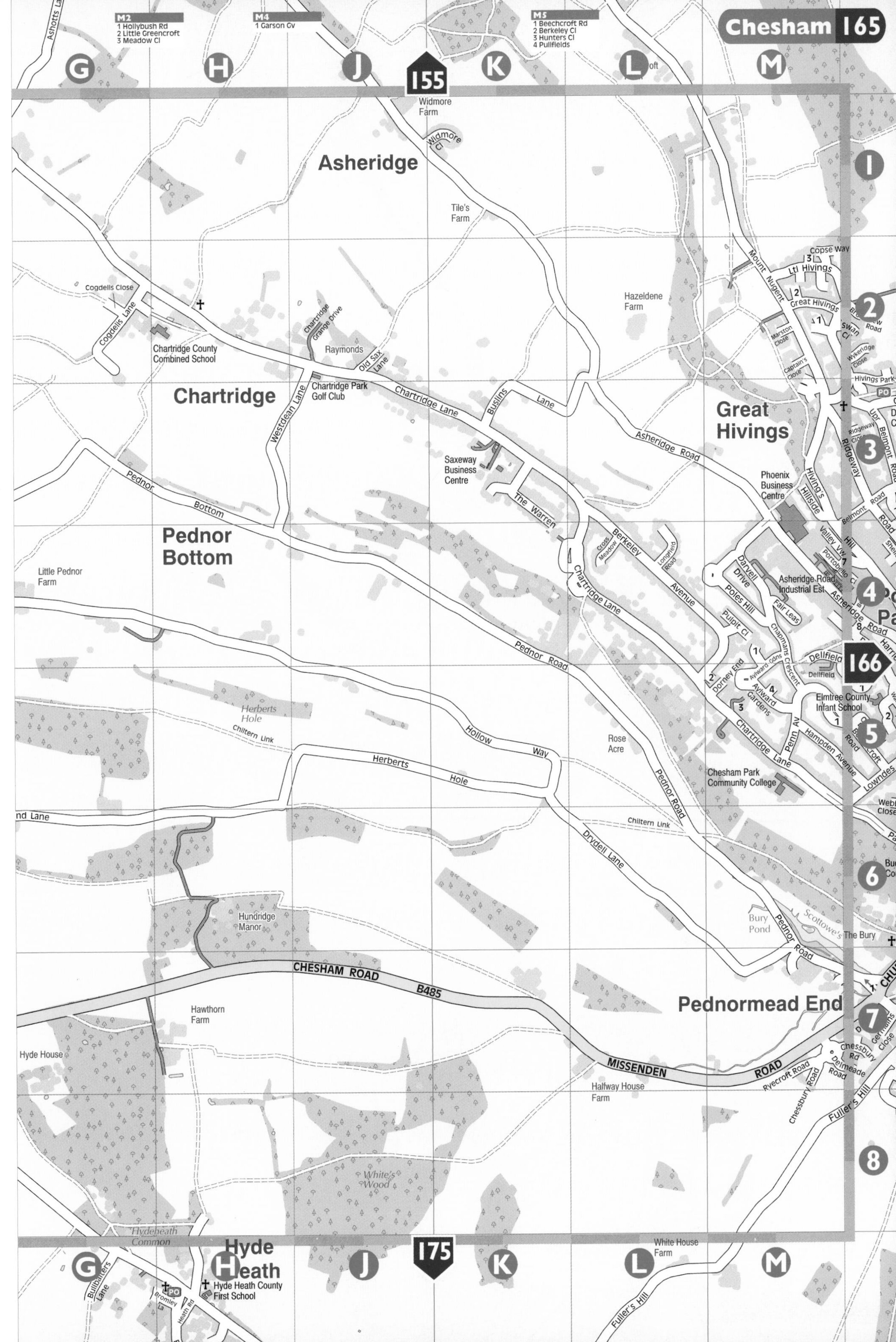
M2
1 Hollybush Rd
2 Little Greencroft
3 Meadow Cl
M4
1 Garson Gv
M5
1 Beechcroft Rd
2 Berkeley Cl
3 Hunters Cl
4 Pullfields
155
Widmore Farm
Widmore Cl
Asheridge
Tile's Farm
Hazeldene Farm
Mount Nugent
Copse Way
Ltl Hivings
Great Hivings
Marston Close
Captain's Close
Hivings Park
Cogdells Close
Cogdells Lane
Chartridge County Combined School
Chartridge Grange Drive
Raymonds
Old Sax Lane
Chartridge Park Golf Club
Chartridge
Westdean Lane
Chartridge Lane
Buslins Lane
Asheridge Road
Great Hivings
Saxeway Business Centre
Phoenix Business Centre
Hivings Hillside
Ridgeway
Belmont Road
Pednor Bottom
The Warren
Cross Meadow
Berkeley Avenue
Longfield Road
Valley Vw
Darvell Drive
Asheridge Road Industrial Est
Little Pednor Farm
Poles Hill
Fair Leas
Chartridge Lane
Pulpit Cl
Pednor Road
Dorney End
Aylward Gdns
Aylward Gardens
Chapmans Crescent
Dellfield
166
Elmtree County Infant School
Herberts Hole
Chiltern Link
Hollow Way
Rose Acre
Penn Av
Hampden Avenue
Lowndes
Herberts Hole
Chesham Park Community College
Pednor Road
Webb Close
Chiltern Link
Drydell Lane
Hundridge Manor
Bury Pond
Scottowe's
The Bury
Pednor Road
CHESHAM ROAD
B485
Pednormead End
Hawthorn Farm
Hyde House
MISSENDEN ROAD
Chessbury Rd
Germains Close
Delmeade Road
Ryecroft Road
Chessbury Road
Halfway House Farm
Fuller's Hill
White's Wood
Hydeheath Common
175
Hyde Heath
White House Farm
Bullbaiters Lane
Bromley La
Heath Rd
Hyde Heath County First School
Fuller's Hill
G H J K L M
I 2 3 4 5 6 7 8

B6
1 Albert Rd
2 The Broadway
B4
1 Britannia Rd
A5
1 Benham Cl
2 Elmtree Hl
3 Upper Meadow
4 Wesley Hl
A3
1 Mansefield Cl
2 Wil'm Moulder Ct
156
165
176
C8
1 Box Tree Cl
2 Gawdrey Cl
A4, A6, A7
Street names for these grid squares are listed at the back of the index
B5, B7, C4, C5
Street names for these grid squares are listed at the back of the index
HP5
Lye Green
Pond Park
Newtown
Hilltop
Codmore
Botley
CHESHAM
Tyler's Hill
Chessmount
Waterside
Lower Bois
Chesham Vale
Pressmore Farm
Broadview Farm
Nashleigh Farm
Chesham Preparatory School
Brushwood Middle School
Brockhurst Farm
Greenway CP School
Durrant CP School
Howard Industrial Estate
Crown Business Estate
Elmtree County Infant School
Heritage House School
Chesham High School
Chesham Leisure Centre
Buckinghamshire Co Council
Chesham Station
Dungrove Farm
Prospect Industrial Estate
Chesham Community Hospital
New Elgiva Theatre
Orchard House Industrial Estate
Chesham Health Cen
Middle Sch
Chesham United Football Club
Combined School
The Bury
Town Hall
The Surgery
The New Surgery
Cemetery
ASHLEY GREEN ROAD
NASHLEIGH HILL A416
BERKHAMPSTEAD ROAD
BROAD STREET
LYE GREEN ROAD
B4505
ESKDALE AVENUE
Botley Road
AMERSHAM ROAD
RED LION STREET
ST MARY'S WY
CHURCH ST
Vale Road
Lycrome Road
Two Dells Lane
Sunnyside Road
Lowndes Avenue
Cameron Road
Tylers Hill Road
Moor Road
Waterside
Cresswell Road
Latimer Road
Pump Lane
1 grid square represents 500 metres

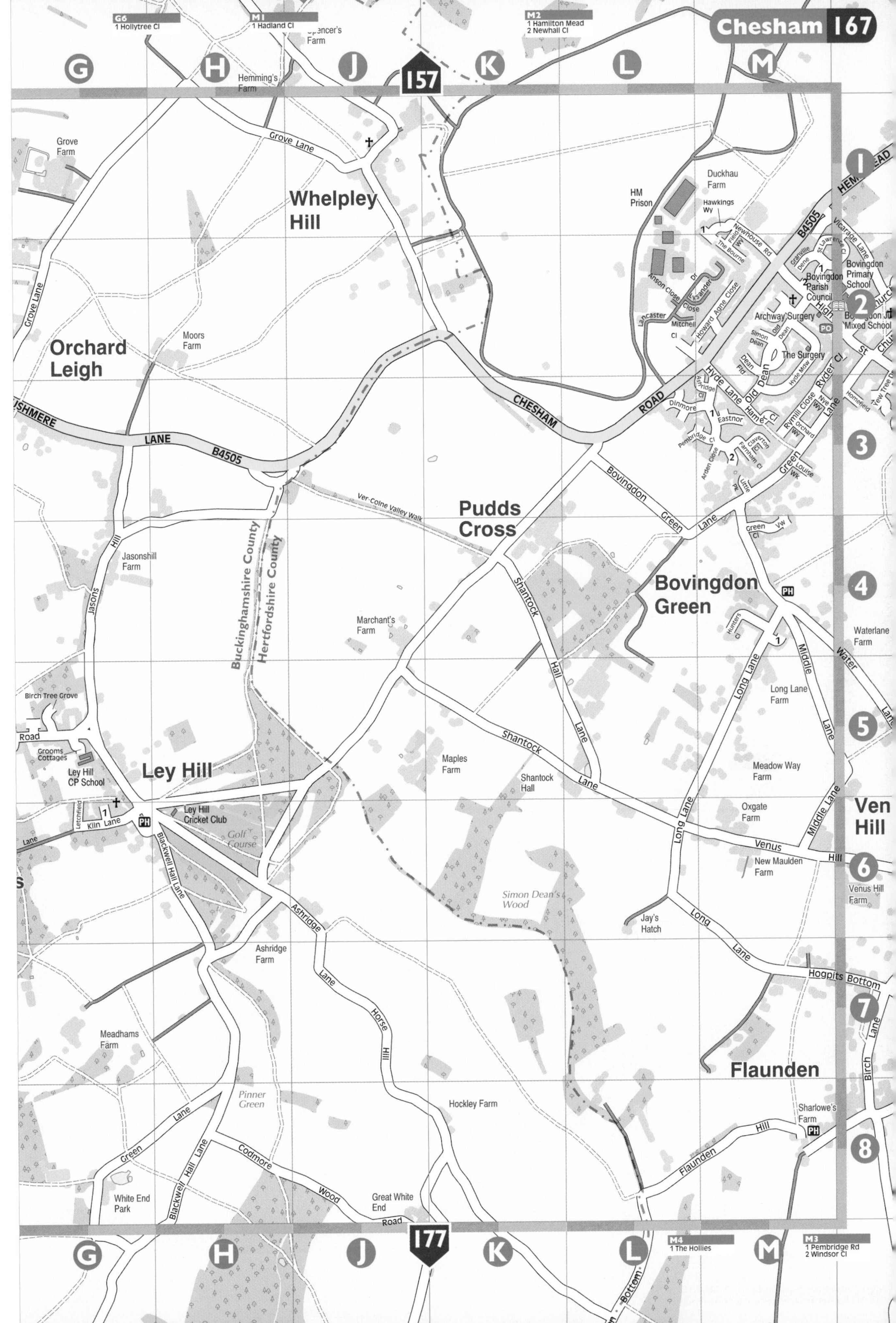
G6 1 Hollytree Cl
M1 1 Hadland Cl
M2 1 Hamilton Mead 2 Newhall Cl
157
Whelpley Hill
Orchard Leigh
Pudds Cross
Bovingdon Green
Ley Hill
Flaunden
Ven Hill
Grove Farm
Hemming's Farm
Moors Farm
Jasonshill Farm
Marchant's Farm
Maples Farm
Shantock Hall
Ashridge Farm
Meadhams Farm
Hockley Farm
Great White End
White End Park
Pinner Green
Simon Dean's Wood
Jay's Hatch
Long Lane Farm
Meadow Way Farm
Oxgate Farm
New Maulden Farm
Venus Hill Farm
Waterlane Farm
Sharlowe's Farm
Duckhau Farm
HM Prison
Bovingdon Primary School
Bovingdon Parish Council
Archway Surgery
The Surgery
Ley Hill CP School
Ley Hill Cricket Club
Golf Course
Grooms Cottages
Birch Tree Grove
Grove Lane
Chesham Road
B4505
Lane
Ver-Colne Valley Walk
Buckinghamshire County
Hertfordshire County
Bovingdon Green Lane
Shantock Hall Lane
Shantock Lane
Long Lane
Middle Lane
Venus Hill
Hogpits Bottom
Flaunden Hill
Horse Hill
Ashridge Lane
Blackwell Hall Lane
Codmore Wood Road
Green Lane
Jasons Hill
Kiln Lane
Birch Lane
177
M4 1 The Hollies
M3 1 Pembridge Rd 2 Windsor Cl

F2
1 Pleck La
C3
1 Aston Gdns
158
180
Kingston Blount
Aston Rowant
Aston Rowant C of E Primary School
School Lane
Plowden Park
Church La
Aston Rowant Cricket Club
Kingston House
Park Lane
HIGH STREET
B4009
Brook Street
Baker's Piece
Pleck Lane
Old Cft Cl
Icknield Cl
Stert Road
OX9
A40
Aston Park Stud
CHINNOR ROAD
Woodway Farm
Butts Way
Swan's Way
Kingston
Kingston Grove
Grove Wood
Aston Wood
ASTON HILL
Hill Farm
Lewknor C of E School
PO
Church Rd
High Street
Weston Rd
Watlington Road
Hill Rd
M40
Junction 6
The Knapp
Hill Road
Nature Reserve
Hailey Wood
1 grid square represents 500 metres

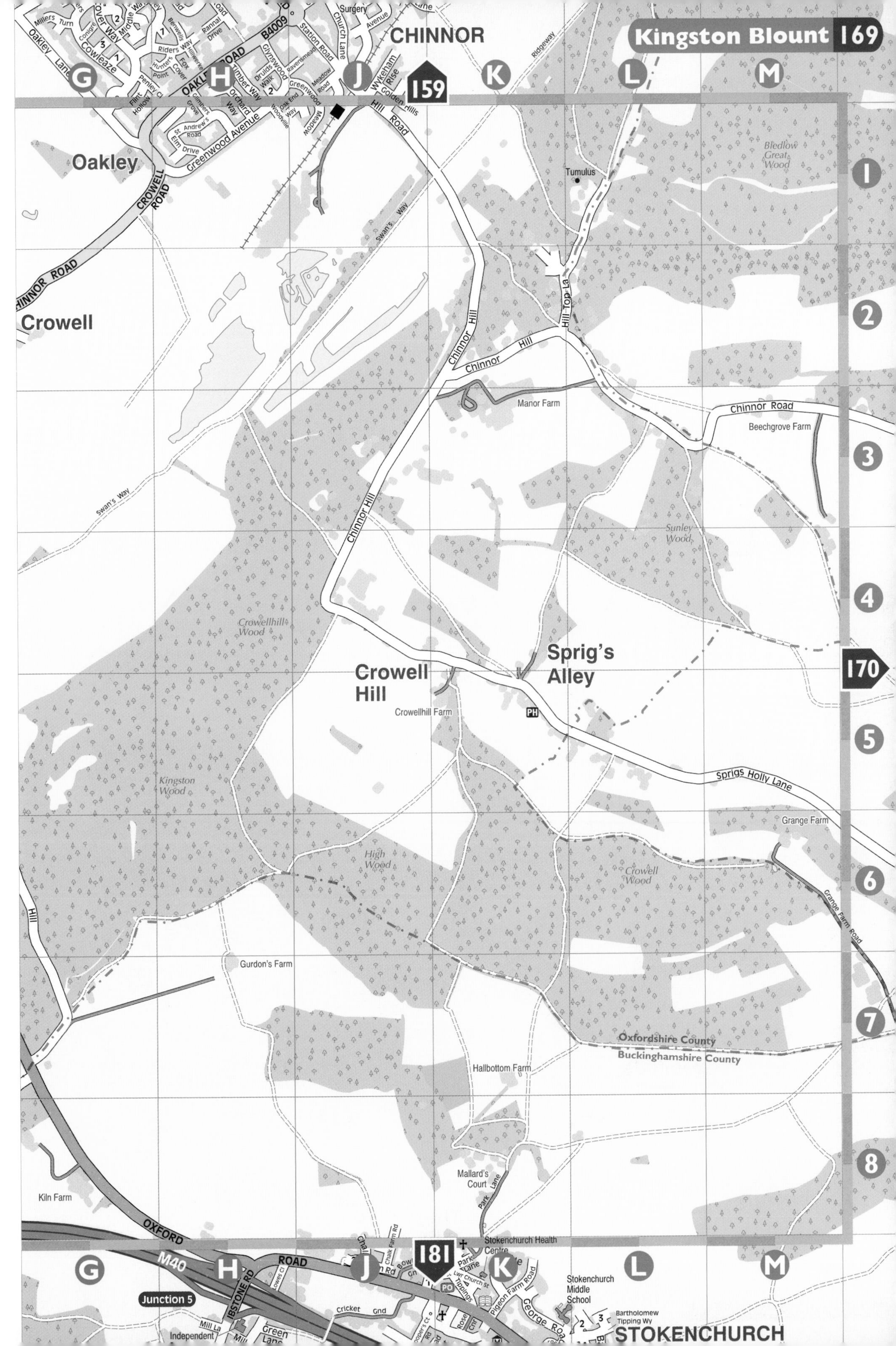
CHINNOR
Oakley
Crowell
Crowell Hill
Sprig's Alley
STOKENCHURCH
Chinnor Hill
Chinnor Road
Sprigs Holly Lane
Hill Top La
Manor Farm
Beechgrove Farm
Sunley Wood
Crowellhill Wood
Crowellhill Farm
Kingston Wood
High Wood
Crowell Wood
Grange Farm
Grange Farm Road
Gurdon's Farm
Hallbottom Farm
Mallard's Court
Park Lane
Kiln Farm
Bledlow Great Wood
Tumulus
Swan's Way
Ridgeway
Oxfordshire County
Buckinghamshire County
OXFORD ROAD
M40
Junction 5
Stokenchurch Health Centre
Stokenchurch Middle School
Cricket Gnd
Greenwood Avenue
CROWELL ROAD
OAKLEY ROAD
B4009
Station Road
Church Lane
Wykeham Rise
Golden Hills
Hill Road
159
170
181

170
160
169
182
A
B
C
D
E
F
1
2
3
4
5
6
7
8
Risborough Golf Club
Ridgeway
Ridgeway
Ridgeway
Wigan's Farm
Wigan's Lane
Lee
Road
Saund Lee
Callow Down Farm
Harper's
Lodge Hill Farm
Radnage Lane
Retreat Lane
Radnage Bottom Farm
Chinnor Road
Chapel Lane
Rout's Green
Haw Lane
Bledlow Ridge
Daws Hill Farm
Church Lane
Town End
Radnage
Grange Farm
Town End Road
Ford's Cl
Church Lane
Rdg Side
Virginia Gdns
Chinnor Road
The Road
Crest
Haw Lane
Bledlow Ridge
Grange Farm Road
Rd
Horseshoe
Town End Road
Bledlow Ridge County Combined School
PO
Bottom Road
Bennett End Road
Grange Farm Road
Bower's Lane
Bennett End
Morlands Farm
Pophley's Wood
Bottle Sq. Lane
Radnage C of E First School
City Road
Green Lane
The City
Green End Road
Loxborou House
Radnage House
I grid square represents 500 metres

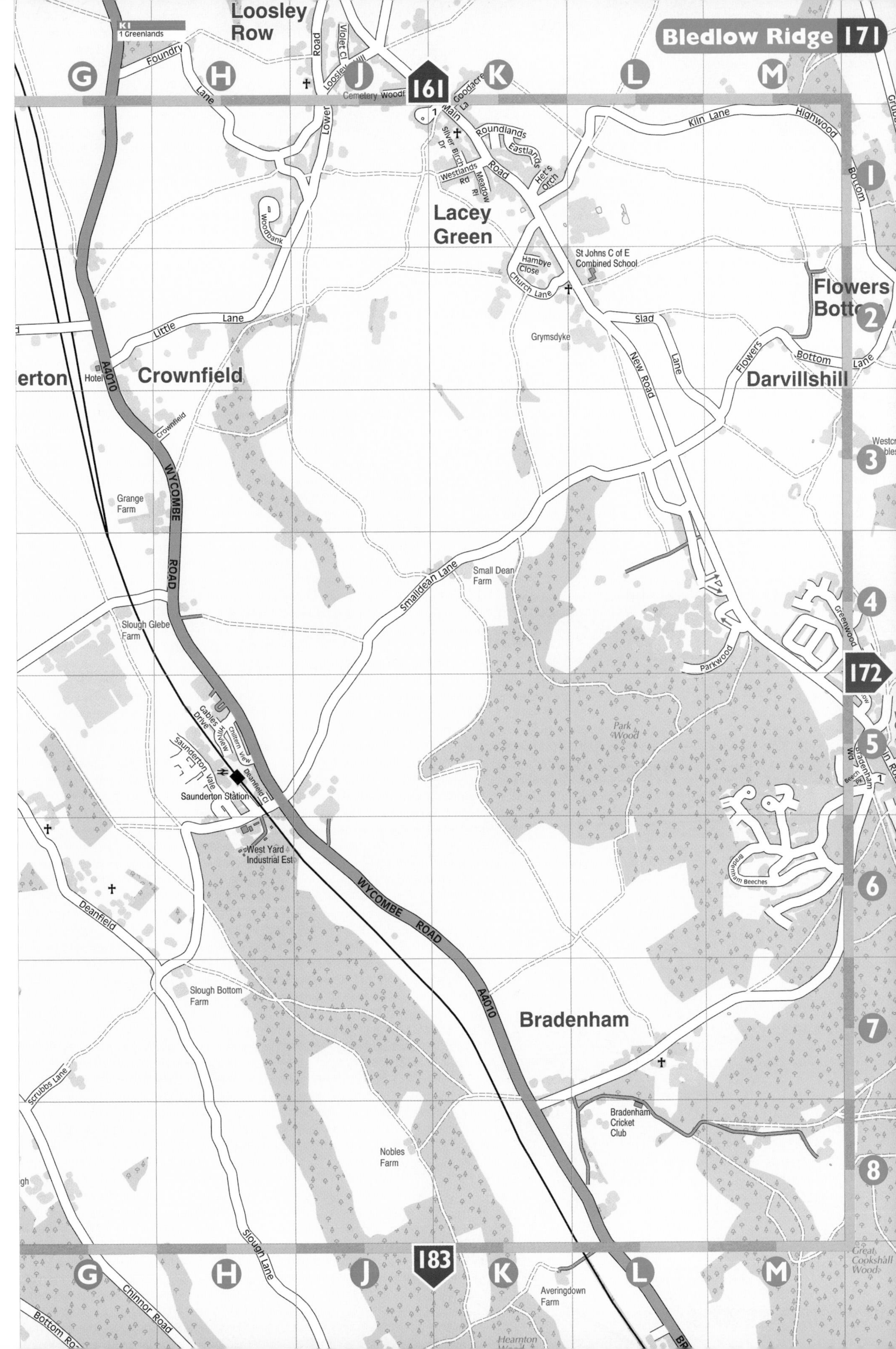
Loosley Row
K1
1 Greenlands
Foundry
Lane
Road
Violet Cl
Loosley
Lower
Cemetery
Woodf
161
Goodacre La
Main
Road
Silver Birch Dr
Roundlands
Eastlands
Het's Orch
Westlands Rd
Meadow Ri
Kiln Lane
Highwood
Bottom
Woodbank
Lacey Green
Hambye Close
Church Lane
St Johns C of E Combined School
Flowers Botto
Little Lane
Slad
Lane
New Road
Grymsdyke
Flowers
Bottom Lane
Darvillshill
erton
Hotel
A4010
Crownfield
Crownfield
WYCOMBE ROAD
Grange Farm
Smalldean Lane
Small Dean Farm
Slough Glebe Farm
Greenwood
Parkwood
172
Park Wood
Gables Drive
Hillview
Chiltern View
Saunderton Vale
Deanfield Cl
Saunderton Station
Bradenham Wd
Beech Pk
Bradenham Beeches
West Yard Industrial Est
WYCOMBE ROAD
Deanfield
A4010
Slough Bottom Farm
Bradenham
Scrubbs Lane
Bradenham Cricket Club
Nobles Farm
Slough Lane
183
Great Cookshall Wood
Averingdown Farm
Chinnor Road
Bottom Ro
Hearnton
G
H
J
K
L
M
1
2
3
4
5
6
7
8

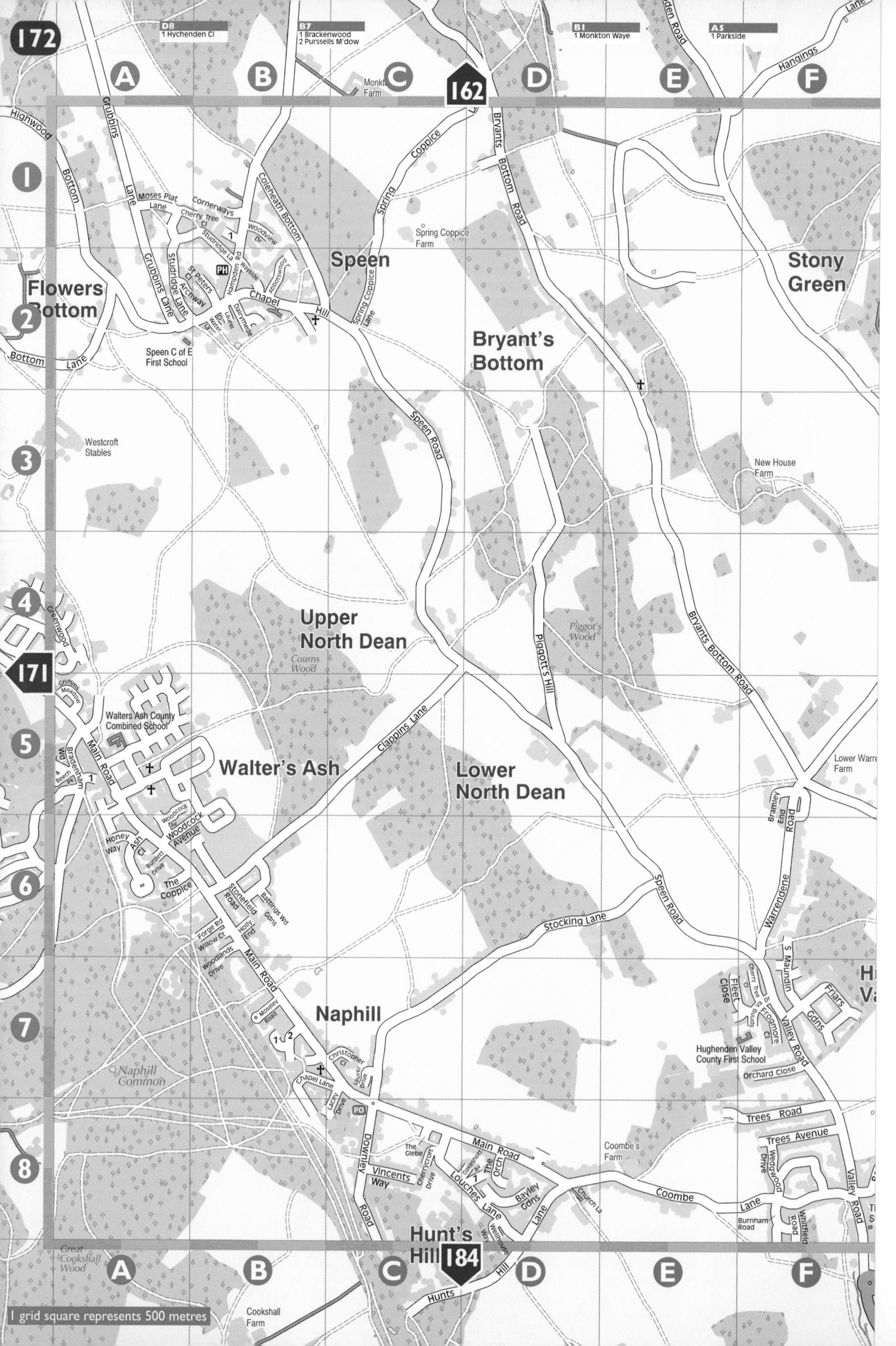
172
D8
1 Hychenden Cl
B7
1 Brackenwood
2 Pursselles M'dow
B1
1 Monkton Waye
A5
1 Parkside
162
171
184
A
B
C
D
E
F
1
2
3
4
5
6
7
8
Flowers Bottom
Speen
Stony Green
Bryant's Bottom
Upper North Dean
Walter's Ash
Lower North Dean
Naphill
Hunt's Hill
Speen C of E First School
Westcroft Stables
Spring Coppice Farm
New House Farm
Lower Warre Farm
Walters Ash County Combined School
Hughenden Valley County First School
Coombe's Farm
Cookshall Farm
Great Cookshall Wood
Naphill Common
Courns Wood
Piggot's Wood
Highwood Bottom
Grubbins Lane
Moses Plat Lane
Cornerways
Cherry Tree Cl
Studridge La
Studridge Lane
St Peters Cl
Archway
Hampden Rd
Woodview Dr
Wayside
Abbotswood
Chapel Hill
Dairymede
Laurel
Water La
Coleheath Bottom
Spring Coppice Lane
Spring Coppice
Bryants Bottom Road
Speen Road
Piggott's Hill
Clappins Lane
Stocking Lane
Bramley End
Warrendene Road
Greenwood
Crimms Meadow
Main Road
Bradenham Wd
Beech Pk
Honey Way
Ash Cl
Burdett Drive
Woodcock Av
Woodcock Avenue
The Coppice
Stonefield Road
Battings Wd Gdns
Holly End
Forge Rd
Willow Ct
Woodlands Drive
Moseley Road
Christopher Cl
Laurel Drive
Chapel Lane
Lacey Drive
PO
PH
Downley Road
Vincents Way
Cherrycroft Drive
The Glebe
Louches Lane
The Orch
Oakeshott Av
Bayley Gdns
Wellhouse Way
Church La
Coombe Lane
Hunts Hill
S Maundin
Fleet Close
Cherry Tree Cl
Friars Gdns
Frogmore Cl
Valley Road
Orchard Close
Trees Road
Trees Avenue
Wedgwood Drive
Burnham Road
Whitfield Road
Hangings Lane
Monkton Farm
1 grid square represents 500 metres

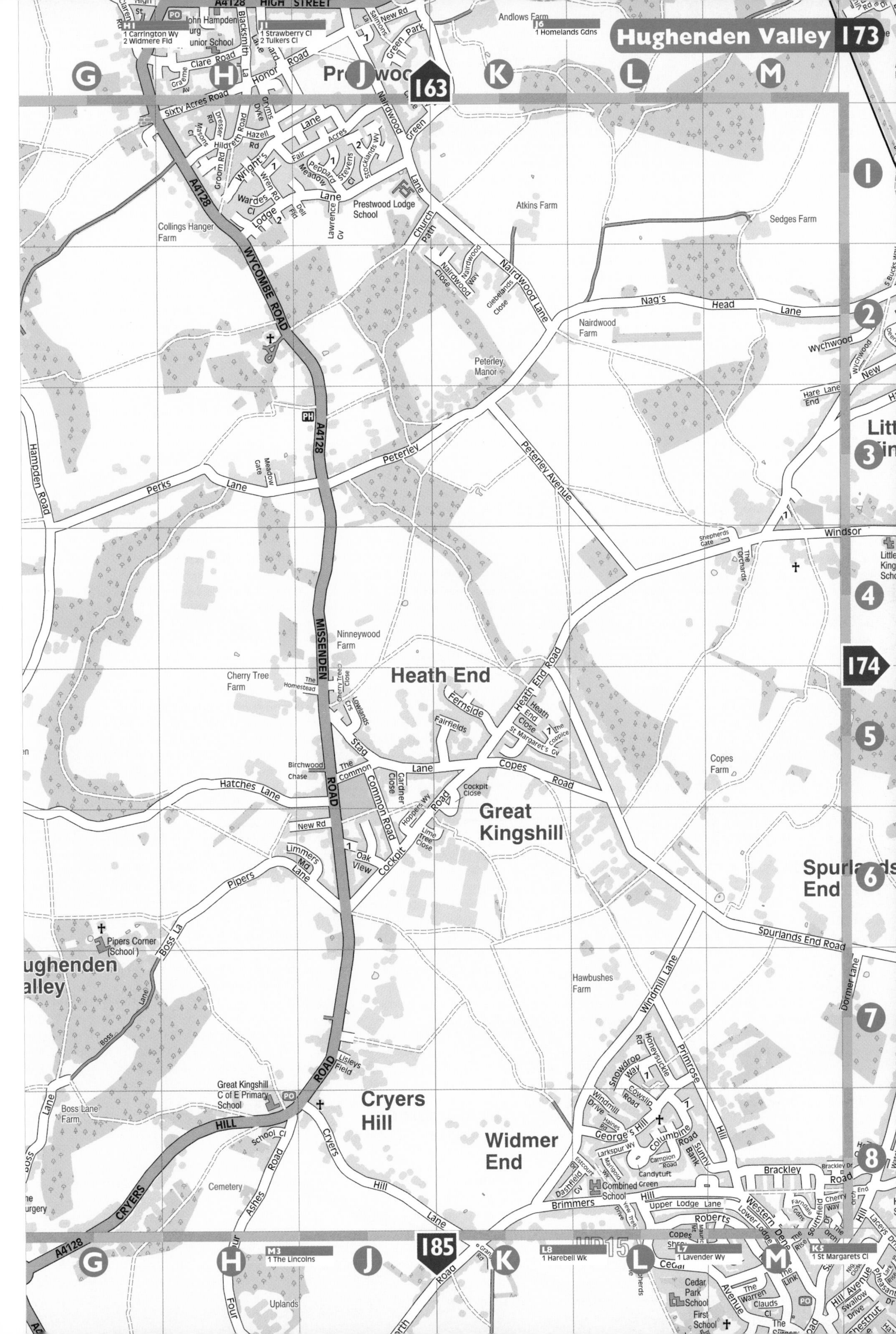
A4128 HIGH STREET
H1 1 Carrington Wy 2 Widmere Fld
J1 1 Strawberry Cl 2 Tulkers Cl
J6 1 Homelands Gdns
Andlows Farm
Prestwood
163
Sixty Acres Road
Clare Road
Honor Road
Nairdwood Lane
Green Park
Collings Hanger Farm
Prestwood Lodge School
Atkins Farm
Sedges Farm
WYCOMBE ROAD
A4128
Nag's Head Lane
Nairdwood Farm
Peterley Manor
Wychwood
Hare Lane End
Peterley Lane
Perks Lane
Hampden Road
Meadow Gate
Peterley Avenue
Windsor
Shepherds Gate
The Orchards
Little Kingshill
174
MISSENDEN ROAD
Ninneywood Farm
Cherry Tree Farm
Heath End
Heath End Road
Fernside
Fairfields
Lowlands
Stag Lane
Copes Road
Copes Farm
Birchwood Chase
The Common
Hatches Lane
Common Road
Gardner Close
Cockpit Close
Cockpit Road
New Rd
Great Kingshill
Limmers Mead
Pipers Lane
Oak View
Lime Tree Close
Spurlands End
Spurlands End Road
Pipers Corner (School)
Boss Lane
Hughenden Valley
Hawbushes Farm
Windmill Lane
Dormer Lane
Lisleys Field
Great Kingshill C of E Primary School
Cryers Hill
Widmer End
Boss Lane Farm
HILL
School Cl
Ashes Road
Cryers Hill Lane
Cemetery
Snowdrop Way
Honeysuckle Rd
Primrose Hill
Windmill Drive
Cowslip Road
George's Hill
Columbine Road
Larkspur Wy
Campion Road
Candytuft Green
Sunny Bank
Combined School
Dashfield Gv
Brimmers Hill
Upper Lodge Lane
Brackley Road
Roberts
Western Dene
Lower Lodge
Southfield Dr
Cherry Way
A4128 CRYERS
Uplands
185
Four Ashes
M3 1 The Lincolns
L8 1 Harebell Wk
L7 1 Lavender Wy
K5 1 St Margarets Cl
HP15
Cedar Park School
First School
The Warren
Clauds Cl
Hill Avenue
Swallow Drive

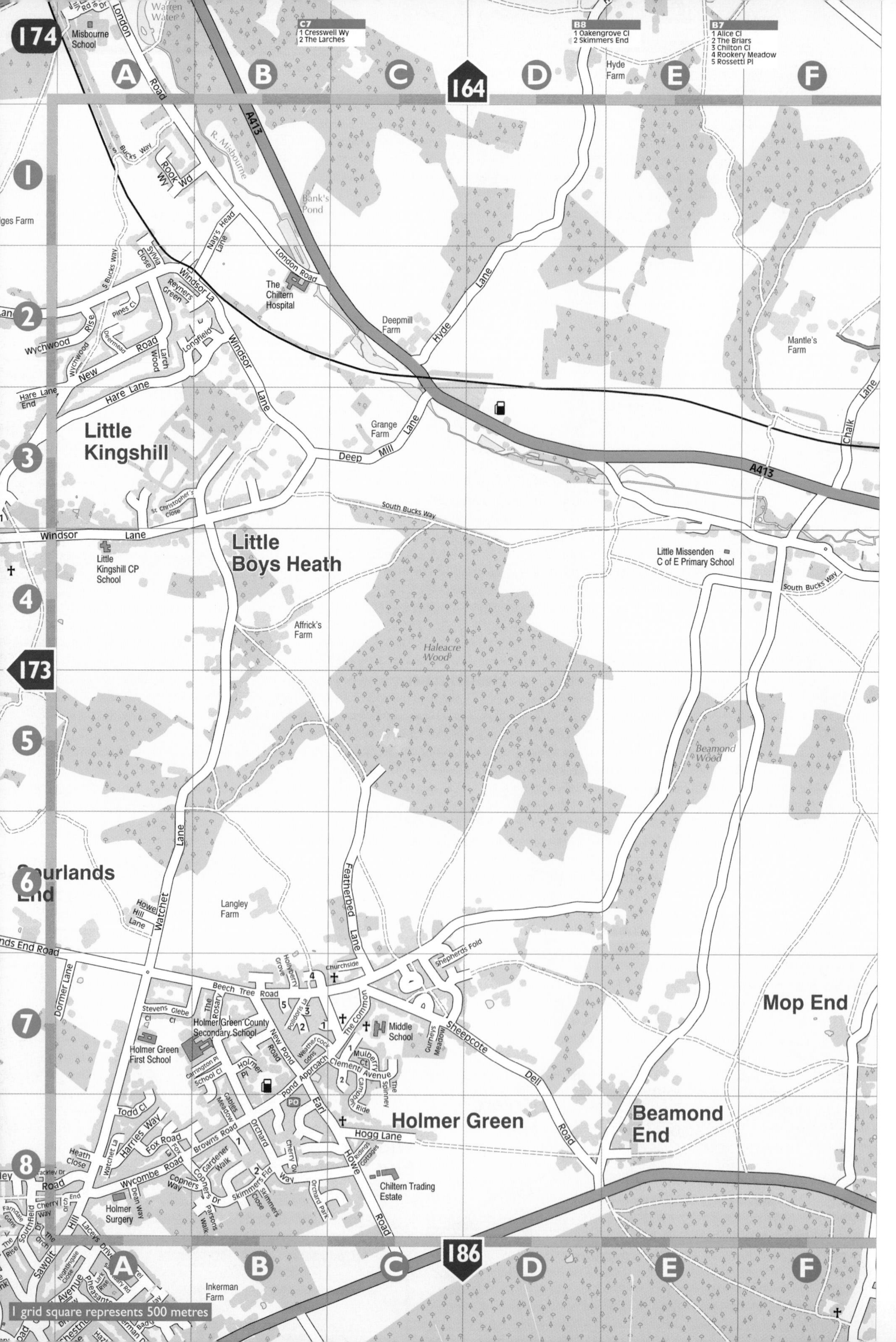
174
Misbourne School
London Road
Warren Water
C7
1 Cresswell Wy
2 The Larches
B8
1 Oakengrove Cl
2 Skimmers End
B7
1 Alice Cl
2 The Briars
3 Chilton Cl
4 Rookery Meadow
5 Rossetti Pl
Hyde Farm
164
A413
R. Misbourne
Bucks Way
Rook Wy
Wd
Bank's Pond
Nag's Head Lane
Sylvia Close
S Bucks Way
London Road
The Chiltern Hospital
Reyners Green
Windsor La
Pines Cl
Wychwood Rise
Deermead
New Road
Larch Wood
Longfield
Windsor Lane
Deepmill Farm
Hyde Lane
Mantle's Farm
Hare Lane End
Hare Lane
Little Kingshill
Grange Farm
Deep Mill Lane
Chalk Lane
St Christopher's Close
South Bucks Way
Windsor Lane
Little Kingshill CP School
Little Boys Heath
Little Missenden C of E Primary School
South Bucks Way
Affrick's Farm
Haleacre Wood
173
Beamond Wood
Spurlands End
Howe Hill Lane
Watchet Lane
Langley Farm
Featherbed Lane
Shepherds Fold
Dormer Lane
Churchside
Hollyberry Grove
Beech Tree Road
Stevens Cl
Glebe Cl
The Rosary
Holmer Green County Secondary School
Polidoris La
The Common
Middle School
Gurneys Meadow
Sheepcote Dell Road
Mop End
Holmer Green First School
Carrington Pl
School Cl
Holmer Pl
New Pond Road
Pond Approach
Weathercock Gdns
Mulberry Ct
Clementi Avenue
Campion Ride
The Spinney
Todd Cl
Cables Meadow
Earl Howe Road
Holmer Green
Beamond End
Harries Way
Fox Road
Browns Road
Orchard
Hogg Lane
Heath Close
Watchet La
Gardener Walk
Cherry Tree Way
Ridings Cottages
Wycombe Road
Copners Way
Copners Dr
Skimmers Fld
Skimmers Close
Orchard Park
Chiltern Trading Estate
Holmer Surgery
Dean Way
Parsons Walk
Cherry Way
Orch End
Hill
Laceys Drive
Southfield
Sawpit
The Rise
Pheasant
Avenue
186
Inkerman Farm
1 grid square represents 500 metres

H2
1 Meadow Wy
2 Stonecroft
White's Wood
165
Hydeheath Common
Hyde Heath
Hyde Heath County First School
Bullbaiters Lane
Bromley
Heath Rd
Brays Lane
Cedars Ridge
Saunders End
Brays Meadow
Westfield
Harvest Bank
Walnut Way
Brays Close
Brays Green Lane
White House Farm
Fuller's Hill
Weedon Hill Farm
Weedon Hill
Mayhall Farm
Deep Acres
The Willows
Bois Avenue
Weedonhill Wood
Amersham & Chiltern Rugby Club
Weedon Lane
Ash Grove
Windmill Wood
Woodfield Park
Berry Fld
Butlers Close
Reddin Drive
Lime Farm
Little Missenden
River Misbourne
South Bucks Way
A413
176
Mantles Green
School Lane
Amersham Town Football Club
High St
Mill Lane
Hawker Galleries
Coldmoreham Yard
Little Shardeloes
High Street
Shardeloes
Cherry Lane
Amersham Old Town
The Plat
Shardeloes Farm
Whielden
South Buckinghamshire NHS Trust
Woodrow High House
Second Wood
Whielden Lane
187
Curzon C of E Primary Sch
School La
Chancellors
Penn Street
Woodrow
HP7
A404

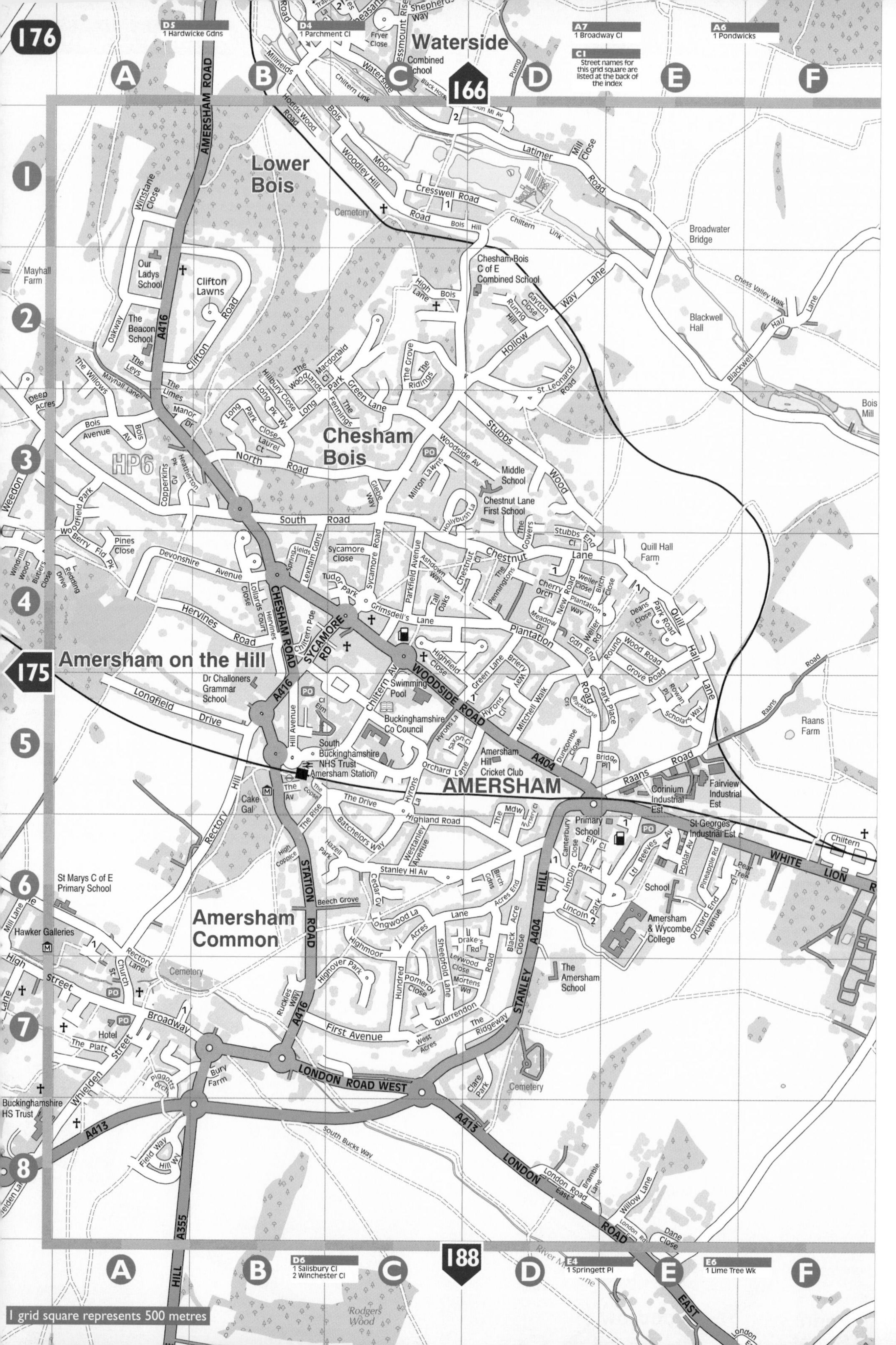
D5
1 Hardwicke Gdns
D4
1 Parchment Cl
A7
1 Broadway Cl
C1
Street names for this grid square are listed at the back of the index
A6
1 Pondwicks
Waterside
Combined School
166
Shepherds Way
Fryer Close
Millfields
Hodds Wood Road
Chiltern Link
Lower Bois
AMERSHAM ROAD
Winstane Close
Woodley Hill
Moor
Cresswell Road
Latimer
Mill Close
Road
Bois Hill
Chiltern Link
Cemetery
Broadwater Bridge
Mayhall Farm
Our Ladys School
Clifton Lawns
Clifton Road
Chesham Bois C of E Combined School
High Lane
Bois
Cayton Close
Runrig Hill
Hollow Way Lane
Chess Valley Walk
Blackwell Hall
Hall Lane
Blackwell
The Beacon School
Oakway
A416
The Leys
The Willows
Mayhall Lane
Deep Acres
The Limes
Manor Dr
Bois Avenue
Bois Av
Hillbury Close
The Woodlands
Macdonald Cl
Park
Long Pk Wy
Long Park Close
Laurel Ct
Green Lane
The Grove
The Ridings
The Fennings
St Leonards Road
Stubbs
Bois Mill
Chesham Bois
HP6
North Road
Heatherton Pk
Copperkins Ln
Weedon
Woodfield Park
Woodside Av
Milton Lawns
Middle School
Chestnut Lane First School
Hollybush La
Glebe Way
Wood
South Road
Berry Fld Pk
Pines Close
Windmill Wood
Butlers Close
Reading Drive
Devonshire Avenue
Lollards Close
Springfields
Lexham Gdns
Sycamore Close
Sycamore Road
Parkfield Avenue
Ashdown Way
Chestnut Cl
The Gowers
Stubbs Cl
Stubbs End
Chestnut Lane
Quill Hall Farm
The Penningtons
Cherry Orch
New Road
Weller Close
Birch Close
Plantation Way
Deans Close
Park Road
Quill Hall Lane
Hervines Road
Hervines Court
CHESHAM ROAD
Tudor Park
Grimsdell's Lane
Tall Oaks
Meadow Dr
Weller Rd
Plantation Gdn End
Round Wood Road
Grove Road
Rowan Way
Scholars Way
Amersham on the Hill
175
Chiltern Pde
SYCAMORE RD
Highfield Close
Green Lane
Briery Way
Hyrons Cl
Mitchell Walk
Blackhorse Cres
Park Place
Dr Challoners Grammar School
Longfield Drive
Hill Avenue
Elm Cl
Chiltern Av
WOODSIDE ROAD
Swimming Pool
Buckinghamshire Co Council
Hyrons La
Saxon Cl
Duncombe Close
Raans Road
Raans Farm
South Buckinghamshire NHS Trust
Amersham Station
Amersham Hill Cricket Club
A404
Orchard Lane
Bridge Pl
Corinium Industrial Est
Fairview Industrial Est
Rectory Hill
Cake Gal
The Av
The Copse
The Drive
Hyrons La
AMERSHAM
The Mdw
Nursery Cl
Primary School
St Georges Industrial Est
Chiltern
WHITE LION
The Rise
Highland Road
Hazell Park
Batchelors Way
Westanley Avenue
High Coppice
STATION ROAD
Stanley Hl Av
Birch Gdns
Canterbury Close
Ely Cl
Lincoln Park
Ltl Reeves Av
Poplar Av
Pineapple Rd
Pear Tree Cl
St Marys C of E Primary School
Beech Grove
Cedar Gv
Acres End
HILL
School
Orchard End Avenue
Amersham Common
Hawker Galleries
Mill Lane
Longwood La
Acres
Lane
Drake's Rd
Sheepfold Lane
Black Acre Close
Lincoln Park
Amersham & Wycombe College
Highmoor
Leywood Close
Mortens Wd
Road
A404
The Amersham School
High Street
Rectory Lane
Church St
Cemetery
Highover Park
Hundred Acres
Pomeroy Close
STANLEY
Broadway
Ruckles Way
A416
Quarrendon
The Ridgeway
Hotel
The Platt
Street
First Avenue
West Acres
Bury Farm
Piggotts Orch
LONDON ROAD WEST
Clare Park
Cemetery
Buckinghamshire HS Trust
Whielden Street
A413
A413
South Bucks Way
Field Way
Hill Wy
LONDON
London Road East
Bramble Lane
Willow Lane
ROAD
London Rd
Dane Close
A355
HILL
D6
1 Salisbury Cl
2 Winchester Cl
188
E4
1 Springett Pl
E6
1 Lime Tree Wk
EAST
Rodgers Wood
Whielden La
London
1 grid square represents 500 metres

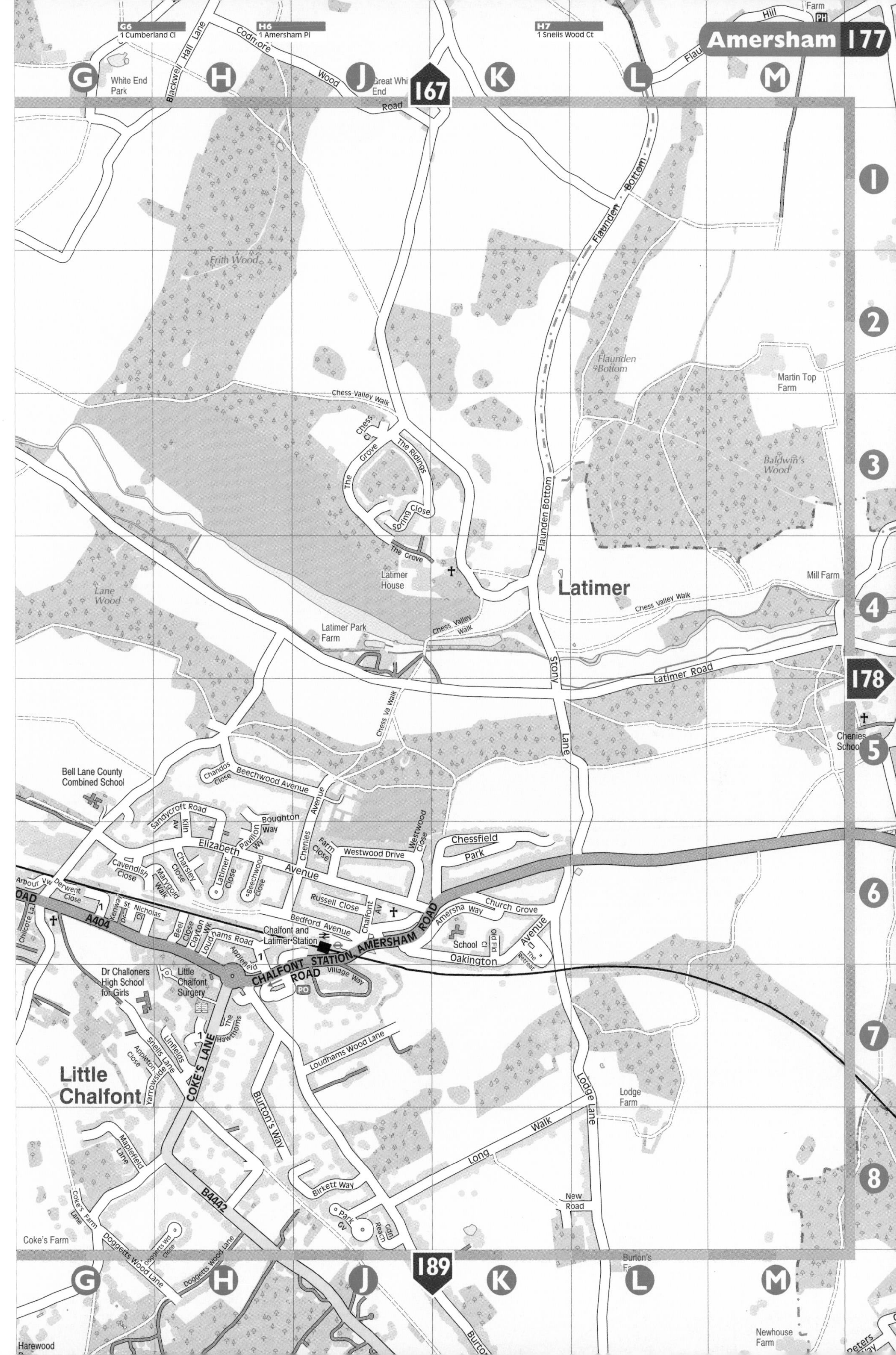
G6
1 Cumberland Cl
H6
1 Amersham Pl
H7
1 Snells Wood Ct
White End Park
Blackwell Hall Lane
Codmore Wood Road
Great Whi End
167
Flaunden Bottom
Frith Wood
Flaunden Bottom
Martin Top Farm
Chess Valley Walk
Chess Cl
The Grove
The Ridings
Spring Close
Baldwin's Wood
The Grove
Latimer House
Latimer
Mill Farm
Lane Wood
Chess Valley Walk
Latimer Park Farm
Chess Valley Walk
Stony Lane
Latimer Road
178
Chess Va Walk
Chenies School
Bell Lane County Combined School
Chandos Close
Beechwood Avenue
Chenies Avenue
Sandycroft Road
Kiln Av
Boughton Way
Pavilion Wy
Elizabeth Avenue
Westwood Close
Chessfield Park
Cavendish Close
Charsley Close
Marigold Walk
Latimer Close
Beechwood Close
Farm Close
Westwood Drive
Arbour Vw
Derwent Close
Kenway Dr
St Nicholas Cl
Russell Close
Chalfont Av
Church Grove
Amersha Way
ROAD
A404
Chilcote La
Beel Close
Clayton Wk
Loudhams Road
Bedford Avenue
Chalfont and Latimer Station
Appletield
AMERSHAM ROAD
School
Old Fld Cl
Avenue
The Retreat
Oakington
CHALFONT STATION ROAD
Village Way
PO
Dr Challoners High School for Girls
Little Chalfont Surgery
The Hawthorns
Linfields
Snells Lane
Appleton Close
Yarrowside
COKE'S LANE
Loudhams Wood Lane
Little Chalfont
Burton's Way
Lodge Lane
Lodge Farm
Long Walk
Maplefield Lane
B4442
Birkett Way
Park Gv
Gdn Reach
New Road
Coke's Farm Lane
Coke's Farm
Doggetts Wood Lane
Doggetts Wd Close
Doggetts Wood Lane
189
Burton's Fa
Harewood
Newhouse Farm
G
H
J
K
L
M
1
2
3
4
5
6
7
8

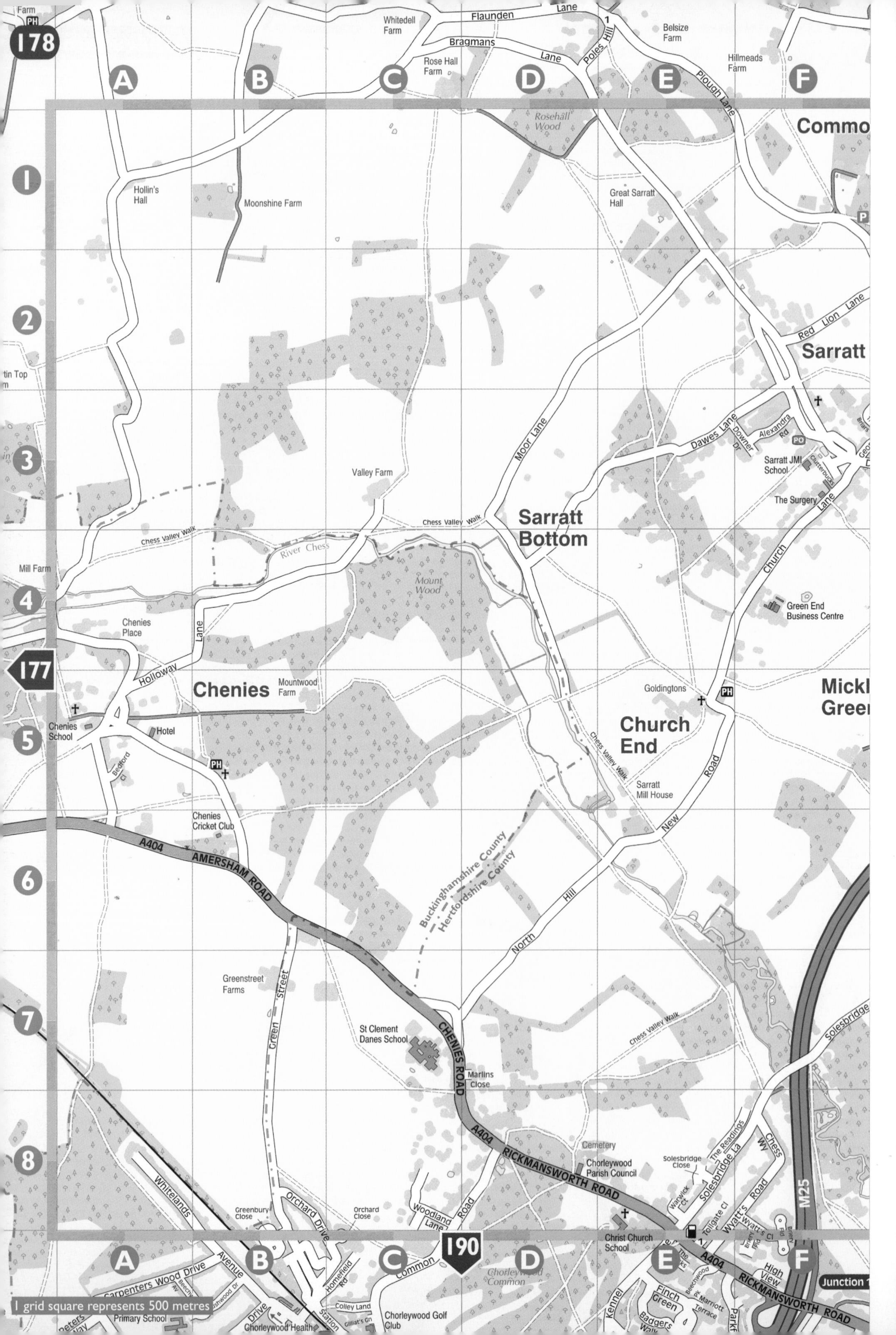
178
177
190
Whitedell Farm
Flaunden Lane
Bragmans Lane
Rose Hall Farm
Poles Hill
Belsize Farm
Hillmeads Farm
Plough Lane
Rosehall Wood
Common
Hollin's Hall
Moonshine Farm
Great Sarratt Hall
Red Lion Lane
Sarratt
Moor Lane
Dawes Lane
Downer Dr
Alexandra Rd
PO
Sarratt JMI School
The Surgery
Church Lane
Valley Farm
Chess Valley Walk
Sarratt Bottom
River Chess
Mount Wood
Mill Farm
Green End Business Centre
Chenies Place
Lane
Holloway
Chenies
Mountwood Farm
Goldingtons
PH
Church End
Chenies School
Hotel
Bedford
Chess Valley Walk
Sarratt Mill House
New Road
Chenies Cricket Club
A404 AMERSHAM ROAD
Buckinghamshire County
Hertfordshire County
North Hill
Greenstreet Farms
Green Street
St Clement Danes School
CHENIES ROAD
Chess Valley Walk
Solesbridge
Marlins Close
M25
A404 RICKMANSWORTH ROAD
Cemetery
Chorleywood Parish Council
Solesbridge Close
The Readings
Solesbridge La
Chess Wy
Warwick Ct
Whitelands
Greenbury Close
Orchard Drive
Orchard Close
Woodland Lane
Road
Tollgate Cl
Wyatt's Road
Wyatt's Cl
Christ Church School
Carpenters Wood Drive
Avenue
Common
Homefield Rd
Chorleywood Common
High View
Junction
Finch Green
Marriott Terrace
Kennel
Parkf
Badgers Walk
Colley Land
Chorleywood Golf Club
Primary School
Chorleywood Health
Station
1 grid square represents 500 metres

Quickmoor Lane
Baytree Farm
Jeffery's Farm
Berrybushes Wood
Model Farm
Bucks Hill
Great Westwood
Old House Lane
Bottom Lane
Deadman's Ash Lane
Caroon Drive
Buck's Hill Bottom
Tom's Hill
Newhall Farm
Junction 19
Templepan Lane
Yew Court Farm
White House
Chandler's Lane
M25
White Shack Lane
Fir Tree Hill
Chandler's Cross
Sarratt Road
Rousebarn Lane
Redhall Lane
Harrocks Wood
Redhall
Solesbridge Lane
Sarratt Lane
Cherry Walk
Beechengrove Wood
Redheath
York House School
Ladywood Close
Whisper Wood
Loudwater Hts
Bridle Lane
Lower Plantation
Wagon Way
Trout Rise
Cherry Hl
Farm La
River Chess
Loudwater
Waterdell House
Little Green Lane
Thurlwood House
Little Green CP School
Sarratt Lane
Lodge Dr
Timber Rdg
Rooks Hill
Arm Close
Chess Cl
Chess Hill
Loudwater Lane
Croxley Green
Loudwater Drive
Troutstream
Overstream
Dugdale
Lovatts
Grove Crs
Baldwins Lane
Whitegates Cl
Manor Way
Lincoln Way
Rochester Way
191
G
H
J
K
L
M
1
2
3
4
5
6
7
8

168
Hill Farm
Hill Ro
Nature Reserv
M40
Hailey Wood
Upper Vicar's Farm
Lower Vicar's Farm
Cowleaze Wood
Lydall's Wood
Wellground Farm
Shirburn Wood
Portobello Farm
Wormsley Park
Buckinghamshire County
Oxfordshire County
Shirburn Lodge
Hungryhill Wood
Shotridge Wood
Portways
Blackmoor Wood
Hale Wood
Northend
Launder's Farm
Queen Wood
192
A
B
C
D
E
F
1
2
3
4
5
6
7
8
1 grid square represents 500 metres

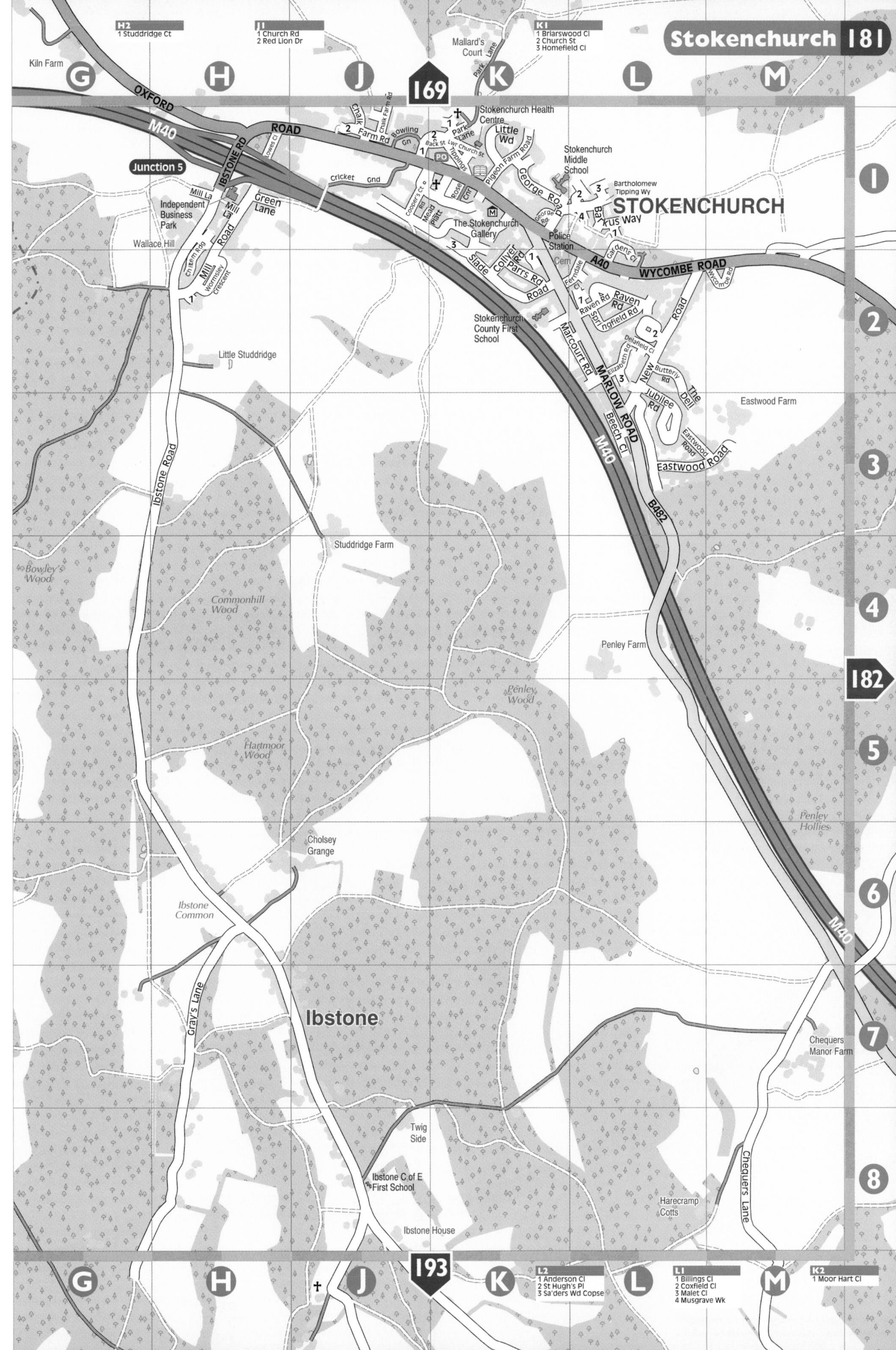
H2
1 Studdridge Ct
J1
1 Church Rd
2 Red Lion Dr
K1
1 Briarswood Cl
2 Church St
3 Homefield Cl
169
182
193
L2
1 Anderson Cl
2 St Hugh's Pl
3 Sa'ders Wd Copse
L1
1 Billings Cl
2 Coxfield Cl
3 Malet Cl
4 Musgrave Wk
K2
1 Moor Hart Cl
Kiln Farm
Mallard's Court
Park Lane
Stokenchurch Health Centre
OXFORD ROAD
M40
Junction 5
IBSTONE RD
Chalk Farm Rd
Bowling Gn
Back St
Lwr Church St
Tippings
Little Wd
Pigeon Farm Road
Stokenchurch Middle School
Bartholomew Tipping Wy
STOKENCHURCH
Barkus Way
George Road
Mill La
Independent Business Park
Green Lane
Cricket Gnd
Cooper's Ct
Mead Platt
Rose Cnr
The Stokenchurch Gallery
Police Station
Wallace Hill
Chiltern Rdg
Mill Road
Wormsley Crescent
Slade
Collyer Rd
Parrs Rd
Road
Cem
A40
WYCOMBE ROAD
Gardens Cl
Ferndale Cl
Raven Rd
Springfield Rd
Stokenchurch County First School
Marcourt Rd
MARLOW ROAD
Delafield Cl
Elizabeth Rd
New Road
Buttery Rd
The Dell
Jubilee Rd
Eastwood Farm
Beech Cl
Eastwood Road
Little Studdridge
Ibstone Road
B482
Studdridge Farm
Bowley's Wood
Commonhill Wood
Penley Farm
Penley Wood
Hartmoor Wood
Penley Hollies
Cholsey Grange
Ibstone Common
Gray's Lane
Ibstone
Chequers Manor Farm
Twig Side
Ibstone C of E First School
Harecramp Cotts
Chequers Lane
Ibstone House
G
H
J
K
L
M
1
2
3
4
5
6
7
8

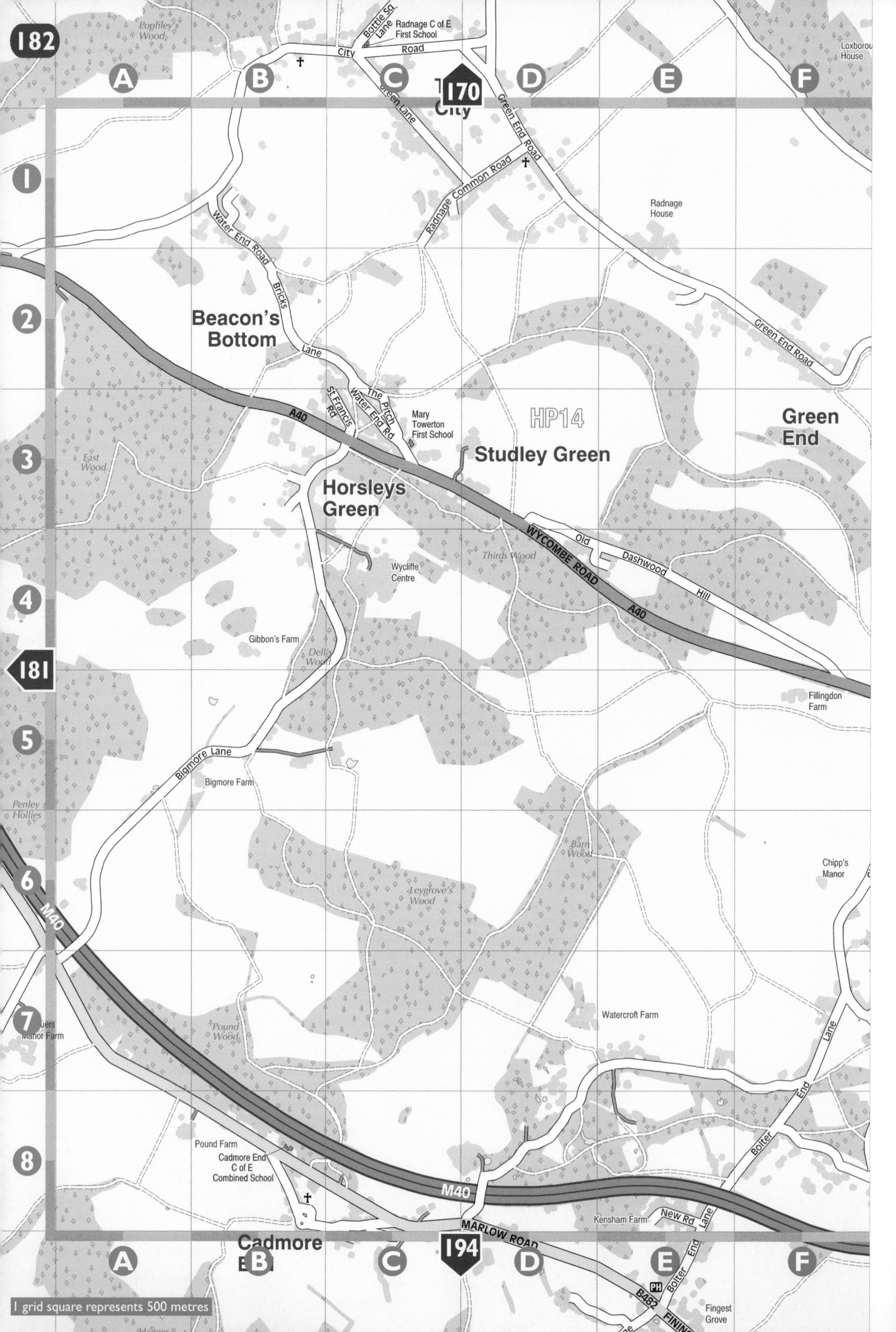
182
170
181
194
A
B
C
D
E
F
1
2
3
4
5
6
7
8
Poptley's Wood
Radnage C of E First School
Bottle Sq.
Lane
City
Road
Green Lane
City
Green End Road
Radnage Common Road
Loxborough House
Radnage House
Water End Road
Bricks
Lane
Beacon's Bottom
Green End Road
St Francis Rd
The Pitch
Water End Rd
A40
Mary Towerton First School
HP14
Green End
Studley Green
East Wood
Horsleys Green
WYCOMBE ROAD
Old
Dashwood
Hill
Thirds Wood
Wycliffe Centre
A40
Gibbon's Farm
Dell's Wood
Fillingdon Farm
Bigmore Lane
Bigmore Farm
Penley Hollies
Barn Wood
Chipp's Manor
M40
Leygrove's Wood
Watercroft Farm
Manor Farm
Pound Wood
Lane
End
Bolter
Pound Farm
Cadmore End C of E Combined School
M40
Kensham Farm
New Rd
Lane
MARLOW ROAD
Cadmore End
Bolter End
PH
B482
Fingest Grove
1 grid square represents 500 metres

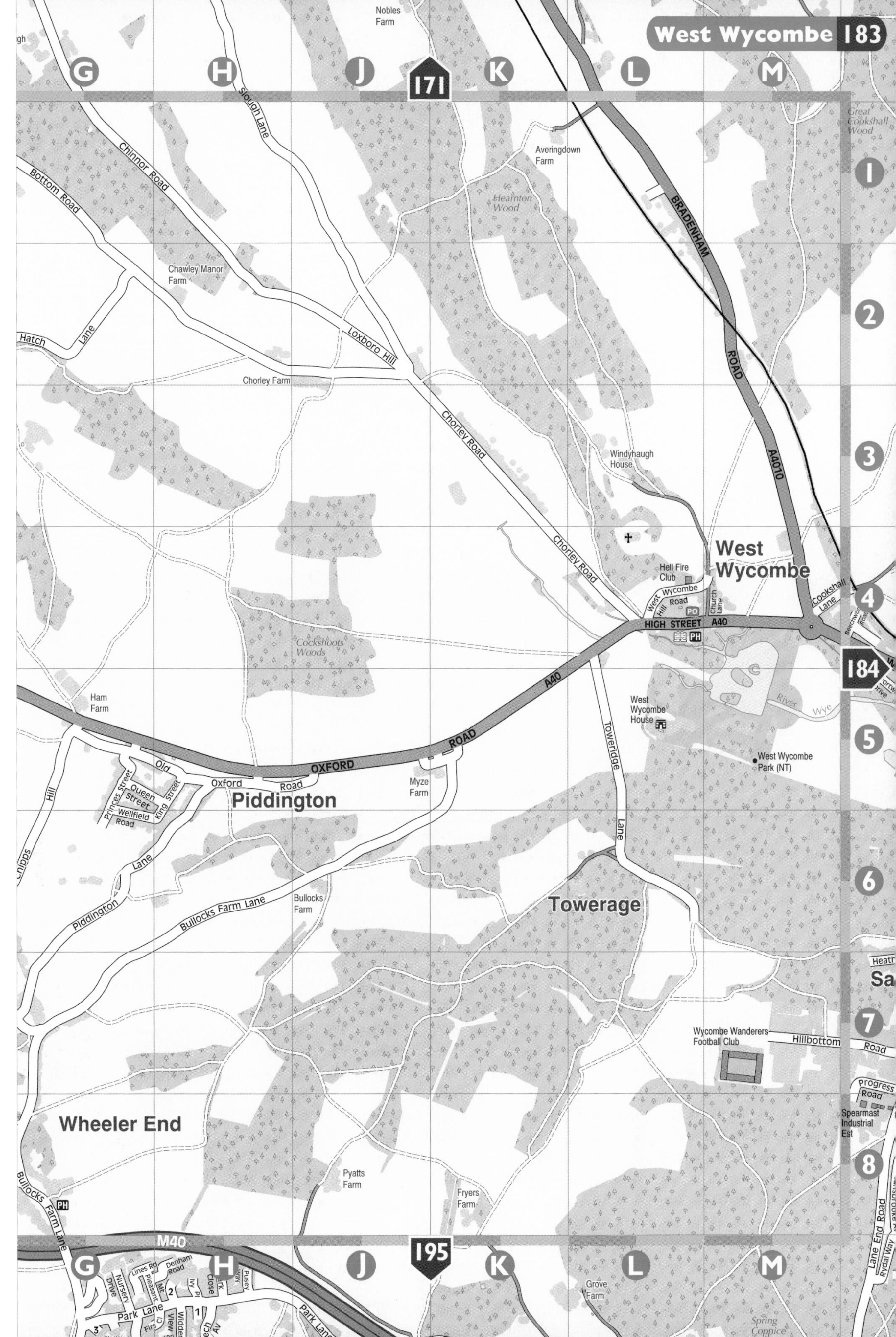
G
H
J
K
L
M
171
195
184
1
2
3
4
5
6
7
8
Nobles Farm
Great Cookshall Wood
Averingdown Farm
Hearnton Wood
Chinnor Road
Bottom Road
Slough Lane
BRADENHAM ROAD
A4010
Chawley Manor Farm
Hatch Lane
Loxboro Hill
Chorley Farm
Chorley Road
Windyhaugh House
West Wycombe
Hell Fire Club
West Wycombe Hill Road
Church Lane
Cookshall Lane
HIGH STREET A40
Cockshoots Woods
A40
OXFORD ROAD
Ham Farm
West Wycombe House
River Wye
West Wycombe Park (NT)
Toweridge Lane
Old Oxford Road
Princes Street
Queen Street
King Street
Wellfield Road
Piddington
Myze Farm
Chipps Hill
Piddington Lane
Bullocks Farm Lane
Bullocks Farm
Towerage
Wycombe Wanderers Football Club
Hillbottom Road
Progress Road
Spearmast Industrial Est
Wheeler End
Pyatts Farm
Fryers Farm
Bullocks Farm Lane
M40
Lines Rd
Denham Road
Nursery Drive
Pleasant
Ivy Pl
Close
Pusey Way
Park Lane
View
Widden
Grove Farm
Spring Coppice
Lane End Road
Rydal Way

D5
1 The Acres
C7
1 Bevelwood Gdns
2 Whitelands Wy
B8
1 The Middleway
C3
Street names for these grid squares are listed at the back of the index
B6
1 Applewick La
A
B
C
D
E
F
1
2
3
4
5
6
7
8
172
183
196
Hunts Hill
Great Cookshall Wood
Cookshall Farm
Common Wood
Downley Common
Downley
Wycombe West School
Hughendon Manor (NT)
Manor Farm
Church Farm
Common Side
Coates Lane
Plomer Green
Moor Lane
High St
Chapel St
School Close
Narrow Lane
Littleworth Road
Jubilee Rd
Turners Field
The Downley School
Avery Avenue
Plomer Green Av
Gray's Lane
South View
Sunny Croft
Talbot Avenue
Curlew Close
Partridge Way
Kestrel Close
Pheasant Drive
Lyndhurst Close
Westover Road
Plomer Hill
Old Farm Road
Hillfield Close
Downs Park
Hithercroft
Tinkers Wood Road
The Pastures
Tinkers Wood CP School
Wyndham Av
Calverley Crescent
Disraeli Crs
Coates La
Tancred Road
Rennie Close
Telford Way
Hinton Close
Hughenden Avenue
Fulton Close
Disraeli County Combined School
Kelvin Close
Garratts Way
Gibbs Cl
Mendip Way
Cumbrian Way
Brecon Way
Cotswold Way
Malvern Cl
Middlebrook Road
Southfield Road
White Close
Merry Down
WEST WYCOMBE ROAD
A40
Floras Temple
Copperfields
CHAPEL LANE A4010
Gilletts Lane
Sands County Middle School
Fryers Lane
Birches Rise
Pilot Trading Est
Parkhouse Business Centre
Eaton Avenue
Grafton Street
Dashwood Works Industrial Cen
Desborough Park Road
Abercromby Avenue
Dashwood Av
Mill End Road
Gallows Lane
Heathfield
Sands
Stanley Road
Sands County First School
Pinewood Road
Hylton Road
Combe Rise
Hillbottom Road
Lane End Road
Roundwood Road
Barn Court
NEW ROAD
Britannia Ind Park
Ogilvie Road
Copyground Lane
Lindsay Av
Riverside Business Cen
Wye Valley Surg
Riverside Surg
Avocet Trading Est
First School
Doctors Surg
Desborough Road
West End Road
Kitchener Road
Berber Business Cen
Oakridge Road
Oakridge CP School
Plumer Road
Wendover Street
Suffield Road
Newlands Bus Station
Buckinghamshire Coll
OXFORD ROAD
A40 ABBEY WAY
Central Park Business Cen
Bellfield Road
Progress Road
Spearmast Ind Park
Spearmast Industrial Est
Warwick Av
Highwood Crs
Mentmore Rd
Booker Hill Combined School
Castlefield School
HP12
Lincolns Park Business Cen
Desborough Avenue
Colville Road
The Chimes
Deeds Grove
Baronsmead Road
Kingsley Crs
Alexandra Road
Wycombe General Hospital
A&E
Rutland Avenue
Booker Lane
Whitelands Road
Carrington Road
Cross Road
Spearing Road
Chiltern Av
England Way
Pettifer Way
Crusader Industrial Est
College
D7
1 Copy Ground Ct
E7
1 Cedar Ter
2 George St
3 Mill St
4 Richardson St
F7
1 Queen Sq
2 Ship St
1 grid square represents 500 metres

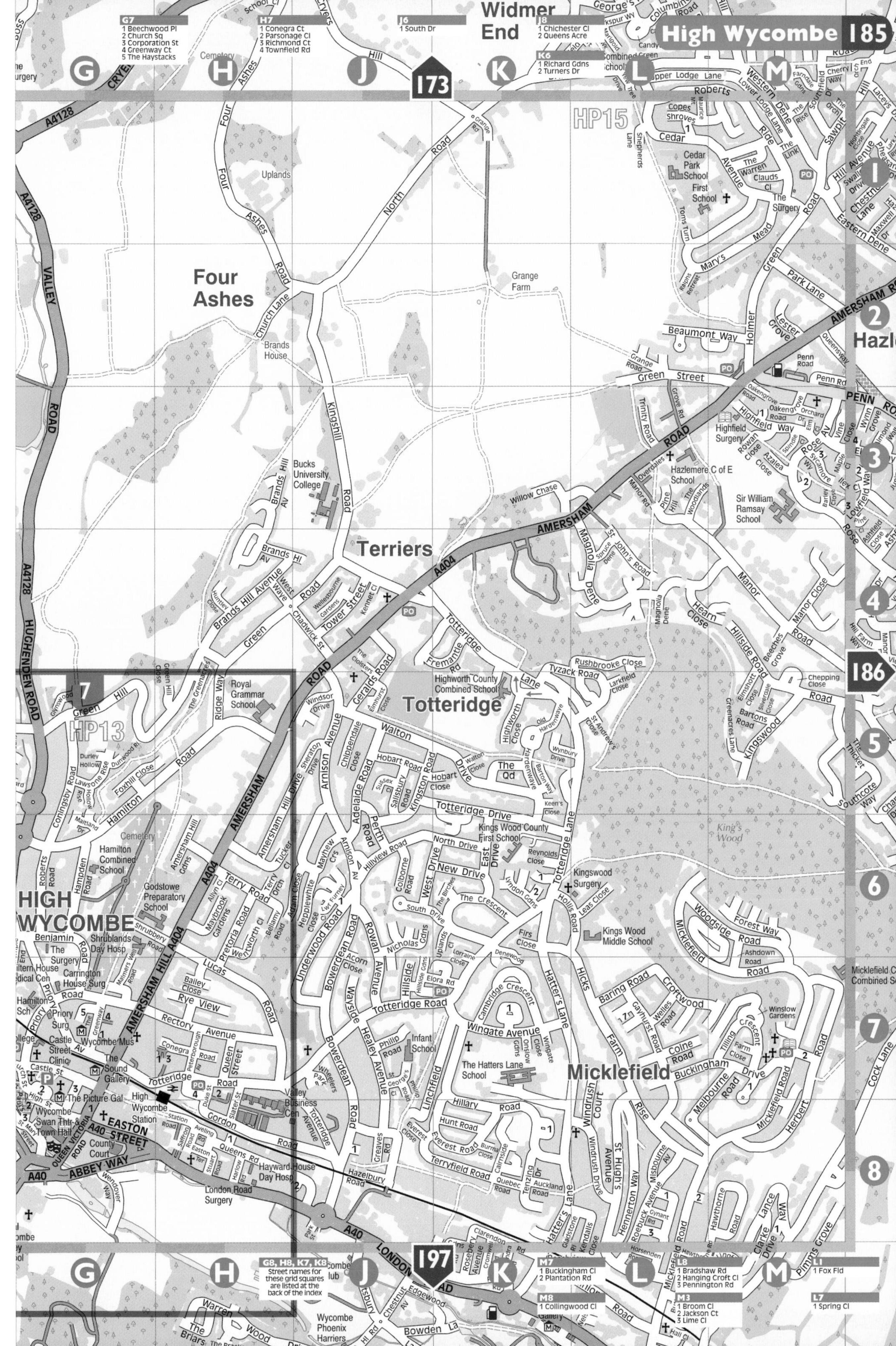
G7
1 Beechwood Pl
2 Church Sq
3 Corporation St
4 Greenway Ct
5 The Haystacks
H7
1 Conegra Ct
2 Parsonage Cl
3 Richmond Ct
4 Townfield Rd
J6
1 South Dr
Widmer End
J8
1 Chichester Cl
2 Queens Acre
K6
1 Richard Gdns
2 Turners Dr
173
HP15
Four Ashes
Uplands
Grange Farm
Brands House
Bucks University College
Terriers
A4128
VALLEY ROAD
HUGHENDEN ROAD
AMERSHAM ROAD
A404
Cedar Park School
First School
The Surgery
Highfield Surgery
Hazlemere C of E School
Sir William Ramsay School
Penn Road
PENN RD
Hazl
186
Totteridge
Highworth County Combined School
Royal Grammar School
HP13
Hamilton Combined School
Cemetery
Godstowe Preparatory School
HIGH WYCOMBE
Shrublands Day Hosp
Carrington House Surg
Wycombe Mus
The Sound Gallery
The Picture Gal
High Wycombe Station
Wycombe Swan Thtr & Town Hall
County Court
EASTON STREET
A40
ABBEY WAY
Hayward House Day Hosp
London Road Surgery
Valley Business Cen
Kings Wood County First School
Kingswood Surgery
Kings Wood Middle School
King's Wood
Micklefield
Micklefield Combined Sch
The Hatters Lane School
Infant School
LONDON ROAD
197
G8, H8, K7, K8
Street names for these grid squares are listed at the back of the index
M7
1 Buckingham Cl
2 Plantation Rd
M8
1 Collingwood Cl
L8
1 Bradshaw Rd
2 Hanging Croft Cl
3 Pennington Rd
M3
1 Broom Cl
2 Jackson Ct
3 Lime Cl
L1
1 Fox Fld
L7
1 Spring Cl
Wycombe Phoenix Harriers

186
174
185
198
Hazlemere
Tylers Green
Penn Bottom
Penn
Beacon Hill
Penn Wood
Common Wood
Inkerman Farm
Hazlemere Golf & Country Club
Puttenham Place Farm
Chiltern Trading
B6
1 Glebelands
2 Katherine Cl
3 St Margaret's Cl
4 Stretton Cl
B4
1 Coppice Farm Rd
2 Curzon Cl
A7
1 Greenridge
A3
1 Briarswood
2 Cornel Cl
3 Lowfield Cl
4 Redwood Cl
AMERSHAM ROAD
A404
PENN ROAD
B474
HAZLEMERE ROAD
ELM ROAD
CHURCH ROAD
WITHERIDGE
Middle School
Tylers Green County Junior School
Tylers Green County First School
Penn School
Micklefield County Combined School
Penn Surgery
Cemetery
Penbury Grove
Underwood
Town Farm
Parsonage Farm
1 grid square represents 500 metres

175
188
199
HP7
Penn Street
Woodrow
Winchmore Hill
Coleshill
Knotty Green
Curzon C of E Primary School
School Lane
Chancellors
Winchmore Hill Cricket Club
Penn House
Nelson Cl
The Hill
Pond Close
Coleshill Lane
Fagnall Farm
Glory Farm
Whielden Lane
WHIELDEN LANE A404
New Road
Coleshill House
Chase Close
Tower Road
Meadow Hl
Village Road
Meadow Cott Lane
Coleshill C of E First School
Barracks Hill
Sampsons Hill
Chalk Hill
Windmill Hl
Rushymead
Luckings Farm
Hertfordshire House
Magpie Lane
Bowers Farm
Ongar Hill Farm
Marrod's Bottom
Great Beard's Wood
Seagrave's Farm
Witheridge Wood
Second Wood
LANE
B474
Drews Pk
Alfriston School
Latimer Way
Woodchester Pk
Shrimpton Close
Shrimpton Rd
Berkley Rd
Natwoke Close
The Grange
Brown's Wood
AMERSHAM ROAD
A355
Birchen Spring
Red Farm
Finch La
Knottocks Close
Knottocks Drive
Old Farm Cl
Oldbury Grove
Wyngrave Place
Road
PENN
Churchill
Upper Drive
Sandelswood
Howe Drive
1 Mynchen End

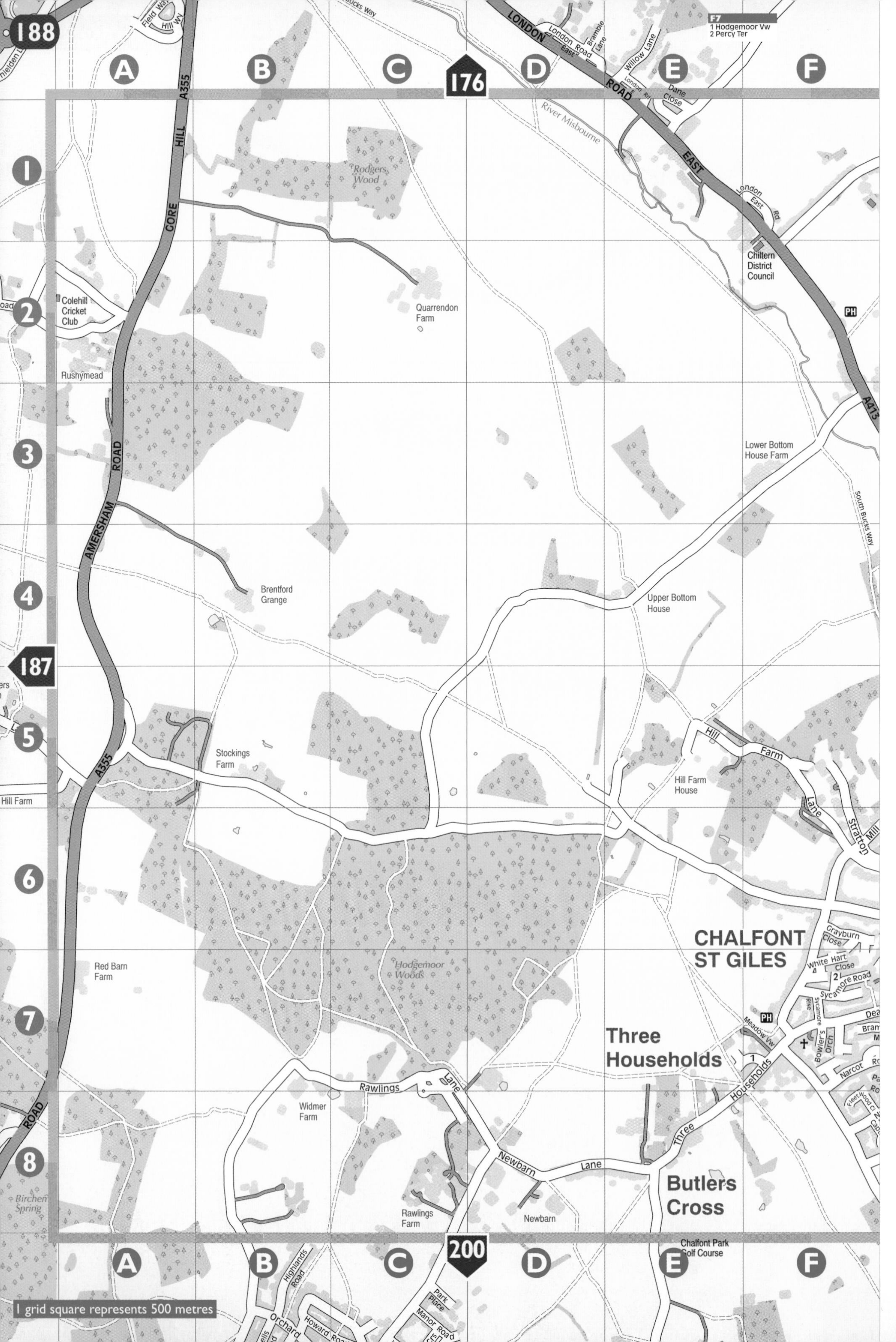

188
176
187
200
A
B
C
D
E
F
1
2
3
4
5
6
7
8
F7
1 Hodgemoor Vw
2 Percy Ter
LONDON
ROAD
EAST
London Road East
Bramble Lane
Willow Lane
Dane Close
River Misbourne
London East Rd
Chiltern District Council
PH
A413
A355
GORE HILL
AMERSHAM ROAD
Colehill Cricket Club
Rushymead
Rodgers Wood
Quarrendon Farm
Brentford Grange
Lower Bottom House Farm
South Bucks Way
Upper Bottom House
Stockings Farm
Hill Farm
Hill Farm Lane
Hill Farm House
Stratton
Mill
CHALFONT ST GILES
Grayburn Close
White Hart Close
Sycamore Road
Sycamore Rise
Bowler's Orch
Meadow Vw
Narcot Rd
Fleetwood Cl
Red Barn Farm
Hodgemoor Woods
Three Households
Rawlings Lane
Widmer Farm
Newbarn Lane
Newbarn
Rawlings Farm
Butlers Cross
Chalfont Park Golf Course
Birchen Spring
Highlands Road
Orchard
Howard Rd
Park Place
Manor Road
1 grid square represents 500 metres

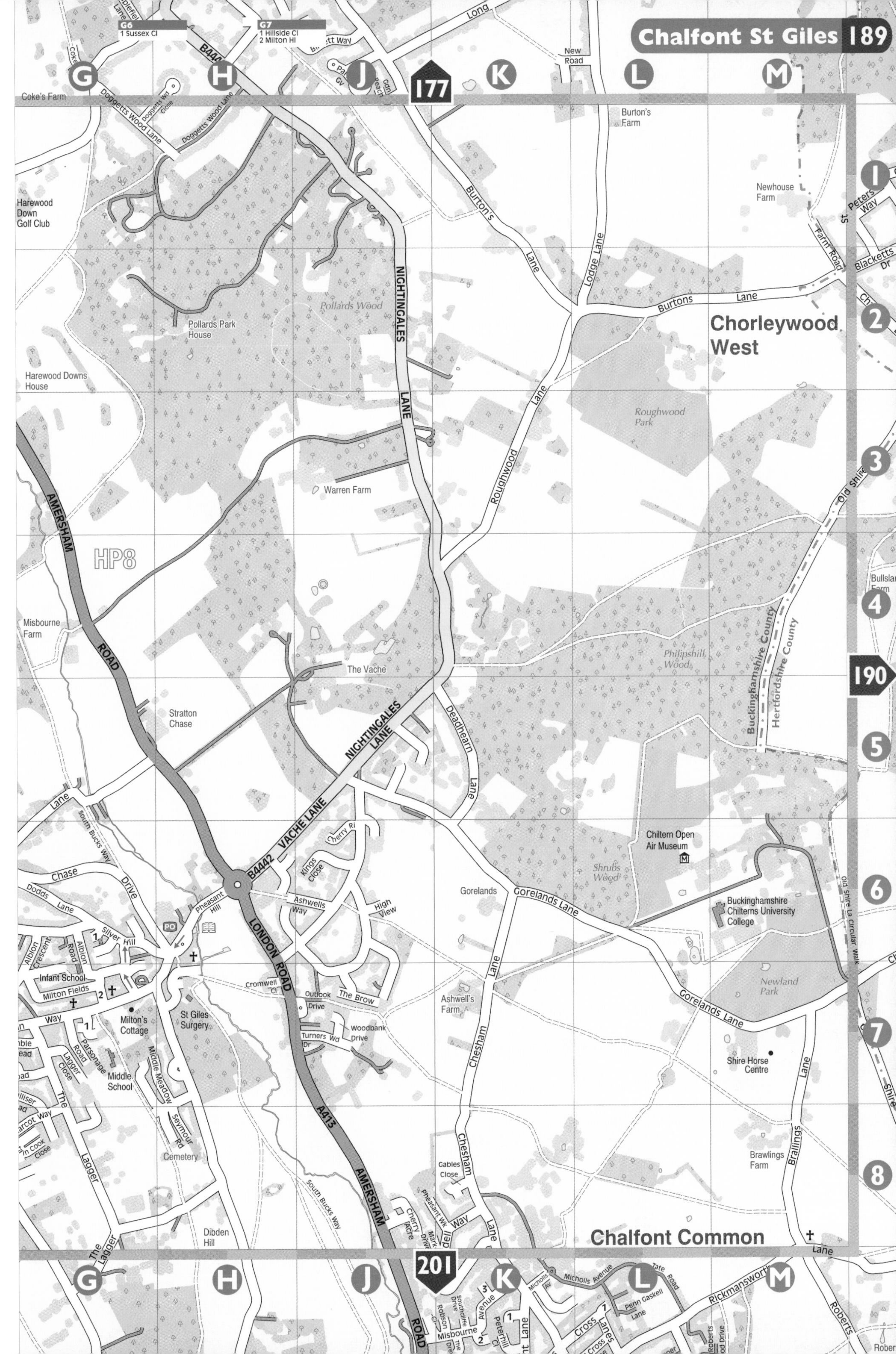

G6
1 Sussex Cl
G7
1 Hillside Cl
2 Milton Hl
G
H
J
K
L
M
177
201
190
1
2
3
4
5
6
7
8
Coke's Farm
Doggetts Wood Lane
Doggetts Wood Close
New Road
Burton's Farm
Newhouse Farm
St Peters Way
Farm Road
Blacketts Dr
Harewood Down Golf Club
Burton's Lane
Lodge Lane
Burtons Lane
Chorleywood West
Pollards Wood
Pollards Park House
Harewood Downs House
NIGHTINGALES LANE
Roughwood Lane
Roughwood Park
Warren Farm
Old Shire
AMERSHAM ROAD
HP8
Bullslan Farm
Misbourne Farm
Philipshill Wood
Buckinghamshire County
Hertfordshire County
The Vache
Stratton Chase
NIGHTINGALES LANE
Deadhearn Lane
B4442 VACHE LANE
Lane
South Bucks Way
Cherry Ri
Kings Close
Chiltern Open Air Museum
Chase
Drive
Dodds Lane
Pheasant Hill
Shrubs Wood
Gorelands
Gorelands Lane
Ashwells Way
High View
Buckinghamshire Chilterns University College
PO
Silver Hill
Albion Crescent
Albion Road
Infant School
Milton Fields
LONDON ROAD
Cromwell Cl
Outlook Drive
The Brow
Chesham Lane
Ashwell's Farm
Newland Park
Gorelands Lane
Old Shire La Circular Walk
Way
Milton's Cottage
St Giles Surgery
Woodbank Drive
Turners Wd Dr
Parsonage Road
Lagger Close
Middle School
Middle Meadow
Shire Horse Centre
Lane
The Lagger
A413
Seymour Rd
Cemetery
AMERSHAM
Chesham
Brawlings Farm
Brawlings Lane
Gables Close
South Bucks Way
Pheasant Wk
Cherry Acre
Dell Way
Chalfont Common
Dibden Hill
The Lagger
ROAD
Micholls Avenue
Micholls Av
Tate Road
Penn Gaskell Lane
Rickmansworth
Roberts Lane
Robson Cl
Southcliffe Drive
Avenue
Peterhill Cl
Misbourne
Cross Lanes
Robert

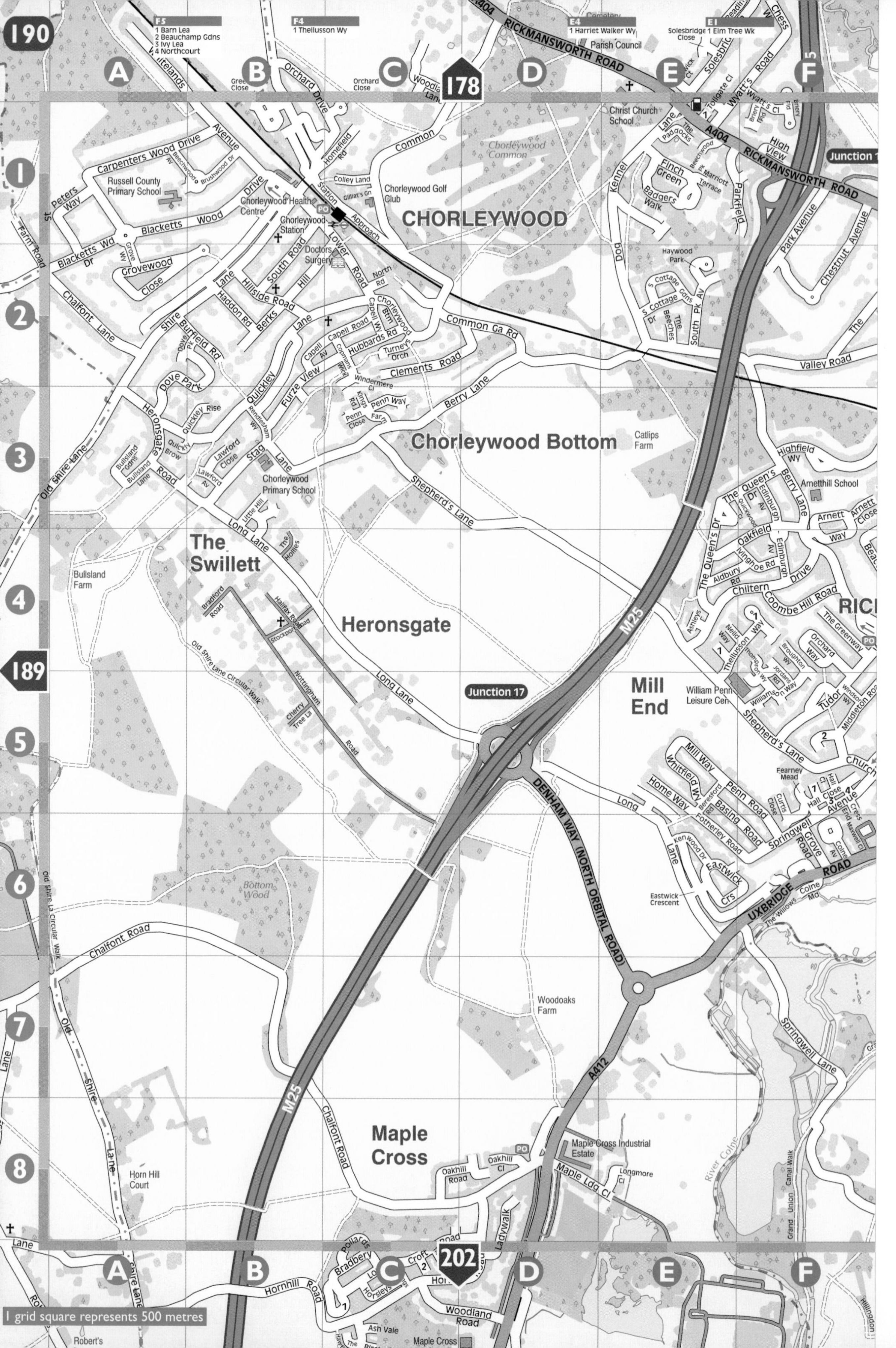

190
F5
1 Barn Lea
2 Beauchamp Gdns
3 Ivy Lea
4 Northcourt
F4
1 Thellusson Wy
E4
1 Harriet Walker Wy
E1
Solesbridge Close
1 Elm Tree Wk
178
189
202
A
B
C
D
E
F
1
2
3
4
5
6
7
8
RICKMANSWORTH ROAD
A404
Parish Council
Christ Church School
Chorleywood Common
Chorleywood Golf Club
CHORLEYWOOD
Russell County Primary School
Chorleywood Health Centre
Chorleywood Station
Doctors Surgery
Carpenters Wood Drive
Blacketts Wood Drive
Grovewood Close
Chalfont Lane
Shire Lane
Hillside Road
South Road
Lower Road
Common Ga Rd
Clements Road
Berry Lane
Dove Park
Quickley Lane
Furze View
Heronsgate Road
Old Shire Lane
Chorleywood Bottom
Catlips Farm
Chorleywood Primary School
Shepherd's Lane
Long Lane
The Swillett
Bullsland Farm
Heronsgate
Nottingham Road
Old Shire Lane Circular Walk
Junction 17
M25
Mill End
William Penn Leisure Cen
Haywood Park
Valley Road
Park Avenue
Chestnut Avenue
Arnetthill School
Chiltern Drive
Coombe Hill Road
Junction 18
DENHAM WAY (NORTH ORBITAL ROAD)
A412
UXBRIDGE ROAD
Eastwick Crescent
Bottom Wood
Chalfont Road
Woodoaks Farm
Springwell Lane
River Colne
Grand Union Canal Walk
Maple Cross
Maple Cross Industrial Estate
Maple Ldg Cl
Oakhill Road
Horn Hill Court
Hornhill Road
Woodland Road
Ladywalk
Robert's
Maple Cross
1 grid square represents 500 metres

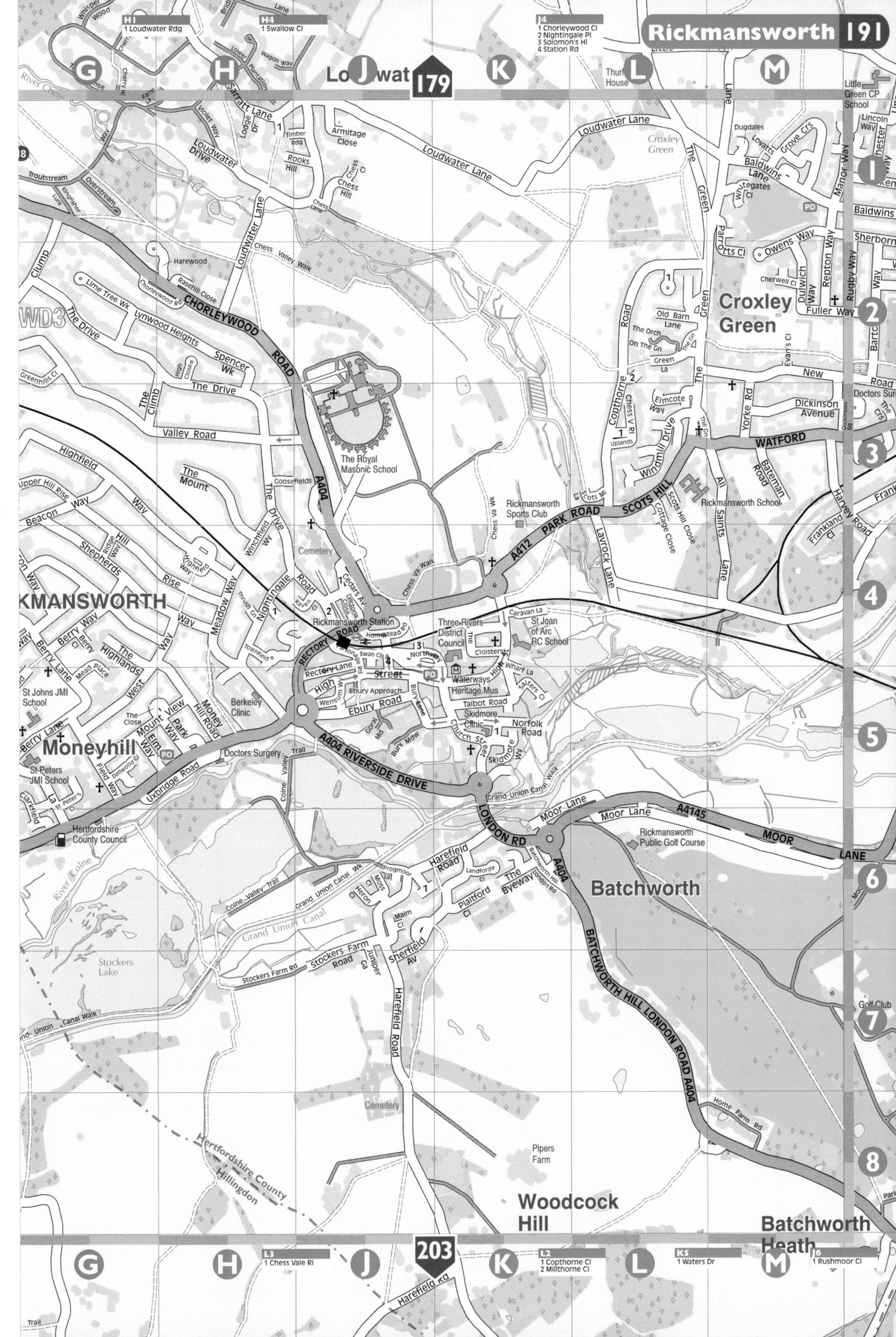
H1 1 Loudwater Rdg
H4 1 Swallow Cl
J4 1 Chorleywood Cl 2 Nightingale Pl 3 Solomon's Hl 4 Station Rd
179
Croxley Green
Rickmansworth
Moneyhill
Batchworth
Woodcock Hill
Batchworth Heath
The Royal Masonic School
Rickmansworth Station
Three Rivers District Council
Rickmansworth School
Rickmansworth Sports Club
Rickmansworth Public Golf Course
St Joan of Arc RC School
St Johns JMI School
St Peters JMI School
Hertfordshire County Council
Berkeley Clinic
Skidmore Clinic
Waterways Heritage Mus
Doctors Surgery
Stockers Lake
Pipers Farm
Cemetery
Grand Union Canal
River Colne
River Chess
Hertfordshire County
Hillingdon
CHORLEYWOOD ROAD
A404 RIVERSIDE DRIVE
A412 PARK ROAD
SCOTS HILL
A4145 MOOR LANE
BATCHWORTH HILL LONDON ROAD A404
LONDON RD
RECTORY ROAD
Loudwater Lane
Harefield Road
Stockers Farm Road
203
L3 1 Chess Vale Ri
L2 1 Copthorne Cl 2 Millthorne Cl
K5 1 Waters Dr
J6 1 Rushmoor Cl

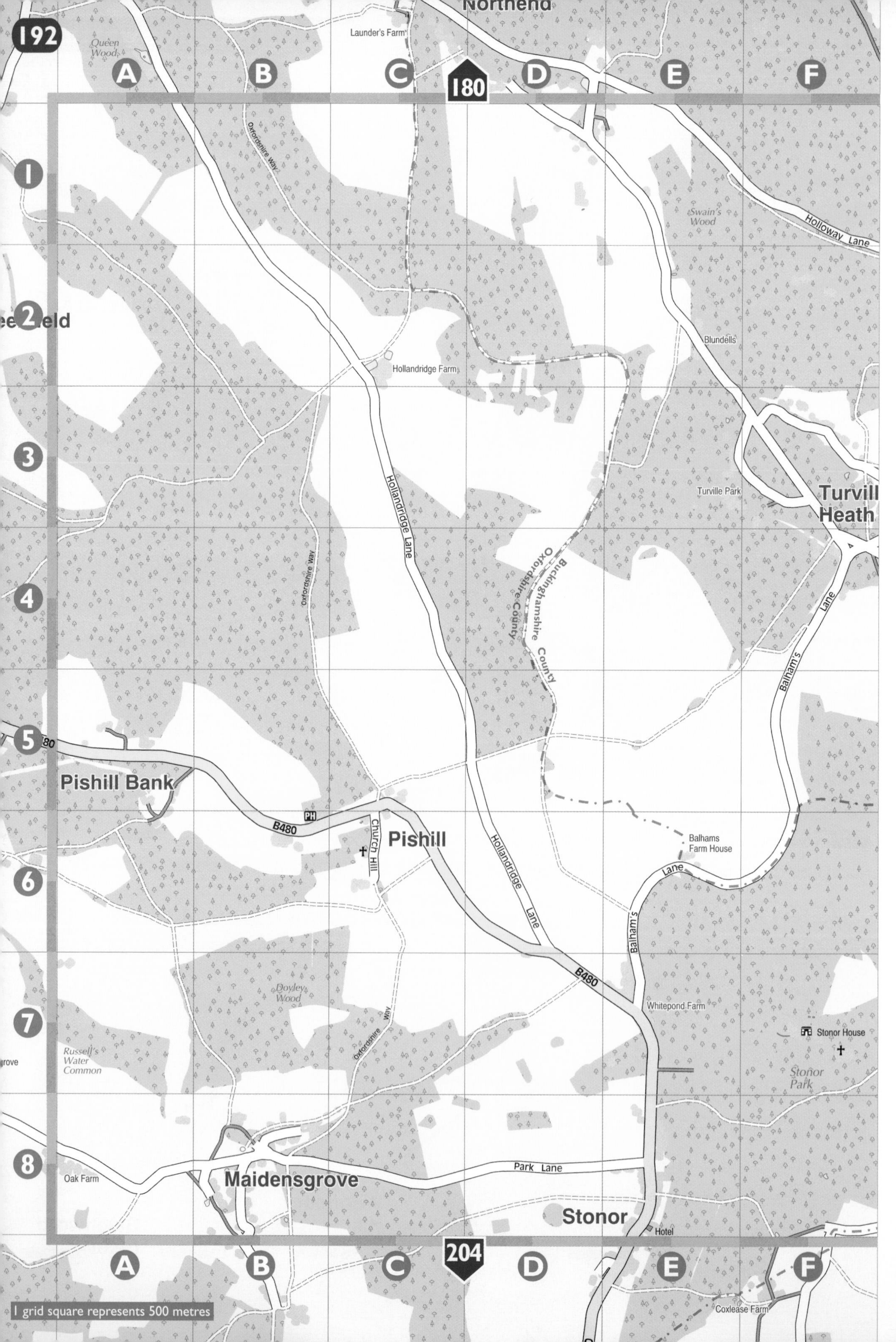

192
180
204
Northend
Launder's Farm
Queen Wood
Oxfordshire Way
Swain's Wood
Holloway Lane
Blundells
Hollandridge Farm
Hollandridge Lane
Turville Park
Turvill Heath
Oxfordshire County
Buckinghamshire County
Balham's Lane
Pishill Bank
B480
PH
Church Hill
Pishill
Balhams Farm House
Doyley Wood
Whitepond Farm
Stonor House
Stonor Park
Russell's Water Common
Park Lane
Oak Farm
Maidensgrove
Stonor
Hotel
Coxlease Farm
1 grid square represents 500 metres

G
H
J
K
L
M
181
Ibstone C of E
First School
Harecramp
Cotts
Manor Farm
Ashfield
Barn
Holloway Lane
Turville
School La
PH
Turville
Grange
Turville
Court
Summer
Heath
Dolesden Lane
Dolesden
Watery
Lane
194
Poynatts Farm
Fingest
Drovers Lane
Southend
Balham's
Wood
Great
Wood
Elmdown
Kimble Farm
Gussetts
Wood
Luxters Farm
Dudley
Lane
Henleyhill
Wood
Upper
Woodend Farm
Howe Farm
205
1
2
3
4
5
6
7
8

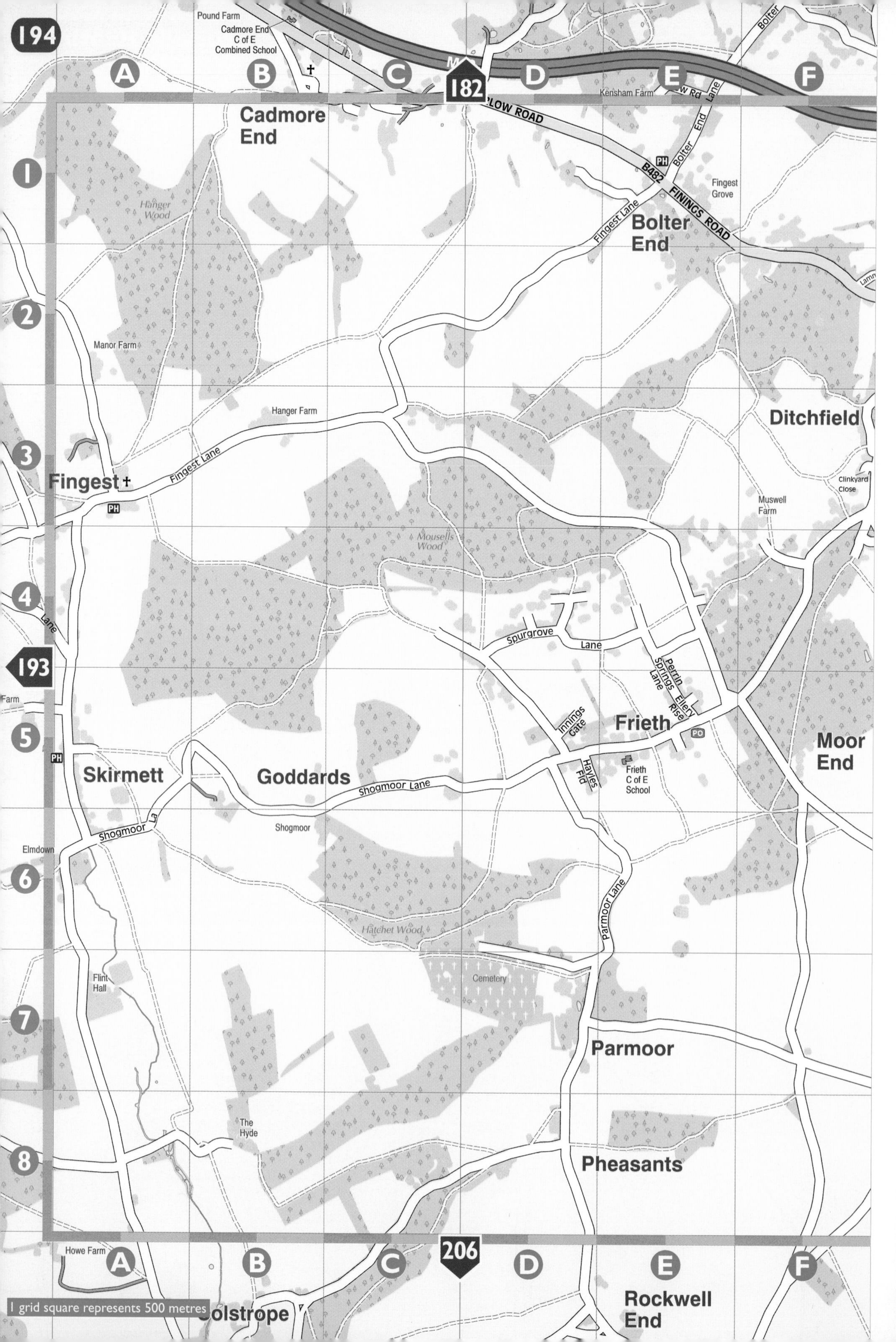
Pound Farm
Cadmore End C of E Combined School
182
A
B
C
D
E
F
Kensham Farm
Bolter
Cadmore End
MARLOW ROAD
B482
PH
Bolter End Lane
Fingest Grove
FININGS ROAD
Fingest Lane
Bolter End
Hanger Wood
1
2
Manor Farm
Hanger Farm
Ditchfield
3
Fingest
Fingest Lane
PH
Clinkyard Close
Muswell Farm
Mousells Wood
4
Lane
Spurgrove
Lane
193
Perrin Springs Lane
Ellery Rise
Farm
Innings Gate
Frieth
PO
Moor End
5
PH
Skirmett
Goddards
Hayles Fld
Frieth C of E School
Shogmoor Lane
Shogmoor La
Shogmoor
Elmdown
6
Parmoor Lane
Hatchet Wood
Cemetery
Flint Hall
7
Parmoor
The Hyde
8
Pheasants
206
Howe Farm
A
B
C
D
E
F
Rockwell End
Colstrope
1 grid square represents 500 metres

G1
1 Harris Rd
2 Johnson Rd
3 Wrights Cl
G2
1 James Rd
H1
1 Park Farm Wy
2 Rustlings Ga
Pyatts Farm
Fryers Farm
183
M40
Bullocks Farm Lane
Nursery Drive
Lines Rd
Denham Road
Pleasant
Mt
Ivy Pl
Close
Park
Pusey Way
Park Lane
Firs Cl
View
Widdenton
Coronation Crescent
Beech Av
Blackwell Road
Prospect Court
Sandage Rd
Archers Way
The Row
Edmonds Road
Thorne Rd
Forgetts Rd
Shotfield Rd
Oak Tree Drive
Saxhorn Road
Slayter Road
Cater Rd
Philps Rd
The Surgery
Francis Edmonds CP School
Simmons Way
Ridge Cl
Ellis Way
B482 HIGH STREET
Lane End
Church Road
Grove Farm
Spring Coppice
Lane End Road
Lane End Road
Rydal Way
Booker Common
Horns Lane
Willow Av
Glade Vw
Catkin Cl
Limmer Lane
Linnet Cl
The Paddocks
Cressex Road
Old Horns La
MARLOW ROAD
B482
Moor Farm
Moor Common
Wycombe Air Park
Clay Lane Farm
High Wycombe Squash Club
Claymoor
Clayhill
Clay Lane
196
Beacon Lane
Red Barn Farm
Moor Wood
Beacon Farm
B482
MARLOW
Bluey's Farm
Widmere Lane
Widmere Farm
Chisbridge
Chisbridge Cross
Frieth Road
Shillingridge Wood
Holme Wood
207
Copy Farm
Mundaydean Lane
Mundaydean Bottom
H2
1 Basset Rd
2 Elwes Rd
3 Hobbs Rd
4 Tapping Rd
G H J K L M
1 2 3 4 5 6 7 8

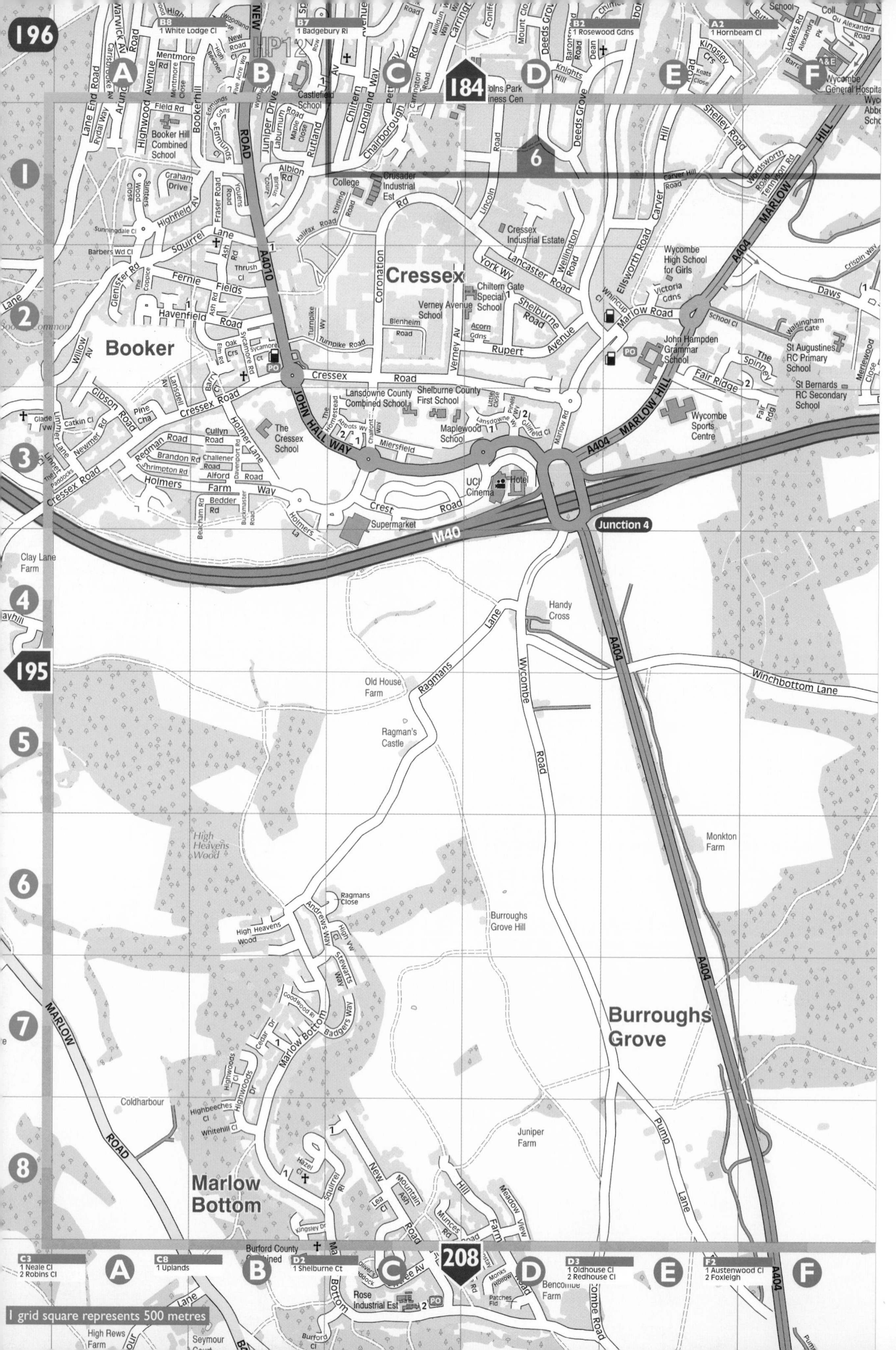
B8 1 White Lodge Cl
B7 1 Badgebury Ri
B2 1 Rosewood Gdns
A2 1 Hornbeam Cl
184
6
Booker
Cressex
Booker Hill Combined School
Castlefield School
College
Crusader Industrial Est
Cressex Industrial Estate
Wycombe High School for Girls
Chiltern Gate Special School
Verney Avenue School
John Hampden Grammar School
St Augustines RC Primary School
St Bernards RC Secondary School
Lansdowne County Combined School
Shelburne County First School
Maplewood School
The Cressex School
Wycombe Sports Centre
UCI Cinema
Hotel
Supermarket
Junction 4
M40
A404
A4010
JOHN HALL WAY
MARLOW HILL
Wycombe General Hospital
Clay Lane Farm
Handy Cross
Old House Farm
Ragman's Castle
Winchbottom Lane
Ragmans Lane
Wycombe Road
High Heavens Wood
Monkton Farm
Burroughs Grove Hill
Burroughs Grove
Coldharbour
Juniper Farm
Marlow Bottom
MARLOW ROAD
Pump Lane
Burford County Combined
Rose Industrial Est
Bencombe Farm
High Rews Farm
Seymour
195
208
C3 1 Neale Cl 2 Robins Cl
C8 1 Uplands
D2 1 Shelburne Ct
D3 1 Oldhouse Cl 2 Redhouse Cl
F2 1 Austenwood Cl 2 Foxleigh
1 grid square represents 500 metres

G2
1 Alaska St
2 Arizona St
3 Birch St
4 Westminster Cl
H2
1 Oak St
L1
1 Charnwood Cl
2 Kaybridge Cl
L2
1 Beech Cl
2 Ford St
3 Grapevine Cl
185
7
198
209
G
H
J
K
L
M
1
2
3
4
5
6
7
8
A40
ABBEY WAY
LONDON ROAD
London Road
Hazelbury Road
Queens Rd
High Wycombe Tennis Club
Bassetsbury
Chestnut Av
Edgewood
Bowden La
Lane
Wycombe Phoenix Harriers
Keep Hill Rd
Warren Wood Drive
The Briars
The Brackens
Kennedy Avenue
Daws Hill House
London Central High School
Sixth St
Fifth St
Fourth Street
Third St
Second St
First St
Beech St
Florida Street
HP11
Templar Wy
Wallingford Gdns
Sandford Gdns
Knights
Romsey Wy
Hill
Kew Cv
Lane
Bellwood Ri
Daws Lea
Alabama Cir
Alabama Dr
California Cir
Lime Av
Gyspy La
Lowdon Close
Keep Hill Dr
Wycombe Theatre Co
Deangarden Wood
Deangarden Rise
Willow Ct
Clarendon Rd
Spring Gdns
Rosebery Avenue
Cromwell Road
Alexandra Rd
Pinions Rd
Beechview Middle School
Guinions Road
The Sound Gallery
Wye Industrial Est
PO
Wycombe Marsh
Marsh County Infant School
Abbey Barn Rd
Mead Wy
Meadow Cl
Beech Rd
King's Rd
Fennels
Tannery Road Industrial Est
Fairview Estate
Hill St
Bank St
Orchard Rd
Gomm Road
Gomm Rd
Md St
Peregrine Business Park
Hall Cl
Forest Point
Micklefield Road
Hawthorne Rd
Hunters Hill
Butlers Ct
Horsenden Road
Clarke Drive
Pimms Grove
Old Coach Dr
The Pentlands
Hammersley La
Brambleside
River Wye
High Wycombe Rugby Union Football Cl
Kingsmead Road
Bridge Bank Cl
Holly Pl
M40
Heath End Road
Abbey Barn Lane
Ski Slopes
Abbey Barn Farm
Cobbles Farm
Spring Lane
Winchbottom Lane
Winchbottom Farm
Hard to Find Farm
Amersham & Wycombe College
Loudwater Co Combined Sc
Wycombe View
Beech Cl
Oakwood
St Hilda's Wy
St Birinus
Hawthorne Gdns
Ring Rd
Seymour Close
Rugwood Road
Woodlane Cl
Buckingham Way
Bernards Wy
Oakland Way
Fennels Farm Road
Fennels Way
Heath End Rd
Fairview La
Magpie Cl
Magpie La
Southfield Rd
Junior School
Halls Corner
Swains Lane
Carrington First School
Common Rd
Chapel Road
Old Kiln Road
Cherrywood Gardens
Sedgmoor
Carrington Av
Highlea Avenue
Highfield Road
Sedgmoor Gdns
Sedgmoor Close
Sedgmoor La
Sheepridge Lane
New Farm
Sheepridge
Flackwell Heath
Horton Wood
Bloom Wood
Bloom Farm
Pigeon House Farm
Parkview
The Close
M6
1 Chiltern Gn
M5
1 Fernlea Cl
2 Woodlane Gdns
M4
1 Glenmore Cl
M3
1 Rivers Edge
M2
1 Cherry St
2 Ludlow Ms
3 Pentlands Ct
Wilton Farm
MARLOW ROAD
A4155
Chapman Lane
Well End
Claytons Combined School
Winchbottom Lane

D6
1 Cleveland Cl
2 Old Watery
3 Shelley Cl
4 Spring Gdns
5 Thornaby Pl
B7
1 Jennings Fld
2 Northend Cl
3 Strathcona Cl
4 Tower Cl
B5
1 Snakeley Cl
B4
1 Thanestead Copse
A
B
C
186
D
E
F
Town Farm
Parsonage Farm
Magpie Lodge
Lude Farm
Hammersley Lane
Clearbrook Cl
Forty Green
Upper Dearham's Farm
Ravners Avenue
Robinson Road
Walkham Cl
London Rd
LONDON ROAD
High Wycombe Rugby Football Club
Kingsmead Business Park
Derehams Avenue
Altona Road
Loudwater
Loudwater County Combined School
Fassetts Road
Norwood Rd
LONDON ROAD
HP10
Berkeley Road
Station Rd
Loudwater Surg
Treadaway Business Cen
Knaves Beech Industrial Est
KNAVES BEECH WY
Junction 3
Woodburn Moor
Whitehouse Lane
Holtspur
Cherry Tree
Combined School
Treadaway Hill
Flackwell Heath Golf Club
Swains Lane
Knaves Beech Business Centre
BOUNDARY ROAD
M40
A40
WHITE HILL
Top Farm Cl
Holtspur Way
Ivins Rd
Heath Rd
Warwick Gallery
Skelton Cl
The Meadow
Straight Bit
Links Rd
Golf Course
Clapton Ap
Boundary Place
Millstream Way
Falcons Cft
Wye Road
Old Moor Lane
Glory Hill Lane
Glory Hill Farm
Cemetery
WOOBURN GN LA
Watery Lane
Highfield Road
Sedgmoor Road
Chapman Lane
River Vw
Highlands
Greenlands
School
Norland Dr
The Fairway
Juniper Lane
Tudor Drive
Glory Mill Lane
Glory Cl
Wooburn Green
Five Acres
Strathcona Way
Churchill Cl
Northern Woods
Green Dragon Lane
Bekings Way
Georges Dr
Green Crs
Philip Drive
Home Meadow Drive
Parkview
Farm Lea
Hill Close
Hickox Avenue
HOLTSPUR LANE B4440
Broad Lane
North Croft
Rush Burn
WYCOMBE LANE
A4094
School Road
Mayfield Road
The Meadows County Combined School
Woodside
Little Close
Willow Cl
Blind Lane
Wilfrids Wd Close
Whitepit Lane
Goodwin Mdw
Red Lion Way
Pound House Surgery
The Hawthornes
River Wye
197
1
2
3
4
5
6
7
8
D7
1 Waterside
D8
1 Walnut Gv
E6
1 Longview
210
E7
1 Hill Farm Ap
F6
1 Edmund Ct
2 Holtspur Cl
3 Kings Cl
4 South Wy
1 grid square represents 500 metres

G2 1 Roundheads End
H1 1 Robinswood Cl
H2 1 Crispin Cl
Knotty Green
Alfriston School
187
Brown's Wood
Birchen Spring
AMERSHAM ROAD
A355
Oldfields Farm
Wyngrave Place
PENN ROAD
B474
Knottocks Drive
Sandelswood End
Netherwood Road
Howe Drive
Copperfields
Upper Drive
Middle Drive
Lower Drive
Eastergate
Dower Close
Cherry Drive
Red House Close
Forty Green
Eghams Cl
Brownswood Road
Bearswood End
Curzon Av
High March School
Assheton Road
Ledborough Lane
Ledborough Wood
Woodlands Drive
Seeleys Road
Hogback Wood Road
Owlsears Close
Blyton Close
Wilton Road
Grenfell Road
Beconscot Model Village
Warwick Road
Reynolds Road
Woodside Avenue
Woodside Road
Malkin Dr
Caledon Road
One Tree Lane
Baring Road
STATION RD
Beaconsfield Station
Simpson Health Centre
Gregories Road
Maxwell Road
Hyde Green
Hyde Gn
Waller Road
Primary School
Garvin Avenue
Chesterton Gn
Cambridge Road
Beechwood Road
Gurney Close
Gregories Farm Lane
Davenies Boys Preparatory School
Candlemas Mead
Fernhurst
Ronald Rd
Hampden
Chiltern Hills Rd
Burkes Crs
Burkes Road
Bon Secours Hospital
Candlemas Lane
Meadow Lane
B474 STATION ROAD
Grove Road
HP9
Burgess Wd Rd
Westfield Road
BEACONSFIELD
Butlers Court County First & Middle School
Cemetery
PARK LANE
Minerva Way
Maude Road
Maude Close
200
Butlers Court
Beaconsfield High School
Beaconsfield School
Rolfe Close
The Gallery
Millbarn Medical Cen
Shepherds Lane
Crossways
Holtspur
Maplewood Gdns
South Road
Ellwood Road
Chestnut Road
Butlers Court Road
Tilsworth Road
Wattleton Road
The Spinney
AYLESBURY WAY
A40
LONDON ROAD
Beaconsfield Cricket Club
Burnham Av
Pennington Road
Burkes Road
Walk Wood Rise
WYCOMBE END
Malthouse Square
Lakes Lane
PH
PO
Burkes Close
A40
South Drive
Windsor End
Hedgerley Lane
Beaconsfield Rugby Football Club
Cross Lane
Pyebush Lane
Hall Barn
Junction 2
The Grove
Over's Farm
Burtley Wood
Rare Breeds Centre
Burnham Road
Fairview House
211
L6 1 Crosby Cl
J3 1 Calumet 2 Hubert Day Cl 3 Somerford Pl
J1 1 Bealings End 2 Chacombe Pl 3 Knottocks End
H6 1 Tilsworth Rd
Dipple Wood
Woodlands
DORNEY
G H J K L M
1 2 3 4 5 6 7 8

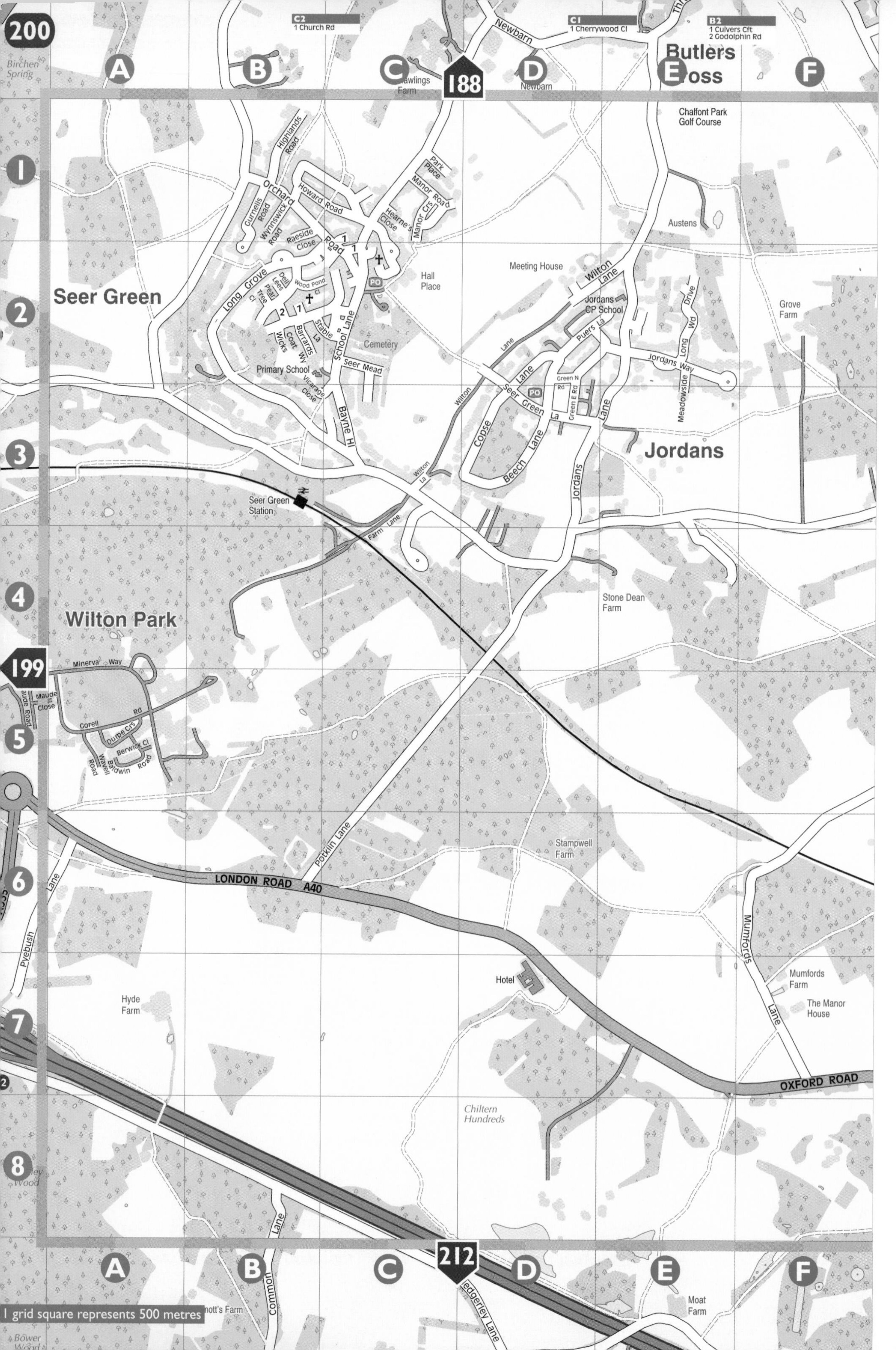

C2 1 Church Rd
C1 1 Cherrywood Cl
B2 1 Culvers Cft 2 Godolphin Rd
188
199
212
Butlers Cross
Chalfont Park Golf Course
Newbarn
Seer Green
Jordans
Wilton Park
Austens
Meeting House
Hall Place
Jordans CP School
Grove Farm
Cemetery
Primary School
Seer Green Station
Stone Dean Farm
Stampwell Farm
Hotel
Hyde Farm
Mumfords Farm
The Manor House
Chiltern Hundreds
Moat Farm
Highlands Road
Orchard Road
Howard Road
Park Place
Manor Road
Manor Crs
Hearne's Close
Gurnells Road
Wynnswick Road
Raeside Close
Long Grove
Dell Lees
Pearl Tree Cl
Wood Pond Cl
Stable La
School Lane
Wicks Coat Wy
Barrards
Seer Mead
Vicarage Close
Bayne Hl
Wilton Lane
Puers La
Jordans Way
Long Wd Drive
Meadowside
Green N Rd
Green E Rd
Copse Lane
Seer Green La
Beech Lane
Jordans Lane
Wilton La
Farm Lane
Minerva Way
Maude Close
Maude Road
Corell Rd
Dumbe Crs
Berwick Cl
Wavell Road
Baldwin Road
Potkiln Lane
LONDON ROAD A40
OXFORD ROAD
Pyebush Lane
Mumfords Lane
Common Lane
Hedgerley Lane
1 grid square represents 500 metres

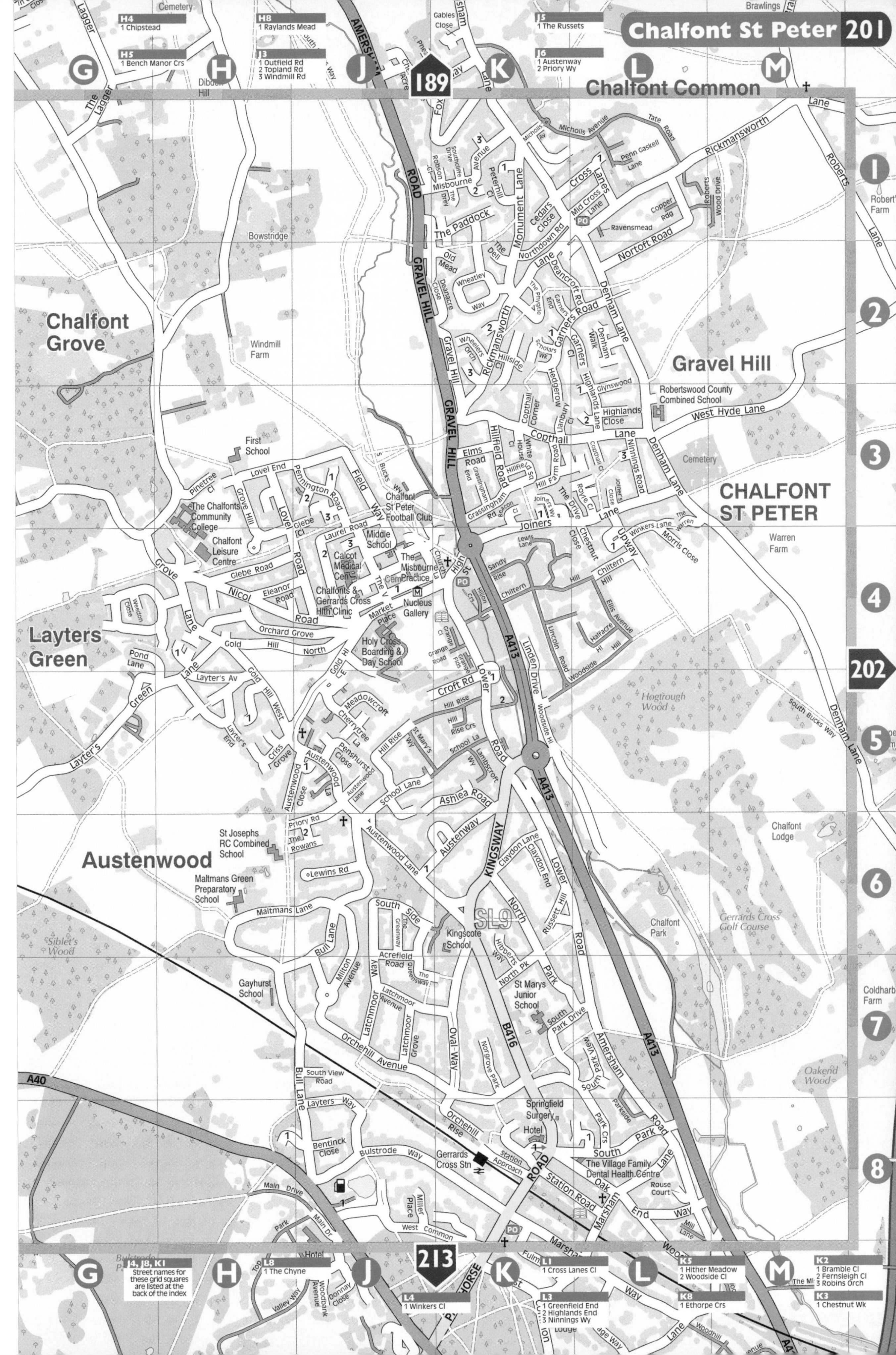
H4
1 Chipstead
H5
1 Bench Manor Crs
H8
1 Raylands Mead
J3
1 Outfield Rd
2 Topland Rd
3 Windmill Rd
J5
1 The Russets
J6
1 Austenway
2 Priory Wy
189
Chalfont Common
Chalfont Grove
Windmill Farm
Bowstridge
Gravel Hill
CHALFONT ST PETER
Layters Green
Austenwood
Robertswood County Combined School
The Chalfonts Community College
Chalfont Leisure Centre
Chalfont St Peter Football Club
Middle School
Calcot Medical Cen
The Misbourne Practice
Chalfonts & Gerrards Cross Hlth Clinic
Nucleus Gallery
Holy Cross Boarding & Day School
St Josephs RC Combined School
Maltmans Green Preparatory School
Kingscote School
Gayhurst School
St Marys Junior School
Springfield Surgery
Hotel
Gerrards Cross Stn
The Village Family Dental Health Centre
Rouse Court
Hogtrough Wood
Siblet's Wood
Gerrards Cross Golf Course
Chalfont Park
Chalfont Lodge
Warren Farm
Oakend Wood
Coldharbo Farm
Robert's Farm
Cemetery
SL9
AMERSHAM ROAD
GRAVEL HILL
A413
A40
B416
KINGSWAY
202
213
Street names for these grid squares are listed at the back of the index
L8
1 The Chyne
L4
1 Winkers Cl
L1
1 Cross Lanes Cl
L3
1 Greenfield End
2 Highlands End
3 Ninnings Wy
K5
1 Hither Meadow
2 Woodside Cl
K8
1 Ethorpe Crs
K2
1 Bramble Cl
2 Fernsleigh Cl
3 Robins Orch
K3
1 Chestnut Wk

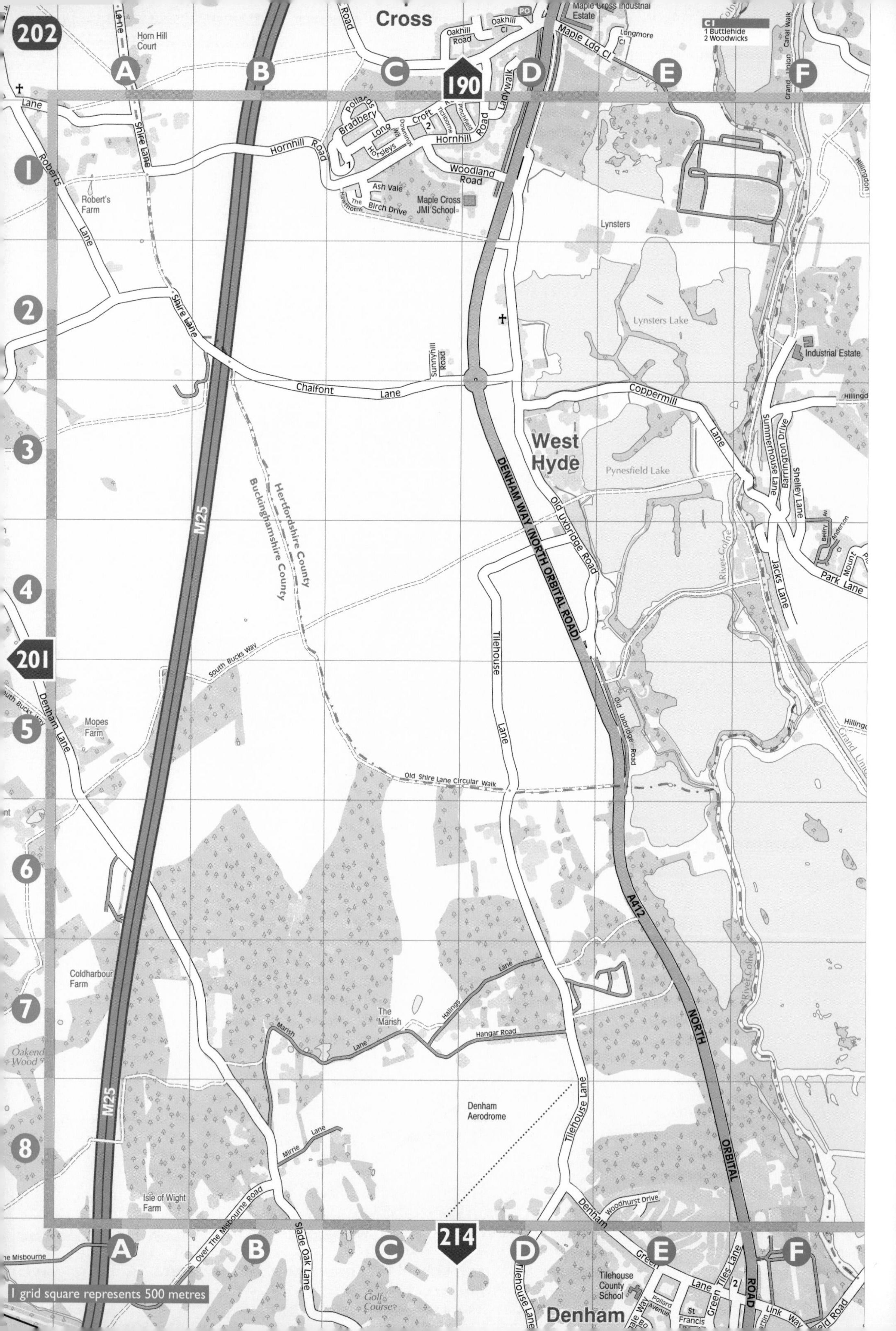
Cross
Horn Hill Court
Maple Cross Industrial Estate
Oakhill Road
Oakhill Cl
Maple Ldg Cl
Longmore Cl
C1
1 Buttlehide
2 Woodwicks
Canal Walk
190
Shire Lane
Roberts Lane
Hornhill Road
Pollards
Bradbery
Long
Horsleys
Croft
Tichborne
Pinchfield
Ladywalk
Woodland Road
Ash Vale
The Hawthorns
Birch Drive
Maple Cross JMI School
Robert's Farm
Lynsters
Hillingdon
Lynsters Lake
Industrial Estate
Sunnyhill Road
Chalfont Lane
Coppermill Lane
West Hyde
Pynesfield Lake
Summerhouse Lane
Barrington Drive
Shelley Lane
Belfry Av
Anderson Cl
Mount
Park Lane
Jacks Lane
River Colne
M25
Hertfordshire County
Buckinghamshire County
DENHAM WAY (NORTH ORBITAL ROAD)
Old Uxbridge Road
Tilehouse Lane
South Bucks Way
201
Denham Lane
Mopes Farm
Grand Union
Old Shire Lane Circular Walk
A412
Coldharbour Farm
Lane
Hallings
The Marish
Marish Lane
Hangar Road
NORTH ORBITAL ROAD
Oakend Wood
Denham Aerodrome
Tilehouse Lane
Mirrie Lane
Isle of Wight Farm
Over The Misbourne Road
Slade Oak Lane
Denham
Woodhurst Drive
214
The Misbourne
Green Lane
Green Tiles Lane
Tilehouse County School
Golf Course
Pollard Avenue
St Francis
Link Way
Denham
1 grid square represents 500 metres

H5 1 Countess Cl
H7 1 Harvil Rd 2 Priory Cl
J4 1 Springwood Cl
Hertfordshire County
Hillingdon
G H J K L M
191
Woodcock Hill
Batchworth Heath
Springwell Lane
Cripps House Farm
Weybeards Farm
Hillingdon Trail
Hill End
Hill End Road
Plough Lane
Rickmansworth Road
Harefield Rd
Woodcock Hill
Bishop's Wood
Bishops Wood Hospital
White Hill
Jackets Lane
Harefield Grove
Sanctuary Close
Hospital Annexe
Mount Pleasant
Harefield Hospital
Harefield Health Centre
Harefield Junior School
Harefield Infant School
Colney Farm
Dunster Cl
Northwood Road
Shepherds Hill House
John Penrose School
Newdigate Road
Vernon Drive
Ash Grove
Olivia Gdns
Wickham Cl
Savoy Cl
Gilbert Road
Sullivan Crescent
Pond Close
Harefield Cricket Club
Merle Av
Dovedale Cl
High Street
Lewis Cl
Dexter Rd
Morse Cl
Childs Av
Manor Ct
Harefield
Knightscote Farm
Holland & Holland Shooting School
Ducks Hill Rd
Lovett Road
Grand Union Canal Walk
Breakspear Road North
Bourne Farm
Breakspear House
St Mary's Road
St Anne's Road
Church Road
Church Hill
St Mary's Close
Broadwater Lane
Sedley Gv
Broadwater Gdns
Hinkley Close
Priory Gdns
Harvil Road
Truesdale Drive
Peerless Dr
Peerless Drive
Park Lodge Farm
South Harefield
Hillingdon Trail
Bayhurst Wood Country Park
Dellside
Hillside
Moorhall Road
215
J5 1 Penzance Cl
Newyears Green Lane
1 2 3 4 5 6 7 8

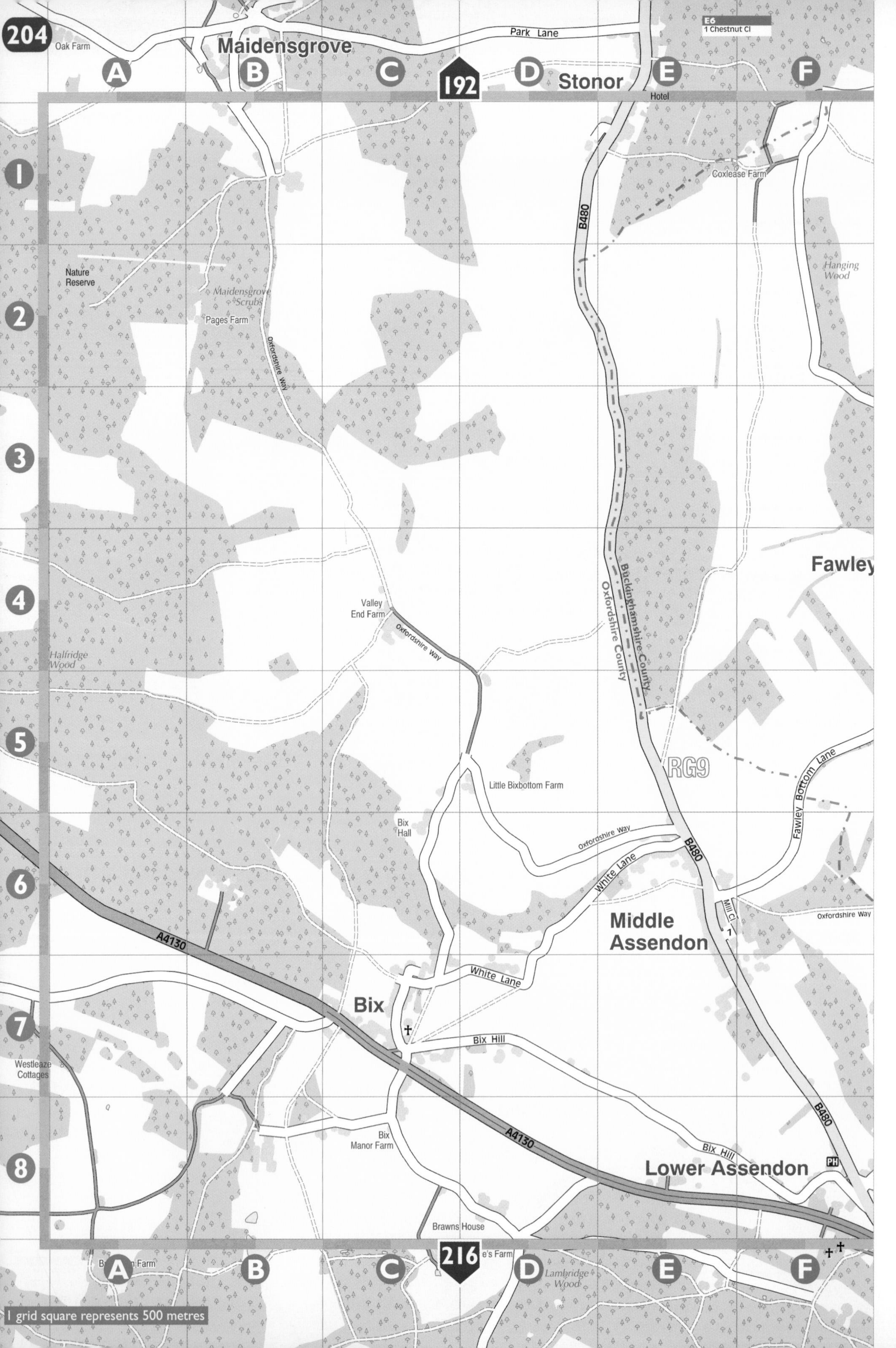

204
Oak Farm
Maidensgrove
Park Lane
E6
1 Chestnut Cl
A
B
C
192
D
Stonor
E
F
Hotel
Coxlease Farm
B480
Nature Reserve
Maidensgrove Scrubs
Pages Farm
Oxfordshire Way
Hanging Wood
Fawley
Valley End Farm
Oxfordshire Way
Halfridge Wood
Buckinghamshire County
Oxfordshire County
RG9
Little Bixbottom Farm
Bix Hall
Oxfordshire Way
Fawley Bottom Lane
B480
White Lane
Mill Cl
1
Oxfordshire Way
Middle Assendon
A4130
White Lane
Bix
Bix Hill
Westleaze Cottages
B480
Bix Manor Farm
A4130
Bix Hill
Lower Assendon
PH
Brawns House
216
A
B
C
D
E
F
Lambridge Wood
1
2
3
4
5
6
7
8
1 grid square represents 500 metres

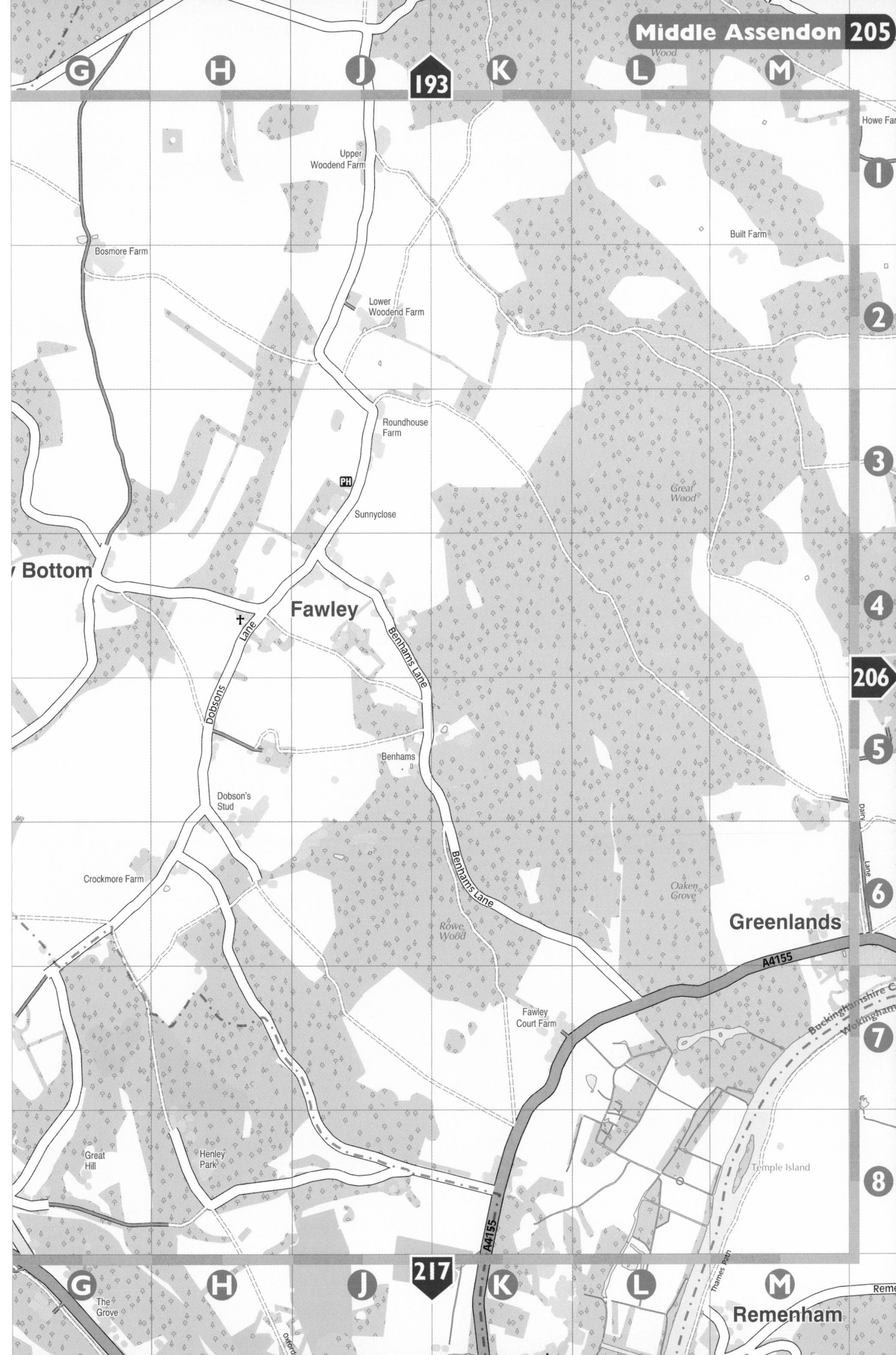
G
H
J
193
K
L
M
Upper Woodend Farm
Howe Farm
Bosmore Farm
Built Farm
Lower Woodend Farm
Roundhouse Farm
PH
Sunnyclose
Great Wood
Bottom
Fawley
Lane
Benhams Lane
Dobsons
206
Benhams
Dobson's Stud
Dairy Lane
Crockmore Farm
Benhams Lane
Oaken Grove
Rowe Wood
Greenlands
A4155
Fawley Court Farm
Buckinghamshire
Wokingham
Temple Island
Great Hill
Henley Park
A4155
217
Thames Path
The Grove
Remenham
1
2
3
4
5
6
7
8

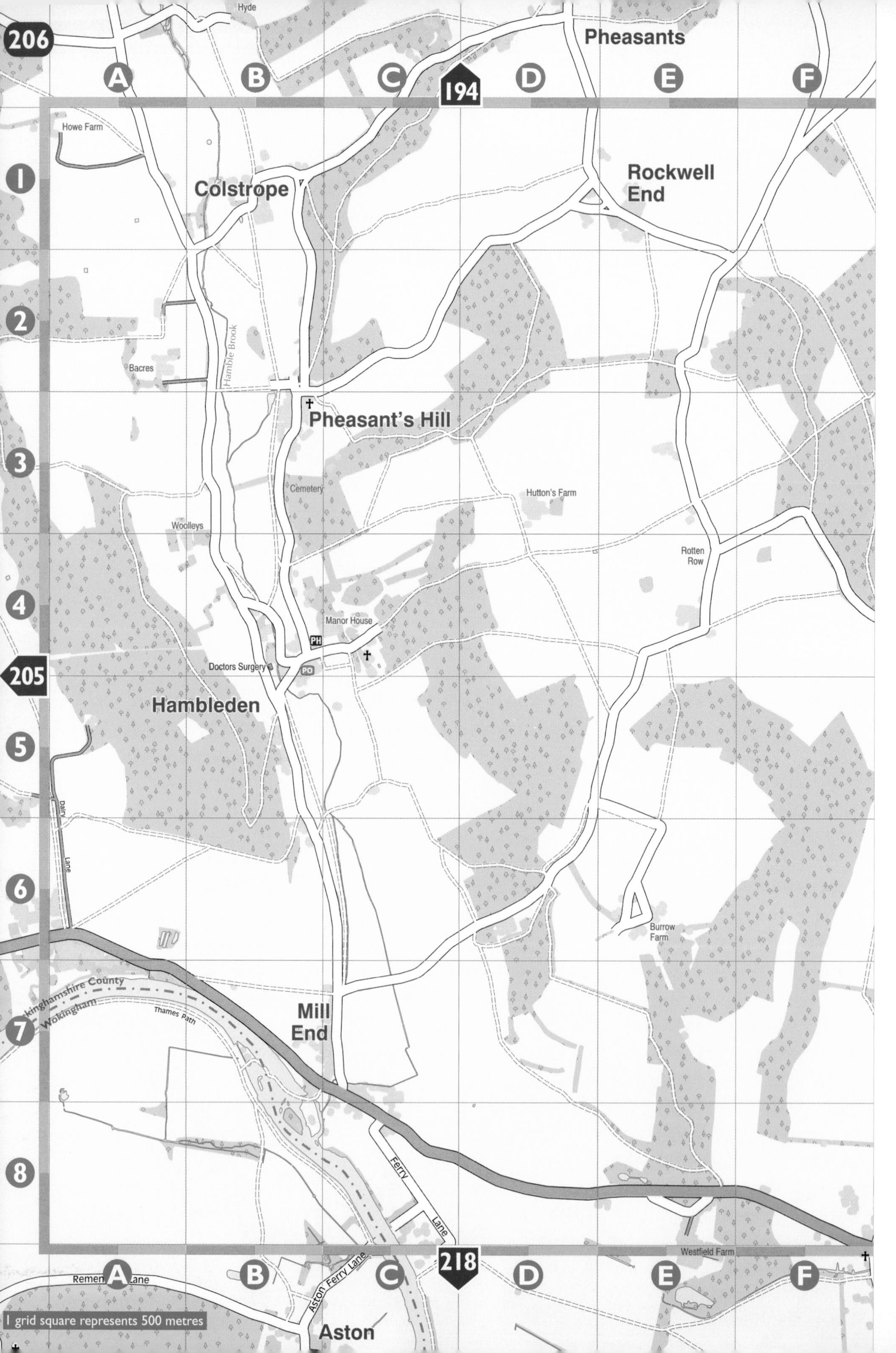
206
Hyde
Pheasants
194
A
B
C
D
E
F
Howe Farm
1
Colstrope
Rockwell End
2
Hamble Brook
Bacres
Pheasant's Hill
3
Cemetery
Hutton's Farm
Woolleys
Rotten Row
4
Manor House
PH
Doctors Surgery
PO
205
Hambleden
5
Dairy Lane
6
Burrow Farm
Thames Path
7
Mill End
8
Ferry Lane
Westfield Farm
218
Remenham Lane
Aston Ferry Lane
Aston
1 grid square represents 500 metres

Cross
J7
1 Chestnut Cl
2 Kings Wd
3 Shelley Cl
G
H
J
K
L
M
195
Frieth Road
Holme Wood
Shillingridge
Copy Farm
Mundaydean Lane
Mundaydean Bottom
Hawkins Farm
Woodend House
Woodend Farm
Holywick
Frieth Road
Lower Woodend
Marlow Common
Marlow Common
Bovingdon Green
Blount
Chalkpit
Heath Wood
Homefield Wood
Davenport Wood
Bovingdon Hts
208
Bockmer End
Spinfield
Hook's Farm
Bockmer House
Bockmer Lane
Widefield Wood
A4155
Rassler Wood
Danesfield County Combined School
Buckingham Gate
South
Kings Barn Farm
Harleyford
Harleyford Lane
Low Farm
Home Copse
School Lane
Bockmer Lane
A4155
Danesfield
Harleyford Golf Club
A4155
219
Harleyford Manor
Buckinghamshire County
Windsor and Maidenhead
Thames Path
Hot
Medmenham
Ferry
River Thames
1
2
3
4
5
6
7
8

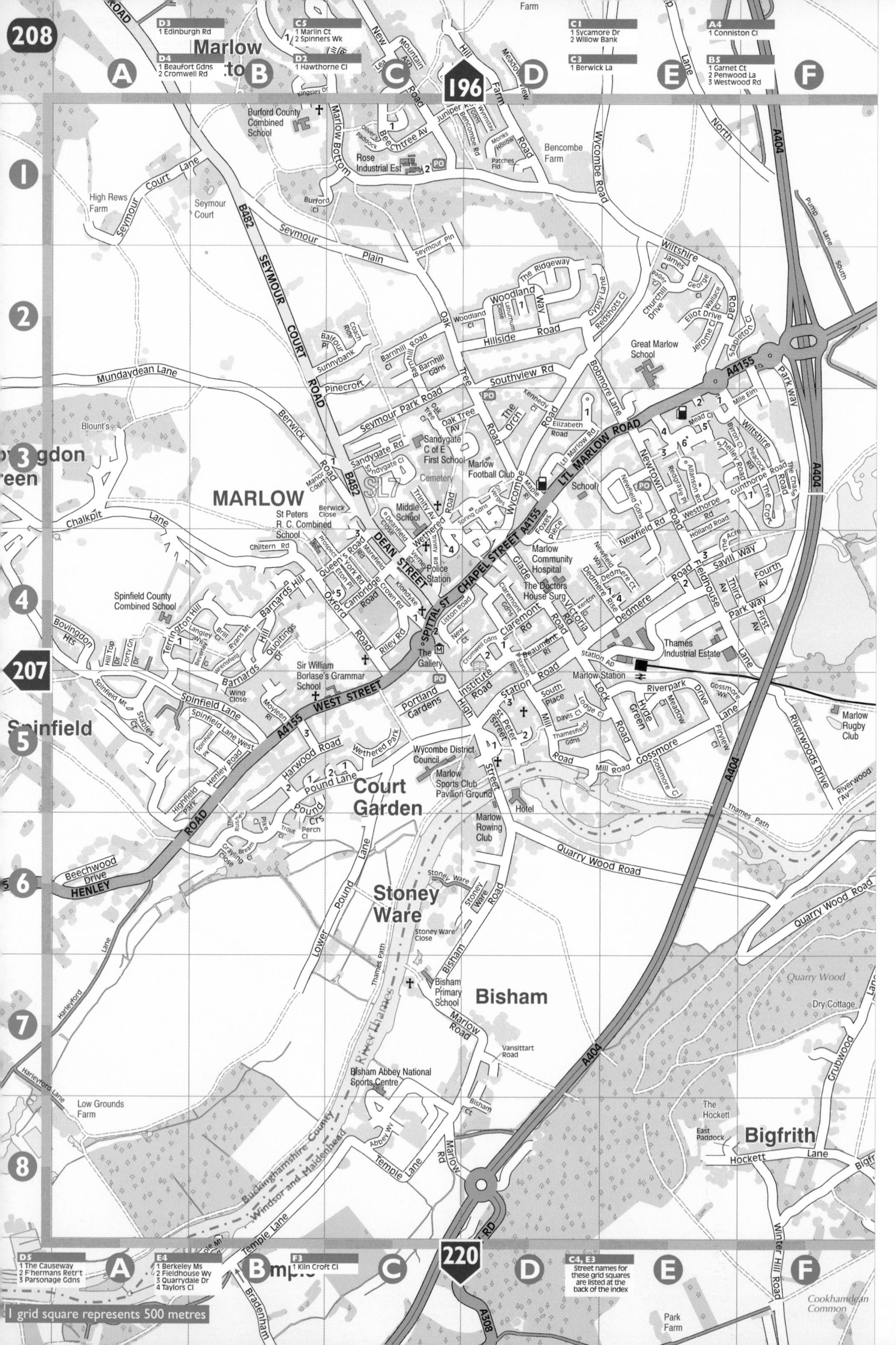
208
196
207
220
D3
1 Edinburgh Rd
D4
1 Beaufort Gdns
2 Cromwell Rd
C5
1 Marlin Ct
2 Spinners Wk
D2
1 Hawthorne Cl
C1
1 Sycamore Dr
2 Willow Bank
C3
1 Berwick La
A4
1 Conniston Cl
B5
1 Garnet Ct
2 Penwood La
3 Westwood Rd
Marlow
Burford County Combined School
Rose Industrial Est
Bencombe Farm
High Rews Farm
Seymour Court
Seymour Court Lane
Seymour Plain
B482
SEYMOUR COURT ROAD
Mundaydean Lane
Blount's
MARLOW
Chalkpit Lane
St Peters R. C. Combined School
Spinfield County Combined School
Sir William Borlase's Grammar School
Spinfield
Great Marlow School
Sandygate C of E First School
Marlow Football Club
Cemetery
SL7
Middle School
Police Station
Marlow Community Hospital
The Doctors House Surg
The Gallery
Thames Industrial Estate
Marlow Station
LTL MARLOW ROAD
A4155
CHAPEL STREET
SPITTAL ST
DEAN STREET
WEST STREET
HENLEY ROAD
Wycombe District Council
Marlow Sports Club Pavilion Ground
Court Garden
Hotel
Marlow Rowing Club
Quarry Wood Road
Marlow Rugby Club
Riverwoods Drive
A404
Stoney Ware
Bisham
Bisham Primary School
Bisham Abbey National Sports Centre
River Thames
Thames Path
Low Grounds Farm
Quarry Wood
Dry Cottage
The Hockett
Bigfrith
Hockett Lane
Temple Lane
Winter Hill Road
Cookhamdean Common
Park Farm
A308
D5
1 The Causeway
2 F'hermans Retr't
3 Parsonage Gdns
E4
1 Berkeley Ms
2 Fieldhouse Wy
3 Quarrydale Dr
4 Taylors Cl
F3
1 Kiln Croft Cl
C4, E3
Street names for these grid squares are listed at the back of the index
1 grid square represents 500 metres

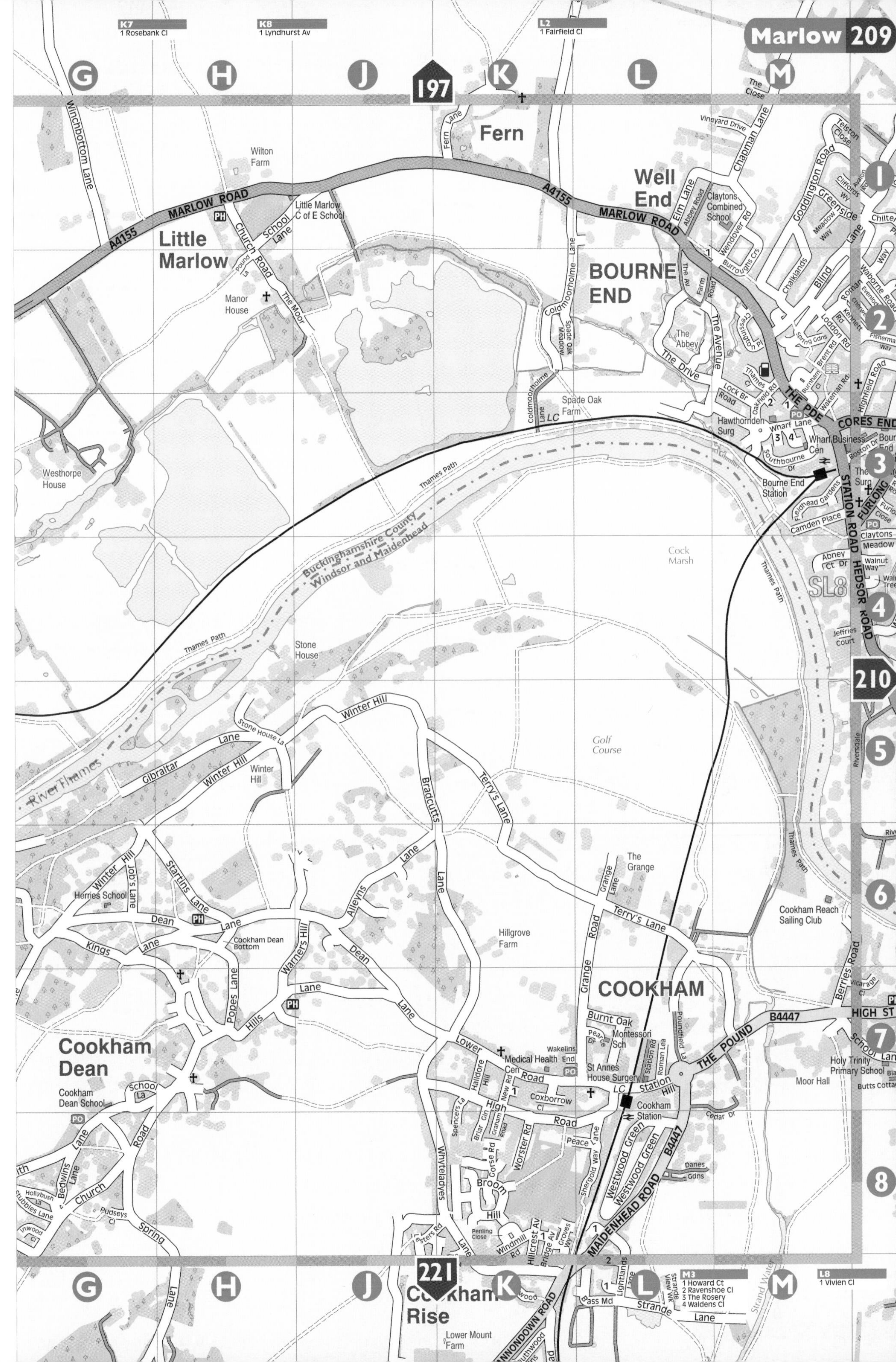
K7 1 Rosebank Cl
K8 1 Lyndhurst Av
L2 1 Fairfield Cl
197
Fern
Fern Lane
Wilton Farm
Winchbottom Lane
A4155
MARLOW ROAD
Little Marlow
Little Marlow C of E School
School Lane
Church Road
Pound La
Manor House
The Moor
Well End
Elm Lane
Abbey Road
Claytons Combined School
Chapman Lane
Vineyard Drive
The Close
Wendover Rd
Burroughs Crs
BOURNE END
Coldmoorholme Lane
Spade Oak Meadow
The Abbey
The Avenue
The Drive
Farm Road
The Av
Cressington Pl
Goddington Road
Greenside
Meadow Way
Chalklands
Blind Lane
Telston Close
Cliffords Wy
Chiltern Pk
Waborne Road
Kennett Rd
Loddon Rd
Brent Rd
Spring Gdns
Burnham Cl
Fisherman's Way
Highfield Road
Wakeman Rd
THE PDE
CORES END
Spade Oak Farm
LC
Lock Br Road
Thames Cl
Oakfield Rd
Hawthornden Surg
Wharf Lane
Southbourne Dr
Wharf Business Cen
Boston Dr
Bourne End Station
STATION ROAD
FURLONG
The Surg
Furlong Close
Fieldhead Gardens
Camden Place
Claytons Meadow
Abbey Ct Dr
Walnut Way
Walnut Tree
HEDSOR ROAD
SL8
Jeffries Court
Westhorpe House
Thames Path
Buckinghamshire County
Windsor and Maidenhead
Cock Marsh
Stone House
210
Golf Course
Winter Hill
Stone House La
Gibraltar Lane
River Thames
Bradcutts Lane
Terry's Lane
Riversdale
Thames Path
The Grange
Grange Lane
Cookham Reach Sailing Club
Herries School
Job's Lane
Startins Lane
Dean Lane
Alleyns Lane
Kings Lane
Cookham Dean Bottom
Warners Hill
Dean Lane
Popes Lane
Hills Lane
Hillgrove Farm
Grange Road
COOKHAM
Burnt Oak
Montessori Sch
Pearce Dr
Berries Road
Vicarage Cl
HIGH ST
B4447
THE POUND
Poundfield La
School Lane
Holy Trinity Primary School
Moor Hall
Butts Cottage
Cookham Dean
Lower Road
Medical Health Cen
Wakelins End
St Annes House Surgery
Station Rd
Roman Lea
Station Hill
Cookham Station
Cedar Dr
Cookham Dean School
School La
Halldore Hill
New Rd
High Road
Coxborrow Cl
Spencers La
Briar Gln
Graham Road
Worster Rd
Peace Lane
Shergold Way
Westwood Green
MAIDENHEAD ROAD
Danes Gdns
Bedwins Lane
Hollybush La
Church Road
Stubbles Lane
Inwood Cl
Pudseys Cl
Spring Lane
Whyteladyes Lane
Gorse Rd
Broom Hill
Penling Close
Windmill Rd
Hillcrest Av
Bridge Av
Groves Wy
Peters Rd
221
Cookham Rise
Lower Mount Farm
Lane
Lightlands Lane
Strande View Wk
Strande Lane
Bass Md
Strand Water
M3 1 Howard Ct 2 Ravenshoe Cl 3 The Rosery 4 Waldens Cl
L8 1 Vivien Cl
G H J K L M
1 2 3 4 5 6 7 8

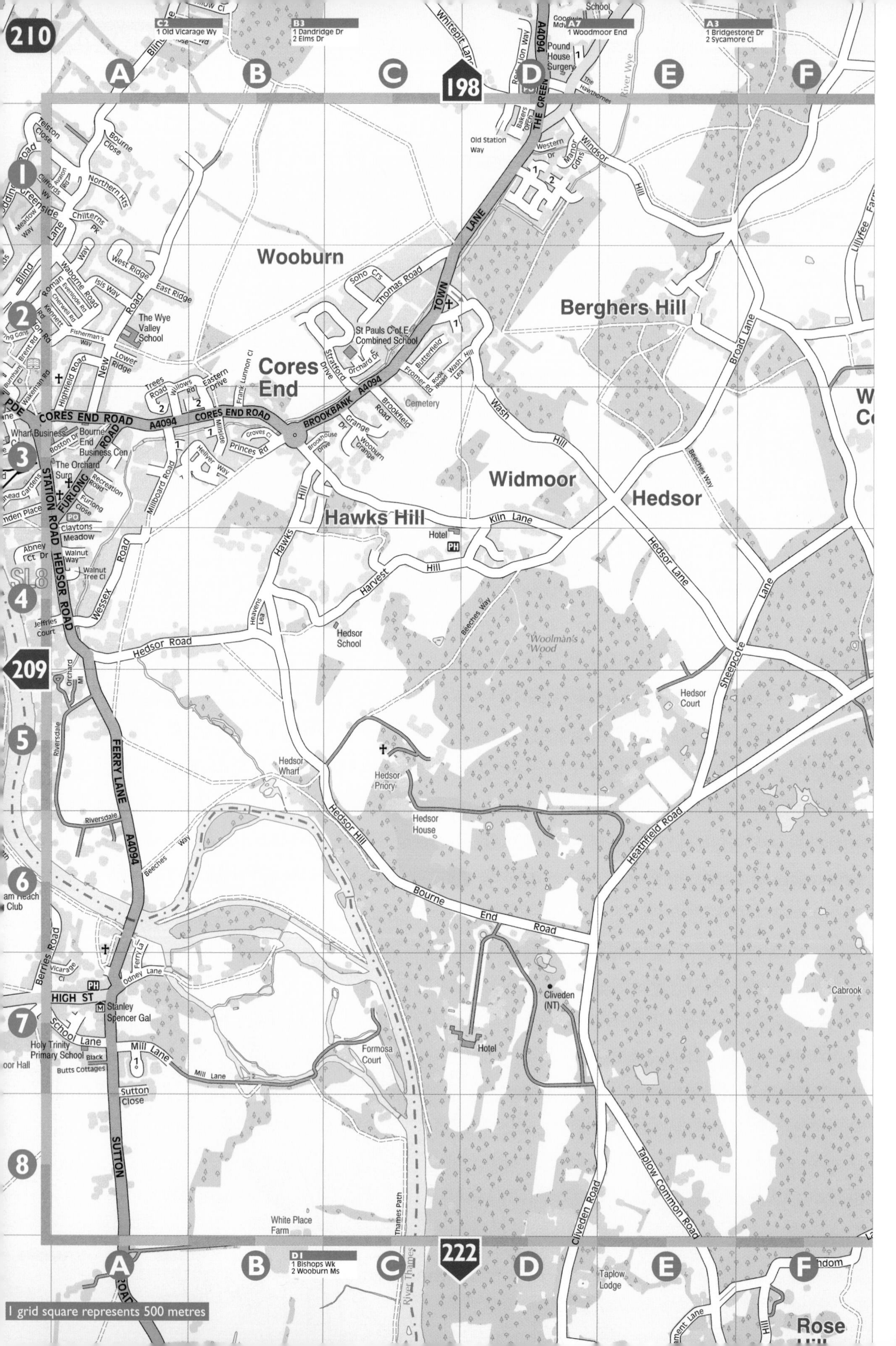
C2
1 Old Vicarage Wy
B3
1 Dandridge Dr
2 Elms Dr
A7
1 Woodmoor End
A3
1 Bridgestone Dr
2 Sycamore Cl
198
209
222
D1
1 Bishops Wk
2 Wooburn Ms
Wooburn
Berghers Hill
Cores End
Widmoor
Hedsor
Hawks Hill
Woolman's Wood
Pound House Surgery
The Wye Valley School
St Pauls C of E Combined School
Hedsor School
Hedsor Wharf
Hedsor Priory
Hedsor House
Hedsor Court
Cliveden (NT)
Hotel
Cemetery
Formosa Court
White Place Farm
Taplow Lodge
Cabrook
Stanley Spencer Gal
Holy Trinity Primary School
Butts Cottages
The Orchard Surg
Wharf Business
Bourne End Business Cen
CORES END ROAD
A4094
BROOKBANK
TOWN LANE
THE GREEN
STATION ROAD
HEDSOR ROAD
FERRY LANE
SUTTON ROAD
HIGH ST
Hedsor Road
Hedsor Lane
Hedsor Hill
Bourne End Road
Heathfield Road
Cliveden Road
Taplow Common Road
Kiln Lane
Harvest Hill
Hawks Hill
Wash Hill
Windsor Hill
Broad Lane
Sheepcote Lane
Beeches Way
Mill Lane
School Lane
Thames Path
River Thames
River Wye
Rose Hill
SL8
1 grid square represents 500 metres

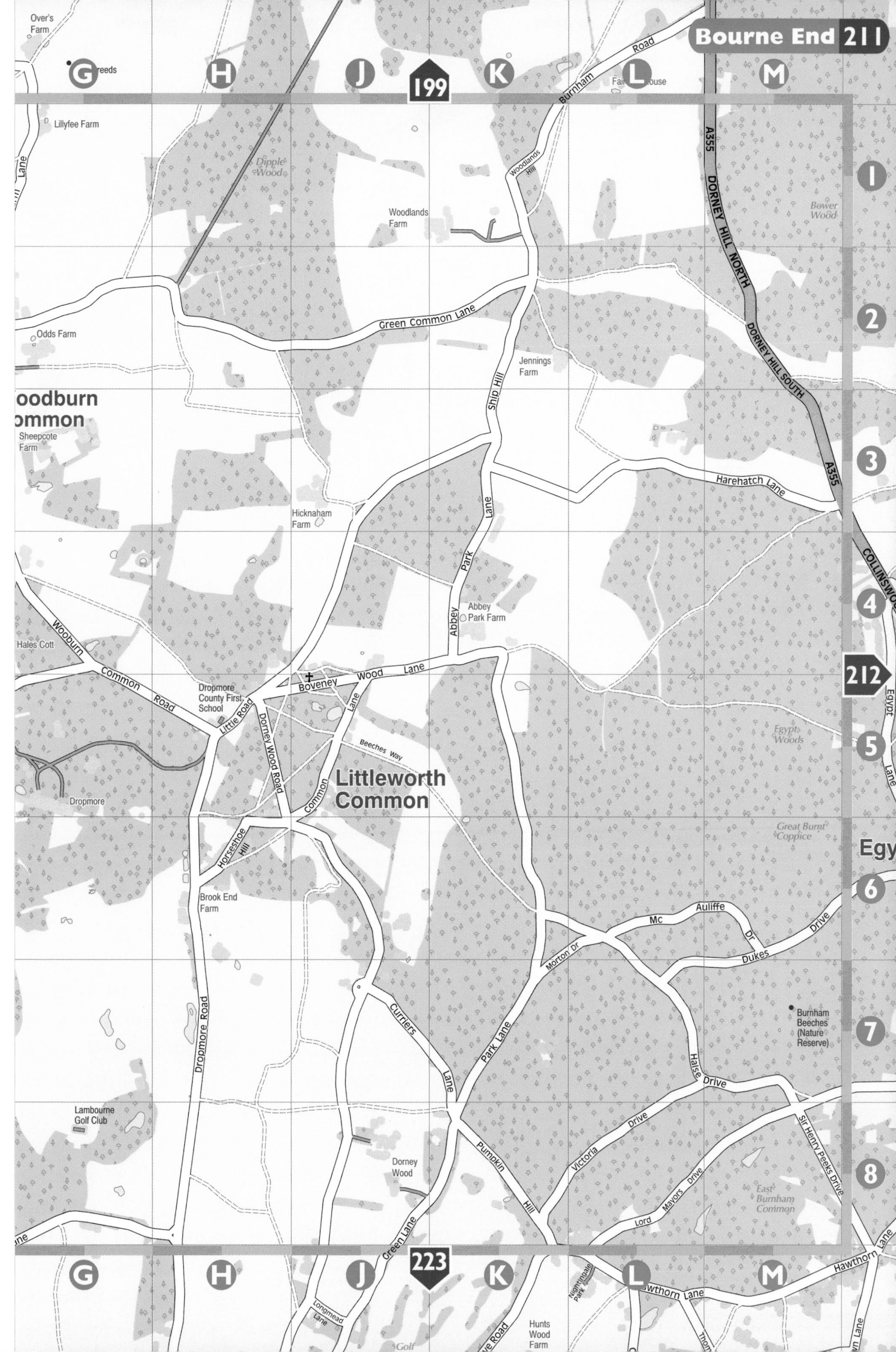

Over's Farm
Greeds
Lillyfee Farm
Dipple Wood
Woodlands Farm
Burnham Road
Woodlands Hill
A355
DORNEY HILL NORTH
DORNEY HILL SOUTH
Bower Wood
Green Common Lane
Odds Farm
Woodburn Common
Sheepcote Farm
Jennings Farm
Ship Hill
Harehatch Lane
Hicknaham Farm
Park Lane
Abbey Park Farm
Abbey Park Lane
COLLINSWOOD
Hales Cott
Wooburn Common Road
Boveney Wood Lane
Dropmore County First School
Little Road
Dorney Wood Road
Beeches Way
Common Lane
Littleworth Common
Egypt Lane
Egypt Woods
Dropmore
Great Burnt Coppice
Egy
Horseshoe Hill
Brook End Farm
Mc Auliffe Dr
Dukes Drive
Morton Dr
Burnham Beeches (Nature Reserve)
Curriers Lane
Park Lane
Halse Drive
Dropmore Road
Lambourne Golf Club
Victoria Drive
Sir Henry Peeks Drive
Pumpkin Hill
Dorney Wood
Lord Mayors Drive
East Burnham Common
Green Lane
Hawthorn Lane
Nightingale Park
Longmead Lane
Hunts Wood Farm
Golf
G H J K L M
1 2 3 4 5 6 7 8
199
212
223

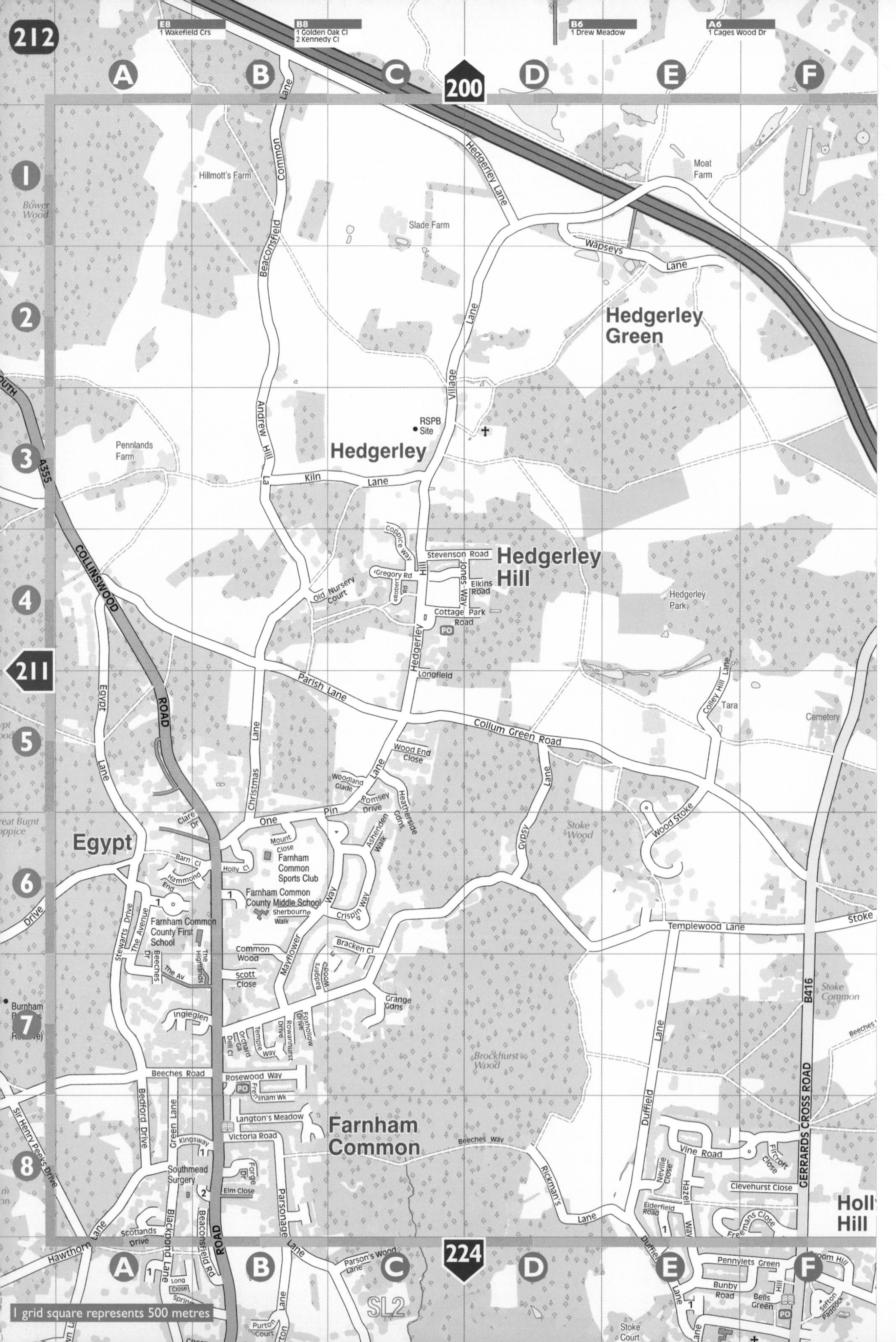
E8 1 Wakefield Crs
B8 1 Golden Oak Cl 2 Kennedy Cl
B6 1 Drew Meadow
A6 1 Cages Wood Dr
200
211
224
Hillmott's Farm
Beaconsfield Common Lane
Hedgerley Lane
Slade Farm
Moat Farm
Wapseys Lane
Hedgerley Green
Village Lane
Andrew Hill La
RSPB Site
Hedgerley
Pennlands Farm
Kiln Lane
A355
COLLINSWOOD ROAD
Coppice Way
Stevenson Road
Hedgerley Hill
Gregory Rd
Robert Rd
Jones Way
Elkins Road
Old Nursery Court
Cottage Park Road
PO
Hedgerley Park
Longfield
Parish Lane
Egypt Lane
Christmas Lane
Collum Green Road
Colley Hill Lane
Tara
Cemetery
Wood End Close
Woodland Glade
Pin Lane
Romsey Drive
Heatherside Gdns
Ashenden Walk
Gypsy Lane
Stoke Wood
Wood Stoke
One Pin
Clare Dr
Mount Close
Farnham Common Sports Club
Egypt
Barn Cl
Hammond End
Holly Cl
Farnham Common County Middle School
Sherbourne Walk
Crispin Way
Mayflower Way
Drive
Stewarts Drive
The Avenue
Farnham Common County First School
Beeches Dr
The Av
The Highlands
Common Wood
Scott Close
Bracken Cl
Badgers Wood
Grange Gdns
Templewood Lane
Stoke
Stoke Common
B416
Inglegien
Dell Cl
Orchard Ga
Temple Way
Rowanhurst Drive
Foxhollow Drive
Brockhurst Wood
Duffield Lane
GERRARDS CROSS ROAD
Beeches Road
Rosewood Way
Fresham Wk
Langton's Meadow
Farnham Common
Bedford Drive
Green Lane
Kingsway
Victoria Road
Beeches Way
Vine Road
Fircroft Close
Neville Close
Hazell Way
Clevehurst Close
Sir Henry Peeks Drive
Southmead Surgery
Forge Dr
Elm Close
Parsonage Lane
Rickman's Lane
Elderfield Road
Freemans Close
Holly Hill
Scotlands Drive
Blackpond Lane
Beaconsfield Rd
ROAD
Hawthorn Lane
Long Close
Springs
Parson's Wood Lane
Duffield Lane
Pennylets Green
Bunby Road
Bells Green
Hill
Sefton Paddock
SL2
Purton Court
Lane
Stoke Court
Bower Wood
Burnham Beeches
1 grid square represents 500 metres
A B C D E F
1 2 3 4 5 6 7 8

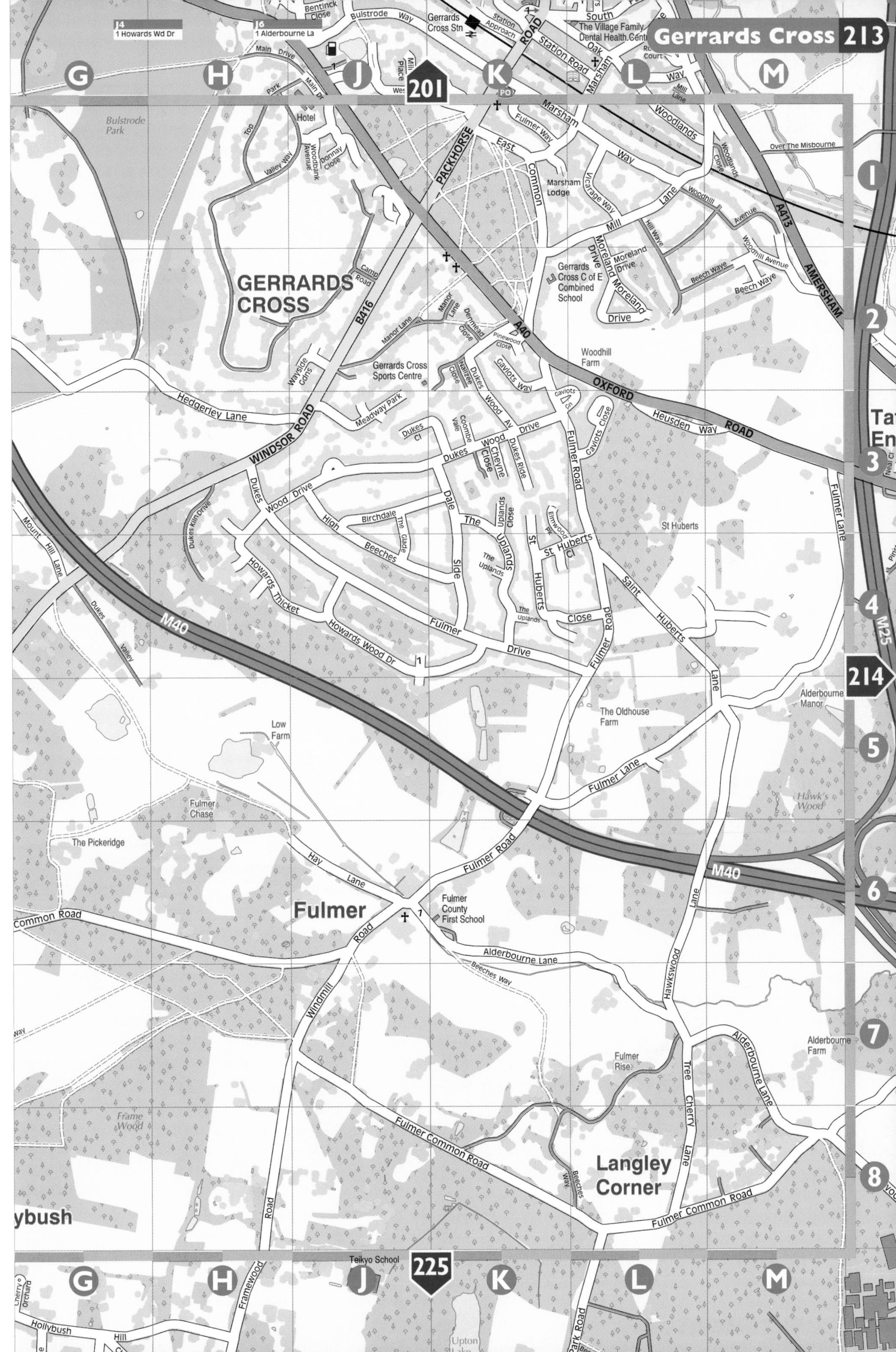
GERRARDS CROSS
Fulmer
Langley Corner
Bulstrode Park
Gerrards Cross Stn
Gerrards Cross Sports Centre
Gerrards Cross C of E Combined School
Marsham Lodge
Woodhill Farm
St Huberts
The Oldhouse Farm
Alderbourne Manor
Low Farm
Fulmer Chase
The Pickeridge
Fulmer County First School
Fulmer Rise
Alderbourne Farm
Frame Wood
Hawk's Wood
Teikyo School
Upton Lake
The Village Family Dental Health Centre
Hotel
OXFORD ROAD
WINDSOR ROAD
PACKHORSE ROAD
AMERSHAM
A40
A413
B416
M40
M25
Bulstrode Way
Station Road
Station Approach
Marsham Way
East Common
Mill Lane
Fulmer Road
Fulmer Drive
Dukes Wood Drive
Hedgerley Lane
Fulmer Lane
Hay Lane
Windmill Road
Alderbourne Lane
Fulmer Common Road
Hawkswood Lane
Tree Cherry Lane
Saint Huberts Lane
Howards Thicket
Howards Wood Dr
Heusden Way
Mount Hill Lane
Dukes Valley
J4 1 Howards Wd Dr
J6 1 Alderbourne La
201
214
225
G H J K L M
1 2 3 4 5 6 7 8

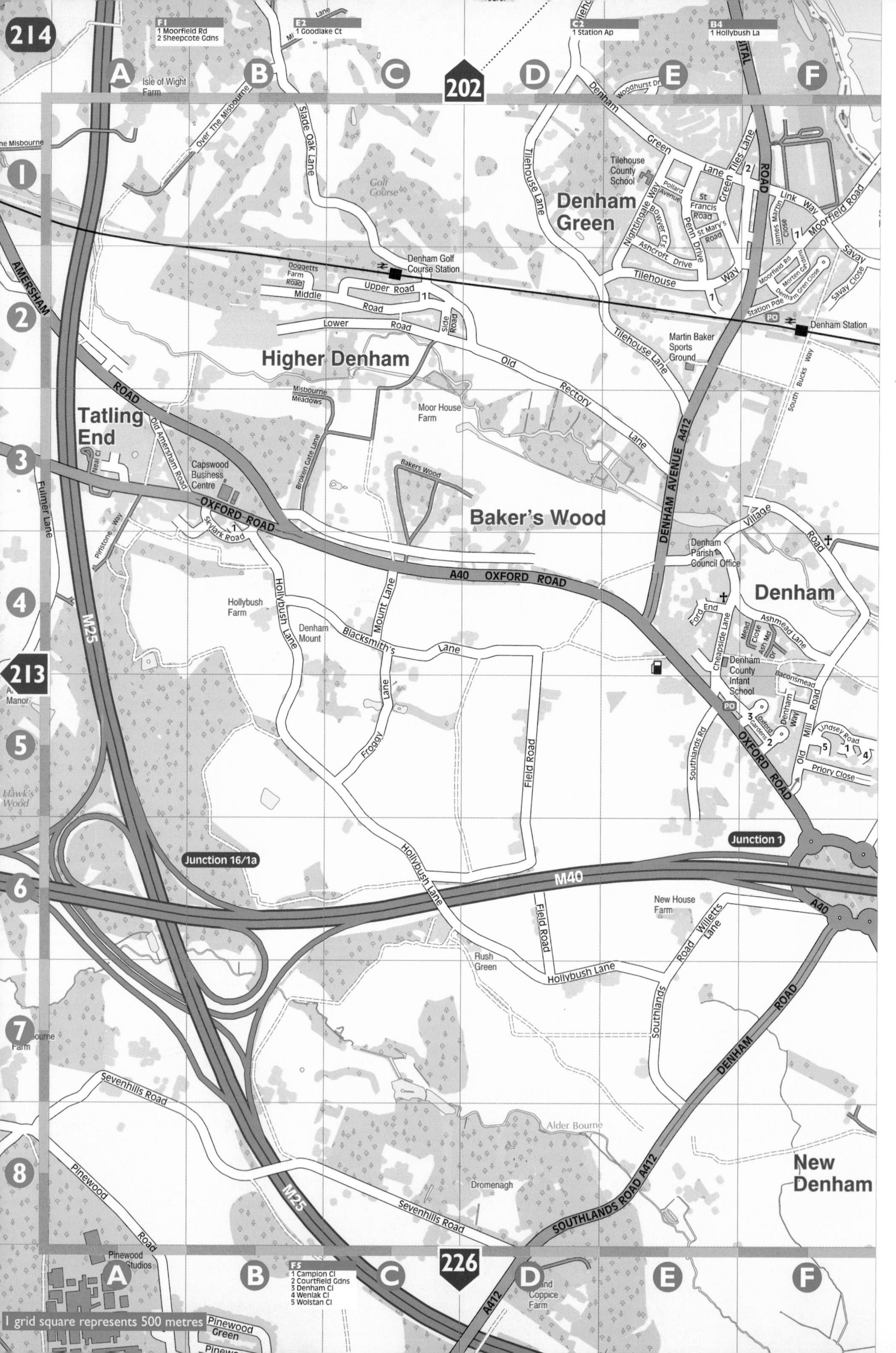
F1
1 Moorfield Rd
2 Sheepcote Gdns
E2
1 Goodlake Ct
C2
1 Station Ap
B4
1 Hollybush La
202
Isle of Wight Farm
Over The Misbourne
Slade Oak Lane
Golf Course
Denham Golf Course Station
Doggetts Farm Road
Upper Road
Middle Road
Lower Road
Side Road
Higher Denham
Old Rectory Lane
Misbourne Meadows
Moor House Farm
Broken Gate Lane
Bakers Wood
Baker's Wood
Tatling End
Neal Cl
Old Amersham Road
Capswood Business Centre
AMERSHAM ROAD
OXFORD ROAD
Skylark Road
Pinstone Way
Fulmer Lane
A40 OXFORD ROAD
Hollybush Farm
Hollybush Lane
Denham Mount
Blacksmith's Lane
Mount Lane
Froggy Lane
Field Road
M25
Junction 16/1a
Junction 1
M40
Hollybush Lane
Rush Green
New House Farm
Willetts Lane
Southlands Road
DENHAM ROAD
A40
Denham Green
Tilehouse County School
Tilehouse Lane
Nightingale Way
Pollard Avenue
Bowyer Cres
Ashcroft Drive
Tilehouse Way
St Francis Road
St Mary's Road
Penn Drive
Green Tiles Lane
Denham Green Lane
Woodhurst Dr
Link Way
Moorfield Road
James Martin Close
Savay Lane
Savay Close
Moorfield Rd
Morten Gardens
Denham Green Close
Station Pde
PO
Denham Station
Martin Baker Sports Ground
Tilehouse Lane
DENHAM AVENUE A412
South Bucks Way
Village Road
Denham Parish Council Office
Denham
Ford End
Cheapside Lane
Mead Close
Ash Md
Ashmead Lane
Denham County Infant School
Baconsmead
Denham Way
Oxford Gardens
Old Mill Road
Lindsey Road
Priory Close
Southlands Rd
OXFORD ROAD
Manor
Hawk's Wood
Sevenhills Road
Pinewood Road
Pinewood Studios
Alder Bourne
Dromenagh
SOUTHLANDS ROAD A412
New Denham
A412
Coppice Farm
Pinewood Green
213
226
F5
1 Campion Cl
2 Courtfield Gdns
3 Denham Cl
4 Wenlak Cl
5 Wolstan Cl
1 grid square represents 500 metres

G8
1 Nine Stiles Cl
J8
1 Blackmore Wy
2 Fairlight Dr
3 The Hermitage
4 Lancresse Cl
K6
1 Hetherington Wy
203
227
L6
1 Shipton Rd
L5
1 Swakeleys Rd
K8
1 Brearley Cl
Newyears Green
Ickenham
Willowbank
Newyears Green Lane
Harvil Road
Highway Farm
Savay Farm
UB9
Buckinghamshire County
Hillingdon
Grand Union Canal Walk
Buckinghamshire Golf Club
Golf Course
Copthall Farm
Breakspear Road
Breakspear Road South
Copthall Road West
Copthall Road East
Breakspear Junior School
Swakeleys Road
Western Avenue
A40(T)
Oxford Road
A4020
Park Road
B483
B467
Harefield Road
Uxbridge Common
Uxbridge Cricket Club
Dry Ski Slope
Uxbridge Swimming Pool
Uxbridge College
Vyners School
Hillingdon Station
Long Lane
The Lea
South Bucks Way
Colne Valley Trail
Ivy House Farm
Highbridge Industrial Estate
Frays College
Magistrates Court
Uxbridge Co Court
Hermitage Primary
Med Centre
Honeycroft Hill
Warren Road
Woodstock Drive
Halford Road
The Chase
Tudor Way
Lodore Green
Denham Court Drive
Moorhall Road

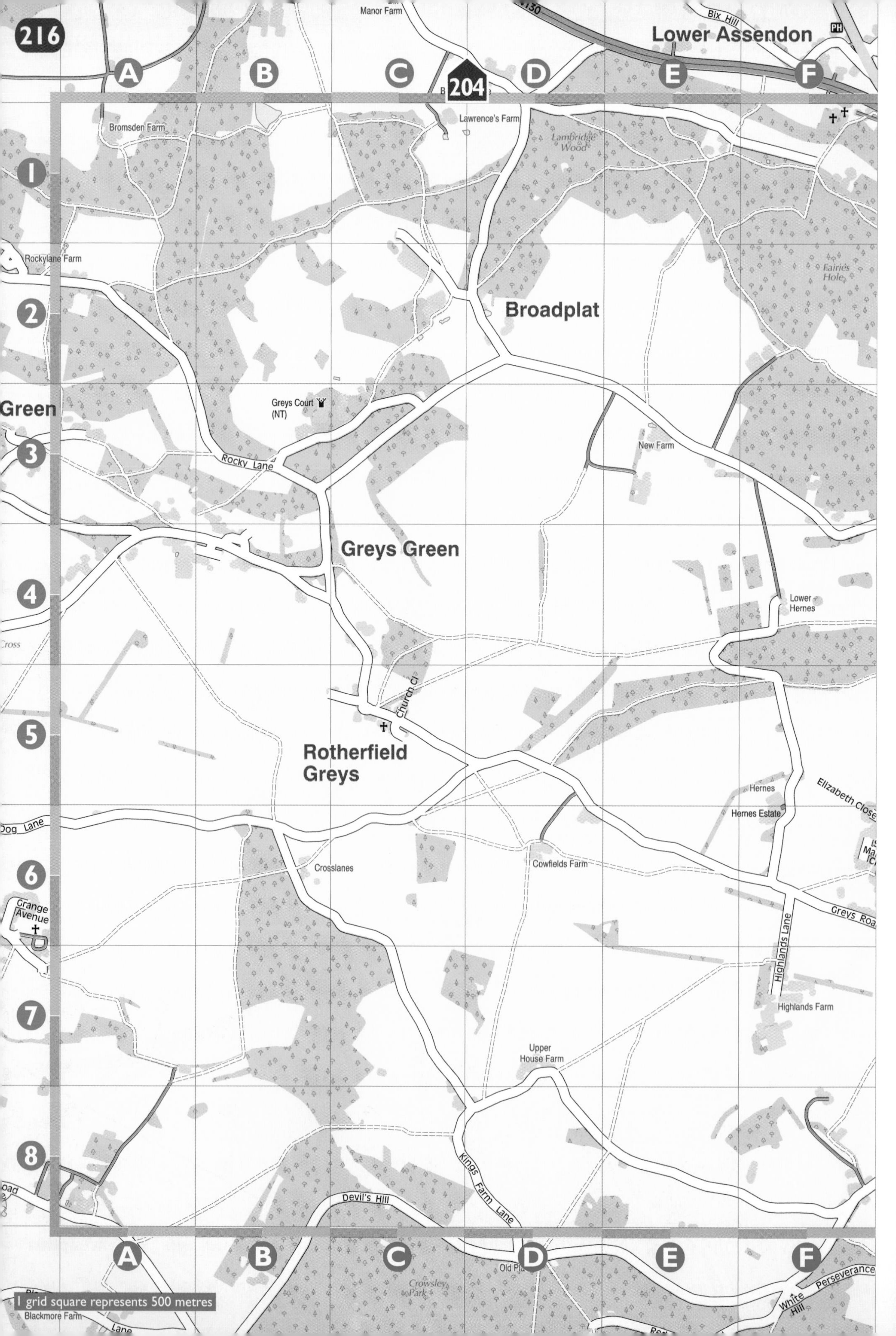

1 grid square represents 500 metres

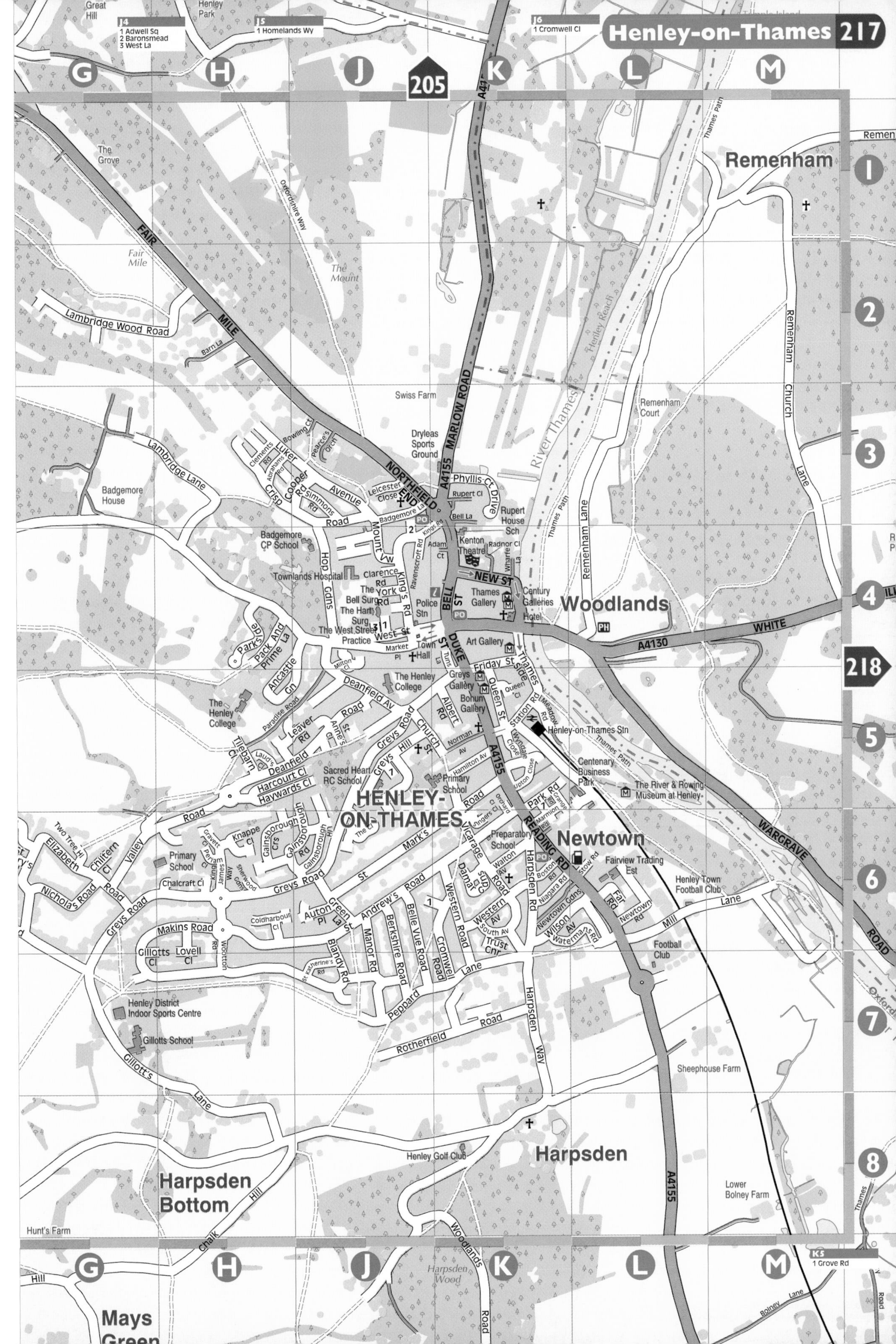
J4
1 Adwell Sq
2 Baronsmead
3 West La
J5
1 Homelands Wy
J6
1 Cromwell Cl
205
218
K5
1 Grove Rd
Remenham
Woodlands
HENLEY-ON-THAMES
Newtown
Harpsden
Harpsden Bottom
Mays Green
FAIR MILE
MARLOW ROAD
A4155
A4130
WHITE
WARGRAVE ROAD
River Thames
Henley Reach
Thames Path
Oxfordshire Way
The Grove
Fair Mile
The Mount
Lambridge Wood Road
Lambridge Lane
Barn La
Badgemore House
Swiss Farm
Dryleas Sports Ground
Remenham Court
Remenham Lane
Remenham Church Lane
NORTHFIELD END
Phyllis Ct Drive
Rupert Cl
Bell La
Rupert House Sch
Kenton Theatre
Radnor Cl
NEW ST
BELL ST
DUKE ST
Thames Gallery
Century Galleries
Hotel
Art Gallery
Town Hall
Market Pl
Police Stn
Badgemore CP School
Townlands Hospital
Bell Surg
The Hart Surg
The West Street Practice
The Henley College
Greys Gallery
Bohun Gallery
Friday St
Thames Side
Queen St
Queen Cl
Station Rd
Meadow Rd
Henley-on-Thames Stn
Centenary Business Park
The River & Rowing Museum at Henley
Sacred Heart RC School
Primary School
Preparatory School
Fairview Trading Est
Henley Town Football Club
Football Club
Mill Lane
Henley District Indoor Sports Centre
Gillotts School
Gillott's Lane
Henley Golf Club
Sheephouse Farm
Lower Bolney Farm
Bolney Lane
Hunt's Farm
Chalk Hill
Harpsden Wood
Woodlands Road
Harpsden Way
Harpsden Rd
Rotherfield Road
Peppard Lane
READING RD
Greys Road
St Mark's Road
St Andrew's Road
Vicarage Road
Western Road
Cromwell Road
Belle Vue Road
Berkshire Road
Manor Rd
Blandy Rd
Makins Road
Gillotts Cl
Lovell Cl
Chalcraft Cl
Nicholas Road
Elizabeth Rd
Chiltern Cl
Valley Road
Two Tree Hill
Deanfield Av
Deanfield Road
Harcourt Cl
Haywards Cl
Tilebarn Cl
Paradise Road
Parkside
Pack And Prime La
Ancastle Gn
Leaver Rd
St Anne's Cl
Greys Hill
Church St
Albert Rd
Norman Av
Hamilton Av
Park Rd
Marmion Rd
Stow Rd
Boston Rd
Niagara Rd
Newtown Gdns
Newtown Rd
Wilson Av
Watermans Rd
Far Rd
Damer Gdns
Walton Av
South Av
Western Av
Trust Cnr
Coldharbour Cl
Auton Pl
Green La
St Katherine's Rd
Wootton Rd
Gainsborough Hill
Gainsborough Crs
Gainsborough Rd
Knappe Cl
Sherwood Gdns
Kings Rd
Clarence Rd
York Rd
Ravenscroft Rd
Mount Vw
Hop Gdns
Avenue Road
Simmons Rd
Cooper Rd
Crisp Rd
Luker Av
Clements Rd
Abrahams Rd
Bowling Ct
Pearce's Orch
Leicester Close
Badgemore La
Adam Ct
Wharfe La
Wyndale Close
Upton Close
Orchard Cl
Singers Cl
Milton Cl
Laud's Cl
Great Hill
Henley Park
Hill
Thames Path

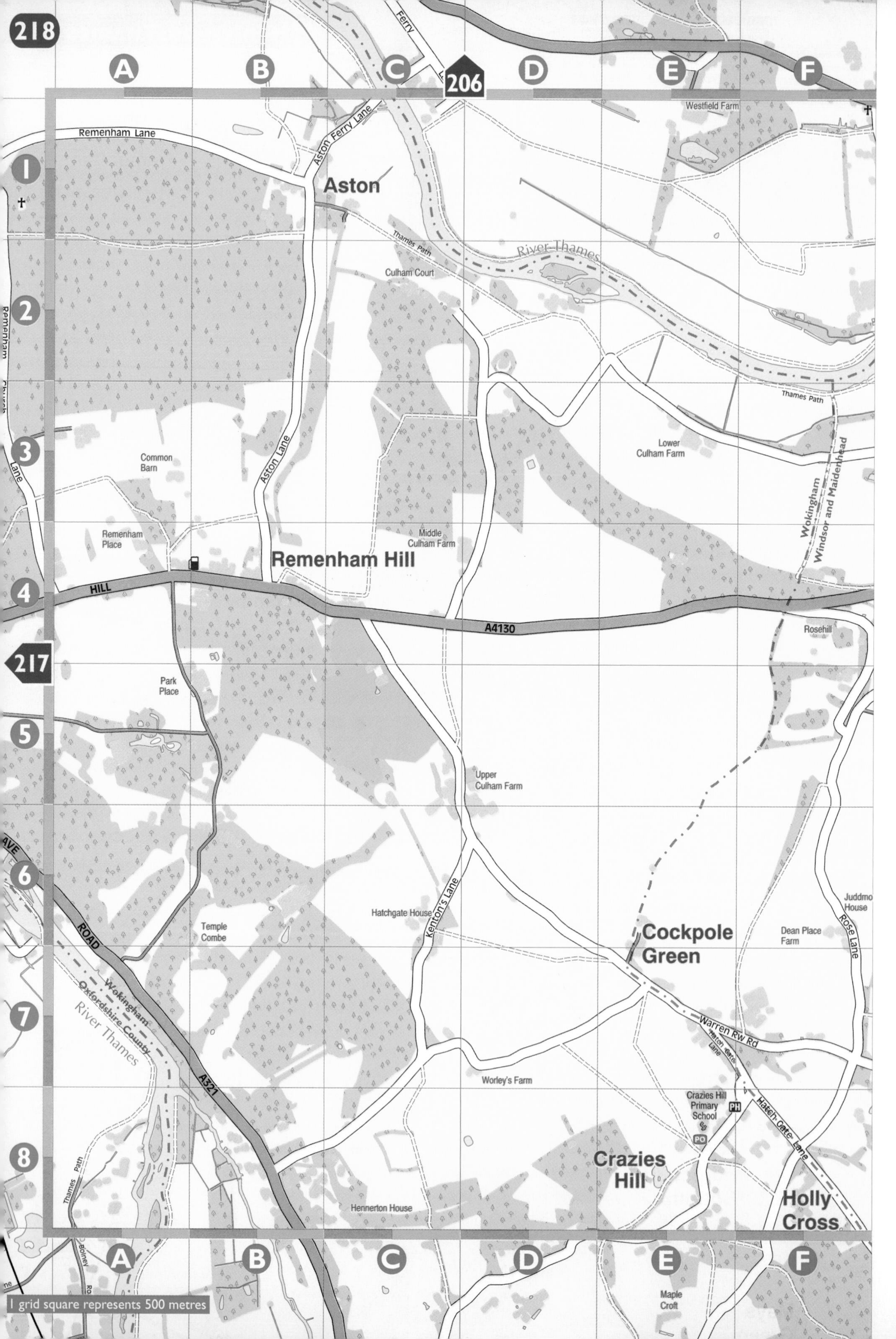
A
B
C
D
E
F
206
217
1
2
3
4
5
6
7
8
Ferry
Westfield Farm
Remenham Lane
Aston Ferry Lane
Aston
Thames Path
River Thames
Culham Court
Remenham Church Lane
Thames Path
Lower Culham Farm
Wokingham
Windsor and Maidenhead
Common Barn
Aston Lane
Remenham Place
Middle Culham Farm
Remenham Hill
HILL
A4130
Rosehill
Park Place
Upper Culham Farm
AVE
Kenton's Lane
Hatchgate House
Juddmo House
Cockpole Green
Dean Place Farm
Rose Lane
ROAD
Temple Combe
Wokingham
Oxfordshire County
River Thames
Warren Rw Rd
Hatch Gate Lane
A321
Worley's Farm
Crazies Hill Primary School
PH
PO
Hatch Gate Lane
Thames Path
Crazies Hill
Hennerton House
Holly Cross
Bolney Rd
Maple Croft
1 grid square represents 500 metres

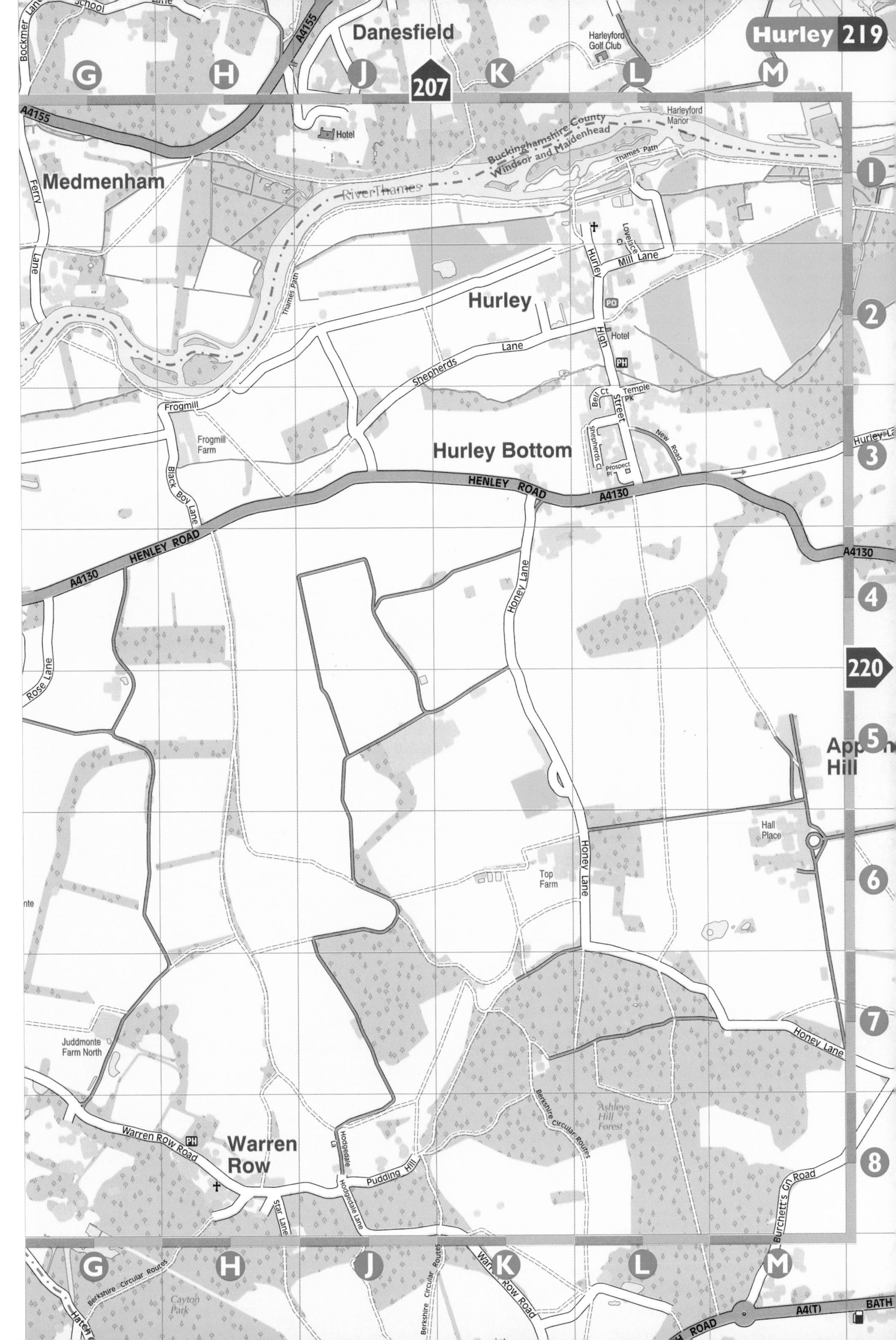
Danesfield
Harleyford Golf Club
207
G
H
J
K
L
M
A4155
Hotel
Harleyford Manor
Buckinghamshire County
Windsor and Maidenhead
Thames Path
Medmenham
River Thames
Ferry Lane
Lovelace Cl
Hurley
Mill Lane
Hurley
Thames Path
PO
Hotel
High
PH
Shepherds
Lane
Temple Pk
Bell Ct
Street
Frogmill
Frogmill Farm
Shepherds Cl
New Road
Hurley Bottom
Prospect Pl
Hurley La
Black Boy Lane
HENLEY ROAD
A4130
HENLEY ROAD
A4130
A4130
Honey Lane
Rose Lane
220
App
Hill
Hall Place
Top Farm
Honey Lane
Honey Lane
Juddmonte Farm North
Berkshire Circular Routes
Ashley Hill Forest
Warren Row Road
PH
Warren Row
Hodgedale La
Pudding Hill
Hodgedale Lane
Star Lane
Burchett's Gn Road
Berkshire Circular Routes
Cayton Park
Berkshire Circular Routes
Warren Row Road
ROAD
A4(T)
BATH
1
2
3
4
5
6
7
8

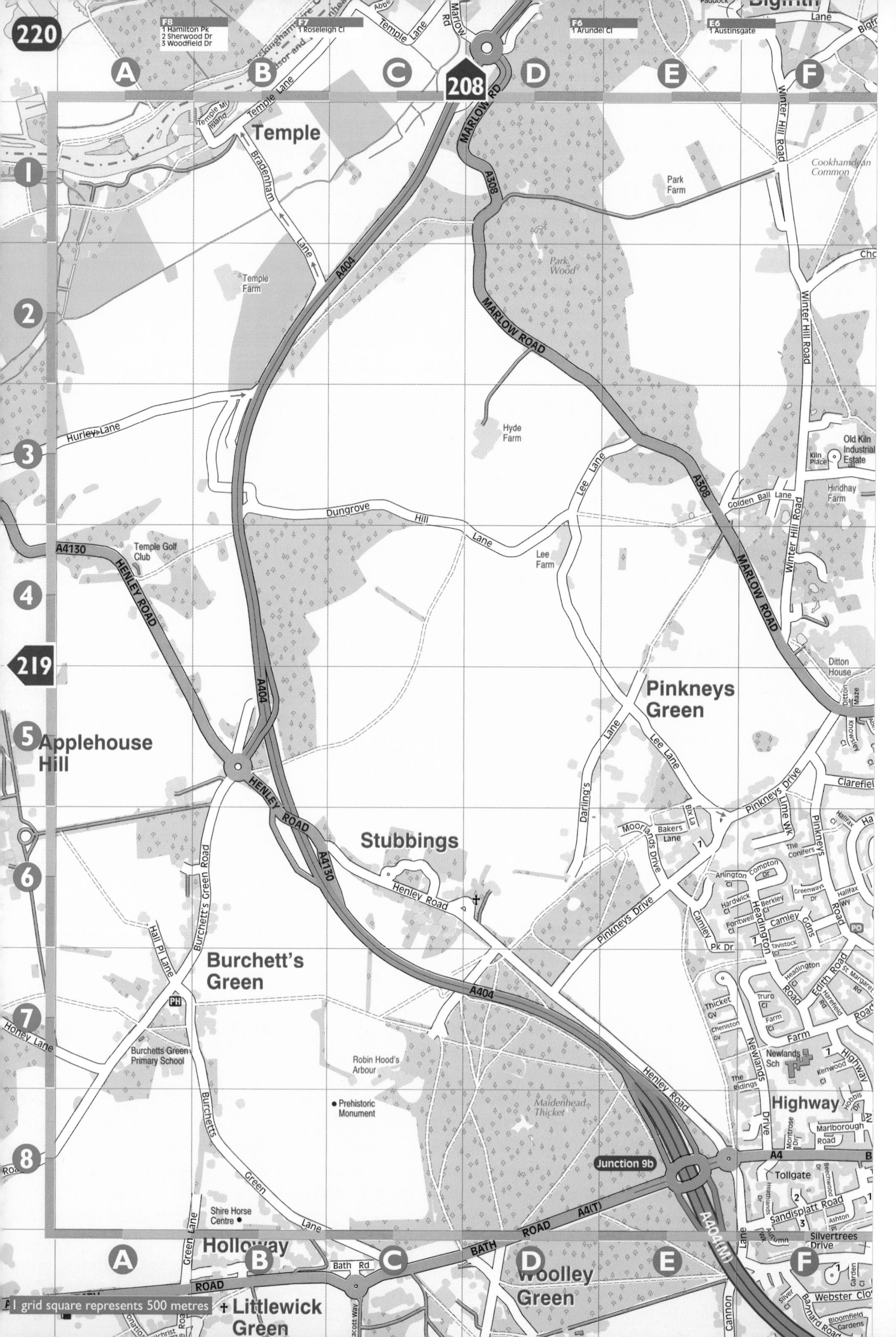
F8 1 Hamilton Pk 2 Sherwood Dr 3 Woodfield Dr
F7 1 Roseleigh Cl
F6 1 Arundel Cl
E6 1 Austinsgate
208
219
Temple
Temple Lane
Bradenham Lane
Temple Farm
Hurley Lane
A404
MARLOW RD
A308
MARLOW ROAD
Park Farm
Park Wood
Cookhamdean Common
Winter Hill Road
Hyde Farm
Old Kiln Industrial Estate
Kiln Place
Hindhay Farm
Golden Ball Lane
Lee Lane
Dungrove Hill Lane
Lee Farm
A4130
HENLEY ROAD
Temple Golf Club
Ditton House
Pinkneys Green
Applehouse Hill
Darling's Lane
Pinkneys Drive
Lime Wk
Stubbings
Henley Road
Moorlands Drive
Bakers Lane
Blix La
Burchett's Green Road
Hall Pl Lane
Burchett's Green
Camley Pk Dr
Headington Road
Highway Road
Highway
Honey Lane
Burchetts Green Primary School
Robin Hood's Arbour
Prehistoric Monument
Maidenhead Thicket
Newlands Drive
Newlands Sch
Junction 9b
A4
A4(T)
BATH ROAD
A404(M)
Tollgate
Sandisplatt Road
Silvertrees Drive
Burchetts Green Lane
Shire Horse Centre
Holloway
Green Lane
Bath Rd
Woolley Green
Littlewick Green
Webster Cl
Barnard Road
Bloomfield Gardens
Cannon Lane
Marlborough Road
1 grid square represents 500 metres

Numbered streets
The names of all numbered streets on this page are listed at the back of the index
209
222
Cookham Rise
Lower Mount Farm
Long Lane
Mount Farm
Cemetery
CANNONDOWN ROAD
SWITCHBACK ROAD NORTH
Maidenhead Road
Strande Lane
Bass Md
Lightlands Lane
Malders Lane
Nightingale Lane
Cannon Court Farm
Hindhay Lane
Hungerford Drive
Kinghorn Park
Burcot Gdns
Shifford Crescent
GARDNER ROAD
Furze Platt
FURZE PLATT ROAD A308
Furze Platt Comprehensive School
Furze Platt Junior & Infant School
Malvern Road
Furze Platt Station
North Town
North Maidenhead Cricket Club
Maidenhead Sailing Club
Summerleaze
Oaken Grove
Linden Medical Cen
Alwyn County Infant School
Court House Junior School
GRINGER HILL A308
COOKHAM ROAD
Ray Mill Road West
Blackamoor Lane
Gladstone Industrial Estate
Doctors Surgery
Cemetery
St Marks Hospital
St Mark's Crescent
Berkshire College of Art & Design
College Avenue
CRAUFURD RISE
MARLOW RD
BAD GODESBERG WY
SAINT-CLOUD WAY
Wilderness Medical Centre
Superbowl Leisure Centre
Ivyleaf W.M. Club
CASTLE HILL
High Street
Maidenhead Clinic
Broadway
Maidenhead Synagogue
The Symonds Medical Cen
Redroofs Theatre School
Highfield Sch
A4 BATH ROAD
Kings Grove Industrial Est
Boyn Valley Industrial Est
East Berkshire College
Maidenhead United Football Club
Maidenhead Station
KING ST
Tittle Row
St Edmund Campion RC Primary School
SL6 MAIDENHEAD
Fishery
Altwood C of E School
Boyn Hill
Desborough School
Maidenhead Golf Club
BRAYWICK ROAD
Reform Road
OLDFIELD
Bell St
Stafferton Way
Ludlow Road
G
H
J
K
L
M
1
2
3
4
5
6
7
8

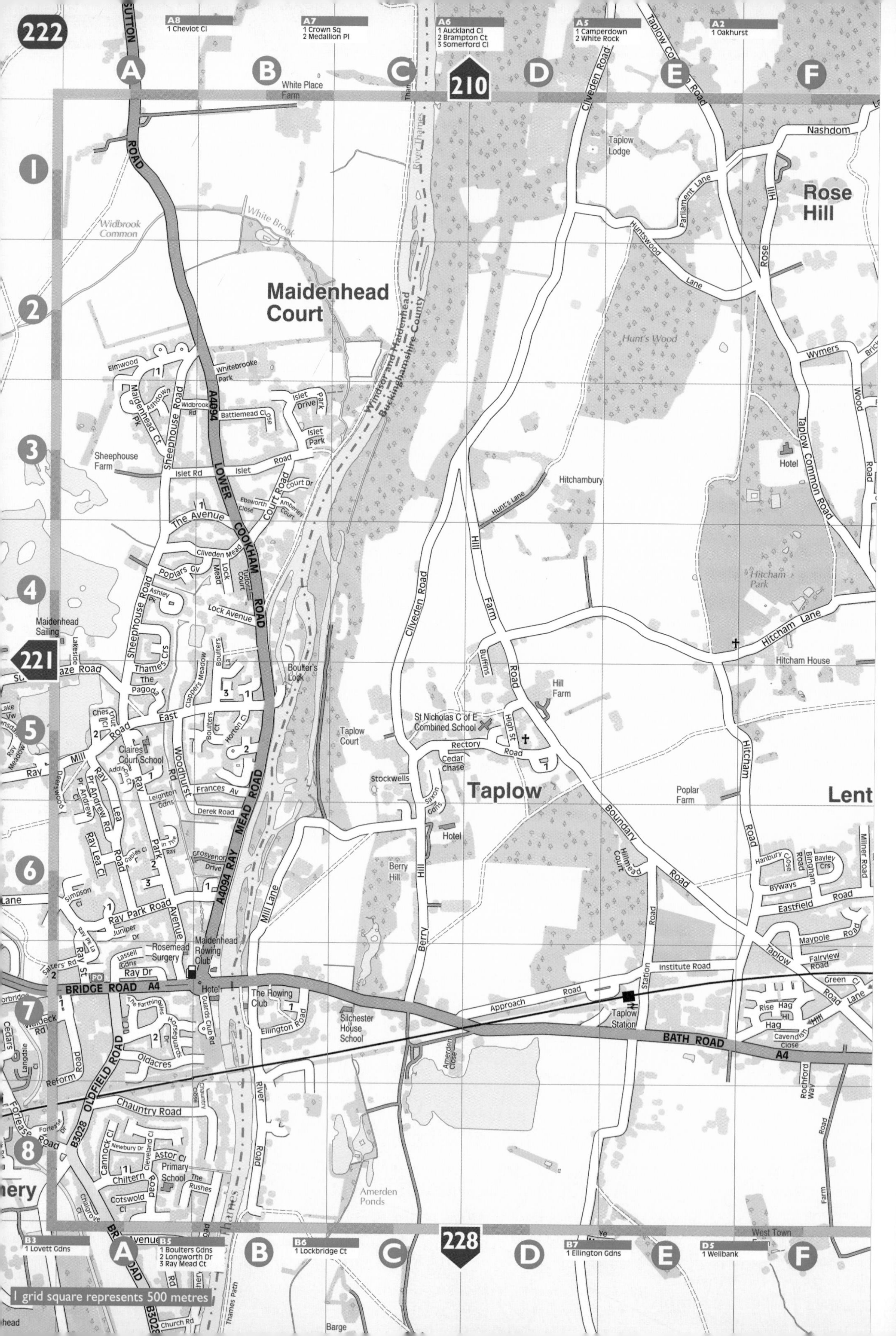
A8
1 Cheviot Cl
A7
1 Crown Sq
2 Medallion Pl
A6
1 Auckland Cl
2 Brampton Ct
3 Somerford Cl
A5
1 Camperdown
2 White Rock
A2
1 Oakhurst
210
White Place Farm
Maidenhead Court
Rose Hill
Taplow Lodge
Nashdom
Parliament Lane
Huntswood Lane
Rose Hill
Widbrook Common
White Brook
River Thames
Windsor and Maidenhead
Buckinghamshire County
Hunt's Wood
Wymers Wood
Taplow Common Road
Hotel
Hitchambury
Hunt's Lane
Cliveden Road
Hill Farm Road
Hitcham Park
Hitcham Lane
Hitcham House
Elmwood
Maidenhead Ct
Ashdown
Sheephouse Road
Whitebrooke Park
Widbrook Rd
Battlemead Cl
Islet Drive
Islet Park
Sheephouse Farm
Islet Rd
Islet Road
Court Dr
Court Road
Ebsworth Close
Amberley Court
The Avenue
A4094 LOWER COOKHAM ROAD
Cliveden Mead
Poplars Gv
Lock Mead
Tudor Court
Ashley Pk
Lock Avenue
Maidenhead Sailing
221
Lakeside
Sheephouse Road
Thames Crs
Boulters La
Clappers Meadow
Boulter's Lock
The Pagoda
East Road
Boulters Ct
Horton Cl
Woodhurst Rd
Claires Court School
Mill Rd
Ray Mill Road
Chestnut Cl
Addison Ct
Ray Park
Pr Andrew Cl
Pr Andrew Rd
Lea Road
Leighton Gdns
Frances Av
Derek Road
Ray Lea Cl
In The Ray
Grosvenor Drive
A4094 RAY MEAD ROAD
Simpson Cl
Ray Park Road
Ray Park Avenue
Juniper Dr
Ray Park La
Rosemead Surgery
Maidenhead Rowing Club
Lassell Gdns
Ray Dr
Ray St
Salters' Rd
PO
BRIDGE ROAD A4
Hotel
Guards Club Rd
The Rowing Club
Ellington Road
Silchester House School
The Farthingales
Horseguards Dr
Oldacres
OLDFIELD ROAD
Reform Road
Langdale Cl
Chauntry Road
Chauntry Close
River Road
B3028
Forlease Road
Forlease Dr
Cannock Cl
Newbury Dr
Cleveland Cl
Astor Cl
Primary School
The Rushes
Chiltern Road
Cotswold Cl
Challow Cl
Thames
Amerden Ponds
Amerden Close
Taplow Court
Stockwells
Mill Lane
St Nicholas C of E Combined School
High St
Rectory Road
Cedar Chase
Saxon Gdns
Taplow
Hotel
Berry Hill
Boundary Road
Hillmead Court
Station Road
Institute Road
Approach Road
Taplow Station
BATH ROAD A4
Hitcham Road
Poplar Farm
Lent
Hanbury Close
Bingham Road
Bayley Crs
Milner Road
Byways
Eastfield Road
Maypole Road
Fairview Road
Taplow Road
Green Cl
Lane
Rise Hag Hill
Hag
Cavendish Close
Rochford Way
Farm Road
Hill Farm Road
West Town
228
B3
1 Lovett Gdns
B5
1 Boulters Gdns
2 Longworth Dr
3 Ray Mead Ct
B6
1 Lockbridge Ct
B7
1 Ellington Gdns
D5
1 Wellbank
1 grid square represents 500 metres
Thames Path
Church Rd
Barge

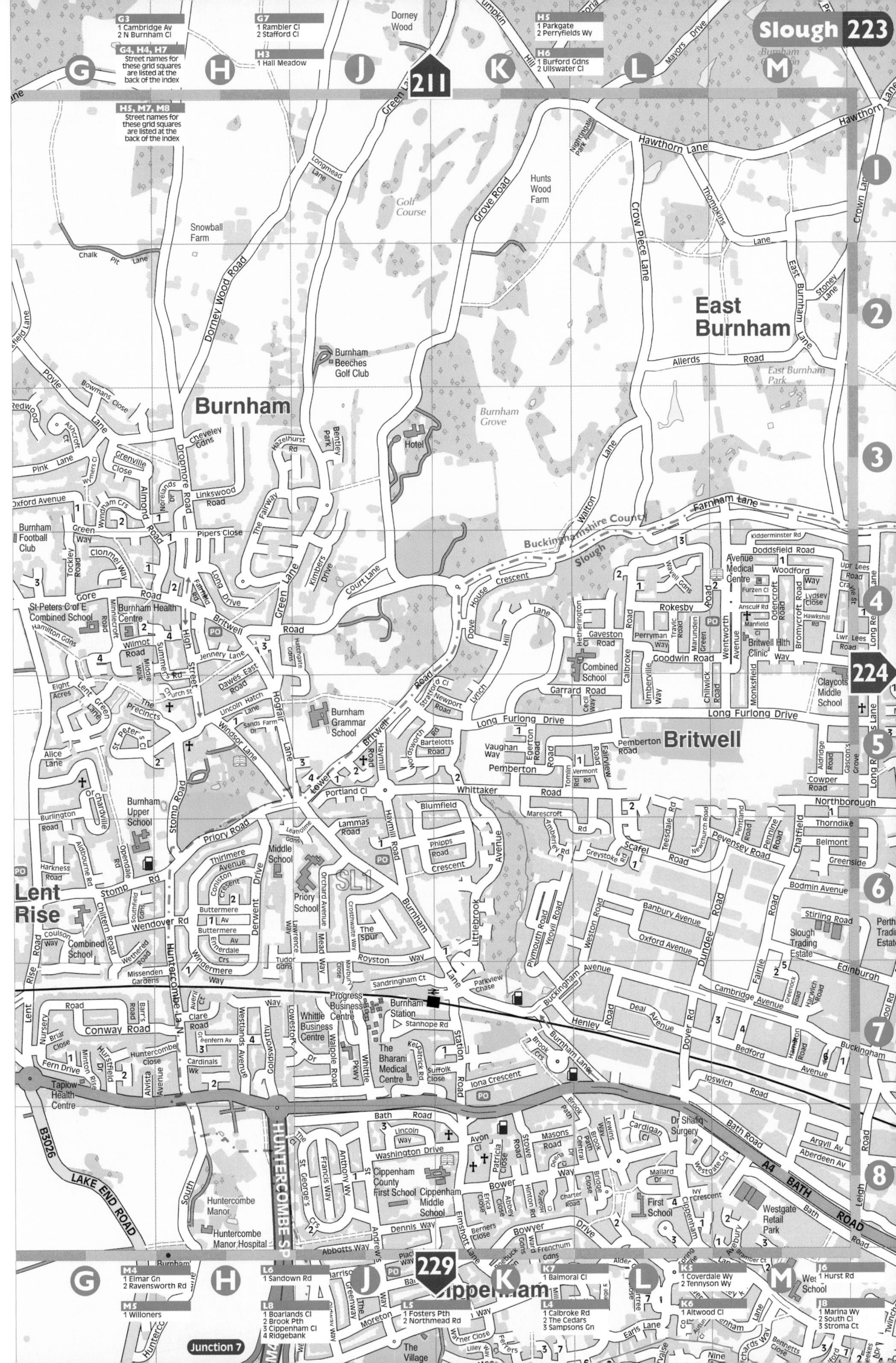
G3
1 Cambridge Av
2 N Burnham Cl
G4, H4, H7
Street names for these grid squares are listed at the back of the index
H5, M7, M8
Street names for these grid squares are listed at the back of the index
G7
1 Rambler Cl
2 Stafford Cl
H3
1 Hall Meadow
H5
1 Parkgate
2 Perryfields Wy
H6
1 Burford Gdns
2 Ullswater Cl
211
224
229
Burnham
East Burnham
Britwell
Lent Rise
Cippenham
Junction 7
M4
1 Elmar Gn
2 Ravensworth Rd
M5
1 Willoners
L6
1 Sandown Rd
L8
1 Boarlands Cl
2 Brook Pth
3 Cippenham Cl
4 Ridgebank
L5
1 Fosters Pth
2 Northmead Rd
K7
1 Balmoral Cl
L4
1 Calbroke Rd
2 The Cedars
3 Sampsons Gn
K5
1 Coverdale Wy
2 Tennyson Wy
K6
1 Altwood Cl
J6
1 Hurst Rd
J8
1 Marina Wy
2 South Cl
3 Stroma Ct

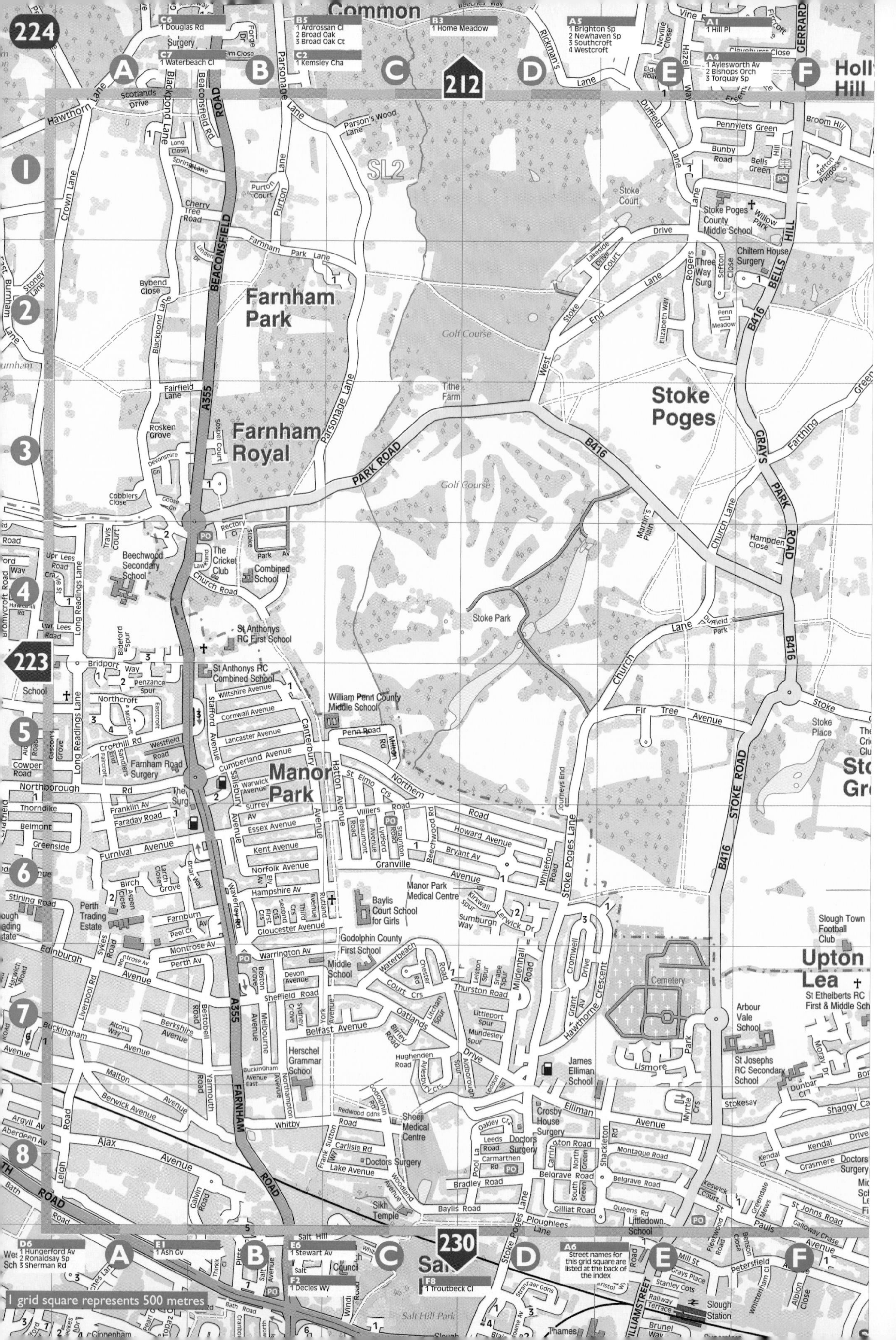
Common
C6 1 Douglas Rd
C7 1 Waterbeach Cl
B5 1 Ardrossan Cl 2 Broad Oak 3 Broad Oak Ct
C2 1 Kemsley Cha
B3 1 Home Meadow
A5 1 Brighton Sp 2 Newhaven Sp 3 Southcroft 4 Westcroft
A1 1 Hill Pl
A4 1 Aylesworth Av 2 Bishops Orch 3 Torquay Sp
212
Holly Hill
A B C D E F
1 2 3 4 5 6 7 8
Hawthorn Lane
Scotlands Drive
Blackpond Lane
Beaconsfield Rd
BEACONSFIELD ROAD
Parsonage Lane
Parson's Wood Lane
Rickman's Lane
Duffield Lane
Hazell Way
Pennylets Green
Bunby Road
Bells Green
Broom Hill
Sefton Paddock
GERRARDS
Crown Lane
Long Close
Spring Lane
Purton Court
Purton Lane
Cherry Tree Road
SL2
Stoke Court
Stoke Poges County Middle School
Willow Park
Drive
Lakeside Drive Court
Farnham Park Lane
Stoney Lane
East Burnham Lane
Bybend Close
Farnham Park
Three Way Surg
Rogers Lane
Sefton Close
Chiltern House Surgery
BELLS HILL
B416
Elizabeth Way
Penn Meadow
Stoke End Lane
West
Golf Course
Burnham
Fairfield Lane
A355
Tithe Farm
Stoke Poges
Rosken Grove
Gospel Court
Farnham Royal
PARK ROAD
Devonshire Gn
Cobblers Close
Goose Gn
Golf Course
GRAYS PARK ROAD
Farthing Green
Travis Court
Rectory Cl
Stoke Park Av
The Cricket Club
Combined School
Martin's Plain
Church Lane
Hampden Close
Beechwood Secondary School
Church Road
Upr Lees Road
Long Readings Lane
Hawkshill Rd
Lwr Lees Road
Bromycroft Road
Stoke Park
St Anthonys RC First School
Bideford Spur
Duffield Park
223
Bridport Way
Penzance Spur
St Anthonys RC Combined School
Wiltshire Avenue
Cornwall Avenue
Stafford Avenue
Lancaster Avenue
Cumberland Avenue
Canterbury Avenue
William Penn County Middle School
Penn Road
Milton Rd
Fir Tree Avenue
Stoke Place
Northcroft
Eastcroft
Crofthill Rd
Westfield Road
Farnham Road Surgery
Sandlers End
Cowper Road
Northborough Rd
Manor Park
Warwick Avenue
Salisbury Avenue
Hatton Avenue
St Elmo Crs
Northern Road
Journeys End
STOKE ROAD
Thorndike
Belmont
Franklin Av
Faraday Road
Surrey Av
Essex Avenue
Kent Avenue
Norfolk Avenue
Villiers Road
Beaumont Road
Lydford Avenue
Staunton Road
Beechwood Rd
Howard Avenue
Bryant Av
Granville Avenue
Whiteford Road
Stoke Poges Lane
Greenside
Furnival Avenue
Briar Way
Birch Grove
Larch Close
Aspen Close
Hampshire Av
Ely Av
Manor Park Medical Centre
Kirkwall Spur
Sumburgh Way
Lerwick Dr
Stirling Road
Perth Trading Estate
Farnburn Av
Peel Ct
Waverley Rd
Third Crs
Second Crs
First Crs
Rutland Avenue
Baylis Court School for Girls
Gloucester Avenue
Cromwell Drive
Slough Town Football Club
Edinburgh Avenue
Sykes Road
Montrose Av
Perth Av
Warrington Av
Godolphin County First School
Middle School
Waterbeach Road
Chester Rd
Leiston Spur
Snape Spur
Mildenhall Road
Hawthorne Crescent
Cemetery
Upton Lea
St Ethelberts RC First & Middle School
Liverpool Rd
Boston Grove
Devon Avenue
Sheffield Road
Court Crs
Thurston Road
Grant Av
Sydney Grove
York Avenue
Littleport Spur
Arbour Vale School
Buckingham Avenue
Altona Way
Berkshire Avenue
Bestobell Road
Melbourne Avenue
Belfast Avenue
Oatlands Drive
Litcham Spur
Mundesley Spur
Birley Road
Park
Lismore
Moray Dr
Herschel Grammar School
Hughenden Road
Aylesbury Crs
Aldborough Spur
Loddon Spur
James Elliman School
St Josephs RC Secondary School
Dunbar Cl
Malton Avenue
Yarmouth Road
Buckingham Avenue East
Northampton Avenue
Godolphin Rd
Elliman Avenue
Myrtle Crs
Stokesay
Shaggy Calf
Berwick Avenue
Whitby Road
Redwood Gdns
Sheeji Medical Centre
Oakley Crs
Crosby House Surgery
Shackleton Rd
Argyll Av
Aberdeen Av
Ajax Avenue
Leigh Road
FARNHAM ROAD
Frank Sutton Way
Carlisle Rd
Doctors Surgery
Leeds Road
Carmarthen Rd
Doctors Surgery
Carrington Road
North Green
Montague Road
Kendal Drive
Grasmere
Doctors Surgery
Bath Road
Lake Avenue
Woodland Avenue
Pool La
Bradley Road
Belgrave Road
South Green
Kendal Cl
Galvin Road
Sikh Temple
Baylis Road
Gilliat Road
Queens Rd
Keswick Court
Greendale Mews
St Pauls Avenue
St Johns Road
Ploughlees Lane
Littledown School
Galloway Chase
D6 1 Hungerford Av 2 Ronaldsay Sp 3 Sherman Rd
E1 1 Ash Gv
E6 1 Stewart Av
Salt Hill
Council
F2 1 Decies Wy
230
F8 1 Troutbeck Cl
A6 Street names for this grid square are listed at the back of the index
Mill St
Grays Place
Stanley Cots
Railway Terrace
Fleetwood Road
Benson Close
Petersfield Avenue
Whittenham Cl
Albion Close
WILLIAMSTREET
Slough Station
Brunel Way
Salt Hill Park
Stranraer Gdns
Thames
Bath Road
Cippenham
1 grid square represents 500 metres

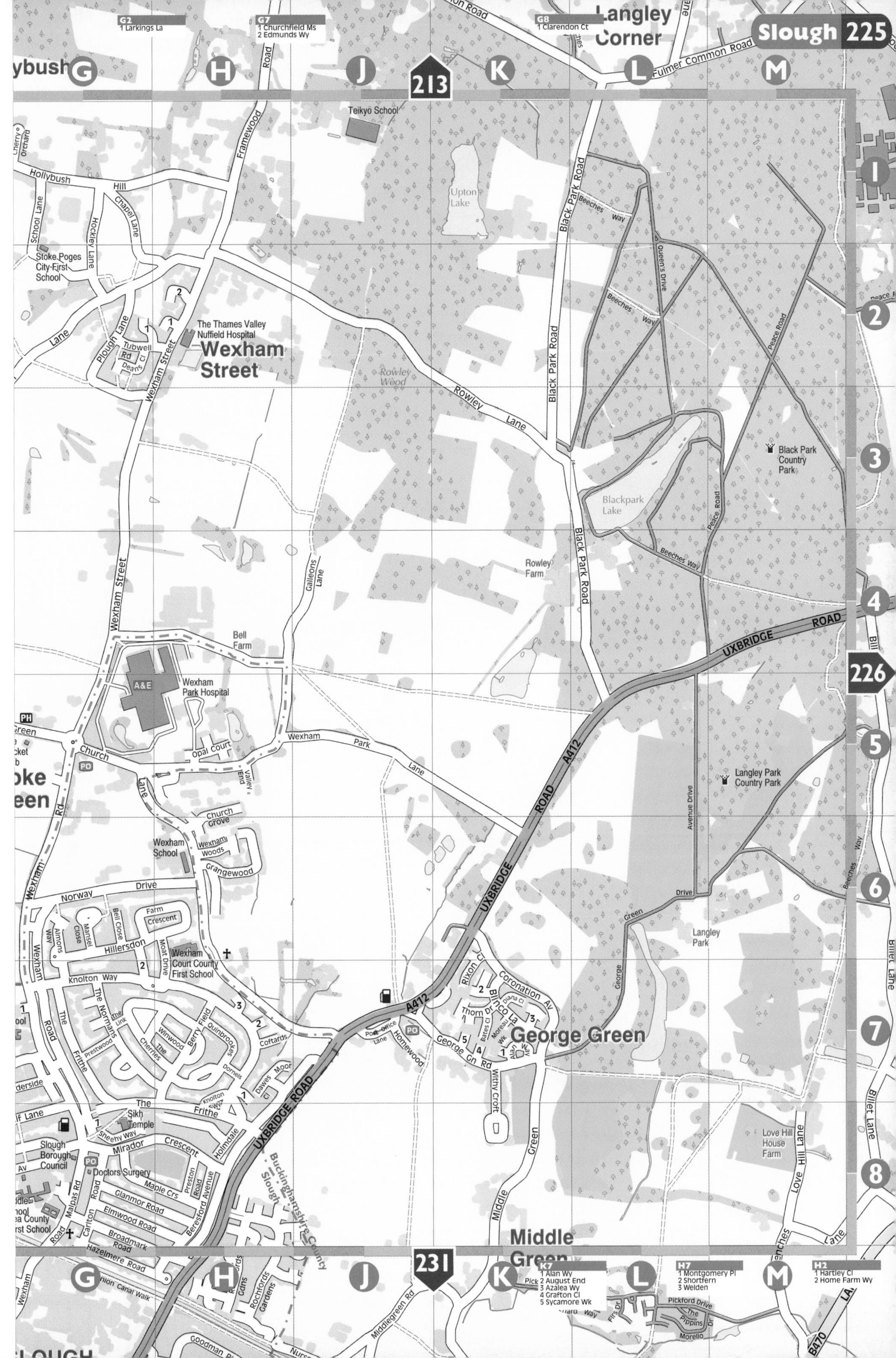
G2
1 Larkings La
G7
1 Churchfield Ms
2 Edmunds Wy
G8
1 Clarendon Ct
Langley
Corner
Fulmer Common Road
213
Teikyo School
Framewood Road
Hollybush Hill
School Lane
Hockley Lane
Chapel Lane
Stoke Poges
City First
School
Upton
Lake
Black Park Road
Beeches Way
Queen's Drive
Peace Road
Plough Lane
Tubwell Rd
Deans Cl
Wexham Street
The Thames Valley
Nuffield Hospital
Wexham
Street
Rowley
Wood
Rowley Lane
Black Park
Country
Park
Blackpark
Lake
Rowley
Farm
Galleons Lane
Bell
Farm
UXBRIDGE ROAD
226
A&E
Wexham
Park Hospital
Wexham Park Lane
Church
Opal Court
Valley End
A412
Langley Park
Country Park
Avenue Drive
Church
Grove
Wexham
School
Wexham Woods
Grangewood
Norway Drive
Farm
Crescent
Bell Close
Mansel Close
Almons Way
Hillersdon
Moat Drive
Wexham
Court County
First School
Knolton Way
The Normans
The Link
Berry Field
Winwood
Quinbrookes
Cherries
Prestwood
Coftards
Dornels
Dawes Moor
Green Drive
George Green
Langley
Park
Rixon Cl
Coronation Av
Blinco La
Thorn Dr
Bates Cl
Moreau Wk
Diana Cl
Post Office Lane
Homewood
George Gn Rd
George Green
Withy Croft
The Frithe
Knolton Way
Sikh
Temple
Sheehy Way
Slough
Borough
Council
Mirador Crescent
Doctors Surgery
Preston Road
Maple Crs
Glanmor Road
Elmwood Road
Broadmark Road
Beresford Avenue
Holmdale
Malpas Rd
Carlton Road
Hazelmere Road
Buckinghamshire County
Slough
Middle Green
Love Hill
House
Farm
Love Hill Lane
Billet Lane
Middle
Green
231
Middlegreen Rd
K7
1 Alan Wy
2 August End
3 Azalea Wy
4 Grafton Cl
5 Sycamore Wk
H7
1 Montgomery Pl
2 Shortfern
3 Welden
H2
1 Hartley Cl
2 Home Farm Wy
Pickford Drive
The Pippins
Morello
Rochfords Gardens
Union Canal Walk
Goodman Pk
B470
SLOUGH
G H J K L M
2 3 4 5 6 7 8

226
D7 1 Gilliatt Cl
C4 1 Slough Rd 2 Whitehouse Wy
C3 1 Keensacre 2 Trewarden Av
B4 1 Hawthorn Cl
B3 1 Glaisyer Wy 2 Rowan Gdns 3 Warren Fld
New Denham
214
Pinewood Film Studios
Pinewood Green
Pinewood Close
Ashford Rd
Cedar Cl
Thornbridge Road
Heatherden Green
Peace Road
Pinewood Road
DENHAM ROAD
SOUTHLANDS ROAD A412
Round Coppice Farm
Iver Heath
The Parkway
Longstone Rd
St David's Close
Bangors Road N
Aysgarth Medical Centre
Birch Cl
Anslow Gdns
Trewarden Av
Templewood Surgery
CHURCH ROAD
Iver Heath Hlth Centre
St Margaret's Close
Heath Way
Laurels Rd
Oak End Dr
Alder Rd
Iver Heath Middle School
Warren House
SLOUGH ROAD
A4007
A412
First School
Post Meadow
Lower Md
Potters Cross
Swallowdale
The Close
Park Lodge
Mansfield Farm
Cherrytree Lane
Cowley Industrial
Unit 5 Trading
M25
Moorwards
Wood Lane Close
225
Hardings Row
Coopers Row
White Lodge
Bangors Road South
Swallow Street
Billet Lane
Norwood Lane
Martindale
Palmer's M
Beeches Way
St Johns
Coppins Lane
Coppins
SL0
Colne Brook
Love Green Lane
Bellswood Lane
Heath Lodge
Love Green
Wood Lane
Love Lane
Barnfield
Evreham Road
Stonecroft Av
Widecroft Rd
Junior School
Cecil Rd
Iver
HIGH ST
B470
Swan Road
Ford Lane
Colne Valley
Iver Doctors Surgery
Infant School
Leas Drive
Leacroft Road
Reed Cl
Grange Way
Blythe Cl
Ward Close
Thorney
Holmsdale
Colne Orch
Victoria Crs
Barnes Way
Marina Way
North Lane
Shreding Green
Honeysuckle Close
Hollybush Lane
LANGLEY PARK ROAD
Lossie Dr
Iverdale Cl
Langley Pk Road
Hollow Hill
Mansion Lane
Ridge Way
Court Lane
Love Hill Lane
D8 1 Addison Cl
232
E7 1 Bangors Cl 2 Chequers Orch
F7 1 Delaford Cl
Grand Union Canal
LANGLEY
1 grid square represents 500 metres

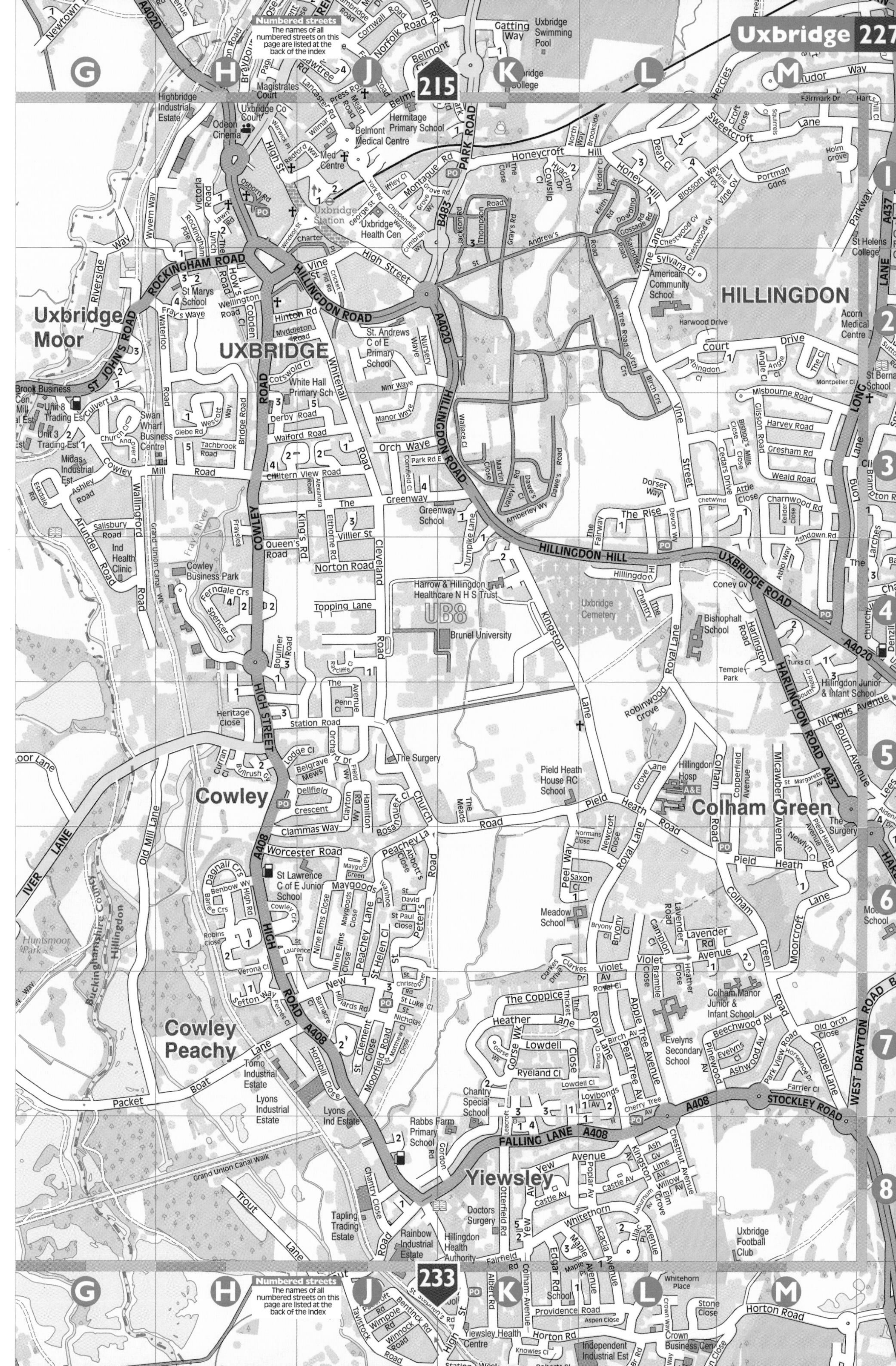

Numbered streets
The names of all numbered streets on this page are listed at the back of the index
215
233
UXBRIDGE
Uxbridge Moor
HILLINGDON
Cowley
Cowley Peachy
Colham Green
Yiewsley
UB8
Brunel University
Harrow & Hillingdon Healthcare N H S Trust
Uxbridge Cemetery
Hillingdon Hosp
A&E
HILLINGDON HILL
HILLINGDON ROAD
UXBRIDGE ROAD
HARLINGTON ROAD
COWLEY ROAD
HIGH STREET
HIGH ROAD
FALLING LANE
STOCKLEY ROAD
WEST DRAYTON ROAD
ROCKINGHAM ROAD
ST JOHN'S ROAD
IVER LANE
PARK ROAD
LONG LANE
Packet Boat Lane
Grand Union Canal Walk
Horton Road
Uxbridge Football Club
Uxbridge Swimming Pool
Hermitage Primary School
Uxbridge Station
American Community School
Acorn Medical Centre
St Helens College
Bishophalt School
Evelyns Secondary School
Colham Manor Junior & Infant School
Greenway School
St Lawrence C of E Junior School
Rabbs Farm Primary School
Chantry Special School
Meadow School
Pield Heath House RC School
Hillingdon Junior & Infant School
Cowley Business Park
Tomo Industrial Estate
Lyons Industrial Estate
Tapling Trading Estate
Rainbow Industrial Estate
Hillingdon Health Authority
Yiewsley Health Centre
Independent Industrial Est
Crown Business Cen
Odeon Cinema
Magistrates Court
Uxbridge Co Court
Highbridge Industrial Estate
Swan Wharf Business Centre
Midas Industrial Est
Huntsmoor Park
Buckinghamshire County
Hillingdon

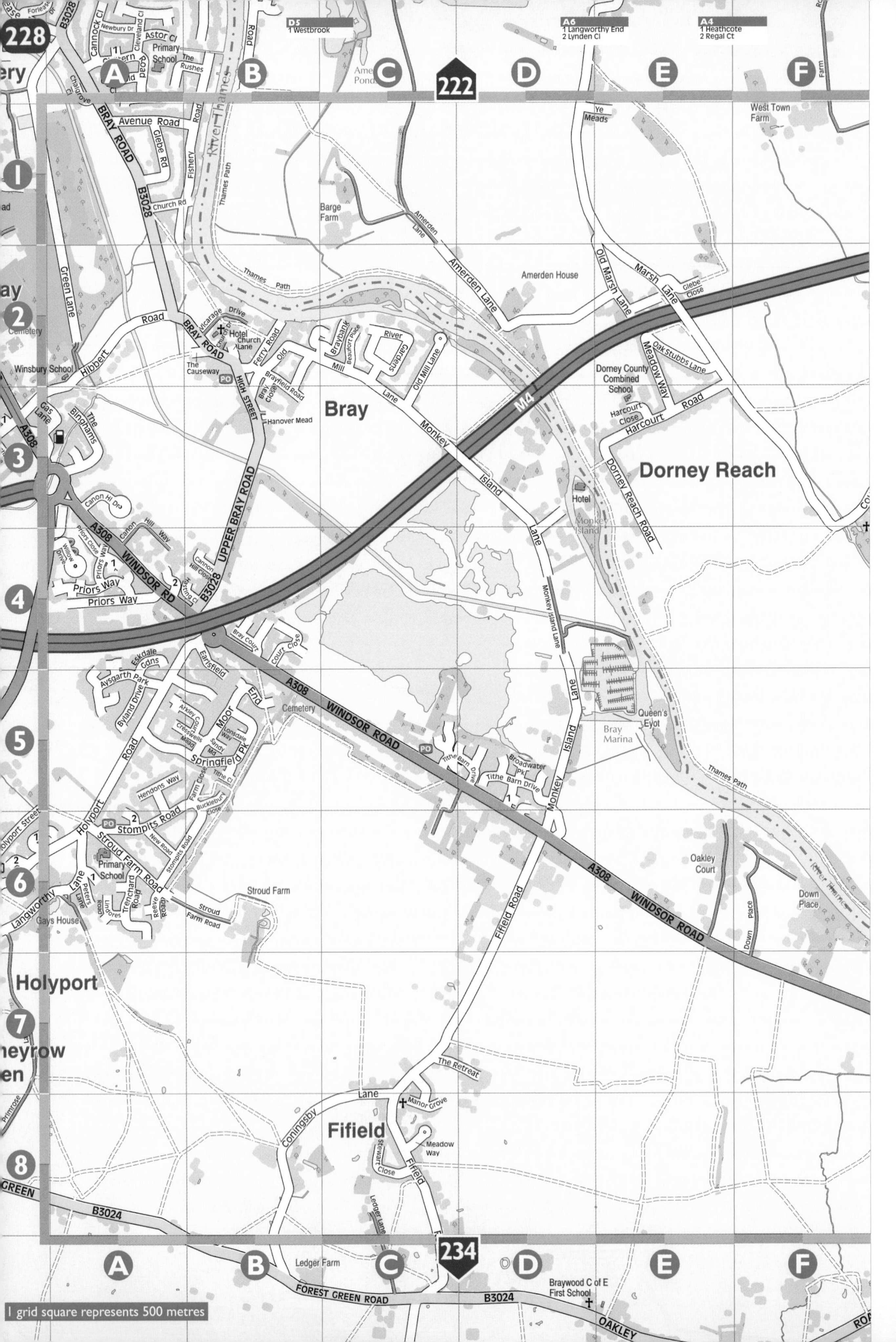

228
D5
1 Westbrook
A6
1 Langworthy End
2 Lynden Cl
A4
1 Heathcote
2 Regal Ct
222
A B C D E F
1 2 3 4 5 6 7 8
B3028
Cannock Cl
Newbury Dr
Cleveland Cl
Astor Cl
Primary School
The Rushes
Road
Chalgrove Cl
BRAY ROAD
Avenue Road
Glebe Rd
Fishery Road
River Thames
Thames Path
Church Rd
Ame Pond
Barge Farm
Amerden Lane
Amerden House
Ye Meads
West Town Farm
Old Marsh Lane
Marsh Lane
Glebe Close
Green Lane
Cemetery
Hibbert Road
Vicarage Drive
Hotel
Church Lane
Ferry Road
Braybank
Beaufort Place
River Gardens
Old Mill Lane
Old Mill Lane
Bray
Winsbury School
The Causeway
PO
HIGH STREET
Brayfield Road
Bray Close
Hanover Mead
Monkey Island Lane
M4
Oak Stubbs Lane
Meadow Way
Dorney County Combined School
Harcourt Close
Harcourt Road
Dorney Reach
Dorney Reach Road
Monkey Island
Gas Lane
The Binghams
A308
Canon Hill Dr
Canon Hill Way
Priors Close
Willow Drive
Priors Way
WINDSOR RD
Cannon Hill Close
UPPER BRAY ROAD
Bray Court
Court Close
Eskdale Gdns
Aysgarth Park
Byland Drive
Earlsfield
Moor End
Arkley Ct
Cresswells Mead
Sandy Mead
Lonsdale Way
Springfield Pk
Tithe Cl
Cemetery
WINDSOR ROAD
Queen's Eyot
Bray Marina
Tithe Barn Drive
Broadwater Pk
Hendons Way
Farm Close
Bucklebury Close
Holyport Road
Stompits Road
New Road
Stroud Farm Road
Primary School
Trenchard Road
Reeve Road
Langworthy Lane
Peters Lane
Lindores Road
Gays House
Holyport Street
Stroud Farm
Stroud Farm Road
Thames Path
Oakley Court
Down Place
Fifield Road
Holyport
Holyport Street
neyrow
en
Primrose
The Retreat
Coningsby Lane
Manor Grove
Fifield
Meadow Way
Stewart Close
Fifield
Ledger Lane
GREEN
B3024
Ledger Farm
234
FOREST GREEN ROAD
Braywood C of E First School
OAKLEY
1 grid square represents 500 metres

G7
1 Oakley Green Rd
K7, K8
Street names for these grid squares are listed at the back of the index
J8
1 Andermans
2 Copper Beech Cl
3 Kingsfield
K1
1 Biddles Cl
2 Chapels Cl
3 Duchess St
4 Molyns Ms
5 Nicholas Gdns
6 Roxwell Cl
7 Waterman Ct
223
G
H
J
K
L
M
Huntercombe Manor Hospital
Burnham Abbey
Huntercombe Lane
Washington Drive
Cippenham County First School
Cippenham Middle School
Abbotts Way
Plackett Way
Harrison Way
Greenway
Barnfield
Cippenham
Moreton Way
Mercian Way
Oldway Way
Langton Cl
West Point
Warner Close
Lilley Way
Ferrers Cl
Moor Furlong
The Village Medical Centre
Hunters Way
Two Mile Dr
Dupre Cl
Eltham Avenue
Elmshott Lane
Bower Way
Bowyer Drive
Frenchum Gdns
Roebuck Green
Millstream La
Robin Hood Close
College Rd
Peartree Close
Alder Cl
Earls Lane
Gervaise Cl
Copse Cl
Nine Acres
Richards Way
Gladstone Way
Lower Cippenham Lane
Bentley Rd
Spring Lane
Avebury
Mallard Dr
Ivy Crescent
Westgate Crs
First School
Westgate School
Bath Road
Bramber Ct
Bennetts Close
Telford Drive
Wade Dr
Amerden Way
Frogmore Cl
Braemar Gdns
Flamborough Spur
Telford Drive
Baird Cl
Moore Cl
Garnet Close
Mitchell Close
Ruby Close
Superstore
Wood Lane
Junction 7
M4
Lake End
Lake End Road
Ashford Lane
B3026 LAKE END ROAD
Dorney
Lane
VILLAGE ROAD
PH
Dorney Court
South Field Close
Slough
Buckinghamshire County
COMMON B3026 ROAD
Dorney Common
Boveney Road
Colenorton Crescent
Boveney Close
New Road
Northfield Road
Moores Lane
Inkerman Rd
Alma Road
Eton Wick Road
Eton Wick
B3026
Tilstone Close
Tilstone Avenue
Leeson Gdns
Cornwall Cl
Victoria Road
Queens Road
Princes Close
Haywards Mead
Eton Wick Football & Social Club
Common Road
Manor Farm
Sheepcote Rd
The Walk
Eton Wick C of E Combined School
ETON WICK
230
South Field
Thames Path
River Thames
Boveney Court
Lock Path
Boveney Lock
Windsor Racecourse
Boveney
Buckinghamshire County
Windsor & Maidenhead
Thames Path
Windsor Marina
Marina
Clewer Village
Mill Lane
Clewer Park
Clewer Court Road
A308 WINDSOR ROAD
Cemetery
The Hatch
Maidenhead Road
A308 MAIDENHEAD ROAD
Whiteley
Aston Mead
Hanley Close
Hayse Hill
Alden View
Clifton Rise
Redford Road
Ruddlesway
Testwood Road
Dedworth
Longmead
Clinic
Holmers First School
Marbeck Close
Lockets Close
Dedworth County Middle School
Pierson Road
Gallys Road
Knights Close
Smith's Lane
Tudor Way
Dedworth Drive
Hanover Way
Sawyer's Close
Buckland Crescent
Vale Road
VALE RD B3025
Rutherford Close
Shirley Avenue
Cemetery
St Edwards Royal Free Ecumenical Middle School
St Edwards RC First School
Errington Drive
Parsonage Lane
Oak Lane
CLARENCE ROAD
Trevelyan Middle School
OAKLEY GREEN ROAD
Bishops Farm Close
DEDWORTH ROAD
Martin Cl
Birch Grove
235
M2
1 Boulters Cl
2 Galahad Cl
M1
1 Adam Cl
2 Egremont Gdns
3 Raleigh Cl
4 Tamarisk Wy
L5
1 Eton Wick Rd
L4
1 Stockdales Rd
2 The Wheatbutts
L1
1 Cobham Cl
2 Manor Ct
3 Marcia Ct
4 Palace Cl
5 Plaines Cl
6 Streamside
7 Trumper Wy
Selwyn Close
Forest Road
Ash Lane
Tinkers Lane
Fairacres Industrial Estate
Greenacre
Cranbourne Avenue
St Johns Drive
Dawson Close
Bridgeman Drive
1
2
3
4
5
6
7
8

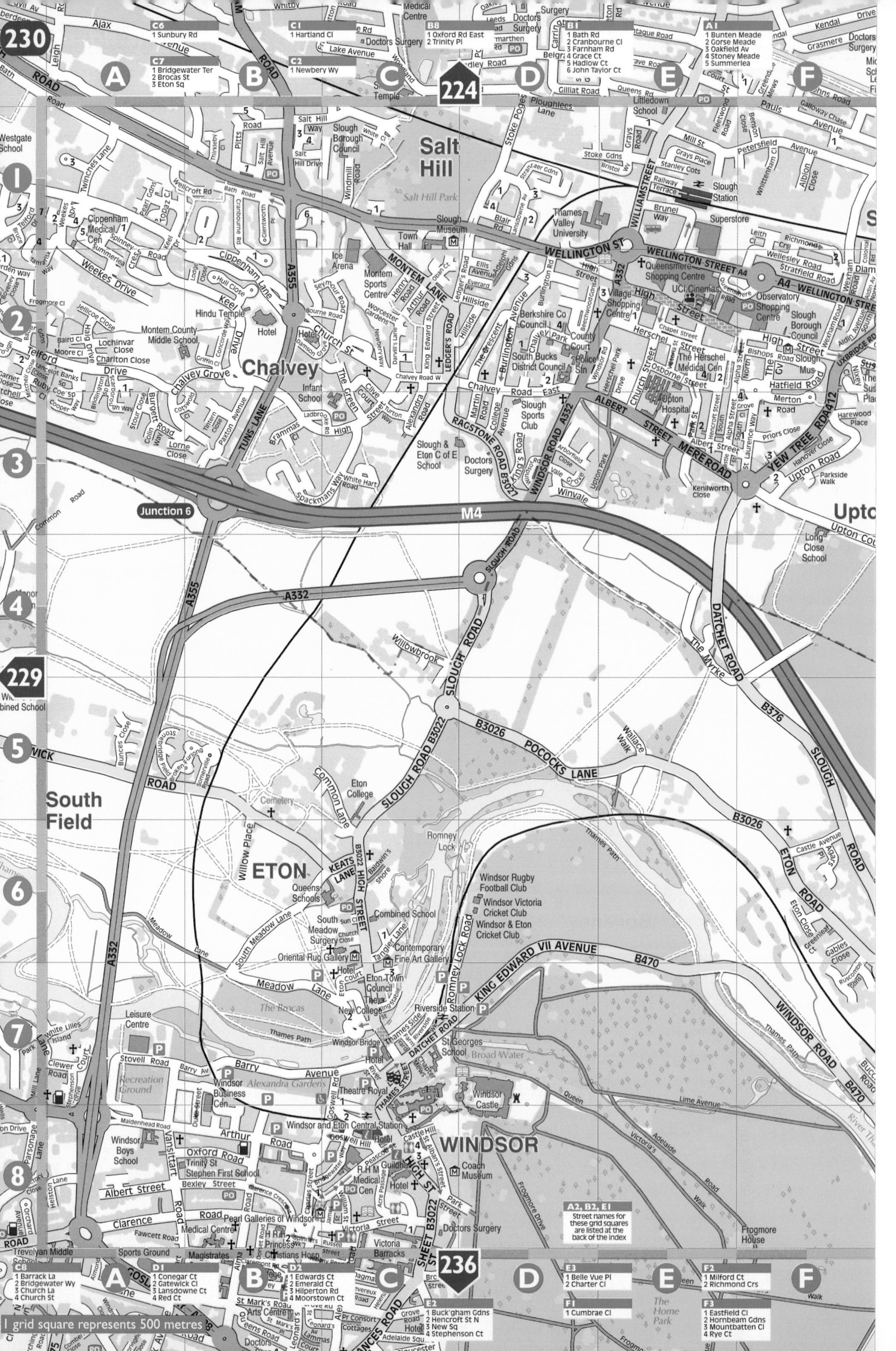

230
224
229
236
C6
1 Sunbury Rd
C7
1 Bridgewater Ter
2 Brocas St
3 Eton Sq
C1
1 Hartland Cl
C2
1 Newbery Wy
B8
1 Oxford Rd East
2 Trinity Pl
B1
1 Bath Rd
2 Cranbourne Cl
3 Farnham Rd
4 Grace Ct
5 Hadlow Ct
6 John Taylor Ct
A1
1 Bunten Meade
2 Gorse Meade
3 Oakfield Av
4 Stoney Meade
5 Summerlea
Salt Hill
Chalvey
Junction 6
M4
South Field
ETON
WINDSOR
Upton
Slough Station
Thames Valley University
Slough Museum
Town Hall
Salt Hill Park
Ice Arena
Montem Sports Centre
Hindu Temple
Montem County Middle School
Queensmere Shopping Centre
UCI Cinemas
Observatory Shopping Centre
Slough Borough Council
Berkshire Co Council
South Bucks District Council
County Court
Police Stn
Upton Hospital
The Herschel Medical Cen
Slough Sports Club
Slough & Eton C of E School
Long Close School
Eton College
Romney Lock
Windsor Rugby Football Club
Windsor Victoria Cricket Club
Windsor & Eton Cricket Club
Queens Schools
Combined School
Contemporary Fine Art Gallery
Oriental Rug Gallery
Eton Town Council
New College
Riverside Station
St Georges School
Windsor Castle
Theatre Royal
Windsor and Eton Central Station
Windsor Boys School
Trinity St Stephen First School
Coach Museum
Guildhall
Victoria Barracks
Frogmore House
Leisure Centre
Recreation Ground
Alexandra Gardens
The Brocas
Broad Water
The Home Park
Trevelyan Middle School
Sports Ground
Magistrates
A2, B2, E1
Street names for these grid squares are listed at the back of the index
C8
1 Barrack La
2 Bridgewater Wy
3 Church La
4 Church St
D1
1 Conegar Ct
2 Gatewick Cl
3 Lansdowne Ct
4 Red Ct
D2
1 Edwards Ct
2 Emerald Ct
3 Hilperton Rd
4 Moorstown Ct
E2
1 Buck'gham Gdns
2 Hencroft St N
3 New Sq
4 Stephenson Ct
E3
1 Belle Vue Pl
2 Charter Cl
F1
1 Cumbrae Cl
F2
1 Milford Ct
2 Richmond Crs
F3
1 Eastfield Cl
2 Hornbeam Gdns
3 Mountbatten Cl
4 Rye Ct
1 grid square represents 500 metres

G2
1 Chichester Ct
2 Clements Cl
3 Connaught Rd
G7
1 Hall Ct
G8
1 Queensmead
H3
1 La Roche Cl
2 Starwood Ct
H7
1 Leigh Pk
J4
1 Blandford Rd South
225
Middle Green
Trenches Farm
Pickford Dr
Orchard Way
Firs Dr
Pickford Drive
The Pippins
Morello
Middlegreen Rd
Nursery Lane
Goodman Pk
SLOUGH
Rochfords Gdns
Rochfords Gardens
Grand Union Canal Walk
Hazelmere Road
Broadmark Road
Elmwood Road
Glanmor Road
Beresford Avenue
Doctors
Slough Borough Council
Uxbridge Road
Victoria
Eastbridge
Grand Union Canal Wk
Manor School
Middlegreen Trading Estate
Middlegreen Trading Est
Cherry Avenue
Halkingcroft
Ravens Field
Brackenforde
Gilmore Close
Locke Gardens
Foxherne
Dolphin Road
Hawtrey Close
Fishguard Spuare
Dolphin Rd
Dolphin Court
Sussex Place
Sussex Close
A4
SUSSEX PL
St Bernards Convent School
Fielding Gardens
Turner Road
Sutton Avenue
Downs Road
Middlegreen Road
Mina Avenue
Chestnut Av
The Drive
Laurel Av
Beech Road
Hillary Road
Springate Field
Bannister Cl
St Mary's Road
Marys/de
Minster Way
Barchester Rd
SL3
Langley Road
Amanda Ct
Lambert
Langley
Slough Grammar School
Palmerston Avenue
Hermitage
Blackthorn Dell
Hempson Avenue
Appletree Lane
St Bernards Road
Red Cottage Mews
Rambler Lane
Kaywood Close
Lynwood Avenue
Blandford Cl
Blandford Road North
Blandford Road South
Ryvers County First & Middle School
Gosling Road
Gosling Green
Cockett Road
Langleywood Secondary School
Trelawney Av
Mortimer Road
Warren Cl
LONDON ROAD
Quaves Road
Kendrick Road
Wheatlands Road
Buckland Avenue
Lascelles Road
Park Lane
London Rd
Glenavon Gardens
The Glen
Dashwood Close
Dandridge Cl
Upton Court Road
Stile Road
Broad Platts
Hubert Road
Fox Road
Webb Cl
Sherwood Close
Meadow Road
Randolph Road
Rossiter Cl
Wilford Road
Darrell Close
Paget Road
Churchill
Stanley Gn E
Drive
Reddington
Langley Grammar School
Arundel Court
Nelson Close
Marlborough Road
Castleview Road
Castleview School
Blenheim Road
Woodstock Avenue
Parkland Avenue
Courtlands Av
Drake Av
Stanton Way
Radnor Way
Bouverie Wy
Cedar Wy
Mulberry Dr
LONDON RD
Alderbury Road West
Alderbury Road
Darwin Road
Saxon Close
Morley Close
Close
Barton Road
Newton Cl
Talbot Avenue
East Berkshire College
Harrow Road
Hampden Road
Ryvers End
Ryvers Road
Spencer Road
Romsey Close
Ives Road
Marish County Middle School
Langley
Grand Union Canal Wk
Waterside Drive
Waterside Dr
Langley Station
STATION ROAD
B470
LANGLEY
Buckinghamshire County Council
Canal Wharf Whf
Langley Business Cen
Mead Av
Mead Wk
Mead Cl
Meadfield Av
Meadfield
Harvey
New Road
Willoughby Road
Elmhurst Road
Raymond Rd
Pantile Rw
Tithe Ct
Hinksey Cl
Sharney Av
Thames Road
Humber Way
Verney Rd
Morrice Cl
Swabey Road
Trelawney Avenue
HIGH STREET
Slough Community Mental Health Cen
Wyland Rd
Bridgewater Ct
Harrogate Ct
Common Road
Mendip Cl
Langley Health Centre
Foxborough School
Folkestone Ct
Quantock Cl
Cheviot Road
Eden Cl
Shelley Cl
Foxborough Cl
Peterhead Ms
Crampian Way
Kimberley Cl
Langley Broom
The Briars
Fid Hurst
Randall Close
Nash Rd
Holy Family RC School
Gibson Court
Hotel
232
Ditton Park
Slough Rugby Club
Conduit La
Calder Ct
Park Road
Ditton Road
Riding Court Farm
Whites Lane
M4
Ditton Road
Riding Court Road
Court Road
Junction 5
Welland
Tweed Rd
Trent
LONDON RD
Hillrise
Laburnum Gv
Brands Hill
MAJOR'S FARM RD
SLOUGH ROAD
Churchmead School
Datchet Sports Club
Deep Field
Riding
B470 LONDON RD
Fairfield Avenue
Montrose Avenue
B376
Old Bank Gallery
Century Gallery
Priory Wy
Hall Ct
Randolph Medical Centre
C of E School
Queen's Rd
Portland Business Centre
Percy Place
Datchet Place
Green Lane
Lawn Close
Link Road
Linchfield Road
Montrose Way
DITTON ROAD
Cemetery
HIGH ST
Datchet Station
Manor House Lane
HORTON
DATCHET
Montagu Road
The Avenue
B3021 SOUTHLEA ROAD
The Paddock
The Drive
Saffron Close
Elm Cft
Beaulieu Close
Holmlea Road
Holmlea Walk
Talbot Pl
Marshfield
Walk
Cobb Close
New Road
Penn Road
ROAD
The Queen Mother Reservoir
237
Mill Place
B376
Datchet Common
M4
1 Blacksmith Rw
2 Horsemoor Cl
3 Jefferson Cl
4 Parry Gn South
5 Simmons Cl
6 Thompson Cl
7 Wildgreen North
8 Wildgreen South
L5
1 Haynes Cl
L4
1 Denny Rd
2 Parry Gn North
3 Stanley Gn West
K4
1 Ripley Cl
K3
1 Padstow Cl

C8
1 Rudsworth Cl
C7
1 St Thomas Wk
B7
1 Brookside
2 Moreland Cl
3 Willow Cl
B4
1 Formby Cl
2 Kempe Cl
A6
1 Cherwell Cl
2 Colnbr'k By-pass
3 Disraeli Ct
4 Merlin Cl
226
Parsonage Farm
Iver Golf & Leisure Centre
Buckinghamshire County Council
Grand Union Canal
Grand Union Canal Walk
Iver Station
Richings Park
Richings Park Sports Club
Thorney House
Parlaunt Park County Combined School
Langley Business Cen
Sutton
Junction 15/4b
Buckinghamshire County
Slough
M4
M25
Lakeside Industrial Estate
Brands Hill
Colnbrook
Colnbrook C of E Combined School
Colnbrook Sports Club
Coln Industrial Estate
Poyle
Mildridge Farm
Hotel
Mckay Trading Est
Polygon
COLNBROOK BY-PASS
LONDON ROAD
231
238
D8
1 Myrtle Cl
E8
1 Ingleside
1 grid square represents 500 metres

West Drayton 233
G8 1 The Square
J1 1 Heathcote Wy 2 Peplow Cl
J2 1 Caroline Cl 2 Catherines Cl 3 Hatton Gv
J3 1 Rickard Cl 2 Wren Dr
J5 1 Verbena Cl
J6 1 Wilton Cl
J8 1 Northwood Rd
K2 1 Classon Cl 2 Swains Cl
Grand Union Canal Walk
Yiewsley
Doctors Surgery
Tapling Trading Estate
227
Football Club
Trout Lane
Chantry Close
Whitehorn Place
Primary School
Albert Rd
Fairfield Rd
Colham Avenue
Edgar Rd
Maple Avenue
Providence Road
Aspen Close
Stone Close
Horton Road
Horton Rd
Yiewsley Health Centre
Knowles Cl
Roberts Cl
Independent Industrial Est
Horton Br Rd
Crown Business Cen
Horton Close
Horton Ind Park
Uxbridge Way
Iron Bridge Road North
Tavistock Road
Winnock Road
Wimpole Rd
Bentinck Rd
St Stephen's Rd
High St
Station Ap
West Drayton Station
Warwick Rd
Fairway Avenue
Colne Av
Sunray Av
Lawn Avenue
Frays Avenue
Ferrers Avenue
Swan Road
Cherry Orch
Furzeham Road
Bellclose Road
Brandville Rd
Station Road
Primary School
Kingston Lane
Holly Cl
Hawthorne Crs
Iron Br Road S
Emden Cl
Rutters Close
Mulberry Crs
Briar Way
Lavender Rise
Jasmine Ter
Stockley Road
Coine Valley Way
Thorney
Buckinghamshire County
Hillingdon
Old Farm Rd
Wren Dr
Drayton Gdns
St Catherines RC Primary School
Medical Centre
Church Road
Kings Rd
Porters Way
Mulberry Pde
Money La
Brooklyn Wy
The Green
Copse Close
Pippins Cl
Church Close
Bagley Close
West Drayton Park Avenue
Hanson Cl
Percy Bush Rd
Brickfields Wy
South Cl
West Road
Almond Av
Oak Av
Hazel Av
Golf Course
Thorney Mill Road
Frays Cl
Mill Cl
Avenue Close
Thornton Av
Walnut Av
Fir Tree Av
Smaldon Cl
West Drayton
St Martin's Cl
Mill Road
Elruge Cl
Rowlheys Place
Sipson Cl
North Road
Thornton Avenue
Chapman Cl
Bell Av
Myrtle Cl
Beech Cl
Blackthorn Av
Crown Plaza Hotel
Cricketfield Road
West Drayton Cricket Club
Wise Lane
Treeside Close
Longmead Junior & Infant School
Cemetery
Dell Road
Maxwell Road
East Road
Laurel Lane
Cherry Lane
Novotel Hotel
Roseary Close
Berberis Walk
Benty
The Glebe
UB7
Cherry Lane Junior School
Blossom Way
Holloway Lane
Magnolia Street
Wise La
Rowan Road
Great Brambles
Harmondsworth
Byron Wy
Scott Close
Coleridge Way
Keats Way
Sipson Rd
Vine Close
Milton Wy
Wordsworth Way
M4
Lupin Cl
Little Benty
The
Junction
Forte Crest Hotel
Holloway Lane
Holloway Close
Sipson
Russell Gdns
Harmondsworth
Saxon Way
River Colne
Heathrow School
Vineries Cl
Sipson La
Blondell Close
Acacia Mews
Meadowlea Cl
Priory Wy
Harmondsworth Lane
A3044
High St
Hollycroft Close
Vincent Cl
Moor Lane
Cambridge Cl
Chambers Business Park
Hollycroft Gardens
Accommodation Lane
Moorland Road
School Rd
Summerhouse La
Sipson Cl
Candover Close
Duke of Northumberland's River
Tarmac Way
Hatch Lane
Sipson Road
Bomer Close
Ashby Way
Sipson Way
Speedbird Wy
Skyport Dr
Zealand Av
Colnbrook By-Pass
A4(T)
Junction 4a
Pinglestone Close
Blunts Avenue
Baysfarm Ct
Heathrow Airport Ltd
Bath Road
Stanwell Moor Road
Bath Road
Northolt Rd
Newton Rd
Newbury Rd
Nelson Rd
West Ramp
Longford
Heathrow Cl
Napier Rd
Northern Perimeter Rd (West)
Western Perimeter Road
G H J K L M
1 2 3 4 5 6 7 8
239
K1 Street names for this grid square are listed at the back of the index
M6 1 Kenwood Cl 2 Wykeham Cl
L3 1 Pocock Av
K4 1 Great Benty
M7 1 Chitterfield Ga
M8 1 Newport Rd
M3 1 Fir Tree Av
L1 1 Cedar Av
TW6
Perry Oaks Dr
Wessex Road
Perry Oak Drive
London Heathrow Airport

1 grid square represents 500 metres

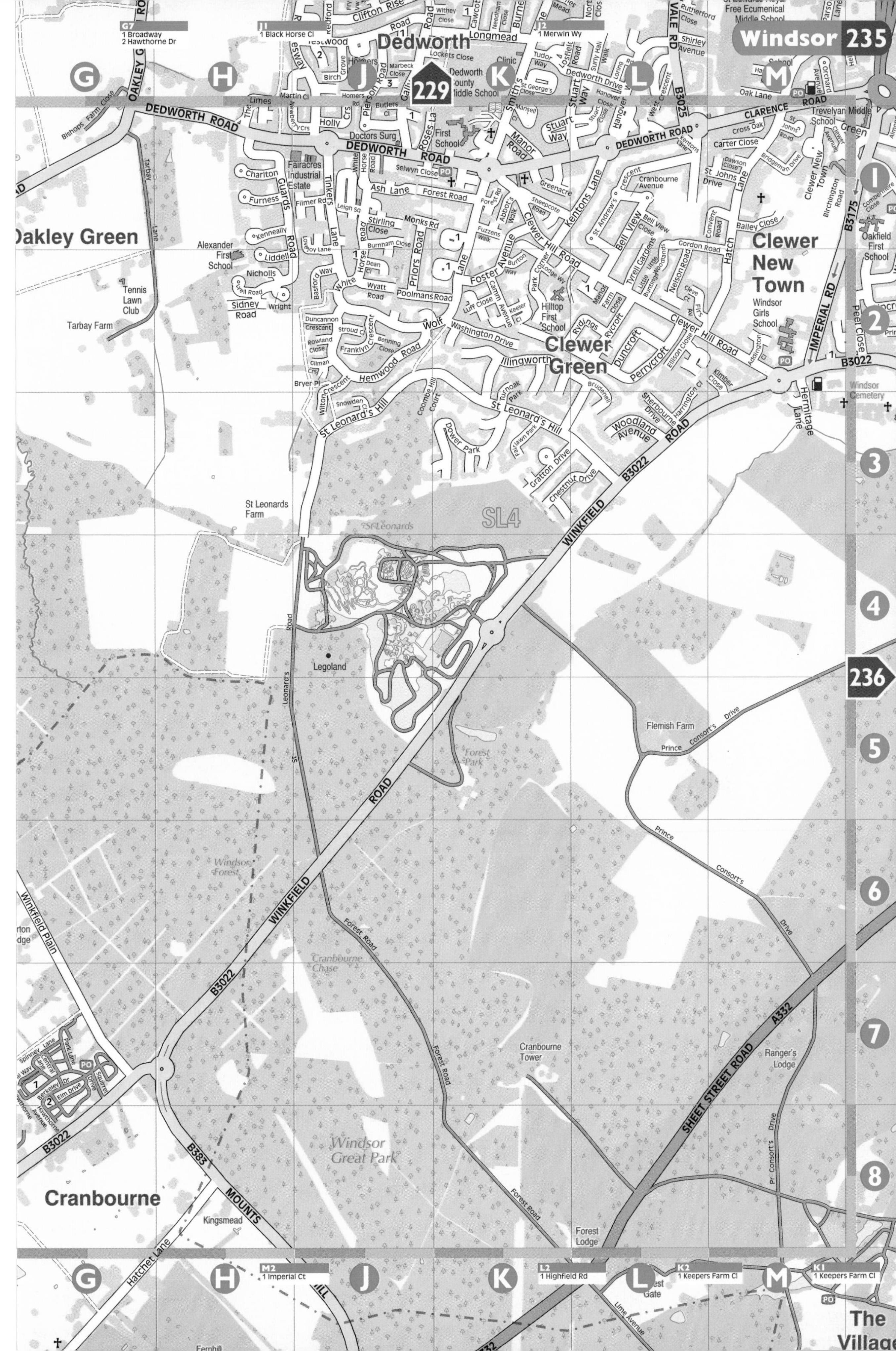
G7
1 Broadway
2 Hawthorne Dr
J1
1 Black Horse Cl
J2
1 Merwin Wy
Dedworth
229
Clifton Rise
Longmead
Lockets Close
Dedworth County Middle School
Clinic
Rutherford Close
Shirley Avenue
Free Ecumenical Middle School
Oak Lane
Clarence Road
Trevelyan Middle School
DEDWORTH ROAD
Bishops Farm Close
Oakley Green
Doctors Surg
Fairacres Industrial Estate
First School
Selwyn Close
Ash Lane
Forest Road
Chariton
Furness
Guards Road
Tinkers Lane
Filmer Rd
Stirling Close
Monks Rd
Priors Road
Alexander First School
Kenneally
Liddell
Nicholls
Sidney Road
Wright
Tennis Lawn Club
Tarbay Farm
Tarbay Lane
White Horse Road
Burnham Close
Wyatt Road
Poolmans Road
Basford Way
Dean Cl
Duncannon Crescent
Stroud Cl
Rowland Close
Franklyn Crescent
Benning Close
Cilman Crs
Hemwood Road
Bryer Pl
Wilton Crescent
Snowden Cl
St Leonard's Hill
Coombe Hill Court
Dower Park
Wolf
Washington Drive
Illingworth
Foster Avenue
Fuzzens Walk
Abbot's Walk
Luff Close
Camm Avenue
Keeler Cl
Clewer Hill Road
Hilltop First School
Clewer Green
Ryecroft
Duncroft
Perrycroft
Manor Road
Kentons Lane
Greenacre
Sheepcote Road
Cranbourne Avenue
St Andrew's Crescent
Bell View
Bell View Close
Tyrell Gardens
Gordon Road
Nelson Road
St Johns Drive
Hatch Lane
Convent Road
Carter Close
Cross Oak
Dawson Close
Bailey Close
Clewer New Town
Windsor Girls School
IMPERIAL RD
B3175
Oakfield First School
Peel Close
B3022
Ellison Close
Kimber Close
Harrington Cl
Sherbourne Drive
Woodland Avenue
Windsor Cemetery
Hermitage Lane
Brudenell
Turnoak Park
Fairlawn Park
Gratton Drive
Chestnut Drive
WINKFIELD ROAD
SL4
St Leonards Farm
St Leonards
St Leonard's Road
Legoland
Forest Park
Flemish Farm
Prince Consort's Drive
Windsor Forest
Winkfield Plain
Cranbourne Chase
Forest Road
Cranbourne Tower
SHEET STREET ROAD
A332
Ranger's Lodge
Pr Consort's Drive
Windsor Great Park
Forest Lodge
Spinney Lane
Park Lane
Central Drive
Berkeley Dr
Elm Drive
Squirrel Drive
B3022
B383
MOUNTS HILL
Cranbourne
Kingsmead
Hatchet Lane
Fernhill
M2
1 Imperial Ct
L2
1 Highfield Rd
K2
1 Keepers Farm Cl
K1
1 Keepers Farm Cl
Lime Avenue
The Village
236

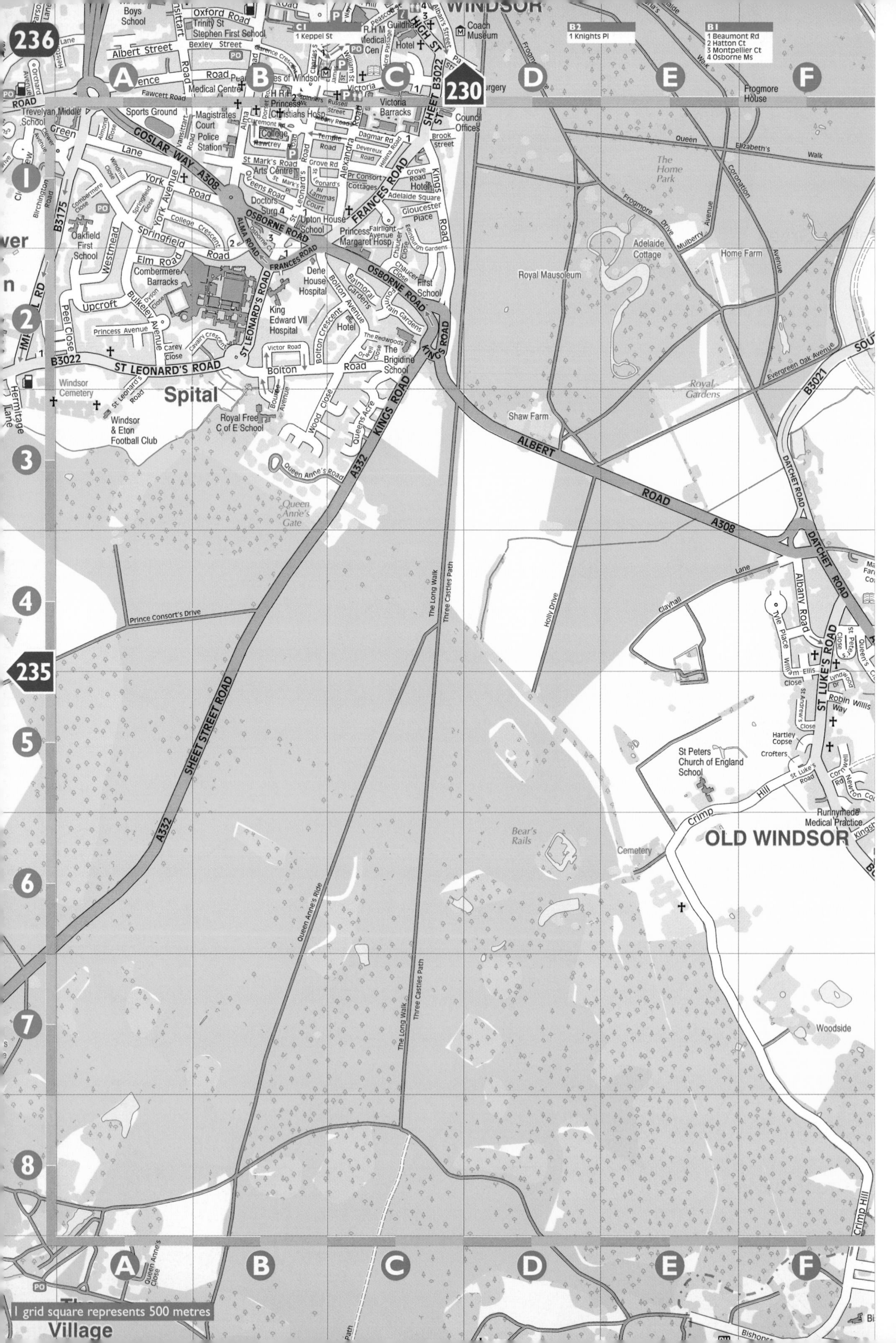
WINDSOR
C1
1 Keppel St
B2
1 Knights Pl
B1
1 Beaumont Rd
2 Hatton Ct
3 Montpellier Ct
4 Osborne Ms
230
235
Spital
OLD WINDSOR
Frogmore House
The Home Park
Royal Mausoleum
Adelaide Cottage
Home Farm
Royal Gardens
Shaw Farm
ALBERT ROAD
A308
DATCHET ROAD
B3021
SHEET STREET ROAD
A332
KINGS ROAD
ST LEONARD'S ROAD
B3022
OSBORNE ROAD
FRANCES ROAD
GOSLAR WAY A308
Queen Elizabeth's Walk
Prince Consort's Drive
The Long Walk
Three Castles Path
Queen Anne's Ride
Queen Anne's Gate
Holly Drive
Clayhall Lane
Crimp Hill
Bear's Rails
Cemetery
St Peters Church of England School
Runnymede Medical Practice
Woodside
King Edward VII Hospital
Combermere Barracks
Victoria Barracks
Windsor Cemetery
Windsor & Eton Football Club
Royal Free C of E School
The Brigidine School
Dene House Hospital
Princess Margaret Hosp
Oakfield First School
Trevelyan Middle School
Magistrates Court
Police Station
Council Offices
Coach Museum
Village
1 grid square represents 500 metres

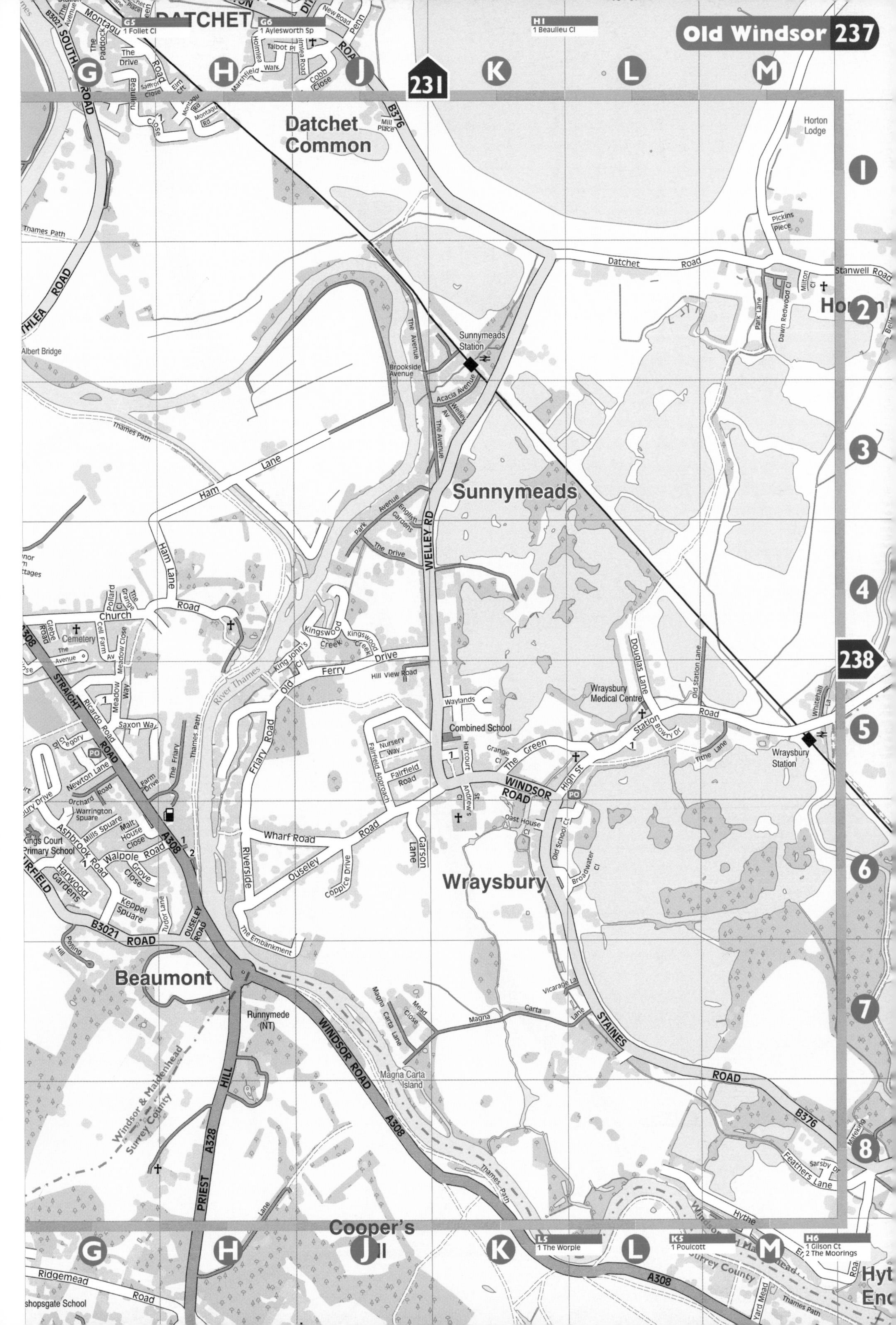
DATCHET
G5 1 Follet Cl
G6 1 Aylesworth Sp
H1 1 Beaulieu Cl
231
238
Datchet Common
Horton Lodge
Pickins Piece
Datchet Road
Stanwell Road
Park Lane
Dawn Redwood Cl
Milton Cl
Sunnymeads Station
Brookside Avenue
Acacia Avenue
Welley Av
The Avenue
Ham Lane
Thames Path
Albert Bridge
Sunnymeads
WELLEY RD
Park Avenue
English Gardens
The Drive
Church Road
Cemetery
Kingswood Creek
Ferry Drive
Hill View Road
King John's Cl
Old Ferry Drive
River Thames
Douglas Lane
Old Station Lane
Wraysbury Medical Centre
Station Road
Bowry Dr
Whitehall La
Wraysbury Station
Tithe Lane
Waylands
Combined School
Nursery Way
Fairfield Approach
Fairfield Road
Harcourt
Grange Cl
The Green
High St
WINDSOR ROAD
Andrew's Cl
St
Oast House Cl
Old School Ct
Broadwater Cl
Friary Road
Wharf Road
Riverside
Ouseley Road
Coppice Drive
Garson Lane
The Embankment
Wraysbury
STRAIGHT ROAD
Ricardo Road
Meadow Way
Saxon Way
Gregory Dr
Newton Lane
Orchard Road
Warrington Spuare
Mills Spuare
Malt House Close
Ashbrook Road
Kings Court Primary School
Walpole Road
Grove Close
Harwood Gardens
Keppel Spuare
Tudor Lane
B3021 ROAD
OUSELEY ROAD
The Friary
Farm Drive
A308
Beaumont
Runnymede (NT)
Magna Carta Lane
Mead Close
Magna Carta Lane
Vicarage La
Magna Carta Island
STAINES ROAD
B376
WINDSOR ROAD
A308
Windsor & Maidenhead
Surrey County
PRIEST HILL
A328
Cooper's Hill
Feathers Lane
Sarsby Dr
Hythe
L5 1 The Worple
K5 1 Poulcott
H6 1 Gilson Ct 2 The Moorings
Ridgemead Road
Bishopsgate School
Yard Mead
Thames Path
G H J K L M
1 2 3 4 5 6 7 8

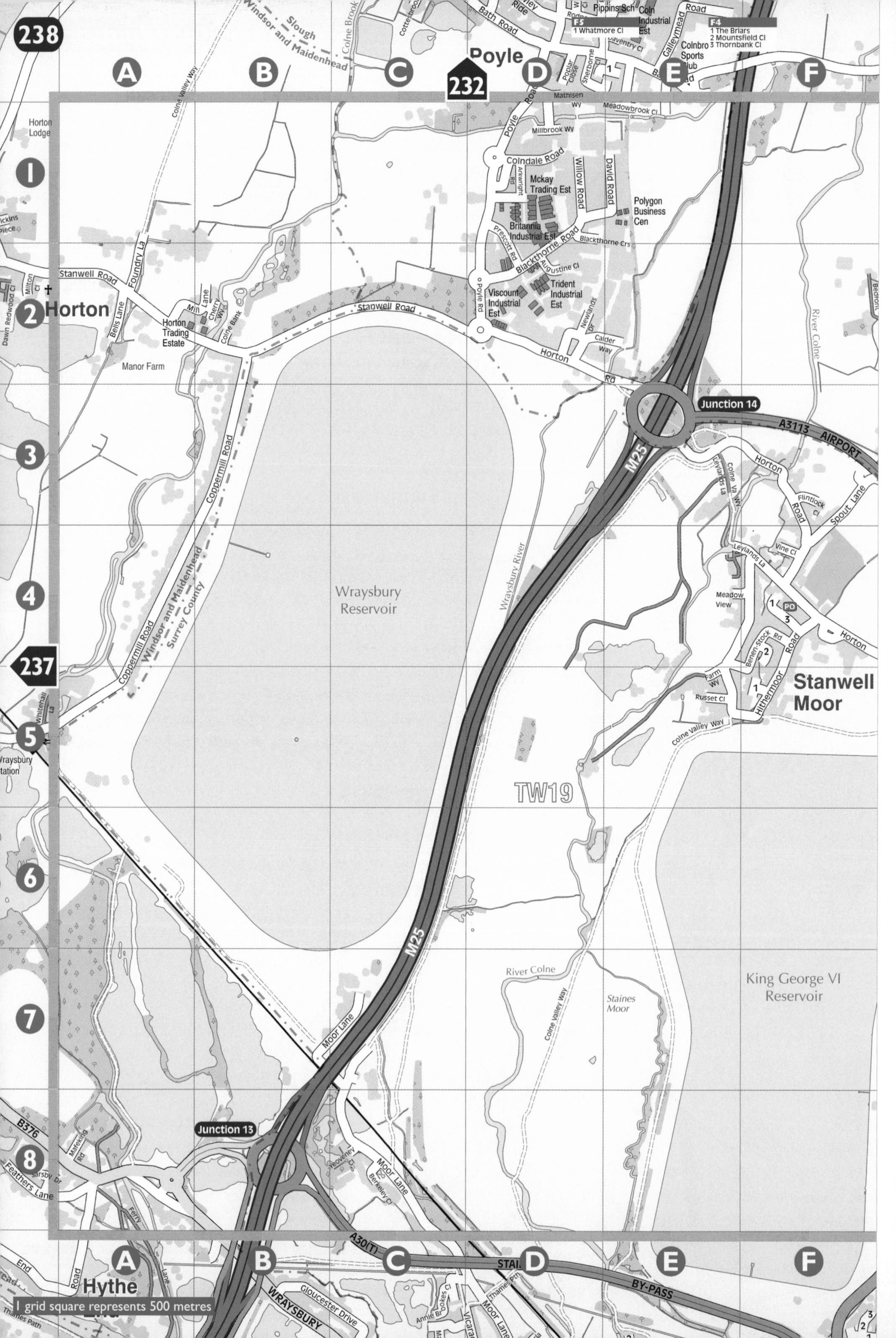


1 grid square represents 500 metres

Longford
H5
1 Selwood Cl
2 Stanhope Heath
3 Stanhope Wy
J5
1 Atherton Cl
2 Chrislaine Cl
3 Douglas Rd
4 Pinewood Ms
5 Stanwell Cl
J7
1 Buttercup Sq
2 Windermere Cl
J6, K5, K6
Street names for these grid squares are listed at the back of the index
Western Perimeter Road
Northern Perimeter Rd
West Ramp
East Ramp
233
G
H
J
K
L
M
TW6
London Heathrow Airport
Tunnel Road West
Tunnel Road East
Wessex Road
Perry Oak Drive
Perry Oaks Dr
Longford River
Burrows Hill Close
Spout Lane North
Court
STANWELL MOOR ROAD
Western Perimeter Rd
Southern Perimeter Road
Terminal 3
Heathrow Terminals 1,2,3 Stn
Cromer Rd
Camberley Rd
Camborne Cl
Control Tower Rd
Heathrow World Cargo Centre
The Britis
Shoreham Road (West)
Shoreham Road (East)
Seaford Rd
Sandringham Rd
Short Rd
Southampton Road
Solent Road
Sealand Road
Tunnel Link Road
Bedfont Road
Sanctuary Rd
Crane Road
Beacon Rd
Longford Rd
Stanwell
Stanwell Place
Gibson Place
Roberts Close
Gleneagles Cl
Russell Dr
Stanwell Gdns
Lowlands Road
Oaks Road
Lindsay Cl
Hendon Wy
Linton Ct
Riverside Road
Riverside Pl
Callis Farm Cl
De Havilland Wy
Dutch Barn Cl
High St
Christ the King RC First School
Whitley Close
Clare Road
Northumberland Close
Blackburn Trading Estate
PARK ROAD
Selwood Gdns
Heath Cl
Lord Knyvett Cl
B378
Hadfield Road
Falcon Dr
Everest Road
Trinity Close
St Mary's Crs
St Davids Health Centre
Town Farm County Primary School
Comet Rd
Corsair Rd
Britannia Way
Hannibal Road
Frobisher Crs
Cordelia Rd
Cordelia Gdns
Cambria Gdns
St Annes Primary School
Jubilee Cl
Lauser Road
Cemetery
Jordans Close
Beech Cl
Rose Gdns
St. Anne's Av
Diamedes Avenue
Vivia Close
Elizabethan Wy
Argosy
Hadrian Way
Canopus Way
Caledonia Rd
Cranford Av
Pk Ms
Hillingdon Av
Osborne Av
Ravensbourne Av
Explorer Av
Longford Way
Longford Av
Clare Road
Viscount Road
Ensign Wy
Ensign Cl
Clyde Road
Elm Cl
Mulberry Avenue
Holywell Way
Holywell Cl
Genesis Cl
Masefield Way
West Bedfont
Brook Cl
Long Lane
Short Lane
Staines Reservoirs
A3044
TOWN LANE
Kingsway
Scots Cl
Viola Avenue
Ashford Sports Club
H & S Community & NHS Trust
Ashdale Cl
Willowbrook
Albain Crs
Ashford Hospital A&E
Ellies Ms
Lodge Way
A30(T)
LONDON ROAD
London Rd
Edward Way
Orchard Way
Desford Way
Harrow Road
Ascot Road
Seaton Dr
Seaton Road
I
2
3
4
5
6
7
8
M2
1 Chester Rd
2 Courtney Rd
3 Courtney Wy
M1
1 Calshot Wy
L7
1 Chesterton Dr
2 Laburnum Wy
3 Milton Gdns
4 The Nightingales
L6
1 The Heathers
K8
1 Maple Gdns
Cumberland Road
Rennie Cl
Ashford Crescent
STANWELL ROAD
Ashford Clinic
St Davids
Midway Cl
CLOCKHOUSE

## USING THE STREET INDEX

Street names are listed alphabetically. Each street name is followed by its postal town or area locality, the Postcode District, the page number, and the reference to the square in which the name is found.

Example: **Abbey Rd** *EAG/OLD/WT* MK6 **61** K1 1

Some entries are followed by a number in a blue box. This number indicates the location of the street within the referenced grid square. The full street name is listed at the side of the map page.

## GENERAL ABBREVIATIONS

ACC ACCESS
ALY ALLEY
AP APPROACH
AR ARCADE
ASS ASSOCIATION
AV AVENUE
BCH BEACH
BLDS BUILDINGS
BND BEND
BNK BANK
BR BRIDGE
BRK BROOK
BTM BOTTOM
BUS BUSINESS
BVD BOULEVARD
BY BYPASS
CATH CATHEDRAL
CEM CEMETERY
CEN CENTRE
CFT CROFT
CH CHURCH
CHA CHASE
CHYD CHURCHYARD
CIR CIRCLE
CIRC CIRCUS
CL CLOSE
CLFS CLIFFS
CMP CAMP
CNR CORNER
CO COUNTY
COLL COLLEGE
COM COMMON
COMM COMMISSION
CON CONVENT
COT COTTAGE
COTS COTTAGES
CP CAPE
CPS COPSE
CR CREEK
CREM CREMATORIUM
CRS CRESCENT
CSWY CAUSEWAY
CT COURT
CTRL CENTRAL
CTS COURTS
CTYD COURTYARD
CUTT CUTTINGS
CV COVE
CYN CANYON
DEPT DEPARTMENT
DL DALE
DM DAM
DR DRIVE
DRO DROVE
DRY DRIVEWAY
DWGS DWELLINGS
E EAST
EMB EMBANKMENT
EMBY EMBASSY
ESP ESPLANADE
EST ESTATE
EX EXCHANGE
EXPY EXPRESSWAY
EXT EXTENSION
F/O FLYOVER
FC FOOTBALL CLUB
FK FORK
FLD FIELD
FLDS FIELDS
FLS FALLS
FLS FLATS
FM FARM
FT FORT
FWY FREEWAY
FY FERRY
GA GATE
GAL GALLERY
GDN GARDEN
GDNS GARDENS
GLD GLADE
GLN GLEN
GN GREEN
GND GROUND
GRA GRANGE
GRG GARAGE
GT GREAT
GTWY GATEWAY
GV GROVE
HGR HIGHER
HL HILL
HLS HILLS
HO HOUSE
HOL HOLLOW
HOSP HOSPITAL
HRB HARBOUR
HTH HEATH
HTS HEIGHTS
HVN HAVEN
HWY HIGHWAY
IMP IMPERIAL
IN INLET
IND EST INDUSTRIAL ESTATE
INF INFIRMARY
INFO INFORMATION
INT INTERCHANGE
IS ISLAND
JCT JUNCTION
JTY JETTY
KG KING
KNL KNOLL
L LAKE
LA LANE
LDG LODGE
LGT LIGHT
LK LOCK
LKS LAKES
LNDG LANDING
LTL LITTLE
LWR LOWER
MAG MAGISTRATE
MAN MANSIONS
MD MEAD
MDW MEADOWS
MEM MEMORIAL
MKT MARKET
MKTS MARKETS
ML MALL
ML MILL
MNR MANOR
MS MEWS
MSN MISSION
MT MOUNT
MTN MOUNTAIN
MTS MOUNTAINS
MUS MUSEUM
MWY MOTORWAY
N NORTH
NE NORTH EAST
NW NORTH WEST
O/P OVERPASS
OFF OFFICE
ORCH ORCHARD
OV OVAL
PAL PALACE
PAS PASSAGE
PAV PAVILION
PDE PARADE
PH PUBLIC HOUSE
PK PARK
PKWY PARKWAY
PL PLACE
PLN PLAIN
PLNS PLAINS
PLZ PLAZA
POL POLICE STATION
PR PRINCE
PREC PRECINCT
PREP PREPARATORY
PRIM PRIMARY
PROM PROMENADE
PRS PRINCESS
PRT PORT
PT POINT
PTH PATH
PZ PIAZZA
QD QUADRANT
QU QUEEN
QY QUAY
R RIVER
RBT ROUNDABOUT
RD ROAD
RDG RIDGE
REP REPUBLIC
RES RESERVOIR
RFC RUGBY FOOTBALL CLUB
RI RISE
RP RAMP
RW ROW
S SOUTH
SCH SCHOOL
SE SOUTH EAST
SER SERVICE AREA
SH SHORE
SHOP SHOPPING
SKWY SKYWAY
SMT SUMMIT
SOC SOCIETY
SP SPUR
SPR SPRING
SQ SQUARE
ST STREET
STN STATION
STR STREAM
STRD STRAND
SW SOUTH WEST
TDG TRADING
TER TERRACE
THWY THROUGHWAY
TNL TUNNEL
TOLL TOLLWAY
TPK TURNPIKE
TR TRACK
TRL TRAIL
TWR TOWER
U/P UNDERPASS
UNI UNIVERSITY
UPR UPPER
V VALE
VA VALLEY
VIAD VIADUCT
VIL VILLA
VIS VISTA
VLG VILLAGE
VLS VILLAS
VW VIEW
W WEST
WD WOOD
WHF WHARF
WK WALK
WKS WALKS
WLS WELLS
WY WAY
YD YARD
YHA YOUTH HOSTEL

## POSTCODE TOWNS AND AREA ABBREVIATIONS

AMS Amersham
AMSS Amersham south
ASHF Ashford (Surrey)
AYL Aylesbury
AYLS Aylesbury south
AYLW Aylesbury west
BDWL Bradwell
BEAC Beaconsfield
BERK Berkhamsted
BIC Bicester
BNEND Bourne End
BNFD Binfield
BOZ/IR/WOL Bozeat/Irchester/Wollaston
BRACKY Brackley
BTCHLY Bletchley
BUCK/WIN Buckingham/Winslow
CAV/SC Caversham/Sonning Common
CFSP/GDCR Chalfont St Peter/Gerrards Cross
CHNR Chinnor
CMK Central Milton Keynes
CNH/GTH/TMA Crownhill/Great Holm/Two Mile Ash
CSHM Chesham
CSTG Chalfont St Giles
DBGH Denbigh
DEN/HRF Denham/Harefield
DTCH/LGLY Datchet/Langley
DUN/HR/TOD Dunstable/Houghton Regis/Toddington
DUN/WHIP Dunstable/Whipsnade
EAG/OLD/WTN Eaglestone/Oldbrook/Woughton
EGH Egham
EMV/FZ Emerson Valley/Furzton
FLKWH Flackwell Heath
GTLIN Great Linford
GTMIS/PWD Great Missenden/Prestwood
HADM Haddenham
HAZ/HG Hazlemere/Holmer Green
HEAD Headington
HEN Henley-on-Thames
HGDN/ICK Hillingdon/Ickenham
HHS/BOV Hemel Hempstead south/Bovingdon
HHW Hemel Hempstead west
HTHAIR Heathrow Airport
HWYN High Wycombe north
HWYW High Wycombe west
IVER Iver
KGLGY Kings Langley
KID Kidlington
LBUZ Leighton Buzzard
MDHD Maidenhead
MKV Milton Keynes Village
MLW Marlow
NPAG Newport Pagnell
NTHWD Northwood
OLN Olney
PRRI Princes Risborough
RAYLNE/WEN Rural Aylesbury north & east/Wendover
RAYLW Rural Aylesbury west
RBEDW Rural Bedford west
RBICN Rural Bicester north
RBICS/W Rural Bicester south & west
RKW/CH/CXG Rickmansworth/Chorleywood/Croxley Green
RMKN Rural Milton Keynes north
RMKS/WB Rural Milton Keynes south/Woburn
RNHPTN Rural Northampton
SHEN Shenley
SKCH Stokenchurch
SL Slough
SLN Slough north
STSTR Stoney Stratford
STWL/WRAY Stanwell/Wraysbury
THAME Thame
TOW Towcester
TRING Tring
UX/CGN Uxbridge/Colham Green
WAR/TWY Wargrave/Twyford
WDR/YW West Drayton/Yiewsley
WDSR Windsor
WEAT Water Eaton
WHLY Wheatley
WLLN Willen
WOLV Wolverton
WTLGN Watlington
WTR/OFPK Walnut Tree/Old Park Farm
WYM Wycombe Marsh

## Index - streets



## A

## B

## E

## H

## I



## J

## M

## N



## O

## P

## S

# T

## W

## Y



## Z

Notes

Notes

# Notes

# Notes

**Notes**

## Notes